A History of Corporate Governance around the World

**A National Bureau
of Economic Research
Conference Report**

A History of Corporate Governance around the World

Family Business Groups to Professional Managers

Edited by **Randall K. Morck**

The University of Chicago Press

Chicago and London

The University of Chicago Press, Chicago 60637
The University of Chicago Press, Ltd., London
© 2007 by The University of Chicago
All rights reserved. Published 2005
Paperback edition 2007
Printed in the United States of America
16 15 14 13 12 11 10 09 08 07   2 3 4 5 6
ISBN-13: 978-0-226-53680-4 (cloth)
ISBN-13: 978-0-226-53681-1 (paper)
ISBN-10: 0-226-53680-7 (cloth)
ISBN-10: 0-226-53681-5 (paper)

Library of Congress Cataloging-in-Publication Data

A history of corporate governance around the world : family business
    groups to professional managers / edited by Randall K. Morck.
        p.   cm. — (A National Bureau of Economic Research
    conference report)
      Includes bibliographical references and index.
      ISBN 0-226-53680-7 (alk. paper)
      1. Corporate governance—History. I. Morck, Randall. II. Series.

HD2741 .H568 2005
658.4′09—dc22

                                                                                2005010526

Relation of the Directors to the
Work and Publications of the
National Bureau of Economic Research

1. The object of the NBER is to ascertain and present to the economics profession, and to the public more generally, important economic facts and their interpretation in a scientific manner without policy recommendations. The Board of Directors is charged with the responsibility of ensuring that the work of the NBER is carried on in strict conformity with this object.

2. The President shall establish an internal review process to ensure that book manuscripts proposed for publication DO NOT contain policy recommendations. This shall apply both to the proceedings of conferences and to manuscripts by a single author or by one or more co-authors but shall not apply to authors of comments at NBER conferences who are not NBER affiliates.

3. No book manuscript reporting research shall be published by the NBER until the President has sent to each member of the Board a notice that a manuscript is recommended for publication and that in the President's opinion it is suitable for publication in accordance with the above principles of the NBER. Such notification will include a table of contents and an abstract or summary of the manuscript's content, a list of contributors if applicable, and a response form for use by Directors who desire a copy of the manuscript for review. Each manuscript shall contain a summary drawing attention to the nature and treatment of the problem studied and the main conclusions reached.

4. No volume shall be published until forty-five days have elapsed from the above notification of intention to publish it. During this period a copy shall be sent to any Director requesting it, and if any Director objects to publication on the grounds that the manuscript contains policy recommendations, the objection will be presented to the author(s) or editor(s). In case of dispute, all members of the Board shall be notified, and the President shall appoint an ad hoc committee of the Board to decide the matter; thirty days additional shall be granted for this purpose.

5. The President shall present annually to the Board a report describing the internal manuscript review process, any objections made by Directors before publication or by anyone after publication, any disputes about such matters, and how they were handled.

6. Publications of the NBER issued for informational purposes concerning the work of the Bureau, or issued to inform the public of the activities at the Bureau, including but not limited to the NBER Digest and Reporter, shall be consistent with the object stated in paragraph 1. They shall contain a specific disclaimer noting that they have not passed through the review procedures required in this resolution. The Executive Committee of the Board is charged with the review of all such publications from time to time.

7. NBER working papers and manuscripts distributed on the Bureau's web site are not deemed to be publications for the purpose of this resolution, but they shall be consistent with the object stated in paragraph 1. Working papers shall contain a specific disclaimer noting that they have not passed through the review procedures required in this resolution. The NBER's web site shall contain a similar disclaimer. The President shall establish an internal review process to ensure that the working papers and the web site do not contain policy recommendations, and shall report annually to the Board on this process and any concerns raised in connection with it.

8. Unless otherwise determined by the Board or exempted by the terms of paragraphs 6 and 7, a copy of this resolution shall be printed in each NBER publication as described in paragraph 2 above.

To the boss

Contents

Preface   xi

The Global History of Corporate Governance:
An Introduction   1
Randall K. Morck and Lloyd Steier

1. **The Rise and Fall of the Widely Held Firm:**
A History of Corporate Ownership in Canada   65
Randall K. Morck, Michael Percy, Gloria Y. Tian,
and Bernard Yeung
Comment: Jordan Siegel

2. **The History of Corporate Ownership in China:**
State Patronage, Company Legislation, and the
Issue of Control   149
William Goetzmann and Elisabeth Köll
Comment: Dwight H. Perkins

3. **Corporate Ownership in France: The Importance**
of History   185
Antoin E. Murphy
Comment: Daniel Raff

4. **The History of Corporate Ownership and Control**
in Germany   223
Caroline Fohlin
Comment: Alexander Dyck

5.   **The Evolution of Concentrated Ownership in India:
      Broad Patterns and a History of the Indian
      Software Industry**   283
      Tarun Khanna and Krishna G. Palepu
      Comment: Ashoka Mody

6.   **The History of Corporate Ownership in Italy**   325
      Alexander Aganin and Paolo Volpin
      Comment: Daniel Wolfenzon

7.   **A Frog in a Well Knows Nothing of the Ocean:
      A History of Corporate Ownership in Japan**   367
      Randall K. Morck and Masao Nakamura
      Comment: Sheldon Garon

8.   **Financing and Control in The Netherlands:
      A Historical Perspective**   467
      Abe de Jong and Ailsa Röell
      Comment: Peter Högfeldt

9.   **The History and Politics of Corporate Ownership
      in Sweden**   517
      Peter Högfeldt
      Comment: Ailsa Röell

10.   **Spending Less Time with the Family: The Decline of
      Family Ownership in the United Kingdom**   581
      Julian Franks, Colin Mayer, and Stefano Rossi
      Comment: Barry Eichengreen

11.   **Why Has There Been So Little Block Holding in
      America?**   613
      Marco Becht and J. Bradford DeLong
      Comment: Richard Sylla

      Contributors   667
      Author Index   671
      Subject Index   679

Preface

Let the reader beware that this book differs from most conference volumes, for it is not a collection of more or less independent research articles. Rather, each set of authors was asked to provide a history of corporate governance in a given country, beginning as early as necessary to explain how that country came to its current state. Inevitably, great mercantile families, politics, and institutional development interact. Each chapter went through repeated revisions, as one set of authors embraced ideas raised by another in a long process that ultimately converged on the pages that follow. I am deeply grateful to the esteemed authors and discussants of this volume, some of the world's very best financial economists and economic historians, who took up my challenge to explore this little-known but critically important research frontier. This volume, quite literally, capitalizes thousands of hours of their work.

This volume would have been impossible without the financial support of the University of Alberta School of Business and especially its much acclaimed Centre for Entrepreneurship and Family Enterprise. Logistic and organizational support from the National Bureau of Economic Research was also critical to the project's success, especially to the successful preconference in September 2002 in Cambridge, Massachusetts, and the authors' and discussants' conference at Lake Louise, Alberta, in June 2003. Special thanks are due Helena Fitz-Patrick for stalwartly herding the many busy contributors toward final versions, and to Brett Maranjian for flawlessly organizing the Cambridge and Lake Louise conferences.

Further financial support permitted the presentation of the papers in this volume at a second conference in Fontainebleau, France, in January 2004. For this, many thanks are due the Center for Economic Policy Research (CEPR), the European Corporate Governance Institute (ECGI), and IN-

SEAD. Thanks are due Gordon Redding, Silvia Giacomelli, Rosa Nelly Travino, Javier Suárez, Christine Blondel, Yishay Yafeh, Mark Roe, Erik Berglöf, Bruce Kogut, Ronald Anderson, Enrico Perotti, Xavier Vives, and Sabine Klein for serving as discussants of the papers and discussants at large in Fontainebleau.

The *Times* of London kindly ran synopses of several of the chapters in this volume, and many thanks are due their staff, especially Brian Groom and Paul Betts.

Encouragement throughout from Martin Feldstein, president and CEO of the National Bureau of Economic Research; Michael Percy, the dean of the University of Alberta School of Business; and Lloyd Steier, the director of the Centre for Entrepreneurship and Family Enterprise, was also invaluable. Also providing indispensable help at critical junctures were Marco Becht, director of the European Corporate Governance Institute; Christine Blondel, senior research program manager of INSEAD's Research Initiative for Family Enterprise; Barry Eichengreen, George C. Pardee and Helen N. Pardee Professor of Economics and Political Science at the University of California at Berkeley; Ludo van der Heyden, Wendel Chaired Professor for the Large Family Firm and Solvay Professor in Technology Innovation at INSEAD; and Andrei Shleifer, Whipple V. N. Jones Professor of Economics at Harvard. I am also grateful to Stephen Jarislowsky for his intellectual encouragement and financial support.

Two anonymous manuscript reviewers provided insightful and keenly critical comments that greatly improved many of the chapters, especially those in which I had a hand. More thanks are due Helena Fitz-Patrick of the National Bureau of Economic Research for patiently guiding us all toward publication, and to Peter Cavagnaro of the University of Chicago Press for expertly overseeing the publication process.

Finally, my wife deserves boundless gratitude for her patience and support throughout.

The Global History of Corporate Governance
An Introduction

Randall K. Morck and Lloyd Steier

To Whom Dare We Entrust Corporate Governance?

Capitalism at the beginning of the twenty-first century is a variegated collection of economic systems. In America, *capitalism* is a system where a huge number of independent corporations compete with each other for customers. Monopolies are illegal, though the courts are sometimes an imperfect safeguard against them. Each corporation has a chief executive officer (CEO) who dictates corporate policies and strategies to a largely passive board of directors. The true owners of America's great corporations, millions of middle-class shareholders, each owning a few hundred or a few thousand shares, are disorganized and generally powerless. Only a handful of institutional investors accumulate large stakes—3 or even 5 percent of an occasional large firm's stock—that give them voices loud enough to carry into corporate boardrooms. Corporate CEOs use or abuse

Randall K. Morck is the Stephen A. Jarislowsky Distinguished Professor of Finance at the University of Alberta School of Business and a research associate at the National Bureau of Economic Research. Lloyd Steier is professor of Strategic Management and Organization, chair in Entrepreneurship and Family Enterprise, and academic director of the Centre for Entrepreneurship and Family Enterprise at the University of Alberta School of Business.

We are grateful for helpful comments, insights, and suggestions from Philippe Aghion, Lucien Bebchuk, Daniel Berkowitz, Brian Cheffins, Stijn Claessens, Paul Frentrop, Brad DeLong, Alexander Dyck, Barry Eichengreen, Lucas Enriques, Merritt Fox, Rafael La Porta, Ross Levine, Florencio López-de-Silanes, Marco Pagano, Enrico Perotti, Katharina Pistor, Mark Rameseyer, Andrei Shleifer, Richard Sylla, and Bernard Yeung, as well as participants at the University of Alberta/NBER conference at Lake Louise, Alberta, the CEPR/ECGN/INSEAD/University of Alberta/NBER conference in Fontainebleau, France, the Corporate Governance Forum of Turkey in Istanbul, and the Academy of International Business conference in Stockholm. This research was supported by the University of Alberta School of Business and the University of Alberta Centre for Entrepreneurship and Family Enterprise in cooperation with the National Bureau of Economic Research.

their considerable powers in accordance with their individual political, social, and economic beliefs. In much of the rest of the world, *capitalism* is a
system where a handful of immensely wealthy families control almost all of
a country's great corporations, and often its government to boot. Competition is largely a mirage, for few firms are genuinely independent. Professional managers are hired help, subservient to oligarchic family dynasties
that jealously safeguard their power, sometimes at great cost to their host
economies.

The purpose of this volume is to explore how capitalism came to mean,
and to be, such different things in different parts of the world. How did
some economies come to entrust the governance of their great corporations to a handful of old moneyed families, while others place their faith in
professional CEOs?

Such different usages of the word *capitalism* make for difficult communication. American economists are often baffled by the reluctance of seemingly well-educated foreigners to embrace the tenets of free enterprise, and
foreign economists marvel at the naive simplicity of their American colleagues. In fact, each would do well to take the other more seriously. The
rest of the world is not simply like America, but usually poorer to varying
degrees. Different countries' economies are organized in very different
ways, and corporate governance—that is, decisions about how capital is
allocated, both across and within firms—is entrusted to very different sorts
of people and constrained by very different institutions.

A key study that forces this point upon the economics profession is by
La Porta et al. (1999), who contrast the ownership of large and medium-
sized companies across countries. Figure 1 illustrates their findings.[1] The
central message of figure 1 is how very different different countries are. The
large corporate sector of Mexico is entirely controlled by a few enormously
wealthy families, whereas all the largest British companies get by with no
controlling shareholders at all. Most Argentine firms are controlled by
wealthy families, but most great American corporations are not. Wealthy
family domination of great corporations is not restricted to poor countries
but also characterizes relatively rich economies like Israel, Hong Kong,
and Sweden.

Nonetheless, Claessens, Djankov, and Lang (2000), Khanna and Rivkin (2001), and many others document the ubiquity of family-controlled

---

1. La Porta et al. (1999) list several large German and Japanese firms as having no controlling shareholder. However, because German banks typically vote the shares of small investors, Baums (1995) shows that these firms are actually controlled by banks. All the large
Japanese firms La Porta et al. list as having no controlling shareholder are members of corporate groups called *keiretsu,* in which each firm is controlled collectively by other firms in the
group. Although each group firm's stake in every other group firm can be small, these stakes
accumulate to control blocks. Figure 1 is based on La Porta et al. for all other countries. We
are grateful to Raphael La Porta for making the names of the top firms in each country available to us.

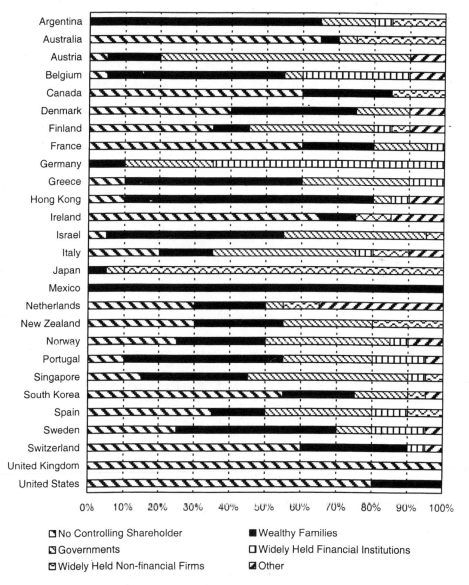

Fig. 1   Who controls the world's great corporations?

Sources: La Porta et al. (1999) with Japanese data augmented by Morck and Nakamura (1999) to account for combined *keiretsu* stakes and German data augmented with information from Baums (1995) to account for bank proxy voting.

Notes: Fraction of top ten firms with different types of controlling shareholders is shown for each country. Control is assumed if any shareholder or group of shareholders believed to work in consort controls 20 percent of the votes in a company's annual shareholder meeting.

corporate groups in poor countries. In general, poor economies have corporate sectors controlled by some mixture of state organs and wealthy families. The variety illustrated in figure 1 is primarily a feature of the developed world.

The fact that most large U.K. and U.S. firms are widely held, while most large firms elsewhere are controlled by a few wealthy families, is perhaps insufficient to explain the different perceptions of capitalism that hold force in different countries, for independent firms that compete with each other still lead to economic efficiency regardless of who controls them. However, a second feature of corporate governance in most countries, the *pyramidal business group* or *pyramid* for short, magnifies the economic importance of this difference enough to create genuinely different economic systems, all of which go by the name of capitalism.

A pyramid is a structure in which an apex shareholder, usually a very wealthy family, controls a single company, which may or may not be listed. This company then holds control blocks in other listed companies. Each of these holds control blocks in yet more listed companies, and each of these controls yet more listed companies. Structures such as these are ubiquitous outside the United Kingdom and United States. They can contain dozens or hundreds of firms, listed and private, and put vast sweeps of a nation's economy under the control of a single family. These are the structures that permit tiny elites to control the greater parts of the corporate sectors of many countries.

Berle and Means (1932), Bebchuk, Kraakman, and Triantis (2000), Morck, Stangeland, and Yeung (2000), Claessens, Djankov, and Lang (2000), and many others demonstrate the severe corporate governance problems that can occur in pyramidal business groups. However, these problems are only of interest in this volume to the extent that they motivate the formation of business groups, or their dissolution. Our focus is on how the differences in corporate control illustrated in figure 1 came to be.

The remainder of this chapter is laid out as follows: section 2 explains why the differences outlined in figure 1 matter. Indeed, they are the key distinguishing features that define different forms of capitalism. Section 3 then briefly describes the key arguments and findings of each chapter. Section 4 then sorts through these findings, highlighting common threads that connect to current thinking about corporate governance. Section 4 goes on to consider the implications of these threads, and section 5 provides a summary.

Does It Matter?

Capitalism is thus called because it is an economic system organized around the production and allocation of capital. The savings of individuals are the basis of all capital. Yet the ways in which economies accumulate and allocate capital are quite different in different countries, and seem closely related to how each country handles corporate governance issues.

Individuals can save by investing in corporate stocks and bonds. Companies they view as good bets can raise huge amounts of money by issuing securities—as when Google raised $1.67 billion by selling new shares to the public in 2004.[2] A company that investors feel is a poor bet has difficulty raising any substantial amount by issuing securities. For instance, the Internet-based sales intermediary deja.com withdrew from its proposed share issue in 2000, after it became clear that investors were not likely to pay the sort of price management hoped for.[3]

If investors know what they are doing, capital is allocated to firms that can use it well and is kept away from firms that are likely to waste it. This process underlies *shareholder capitalism,* as practiced in the United Kingdom and United States. Firms in those countries that can issue stock and bonds to investors acquire funds to build factories, buy machinery, and develop technologies.

For investors to trust a company enough to buy its securities, they need reassurance that the company will be run both honestly and cleverly. This is where corporate governance is critical. The corporate governance of large corporations in these countries is entrusted to CEOs and other professional managers. Investors collectively monitor the quality of governance of each listed firm, and its share price reflects their consensus.

This system has costs. Monitoring the quality of corporate governance in every firm in the economy eats up resources. American and British capital markets and regulators try to shift this cost away from investors by mandating that firms disclose detailed financial reports, insider share holdings, management pay, and any conflicts of interest. Other rules proscribe stock manipulation, certain trading, and other self-dealing by corporate insiders. Shareholders can sue the directors and officers of any company that violates these rules. These prohibitions aim to help investors by adding regulatory and judicial oversight to the mix. And raiders and institutional investors stand ready to toss out managers who seem either inept or dishonest. These deep-pocketed investors can afford to bear a disproportionate share of the cost of monitoring corporate governance and of cleaning up governance problems when they arise.

This system is certainly imperfect. Good managers are penalized and poor ones rewarded if investors get things wrong, and this seems to happen with some regularity, as during the dot.com boom of 1999 when investors bought Internet-related company shares with apparently irrational enthusiasm. But over the longer term, through the ebbs and rises of the busi-

---

2. See "Google's Stock Offering Didn't Follow Script," *Billings Gazette,* 20 August 2004.
3. See "After failed IPO, Deja.Com Attempts to Reanimate," by Jason Chervokas, at NewYork.com, 4 February 2000.

ness cycle, Anglo-American capitalism seems to deliver high standards of living.

But Anglo-American shareholder capitalism is exceptional. Other systems predominate, and La Porta et al. (1999) find that the most common system of corporate governance in the world is *family capitalism,* in which the governance of a country's large corporations is entrusted to its wealthiest few families. This situation might arise if investors are deeply mistrustful of most companies and prefer to invest by entrusting their savings to persons of good reputation. Family firms constitute larger fractions of the stock markets of countries that provide investors with fewer legal rights. Respected business families can leverage their reputations by controlling many listed companies, and by having listed companies they hold control blocks of other listed companies, in successive tiers of intercorporate ownership. Such pyramidal business groups are also more common where investors' legal rights are weaker.

Yet family capitalism also has its problems. Corporate governance in many countries is remarkably concentrated in the hands of a few wealthy families. Governance can deteriorate over a wide swathe of the economy if the patriarch, or heir, controlling a large business group grows inept, excessively conservative, or overly protective of the status quo. Since the status quo clearly has advantages to these families, the last possibility is especially disquieting. For example, they might lobby to keep shareholder rights weak so that upstarts cannot compete for public investors' savings.

Another way investors can save is by putting money in a bank or other financial institution. The bank then lends the money to companies to buy factories, machinery, and technologies. Or sometimes the bank actually invests in other companies by buying their shares or bonds. This constitutes another way in which economies can accumulate and allocate capital. Banks play much greater capital allocation roles in German and Japanese capitalism than in the Anglo-American variant, although, as Morck and Nakamura (1999) and Fohlin (chap. 4 in this volume) show, their role may have been somewhat overstated in both countries.

In *bank capitalism,* oversight by bankers substitutes for shareholder diligence. Bankers monitor the governance of other firms and intervene to correct governance mistakes. If errant managers refuse to change their ways, banks withhold credit, starving the misgoverned firm of capital. As long as the bankers are altruistic and competent, this system can allocate capital efficiently. However, if a few key banks are themselves misgoverned, the ramifications are much worse and can create problems across all the firms that depend on that bank for capital. Bank capitalism delivered solid growth in postwar Germany and Japan, and in emerging economies like Korea. But in all three, overenthusiastic lending by a few top bankers to misgoverned firms created financial problems that continue to hinder macroeconomic growth.

Yet another way investors can save is by paying taxes and letting the state provide capital to businesses. In its extreme form, this is the guiding principle of socialism. But industrial policies—state-guided capital accumulation and allocation—are important in many free-market economies as well, especially historically. For example, the Fascist governments of Germany, Italy, and Japan all imposed this form of corporate governance upon virtually all their large corporations. More democratically formulated industrial policies played large roles in the economies of Canada, Japan, India, and all major continental European economies, as well as in many emerging-market economies. Nationalized industries in mid-twentieth-century Britain and massive defense and public works investments in the United States also count as industrial policies.

In *state capitalism,* public officials supervise corporate managers and intervene to correct any governance problems. If the bureaucratic overseers are able and altruistic, they can direct corporate decision making down paths that promote the general good. But intractable governance problems arise if the public officials have inadequate ability or knowledge to make such decisions or if they skew decisions to benefit politically favored persons or groups. State capitalism delivered brief periods of high growth in many countries, but it seems prone to serious governance problems of these sorts over the longer run.

Finally, investors can save by hoarding gold and silver coins. If people mistrust financial markets, wealthy families, bankers, and politicians, this may be the only option left. Murphy (chap. 3 in this volume) argues that a series of financial scandals and crises in France actually did reduce generations of Frenchmen to burying coins in their yards to provide for their futures, and that this mistrust retarded French financial development severely. When the savings of the broader public are unavailable to business, each company must grow using its earnings alone. This automatically allocates additional capital to those who already control companies, which is unlikely to be economically efficient. It also makes getting started very difficult for impecunious entrepreneurs.

Of course, no country is a pure example of any of these flavors of capitalism. Each variant of capitalism accounts for part of the capital formation in all the countries covered in this book. But the different variants clearly have different relative importance—both across countries and over time—and these differences are of great moment. Entrusting corporate governance to wealthy families, a few powerful bankers, or a cadre of bureaucrats might seem profoundly undemocratic to some. Entrusting it to anyone but civil servants, chosen by elected officials, might seem undemocratic to others. And entrusting corporate governance to anyone but reputable leading families might seem rashly irresponsible to still others. Moreover, as the chapters of this book show, impersonal stock markets, banks, wealthy families, and government bureaucrats each arise from different circumstances, operate in different ways, and bring different sets of issues to the fore.

Why Did Different Countries Follow Different Paths?

This volume contains one chapter describing the history of corporate governance in each member country in the Group of Seven (G7) of leading industrialized nations: Canada, France, Germany, Italy, Japan, the United Kingdom, and the United States. To these we add a chapter on the Netherlands, because it is the oldest capitalist economy, and many of the institutions that determine corporate control elsewhere originated there. We also add a chapter on Sweden because it is the standard bearer of an alternative *Swedish model* of capitalism tempered by social democracy. Finally, we add a chapter each on India and China—the world's two largest developing economies. This list is incomplete—omitting such important countries as Australia, Russia, Spain, and Switzerland, not to mention much of Asia and all of Latin America, Africa, and the Middle East. It is our hope that other students of corporate finance or economic history will fill in these gaps.

Early stages of the research that led to this volume showed that the first large corporations almost everywhere were family businesses, and that family firms predominate in most countries whose industrial histories are short. We therefore chose the countries enumerated above not because we believe they are more important, but because they all have reasonably long histories as industrial economies. Countries whose industrial histories go back only a generation or two, such as Korea, Malaysia, and Singapore, provide insufficient time for the forces that change corporate governance to act. While these countries are profoundly interesting from many perspectives, they are less able to provide insight into the evolution of corporate control than older industrial economies.

The authors of each study were invited to write a historical account of the evolution of control over their assigned country's large firms. The focus is primarily on large firms, for small firms everywhere tend to have controlling shareholders. Mom-and-pop stores in India, Italy, and the United States all tend to be owned by mom and pop. The different connotations of capitalism that spice political debates in different countries so differently are mainly due to differences in who controls countries' large corporations.

This section now summarizes the key results of each chapter. The next section condenses these findings into a general account of how corporate governance diverged as it did.

Canada

In chapter 1, Morck, Percy, Tian, and Yeung describe Canada's pre-industrial history—first as a French colony of resource extraction built around the fur trade, and then as first a French and then a British colony of settlement. Their theme is how the institutions built up during these colonial periods affected Canada's subsequent industrial development.

This study has two key points. The first is that Canada was a remarkably corrupt country until a few generations ago. Canada inherited from her French colonial history a disposition to mercantilist policies that invite official abuse. Indeed, the country was a veritable laboratory for Jean Baptiste Colbert, the father of French mercantilism. Subsequent British and Canadian elites preserved this disposition in the Canadian government, economy, and culture.

Their second key point is a remarkable pattern in Canadian corporate control. A full century ago, the large corporate sector looked much as it does now: a slight predominance of family-controlled pyramidal business groups supplemented by a large phalanx of freestanding widely held firms. However, half a century ago, the Canadian large corporate sector was composed mainly of freestanding widely held firms.

Through the first half of the twentieth century, wealthy Canadian families sold out into stock market booms, went bankrupt during recessions, diluted their stakes by issuing stock to fund takeovers, and liquidated corporate empires to pay estate taxes. The net effect was a marked eclipse of family control and pyramids. By the mid-twentieth century, Canada looked much like the United States does in Figure 1. Then, in the late 1960s and early 1970s, pyramidal groups resurged, and they had regained their gilded-age proportions by the century's end. The reasons for this are not fully clear. The authors speculate that an emasculation of the estate tax and a dramatic expansion of state intervention in the economy may have been factors. The erosion of the estate tax permitted large fortunes to survive and grow. Government intervention made political connections more valuable corporate assets than in the past, and pyramidal business groups may have been better than freestanding, widely held, and professionally managed firms at building and exploiting such connections.

Siegal's discussion of this chapter introduces an especially insightful division of institutional development into three stages. First come institutions, such as universal education, necessary for the production of entrepreneurial ideas. Then come institutions, such as financial systems, necessary to realize these ideas. Finally come institutions, such as public policy regarding inheritances, that prevent one period's entrepreneurs from entrenching themselves and blocking entrepreneurship by others.

China

Chapter 2, by Goetzmann and Köll, examines Chinese corporate governance in the late nineteenth and early twentieth centuries. This period is of interest because it corresponds to the beginning of China's industrialization and sees the attempted transplanting of Western institutions into a non-Western economy. Pre-Communist China's industrial development may thus offer more interesting lessons for modern emerging economies than does post-communist China, scraped clear of its non-Western traditions by decades of totalitarian Marxism. Certainly, for China herself, pre-revolutionary capitalism also provides a model of a "market economy with Chinese characteristics."

Late nineteenth-century China's first generation of industrial firms floated equity yet remained under state control. Modeled on the imperial salt monopoly, these ventures were financed and operated by private merchants, but ultimately controlled by imperial bureaucrats. Intended to re-assert China's pride and prestige, they sought to free China of foreign arms makers, shippers, and manufacturers. Industrialization was a means to this end, and to restoring China's traditional economic balance, but not an end in itself.

Imperial bureaucrats were accustomed to buying and selling offices and favors. Profitable businesses thus attracted more intensive bureaucratic oversight, and their earnings were quickly bled away. Although bureaucratic intervention protected these firms from competition, their merchant investors and managers became increasingly dissatisfied with the fees and bribes their civil service overlords demanded.

Having lost the Sino-Japanese War in 1895, the imperial government was forced to permit private foreign industry in treaty ports, which were subject to foreign law, and so could no longer prevent Chinese from establishing private industrial firms. New industrial businesses proliferated rapidly.

To regulate these, the imperial government enacted a new Corporations Law in 1904. An abbreviated version of contemporary English and Japanese law, it permitted limited liability and mandated shareholder meetings, elected boards, auditors, and detailed annual reports. Shares had traded in Shanghai since the 1860s, and equity participation was a long-established business principle. The 1904 code was thus a top-down revision of established practices, not a de novo introduction of business corporations. Its main innovation was the replacement of official patronage by a rules-based code of conduct designed to attract investment by public shareholders.

It was remarkably ineffective. Goetzmann and Köll examine a large industrial concern, Dasheng No. 1 Cotton Mill, to see how the 1904 law altered its governance and find virtually no effect. The founder and general manager, Zhang Jian, continued intermingling company and personal funds, ignored shareholder criticism of his donations of company money to political causes, and could not be removed because the corporate charter contained numerous provisions protecting his power. The absence of standard accounting rules made the disclosed financial accounts of minimal use.

The reasons beneath this failure are not fully clear. Perhaps cultural inertia prevented real change, and China's long culture of family business paying for the patronage of imperial bureaucrats proved too deeply ingrained. But the top-down reformers also saw capital markets only as sources of funds, overlooking their use as mechanisms for disciplining errant corporate insiders. Portfolio investors, unable to influence corporate governance after the fact, moved out of stocks. This kept the Chinese stock market illiquid and subject to severe boom-and-bust cycles. This, in turn, kept insiders from selling out and diversifying, underscoring the value of their private benefits of control.

In his discussion of this chapter, Perkins argues that China's traditional legal system was also an important factor. By empowering each county's magistrates as representative of the central government, judge, and prosecutor, this system prevented the disinterested enforcement of any laws, no matter how well written. Perkins stresses that the real lesson modern emerging economies should take from pre-Communist Chinese economic history is the critical importance of an independent and trustworthy judiciary.

France

The chapter on France by Murphy (chap. 3) stresses the importance of history. Its theme is that historical trauma generates strong aftershocks that affect the economy for generations, shaping the collective psyche to constrain the course of subsequent events. This chapter is an eloquent restatement of "path dependence"—the thesis that a simple historical accident can set the economy on one of many previously equally probable paths.

The shock that set the course of future French corporate governance was the implosion of the Mississippi Company in 1720. John Law (1671–1729), a Scottish convicted murderer, rescued France from the financial ruin wrought by the wars and court extravagance of Louis XIV. Law's Compagnie de l'Occident took on all French government debt in return for a monopoly on trade with Louisiana. Law's company issued shares and hyped their value, stimulating investment demand, which pushed their value up further, stimulating even more demand.

This bubble imploded in 1720, ruining the finances not only of the French kingdom but of much of her aristocracy and merchant elite. Joint stock companies were banned, and wise Frenchmen shunned financial markets and passed this wisdom on to their children.

The South Sea Company, a deliberate imitation of Law's French experiment in Britain, burst at about the same time and to somewhat the same effect. The Bubble Act of 1722 banned joint stock companies in Britain unless they secured a parliamentary charter. This meant that establishing each new joint stock company required an act of Parliament. The London Stock Exchange survived because preexisting sound British companies, such as the British East India Company and the Hudson's Bay Company, were grandfathered.

The reaction in France was much more severe—a profound rejection of banks, credit, and financial innovation and a retreat to the traditional French financial system, regulated by religious directives, which controlled methods of borrowing and lending, with the state constituting the main borrower. Religious prohibitions against interest meant that contracts had to separate the ownership of savings from the streams of revenue they produced. The notaries who drew up these contracts became surrogate bankers, but only in a very limited sense. While they arranged for the state to borrow by issuing annuities, Murphy argues that their role in financing the private sector was mainly limited to mortgages for real estate purchases. While they had some leeway around the usury laws, the notaries were unable to arrange the sorts of high-interest speculative debt appropriate to finance an industrial revolution. British companies needed parliamentary approval to issue shares, but French businesses had even more difficulty issuing shares, had no access to debt in the ordinary sense, and had to get by without a formal banking system.

In October 1789, the revolutionary government repealed the usury laws and resurrected Law's economic system, now issuing *assignats*. The only real difference was that these securities were backed by seized church estates, rather than a monopoly on trade with Louisiana. John Law was a central topic in the National Assembly debates. Murphy describes how the Abbé Maury produced a fistful of Law's banknotes, denouncing them as "fictive pledges of an immense and illusory capital, which I drew from a huge depot where they have been held for the instruction of posterity. With sorrow I look at these paper instruments of so many crimes, I see them still covered with the tears and blood of our fathers and I offer them today to the representatives of the French nation as beacons placed on the reefs so as to perpetuate the memory of this massive shipwreck."

Maury was ignored, and the Revolutionary government issued ever more *assignats* to cover its escalating expenses. France soon experienced full-blown hyperinflation and financial collapse. Kindleberger (1984, p. 99) writes that *assignats* "embedded paranoia about paper money and banks more deeply in the French subconscious."

The hyperinflation nourished the popular distrust of finance that Law had sown, and the French public took to hoarding gold and silver. Through most of the nineteenth century, most transactions were in specie, and coins still composed more than half of the money supply in 1885.

The French banking system was reinvigorated with the rise of the Crédit Mobilier, a universal bank established by Emile and Isaac Pereire, inspired by the utopian socialist ideals of Claude-Henri, comte de Saint-Simon, who saw banks as irrigation systems to bring capital from areas of overabundance to areas of drought. Hobbled by a portfolio of disastrous investments, the Crédit Mobilier collapsed in 1867, taking much of the French and European banking system down with it, and wise Frenchmen continued hoarding gold and silver coins.

The Paris bourse would occasionally achieve brief periods of activity in the late nineteenth and early twentieth centuries, but it would never again rival the economic importance of the London Stock Exchange. Kindleberger (1984, p. 113) estimates that "France lagged behind Britain in financial institutions and experience by a hundred years or so."

French businesses expanded, using the retained earnings of one company to build others, and the founding families of these business groups remained in control generation after generation. French Civil Law facilitated this course by making it virtually impossible for the owner of a business to bequeath it to anyone but his children. French tycoons with families cannot leave their fortunes to charitable foundations. Landes (1949) argues that France fell behind Britain because a preponderance of family control made large French corporations more conservative and reliant on government connections.

Severe financial trauma thus set France on a course of economic development that left wealthy families controlling her corporate sector under the watchful guidance of the state. Psychologists have only the vaguest understanding of why a similar trauma shatters some individuals' lives and barely affects others. Economists, likewise, need a deeper understanding of how economic trauma shapes institutional development. Murphy's chapter is a first step in that direction.

Daniel Raff, in his discussion of this chapter, raises a series of penetrating questions arising from Murphy's central ideas, and argues that we need much additional work along these lines.

Germany

In chapter 4, Fohlin argues that Germany's large universal banks were less important to its history of corporate governance than is commonly believed. German industrialization advanced rapidly in the late nineteenth century, financed by wealthy merchant families, foreign investors, small shareholders, and private banks. Industrial firms with bankers on their boards did not perform better than other firms.

German corporate governance appears thoughtfully developed in this era. The Company Law of 1870 created the current dual-board structure explicitly to protect small shareholders and the public from self-serving insiders. It also required greater uniformity and consistency in accounting, reporting, and governance. The Company Law of 1884 proscribed sitting on the same company's supervisory and management boards and thrust a "duty to become informed" on supervisory board directors. In the two decades before World War I, managerial turnover was highly sensitive to firm performance, suggesting that some form of disciplinary governance mechanism was functioning. Firms listed in Berlin stock exchange, which were most likely to be owned mainly by public shareholders, rather than founding families or other block holders, replaced management even more readily in response to poor performance.

German universal banks' proxy-voting powers arose from their role in placing new securities and in lending with shares as collateral. The Company Law of 1884 required a minimum turnout at a company's first shareholders meeting, and banks could accomplish this by holding proxies for small shareholders. Banks thus ended up voting the shares of companies that used their underwriting services. The Company Law of 1897 made exchange trading cumbersome, and this apparently moved share trading inside the big banks.

Under the Weimar Republic, ownership seems to have grown more dispersed, instilling fears of corporate takeovers in both founding families and their hired managers. To prevent such events, multiple voting shares and voting caps came into widespread usage.[4] Multiple voting shares were often bestowed on family members serving on supervisory boards and on the family's bank. Voting caps cap nonfamily shareholders' voting rights regardless of their actual ownership. Pyramids do not seem to have gained prominence, perhaps because these other devices permitted firms to tap public equity markets for capital without risking takeovers.

The National Socialist government established much of the modern foundations of German corporate governance. Invoking the *Führerprinzip* or *leader principle,* the Nazis' Shareholder Law of 1937 freed corporate managers and directors of their specific fiduciary duty to shareholders and substituted a general duty to all stakeholders—especially to the Reich. It banned voting by mail, and forced shareholders who could not vote in person to register their holdings with banks and entrust banks with proxy voting rights. This bestowed the large banks with voting control over much of the German large corporate sector. The Reich then took control of the banks.

Following the war, the banks were privatized, but the Nazi innovations of stakeholder rights and proxy voting by banks remained. Codetermination gave workers half the supervisory board, though Roe (2002) argues that companies simply shifted decisions out of the supervisory boards. Reforms in 1965 abolished the *Führerprinzip,* required banks to have written permission to vote proxies, and required that banks inform shareholders of how they voted. Shareholders could be anonymous again. Reforms in 1998 abolished voting caps, and the stock prices of affected companies rose sharply. Multiple voting shares remained unimportant.

Pyramiding apparently arose mainly after WWII. German households' ownership of shares declined sharply, from 48.6 percent of all shares in

---

4. Though Dunlavy (2004) argues for a much earlier provenance.

1950 to 17 percent in 1996. Meanwhile, intercorporate equity blocks rose from 18 percent in 1950 to 41 percent in 1996. The use of pyramids is far more extensive in the last few decades of the twentieth century than before. With multiple voting shares banned, pyramids may have become the preferred mechanism for retaining control while also using public shareholders' money.

The modern German economy thus consists primarily of family-controlled pyramidal groups and nominally widely held firms that are actually controlled by the top few banks via proxies. The leading banks collectively also control dominant blocks of their own shares. Bank voting control is less evident in smaller firms, which tend to have family control blocks. Recent reforms require banks to inform shareholders of their right to vote their own shares annually and to erect Chinese Walls around staff who decide how to vote at shareholder meetings.

Fohlin argues that patterns of corporate control in Germany are best explained by "a string of disastrous political institutions and movements in the aftermath of World War I, culminating in the Nazi regime, dismantled the rich, highly functioning, hybrid financial system of the Second Reich. The postwar political and legal climate, one that continues to suppress the liberal tradition of the pre–World War I era, seemingly prevents the old dual system from reemerging."

Dyck's discussion commends Fohlin for documenting the aborted dispersion of German shareholdings, but argues that a complete explanation needs further work. Dyck is unswayed by arguments diminishing the role of banks in German corporate governance, and argues that Germany's economic success warrants further study of how German firms avoid classic governance traps.

India

Chapter 5, by Khanna and Palepu, highlights India's long business history. Large-scale trading networks of merchants belonging to particular ethnic and sectarian groups go back centuries, and modern Indian business groups often correspond to these same groupings. When India began industrializing under the British Raj, these groups had the capital both to compete and to cooperate with Indian subsidiaries of the great British business groups of the era.

The Tata family, of priestly Parsi origin, controlled the largest business group in India for the past sixty years. The group grew to prominence under the Raj, nurtured by colonial government contracts and protected by imperial tariffs. The Tatas were neutral on independence, and so they lost favor when the Congress party took charge.

The Birla family, of the prosperous Marwari community, financed Mohandas Gandhi and the Congress party generously. Khanna and Palepu quote Sarojini Naidu, a Congress activist and poet, who quipped, "It took all Birla's millions to enable Gandhi to live in poverty. And he gave for free." The Birla group expanded dramatically in the postindependence period and by 1969 was the second largest Indian business group.

Thus, the early histories of India's two greatest business groups align with two theses of Ghemawat and Khanna (1998) and Khanna (2000): that such groups excel at doing deals with politicians and attain their position through political connections, and that they confer genuine economic advantages. Khanna and Palepu's finding that group firms are typically older and larger than independent firms is consistent with both.

Khanna and Palepu's key point is that the rankings of smaller Indian business groups are quite volatile, with groups appearing, rising, falling, and disappearing. Turnover around independence doubtless reflects the withdrawal from India of British business groups such as Martin Burn, Andrew Yule, and Inchcape. But volatility actually increases after independence, clearly showing that business groups did not always entrench their owners' economic positions. Such volatility speaks of a more entrepreneurial economy than is generally credited to postindependence India.

Thus, business groups as an organizational form persisted, but many individual business groups, especially smaller ones, did not. In the 1960s, Prime Minister Jawarharlal Nehru led India down a distinctly socialist path, building a dense thicket of regulation and bureaucratic oversight that came to be called the License Raj. Nehru's original motive seems to have been a desire to curb the power of India's large business groups following a series of official reports that documented evidence of big business houses exerting significant influence over the economy and exploiting growth opportunities through favorable access to finance and government permits. Nehru's daughter, Prime Minister Indira Gandhi, asserted even greater state control over private-sector firms' pursuit of growth opportunities, access to finance, and collaboration with foreign partners and forced many multinational companies out of the country. This policy proved economically disastrous, and a period of slow deregulation began in the mid-1980s. A financial crisis spurred a much more radical liberalization in the 1990s.

Turnover among smaller business groups during all of this might indicate an entrepreneurial economy, in which innovative new businesses arise and old ones die out. Khanna and Palepu argue that business groups retained an advantage over individual firms throughout because they could better bridge institutional gaps—like dysfunctional capital, labor, and product markets. But these benefits certainly accrue mostly to very large business groups. Smaller ones containing only a few firms cannot avoid markets as well as huge groups containing larger reservoirs of capital, labor, and products of all kinds that can be allocated internally.

But the larger groups also devoted huge resources, establishing de facto embassies in New Delhi staffed by legions of experts in all manner of bureaucratic red tape. The License Raj was clearly constructed to tie down the great business groups, but its actual effect may have been the opposite. Only the largest groups could absorb the huge fixed cost of retaining the bureaucratic expertise needed to navigate the maze.

Under Indira Gandhi, the Birla group was accused of manipulating the licensing system. Stung by this unexpected criticism, the Birlas shifted their expansion plans overseas. Given India's strict foreign exchange controls at the time, this surely required official acquiescence. A string of profitable overseas subsidiaries put substantial group cash flows well beyond the reach of the minions of New Delhi, enabling the group to expand rapidly within India once the License Raj was dismantled. One interpretation of all this is that the size and prominence of the Birla group reflects their entrepreneurial tendencies in handling the licensing restrictions, rather than simple political rent seeking.

The Tatas felt discriminated against under the License Raj, and this may well have been so. Nonetheless, they survived and prospered, and grew increasingly entrepreneurial and innovative to compensate for their relative lack of political influence. By remaining economically dominant, the Tata group confirms that government connections are but one factor underlying the success of Indian businesses.

Ultimately, the chapter argues that large family business groups likely persisted because they bridged institutional voids created by dysfunctional markets and weak economic institutions. But even beyond this, the chapter argues that the Tata group in particular survives and prospers because of genuine entrepreneurship. They stress the role of the Tatas in developing India's software industry. This industry is thought to prosper precisely because it is less dependent on India's creaking domestic institutions and markets, so groups' advantage in this sector should be minimal. Perhaps the Tatas supply entrepreneurial activity and prosper because this is in short supply in emerging economies like India.

Mody's discussion of this chapter begins with a comparison of Korea, whose development depended on large family-controlled business groups, and Taiwan, whose development was mainly due to smaller firms. He points out that both countries grew rapidly, but he suggests that Korean groups eventually became a problem because they made entrepreneurship by outsiders difficult. Mody recounts the Bombay Plan, in which the leaders of India's most powerful business families "called on government support for industrialization, including a direct role for the government in the production of capital goods, foreshadowing postindependence Indian planning, typically considered an outgrowth of socialist ideas drawn either from the Soviet Union or the so-called Fabian socialists." He argues that this plan, proposed just before independence, shows that its sponsors, including the Tata and Birla families, did actively seek partnership with the Congress party government they saw approaching.

Italy

Chapter 6, by Aganin and Volpin, shows that family-controlled business groups were more powerful in the middle of the century than at either end of it, and that the stock market was more important at either end of the century than at its midpoint.

Laws and politics clearly have some explanatory power. At the beginning of the century, the Italian government had little interest in direct intervention in the economy. However, all three major Italian investment banks collapsed in 1931, and the Fascist government took on their holdings of industrial shares and imposed a legal separation of investment from commercial banking. The shares were turned over to the Istituto per la Riconstruzione Italiana (IRI), which would persist as a large state-controlled pyramidal group. After the Second World War, Italy's governments maintained a direct role in the economy, propping up financially troubled companies and using its corporate governance power to direct economic growth, especially in capital-intensive sectors. Postwar governments founded the Ente Nazionale Idrocarburi (ENI) in 1952 to control firms in the chemical, oil, and mining sectors; the Ente Partecippazioni e Finanziamento Industrial Manifatturiera (EFIM) in 1962 to control electric and other companies; and the Società di Gestioni e Partecipazioni Industriali (GEPI) in 1972 to intervene in the Southern Italian economy. Each of these business groups controlled numerous listed companies and was directed by a forceful, politically appointed CEO.

Aganin and Volpin thus argue that, since postwar Italian politicians opted to allocate capital via an industrial policy rather than via the financial system, they saw no great need for investor protection. Investors opted for government bonds, rather than shares, and the Italian stock market shrank steadily through the middle of the century. New entrants found public share issues very expensive, while politicians assisted established large business groups with cheap capital. New publicly traded family groups emerged rarely, and always with strong political support. Most Italian firms remained unlisted and were operated by founding families in small-scale niche markets.

This locked in a sort of *state and family capitalism*. Listed firms were mostly organized into pyramidal groups controlled by either the state or old families. The corporate governance of Italy's large listed firms was thus entrusted either to politically appointed bureaucrats or to wealthy old families who transmitted power from generation to generation.

Italy's industrial policies directed subsidized capital to both sorts of business groups, which raised public debt and taxes to unsustainable levels by the 1990s. A sweeping privatization program and improved legal protection for public shareholders reinvigorated the stock market. Formerly unlisted companies opted to go public, and the stock market grew further.

Investors, increasingly conscious of the need for good corporate governance, continue to demand stronger property rights protection.

Japan

The history of corporate governance in Japan is more complicated and variegated than in any other major country. Consequently, chapter 7, by Morck and Nakamura, takes the form of a narrative history more than do many of the other contributions to this volume.

Prior to 1868, Japan was a deeply conservative and isolationist country. Business families were at the bottom of a hereditary caste system—beneath priests, warriors, peasants, and craftsmen. Unsurprisingly, this moral inversion led to stagnation. Yet the necessity of running a densely populous country forced Japan's feudal shoguns to give prominent mercantile families, like the Mitsui and Sumitomo, steadily greater influence.

When Admiral Perry, in an early example of American unilateralism, bombarded Tokyo until Japan opened her markets to American traders, the shogun acquiesced and a cadre of rash young samurai warriors seized power, justifying their coup as the restoration of the Meiji emperor, who nonetheless remained a figurehead. The Meiji Restoration leaders planned to defeat the foreigners and restore Japan's splendid isolation, but they soon realized that beating the foreigners meant learning their ways. The Meiji leadership sent Japan's best students to universities throughout the world to learn about foreign technology, business, and governments, and to report back. The result was a cultural, economic, and political reinvention of Japan, in which the reformers cobbled together a new system based on what they saw as global best practice in legal, economic, and social institutions. The government founded state-owned enterprises to bring all manner of Western industry to Japan, and built up huge debts in the process. To extricate itself, the Meiji government conducted a mass privatization, in which most of these enterprises were sold to the Mitsui and Sumitomo families and to a few other family-controlled business groups that were gaining prominence, such as Mitsubishi. These groups, called *zaibatsu,* were family-controlled pyramids of listed corporations, much like those found elsewhere in the world. Later, other groups like Nissan, a pyramidal business group with a widely held firm at its apex, joined in as Japan's economy roared into the twentieth century. Thus, Japan began its industrialization with a mixture of family and state capitalism. Shareholders eagerly bought shares, especially in numerous subsidiaries floated by these great business groups.

The 1920s and early 1930s were depressionary periods and exposed the weaknesses and strengths of different pyramidal structures. Groups like the Mitsui, Sumitomo, and Mitsubishi pyramids, whose banks (or de facto banks) were located near their apexes, survived. Groups like the Suzuki pyramid, whose bank was controlled but not owned by the Suzuki family, failed. It seems likely that the Suzuki structure disposed the controlling family to transfer funds out of the bank and into firms whose financial fate affected family wealth, and that this rendered such groups financially unstable during downturns. The prolonged economic stagnation eroded the public's appreciation of family capitalism, and economic reformers lambasted the wealthy families for putting their rights as shareholders ahead of the public interest and for their fixation on short-term earnings and dividends rather than long-term investment.

In the 1930s, the military slowly consolidated power by strategically assassinating civilian government leaders and replacing them with military officers. Although Japan's military government was decidedly fascist, its economic policies borrowed unblushingly from Soviet practices. The government freed corporate boards of their duty to shareholders—meaning the families and corporate large shareholders—and limited dividends. Military representatives sat on all major boards and supervised the implementation of centrally directed production quotas. Prices and wages were also determined by central planners. Although the de jure ownership rights of Japanese shareholders were never formally annulled, the 1945 American occupation force took charge of an economy not greatly different from the post-Socialist economies of Eastern Europe in the early 1990s.

The American occupation government, though led by General MacArthur, was staffed with Roosevelt "New Dealers." As the chapter by Becht and De Long shows, the Roosevelt administration had successfully forced the dismantlement of America's *zaibatsu,* the great family-controlled pyramidal groups that had previously dominated its economy. The New Dealers resolved to do the same in Japan. Family and intercorporate equity blocks were confiscated and sold to the public. The families received nominal compensation in bonds, and the proceeds from the equity sales accrued to the government. By 1952, Japan's great corporations were almost all freestanding and widely held, just as those of the United Kingdom and United States are at present. Corporate raiders soon emerged and launched two major waves of hostile takeovers of firms they viewed as misgoverned. As in the United Kingdom and United States today, hostile takeovers were only a small fraction of total merger activity, but they affected large firms and drew disproportionate publicity. As Morck, Shleifer, and Vishny (1988) stress, the threat of a hostile takeover is probably more important to promoting good governance than its occurrence.

But takeovers did not lead to the improved governance the raiders desired. The professional managers now governing Japan's great corporations were not constrained by regulations, laws, or customs to protect the property rights of public shareholders. Initially, a popular takeover defense was *greenmail*—the target firm's managers would pay the raider (with shareholders' money) to back off. These payments likely only emphasized the target firms' poor governance to other potential raiders.

Ultimately, a more effective takeover defense was devised—the *keiretsu.* In the United States, target firms sometimes obstruct a raider by placing a block of stock with a friendly shareholder, called a *white squire,* or by bringing in a rival acquirer, a *white knight,* whose management is friendly to the target's managers. The *keiretsu* defense, a variant along the same lines, involves a group of firms run by mutually friendly managers exchanging small blocks of stock with each other. Even though each firm holds only a tiny stake in every other firm, these stakes collectively sum to effective control blocks. Every firm in the *keiretsu* group is thus controlled collectively by all the other firms in the group. *Keiretsu* groups arose in two waves, first in the 1950s and then in the 1960s. Japan's experiment with Anglo-American shareholder capitalism was short-lived, and the *keiretsu* system remains in place today.

Although their primary functions were to lock in corporate control rights, both *zaibatsu* and *keiretsu* were probably also rational responses to a variety of institutional failings. Successful *zaibatsu* and *keiretsu* were enthusiastic political rent seekers, raising the possibility that large corporate groups are better at influencing government than freestanding firms. In the case of some *zaibatsu* and many *keiretsu,* this rent seeking probably retarded financial development. This, and the probable misallocation of substantial amounts of capital by poorly governed *keiretsu* firms, appears to have created long-term economic problems that slowed Japan's growth through the 1990s.

Sheldon Garon's discussion argues that more attention should be paid to precisely who made which decisions in importing Western institutions. He also points out that little is said in the chapter about small and medium-sized firms, despite their importance. He also takes issue with the view that Tokugawa Japan isolated itself from the rest of the world and that Japan's wartime economy resembled Soviet central planning. He points out that recent thinking stresses Tokugawa Japan's contacts via foreigners in Nagasaki and rightly argues that wartime Japan imitated National Socialist central planning, which is described in detail in the chapter by Fohlin. We recognize this but remain impressed by the remarkable similarity of National Socialist, Fascist, and Soviet socialist central planning, as described by Silverman (1998), Guerin (1945), and Hosking (1985), respectively, among others.

The Netherlands

The Netherlands has the oldest stock market in the world, and its entrepreneurs largely invented the joint-stock corporation. Chapter 8, in which de Jong and Röell discuss the history of corporate governance in the Netherlands, is therefore especially enlightening. The world's first great limited-liability, widely held, joint-stock company, the Dutch East Indies Company, or Vereenigde Oostindische Compagnie, was founded in 1602.

The world's first great corporate governance dispute quickly followed in 1622, when the managers, who had floated the stock as participation in a limited-term partnership with a liquidating dividend in twenty years, decided to keep the "astonishingly lucrative" enterprise continuing indefinitely. The investors were outraged, but the government of the Dutch Republic saw the company as a weapon in its conflicts with Spain and supported management. The dividend stream was large enough that investors who wanted out could sell their shares to others. This was perhaps better than a liquidating dividend since the seller need not wait for the company's fixed lifetime to expire. Nonetheless, vociferous shareholder complaints about inadequate disclosure and dividend payouts continued and are preserved in the company archives. Other widely held firms followed suit, and the Dutch stock markets remained Europe's financial heart for a century.

Among other things, spillovers from the series of French financial crises, which Murphy discusses in chapter 3, undermined Dutch investors' confidence in financial markets—slowly through the eighteenth century, and then quite rapidly during the French occupation (1795–1813). In 1804, the French imposed a version of their civil code. This was widely viewed as less sophisticated than the indigenous legal system. It jettisoned two centuries of Dutch accumulated legal wisdom and inflicted French investors' aversion of financial markets upon the Netherlands. The French civil code, along with a public debt (bequeathed by the French administration) of more than four times national income, and a prolonged industrial dislocation caused by the carve-out of Belgium as a separate state, made the first part of the nineteenth century a period of slow growth.

Industrial development in the second half of the nineteenth century was financed mainly with retained earnings from family firms that had slowly accumulated wealth over the previous half-century. Wealthy families often bought into new firms' commercial paper, or *prolongatie,* and were expected to roll these investments over indefinitely. Listed domestic shares played a role toward the century's end, but repeated egregious looting of listed companies by insiders limited public investors' appetites. Many small Dutch investors, whose families had lost heavily in the official defaults of the French revolutionary era, apparently preferred to save by hoarding coins. Although Dutch markets were energetic throughout the nineteenth century, their most active listings were foreign government bonds and American railroad and industrial stocks.

During the twentieth century, a clear trend away from family control and toward professional management is evident. Public equity issues and long-term bank loans played an important role in an industrialization boom from 1895 to roughly 1920, reinvigorating the stock markets. Unlike Germany, the Dutch kept bankers to a secondary role in the governance and financing of industrial firms. Workers' corporate governance voices grew louder in the final decades of the twentieth century, but they remain more muted than in Germany.

Despite the rise of public equity participation in Dutch firms, de Jong and Röell conclude that real decision-making power remains with self-perpetuating top corporate executives, entrenched behind formidable takeover defenses. These defenses differ from those in Anglo-American finance and so merit mention. Reforms emulating German codetermination mandated that companies establish supervisory boards but gave shareholders no real role in choosing their members. These self-perpetuating supervisory boards thus severed managers' responsibility to shareholders. Another entrenchment device is *priority shares,* to whose owners are relegated key corporate governance decisions, such as board appointments. Other so-called *oligarchic devices* relegate power over key decisions, like payout policies, to organs other than the management board. Voting caps, restricted voting shares, and super-voting shares are also widely used. From the end of World War II through the 1970s, another popular entrenchment device was *preference shares,* issued to white squire shareholders at deep discounts and often carrying superior voting rights. Yet another device is to place all voting shares with an income trust and then let public investors buy units in that trust. Finally, interlocking directorships are commonplace, apparently giving the Dutch corporate sector a clubby air.

De Jong and Röell find that these devices are associated with depressed shareholder value. Many of these entrenchment devices have come (or are) in conflict with European Union directives, and they suggest that other entrenchment devices, like pyramidal groups, will grow more popular in their place.

Högfeldt's discussion compares the Netherlands to Sweden, stressing the remarkably reticent role of Dutch banks compared to Swedish ones, the remarkable array of takeover defenses in Dutch listed firms, and the apparent acquiescence of Dutch politicians to these defenses.

Sweden

Swedes are justly proud of their unique model of highly egalitarian social democracy. Yet chapter 9, by Peter Högfeldt, shows that Swedes also entrust their wealthiest families with an extraordinary concentration of corporate governance power.

Högfeldt argues that this concentration occurs because of persistent Social Democratic political influence, not despite it. The Social Democrats became de facto guarantors of family capitalism because of a surprising commonality of interests. Social Democratic politicians wanted a stable large corporate sector controlled by Swedes, who were thought more susceptible than foreign owners to political pressure and hence more likely to buy into Social Democracy eventually. Sweden's wealthy families, who used small blocks of super-voting shares to hold together their vast pyramidal business groups, wanted to preserve the status quo. Buying into Social Democracy apparently seemed a reasonable price for policies that locked in their corporate governance powers.

Högfeldt argues that the extensive separation of ownership from control in these pyramidal structures makes external financing expensive relative to retained earnings, and so encourages existing firms to expand and discourages new firms from listing. He calls this a political pecking order theory of financing. To this, the Social Democrats added tax subsidies for firms that finance expansions with retained earnings and heavy taxation of returns to public shareholders.

These entrenched mutually supportive political and corporate elites provided Swedes solid growth until the 1970s, when the economy proved unexpectedly inflexible in dealing with external shocks. Institutions designed to stabilize the largest firms and prevent upstarts from arising to challenge them were ill suited to dealing with a rapidly shifting comparative advantage in the global economy. Social Democracy had redistributed income dramatically but could not manage the necessary redistribution of property rights and wealth.

The result, according to Högfeldt, is an increasingly frail economy dominated by elderly and infirm companies, still controlled by the same wealthy families that bought into the Social Democratic experiment more than half a century ago.

Röell's discussion stresses the differences between Sweden and the Netherlands—both small, northern European social democracies. She argues that voting caps and other residues of Napoleonic civil law entrenched insiders in the Netherlands while dual class shares and pyramids entrenched Swedish insiders. Both sorts of entrenchment are costly, and tallying up these costs is an important research problem.

The United Kingdom

The chapter on the United Kingdom by Franks, Mayer, and Rossi compares a cadre of firms founded in 1900 to another founded in 1960. The authors find that ownership grows diffuse in both sets of firms at roughly the same rate. Based on this, they argue that the forces that made founding families withdraw from corporate governance in the modern United Kingdom also operated a century ago.

They argue that shareholder rights in the United Kingdom were extremely weak until the latter part of the twentieth century and so dispute the contention of La Porta et al. (1999) that shareholder legal protection permits diffuse ownership in the United Kingdom. If this were true, they argue that corporate ownership should have been highly concentrated earlier in the century, which they do not observe.

Providing a descriptive summary of United Kingdom corporate governance in greater generality, they further argue that pyramids gained importance at the middle of the century. They suggest that improved corporate disclosure, implemented in 1948, made hostile takeovers less risky for raiders, and that pyramids developed as a defense against hostile takeovers. However, they argue that institutional investors saw serious governance problems in these structures and lobbied to have them undone. British institutional investors successfully pressed the London Stock Exchange to adopt a takeover rule whereby any bid for 30 percent or more of a listed firm must be a bid for 100 percent. Franks et al. propose that this rule made pyramidal business groups untenable as takeover defenses and that continued pressure from institutional investors on boards rapidly rid Britain of these structures.

Franks et al. also argue that concentrated corporate control and pyramidal groups are of more value to insiders elsewhere than in Britain. This is because these ownership structures permit corporate insiders to extract private benefits of control. However, they propose that British corporate insiders were and are governed by higher standards of ethical conduct, which preclude the extraction of such private benefits. Given this, British corporate insiders were more readily convinced to sell their control blocks and dismantle their pyramids. Thus, the current diffuse ownership of British corporations came to prevail early in the twentieth century and still persists.

Eichengreen's discussion raises further questions. The Great Depression was a critical juncture in the evolution of corporate governance in many countries, yet it is little discussed. Why were British banks content without the corporate governance powers of their German or Swedish peers? He notes that Sylla and Smith (1995) emphasize the Directors Liability Act of 1890, which made company directors liable for statements in prospectuses soliciting buyers for company shares, and the Companies Act of 1900, which strengthened the principle of compulsory corporate disclosure, as the explanation for why British financial markets developed so rapidly around the turn of the century. He speculates that shareholder rights might have been stronger in early twentieth-century Britain than Franks et al. admit.

The United States

The chapter on the United States by Becht and DeLong explores how that country came to have the atypically diffuse corporate ownership evident in figure 1. The great corporations of other countries are usually organized into business groups that are controlled by wealthy, old families or powerful financial intermediaries. Great corporations in the United States are, for the most part, managed by career professionals and freestanding—they do not have listed subsidiaries or parents.

These differences are developments of the twentieth century, for Moody (1904) describes an America that was more "normal." Powerful banking houses and plutocratic families controlled much of the large corporate sector, wielding their corporate governance power robustly, monitoring, choosing, and replacing managers and setting corporate direction.

But by the 1930s, all of this had changed. A remarkable democratization of shareholding took place between World War I and the end of World War II. The benefits of diversification depend on the depth of the stock market. High-pressure war-bond sales campaigns in 1917–18, popular magazines on share ownership, and popular media coverage of Wall Street celebrities brought middle American wealth into the stock market, vastly deepening it and thus making the sacrifice of control for diversification more attractive than elsewhere.

The burgeoning Progressive Movement deplored both the concentration of economic power and the way business oligarchs like J. P. Morgan, the Rockefellers, and others ruling vast pyramidal groups "turned conflict of interest into a lifestyle." Progressive politicians pilloried the "robber barons" of industry, their heirs, and J. P. Morgan.

Both to obtain the benefits of diversification and to relieve their pummeling by the progressive press, many wealthy families sold majorities of their firms' shares into the stock markets. Of course, most of these families at first retained control through voting trusts, staggered boards, larger and more complicated pyramidal holding companies with multiple classes of stock, and other entrenchment devices.

But progressive politicians were on a roll, and they pressed antitrust regulators into service. In 1911, they succeeded in breaking up the Standard Oil Trust, a huge group of petroleum and industrial companies formerly controlled by the Rockefeller family. Over the subsequent decades, these emerged as freestanding, widely held, and professionally managed entities. Becht and DeLong track this process in detail for Standard Oil of New Jersey.

America's response to the Great Depression then razed much of what *family capitalism* remained. Two great pyramids, the Insull and van Sweringen business groups, collapsed after the 1929 crash. These high-profile collapses appear to have linked the Depression with highly concentrated corporate control in the public mind, justifying a barrage of progressive reform. The Glass-Steagall Act of 1933 pared commercial from investment banking. The Public Utility Company Holding Companies Act of 1935 forbade pyramidal control of utility companies. A series of regulatory reforms governing banks, insurance companies, mutual funds, and pension funds prevented any of these organizations from accumulating any serious corporate governance influence either.

The activist U.S. courts intervened further to keep shareholdings dispersed. For example, in 1957 the Supreme Court ordered the DuPont family to sell its equity block in General Motors to prevent DuPont from obtaining "an illegal preference over its competitors in the sale to General Motors of its products."

Becht and DeLong then explore 1937 data on blockholdings in the top listed 200 U.S. firms. Of these, 24 are subsidiaries in pyramids and only 34 have no controlling shareholder. They explore the history of the last and find that they became widely held when their founding families sold out, either directly or with trust promoters as intermediaries. Some of this might have been market timing—selling stocks for more than their fundamental values during bubbles. Most of it was probably founding families appreciating the value of diversification in a deep stock market. These wealthy families often retained influence on their boards without holding control blocks.

Stung by progressive-era condemnation, they often turned to philanthropy, distancing themselves and their heirs even further from governance issues. Thus, modern Americans associate the names Rockefeller, Harkness, Carnegie, and Guggenheim with the performing arts, universities, and museums, not with the great business groups that built those fortunes.

Activist judges and progressive politicians, aided by fortune, thus effectively entrusted the governance of America's great corporations to professional managers. The Securities and Exchanges Act of 1934 relegated to management control over who can stand for election to boards, and left boards to monitor management. Although the hostile takeovers of the 1980s disrupted this arrangement for some firms, and some U.S. institutional investors are clearing their throats, this situation has kept most American firms freestanding and professionally run ever since.

Richard Sylla's discussion contrasts Becht and DeLong's arguments with those of Dunlavy (2004), who contends that by 1900 American firms were already exceptional in having one-vote-per-share voting rights, giving large shareholders more say in corporate affairs than small shareholders. In Europe, Dunlavy argues, shareholder voting rights were more "democratic" in limiting the power of large shareholders, as was the case earlier in the United States. Sylla notes that Alexander Hamilton proposed such limits on large blockholder votes as necessary to prevent a few large players from dominating corporate policies. We are impressed that Hamilton was clearly more concerned about entrenched large blockholders, not professional managers, abusing small shareholders, as are students of corporate governance in most modern countries other than the United Kingdom and United States.

What Are the Common Factors?

Each chapter highlights the intricate complexity of financial history. Yet there are common threads spanning many countries. This section tracks some of the most visible of these threads and ties them to current thinking about the reasons why corporate governance is so different in different countries.

Accidents of History

The clearest lesson, evident in every chapter, is that "things happen," and constrain what can happen next. The history of corporate governance, like other historical processes, is *path dependent.*

Had France not suffered repeated financial collapses at the hands of John Law, the Revolutionary Assembly, and the Crédit Mobilier, shareholder rights in that country might have solidified much earlier and much harder. Murphy argues that the formation of new joint-stock companies and other large enterprises essentially ceased in France until 1840 and resumed only very slowly thereafter. Other students of European history make similar points—Frentrop (2003, p. 137) writes that "following the experience of 1720, French public opinion developed a violent distaste for anything to do with financial markets." He goes on to argue that "A similar opinion was expressed in the Netherlands." Frentrop argues that the Napoleonic Code, which French armies spread across the continent in the early nineteenth century, carried that distaste, and was far less conducive to large business undertakings than was the previous Dutch legal system. Perhaps accidents of history explain the findings of La Porta et al. (1999) that countries with legal systems based on the Napoleonic Code have stunted financial systems.

Yet other countries underwent financial crises and responded entirely differently. Britain's South Sea bubble closely paralleled Law's Mississippi bubble, and its response, the Bubble Act, hampered equity markets for generations afterward. But sound ventures like the British East India Company and the Hudson's Bay Company sustained a financial sector that soon boasted sophisticated merchant banks.[5] Psychologists puzzle over why some people are devastated by emotional traumas that others recover from on their own. Economists, too, understand little about how crises affect institutional development. The histories in this volume show this to be an important fault in our discipline.

China's stock market, founded in the 1870s, saw the same sorts of manipulation and insider trading that characterized other markets around the world, and collapsed in 1883—and again in 1922. Perhaps these misfortunes pushed China off a path to free market democracy she might otherwise have followed. Chinese capitalism never recovered, shares in Chinese companies grew illiquid, and the faltering free market economy fell to Mao's Socialist revolution.

In 1933, a committee of experts assembled under the Weimar Republic completed its deliberations on separating commercial from investment banking. Had it favored this separation, German banks would have relinquished most of their corporate governance influence over nonfinancial

5. See Kindleberger (1978).

firms, and German capitalism would have developed far differently than it did. However, the committee favored the status quo—possibly because its chairman, Reichsbank President Hjalmar Horace Greeley Schacht feared setting a berserker like Gottfried Feder loose to reform the system.[6] Feder, a founding member of the National Socialist Party and Hitler's banking advisor, was famous for his 1919 *Manifesto on Breaking the Shackles of Interest* and advocated the nationalization of all banks and the total abolishment of interest.

Perhaps China, Germany, Japan, and Italy might have evolved ingrained cultures of shareholder capitalism had they avoided prolonged economic collapses in the 1920s and 1930s—and if Fascism and Socialism had been less entrancing. Had Socialism been less in vogue in the mid-twentieth century, perhaps India, the Netherlands, and Sweden might have gone the route of American corporate governance. If Colbert had been British, the English-speaking world had had a few more financial crises, or Fascism and Socialism had had more persuasive English-speaking advocates, would America and Britain be dominated by large family-controlled business groups?

But concluding that everything is a concordance of accidents is too simple. However satisfying that view to pure historians of individual countries, economic history is about patterns and regularities amid those accidents. Fortunately, many issues that ought to affect corporate governance are already highlighted in the literature. Even more fortunately, the chapters in this volume present a wealth of detail that helps fill in the gaps. It would be wonderful for economists if we could conclude that one theory is correct and discard the others, but economics is rarely so simple. All of the major theories that purport to explain historical and cross-country differences in corporate control find support, though some require modification in passing.

Ideas

Wars, upheavals, and many other catastrophes affected many countries simultaneously but triggered different reactions in different countries—perhaps depending on the popularity or unpopularity of certain ideologies at that point in time. Rarely, as after the English Civil War and American Revolution, private property rights coalesced. Perhaps more typically, French economic and political turmoil in the 1720s resurrected traditional Catholic restraints on business. More turmoil at the end of the eighteenth century institutionalized a suspicion of all things financial, and wars exporting the French Revolution spread this to the Netherlands and elsewhere. The chapters in this book collectively suggest the importance, for good and ill, of ideologies at critical moments when economies are ripe for institutional transformations.

One such critical moment was the Great Depression of the 1930s, when

---

6. See Kleeberg (1987) for details.

different countries set off in different directions that wrought today's differences in corporate governance. Financial catastrophes in many countries in the 1920s and 1930s, and ideological reactions to them, deeply affected their subsequent evolution of corporate control.

In the 1930s, the United States was deeply influenced by the progressive ideology of Louis Brandeis, Thorsten Veblen, and others. Roosevelt's New Dealers realigned American institutions to this ideology when the Great Depression undermined popular faith in America's older institutions. Dispersing economic power as widely as possible was a key part of this. Thus, the American government undertook to break up that country's great pyramidal corporate groups by banning large pyramidal groups from controlling public utility companies, applying taxes to intercorporate dividends, and strengthening public shareholders' property rights over their investments.[7] This fortuitous coincidence of ideology and opportunity to act created America's exceptional large corporate sector composed mainly of freestanding widely held firms.

In Sweden, the same Great Depression had completely different results. The ideology waiting in the wings in Sweden was Social Democracy. When Swedish voters lost faith in their traditional institutions, Social Democrats took power and radically concentrated economic power in two ways. First, the state assumed power over the commanding heights of the Swedish economy. Second, widespread corporate bankruptcies left large banks, like that owned by the Wallenberg family, holding control blocks in most large Swedish companies. These banks reorganized these companies into the large pyramidal groups that currently dominate the Swedish economy. Högfeldt (chap. 9 in this volume) argues that the Social Democrats and these powerful families developed a symbiotic relationship—the families supported the Social Democrats, who enacted policies that favored large old firms and hampered upstart firms.

Mixtures of Socialist and nationalist ideologies emerged in Germany, Italy, and Japan during the Great Depression. Ultimately, radical nationalists won in all three, but not without adopting many Socialist policies. In the 1920s and 1930s, the major German banks had accumulated huge holdings of their own shares in efforts to stabilize their own stock prices. The National Socialists confiscated these holdings, effectively nationalizing the banks and imposing party control over their proxy voting processes. Multiple voting shares were nullified, except of family firms controlled by gentiles, and voting caps did not apply to banks voting the holdings of individual shareholders by right of proxy. In this way, the Reich de facto nationalized the greater part of the German economy while leaving the formalities of private ownership in place.[8] The Fascist government

---

7. See Morck (2004b).
8. See Kleeberg (1987, p. 83).

of Italy nationalized the banks, which had seized control blocks in many large bankrupt companies. Italy's postwar governments retained many aspects of Mussolini's economic system, including large pyramidal groups of listed companies with state holding companies at their apexes. Japan's military government likewise placed military representatives on all boards to ensure that large firms were managed patriotically and not for mere profit.

In Canada, socialists and progressives trumpeted opposing visions of reform in the 1930s, letting old-line parties hold the center and retain power. This preserved its prewar system of pyramidal groups. The corporate governance of large Canadian firms changed only gradually over the subsequent decades. Britain, France, and the Netherlands also seem to have preserved their pre-Depression systems of corporate governance.

Another example arises in connection with India and other postcolonial economies. Das (2002) and others argue that intellectual fashions at the London School of Economics adversely affected India's economic policies, including corporate governance. Similar effects elsewhere in the third world seem highly plausible.

Families

A purpose of this book was to provide a richer rendering of corporate governance systems throughout the world. The geographic and chronological scope of the project allows us to make observations as well as raise important questions regarding how enterprise is organized in different parts of the world. Importantly, the book speaks to the neglect of family enterprise relative to its role in capitalist economies. Family capitalism contributes to the wealth and/or poverty of a nation, with appreciation to Adam Smith and David Landes.

A theme throughout this volume is the importance of large family business groups in most developed economies. This confirms La Porta et al. (1999) and Burkart, Panunzi, and Shleifer (2003), who conclude (p. 2167) that most large businesses throughout the world "are controlled by their founders, or by the founder's families and heirs." Moreover, there is no evidence of a uniform natural transition from family capitalism to managerial capitalism. Franks, Mayer, and Rossi's chapter describes such a transition in the United Kingdom, and in chapter 8 de Jong and Röell describe a form of managerial capitalism that is perhaps native to the Netherlands. In chapter 11 Becht and DeLong describe the transition from family to managerial capitalism in the United States as a convolution of accidents and America's unique progressive ideology. In chapter 4 Fohlin shows that, although Germany developed a variant of managerial capitalism because of banking laws left in place by the National Socialists, large family firms and groups remain very important there. Japan's variant of managerialism was a forced postwar transplant of American institutions. In Canada, managerial capitalism displaced family groups through the first part of the century, and then retreated before a resurgence of family groups. Else-where, family business groups were seldom challenged except by state-owned enterprises. Professional managers, where they exist at all, are merely hired help employed by enormously wealthy families.

The studies in this volume provide abundant evidence of family control encompassing both best and worst practice. How large family groups per-form, and how they affect their economies, seems highly context dependent. Burkart, Panunzi, and Shleifer (2003) stress the legal protection of public shareholders, arguing that heirs relinquish control to better-qualified pro-fessional managers and diversify their wealth across many firms only if they trust the corporate governance of those firms, and conclude (p. 2193) that "the separation of ownership and management is thus an indication of a su-perior corporate governance environment. The lack of such separation, and the prevalence of family firms, is evidence of financial underdevelopment."

But La Porta et al. (1997a, 1998) show that many highly developed econ-omies provide few rights to public shareholders. This might occur naturally if family control offers many advantages. For example, close family bonds might enable a degree of cooperation that is more difficult to sustain among nonkin. Entrusting control over different firms to blood kin might facilitate the transfer of knowledge, roles, and routines from firm to firm as well as from generation to generation. In other words, large family business groups may represent effective ways of organizing enterprises that survive the rigors of economic selection. Khanna and Palepu (chap. 5) stress this naturally cooperative behavior as the glue that holds family groups to-gether and the hard-earned reputations of certain families for their relative success.

But they also show that family business groups rise and fall in India, and other chapters identify analogous change elsewhere. Schumpeter (1951) makes a similar observation about European family enterprises. He posits several factors that alter the relative positions of wealthy families within a ruling class, the breaching of class barriers—upward or downward, and the rise and fall of whole classes. These factors are chance; shrewd man-agement of the families' position, especially via advantageous arranged marriages; differences in the usefulness of families to their feudal superi-ors; and different entrepreneurial ability in successive generations of the family. He argues for a sort of automatism—a family that simply reinvests a proportion of its profits in its business is bound to go under sooner or later. Bad luck strikes, competition emerges, politics shift, and, most im-portant, entrepreneurs die. Schumpeter (1951, p. 122) stresses that rare en-trepreneurial ability is the foundation of most great family fortunes but is an individual trait and does "not coincide with the logical necessity that obtains in the case of family enterprises." This, he continues, means "the complete displacement of powerful family positions as typical phenome-non, not merely the shifting of positions between families." The entry and exit of families is thus "individually effected" (p. 123), so that classes survive, but families come and go. He concludes (p. 130) that "the persistence of class position is an illusion, created by the slowness of change and the stability of class character as such and of its social fluid."

Ultimately, Schumpeter's (1912) notion of creative destruction is an underlying principle of capitalism. But innovation and entrepreneurship need to be nurtured. Oligarchic family elites can use their considerable wealth and connections to maintain their power and control at the expense of economic development. Haber (1999), Morck, Wolfenzon, and Yeung (2004), Olson (1963, 1982), Rajan and Zingales (2003), Thurow (1989), and others call such entrenched elites *oligarchies.* Thurow, for example, distinguishes *establishments* from *oligarchies.* Both are well-educated, wealthy, powerful, intermarried elites who

> run their countries. . . . [But] the central goal of an establishment is to insure that the system works so that the country will in the long run be successful. An establishment is self-confident that if the system works and if their country does well, they will personally do well. . . . In contrast an oligarchy is a group of insecure individuals who amass funds in secret Swiss bank accounts. Because they think that they must always look out for their own immediate self-interest, they aren't interested in taking time and effort to improve their country's long-run prospects. (p. 405)

The studies in this volume provide ample evidence of powerful family business groups behaving as establishments, oligarchies, or first one and then the other.

Business Groups

Conceptualizing economic activity in terms of business groups, as opposed to freestanding firms, is an incompletely understood area—perhaps because groups are rarest in the United States and United Kingdom, where business research is most active. A literature on business groups is coalescing but is probably decades behind that for other issues of similar importance.[9] The literature is probably most developed in connection with Japan, where area studies scholars have long appreciated business groups' importance.[10] However, Japanese business groups, as Morck and Nakamura show in chapter 7, have a history starkly different from groups elsewhere. Most important, large horizontal Japanese *keiretsu* are controlled by managers, not wealthy families.

9. See Bae, Kang, and Kim (2002), Bebchuk, Kraakman, and Triantis (2000), Barca and Becht (2001), Bertrand, Mehta, and Mullainathan (2002), Claessens, Djankov, and Lang (2000), Claessens et al. (2002), Daniels, Morck, and Stangeland (1995), Faccio and Lang (2003), Faccio, Lang, and Young (2001), Faccio (2002), Ghemawat and Khanna (1998, 2000), Granovetter (in press), Khanna and Palepu (2000), Morck et al. (2000, 2004b), and others.
10. See, e.g., Aoki (1988), Hoshi, Kashyap, and Scharfstein (1991), and especially Nakatani (1984).

Humans' tendency to organize activities along patterns of kinship may be biologically innate, as Axelrod and Hamilton (1981) suggest. But this organizing propensity continues long after the biological necessity is removed, and often extends to economic activity. Family and kinship groupings are likely the oldest and most pervasive forms of group behavior. From an economic perspective, Khanna and Palepu (2000) conceptualize family business groups "as a mechanism through which intragroup transaction costs are lowered, by encouraging information dissemination among group firms, reducing the possibility of contractual disputes, and providing a low-cost mechanism for dispute resolution" (p. 271).

Economic welfare, in theory, is greatly enhanced if trade extends beyond kinship groups and even encompasses anonymous transactions. Firms that raise capital from public shareholders at low cost can expand more rapidly than those constrained by family wealth. Family-controlled pyramidal groups arose everywhere as devices to tap public equity financing on a huge scale but retain family control over all key decisions.

Groups that do not fit this pattern, such as modern Japanese *keiretsu,* German bank groups, and groups with widely held or state-owned enterprises at their apexes, are exceptions, but important ones. In every case, they too are structured to preserve public equity financing while locking in control by insiders—professional managers, bankers, or bureaucrats, rather than wealthy families. The broader theme of concentrated control seems to encompass all business groups everywhere.

Why might such concentrated control develop and persist? Why does it most often rest with a handful of wealthy families? At this point we can only speculate.

There is safety in numbers, and as Aristotle wrote in his *Ethics,* "Men journey together with a view to particular advantage." Sociologists have long recognized that "involvement and participation in groups can have positive consequences for the individual and the community" (Portes, 1998, p. 2). Granovetter (in press) speculates that American-style freestanding widely held firms did not last in postwar Japan because the "planners had dramatically underestimated the extent to which the dense web of ties connecting firms within these groups, and the resulting sense of group identity and patterns of customary cooperation, could persist and regenerate even without direction from family owners." Perhaps, but group identity and cooperation need not require intercorporate equity holdings, which Morck and Nakamura's chapter argues were established as takeover defenses in the 1950s and 1960s. In their view, Japanese groups were raised from the dead to protect the positions of top corporate managers.

Khanna and Palepu (1997, p. 41) note that the "diversified business group remains the dominant form of enterprise throughout most emerging markets." They caution economic planners and executives in those countries against imitating Western-style freestanding industrially focused firms. They argue that ties of the sort Granovetter (in press) proposes substitute for markets and institutions that permit anonymous or arm's-length transactions in developed countries. Khanna and Palepu (p. 41) argue that if "a country's product, capital, and labor markets; its regulatory system; and its mechanisms for enforcing contracts" are not trusted, business groups substitute for them. Trust between family members running various group firms substitutes for trust in business contracts, financial markets, or labor market signals.

Trust

Cooperative behavior with blood kin may well be genetically programmed, making families the default junctures of high-trust behavior for the individuals within them. But wider networks of high-trust behavior appear to be important to the creation of an effective system of governance for large organizations and of reliable institutions in general.[11] Mayer, Davis, and Schoorman (1995, p. 712) define trust as "the willingness of a party to be vulnerable to the actions of another party based on the expectation that the other will perform a particular action important to the trustor, irrespective of the ability to monitor or control that other party." Arrow (1974, p. 23) explains the advantages it bestows thus: "Trust is an important lubricant of a social system. It is extremely efficient; it saves people a lot of trouble to have a fair degree of reliance on other people's word." Trust can lower transaction costs and permit effective coordination and control. Macaulay (1963, p. 55) makes a strong case that the governance of business transactions has an important dimension that goes beyond formal agreements and contracts. He argues (p. 58) that formal legal contracts cover a very small portion of all business conducted, and that business people largely prefer to rely on mechanisms such as "a man's word," a "handshake," or "common honesty and decency."

For Fukuyama (1995) a high level of societal trust improves the performance for all the society's institutions. The absence of trust—or, more seriously, distrust—makes coordination and control problematic. In certain situations, such as the grafting of Western capitalism onto a developing economy with low general levels of trust for nonkin, a "mismatch" of trust occurs where people take advantage of the erroneous expectations of others. This is a key theme in the chapter by Goetzmann and Köll, in which Western institutions built on certain assumptions of trust failed abjectly in prerevolutionary China when adjoined to its ancient entrenched bureaucracy.

Although readily destroyed, trust in a society's institutions is not easily

---

11. Regarding trust in large organizations, see Bradach and Eccles (1989), Coase (1937), La Porta et al. (1997b), Powell (1990), Sahlman (1990), Steier (1998), Stinchcombe (1965), and Williamson (1975, 1985). Regarding institutions broadly interpreted, see Coleman (1988), Putman (1993), and Fukuyama (1995).

built up. Putnam (1993) describes how economically important networks of trust in Northern Italy were built through centuries of successful association. The chapter on Canada by Morck et al. describes that country's evolution from a low-trust society in which families were virtually the only instruments of trust reliable enough to finance business ventures. Murphy's chapter on France describes the destruction of popular trust in the institutions of arm's-length finance.

Certain organizational arrangements can substitute to some extent for low trust outside families and can even increase ambient levels of trust, albeit slowly. Khanna and Palepu's chapter on India describes the importance of ethnic minorities in India's early large businesses. The relatively small size of these communities in large markets permitted both relationships of trust between key decision makers and certain economies of scale. In India and other countries, small elites developed within which huge deals could be consummated largely on the basis of trust.

This view of business groups is underscored by the business histories of many of the countries surveyed in this volume. The earliest origins of Japan's family business groups, or *zaibatsu,* were to circumvent low-trust problems. For example, the Mitsui family expanded into commodity trading because their silk business depended on barter deals. They later moved into banking to move Japan beyond barter deals into a real financial system.

It also helps explain the structures of business groups. The relational approach to strategy and economics propounded by Dyer and Singh (1998), Landes (1998), and Portes (1998) suggests that economic success depends on effective network relationships. Burt (1992b, p. 11) thus argues that "something about the structure of the player's network and the location of a player's contacts in the social structure of the arena provides a competitive advantage." In this light, business groups should be structured around critical transactions where trust is important. Effective networks contain enough members to accomplish the task, but not so many as to be unmanageable nor unnecessary or redundant.

Burt (1992a) models effective network ties as links to clusters of resources. The number of ties matters less than the clusters of resources accessed. A bigger network is only more effective if it connects to additional pertinent clusters of resources. An effective network thus contains "structural holes," where the costs of expansion outweigh the benefits (Burt 1992a, p. 65). There are advantages (Burt 1997, p. 343) to "having a contact network rich in structural holes." Business groups should grow to encompass relevant clusters but avoid redundant relationships by economizing on ties. Thus, very early Canadian groups began with timber businesses and expanded into ship building, then shipping, and then insurance.

Business-government relations are also critical links for business groups in many countries. Högfeldt's chapter on Sweden essentially argues that

Socialist politicians viewed family-controlled business groups as effective links to the whole of the private sector. By abetting dynastic family control over wide circles of firms, these politicians established a system where they could negotiate with the greater part of the large corporate sector over a small table. He adds that this may have stymied the development of arm's-length institutions in Sweden. This logic of business groups as second-best solutions impeding movement toward first-best solutions is echoed in several other chapters.

Franks et al. (chap. 10) argue that fear of losing one's reputation spread trustworthy behavior widely across British corporate governance by the early twentieth century. But in the rest of this volume, legal or regulatory sanction as reprisal for unacceptable grasping seems necessary to elevate ambient levels of trust, though exactly which sanctions mattered historically in which countries remains unclear.[12] In the United States especially, Becht and DeLong (chap. 11) see popular disquiet with concentrated economic power as perhaps more important than economic inefficiency in advancing tax, securities law, and other regulations that ultimately destabilized large business groups.[13] And Sylla and Smith (1995) argue that law played a greater role in Britain than Franks et al. allow.

Law

In a fundamental paper, La Porta et al. (1997a) argue that stock market development should be positively correlated with shareholder legal protection. Shleifer and Wolfenzon (2002) formalize this argument with a model in which controlling shareholders sell out to diversify if their rights as portfolio investors are legally protected. Otherwise, they remain undiversified blockholders in the companies they manage and consume what private benefits they can extract from their public shareholders. La Porta et al. (1997a) measure shareholder rights by focusing on six specific legal rights shareholders have in the United States and counting how many of them shareholders have in other countries.[14] They find that in the 1990s countries with stronger shareholder protection were characterized by larger stock markets and more diffusely held large corporations, and that these countries tend to have legal systems derived from British common law. The common-law countries in figure 1 are Australia, Canada, Hong Kong, Ireland, New Zealand, Singapore, the United Kingdom, and the United States, and they clearly do have more widely held large firms than

12. See La Porta, López-de-Silanes, and Shleifer (2003).
13. See Morck (2004b) for detail on these regulatory attacks.
14. This index adds one point if the country lets shareholders mail in proxy votes, does not require shares to be deposited prior to a general shareholders' meeting, allows cumulative voting or proportional representation of minorities in the board, provides an oppressed minority remedy, lets an owner of 10 percent or less of the share capital call an extraordinary shareholders' meeting, or lets shareholders' preemptive rights be voided only by a shareholders' vote.

the other countries, all of which employ civil codes of one form or another. La Porta et al. (1997a, 1999) conclude that diffuse ownership and shareholder capitalism require solid legal protection of public shareholders' property rights in their investments.

Several of the chapters in this volume beg to differ. Murphy remarks in chapter 3 that "in a post Enron, Tyco, WorldCom world, French jurists and financiers might be permitted a wry smile at the implication that the common-law system is linked to a strong system of corporate control." Fohlin argues that her chapter "casts doubt on the notion that civil law traditions per se consistently undermine market functioning" because German stock markets ebbed and rose at various points, while its legal system changed little. She also fails to find any temporal correlation between changes in shareholder protection and ownership diffusion. Franks, Mayer, and Rossi argue that British shareholders had none of the legal rights La Porta et al. (1997a) enumerate until 1948, and only attained their current level of protection in the final third of the twentieth century.[15] Yet they find that the ownership of new British firms dispersed as quickly early in the twentieth century and in its latter decades. Canadian shareholders had few of these same rights until the 1960s, but Morck, Percy, Tian, and Yeung find that Canadian corporate ownership grew widely dispersed by the middle of the twentieth century and that family-controlled pyramidal groups staged a roaring comeback at the century's end and under unprecedentedly strong shareholder rights laws. France, Germany, Italy, Japan, the Netherlands, and Sweden all had economically very important stock markets off and on through their history—especially at the beginning of the twentieth century, as noted by Rajan and Zingales (2003). Becht and DeLong argue in chapter 11 that U.S. shareholders remain vulnerable to many forms of expropriation by corporate insiders despite their statutory legal rights, and Aganin and Volpin (chap. 6) argue that shareholder rights in Italy are a dead letter because of general judicial system inefficiency.

Three general criticisms of La Porta et al. (1997a, 1999) emerge. First, the timing of improved shareholder rights does not match the timing of ownership dispersion in several countries. Second, the correlation between large stock markets and shareholder rights is highly specific to the late twentieth century. Third, the La Porta et al. shareholder rights index is an incomplete proxy for actual shareholder legal protection. The thesis that statutory shareholder rights cause stock market development and ownership diffusion is hard to square with these findings. However, the thesis that a country's legal system, or some other factor highly correlated with this, *predisposes* it to a certain form of capitalism, which is really the funda-

---

15. Cheffins (2001) also argues that British legal developments weaken the thesis of La Porta et al. (1997a, 1998), though Sylla and Smith (1995) argue that late nineteenth-century developments in British law actually did strengthen shareholder rights considerably.

mental point La Porta et al. advance, is harder to challenge. Indeed, the chapters of this book provide fairly solid evidence in its favor.

Murphy (chap. 3) does not argue that the French legal code is unimportant but rather that French public investors grew skeptical of stock markets because of repeated financial crises. Yet the response of French politicians and jurists to each crisis was not to strengthen investor rights. Rather, the response to the Mississippi Company bubble was to reassert Roman Catholic prohibitions on interest and to all but shut down the financial system. Neither the revolutionary government's *assignats* nor the Crédit Mobilier fiasco heralded stronger investor rights. Likewise, the responses of the Dutch, Italian, Japanese, and Swedish governments to the financial crises of the 1920s and 1930s were to substitute various mechanisms of state-controlled capital allocation for their stock markets. In contrast, a not dissimilar succession of financial manias, panics, and crises in Britain, Canada, and the United States ultimately strengthened shareholder rights. Clearly something in their legal systems changed. Why did financial crises trigger fuller disclosure, better regulation, and stronger investor rights in common-law countries but a disconnection of the stock market from the economy in countries with civil law traditions?

Aganin and Volpin (chap. 6) shed light on what happened in Italy. After the crash of 1907, Fiat's shareholders sued the Agnelli family for accounting irregularities and stock price manipulation. The Agnellis were cleared of all wrongdoing, but investor confidence in the stock market was deeply shaken, and Italy remained in a prolonged financial crisis through 1914. Aganin and Volpin argue that "there was a general market perception that universal banks and corporate insiders like the Agnellis used the investment boom early in the century to pump and dump their shares."

Morck and Nakamura (chap. 7) describe how the American occupation force redesigned the ownership structures of Japan's major corporations in the late 1940s to make them widely held. Yet Japanese managers, fearful of hostile takeovers, placed blocks of stock with each other's firms to defend against raiders, forming the current *keiretsu* groups. Recent work in the United States and other countries shows that barriers to takeovers are not in the best interests of shareholders. Yet the Japanese managers acted anyway, for Japanese shareholders had no legal right to object.

One interpretation of the findings in this volume is that both civil law and common-law countries create large financial markets but that common-law countries are better able to *sustain* them over the longer run. Perhaps, from time to time, a new generation in a civil law country discards the advice of its grandparents and invests heavily in stocks. Once it becomes clear that its rights are ill protected, the values of its portfolios collapse and the next generation or two shun the market again until collective memory fades and a new generation of marks is born.

But what is it about common-law systems that sustains large stock markets and makes sustained diffuse ownership possible? If La Porta et al.'s (1997a) shareholder rights are recent statutory innovations in most common-law countries, why are investors in those countries generally more accepting of stocks? One possibility is deeper characteristics distinguishing common law from civil law.

One such difference emerged in the early seventeenth century, when France was exhausted by its Wars of Religion (1562–98) and England was devastated by its Civil War (1625–49). Cardinal Richelieu sought to reunite France by centralizing power in the hands of an absolute monarchy. Bloodied by years of chaos, the French people accepted this as a sort of salvation. The arbitrary Revolutionary Tribunals of the late eighteenth century left the public mistrustful of judicial discretion and probably made the French people, and Napoleon in particular, receptive to the rigid codification of the law and the subjugation of judges to the executive branch of government. Thus, Napoleon replaced France's prerevolutionary civil code with a new, expanded Napoleonic Code, and his armies exported this across the European continent. Meanwhile, England had developed a tradition of an independent judiciary—the Courts of Common Law—as alternatives to the royal courts—the Exchequer and the Court of Star Chamber. This was a reflection of a broader struggle for power between the monarch and Parliament that came to a head with Cromwell's Commonwealth (1649–60). Parliament won both the English Civil War and the battle for the courts that followed. English courts became independent of the executive branch and subject only to Parliament.[16]

This gave English and French jurisprudence very different flavors.[17] To vastly oversimplify, the French courts existed to implement the will of the king, while the English courts existed to protect free Englishmen from abuse by their king. Over time, *government* came to be substituted for *king,* but the difference persists. Common-law systems protect the weak from the strong; civil law systems enforce the edict of the state. This distinction disposes courts in common-law countries to protect public shareholders, even in the absence of explicit statutes.

A second underlying difference is that civil codes provide detailed instructions to judges that try to anticipate all possible cases and specify decisions for each. The judge looks to the letter of the law anew in each case. Merryman (1966, p. 586) describes the resulting dominance of doctrine and how judicial decisions read "more like excerpts from treatises or commentaries on the codes than the reasoning of a court in deciding a concrete case." Under common law, judges base rulings upon general principles and previous cases as well as legislation. This, with the relative independence of the judiciary from political interference, renders *all* common-law courts, to

16. See also Hayek (1960) and Glaeser and Shleifer (2002).
17. See Watson (1981), Pistor et al. (1999), Glaeser and Shleifer (2002), and others.

some extent, activist courts. Decisions are less responsive to the minutia of a legal code and more to the perceived viewpoint of a *reasonable man,* a *prudent man,* or the like. Corporate insiders who pilfer from public share-holders in a common-law jurisdiction, even if they fastidiously avoid breaching all written statutes, can never be entirely certain the courts will not find a precedent or general principle to convict them anyway. This un-certainty might contribute to better general treatment of public investors in common-law countries, even before those countries enacted the specific statutory rights La Porta et al. (1997a) enumerate.

A third difference, which flows from the first two, is the quality of judi-cial decisions. Both common-law and civil code systems can be of high quality, but both also have weak points.[18] Three particular vulnerabilities to which civil law systems are prone are of special concern in cases of cor-porate governance that pit connected corporate insiders against impecu-nious public shareholders. First, because civil law judges are bureaucrats subordinate to the government, ill-functioning courts are malleable to po-litical pressure.[19] Second, because decisions depend on complicated codes rather than broad principles, a poorly functioning civil law system can fa-vor litigants who are better at parsing those codes. Third, because prece-dent is less a guiding principle, civil law judges can shrug off how their judgments affect people's future behavior in the belief that good bureau-crats should defer to politicians.

These differences can all be overstated, of course. The United States has codified its contract law in the Uniform Commercial Code, and its securi-ties laws in the Securities and Exchanges Act and various and sundry leg-islation. These codes are easily as detailed as many civil codes.[20] Mean-while, Enriques (2002) documents how civil codes contain "general clauses" instructing judges to apply certain standards on a case-by-case basis, and civil law judges sometimes even create new standards or extend existing ones. Although these clauses theoretically allow civil law judges latitude to convict wrongdoers who delicately avoid breaking the letter of the law, they seldom exercise it—perhaps because of their doctrinal train-ing. Finally, the executive branch of government appoints high court judges in most common-law countries, and some might see this as subju-gating the courts. There is even disagreement among legal scholars about the degree of protection civil law countries actually accord public share-holders. For example, Ramseyer and Nakazato (1999) argue that Japanese law gives public shareholders fairly strong legal rights. Many legal scholars

18. Berkowitz and Clay (2004) find that U.S. states with civil law colonial legal systems (Florida, Louisiana, and southwestern states taken from Mexico) have more constitutional instability than purely common-law states. Whether this reflects inherent problems in civil law or in switching legal systems is not fully clear, though they favor the latter explanation.
19. See Hayek (1960), Mahoney (2001), and La Porta et al. (2004).
20. See Weiss (2000).

thus regard the distinction between civil and common law as primarily of historical interest.[21]

Nonetheless, these three differences might perhaps coalesce into an explanation.[22] Many common-law and civil code countries had large stock markets to which numerous small investors entrusted their savings at various points in their histories. All of these countries experienced financial panics and crises, but these seem to have devastated shareholder cultures in civil law countries worse than in common-law countries.

Albeit often with very long lags, financial crises induced stronger shareholder legal rights in common-law countries. Coffee (2001) argues that common law created a better environment for self-regulation. Moreover, a succession of British court decisions and laws, beginning with the Joint Stock Companies Registration, Incorporation, and Regulation Act of 1844, steadily expanded investor legal protection. Indeed, the committee that drafted the 1844 act reflected long on past financial crises and stock market bubbles and "classified bubble companies into those naturally unsound, those unsound through bad management, and those clearly fraudulent. For the first nothing could be done, and for the others the great remedy was publicity" (Frentrop 2003, p. 155). In contrast, civil law countries typically responded to such crises by using banks or state investment programs to circumvent the stock market. Thus, Aganin and Volpin (chap. 6) write that "in Italy, the government responded to the Great Depression by becoming a substitute for capital markets. Post war [sic] governments saw no great need to improve capital market regulation." Most other continental European countries and Japan adopted similar policies. This reflects the first intrinsic difference between the two systems. Common-law countries' courts and governments sought to protect the weak from the strong; civil law countries' governments sought alternative ways of implementing the public-policy goal of efficient capital allocation. Their courts, ill equipped to restore faith in capital markets for the reasons outlined above, let matters rest.

Franks, Mayer, and Rossi (chap. 10) write of higher standards of ethics in British than in foreign businesses. This might reflect the second intrinsic difference between common-law and civil code systems, the uncertainty intrinsic to common law. Precedent and general principle can convict wrongdoers who rely overly on the letter of the law. Certainly, Becht and DeLong (chap. 11) ascribe the diffusion of ownership to shareholder rights created by activist common-law courts in the United States. Perhaps small investors in common-law countries factored in the probability of some property rights protection despite an absence of statutory rights, and this sus-

21. See, e.g., Markesinis (2000), and see also Posner (1996).
22. See also Weiss (2000) for the argument that differences, though perhaps overstated by some scholars, exist and are important.

tained their stock markets through rough patches. Sylla and Smith (1995) argue that legal reforms in late nineteenth-century Britain could have permitted this.

Enriques (2002) tracks Italian corporate judicial rulings through the late 1980s and 1990s and finds a bias in favor of corporate insiders and highly formalistic arguments; but no evidence that judges consider the impact of their rulings on the incentives or behavior of firms and managers. Aganin and Volpin (chap. 6) refer to these findings, and to evidence in La Porta et al. (1998) of the low quality of legal enforcement in Italy, to stress that weak Italian corporate governance might reflect a poor-quality judicial system rather than an absence of specific shareholder rights or a civil law system per se. But the third intrinsic difference between common law and civil codes points to judicial dysfunction in these specific areas of law, which matter critically to the corporate governance of diffusely owned firms, as special vulnerabilities of an ill-functioning civil code system.

Overall, the studies in this volume do not undermine the basic argument that differences in legal systems matter. Indeed, de Jong and Röell (chap. 8) present the only discussion of a discrete change in legal system, describing how Napoleon's imposition of his civil code on the Netherlands undid much of its financial development.[23] Frentrop (2003) confirms much of this in more detail. De Jong and Röell clarify the subsidiary importance of lists of statutory shareholder rights and underscore the need to study more fundamental differences between legal systems. Effective shareholder legal protection takes more than a complete checklist of statutory provisions. La Porta et al. (2004) and La Porta, López-de-Silanes, and Shleifer (2005) stress more fundamental legal system differences turning on judicial independence, disclosure, and securities laws.

Origins

Much recent work posits that the institutional differences between modern countries derive, in part at least, from differences in their preindustrial economies.[24] To some extent, these arguments are motivated by econometric considerations. A truly exogenous variable is needed to resolve many of the econometric issues that bedevil empirical economics, and where better to find one than in the distant past? But beneath these technical motivations there lies a genuine belief that past centuries' events and conditions constrain today's decision makers and institution builders.

An extreme thesis of this sort is that economic development is predestined by geography. This is an uncomfortable philosophy to economists, for it diminishes somewhat their trade. Yet Diamond (1997) posits precisely

---

23. Though Mokyr (2000) argues that Dutch laws and institutions needed serious reform at this point anyway because heirs to its earlier economic success had become entrenched and blocked further progress.

24. La Porta et al. (1997a) justify the exogeneity of legal origin on this basis.

this.[25] Others, like Weber (1904) and Stulz and Williamson (2003), argue, in a parallel vein, that deeply ingrained cultural factors predetermine economic prosperity. Weber stresses the unique developments surrounding the Protestant Reformation in Europe and argues that these prepared Europe uniquely for free markets and rapid economic growth. True, the first two economic powerhouses of modern Europe, Britain and the Netherlands, were resolutely Protestant, as were many principalities that became Germany. The religious wars that swept Europe funneled educated refugees and capital into the uniquely tolerant Netherlands as Dutch merchants invented the joint-stock company. The English Civil War, which freed British courts of royal oversight, certainly had a religious side—unfinished business from the Reformation. But German industrial development occurred long after the Reformation, and not much before similar bursts of growth in Catholic Europe in the twentieth century. Högfeldt's chapter on Sweden describes decidedly oligarchic institutions given a modern social democratic sheen. And other Protestant countries, like the Baltic states, remained outside the modern world until quite recently.

An alternate approach to predestination, more conducive to economic analysis, is Haber's (1999) argument that different countries have different economic institutions—customs, cultures, and traditions as well as legal systems—and that these institutions determine how people behave, and hence what sorts of public and private investments are feasible.[26] Sound institutions protect private property rights, encourage the honest payment of taxes, and enforce contractual agreements and other forms of cooperation. In a sound institutional environment, large-scale public and private investment are made possible by freedom from the threats of theft, cheating, and reneging. With varying qualifications, this situation characterizes today's developed economies. In particular, sound institutions of corporate governance permit the existence of large corporations and their ownership by diffuse investors.

But an absence of sound institutions leads to different arrangements. Where the state and investors cannot rely on arm's-length arrangements to protect property rights, one must co-opt the other. To protect their property rights, powerful individuals and families in such countries control the police powers of the state. Or those who control the state appropriate what wealth the economy has, invest it to benefit themselves, and use their po-

---

25. Diamond (1997) argues that the larger land mass of the Eurasia gave rise to more domesticable plants and animals and that its primarily east-to-west orientation permitted their rapid diffusion. This gave its inhabitants a permanent lead in the process of economic development. Our problem with this thesis is that most domesticated plants and animals derive from wild species. Ex post, the ancestors of wheat and cows must have been domesticable. This does not mean New World species, like turkeys and potatoes, could not have been domesticated earlier and more fully too. Who knows how good a beast of burden might have been bred from, say, the plains bison?

26. This work builds upon Olson (1963, 1982) and others.

lice power to protect their investments. Either solution frees investors from the danger of losing to cheaters, thieves, and scoundrels. However, unsurprisingly, these oligarchs see little reason to protect the property rights of others. This leads to *oligarchic institutions*—the governance of most economic activity is entrusted to wealthy oligarchs who use the state to protect their interests, and most of the population lives without meaningful property rights or extensive public goods. Haber (1999) views Latin America as typifying this form of economic organization.

Once oligarchic institutions are in place, oligarchs understandably prefer the status quo and use the state to prevent institutions from changing. Olson (1963), Acemoglu and Robinson (2000), Acemoglu, Johnson, and Robinson (2001, 2002a,b), and Morck, Wolfenzon, and Yeung (2004) all present mechanisms through which this can happen and which give rise to a sort of economic predestination. Once a country has oligarchic institutions, upending them is not easy.

Advanced non-Western economies, according to Acemoglu, Johnson, and Robinson (2002b), had well-developed indigenous institutions that evolved to exploit natural resources for the benefit of the local elite. European colonial rulers and postcolonial independence leaders retained these oligarchic institutions, hampering broad-based economic development. Consequently, the most advanced non-Western societies—Asia, the Islamic world, Mexico, and Peru—have the most problems incorporating modern Western institutions.

This certainly resonates with the chapter on China by Goetzmann and Köll, which describes how the traditional Chinese imperial bureaucracy, acting as it always had, undermined well-intentioned and carefully written legal reforms aimed at establishing the institutions of good corporate governance in late nineteenth-century China. In contrast, Japan, a much younger civilization, whose local institutions were in disrepute at the time of its opening to the West, managed a more successful transplant of Western institutional arrangements.

The chapter on India fits less fully with the thesis of Acemoglu, Johnson, and Robinson (2002a). Khanna and Palepu point to India's ancient precolonial mercantile traditions, carried into the modern world by specific ethnic minorities—especially the Marwari, Gujerati, and Parsi. They document the close ties between India's leading mercantile families and both the British Raj and Congress party, and describe situations similar to Haber's (1999) depiction of Latin American oligarchic institutions and in line with Acemoglu, Johnson, and Robinson. However, Khanna and Palepu go on to describe how the Tata family, which was politically close to the British colonial government, lost much of its political influence after independence, and especially after India embraced Nehruvian Socialism. The family's response was an energetic entrepreneurial strategy that worked around a mainly hostile License Raj and built up sufficient capital and goodwill to finance a large part of India's new software industry.

Acemoglu, Johnson, and Robinson (2001) argue that patterns of European settlement centuries ago determine modern economic institutions and patterns of corporate control in the modern world. They argue that where European settlers could survive, they created institutions that promoted economic development, but that where they could not survive, they created institutions that facilitated the fastest possible extraction of valuable resources. Those oligarchic institutions, once established, were locked in, condemning the latter countries to centuries of poverty and exploitation by colonial and then local elites.

The chapters on Canada, India, and the United States—all former colonies—speak to this thesis. Those on Canada and the United States document early institutions and institutional development not very different from those of their colonial masters, the British and French. Morck et al. (chap. 1) make the point that Canada's longer presettlement history as a French, and then British, fur trade entrepôt gives it some institutional echoes of a colony of resource extraction run in the interests of a tiny elite. Clearly, colonial and traditional institutions do persist, and constrain subsequent institutional development.

Evolution

But this argument can be pressed too far. European countries also have their colonial origins. France was a Roman colony, and the French civil code is essentially a revised version of the code Justinian applied to all parts of the Roman Empire, including Gaul. The Romans adopted Greek ideas, and the Greeks drew from Egypt. Modern European institutions of government, society, and law still echo ancient antecedents, but they have also clearly evolved.

Institutions change—occasionally radically—dooming predestination as a complete explanation of modern institutions. Olson (1982) argues that major institutional changes require major disruptions, like wars or disasters, which weaken the elite sufficiently to interrupt its control of the state. This certainly resonates with several of the chapters in this volume and other work on the history of corporate governance. Frentrop (2003) argues that the Dutch developed the first joint-stock company, the Dutch East Indies Company, founded in 1602, to gain leverage against larger European powers that threatened them.[27] This company pioneered the use of share certificates traded on a stock exchange to raise money. This freed the company from financial dependence on a royal exchequer so that economic logic, rather than court intrigue, might determine strategies. Its commercial success catapulted the small Dutch Republic from obscurity to chal-

27. See Frentrop (2003) for details.

lenging the Spanish Empire, built on New World gold, and the Portuguese domination of the circum-African spice trade. In the seventeenth century, the British imported successful Dutch institutions along with the House of Orange after the Glorious Revolution. In the nineteenth century, the French, Germans, Italians, and Swedes—and even the Dutch—could all look to Britain for model institutions when their own came into disrepute. In the twentieth century, Germany, the Soviet Union, Japan, and the United States each took Britain's place in different decades, with decidedly more mixed results.

The chapters in this book show that institutional change seems to require a crisis in existing institutions and a workable role model for new ones. The Tokugawa shoguns lost face irreparably by capitulating to Admiral Perry and opening Japan to American trade. This loss let the Meiji leaders stage a coup and undertake wholesale changes to every aspect of Japanese society. The American Revolution and the liberal rebellions in 1830s Canada also clearly reshaped institutions. But the financial chaos of the French Revolution, according to Murphy (chap. 3), helped induce institutions that delayed French financial development. Good intentions are certainly no guarantee of good results.

Most important to recent developments in corporate governance, the Great Depression emerges in virtually every chapter as a key formative experience. In the United States, this crisis activated progressive political forces that broke up America's great pyramidal groups. But in Canada, it triggered a return to old mercantilist traditions, as the government cartelized the economy to fight deflation. In Sweden, the Great Depression left scores of firms bankrupt and the Wallenbergs' bank holding control blocks of their shares in lieu of debt repayments. In Germany, Italy, and Japan, the Depression brought in extremist political movements, which subordinated corporate governance to ideology.

Transplants

The histories recounted in this volume contain several instances of one country deliberately adopting institutions developed in another. Generalizations from these few histories must be highly tentative. Nonetheless, a few patterns stand out.

Transplants between Western countries seem healthier than those from Western to non-Western countries. This might be because none of these institutions was totally foreign to the importing country. Thus, the Napoleonic code was successfully transplanted to the rest of continental Europe, including the Netherlands. That most of Europe already used variants of Roman civil law prepared the ground. Sweden adopted first Scottish and then German banking with little difficulty, but Swedes were already quite familiar with each system beforehand. Canada borrowed much of her securities laws from the United States, but many Canadians were already familiar with American securities laws from doing business in the United States.

Transplants to non-Western countries seem less robust. The chapter on China describes a rejected transplant. In the late Qing dynasty, China's entrenched bureaucrats could not comprehend the concept of independent firms, as envisioned in its Westernized corporations law. The bureaucrats' traditional concepts of patronage and loyalty congealed into endemic corruption that replaced Chinese capitalism with Soviet institutions. The chapter on India describes how shoddy Soviet transplants also corroded India's British institutions after independence, though less completely. The Japan chapter describes that country's serial adoption of a sequence of foreign institutions.

All of these observations concur well with the *transplant effect* proposed by Berkowitz, Pistor, and Richard (2003) and Pistor et al. (2003, p. 81), who argue that legal evolution is continuous and gradual in countries with indigenously developed legal systems but that transplanted legal systems stagnate for long periods, with interruptions of radical and even erratic change. Pistor argues that transplanted legal systems that can adapt are more likely to succeed. Without disputing this, Goetzmann and Köll (chap. 2) propose that indigenous Chinese institutions undermined promising transplants. This raises the possibility that operational home-grown institutions might marginalize or capture transplants, rendering them dysfunctional.

Large Outside Shareholders

Corporate governance is an important determinant of the distribution of economic power, and thus a key plank of reform in many political ideologies.

For example, the French Revolution probably injected an important ideological element into European corporate governance. Dunlavy (2004) argues that many corporate shareholder meetings were radically more democratic in the early nineteenth century than they are now. Many corporate charters at that time granted *one vote per shareholder,* rather than *one vote per share,* which Dunlavy calls *plutocratic voting.* Others had scaled voting rights systems, which granted larger shareholders fewer votes per share or capped their voting rights. The one-vote-per-shareholder system may have reflected common legal rules governing business and municipal corporations. However, such voting systems were by no means universal in the early history of capitalism. For example, the 1670 charter of the Hudson's Bay Company provided for one vote per share, not one vote per shareholder. Dunlavy reports that plutocratic voting rapidly came to dominate American shareholder meetings but that more democratic shareholder meetings persisted through much of the nineteenth century on the European continent.

Perhaps the radical democratic ideals of the French Revolution sustained the popularity of one-vote-per-shareholder corporate governance on the continent. Certainly, Frentrop (2003) argues that "the ideal of equality promulgated by the French Revolution made the shareholders' meeting, which provided equal rights for all shareholders, the most powerful body of the company. This was so self-evident that Napoleon's 1807 Code de Commerce does not mention it. Directors were dismissible agents of the shareholders."

An alternative explanation, proposed by de Jong and Röell (chap. 8) in connection with the Netherlands, is that corporate insiders limited the voting power of large outside shareholders to entrench themselves. Certainly, both explanations could be true. Corporate insiders might have cynically exploited popular ideologies to lock in their control rights. Or they might have genuinely subscribed to ideologies that coincidentally entrenched their economic power.

Rajan and Zingales (2003) advance the former thesis to explain why the financial systems of many countries atrophied during the twentieth century. They show that many countries had much larger and more developed financial systems at the beginning of the century than at the end of the cold war era. They propose that a first generation of entrepreneurs raised money to finance industrialization at the beginning of the century and that they or their heirs lobbied for government policies that crippled their countries' financial systems to prevent competitors from raising capital. One way to do this is to support high income taxes and low estate taxes. Another might be checks on the voting power of large outside shareholders, which might have been an ideologically acceptable way to do this.

Shleifer and Vishny (1986, 1997) argue that large outside shareholders, by rendering takeovers credible threats, cause corporate managers in the United States to work harder, and that this raises share prices for small investors. Weakening large outside shareholders would entrench existing insiders by stopping takeovers and would make stocks less attractive to small investors, depriving potential entrants of capital.

However, large outside shareholders may have interests of their own that mesh poorly with small shareholders' interests. Corporate pension funds might be reined in by corporate management to invite reciprocal treatment from their counterparts' pension funds. Public-sector pension funds might be subject to political influence. Nonetheless, Franks, Mayer, and Rossi (chap. 10) argue that institutional investors were clearly a force for good governance in the United Kingdom. Perhaps they are set to play similar roles elsewhere too.

Becht, Bolton, and Röell (2002) stress finding a balance between managerial discretion and small shareholder protection. Systems that lean too far toward protecting small shareholders from blockholders let existing corporate insiders do as they like because small shareholders lack the resources to challenge them. Leaving too much power in the hands of large blockholders exposes shareholders to expropriation and perhaps also subjects managers to unwarranted monitoring.

Financial Development

In a historical study of German universal banks, Kleeberg (1987, p. 112) remarks that "the best advice for a young German industrialist who needed more capital was to marry a rich wife . . . this was the advice which the cologne merchant Friedrich Sölling constantly pressed upon his partner Adolf Krupp. Hence the extremely complicated family trees and numerous intermarriages among the Rhenish Bourgeoisie, grown rich off trade."

Schumpeter (1912) puts less faith in entrepreneurs' ability to procure advantageous marriages. He argues that the social purpose of financial markets and institutions is to put capital in the hands of people with economically viable business plans, and that technology-driven growth is very difficult without tandem financial development. Consistent with this, King and Levine (1993) show that countries with better-developed stock markets and banking systems continually reallocate capital to finance visionary entrepreneurs and thereby grow faster. The studies in this volume largely support King and Levine.

Energetic stock markets are associated with the entry of new firms and corporate governance entrusted to new entrepreneurs. Sleepy stock markets are associated with a freezing of cast. Morck et al. (chap. 1) show that Canadian stock market booms correspond to periods of energetic entrepreneurial activity. Aganin and Volpin (chap. 6) stress the importance of Italy's stock markets a century ago in financing her first generation of great industrial corporate groups. Högfeldt (chap. 9) argues that Sweden's socialist governments weakened her financial system, locking a corporate elite in place, and that this ultimately retarded economic growth. Rajan and Zingales (2003) argue that yesterday's entrepreneurs often lobby to weaken financial markets as a way to deter competitors from arising. While none of the studies in this volume reports direct evidence of such lobbying, the argument is plausible. To distort Mark Twain only slightly, "The radical of one century is the conservative of the next."

Shleifer and Wolfenzon (2002) argue that active stock markets affect corporate governance by letting wealthy heirs sell out, and this is confirmed in several chapters. Becht and DeLong (chap. 11) describe how American stock markets deepened and broadened to finance first railways and then industrial firms too. This permitted trust promoters to float shares to buy out founders or their heirs in a wave of takeovers. Other American families sold out incompletely, keeping a tenuous grip on their companies with relatively small ownership stakes or board seats. Morck et al. (chap. 1) describe similar events in Canada. Aganin and Volpin (chap. 6) describe a boom on the Milan Stock Exchange at the beginning of the twentieth century caused by the Banca Commerciale and Credito Italiano, which helped numerous entrepreneurs raise capital by selling shares on the stock market. They go on to note that, by 1907, 72 percent of the total equity of all Italian limited-liability firms traded on stock markets.

Irrational exuberance in America's stock markets may also have helped disperse corporate ownership in that country. Becht and DeLong (chap. 11) echo Dewing (1919) and argue that the American stock market gave founders and heirs the chance to sell their stock for more than it was worth. "Physicians, teachers, dentists, and clergymen" constituted "the happy hunting ground" of the "sucker list," where people were persuaded to buy "highly speculative and worthless securities" by "devious and dubious" methods. Stock market booms in other countries may have played similar roles. Morck et al. (chap. 1) describe Canadian families selling out into the overheated market of the late 1920s and a consequent increase in the importance of widely held firms.

Where shareholders' property rights are insecure, trust commands a premium. Becht and DeLong (chap. 11) argue that American shareholders at the beginning of the twentieth century had "virtually no statutory legal rights, and so favored companies controlled by men of good repute and accomplishment, such as J. P. Morgan and his partners, who charged handsomely for monitoring services." Under these circumstances, stock markets expand the governance sway of established families. Pagano, Panetta, and Zingales (1998) report that, from 1983 through 1989, the number of listings on the Milan stock market grew more than 50 percent, but that most of the new listings were subsidiaries of traded companies going public to take advantage of booming stock markets. Khanna and Palepu (chap. 5) point to similar developments in postindependence India and argue that established families backed entrepreneurs by helping them build listed companies within established family pyramidal groups.

Where stock markets are ill trusted, banks can channel financing to entrepreneurs and monitor corporate governance. However, this seems to have played an important role in only a few countries. The chapters on Britain, Canada, and the Netherlands highlight how commercial banks in those countries entered the era of industrialization with strong attachments to the *real bills doctrine,* which mandated that banks lend with trade goods as collateral. This let banks enthusiastically fund trade but kept them from financing industrial plant and equipment. Branch banking restrictions and the Glass Steagall Act of 1933 kept American commercial banks to a minimal role in financing large corporations. Memory of the Crédit Mobilier fiasco apparently kept British banks out of investment banking too. In contrast, German, Japanese, and (later) Swedish banks eagerly financed industrial development. In the case of Japanese banks, this was despite an analog of Glass Steagall imposed by Macarthur in the postwar period.

Aoki (1988), Kaplan (1994) and others argue that bankers can be sophisticated monitors of corporate insiders and thus reliable guarantors of good corporate governance. However, Morck and Nakamura (1999), Morck, Nakamura, and Shivdasani (2000), and others argue that bankers' aim in governance oversight is to make sure corporate borrowers repay their debts. This could induce excessive risk aversion and excessive investment in tangible collateralizable assets, rather than knowledge-based assets. Banks and other financial firms are also biased as monitors of corporate governance because they see firms as customers too. De Jong and Röell (chap. 8) make this point succinctly, quoting an insurance company representative thus: "You are in a difficult position if you want to present a new contract to the management board whilst you have voted against one of their proposals the day before."[28]

Fohlin (chap. 4) argues that German banks' contribution to corporate governance is often overstated. Kleeberg (1987, p. 134) agrees, noting that "German industrialization advanced rapidly in the late nineteenth century, but probably depended more on old family wealth than on bank loans." Where bank financing was important, he questions its economic effects, noting (p. 404) that "an unfortunate result has been that often the most successful captains of industry in Germany have not had any particular talent for industry or marketing, but rather were skilled at handling the banks."

Finally, this volume makes it clear that financial development is not a given but depends on politics and history. China's first attempt to develop a modern financial system was a serious initiative that ran afoul of her ancient entrenched bureaucracy. Murphy (chap. 3) argues that France's train of financial crises made her people leery of capital markets and induced her politicians to overregulate them. Pointing to a constricted financial system as an explanation for highly concentrated corporate governance is inadequate, for this begs the question of why a country's financial system is what it is. Chapters 10 and 11 show how politicians responsive to demands by investors made the financial systems of the United States and United Kingdom, respectively, what they are.

Politics

The studies in this volume are unenthusiastic about direct political involvement in corporate governance. But they also testify to the importance of government in establishing and sustaining the legal and regulatory infrastructure needed for sustained good governance.

From a historical perspective, entrusting corporate governance to the state evokes the Axis powers' policies in the 1930s and 1940s, described in this volume by Aganin and Volpin (chap. 6), Fohlin (chap. 4), and Morck

28. D. Brilleslijper, Delta Lloyd spokesman, in *FEM Business,* 20 September 2003.

and Nakamura (chap. 7). While the forms of private ownership survived, effective control rested with party and military representatives on boards. From a theoretical viewpoint, Boycko, Shleifer, and Vishny (1996) argue that state control leads to excessive employment. Krueger (1990) argues that political patronage inflicts inferior governance on state-owned enterprises. Consistent with this, Dewenter and Malatesta (2001) find significantly depressed profitability in state-owned enterprises.

One state role in corporate governance that has not yet attracted much attention from researchers is the pyramidal group of listed companies with a state-owned enterprise at the apex. Aganin and Volpin (chap. 6) argue that the "wasting of resources" by state-controlled pyramidal groups of listed companies in Italy was an important cause of that country's economic crisis in the 1990s. Morck et al. (chap. 1) refer to scandalous governance problems at the Caisse de Dépôt et Placement du Québec, a provincially controlled pyramidal group in Canada. Further work is needed to clarify the political purposes of these structures and to understand better their governance and economic impact.

Despite their skepticism about direct political involvement in corporate decisions, many contributors stress the power of the state to despoil or distort corporate governance. Rajan and Zingales (2003) argue that the stock market can be either fostered or hampered by government action, depending on the balance of powers between pressure groups. Khanna and Palepu (chap. 5) describe the License Raj as a "Kafkaesque maze of controls [having] more to do with a heady fascination with the intellectual cuisine of the London School of Economics and Cambridge . . . and the wonder of the then ascendant Soviet planning machine, than with the actions of India's dominant family businesses. Business groups had to either manipulate it, as some did, or invent themselves around it, as did others." Aganin and Volpin (chap. 6) likewise stress the role of politics in Italian corporate governance through the century.

Ghemawat and Khanna (1998) argue that business families control business groups to extract personal gains and attain their position through directly unproductive economic activities and through their influence over government policies and actions.[29] Pagano and Volpin (2001) and Biais and Perotti (2003) argue that state intervention in the economy should be negatively correlated with financial development, because the state acts as a substitute for financial markets. Högfeldt (chap. 9) proposes a similar history in Sweden, where the Social Democrats let the financial system wither like an unnecessary appendix. Aganin and Volpin (chap. 6) emphasize how little Italian stock markets mattered mid-century, noting that "from 1950 to 1980, between 15 and 20 percent of traded companies in Italy were

---

29. Morck, Wolfenzon, and Yeung (2004) develop several more arguments along these lines and assemble a range of empirical evidence about their scope of applicability.

controlled by the government. The correlation between the two series is –70 percent."

Entrenchment

Finally, the studies in this volume all point to a commonality in human nature. Elites are self-interested and cooperate to entrench themselves— even at considerable cost to their economies and to themselves in forgone opportunities to grow richer. Becht and DeLong (chap. 11) explain how American controlling shareholders and professional managers took control of the board nomination process to all but give themselves ironclad tenure. Morck and Nakamura (chap. 7) describe how the builders of Japanese *zaibatsu* family pyramids viewed those structures as devices to lock in control, and how postwar *keiretsu* groups developed to block hostile takeovers that threatened corporate insiders' positions. De Jong and Röell (chap. 11) argue that Dutch corporate insiders developed an array of *oligarchic devices* to limit shareholders' power to fire them. Franks, Mayer, and Rossi (chap. 10) describe how British corporate insiders tried unsuccessfully to erect pyramidal business groups to similarly entrench a status quo that bestowed privileges upon them. Fohlin (chap. 4) depicts German banks safeguarding their control of corporate proxy voting to entrench the power of leading bankers. Aganin and Volpin (chap. 6) relate how elite Italian business families entrenched themselves. Chapters 2, 3, 5, and 9 describe bureaucrats destroying wealth to lock in their power. In the case of Sweden, Högfeldt argues that wealthy families ultimately cooperated with public officials in a sort of "mutual entrenchment" pact. Mody argues, in his discussion of the chapter on India, that a similar confluence of self-interest occurred in India, and Morck et al. (chap. 1) speculate that something analogous might have happened in Canada in the latter twentieth century.

A predisposition to invest in entrenching one's position is consistent with recent research into the nature of self-interest. *Prospect theory,* proposed by Kahneman and Tversky (1979), holds that individuals view upside and downside risk asymmetrically. A preponderance of empirical and experimental work, surveyed by Shleifer (2000), now supports prospect theory as representative of typical human behavior.

Prospect theory makes people loss averse. That is, people typically place a higher subjective value on avoiding a $100 loss than on gaining $100 of additional wealth.

In this light, pervasive entrenchment seems almost inevitable. For entrenchment is precisely about sacrificing opportunities for further gain to minimize the risk of loss—archetypical self-interested behavior according to prospect theory. The patriarch of a large family firm can either support or oppose institutional reforms, such as more efficient capital markets or courts. These changes might let the patriarch greatly expand his family business group and grow much wealthier, but they also might let competitors arise who might erode or even destroy the family's established wealth. Large risks of this sort, according to prospect theory, are typically rejected even if they entail substantial upside potential. Risking the patrimony is simply unacceptable. In contrast, minor tinkering with institutional change is typically acceptable. Prospect theory thus suggests a conservative bias that would encourage wealthy patriarchs to invest in entrenching themselves and oppose institutional reform that might risk their current wealth and status. If political power is largely in the hands of the currently wealthy, Kuran (1988) predicts a locking in of the status quo. Olson (1963, 1982) suggests that this is likely to be the case, as does Faccio (2003).

But ordinary citizens might also entertain a bias against institutional reform. Murphy (chap. 3) shows how various attempts to reform the French financial system led to repeated disaster. If most people view institutional change as carrying a substantial probability of making things worse, populations as a whole might likewise favor the status quo.

Another key element of human nature, first demonstrated in experimental work by Milgram (1963, 1983), is an apparently reflexive obedience to perceived legitimate authority.[30] It seems likely that this behavioral response stabilizes family capitalism throughout much of the world, especially where wealthy families who control large business groups are closely intertwined with the state and so have reinforced legitimacy.

Third, the economy requires a degree of institutional stability. Commons (1924) argues correctly that business planning is impossible if critical institutions are uncertain. Business is often easier with certain but unfavorable laws than with uncertain favorable laws. Owen and Braeutigam (1978) argue in this vein that people holding uncompleted contracts perceive themselves as having a right to the continuation of existing institutions, and so oppose change.

All of this might explain the one-sided institutional momentum that is evident throughout the studies in this volume. Institutional reform that locks in the status quo seems easy. Institutional reform that brings real change is rare. China's first attempt to import Western legal institutions failed because it threatened the powers of her ancient bureaucracy. The reforms were either ignored or modified to protect the bureaucrats, and so they failed to bring sustainable free enterprise to China. America's attempt to impose freestanding widely held firms on postwar Japan likewise failed because their professional managers saw their status at risk because of threatened hostile takeovers. Those managers reconstituted corporate groups to lock in the status quo. India's License Raj, Sweden's Social Democracy, and perhaps Canada's post-1960s Statism were all arguably attempts at radical reform of various sorts that ultimately entrenched corporate elite families.

30. For a quick summary, see Morck (2004a).

Real reform seems to have succeeded in 1930s America—perhaps because people thought they had little more to lose given the disaster of the Great Depression. A small loss balanced against a large gain can induce people to take the bet and support institutional change. In America, they apparently won. Similar willingness to bet in 1930s Germany, Italy, and Japan turned out less happily.

Prospect theory is not the only possible underpinning for a conservative bias against institutional change. Roe (1996) argues that institutions might suffer from a QWERTY effect, whereby institutions, like keyboards with which everyone is familiar, are retained because the cost of adjusting to new ways exceeds the benefit—at least in the short term.[31] Day (1987), Heiner (1983, 1986, 1988), and others argue for a conservative bias based on bounded rationality and computation costs.

All of this has several implications. First, real institutional change is difficult, but not impossible. Overcoming a popular conservative bias is easiest during crises, when people feel they have less to lose should the reform go wrong. Second, countries will not easily mimic each other, so variation in institutions across countries with different histories will not disappear easily—even if one system appears better. Third, institutional change, even when implemented enthusiastically from above, as in pre-communist China, may fail because of a popular conservative bias. Institutions that sustain great inefficiency, inequality, and even corruption may thus be quite historically stable.

Conclusions

History, like poetry, does not repeat itself, but rhymes. Accidents of history give the rhyme a different starting point in different countries, but there is a common meter throughout.

Financial disasters tainted French confidence in financial securities early on and set corporate governance in that country on a different path from that of Britain, where similar trauma was overcome and forgotten. Why trauma desolates some people and some nations, while others pick up the pieces and move on, is profoundly unclear. But history is more than a string of accidental traumas.

Ideas matter. There is a conservative bias in every country that impedes institutional change. But when crisis strikes, that bias lessens and change is possible. Whatever idea is waiting in the wings at that time can be swept into reality. Thus, American Progressivism, German National Socialism, Italian Fascism, Japanese militarism, and Swedish Social Democracy all became incarnate during the depressions of the 1920s and 1930s.

Families matter. Throughout the world, big business was, at first, family

31. Though see David (1985).

business. It seems likely this arose because blood kin can cooperate more reliably than nonkin. Reliable cooperation is important in countries at early stages in their economic development, when legal and regulatory institutions are unreliable guarantors of trustworthy behavior. But this, too, is admittedly speculation. For families remain overwhelmingly important in the governance of the large business sectors of all but a handful of developed economies. Perhaps this reflects a conservative bias against change, or perhaps many developed countries still do not have institutions that foster an ambient trust. Or perhaps there are other explanations, like inherited talent, that we find intellectually uncomfortable.

Business groups, each encompassing many separately listed firms, became important in almost every country, including the United States, at some point, and they remain important in most developed economies. These groups almost always have a pyramidal structure, with a family, family partnership, or family trust at the apex. To some extent, these structures were probably hierarchical arrangements designed to span dysfunctional markets in the early stages of economic development, and these explanations perhaps retain validity in modern emerging economies. But the ubiquity of large pyramidal family-controlled business groups in Canada, Japan, and most of Western Europe is harder to square with this theory. Those countries have had many decades of high income and could surely have repaired such problems had they wanted to. It seems likely that pyramidal business groups of listed companies survive in wealthy countries because they lock in the corporate governance power of an elite family over capital assets worth far more than the family fortune. That power brings intangible benefits that such families are loath to surrender.

Wealthy families, to lock in their corporate governance, might block the emergence of trustworthy markets and institutions, and so greatly harm their countries. Or they might persist as a sort of corporate governance appendix while institutions and markets develop around them. Or, like constitutional monarchs, they might serve shareholders by providing constitutional guarantees of good governance, and so contribute to higher levels of trust. Or might business acumen sometimes actually pass down through families? Each possibility was probably realized at different times and in different countries.

Law clearly matters, though just how is less than clear. Many current differences between common-law and civil law countries regarding statutory shareholder rights are not long-standing differences.[32] This volume advances our understanding of the different manifestations of capitalism throughout the world. By adopting a historical approach it provides useful insights into how various economic institutions, and institutional configu-

---

32. See Lamoreaux and Rosenthal (2004) regarding the dearth of shareholder rights in the pre-Depression United States.

rations, came to be. It also engenders some general observation regarding varieties of capitalism and economic change.

Legal systems are not the only features that distinguish former Western colonies from each other. Perhaps vestiges of indigenous institutions mount an immune response against transplanted Western institutions. Or perhaps radical changes in institutions invite problems. Patterns in current corporate governance sometimes attributed to legal system origins may reflect other historical antecedents.

Institutions in every country studied evolved through time, and corporate control changed with them. What caused what is often unclear, though. Many countries now considered to have highly trustworthy institutions, including institutions of corporate governance, were profoundly corrupt only a few generations ago. There seems to have been an evolution toward ever less popular tolerance of corrupt elites everywhere, except perhaps in Britain.

Where reformers sought to hasten that evolution by transplanting institutions from one country to another, success has varied. Although Western institutions grafted onto Japan quickly took on a native appearance, the grafts surely did not fail. Japan is a highly prosperous economy, and few countries are so devoid of governance and other scandals as to denounce its institutional experimentation as a failure. Western institutions grafted onto prerevolutionary China failed spectacularly, and those grafted onto India long looked sickly but recently seem invigorated.

Large outside investors, such as pension funds, are becoming important throughout the world and may well have a salubrious effect on corporate governance everywhere. However, it is hard to see how success in influencing the professional managers of widely held firms in the United Kingdom or United States need imply similar success in influencing old moneyed families with control blocks in scores of firms in a more typical country. Yet wonders happen.

Financial development seems intimately tied to corporate governance, with more developed financial systems associated with more professional management, more diffuse shareholders, and less ubiquitous family control. But these correlations are only rough, and many counterexamples arose in the histories of many countries. For example, family groups rose and fell in importance in Italy, while financial development fell and then rose—consistent with the general cross-country pattern. But family groups fell and then rose in importance in Canada, while financial development probably mainly rose.

Politics perhaps explains some of this, for large family groups may be better at dealing with more interventionist governments than multitudinous freestanding firms. Or politicians bent on interventionism may value being able to influence the whole corporate sector with phone calls to a handful of patriarchs.

Perhaps because business elites and political elites tend to overlap, institutions, including those that pertain to corporate governance, seem hard to change, except to lock in more solidly the status quo at any point in time. A common theme through all the countries surveyed is entrenchment—corporate insiders modifying the rules to minimize the chances of becoming outsiders. This is so ubiquitous that we propose that something basic in human nature must be involved.

An ultimate bottom line for this volume is that history is best enjoyed vicariously. Institutional change and, even worse, experimentation, though enlivening the studies in this volume, have often been disastrous to those involved. This too may explain the institutional momentum apparent in every country. Certainly, it cautions against overly optimistic plans for top-down structural reforms to corporate governance in developing countries. But successful reforms dot history, and Japan's wholesale transplanting of Western institutions can scarcely be called a failure. History need not be the handmaiden of authority.

References

Acemoglu, Daron, Simon Johnson, and James A. Robinson. 2001. The colonial origins of comparative development: An empirical investigation. *American Economic Review* 91 (5): 1369–1422.

———. 2002a. Reversal of fortune: Geography and institutions in the making of the modern world income distribution. *Quarterly Journal of Economics* 117 (4): 1231.

———. 2002b. The rise of Europe: Atlantic trade, institutional change, and economic growth. MIT, Department of Economics. Working Paper.

Acemoglu, Daron, and James A. Robinson. 2000. Political losers as a barrier to economic development. *American Economic Review* 90 (2): 126–30.

Aoki, Masahiko. 1988. *Information, incentives, and bargaining in the Japanese economy.* New York: Cambridge University Press.

Arrow, Kenneth. 1974. *The limits of organization.* New York: Norton.

Axelrod, Robert, and William Hamilton. 1981. The evolution of cooperation in biological systems. *Science* 211 (27): 1390–96.

Bae, Kee-Hong, Jun-Koo Kang, and Jin-Mo Kim. 2002. Tunneling or value added? Evidence from mergers by Korean business groups. *Journal of Finance* 57 (6): 2695–2741.

Barca, Fabrizio, and Marco Becht, eds. 2001. *The control of corporate Europe.* European Corporate Governance Network. Oxford, UK: Oxford University Press.

Baums, Theodor. 1995. Universal banks and investment companies in Germany. New York University Salomon Centre Conference on Universal Banking. Working paper.

Bebchuk, Lucien, Reinier Kraakman, and George Triantis. 2000. Stock pyramids, cross ownership and dual class equity: The mechanisms and agency costs of separating control from cash flow rights. In *Concentrated corporate ownership,* ed. Randall Morck, 295–315. Chicago: University of Chicago Press.

Becht, Marco, Patrick Bolton, and Ailsa Röell. 2002. Corporate governance and control. In *Handbook of economics and finance,* ed. George Constantinides, Milton Harris and René Stulz. Amsterdam: North Holland.

Berkowitz, Daniel, and Karen Clay. 2004. American civil law origins: Implications for state constitutions. *American law and economic review symposium on comparative law,* forthcoming.

Berkowitz, Daniel, Katharina Pistor, and Jean-Francois Richard. 2003. Economic development, legality, and the transplant effect. *European Economic Review* 47 (1): 165–95.

Berle, Adolf, and Gardiner Means. 1932. *The modern corporation and private property.* New York: Macmillan.

Bertrand, Marianne, Paras Mehta, and Sendhil Mullainathan. 2002. Ferreting out tunneling: An application to Indian business groups. *Quarterly Journal of Economics* 117 (1): 121–48.

Biais, Bruno, and Enrico Perotti. 2003. Entrepreneurs and new ideas. CEPR Discussion Paper no. 3864. London: Center for Economic Policy Research.

Boycko, Maxim, Andrei Shleifer, and Robert Vishny. 1996. A theory of privatization. *Economic Journal* 106 (435): 309–19.

Bradach, Jeffrey, and Robert Eccles. 1989. Price, authority, and trust: From ideal types to plural forms. *Annual Review of Sociology* 15:97–118.

Burkart, Mike, Fausto Panunzi, and Andrei Shleifer. 2003. Family firms. *Journal of Finance* 58 (5): 2167–2201.

Burt, Ron S. 1992a. The social structure of competition. In *Networks and organizations: Structure, form, and action,* ed. N. Nohria and R. G. Eccles, 57–91. Boston: Harvard Business School Press.

Burt, Ron S. 1992b. *Structural holes.* Cambridge, MA: Harvard University Press.

Burt, Ron S. 1997. The contingent value of social capital. *Administrative Science Quarterly* 42:339–65.

Cheffins, Brian. 2001. Does law matter? The separation of ownership and control in the United Kingdom. *Journal of Legal Studies* 30:459–84.

Claessens, Stjin, Simeon Djankov, Joseph Fan, and Larry Lang. 2002. Disentangling the incentive and entrenchment effects of large shareholdings. *Journal of Finance* 57 (6): 2741–72.

Coase, Ronald. 1937. The nature of the firm. *Economica* 4:386–405.

Coffee, John. 2001. The rise of dispersed ownership: The roles of law and state in the separation of ownership and control. *Yale Law Journal* 111 (1): 1–82.

Coleman, James S. 1988. Social capital in the creation of human capital. *American Journal of Sociology* 94:S95–S120.

Commons, John R. 1924. Legal foundations of capitalism. Madison, WI: University of Wisconsin Press.

Daniels, Ron, Randall Morck, and David Stangeland. 1995. High gear: A case study of the Hees-Edper corporate group. In *Corporate decision making in Canada,* ed. R. Daniels and R. Morck, 223–41. Calgary: Industry Canada and the University of Calgary Press.

Das, Gurcharan. 2002. *India unbound.* Garden City, NY: Anchor.

David, Paul A. 1985. Clio and the economics of QWERTY. *American Economic Review* 75:332–37.

Day, Richard H. 1987. The general theory of disequilibrium and economic evolution. In *Economic evolution and structural adjustment,* ed. D. Batten, J. Casti, and B. Johansson, 46–63. Berlin: Springer-Verlag.

Dewenter, Kathryn, and Paul Malatesta. 2001. State-owned and privately owned firms: An empirical analysis of profitability. *American Economic Review* 91 (1): 320–35.

Dewing, Arthur. 1919. *The financial policy of corporations.* New York: Ronald Press.

Diamond, Jared. 1997. *Guns, germs, and steel: The fates of human societies.* New York: Norton.

Dunlavy, Colleen. 2004. *The plutocratic turn in 19th-century shareholder voting rights: Why the U.S. but not Britain, France, or Germany?* Harvard University Press, forthcoming.

Dyer, Jeffrey H., and Harbir Singh. 1998. The relational view: Cooperative strategy and sources of interorganizational competitive advantage. *Academy of Management Review* 23:660–79.

Enriques, Luca. 2002. Do corporate law judges matter? Some evidence from Milan. *European Business Organization Law Review* 3:765–821.

Faccio, Mara. 2003. Politically connected firms: Can they squeeze the state? Vanderbilt University, Owen Graduate School of Management. Working Paper.

Faccio, Mara, and Larry H. P. Lang. 2003. The separation of ownership and control: An analysis of ultimate ownership in Western European countries. *Journal of Financial Economics* 65 (3): 365–95.

Faccio, Mara, Larry H. P. Lang, and Leslie Young. 2001. Dividends and expropriation. *American Economic Review* 91 (1): 54–78.

Frentrop, Paul. 2003. *A history of corporate governance 1602–2002.* Trans. Ted Alkins,. Amsterdam: De minor.

Fukuyama, Francis. 1995. *Trust, the social virtues and the creation of prosperity.* New York: Free Press.

Ghemawat, Pankaj, and Tarun Khanna. 1998. The nature of diversified business groups: A research design and two case studies. *Journal of Industrial Economics* 46 (1): 35–62.

Glaeser, Edward, and Andrei Shleifer. 2002. Legal origins. *Quarterly Journal of Economics* 117 (4): 1193–1250.

Granovetter, Mark. In press. Business groups and social organization. In *Handbook of economic sociology,* 2nd ed., ed. N. Smelser and R. Swedberg. Princeton, NJ: Princeton University Press.

Guerin, Daniel. 1945. *Fascism and big business.* New York: Pathfinder.

Haber, Stephen. 1999. *Industry and underdevelopment: The industrialization of Mexico, 1890–1940.* Stanford, CA: Stanford University Press.

Hayek, Friedrich. 1960. *The constitution of liberty.* Chicago: University of Chicago Press.

Heiner, Ronald A. 1983. The origin of predictable behavior. *American Economic Review* 83:560–95.

———. 1986. Imperfect decisions and the law: On the evolution of legal precedent and rules. *Journal of Legal Studies* 15:227–61.

———. 1988. Imperfect decisions and organizations: Toward a theory of internal structure. *Journal of Economic Behavior and Organization* 9:25–44.

Hoshi, Takeo, Anil Kashyap, and David Scharfstein. 1991. Corporate structure, liquidity, and investment: Evidence from Japanese industrial groups. *Quarterly Journal of Economics* 106:33–60.

Hosking, Geoffrey. 1985. *The first Socialist society: A history of the Soviet Union from within.* 2nd ed. Cambridge, MA: Harvard University Press.

Kahneman, Daniel, and Amos Tversky. 1979. Prospect theory: An analysis of decision under risk. *Econometrica* 47:263–91.

Kaplan, Steven. 1994. Top executive rewards and firm performance: A comparison of Japan and the U.S. *Journal of Political Economy* 102:510–46.

Khanna, Tarun. 2000. Business groups and social welfare in emerging markets: Existing evidence and unanswered questions. *European Economic Review* 44: 248–61.

Khanna, Tarun, and Krishna Palepu. 1997. Why focused strategies may be wrong for emerging markets. *Harvard Business Review* 75 (4): 41–51.

———. 2000. The future of business groups in emerging markets: Long-run evidence from Chile. *Academy of Management Journal* 43 (3): 268–85.

Khanna, Tarun, and Jan Rivkin. 2001. Estimating the performance effects of business groups in emerging markets. *Strategic Management Journal* 22 (1): 45–74.

Kindleberger, Charles. 1978. *Manias, panics and crashes.* London: Macmillan.

———. 1984. *A financial history of Western Europe.* London: Allen & Unwin.

King, Robert G., and Ross Levine. 1993. Finance and growth: Schumpeter might be right. *Quarterly Journal of Economics* 108 (3): 717–37.

Kleeberg, John. 1987. The Disconto-Gesellschaft and German industrialization: A critical examination of the career of a German universal bank, 1851–1914. PhD diss., University of Oxford.

Krueger, Anne. 1990. Government failures in development. *Journal of Economic Perspectives* 4 (3): 9–23.

Kuran, Timur. 1988. The tenacious past: Theories of personal and collective conservatism. *Journal of Economic Behavior and Organization* 10 (2): 143–72.

Lamoreaux, Naomi, and Jean-Laurent Rosenthal. 2004. Corporate governance and the plight of minority shareholders in the United States before the Great Depression. NBER Working Paper no. 10900. Cambridge, MA: National Bureau of Economic Research.

La Porta, Rafael, Florencio López-de-Silanes, Cristian Pop-Eleches, and Andrei Shleifer. 2004. Judicial check and balances. *Journal of Political Economy* 112 (2): 445–70.

La Porta, Rafael, Florencio López-de-Silanes, and Andrei Shleifer. 2003. What works in securities laws? Tuck School of Business Working Paper no. 03-22. Dartmouth University.

———. 2005. What works in securities law. *Journal of Finance,* forthcoming.

La Porta, Rafael, Florencio López-de-Silanes, Andrei Shleifer, and Robert Vishny. 1997a. Legal determinants of external finance. *Journal of Finance* 52 (3): 1131–50.

———. 1997b. Trust in large organizations. *American Economic Review* 87 (2): 333–39.

———. 1998. Law and finance. *Journal of Political Economy* 106 (6): 1113–57.

———. 1999. Corporate ownership around the world. *Journal of Finance* 54 (2): 471–520.

Landes, David S. 1949. French entrepreneurship and industrial growth in the nineteenth century. *Journal of Economic History* 9:45–61.

———. 1998. *The wealth and poverty of nations: Why some are so rich and some so poor.* New York: W. W. Norton.

Macaulay, Stewart. 1963. Non-contractual relations in business: A preliminary study. *American Sociological Review* 28:55–67.

Mahoney, Paul. 2001. The common law and economic growth: Hayek might be right. *Journal of Legal Studies* 30:503–26.

Markesinis, Basil. 2000. Our debt to Europe: Past, present and future. In *The Clifford Chance millennium lectures: The coming together of the common law and civil law,* ed. Basil Markesinis, 11–42. London: Hart.

Mayer, Roger C., James H. Davis, and F. David Schoorman. 1995. An integrative model of organizational trust. *Academy of Management Review* 20:709–34.

Merryman, John. 1966. The Italian style III: Interpretation. *Stanford Law Review* 18:583–611.

Milgram, Stanley. 1963. Behavioral study of obedience. *Journal of Abnormal and Social Psychology* 67:371–78.

———. 1983. *Obedience to authority: An experimental view.* New York: Harper-Collins.

Mokyr, Joel. 2000. The industrial revolution and the Netherlands: Why did it not happen? *De Economist* 148 (4): 503–20.

Moody, John. 1904. *The truth about the trusts.* New York: Moody's.

Morck, Randall. 2004a. Behavioral finance in corporate governance: Independent directors and non-executive chairs. NBER Working Paper no. 10644. Cambridge, MA: National Bureau of Economic Research.

———. 2004b. How to eliminate pyramidal business groups: The double taxation of inter-corporate dividends and other incisive uses of tax policy. NBER Working Paper no. 10944. Cambridge, MA: National Bureau of Economic Research.

Morck, Randall, and Masao Nakamura. 1999. Banks and corporate control in Japan. *Journal of Finance* 54 (1): 319–40.

Morck, Randall, Masao Nakamura, and Anil Shivdasani. 2000. Banks, ownership, structure, and firm value in Japan. *Journal of Business* 73:539–69.

Morck, Randall, Andrei Shleifer, and Robert Vishny. 1988. Management ownership and market valuation: An empirical analysis. *Journal of Financial Economics* 20 (Jan/Mar): 293–315.

Morck, Randall, David A. Stangeland, and Bernard Yeung. 2000. Inherited wealth, corporate control, and economic growth: The Canadian disease. In *Concentrated corporate ownership,* ed. Randall Morck, 319–69. Chicago: University of Chicago Press.

Morck, Randall, Daniel Wolfenzon, and Bernard Yeung. 2004. Corporate governance, economic entrenchment and growth. NBER Working Paper no. 10692. Cambridge, MA: National Bureau of Economic Research.

Nakatani, Iwao. 1984. The economic role of financial corporate grouping. In *The economic analysis of the Japanese firm,* ed. Masahiko Aoki, 227–64. Amsterdam: North Holland.

Olson, Mancur, Jr. 1963. Rapid growth as a destabilizing force, *Journal of Economic History* 23 (4): 529–52.

———. 1982. *The rise and decline of nations.* New Haven, CT: Yale University Press.

Owen, Bruce M., and Ronald Braeutigam. 1978. *The regulation game.* Cambridge, MA: Ballinger.

Pagano, Marco, Fabio Panetta, and Luigi Zingales. 1998. Why do companies go public? An empirical analysis. *Journal of Finance* 53:27–64.

Pagano, Marco, and Paolo Volpin. 2001. The political economy of finance. *Oxford Review of Economic Policy* 17 (4): 502–19.

Pistor, Katharina, Yoram Keinan, Jan Kleinhelsterkamp, and Mark West. 1999. The evolution of corporate law. *University of Pennsylvania Journal of International Economic Law* 22:791–871.

———. 2003. Evolution of corporate law and the transplant effect: Lessons from six countries. *World Bank Research Observer* 18 (1): 89–112.

Portes, Alejandro. 1998. Social capital: Its origins and applications in modern sociology. *Annual Review of Sociology* 24:1–24.

Posner, Richard. 1996. *Law and legal theory in England and America.* Oxford: Clarendon Press.

Powell, Walter W. 1990. Neither market nor hierarchy: Network forms of organization. In *Research in organizational behavior,* ed. B. M. Staw and L. L. Cummings, 295–396. Greenwich, CT: JAI.

Putnam, Robert. 1993. *Making democracy work.* Princeton, NJ: Princeton University Press.

Rajan, Raghuram, and Luigi Zingales. 2003. The great reversals: The politics of financial development in the twentieth century. *Journal of Financial Economics* 69 (1): 5–50.

Ramseyer, J. Mark, and Minoru Nakazato. 1999. *Japanese law: An economic approach.* Chicago: University of Chicago Press.

Roe, Mark J. 1996. Chaos and evolution in law and economics. *Harvard Law Review* 109 (3): 641–69.

———. 2002. *Political determinants of corporate governance: Political context, corporate impact.* Oxford, UK: Oxford University Press.

Sahlman, William A. 1990. The structure and governance of venture-capital organizations. *Journal of Financial Economics* 27:473–521.

Schumpeter, Joseph A. 1912. *Theorie der Wirtschaftlichen Entwichlung.* Leipzig: Dunker und Humbolt. Translated by R. Opie in 1934 as *The theory of economic development: An inquiry into profits, capital, credit, interest, and the business cycle.* Cambridge, MA: Harvard University Press.

———. 1951. *Imperialism and social classes.* Greenwich, UK: Meridian Books.

Shleifer, Andrei. 2000. *Inefficient markets: An introduction to behavioral finance.* Clarendon Lectures in Economics. Oxford, UK: Oxford University Press.

Shleifer, Andrei, and Robert Vishny. 1986. Large shareholders and corporate control. *Journal of Political Economy* 95:461–88.

———. 1997. A survey of corporate governance. *Journal of Finance* 52 (2): 737–84.

Shleifer, Andrei, and Daniel Wolfenzon. 2002. Investor protection and equity markets. *Journal of Financial Economics* 66 (1): 3–27.

Silverman, Dan. 1998. *Hitler's economy: Nazi work creation programs 1933–1936.* Cambridge, MA: Harvard University Press.

Steier, Lloyd. 1998. Confounding market and hierarchy in venture capital governance: The Canadian immigrant investor program. *Journal of Management Studies* 35 (4): 511–35.

Stinchcombe, Arthur L. 1965. Social structure and organizations. In *Handbook of organizations,* ed. J. G. March, 142–93. Chicago: Rand-McNally.

Stulz, René, and Rohan Williamson. 2003. Culture, openness, and finance. *Journal of Financial Economics* 70 (3): 313–49.

Sylla, Richard, and George David Smith. 1995. Information and capital market regulation in Anglo-American finance. In *Anglo-American financial systems,* ed. Michael Bordo and Richard Sylla, 179–208. New York: Irwin.

Thurow, Lester C. 1989. An establishment or an oligarchy? *National Tax Journal* 42 (4): 405–11.

Watson, Alan. 1981. *The making of the civil law.* Cambridge, MA: Harvard University Press.

———. 1981. *General economic history.* New Brunswick, NJ: Transaction Books.

Weiss, Gunther. 2000. The enchantment of codification in the common-law world. *Yale Journal of International Law* 25:435.

Williamson, Oliver. 1975. *Markets and hierarchies: Analysis and antitrust implications.* New York: Free Press.

———. 1985. *The economic institutions of capitalism.* New York: Free Press.

1

The Rise and Fall of the Widely Held Firm
A History of Corporate Ownership in Canada

Randall K. Morck, Michael Percy, Gloria Y. Tian,
and Bernard Yeung

1.1 Introduction

At the beginning of the twentieth century, large pyramidal corporate groups, controlled by wealthy families or individuals, dominated Canada's large corporate sector, as in modern continental European countries. Over several decades, a large stock market, high taxes on inherited income, a sound institutional environment, and capital account openness accompanied the rise of widely held firms. At mid-century, the Canadian large corporate sector was primarily freestanding widely held firms, as in the modern large corporate sectors of the United States and United Kingdom. Then, in the last third of the century, a series of institutional changes took place. These included a more bank-based financial system, a sharp abate-

Randall K. Morck is Stephen A. Jarislowsky Distinguished Professor of Finance at the University of Alberta School of Business and a research associate of the National Bureau of Economic Research. This work was done, in part, while he was a visiting professor of economics at Harvard University. Michael Percy is Stanley A. Milner Professor and dean at the University of Alberta School of Business. Gloria Y. Tian is a PhD candidate in finance at the University of Alberta School of Business. Bernard Yeung is the Abraham Krasnoff Professor of International Business and professor of economics at the New York University Stern School of Business.

We are grateful for comments from participants in the National Bureau of Economic Research conference on the history of corporate ownership in Lake Louise, the Canadian Economic Association in Ottawa, and the CEPR/ECGN/INSEAD/University of Alberta/National Bureau of Economic Research Conference in Fontainebleau. We also thank seminar participants at the Bank of Canada, Hitotsubashi University, New York University, Queen's University, the University of Minnesota, and the University of Toronto's Olin Lecture. We are especially indebted to John Baldwin, Steven Globerman, Enrico Perotti, Andrei Shleifer, Jordan Siegel, and Javier Suárez for thoughtful comments and suggestions. Financial support from the University of Alberta School of Business, the University of Alberta Centre for Entrepreneurship and Family Enterprise, and the Social Sciences and Humanities Research Council is gratefully acknowledged.

ment in taxes on large estates, a likely rise in the value of superior rent-seeking skills, and foreign investment restrictions. These were accompanied by a decline in the importance of freestanding widely held firms and a commensurate rise in the prevalence of family pyramidal groups.

The reasons for the relative decline in importance of Canada's stock market as compared to its banking system in the last decades of the century are unclear. The introduction of a capital gains tax at the onset of a period of high inflation may have been a factor, but the stock market did not recover its prior level of importance after inflation abated.

The advent of the capital gains tax accompanied the end of succession taxes. After 1972, inherited income became tax exempt. Capital gains taxes were theoretically due on the decedent's assets at death. But the realization of capital gains could be postponed for two generations through family trusts, structures viable only for very large estates. Several large family corporate groups were clearly broken into freestanding widely held firms to pay succession taxes, so the succession tax clearly accounts, in part at least, for the rise of the widely held firm.

The last third of the century actually saw much more profound transformations of public finances. Corporate taxes rose and became intricately complicated, filled with implicit subsidies and intricate incentives and penalties. A proliferation of agencies administered a vast array of subsidies directly and through regional or industrial development funds. In a comprehensive study of Canadian public finances, Savoie (1990) concludes that "especially since the early 1960s . . . in certain areas of the country at least, there is a government subsidy available for virtually every type of commercial activity." He goes on to quote *Canadian Business* thus: "Some firms are in the happy position of being able to employ staff or consultants whose sole function is to sniff out all the juicy morsels the politicians and policy makers throw in the public trough."

Corporate groups are a response to a weak institutional environment. One version of this hypothesis, developed by Khanna and Palepu (2000a,b, 2001), proposes that corporate groups are a second-best solution in economies whose product, labor, and capital markets are underdeveloped and inefficient. Substantial evidence supports this explanation in emerging economies. A second version of this hypothesis, proposed by Morck and Yeung (2004), holds that family-controlled corporate groups have superior political rent-seeking skills. Political rent seeking, corporate investment in political influence, is commonplace in most countries and is usually legal. Family groups' most important advantages include the following: Groups can act more discretely than freestanding firms, for one group firm can invest in influencing a politician while another, perhaps privately held, collects the reward. Family firms have long time horizons, so they can better invest in influence now to reap subsidies in the distant future. Widely held firms, in contrast, change chief executive officers (CEOs) every few years and so require a faster payback. Thus, as political influence became an increasingly important determinant of financial success in the last decades of the century, family-controlled group firms eclipsed freestanding widely held firms.

Finally, this rise of interventionism also entailed restrictions on foreign investment. Nationalist politicians, seeking to safeguard Canadian control of major corporations, perhaps encouraged family groups to serve as white knights. In some sectors, notably energy and cultural industries, this was overt—locking in future subsidies and tax advantages. In others, the rewards may have been more indirect.

This heightened importance of political influence, and the nationalist overtones surrounding it, have resounding echoes through Canada's economic history. Jean-Baptiste Colbert, the intellectual father of French mercantilism, owned Canada and used the colony as a laboratory for mercantilist experiments. Colonial Canada featured state-subsidized ironworks, shipbuilding, canals, brick making, shoe making, beer making, wool production, mining, lumbering, eel packing, sea oil, and cod salting, among many other industries. In general, these were owned by the colonial political elite (and Colbert), and subsidized by the French government. The British conquerors, appreciating the benefits of this system to the colonial elite (now themselves), preserved it. British North America repeatedly bankrupted itself subsidizing all manner of canal and railway projects owned, directly or indirectly, by colonial politicians. Canadian corporate investment continued in this vein long after independence, almost to the twentieth century. Around the turn of the twentieth century, the Liberal prime minister Wilfrid Laurier greatly reduced corruption and adopted laissez-faire policy (until near the end of his last term). The country enjoyed an unprecedented surge of development. After World War II, C. D. Howe, a powerful cabinet minister in a series of Liberal governments, professionalized the civil service and moved the country back toward laissez-faire. He also virtually monopolized the awarding of remaining subsidies and tax favors. In the 1960s, shareholder rights were formalized, and Canada's mercantilist past seemed buried. This corresponded to the greatest extent of large widely held freestanding firms—about 80 percent of the corporate sector by assets.

Two factors changed this in the late 1960s.

One was the Révolution Tranquille in Quebec, which reignited Canada's dormant linguistic quarrels and created a national identity crisis. Separatist politicians sought to build a Quebecois nation with sweeping industrial policies. To counter this, federal politicians nurtured Canadian identity with nationalist rhetoric. This led to concern about foreign control of Canadian companies and probably to Canadian family groups' serving as white knights to safeguard widely held firms from foreign acquirers.

The second factor was a renewed political respectability for state intervention. Each previous political philosophy—the Tory rejection of the American Revolution, nineteenth-century liberalism, the progressive movement, and agrarian socialism in turn—quickly took on mercantilist garb upon touching Canadian soil. The Keynesian and Social Democratic philosophies of the 1970s were especially open to this. Canada's mercantilist undercurrent transformed idealistic plans to improve society into a morass of political rent seeking. In this environment, family-controlled corporate groups had an edge.

Thus, our findings support Burkart, Panunzi, and Shleifer (2002) and La Porta, López-de-Silanes, and Shleifer (1999), who relate widely held ownership of corporations to sound institutions. They also support the general approach of Acemoglu and Johnson (2000) and Acemoglu, Johnson, and Robinson (2001, 2002, 2003), who stress the importance of colonial institutions in determining modern institutions. Our findings also give credence to the arguments of Morck and Yeung (2004) that family-controlled corporate groups have an advantage in weak institutional environments because of superior rent-seeking skills. However, they in no way undermine the thesis of Khanna and Palepu (2000a,b, 2001) that other institutional deficiencies can also confer advantages on groups.

The remainder of the paper is as follows. Section 1.2 describes our ownership data. Section 1.3 describes Canada's colonial institutions. Section 1.4 describes institutions and large corporate ownership structures at the beginning of the twentieth century. Section 1.5 describes the evolution of large corporations' ownership structures and proffers explanations. Section 1.6 concludes.

1.2 Description of Data

To explore the evolution of corporate ownership, we require a picture of its initial conditions on the eve of industrialization. Continuous quantitative data are unavailable until the twentieth century; however, qualitative descriptions of business ownership are possible. Such descriptions are useful in assessing the influence of Canada's colonial heritages on her industrial-era institutions and in interpreting quantitative data in later years when they become available.

These qualitative descriptions summarize relevant parts of the writings of several business historians. Bliss (1986) presents a thorough review of Canadian business history that is broadly sympathetic to the country's business elite, emphasizing their entrepreneurial ventures and risk taking as well as their occasional skulduggery. Francis (1986) describes the increasing importance of business groups as of the early 1980s and provides some historical information about the thirty largest groups. Hedley (1894) provides brief biographies of Canadian business leaders. Unfortunately, many are at too low a level to be of interest to us. Myers (1914) is something of a muckraker, focusing on the rent seeking, unsavory undertakings, and politically incorrect philosophies of the business elite. Naylor (1975) is quite critical of the business elite and often appears sympathetic to leftist views. Taylor and Baskerville (1994) provide a highly useful history of Canadian businesses, though their coverage after 1930 is rushed. Tulchinsky (1977) provides information about colonial Montreal businesses. Parkman (1867) contains much information about Canada's colonial economy. All provide valuable information about ownership and control as asides to their main arguments.

Much of the qualitative description below relies on these sources—especially Bliss and Naylor for broad historical overviews and basic factual information. To avoid repetitive citations, specific references are mainly to other sources. However, a general reference pervades to these authors, and a degree of plagiarism is gratefully acknowledged.

Certain data on the health of the preindustrial and early industrial economy aid us in interpreting changes in corporate control. The Bay's dividend, available from 1670 on, reflects the health of the fur trade and hence the colony's prosperity. Per capita gross domestic product (GDP) growth is available from 1870 on—from Urquhart (1993) prior to 1926, and from Statistics Canada thereafter.

Annual data on merger and acquisition activity from 1885 can be concatenated from several sources. Marchildon (1990) provides a series from 1885 to 1918. Maule (1966) reports data from 1900 to 1963. The Royal Commission of Corporate Concentration provides data for 1970 through 1986. For 1985 through 2000, data are from *Merger and Acquisition in Canada.*

Corporate financial records begin in 1902.[1] Since these are not available from a uniform source over the full history of the country, we combine all available sources for each time period to produce the most accurate representation possible. Data for later years are probably better. For 1965 through 1998 we take the largest 100 companies, as listed in the *Financial Post,* ranked by assets until 1967 and by revenue thereafter. For earlier years, *Financial Post* rankings are unavailable, so we build our own rankings using annual report data, summarized in the *Canadian Annual Financial Review* for 1902 through 1940 and in *Financial Post Corporate Securities* for 1950 through 1960.[2] We do not consider financial companies because these are not included in the top-100 rankings of the *Financial Post*

---

1. Incomplete data for 1901 are available.
2. The only major data problem concerns Hydro One, formerly Ontario Hydro. Though established in 1906 as the Hydro-Electric Power Commission of Ontario (HEPC), and clearly an important state-owned enterprise throughout the century, it appears as a consolidated entity in the rankings only in 1970. From 1920 on, we estimate its assets and revenues by summing sectoral data in its annual reports. Earlier financial data are extremely disorganized and marred by apparent instances of double-counting. We therefore use a geometric mean growth rate, estimated from 1920 on, to infer assets and revenues for earlier years. This certainly adds noise to our early figures for state-owned enterprises.

and because bank ownership structures are explicitly determined by federal legislation.[3] Both state-owned enterprises and multinational corporations constitute significant fractions of the corporate sector through much of the twentieth century. We therefore consider alternative average ownership structures—including and then excluding state-owned enterprises, multinationals, and both.

A second problem is that the *Financial Post* ranks the top hundred firms from 1901 to 1965 by assets and, for later years, by revenues. This appears to be because only consolidated assets are available for many companies in the earlier years. For later years, when both rankings are available, the use of sales and assets generates similar pictures. Consequently, this shortcoming is unlikely to affect our findings.

Our early ownership data are from several sources. Annual reports summarized in the *Canadian Annual Financial Review* and *Financial Post Corporate Securities* list the identity of any controlling shareholder, though not their equity stake. However, we find instances where these data contradict descriptions of corporate ownership in books on Canadian business history—especially Taylor and Baskerville (1994), Bliss (1986), Myers (1914), and Naylor (1975). In such cases, we assume beneficial ownership was not always clear at the time due to obfuscatory holding company structures. We rely on the business historians to have sorted this out. One shortcoming inherent in using these descriptive sources, however, is that we cannot provide a clear-cut definition of precisely what "controlled" or "member" (of a corporate group) means. A company is controlled by a family or belongs to a group if one of our historical sources says so or if its annual report indicates so.

From 1965 on, securities laws require more detailed disclosure. Statistics Canada summarizes this in the *Directory of Inter-Corporate Ownership* (ICO), our primary source for these years. The *Financial Post* also provides the name and stake of the largest shareholder for top Canadian firms from the 1970s on. We define a company as *controlled* if there is a combined direct and indirect voting stake of 10 percent or more, or if the ICO lists it as controlled. The ICO infers control in the absence of a 10 percent stake if board control derives from director selection rules, golden shares, and the like.

Using all these data, we classify each company into one of the following categories: freestanding widely held firms, freestanding family-controlled firms, family-controlled pyramidal group firms, firms in pyramidal groups controlled by widely held companies, firms controlled by a government or government agency, firms with a controlling foreign shareholder, and firms we cannot classify.

---

3. The Bank Act proscribes any shareholder from voting more than 10 percent of the stock in a chartered bank.

1.3 Colonial Origins

Much work on economic and institutional evolution stresses the importance of early colonial institutions to economic and financial development. This literature stresses *path dependence*—the idea that where an economy was long ago defines the possible places it can be now. Recent work highlights several variants of path dependence.

Sokoloff and Engerman (2000, p. 221) argue that colonies with plantation economies, like the Caribbean Islands and Latin America, started off with tiny colonial elites directing large populations of conquered natives or imported slaves. These elites had no incentive to establish institutions, like land reform, education, banking systems, or stock markets, that would help create small businesses and a middle class. In contrast, the United States, especially north of the Chesapeake, was settled by yeoman farmers who demanded precisely those institutions.[4]

Acemoglu, Johnson, and Robinson (2001) explain the difference between such regions with settler mortality rates. They argue that yeoman farmers settled the United States because the climate of that region allowed them to survive. In contrast, European settlers in the Caribbean and much of Latin American died in droves. Consequently, the colonial powers minimized European settlement and built institutions that facilitated natural resource exploitation—mines and plantations. These sorts of institutions, once established, endured because their owners had sufficient wealth to control the political system. Acemoglu, Johnson, and Robinson (2002, 2003) propose a slightly different view—Europeans preserved extractive precolonial institutions where indigenous civilizations were more developed, like parts of Latin America and Asia.

Easterly and Levine (1997) point out that colonial-era boundaries seldom correspond to linguistic or ethnic divisions, and use modern African data to show that ethnic diversity slows development. They find that ethnically divided countries have worse corruption, perhaps because of ethnic rivalry in tapping government coffers. Such countries also invest less in shared public infrastructure, perhaps because members of one group dislike funding projects the other group can share in.

Glaeser and Shleifer (2002), La Porta, López-de-Silanes, and Shleifer (1999, 2000) and La Porta et al. (1997a, 1998, 2000) argue that events in their early history caused England, but not France, to develop laws that restrained elites and hence that checked both official corruption and theft of outside investors' wealth by corporate insiders. In this view, most countries that inherited British law, through colonization or transplantation, like the

---

4. Other work, notably Acemoglu, Johnson, and Robinson (2001, 2002, 2003), Engerman and Sokoloff (1997), Easterly and Levine (2002), and Rajan and Zingales (2003), similarly highlights the importance of an egalitarian distribution of economic power before industrialization, so that institutional development does not entrench a small elite.

United States, developed dispersed corporate ownership, while most countries that inherited French law, like Latin America, developed concentrated ownership. In general, they argue that British common law better facilitates financial development. King and Levine (1993) demonstrate a clear connection between economic growth and financial development. Thus, a legal system that restrains insider power promotes financial development, which permits development.

Finally, Weber (1958) and others argue that elemental religious, cultural, and social factors direct economic development. Here again, Canada fails to fit nicely within any box. Quebec remained profoundly Roman Catholic, and Anglophone Canada mainly Protestant, until the late twentieth century. Both are now stoutly secular. In a variant of this hypothesis, La Porta et al. (1997b) argue that societies in which people are more prone to act cooperatively with strangers are better able to build and sustain the large-scale public and private-sector institutions needed for long-term economic growth.

All of these authors argue that modern institutions, including corporate ownership, reflect these "locked-in" historical factors. Despite their many cultural and historical similarities, Canada's colonial origins differ from those of other European settlements in North America. These differences relate to several of the above path dependence arguments, and exploring them is therefore a good starting point.

1.3.1   L'Ancien Régime

French Canada was initially a colony of resource extraction, not a colony of settlement. During brief periods when settlement became paramount, Canada was a theocratic society, reminiscent of modern Iran. And when settlement and development were finally pushed determinedly, Canada became a laboratory in which Jean-Baptiste Colbert, the father of French mercantilist economics, tested his theories with development schemes similar to third world misadventures in the 1960s. The values and ideals of French Canada still echo these centuries of theocratic and company rule, though in unexpected and sometimes odd ways.

Canada's history as a colony of extraction began in 1534, when Jacques Cartier mapped the St. Lawrence valley and claimed Canada for France. Seven years later, Francis I created Sieur de Roberval Viceroy of Canada. Roberval founded Quebec in 1541 but abandoned it after a single winter. Although France had no permanent colony in Canada, merchants in Atlantic ports, like La Rochelle, ran regular fur-trading ships to Canada. From 1562 to the 1598 Edict of Nantes, bloody wars of religion ruined France. Cut off from Paris, Catholic, Huguenot, and Jewish merchants in the Atlantic ports grew wealthy off a highly competitive fur trade.

The Edict of Nantes ended the civil wars by granting Protestants full rights, but France remained deeply divided. To reunite France, the state was tightly centralized around an absolute monarchy—a structure that persists, through various reincarnations, to the present. This centralization of economic power boded ill for the competitive fur trade.

Henry IV granted a monopoly to a group of merchants in 1600 and a ten-year monopoly to Sieur de Monts in 1604. De Monts sent Samuel de Champlain to found Port Royal (Annapolis, Nova Scotia) in 1605 and rebuild Quebec in 1608. De Monts renewed his monopoly once; then Champlain's Compagnie de Rouen et St. Malo obtained the sole right to trade furs. Rescinded in 1620 as the counterreformation swept France, the monopoly was transferred to Compagnie de Caen, run by the Rouen merchant William De Caen and his nephew. They established the feudal system in Canada, and the first fiefdom was granted in 1623 to Louis Hébert, whose Canadian title was Seigneur de Sault-au-Matelot.

All these monopolies were unenforceable until La Rochelle fell to the Royal Army in 1629. With the competition ruined, Cardinal Richelieu, chief advisor to the King since 1624, assigned his Compagnie des Cent Associés a permanent fur monopoly and limited monopolies on other transatlantic trades. In return, the Compagnie agreed to settle at least 300 habitants (feudal peasants) per year.

Now a province of France, Canada had a provincial government run by the Compagnie des Cent Associés and a Conseil Souverain composed of the governor of Quebec and senior Jesuits. The Conseil had lawmaking power over all Canada and subjected every aspect of the habitants' existence to the feudal order. Habitants were bound to the land, were unable to marry without their seigneur's leave, and held no property save at their seigneur's pleasure. As the Holy Inquisition swept Catholic Europe, the Jesuits added an unforgiving Roman Catholicism to this mixture.

After Richelieu's death in 1642, the Compagnie quickly faded. The independent *coureurs de bois* seized the fur trade within Canada, and many grew rich. The same year, Sieur de Maisonneuve de la Société de Notre Dame de Montréal founded that town as a missionary base. The Montreal clergy placed themselves above civil law and exercised their feudal powers and rights of tithe to accumulate great wealth (Myers 1914, chap. 2). This let the Canadian clergy and seigneurs take charge through a local council, the Communauté des Habitants, which soon controlled the Compagnie des Cent Associés.

This persisted until Jean-Baptiste Colbert, the intellectual father of mercantilism, became controller of finance in 1661. Colbert used Canada to test his economic theories.[5] In 1663, he formally dissolved the Compagnie des Cent Associés and replaced the local council with a new Conseil Souverain, charged with applying La Coutume de Paris, the ancien régime civil

---

5. For details of these subsidized diversification programs, see Fauteux (1927) and Bliss (1986).

code, in Canada.[6] Colbert appointed Jean Talon intendant of Canada in 1665 and ordered him to diversify the economy. Usually with himself as the major shareholder, Talon subsidized brick making, shoe making, beer making, wool production, mining, lumbering, eel packing, sea oil, and cod salting. Talon's Conseil Souverain also imposed import restrictions and wage and price controls. He shipped *les filles du roi,* peasant women, to Canada to promote population growth. All this was subsidized by Colbert's ministry, the Département de Marine, even though Canada was now a *fief et seigneurie* of the Compagnie des Indes Occidentals, controlled by Colbert. Ultimately, none of these initiatives (save perhaps the *filles du roi*) proved viable.

Colbert's mercantilist experiments enriched a few local entrepreneurs. Charles Aubert de la Chesnaye, an agent in Canada for Rouen merchants, was probably the most important. He became a *négociant marchand*—a wholesaler, importer, exporter, financier, and moneylender. He backed loans with negotiable perpetuities, probably the first (informally) traded securities in Canada, and traded in feudal estates. In 1670, Chesnaye died deep in debt after a series of financial misfortunes.

In 1672, Louis de Buade de Frontenac et de Palluau, comte de Frontenac, a young aristocrat seeking to evade his increasingly violent creditors, accepted the governorship of Canada. (His pay was escrowed to his wife at court, who slowly discharged his debts.) Frontenac continued Colbert's mercantilist projects and subsidized the Royal Army Engineers to build a scratchwork of canals.[7]

With Colbert's death in 1683, France focused on her new colony at Louisbourg, Acadia, near the Grand Banks and so more prosperous than Quebec. But Colbert's mercantilist vision endured. The intendants Bégon and Hocquart used state funds to subsidize a rope-making operation, which quickly failed. Hocquart blamed a lack of investment capital among Canadian merchants for the colony's slow growth, and sponsored a shipyard and an ironworks, the latter a 1729 proposal of François Poulin de Francheville, Seigneur de St. Maurice. Both, and the rope works, soon failed due to prohibitive costs and Clouseauesque quality control. Olivier de Vézin, an engineer, redeveloped the ironworks as La Compagnie des Forges du Saint-Maurice with further government money in 1737. Lunn (1942) describes the result:

> Indications of the disaster which was to overtake the enterprise were evident from the beginning. . . . By October 1737, when the establishment was announced to be complete, the total expenditure was 146,588 *livres* instead of the 100,000 estimated. . . . In 1737 Hocquart had made over

6. The Coutume de Paris granted the Canadian nobility the full feudal rights of the nobility in France, including the power of *haute justice* over their habitants.

7. See Bliss (1986).

to the company the remainder of the loan of 100,000 *livres* agreed upon, but the partners declared they must have an additional 82,642 *livres*. Their need was so pressing that Hocquart took it upon himself to advance them 25,233 *livres,* to be deducted from the 82,642 *livres* which he begged the Minister to lend. . . .

The Minister replied in accents of horror and indignation. . . . It seemed clear to the Minister that there had been much waste and extravagance. Nevertheless, he did consent to the new loan. . . .

Further shocks were in store for the Minister. In 1738, the company foresaw that it would not be able to meet its first payment due in 1739 and the King had to agree to yet another year's delay. . . . De Vézin's estimate had proved completely unreliable, for expenses far exceeded and production fell far short of what had been anticipated . . . Constant breakdowns of the furnace interfered seriously with production . . . The Forges were operated by a staff of costly, dilatory, insubordinate and discontented workmen. (qtd. in Bliss 1986, p. 65)

La Compagnie des Forges du Saint-Maurice sank in 1741, pulled down by engineering, managerial, and financial farce. The state took over the forges and shipyards. The latter posted regular losses until long after the conquest. None of these mercantilist projects stopped Canada's drain on the royal treasury. Exports exceed imports only once in the entire history of the colony, in 1741. The most consistently profitable business was the Société du Canada, run by the Huguenot merchant Robert Dugard, which shipped staples to Canada.

Britain and France wrestled for control of Canada in the War of the Austrian Succession (1740 to 1748) and the Seven Years War (1755 to 1763). Louisbourg fell to Britain in 1758, and Quebec in 1759. With the 1763 Treaty of Paris, all Canada passed to Britain. Blamed for the loss in *l'affaire du Canada,* the last governor, de Vaudreuil, the last intendant, Bigot, and other senior Canadian officials moldered in the Bastille for "corruption."

1.3.2   British North America

Henry Hudson's 1610 claim for Britain to the lands around Hudson's Bay lay unexploited until 1670, when Charles II granted his cousin, Prince Rupert, a fur trade monopoly and rechristened the region Rupertsland. Rupert organized "The Company of Adventurers of England trading into Hudsons Bay" (a.k.a. the Hudson's Bay Company, or "the Bay"), a joint-stock company, to raise funds.[8] The forts, trading posts, and ships required—as well as the risks inherent in the fur trade—were beyond the resources of even the wealthiest individual families. Thus, the Hudson's Bay Company, like the British East India Company and the Dutch East Indies

---

8. The Company was empowered to employ an armed force, appoint commanders, erect forts, and take other necessary measures to protect its property; see Myers (1914), chapter 3. The Bay still exists as a chain of department stores.

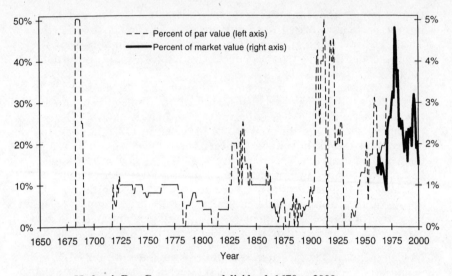

Fig. 1.1   Hudson's Bay Company annual dividend, 1670 to 2000

Source: Newman (1998) and *Financial Post* historical report for Hudson's Bay Company
Note: Dividend is expressed as percent of par value until 1970 and as a percent of equity market value from 1961 to 2000.

Company, was among the first joint-stock companies formed. Figure 1.1, showing the company's annual dividend, is a barometer of the prosperity of the fur trade and, later, of the Canadian economy. From 1670 to the War of the Austrian Succession, British interests in Canada consisted of the Bay's scattered trading posts and little else.

After the Seven Years' War, a deeply corrupt British colonial government took control of Canada.[9] Colonel Talbot, General Brock, and Bishop Mountain all seized vast tracts of Upper Canada (Ontario), while the governor, Henry Hamilton, Judge Elmslie, Judge Powell, and Solicitor General Gray appropriated huge swaths of Lower Canada (Quebec). All of Prince Edward Island was divided up by the Montgomery, Selkirk, Westmoreland, Cambridge, Macdonnell, and Seymour families.

Partially in response to such abuses, London suspended British common law in Canada in 1774, restored the French civil code of the ancien régime in property law and all matters except criminal cases, and extended the boundaries of civil law application to all of British North America north or west of the Appalachians. This seems to be because civil law better restricted land grabs by the local elite. However, French feudal land tenure and civil law were now firmly rooted in British North America.

A tax rebellion, these restrictions on land claims west of the Appalachians, and an elite deeply indebted to British merchant houses combined

9. For details of specific corrupt dealings, see chapter 5 of Myers (1914).

to inspire rebellion in the thirteen coastal colonies in 1776. This conflict was essentially a civil war, with at least a third of the colonial population remaining loyal to the Empire. French intervention allowed a secessionist victory, and revolutionary governments took power in the thirteen colonies. Revolutionary tribunals confiscated the property of those on the losing side and exiled them. In one of history's largest forced displacements, hundreds of thousands of impoverished United Empire loyalist refugees straggled north.[10] In a few short years, Canada was transformed from a Francophone country into a half-English half-French country.

Loyalists settling in Canada disliked the French civil code and coveted land. In 1791, their lobbying partitioned Canada into Upper Canada (Ontario) and Lower Canada (Quebec). In 1793, Chief Justice Osgood restored common law in Upper Canada (Ontario). Upper Canada's governor, Robert Prescott, and lieutenant governor, John Graves Simco, stalwartly upheld directives from London to hold land open for settlement. By 1794, Osgood forced both from office and installed Sir Robert Shore Milnes as governor and Peter Russell as lieutenant governor. Together they apportioned virtually all remaining unclaimed land to a tiny elite of leading loyalist families, later called the Family Compact.

The Family Compact's dominance is hard to exaggerate, as is its success in retarding economic development.[11] As absentee landlords, the families opposed settlement and roads for fear of losing title to squatters. Their control of the legislative and executive councils, the church, and colonial courts let them safeguard their interests regardless of the effect on the economy's overall development.

The influence of the so-called Chateau Clique in Lower Canada was narrower, and so less effective at braking growth. In 1779, British and Loyalist merchants in Montreal established the Northwest Company to compete with the Hudson's Bay Company for the fur trade, contesting the legitimacy of the latter's monopoly. The original founders of the Northwest Company included Simon McTavish, Todd and McGill, Charles Grant, Benjamin and Joseph Frobisher, the firm of McGill and Patterson, and five other merchants and firms.[12] The resulting wealth gave the same names prominence in banking, shipping, and railroad promotion decades later.

Since the Hudson's Bay Company had its own militia, the Northwest Company needed one too. Their battle for market share is best described in military terms. The results are also evident in figure 1.1 in the reduced dividend of the Hudson's Bay Company.

During this period, the most entrepreneurial regions of British North America were the Maritime colonies—Nova Scotia and New Brunswick.

---

10. The precise number of loyalists is disputed by historians.
11. See Myers (1914), chapter 6.
12. See Myers (1914), chapter 4.

Abraham Cunard, a master carpenter, arrived in Halifax in 1783 and rapidly established stores, mills, lumbering, sawmills, shipbuilding, an accounting firm, and other businesses. Despite strong competition from other "timber barons" like Gilmour, Rankin, and Co., Philemon Wright and Sons, William Price, and John Egan, A. Cunard and Son prospered. Many timber barons, including Christopher Scott, John and Charles Wood, and the Cunards, expanded into shipbuilding and shipping. Bliss (1986, p. 135) remarks that all of these fortunes were technically founded on theft, for the timber was almost all harvested from Crown land. The Cunard Line prospered, especially after it obtained a monopoly on delivering the Royal Mail between Britain and the Americas.

In 1812, the Napoleonic War engulfed the Canadas as an American invasion force burned the Parliament Buildings in Toronto and despoiled farms and villages. Figure 1.1 illustrates the disruption of the fur trade in the elimination of Hudson's Bay Company dividends. The French and their American allies having been defeated, the inflow of settlers resumed. Although a new British colony was established in Manitoba in 1811, its remoteness, and the Bay's unwillingness to grant settlers formal property rights, deterred settlement.[13] The Bay viewed farmers as disruptive of its trading relations with Indians, and effectively prevented further westward expansion of settlement. Thus, immigrants remained in the Canadas and the Maritimes.

The economy grew faster in Lower Canada, where the Chateau Clique exercised a looser dominance than did the Family Compact in Upper Canada. Montreal, closer to the Atlantic and the coastal colonies, emerged as the economic center of Canada. In 1821, the Bay absorbed the Northwest Company. The costs of their militarized competition had grown, in both money and death toll, and figure 1.1 illustrates the advantages of a fur trade monopoly. The former principals of the Northwest Company in Montreal—the McGills, MacTavishes, Frobishers, Grants, and others—now had considerable wealth to invest in other ventures.

The House of Phyn, Ellice, and Co. established a branch in Montreal in the late 1770s to finance the staples trade and so became the first bank in Canada. The Napoleonic Wars disrupted this business, and once peace was restored, John Richardson and Horatio Gates, the Montreal principals of Phyn, Ellice, and Co., established the Bank of Montreal as a partnership. The Bank of Montreal subscribed to the *real bills doctrine* and issued dollar banknotes backed by the staples trade, thereby establishing the currency unit for Canada. Rival banks quickly formed in Lower Canada,

13. Myers (1914) describes an 1857 petition signed by Red River settlers to London describing how they had "paid large sums of money to the Hudson's Bay Company for land . . . yet we cannot obtain deeds for the same. The Company's agents have made several attempts to force upon us deeds which would reduce ourselves and our posterity to the most abject slavery under that body. . . ."

but the Bank of Montreal, soon run by Peter McGill, remained dominant. The Bank of Nova Scotia was chartered in 1832 in Halifax as the first limited-liability joint-stock company in what would become Canada.

John Molson, a young Englishman, arrived in Montreal in 1785 and invested his inheritance in a brewery. This continually profitable venture let him finance the first steamship in 1809. Although Molson lobbied for a steamship monopoly, he was unsuccessful, and a brisk competition ensued. Profits from his brewery let him underprice the competition and eventually buy most out.

The main competition would ultimately be the Allan Line, run by Hugh Allan, a partner in his father's Scottish shipbuilding and merchant firm, Edmonstone, Allan, and Co. With family money, Allan launched the Montreal Ocean Steamship Co. in 1852 and immediately reaped great profits transporting troops to the Crimean War. Bliss (1986) reports that "Allan ships sank, ran aground, and broke up with astonishing frequency" but that he courted politicians generously and was a recognized master of political influence. By the 1860s, the Allan Line's safety record was improving, and the family was growing rich bringing steerage immigrants to North America.[14] According to Myers (1914), Allan served as president of fifteen corporations and vice president of six others at the zenith of his career—in industries spanning telegraphy, navigation, iron, tobacco, cotton manufacturing, railways, sewing machines, cattle, rolling mills, paper, cars, elevators, and coal. His Montreal Warehouse Company undertook land speculation (Myers 1914, chap. 12).

In 1838, Joseph Howe, a Nova Scotia colonial leader, lobbied the Royal Mail to switch to steam delivery, and the admiralty invited tenders. Although none of the responses met the admiralty's conditions, Samuel Cunard, Abraham's eldest son, now running the family business, won the contract—apparently through his influential friends in England, including Lady Caroline Norton, the mistress of Lord Melbourne, then the British prime minister. This guaranteed mail business gave the Cunard Line a critical edge over its competition, the Inman and Collins lines. Both modernized rapidly, switching to screw-driven ironclads at great expense, and ultimately failed. Cunard modernized more slowly, and (as Bliss notes) profitably delivered the Royal Mail between London, Halifax, New York, and Boston in wooden steamships.

The Bank of Upper Canada, controlled by the Family Compact, exercised a near monopoly in that colony.[15] In 1825, John Galt, a novelist, or-

---

14. The Allan Line sued the *Montreal Witness,* a newspaper that ran stories about the filth and overcrowding in its steerage compartments, for libel. In 1883, shortly after Allan's death, the jury, after hearing all of the evidence during a trial of eight days, returned a verdict in favor of the *Montreal Witness* on all counts. For details, see *Monetary Times,* 2 November 1883, p. 491.

15. See Baskerville (1987).

ganized the Canada Company to resell land to immigrants, but such entrepreneurial ventures were notable in their rarity (Browde 2002). Some outsiders, notably the Scottish immigrants Isaac and Peter Buchanan and their Ulsterman partner Robert Harris, got Bank of Upper Canada backing and grew rich off the Upper Canadian staples trade. But Isaac recalled that "the wonderful success of my operations in Canada may be to a great extent attributed to my solemn determination not to trust Yankees and my exercising the most vigorous scrutiny before doing business with a man Canadian born" (Bliss 1986, p. 154).

The biggest enterprises in Upper Canada in the early nineteenth century were canals. The government built the Rideau Canal from the Ottawa River to Lake Ontario. William Hamilton Merritt organized the Welland Canal, linking Lake Erie and Lake Ontario, as a joint-stock company controlled by the Family Compact. After providing generous state subsidies and loans, the Upper Canada government finally bought out the owners of the failing venture in 1841. The newspaperman William Lyon Mackenzie charged that the whole project was a scam to enrich the Family Compact. Upper Canada's public finances never recovered.

In 1832, railroad stocks began trading in a café in Montreal that eventually became the Montreal Stock Exchange. The Champlain and St. Lawrence Rail Road was built in 1834 with backing from the Molsons, Horatio Gates, and Peter McGill, then the president of the Bank of Montreal, and financing for other railroads was undertaken.

But complaints about gross corruption and abuse of office by the elites of both Canadas grew louder. Denied political influence and economic opportunities, new immigrants formed an opposition movement that ultimately coalesced into the Reform Party. Francis Bond Head, governor of Upper Canada from 1835 to 1837, cracked down with a policy of "order and discipline." His refusal to permit the suspension of specie payment during the Panic of 1837 caused the Bank of Upper Canada to call in debts ruthlessly throughout the colony, further infuriating the populace. Lower Canada fractured along linguistic lines.

Open rebellion broke out in 1837, as Louis-Joseph Papineau declared a republic in Lower Canada and William Lyon Mackenzie did likewise in Upper Canada.[16] Demanding an end to feudalism, church estates, trade barriers, and land reform, the rebels had strong popular support.[17] Although the army restored order, Upper Canada debentures collapsed. London dispatched a new governor, Lord Durham, whose 1839 report damned decades of fraud and theft by the colonial elite and recommended Responsible Government—democratic home rule.[18]

16. Although Nova Scotians increasingly resented the appointed Council of Twelve (Cunard and other merchants) that ran that colony, democratic reform came peacefully there.
17. See Myers (1914).
18. See Lambton (1838), vol. X, for a description of the abuses.

The end of the Imperial Preference in 1846 exposed Canadian merchants to free trade. The economy collapsed, and Lord Elgin, the governor general of Canada, reported in 1849 that "Property in most Canadian towns, and most especially in the capital [Montreal], has fallen 50 percent in value within the last three years. Three fourths of the commercial men are bankrupt" (Bliss 1986, p. 158). In the London markets Canada's standing, battered by the rebellions of the late 1830s, collapsed.

In 1849, responding to Durham's report (and British bondholders), London merged bankrupt Upper Canada and fiscally sound Lower Canada to form a united, solvent, Province of Canada with home rule. In response, a Tory mob burned Parliament. But Canada now had a prime minister responsible to an elected legislature. Still, since an imperial guarantee was needed to float Canadian debt, the imperial government appointed the London investment houses of Barings and Glyns to oversee the colony's finances.

In 1844, Alexander established the Sherbrooke Cotton Mill, Canada's first industrial joint-stock company, and more investment opportunities emerged as the colony's politics stabilized. Perhaps the most important development policy of the new united province was the new 1849 Patent Act, which forbade Canadian patents on American technology, creating multitudes of openings for local entrepreneurs capable of using such know-how.

The colony's political leaders felt hamstrung by their inability to subsidize such new ventures. Francis Hincks, an entrepreneur and member of Parliament, partially solved this problem with a new Municipalities Act, which let towns float debt. A more complete solution appeared in 1849, when Canada began guaranteeing railroad debt, but only if prominent politicians, such as Hincks and Galt, were on the board to "guarantee good management." After a brief financial crisis in 1849, a boom and bust in railroad stocks ensued, and railroad construction resumed on a grand scale. Although railroads built honest fortunes, like that of the engineer Casimir Gzoski, corruption was endemic.[19] Sir Allan Napier MacNab, president of the Great Western Railway, served Canada as chair of the Parliamentary Standing Committee of Railways and Telegraphs (Bliss 1986, p. 186). The grandest project, the Grand Truck Railroad, run by Prime Minister Hincks, was ineptly built and almost unusable (Myers 1914, chap. 11). A British lobbyist hired by Hincks to lobby members of parliament wrote: "I do not think there is much to be said for Canadians over Turks when contracts, places, free tickets on railways, or even cash was in question" (Bliss 1986, p. 187).

A Barings investigation exposed rampant fraud, kickbacks, and deceit,

---

19. See Myers (1914), chapters 10 and 11, for a detailed description of specific allegations and evidence, including the report of the 1876–77 Select Parliamentary Investigating Committee. Mills (1872), a member of Parliament, writes that "corruption taints the majority of railway enterprises from their inception to completion" and provides details.

and Barings blocked further Canadian listings in London to obtain a veto over additional debt financing and guarantees in 1851. This merely tested the ingenuity of the colonial political elite in circumventing such checks. Railway subsidies became a top government priority. According to Naylor (1975), railroad construction and financing in colonial Canada were "appalling even by the standards of the day." Virtually every important politician now moonlighted as a railway officer or director, and railway subsidies both enriched political insiders and drained government coffers. Current, past, and future prime ministers Francis Hincks, Alexander T. Galt, and John A. MacDonald, respectively, and most of their cabinet ministers all had railway financial ties (Myers 1914, Bliss 1986). In 1858, Alexander Galt, now finance minister, subordinated Canada's sovereign debt to railroad common stock and raised the tariff to obtain funds for larger railway subsidies. By the 1860s, Canada had both a shoddily built, poorly run railroad system and a near-bankrupt government.

Now, only union with the solvent Maritime colonies of Nova Scotia and New Brunswick promised fiscal rescue. When the United States abrogated the Reciprocity Treaty in 1866, Galt lowered the tariff slightly on manufactured goods to match those of the Nova Scotia and New Brunswick colonies, in preparation for their union with Canada. In 1867, British investors blocked New Brunswick and Nova Scotia financing in London to force such a union. The resulting confederation was the Dominion of Canada, a self-governing entity within the British Empire. Canadian independence is usually dated to 1867, though Responsible Government came earlier and Canada remained within the empire long after. Since the Canadian parliament assumed almost all of the powers of the parliament in London in 1867, this date is probably more appropriate than any other.

Despite endemic corruption worthy of the worst modern third world economies, the economy modernized. Alexander Galt formed the British American Land Co. in 1831 to buy feudal estates in Lower Canada and sell small homesteads to English settlers, much as John Galt, his father, had in Upper Canada (Browde 2002).[20] Thus, land reform proceeded through private-sector initiative. The Toronto Stock Exchange, founded in 1854 primarily as a commodity exchange, now traded railroad stocks and even a few other companies. Free trade, though originally disruptive, now let Canada benefit from elevated wheat prices during the Crimean War. An 1854 Reciprocity Treaty (free trade) with the United States further stimulated the economy. Also in 1854, Prime Minister Hincks bought out the remaining seigneurs of Lower Canada, finally ridding Canada of the feudal

---

20. See also Timothy (1977).

21. Myers (1914) makes much of the generous terms of the buyout in contrast to the conditions under which feudalism ended in France in 1789.

system.[21] Although slave sales were abolished in 1797, French Canadian habitants emerged completely from feudal serfdom only a few years before the U.S. Civil War. In 1866, Lower Canada replaced La Coutom de Paris civil code with the Lower Canada civil code, an updated version of the Napoleonic code, and adopted common law for certain commercial and maritime disputes.

1.3.3   Canada on the Eve of Industrialization

All of this invites comparison with the theories, outlined above, of colonial origins determining subsequent institutional and economic development.

Canada, though ultimately a colony of settlement, was long a colony of resource extraction. The core industry through the mid-nineteenth century was the fur trade—natives selling pelts to Europeans stationed in a dispersed network of Bay trading posts. The Bay actively opposed colonization for fear that yeoman farmers would disrupt relations with Indian and Métis trappers. Agriculture in French Canada was organized into feudal estates modeled on those in prerevolutionary France. The early British elite, especially the Family Compact, emulated this by monopolizing land claims. Overall, the early history of Canada thus resembles Sokoloff and Engerman's (2000) description of Caribbean and Latin American colonial economies.

The Canadian climate, though harsh, was not deadly to Europeans, and the French eventually switched their emphasis, in part, to settlement. This was accompanied by extensive mercantilist state intervention and corruption under the French colonial regime. Their British successors preserved much of this institutional heritage, even as loyalist refugees flooded the colony. Thus, an exogenous political event, the secession of the thirteen coastal colonies, irrevocably converted Canada into a colony of settlement, increasingly populated by yeoman farmers who demanded, and ultimately got, legal protection from the colony's elite. Canadian economic history permits a deeper understanding of the results in Acemoglu, Johnson, and Robinson (2002, 2003). An environment in which European settlers could survive did not per se trigger rapid settlement. However, once large-scale British settlement occurred, pressure for British institutions ensued after a few decades, consistent with a broader interpretation of their thesis: institutional development is determined by the settlers' preference.

Easterly and Levine (1997) find that ethnic diversity slows development. The longstanding French-English rivalry in Canada might well have slowed Canada's overall growth, for arguments about each linguistic group's access to government cash flows were central to the debates leading up to Home Rule in 1848 and Confederation in 1867. However, ethnically divided Lower Canada was certainly more dynamic than thoroughly loyalist Upper Canada with its Family Compact earlier in the nineteenth century. Factors other than linguistic divisions were clearly at work as well.

La Porta et al. (1997a, 1998, 2000) and La Porta, López-de-Silanes, and Shleifer (1999) demonstrate a clear correlation between the use of legal systems derived from British common law and fuller financial and institutional development. The early stages of economic development reveal no clear superiority of British over French law. Corruption occurred under both. Although Canada adopted aspects of common law in fields relevant to business corporations, French civil law still remains important in Quebec. Montreal remained the country's economic center of gravity until the twentieth century, so early Canadian businesses functioned in a hybrid legal environment combining civil and common law. La Porta et al. argue that official corruption and insider abuse of investors are more limited by the British than the French legal system. Canada has a venerable tradition of state subsidies to politically connected businesses that we would now characterize as corruption. This may echo Canada's French heritage; but if more than a century of British colonial rule failed to silence these echoes, adopting British legal systems is hardly a viable development strategy for today's emerging economies. Alternatively, the La Porta et al. findings may pertain to an effect of British common law on later stages of industrialization.

Certainly, the half century after widespread British settlement and the establishment of British institutions saw Canada successfully transform from a sparsely populated feudal wilderness into a country with farms, cities, canals, and railways. Land development schemes opened old feudal estates to settlement. The foundations of great business dynasties were laid. While there was clearly enormous waste and theft, this deeply corrupt political economy nonetheless advanced to the earliest stages of industrialization. These observations raise questions about the current condemnation of "corruption" as inimical to development in the third world. Canada's colonial heritage renders the hypothesis that sound institutions are a consequence of growth, rather than its cause, at least worthy of serious thought.

Canadian economic history also provides further insight into the argument of La Porta et al. (1997b) that more hierarchically organized societies have difficulty accommodating institutional development. French Canada once owned by Cardinal Richelieu, was subjected to the full force of the counterreformation, and remained deeply subservient to the Roman Catholic hierarchy until the mid-twentieth century. That hierarchy generally dealt with the English elite on their behalf after the Treaty of Paris. English Canadians whose family histories recall revolutionary tribunals and armed debtors can value "peace, order, and good government" to an extent that foreigners and more recent immigrants find hard to fathom. This deference perhaps allowed the Tory elite to adapt the mercantilist institutions of French Canada to their own needs and the Liberal elite that displaced them after 1837 to do likewise.[22] Only after a vast inflow of immigrants did Canadian voters begin to reject mercantilist policies, and even then with distinctly mixed feelings. Thus, Porter (1965) argues that Canadians, both English and French, still respected established institutions and hierarchies more than their American cousins in the mid-twentieth century. All of this is consistent with a slower development of the institutions of liberal capitalism in the framework of La Porta et al. (1997b).

1.4   Industrialization

The last decade of the nineteenth century and first decade of the twentieth century were Canada's high-growth period. Understanding how corporate ownership and control, and other institutions, evolved during this period is therefore of special interest, as is the institutional structure developed in the prior two decades.

The high-growth period corresponds closely to the governments of Sir Wilfrid Laurier, the first long-serving prime minister unmarred by scandal. Laurier's Liberals took power in 1896 and oversaw a booming economy that lasted until his defeat in 1911. The first Québecois prime minister, Laurier grandly proclaimed, "Canada will fill the twentieth century." This seemed not absurd at the time, for Canada's population and industrial production grew at unprecedented (and unsurpassed) rates. A popular diversion of the time was forecasting when Canada's population would exceed that of the United States by extrapolating the two countries' growth rates. Visionary politicians seriously advocated imperialism, envisioning Canada assuming the burden of weary Britain's worldwide empire. This too seemed not unreasonable, and Laurier was a dedicated imperialist.

The fat Hudson's Bay Company dividends of this era, shown in figure 1.1, as well as the more direct measures of growth in figures 1.2 and 1.3, all also attest to the country's prosperity.

Economic expansion paralleled an immigration boom. Under Laurier, Canada's population rose 44 percent. Western Canada was rapidly populated along the proliferating transcontinental Canadian Pacific Railway (CPR) system. All sectors of the economy grew rapidly and simultaneously to accommodate this infrastructure investment and the millions of new consumers flooding in. The situation thus closely resembles what Murphy, Shleifer, and Vishny (1989) call a *big push*—rapid development sustained by the simultaneous expansion of many interdependent sectors, so demand for intermediate and final goods grows apace with their supply.

The railway, and the immigrant settler farms springing up around it,

---

22. Haber (2002) describes a similar preservation of the institutions of "crony capitalism" by successive new elites in Latin America.

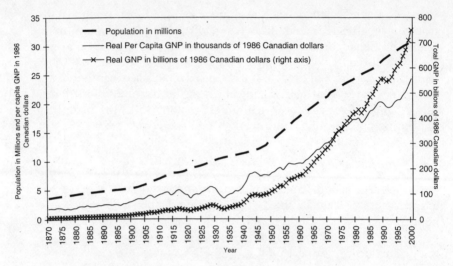

Fig. 1.2   Overall economy growth, 1870 to 2000

Source: Data up to 1926 are from Urquhart (1993). Later data are from Statistics Canada: Historical Statistics of Canada.

Notes: Population in millions and per capita gross national product (GNP) in 1986 Canadian dollars are measured on the left axis. Total GNP in billions of 1986 Canadian dollars is measured on the right axis.

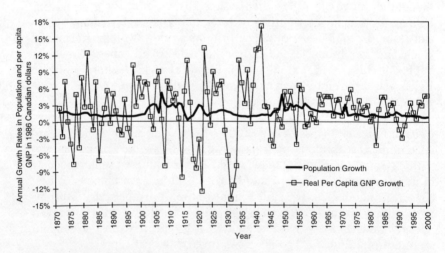

Fig. 1.3   Economic growth, 1870 to 2000

Source: Data up to 1926 are from Urquhart (1993). Later data are from Statistics Canada: Historical Statistics of Canada.

Note: This figure illustrates annual growth rates in population and per capita GNP in 1986 Canadian dollars.

created an economic low-pressure zone. Every sort of new business was needed to supply the railroad, the settlers, and all the other new businesses opening to serve them.

1.4.1   Bracing for the Big Push

Although the actual big push occurred when Laurier was prime minister, the Tory prime minister John A. MacDonald cleared the way over the previous two decades. He did this by managing unfolding political events to divert ever-greater subsidies to the CPR. The successful completion of this transcontinental line created space for immigrants, who raised demand for all manner of goods, which allowed the big push to succeed. The details of this ground clearing are important.

In 1867, Canada's most important business was still the Bay, which still owned Rupertsland—most of the northern half of North America. The chief factor, George Simpson, ruthlessly exploited Rupertsland from the mid-1820s to the 1860s. The bastard son of a Presbyterian minister, Simpson had a profound suspicion of ethics that compensated for the waning European demand for beaver pelts. Nonetheless, the Bay's directors saw an inevitable decline in both the fur trade and the Bay's dividend (in figure 1.1). Through two takeovers, the Bay diversified into lumbering, fishing, livestock, coal mining, buffalo wool, and even a colony in Oregon. All failed, and the dividend slid. Ultimately, a new management team concluded that forsaking the fur trade and selling the Bay's vast landholdings was in the best interests of the shareholders. In 1868, the next chief factor, Donald Smith, sold Canada all of Rupertsland, including the Manitoba colony. The profit maximization decision of a monopoly resource extraction company thus transformed Canada from a colony of extraction into a colony of settlement.

The big push that followed saw no abatement of corruption. Property rights actually grew more unsettled before they became stronger, and the transcontinental line's construction was rife with political kickbacks and self-dealing. The Bay had never assigned formal land titles to the residents of its Manitoba colony. Sold to Canada with no provision for their property rights, the métis and other settlers rose in rebellion in 1869. The poet and philosopher Louis Riel declared a Republic of Manitoba and seceded from Canada.[23] The rebels surrendered in 1870, and President Riel fled. Manitoba rejoined Canada as a province, and the rest of Rupertsland became the Northwest Territories. Property rights were formalized and settlers poured in. But MacDonald concluded that Canada needed a transcontinental railroad to exercise sovereignty over this vast region. In 1871, he convinced the British Pacific coast colonies to join Canada as the

---

23. See Myers (1914), chapter 9, for a detailed description of the conflicting interests behind the rebellion and its suppression.

province of British Columbia by promising them a transcontinental railroad.

Hugh Allan, owner of the Allan Line, founded the Canada Pacific Co. to build the link. The Grand Trunk, fearing competition, lobbied furiously to undermine Allan's company. The Panic of 1873 and subsequent depression—figure 1.3 shows a drop in per capita gross national product (GNP) of almost 8 percent in 1876—stalled these plans. The exposure of a huge kickback from Allan to MacDonald brought down the Tory government, prolonging the stall. The new Liberal government of Alexander Mackenzie cautiously raised the tariff and tried to rehabilitate Canadian debt in London. But a series of bank panics and failures continued through the 1870s.

With no railroad in sight, British Columbia elected a separatist government in 1878. MacDonald recaptured power in 1879 pledging to complete the railroad immediately—as well as raise the tariff and subsidize the Roman Catholic clergy.

The CPR was incorporated in 1881, and its first president, George Stephen, quickly sold his own railways to the CPR. MacDonald provided the CPR a subsidy of millions of acres of former Bay lands. These were assigned to a company controlled by the Bay's chief factor, Donald Smith, and Edmund Osler, the owner of several other railways the CPR bought. In 1883, Smith joined the CPR board and quickly dominated its management. Thus corruption, or at least self-dealing, was central to the CPR from its inception.

To keep railroad construction teams supplied, existing industrial production expanded rapidly. Land prices soared, new coal and natural gas fields were discovered and developed, and settlers moved farther west onto land claimed by Indians and the *métis* descendants of trappers. In 1884, Louis Riel reappeared to declare a republic in Saskatchewan. MacDonald now had to subsidize accelerated CPR construction to move troops to Saskatchewan. Riel was hanged, and no other province has seceded (at writing). The Indian tribes, all repeatedly decimated by disease and aware of the carnage in the western United States, signed treaties and moved peaceably onto reservations. British concepts of property rights replaced communal tribal claims everywhere else.

The CPR finished its transcontinental mainline in 1886 and then diversified into steamships and luxury hotels. It soon displaced the Bay as the dominant business of the land. Presidents of the CPR and prime ministers of Canada renegotiated subsidies (upward, eventually to over 200 million dollars plus land grants) as equals (Myers 1914, chap. 14).

Railroads built the greatest fortunes of the 1890s, enriching Richard Angus, Joseph Hickson, George Cox, Duncan MacIntyre, Lord Strathcona and Mount Royal (formerly Donald Smith), Lord Mount Stephen (formerly George Stephen), and William Van Horne. All but Cox and Hickson grew wealthy building or operating the CPR. Hickson grew rich revitalizing the old Grand Trunk, and Cox by reselling the bankrupt Midland Railway to the Grand Trunk (Myers 1914, chap. 14).

The stage was now set for "big push" development, as in Murphy, Shleifer, and Vishny (1989). Large pools of capital stood ready. The CPR, albeit built for political and military reasons, opened vast new territories. Population could grow rapidly, for the Bay no longer blocked settlement. Rather, its chief factor was set to make a fortune selling land to immigrants.

All this occurred in an economy still mired in both official and private corruption, surrounded by prohibitive tariffs, and hosting a scandal-plagued financial system.

1.4.2 Corruption and the Big Push

Official corruption retards economic development—see Mauro (1995) and many others for empirical evidence. Murphy, Shleifer, and Vishny (1991, 1993) argue that corruption does this by raising the return to investing in political connections above that to investing in ordinary business projects, like plant and equipment or research and development. This diverts talented individuals away from careers as engineers, inventors, and entrepreneurs and into more lucrative careers as politicians and bureaucrats.

Canada was clearly an extremely corrupt country, at least by modern standards, when it began industrializing. However, politicians expected, and were expected, to become wealthy from public office. Behavior that today would clearly constitute corruption was not only legal but anticipated.

An 1875 requirement that insurance companies invest domestically repelled foreign insurers and opened the field for a spate of new Canadian insurers. Confederation Life was run by Sir Francis Hincks, then finance minister. Prime Minister Mackenzie took charge of North American Life after losing power in 1878. Prime Minister MacDonald served as president of Manufacturer's Life while in office. Sun Life was run by Matthew Gault until MacDonald intervened to oust him. The Bay's chief factor, Donald Smith, used his seat in Parliament to promote his steamship and railway investments in Manitoba (Myers 1914, chap. 13).

Thus, members of Parliament and provincial politicians, such as Manitoba premier John Norquay, routinely empowered each other to develop and run coal mines, lumber companies, and land companies (Myers 1914, chaps. 16 and 17). Robert Dunsmuir, wealthy from his Union and Wellington Colliery, Esquimault and Nanaimo Railway, and especially his land grant from the government at the CPR Pacific terminus, an obscure village called Vancouver, served the people of British Columbia in the provincial legislature (Myers 1914, chap. 16).

Municipal politicians also moonlighted as barons of industry.[24] A good example is George Cox, who ran British America Insurance, Canada Life,

---

24. For a detailed list, see Myers (1914), chapter 15.

the Canadian Bank of Commerce (now CIBC), Central Canada Savings and Loan, Canada Landed and National Investment Co., Dominion Coal, Dominion Securities, Imperial Life, Manitoba Northwest, National Trust, Toronto Savings and Loan, and Western Insurance. While thus burdened, Cox served the people as the six-term mayor of Peterborough, Ontario.

However, several factors probably eased the drag of corruption on the economy enough for a big push to succeed under Laurier.

First, some corruption worked for the good. Although MacDonald won and retained power through blatantly corrupt elections, took kickbacks from railroad companies, and continually blurred the boundaries between his private and public duties, he pushed through the transcontinental railway. The CPR, though mired in what today we would call corruption, certainly *raised* the returns to genuine entrepreneurship in numerous other industries, and so shifted talent in that direction.

Second, such corruption grew increasingly unacceptable to the general populace over time. The yeoman farmers of Ontario found the Family Compact's economic stranglehold maddening enough to rise in rebellion in 1837, and the Liberal rebellions of 1837 brought corruption down a notch. Official failures to honor existing property rights caused first Manitoba and then Saskatchewan to secede. Both rebellions were put down, but both also ratcheted respect for private property rights up a notch. MacDonald, though not jailed for demanding kickbacks from railroads, was forced from office temporarily. Future politicians would have to be more honest, or at least more careful. Ultimately the big push came under Laurier, who gave Canada almost two decades of unprecedentedly honest government and hence of abnormally low returns to corruption.

Finally, the returns to genuine business entrepreneurship in Canada probably were very high indeed during the big-push years. Even given a degree of corruption, genuine entrepreneurship was still a very attractive career. This requires a bit of elaboration.

Counterintuitively, the weakness of certain property rights likely encouraged local entrepreneurs. Before 1872, honoring foreign patents was illegal. This let Canadian entrepreneurs freely use the most up-to-date foreign technology. In response to suggestions by some of Canada's trading partners, MacDonald revised the Patent Act in 1872 to permit the honoring of U.S. patents if the holder had a plant in Canada. This was justified as encouraging foreign direct investment. Overall, these policies encouraged new high-technology industries, including steel casting, cement manufacture, farm machinery, and the like.

Fortuitously, many new technologies fit the Canadian economy well. The countryside was designed for hydroelectric power. One important project, by William Mackenzie, momentarily drawn from his railroads and Latin American investments, was turbines under Niagara Falls and lines to transmit the power to Toronto.

Also tailor-made for Canada, another new technology made paper from wood pulp rather than rags. Mills could use hydroelectric power to grind low-grade trees into pulp to produce paper. Hector Clergue built such a mill at Sault Ste. Marie, and the CPR tycoon Van Horne acquired another by squeezing the entrepreneur John Foreman out of his company, Laurentide Pulp. The first prominent Quebecois entrepreneur, Alfred Dubuc, built his Compagnie de Pulpe de Chicoutimi because, as he admitted to his banker, "*Je n'ai pas d'argent* [I have no money]" (Bliss 1986, p. 323). Established lumber barons, including matchmakers Eddy and Booth, also diversified into pulp and paper.

This period also saw the beginnings of Canada's minerals industries. Discovering iron ore near his Sault Ste Marie mill, Clergue formed Algoma Steel Co. to mine and refine it and the Algoma Central Railway to ship it out. Samuel Ritchie gambled on the discovery of low-grade copper and nickel ores in Sudbury, and won hugely when the Boer War pushed prices up sharply. A takeover of Ritchie's mining operation and an amalgamation with several other mining and smelting companies organized by Robert Thompson's smelting firm created International Nickel. When formed in 1902, it was the world's largest nickel producer. The CPR also entered the field, forming the Consolidated Mining and Smelting Company of Canada, or Cominco Ltd.

The CPR diversified, in part, because freight rates fell as the Manitoba entrepreneur William Mackenzie and his partner, Donald Mann, strung bits of railroad together to compete with the CPR in its most lucrative runs. This competition ultimately lowered rail shipping costs substantially, providing further scale economies.

Millions of new immigrant farmers were also soon in business. Canada quickly became the world's largest wheat exporter, and Winnipeg the world's largest commodity exchange. Rising farm income created millions of new aspiring middle-class consumers. The semiliterate Patrick Burns built a huge beef-packing empire based in Calgary.

Selling consumer goods across the much-expanded country built more fortunes. The barely literate Irish immigrant, Timothy Eaton, built a nationwide catalogue department store business that bypassed wholesalers and used the railway system to deliver goods either to branch stores or directly to consumers. Replacing the declining staples wholesale businesses, Eaton's and its imitators—Robert Simpson and Charles Woodward, and of course the Hudson's Bay Company—would dominate Canadian retailing for the next century.

And new information industries arose as the populace grew more educated and economically active. John Bayne Maclean, a clergyman's son, launched the *Canadian Grocer,* Canada's first weekly newspaper. He quickly launched a succession of other newspapers: *Hardware and Metal, Books and Notions, Dry Goods Review,* and *Canadian Printer and Publisher.*

His main surviving ventures are the *Financial Post* and *The Busy Man's Magazine,* reticently renamed *Maclean's.* The Southam family used profits from their *Spectator* to acquire a steel company, printing plants, and a chain of newspapers in other cities.

1.4.3   Finance and Growth

King and Levine (1993) demonstrate a marked correlation between the development of a country's financial system and its economic growth. Canada's financial system under MacDonald consisted of an anemic stock market and banks adhering religiously to the real bills doctrine, lending only for trade credit. Naylor (1975) argues that this adherence had substantially slowed growth by precluding loans for capital. However, by the end of the Laurier years, financial institutions were lending to all manner of businesses and the stock markets had seen two sustained waves of initial public offerings (IPOs).

Up to the late nineteenth century, new ventures were predominantly financed with some mixture of family money, government subsidies, and the retained earnings of existing companies. Both corruption and genuine entrepreneurship had built sizable family fortunes. The largest included Maritime shipping dynasties, heirs of the Montreal fur traders, and a handful of old loyalist families. Hugh Allan made another fortune off his vast ranches in Alberta as meat production shifted west. Alexander Tilloch Galt, whose family had helped settle English immigrants in both Upper and Lower Canada in the nineteenth century by buying land from loyalists and reselling it to settlers, repeated this model in Alberta with more success than in either previous venture. Canadian lumber barons, such as John Hendry of New Brunswick and the Maclaren family of Quebec, began major operations in the new provinces. The tycoons who built, supplied, and operated the CPR and other railroads also acquired vast wealth. And wealth from past government connections created other lasting family fortunes. These assemblages of capital, and their owners' desire to diversify, helped launch new industrial ventures across Canada.

Laurier had originally criticized MacDonald's CPR subsidies and eschewed subsidizing industry until late in his final term. But provincial and municipal governments had no such compunctions. A government-subsidized railway into Northern Ontario in 1902 brought a fabulous return, as minerals were discovered all around it, and it is still used to justify publicly financed development schemes. Gilbert Labline and Noah Timmins developed Hollinger Mines. J. P. Bicksell took over Porcupine Mines after its original owners were imprisoned. These firms, and the new Dome Mines, fueled a second wave of penny mining stock issues. Over five hundred new mining companies were listed in Toronto to meet investor demand at the end of the new century's first decade.

The mining business built more fortunes when gold was discovered, first in British Columbia in the early 1890s and then in the Yukon in 1898. A booming industry of fraudulent penny stock IPOs sprang up in Toronto, fleecing investors from across Canada and around the world. Two additional exchanges were formed in Toronto to handle the boom.[25] Despite the endemic fraud, Canada now had stock markets that attracted capital from all over the world.

Canada's securities markets and financial system had now developed to the point that growth through stock and debt-financed mergers and acquisitions (M&A) became possible. Thus, George Cox and his partner, the former prime minister MacKenzie Bowell, who ruled briefly between MacDonald and Laurier, built National Investment Co. through an M&A program. In fact, the early 1890s constituted Canada's first M&A wave. Figure 1.4 shows M&A activity from the first Canadian records to the present and reveals a distinct surge in this period.

Virtually all of the new companies had controlling shareholders, so a takeover or merger usually required buying a private family company or buying a control block of a traded company from an existing dominant shareholder. Also, much M&A activity involved buying out small-scale family-controlled firms and merging them into growing national companies.

Max Aitken's Montreal Trust and Monty Horne-Payne's British Empire Trust issued bonds in London to finance Canadian M&A. Other M&A entrepreneurs used acquirer company stock to buy targets. A domestic securities industry grew fat off the proceeds of public issues as domestic demand for investments rose.

Venerable family firms seemed in decline. George Cox, despite the obvious incompetence of all his sons, entertained visions of continuing the Cox dynasty. In 1905, James Henry Gundy and George Herbert Wood quit Cox's Dominion Securities to form Wood Gundy Ltd., which quickly grew to dominate the securities industry. Banks and insurance companies, as well as trust companies and the new securities firms, directed Canadian savings into industrial ventures via bonds, preferred stock, and common stock.

These developments permitted a second wave of mergers and acquisitions just before the First World War. By raising cash through bond issues via their securities houses, raiders could finance corporate takeovers. By swapping shares, they could undertake mergers. Figure 1.4 shows a second burst of M&A activity in the early twentieth century.

In 1899, Henry Melville Whitney issued shares to consolidate several collieries into Dominion Coal and then to diversify into steelmaking with Dominion Coal and Steel. The Cox family responded by setting up the country's first pyramidal group, with public shareholders holding minority

25. See Armstrong (1997) for details.

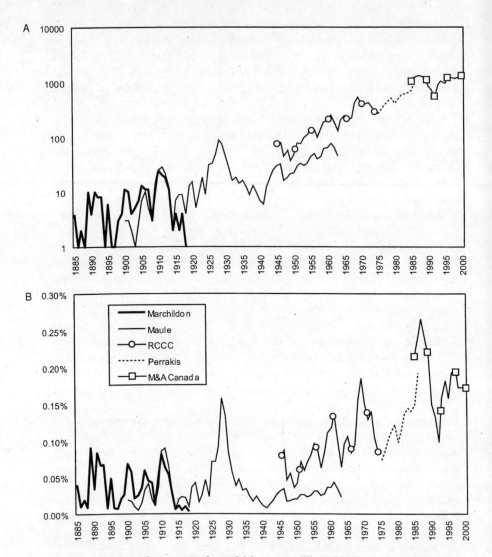

Fig. 1.4   Number of mergers and acquisitions per million 1986 Canadian dollars of GNP: *A,* **raw number of transactions;** *B,* **M&A transactions per million dollars of real 1986 GNP**

Sources: Data for 1885–1918 are from Marchildon (1990), data for 1900–1963 are from Maule (1966), data for 1970–86 are from Globerman (1977, Royal Commission on Corporate Concentration), and data for 1985–2000 are from the Directory of M&A in Canada.

.Note: Because discrepancies exist across different sources, we apply linear transformations to each overlapping period and move different series up or down to generate a single time series.

interests in Crow's Nest Pass Coal, Canada Cycle and Motor Co., and a host of other firms. Panics in 1903 and 1907 soured many of the old families on equity holdings, but public demand continued.

1.4.4   Openness

That trade openness encourages development is well established; see, for example, Bhagwatti (1998). The role of financial openness is more controversial. Bhagwatti cautions that financial openness leads to financial instability and that proponents of globalization should be content with trade openness. However, Henry (2000a,b) shows that modern-day emerging economies experience investment booms upon opening their financial markets and institutions to the global economy.

To subsidize the CPR, MacDonald needed more government revenues. The main source of public funds at this time was the tariff. MacDonald's Tories therefore proclaimed the National Policy—tariffs ultimately averaging 35 percent across the board, ostensibly to promote rapid industrialization by restricting imports. The National Policy is thus a genuinely classical example of import substitution. It remained in effect, in one form or another, until the post–World War II trade liberalizations. Canada's success under this regime is probably the most important argument advanced by later proponents of import substitutions, such as Prebisch (1971).

However, Canada had no major restrictions on capital inflows or outflows during its high-growth period, for the country was on the gold standard. Despite the rapid financial development within Canada, the big push leaned heavily on foreign capital. More foreign investment flowed into Canada per year *in absolute terms* during the Laurier boom than into the United States. This capital, mainly from Britain, but to a lesser extent from the United States, funded waves of startups, expansions, and corporate takeovers that reshaped the economy utterly.

Again, the groundwork for this vast capital inflow lay, to some extent, in the corrupt institutions of the previous two decades. MacDonald's revised Patent Act of 1872 protected U.S. patent holders with operations in Canada, and his National Policy blocked U.S. exports. The result was a sustained wave of foreign direct investment (FDI), as U.S. firms set up shop to protect their patents and then expanded to serve the domestic market. For example, Alexander Graham Bell entrusted his father, Alexander Melville Bell, to set up a Canadian telephone company—American Bell of Boston held Bell's patent from the 1880s on. Thus, trade barriers and selectively weak property rights actually stimulated capital inflow.

Subsidies to foreign capital also played a role. Canadian municipalities everywhere, eager to attract such high-tech ventures, offered increasingly competitive "bonuses"—up-front cash subsidies—to manufacturers. A multitude of bidding wars, often financed with municipal bonds, erupted across the country, with the *Monetary Times* reporting in 1895 that "American firms of every description 'seeking a new site' or 'wishing to extend their business by establishing a Canadian branch' have only to make public their designs and be inundated by letters from Canadian municipal authorities" (qtd. in Bliss 1986, p. 304).

Despite their success in generating foreign capital and branch plants, the overall efficacy of these industrial policies as a development strategy remains a topic of debate. For example, Naylor (1975) argues that their side effect was Canada's marginal position in the wave of technological innovation in the 1890s and early 1900s (vol. 2, p. 47). Bliss (1986) argues that the National Policy "created distorted hot-house growth in manufacturing that had serious, often harmful consequences" and cites a vast overcapacity in chic high-technology industries like textiles and steelmaking. Irwin (2002) argues that rapid growth in Argentina and Canada, two high-tariff, high-growth outliers in the late nineteenth century, depended on commodity exports, not industrialization through import substitution. He argues that the tariff was a revenue source but never a spur to industrialization.

Another distortion was smuggling, which became a major industry. Although this had some beneficial results, such as fueling the growth of Fort Whoop-Up in the part of the Northwest Territories that would become Alberta, its effects were probably mainly negative.

The National Policy also fostered inefficient and high-cost production. Few Canadian firms were capable of exporting. Notable exceptions were the farm machinery firms of Hart Massey and Alanson Harris, both based on Canadian patents and American prototypes. Both prospered as Canadian farming modernized. By 1891, when the two great family firms merged, both had robust export businesses in Argentina, Australia, and Great Britain. Administrative technicalities initially limited their U.S. exports.

But reciprocal trade barriers also stymied creative entrepreneurs. Thus, J. L. Kraft moved his cheese business from Ontario to Chicago in 1905. Over the longer term, the public's identification of tariffs with Canadian nationalism, fueled by the MacDonald Tories and later picked up repeatedly by populists and socialists, would emotionally charge trade and foreign investment policy discussions for a century.

As the big push ended, Canada became a capital and technology exporter. Fresh from building the now world-famous Canadian Pacific Railroad, the longest in the world, other railroad barons looked abroad, setting up railways in Brazil, Cuba, Guatemala, Mexico, Spain, and the West Indies. Once established in those countries, they moved on to trolley systems, electric power and light systems, and sundry other enterprises. Canadian banks followed into these new markets. The old Cox group, now ably managed by the railroad man Mackenzie and advised by the legal virtuoso Zebulon Lash, also rapidly expanded into Latin America, Spain, and the Caribbean. In 1912, Mackenzie and his chief engineer, F. S. Pearson, combined these holdings into Brazilian Traction, also called *o pulve Canadenses* (the Canadian octopus). The Mackenzie family still controls one of Mexico's main pyramidal corporate groups.

1.4.5   Initial Corporate Ownership Structures

As the stock market deepened, widely held industrial firms also appeared. The Hudson's Bay Company generally had no single dominant shareholder, though its chief factor often seemed to rule the company and its shares did not trade on exchange. But Canada now had numerous small, widely held mining companies and two widely held giants. Canadian Pacific was widely held from its inception, and by 1900, Bell Canada too was widely held.

However, many large Canadian firms now belonged to pyramidal corporate groups—structures in which a family or closely held apex firm controls other listed firms, each of which controls yet other listed firms, and so on. The first such group, that of the Cox family, established in 1899, served as a model. Still, Canadian pyramidal groups were usually not terribly complicated, at least relative to their modern descendants. Most had only a few tiers and a handful of firms. The economic motivations of their builders are also fairly straightforward.

Prior to the big-push period, and early into it, old-money families and railroad tycoons diversified their wealth by venturing into different industries. As the stock market developed and public shareholders became a significant source of capital, selling minority interests in these ventures to small investors became increasingly common. Listing its controlled subsidiaries lets a wealthy family leverage its retained earnings into control over much larger pools of capital than its own wealth yet retain complete control. It also let these families diversify more extensively while operating on a larger scale in each industry.[26] Thus began the first corporate groups.

Larger corporate groups were often the result of takeover waves. From 1909 until 1912, when the economy abruptly slowed, 275 of Canada's largest firms coalesced into 58 in half a billion dollars' worth of M&A transactions. The most active corporate acquisitor of this period was Max Aitken, who assembled Canada's largest pyramidal group. The son of a Presbyterian minister, he rose through the ranks of Royal Securities, ultimately running the firm for its controlling shareholder, John Stairs, heir to the old Nova Scotia merchant family. In 1906, he used his earnings to buy Montreal Trust, and he then used that firm to take over Royal Securities. Aitken issued debt in London on a huge scale and used the proceeds to buy steel mills, cement companies, power companies, and other firms all over Canada. In this way, he built the Steel Company of Canada from Montreal Rolling Mills, Hamilton Steel and Iron, Canada Screw, Canada Bolt, and many other smaller firms. Aitken also formed Canada Cement out of

26. See Almeida and Wolfenzon (2003) for a formal model.

twelve of the country's thirteen Portland cement makers. At the end of the big-push years, Aitken, always a passionate imperialist, bought the title Lord Beaverbrook and retired to London.

Larger corporate corporations and groups also resulted from financial distress. The national policy produced enormous overcapacity in stylish industries, with many plants being run by certifiably unskilled managers. Many of these listed to raise capital, but their ongoing overcapacity problems depressed their share prices, inviting the attention of corporate raiders. Thus, A. F. Gault amalgamated about half of the country's cotton mills into Dominion Cotton Mills by 1890, and David Morrice amalgamated most of the rest into Canadian Colored Cotton by 1892. After fairly overtly fixing prices for many years, the two eventually merged into Dominion Textile in 1905.

Acquirers of this era often bought out target controlling shareholders with minority blocks of stock in their other controlled companies. The target insiders who received these shares would sell out to diversify. The result was more complicated structures of less narrowly held listed companies controlling other listed companies. Although Aitken had access to London capital, other Canadian acquirers used the retained earnings of one firm to take over another. Obviously, retained earnings go farther if minimal control blocks are acquired, leaving the target listed after its successful takeover.

It is in this period that we can first construct a broad, though approximate, cross-sectional representation of the ownership structures of large Canadian companies. Figure 1.5 classifies the top sixty-six firms by ownership structure in 1902, midway through the big push, and the top hundred in 1910—near the height of the boom.

It shows that four widely held firms account for 46 percent of large corporate-sector assets in 1902 but that this fell to 29 percent by 1910. In both years, the bulk of these assets belong to two widely held firms—Bell Canada and the CPR. The Bell family had sold out prior to this, and the CPR was widely held from its inception. By 1910, the greatest part of the corporate sector, 40 percent by assets and 45 percent of firms, belonged to pyramids controlled by wealthy individuals or families. A substantial number of smaller firms are independent corporations controlled by a family or individual. About one-fifth of the corporate sector is foreign controlled, primarily by Britons. We are unable to ascertain the ownership of many firms in these early years. We suspect that most of these were indirectly controlled by wealthy families.

1.5   The Evolution of Corporate Ownership

We replicate figure 1.5 for subsequent time periods—every ten years until 1960, and roughly every five years thereafter. We occasionally substitute an adjacent year because of missing data. The main problem is that we do

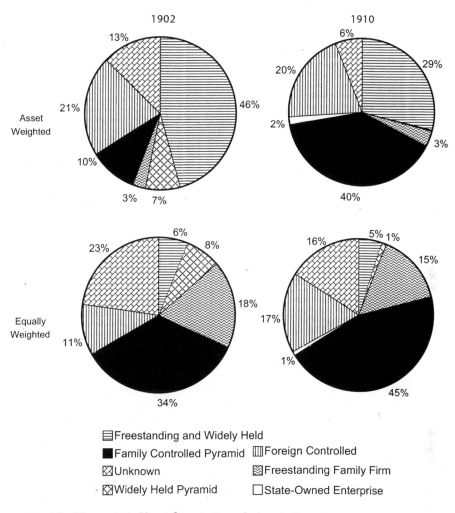

Fig. 1.5   The control of large firms in the early twentieth century

Notes: This figure illustrates the importance of different categories of controlling shareholders in the top 100 firms in 1910 and the top 66 firms in 1902, weighted by total assets and by number of firms. Financial-sector firms are excluded. Assets data are from annual reports. Control is assigned using information in annual reports, corporate histories, and general histories of Canadian business.

not have Statistics Canada Directory of Intercorporate Ownership date for every year. These results are graphed in figure 1.6.

First, the incidence of firms whose control we cannot trace falls off quickly. From 1920 on, the fraction of assets belonging to such firms is near negligible, and the fraction of such firms can be ignored from 1930 on.

State control of corporate assets begins with the First World War and

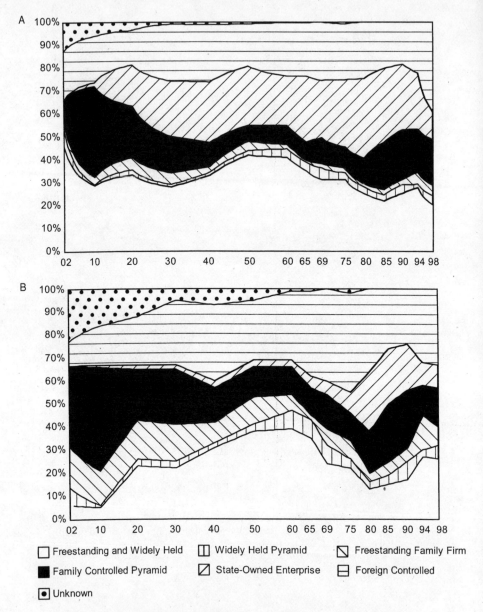

Legend:

□ Freestanding and Widely Held ⊞ Widely Held Pyramid ◺ Freestanding Family Firm

■ Family Controlled Pyramid ◪ State-Owned Enterprise ⊟ Foreign Controlled

⊙ Unknown

Fig. 1.6 The changing control of large firms through the twentieth century:
A, **asset weighted;** *B,* **equally weighted**

Sources: Past issues of Statistics Canada's Directory of Inter-Corporate Ownership, the *Financial Post,* Canadian Annual Financial Review, and *Financial Post* Corporate Securities; supplemented by Taylor and Baskerville (1994), Bliss (1986), Francis (1988), Myers (1914), Naylor (1975), and individual corporate histories.

Note: This figure illustrates the importance of different categories of controlling shareholders in the top 100 firms from 1902 to 1998, weighted by total assets and by number of firms.

steadily grows through the 1990s, when it abruptly falls off. This reflects the privatizations of Air Canada, Canadian National Railways, PetroCanada, and many other state-controlled enterprises by the Mulroney Tories. Note that the number of state-controlled enterprises rose sharply in the 1970s, reflecting the more socialist policies of the Trudeau Liberal governments and the many nationalizations they undertook, and then falls back in the 1990s as the privatizations go ahead.

Multinational firms have always been important in Canada. In 1902, foreigners controlled about 10 percent of the country's large firms, amounting to about 20 percent of corporate assets. Both figures grew to about 30 percent by the 1930s and fluctuate around that figure for the remainder of the century. Foreign control peaks, in terms of number of firms, in the 1970s. This provided the Trudeau Liberals political justification to nationalize numerous companies, as this would keep them out of foreign control. The sharp rise in foreign control in 1998 is due to a few high-profile transactions—the takeover of Labatt's Breweries by the Belgian firm Interbrew and the U.S. firm Verizon's acquisition of a control block in Telus. The nationality of the typical foreign owner also changed. At the beginning of the century, foreign owners were usually British. By the century's end, American owners predominated.

Freestanding widely held firms become more common as the century progresses until the mid-1960s. Thereafter, widely held firms become steadily rarer and account for a diminishing fraction of corporate assets. This pattern is more evident if we drop firms whose controlling shareholder is unknown, foreign-controlled firms, and state-owned enterprises. Figure 1.7 replicates figure 1.6, dropping these.

The importance of family-controlled pyramidal groups, including those controlled by single wealthy individuals, follows precisely the opposite pattern. Family-controlled pyramids are commonplace at the beginning of the century, recede markedly by mid-century, and then resurge at the century's end.

This pattern requires explanation. We first provide more details about the rise and fall of different family- and widely held firms over a century of business cycles. We then consider various reasons why ownership structures might change over time. Since institutional changes and business-cycle conditions often correspond to political events, we refer to periods by the name of the current prime minister. Table 1.1 lists the terms of office of twentieth-century Canadian governments.

1.5.1   Ownership Structure Changes over a Century of Business Cycle[27]

The merger waves, shown in figure 1.4, each correspond to abrupt changes in ownership structures. The main merger waves are the following:

27. What follows is drawn from Bliss (1986), Francis (1986), Khemani, Shapiro, and Stanbury (1988), Maule (1966), Naylor (1975), Newman (1975, 1981, 1991, 1998), and Taylor and Baskerville (1994). The analysis by Bliss is especially useful throughout this section, and a general reference is gratefully acknowledged.

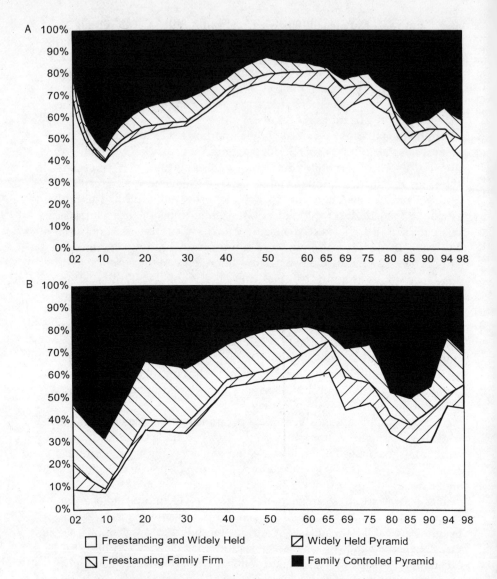

Fig. 1.7   The changing control of domestic private-sector firms: *A,* **asset weighted;** *B,* **equally weighted**

Sources: Past issues of Statistics Canada's Directory of Inter-Corporate Ownership, the *Financial Post,* Canadian Annual Financial Review, and *Financial Post* Corporate Securities, supplemented by Taylor and Baskerville (1994), Bliss (1986), Francis (1988), Myers (1914), Naylor (1975), and individual corporate histories.

Notes: This figure illustrates the importance of different categories of controlling shareholders in the top 100 firms from 1902 to 1998, weighted by total assets and by number of firms. State-owned enterprises, multinational subsidiaries, and firms whose control is unclear are excluded.

Table 1.1   **Canadian prime ministers and governments of the twentieth century**

Prime minister	Party	Elected	Resigned
Martin, Paul Edgar Philippe	Liberal	December 12, 2003	
Chrétien, Jean Joseph Jacques	Liberal	November 4, 1993	December 11, 2003
Campbell, A. Kim	Progressive Conservative	June 25, 1993	November 3, 1993
Mulroney, Martin Brian	Progressive Conservative	September 17, 1984	June 24, 1993
Turner, John Napier	Liberal	June 30, 1984	September 16, 1984
Trudeau, Pierre Elliott	Liberal	March 3, 1980	June 29, 1984
Clark, Charles Joseph (Joe)	Progressive Conservative	June 4, 1979	March 2, 1980
Trudeau, Pierre Elliott	Liberal	April 20, 1968	June 3, 1979
Pearson, Lester Bowles	Liberal	April 22, 1963	April 19, 1968
Diefenbaker, John George	Progressive Conservative	June 21, 1957	April 21, 1963
St. Laurent, Louis Stephen	Liberal	November 15, 1948	June 20, 1957
King, William Lyon Mackenzie	Liberal	October 23, 1935	November 14, 1948
Bennett, Richard Bedford	Conservative	August 7, 1930	October 22, 1935
King, William Lyon Mackenzie	Liberal	September 25, 1926	August 6, 1930
Meighen, Arthur	Conservative	June 29, 1926	September 24, 1926
King, William Lyon Mackenzie	Liberal	December 29, 1921	June 28, 1926
Meighen, Arthur	National Liberal and Conservative Party	July 10, 1920	December 28, 1921
Borden, Robert Laird	Unionist	October 12, 1917	July 9, 1920
Borden, Robert Laird	Conservative	October 10, 1911	October 11, 1917
Laurier, Wilfried	Liberal	November 7, 1896	October 6, 1911

the decades surrounding the beginning of the twentieth century, the late 1920s, the early 1960s, the late 1960s, the late 1980s, and the late 1990s. Figure 1.3 shows that each was also a business-cycle peak. Before considering explicit hypotheses about why ownership structures changed as they did, we provide some background details about conditions over the decades and the associated changes in corporate ownership.

The first merger wave was actually a prolonged period of intermittently high takeover activity spanning the Laurier boom—from the mid-1890s to 1911. Under Laurier's Liberals, new technology and British capital financed waves of takeovers in steel, cement, and other (then) cutting-edge industries. Figure 1.5 shows that these transactions markedly increased in the importance of pyramidal groups—new ones, like the Aitkin group, and pyramids built on old family money, like that of the Coxes.

The subsequent slower-growth period, from 1913 through the mid-1920s, saw a decline in the importance of family pyramids. As figure 1.6 shows, part of this corresponds to an upswing in state-owned enterprises. Ontario businessmen lobbied successfully for a state-owned power company, now called Hydro One, to provide subsidized electricity. Laurier, previously opposed to all business subsidies, grew pragmatic and agreed to subsidize the old Grand Trunk Railway to build a second transcontinental line. William Mackenzie, with Cox money and subsidies from Manitoba, undertook a third. His Tory successor, Prime Minister Borden, poured in more subsidies, and by 1915 the National Transcontinental Grand Trunk Pacific and Canadian Northern were complete. Both were soon hopelessly insolvent, but "too big to fail." After a series of bailouts, Borden bought both in 1917 to form the state-owned Canadian National Railway (CNR).

By the mid-1920s, conditions slowly improved, and new business opportunities emerged. The most significant was Prohibition in the United States, enacted in 1919, which outlawed the manufacture, sale, or transport of alcohol but permitted its consumption. Sam Bronfman, a Saskatchewan innkeeper, set up a mail-order liquor business for thirsty Americans. In a few years, he owned a chain of distilleries along the U.S. border. Bronfman used his newfound wealth to build a new pyramidal group and was soon the most powerful tycoon in Canada.

Takeovers in the late-1920s boom, as in the Laurier years, built new pyramidal groups. Max Aitkin had retired to London as Lord Beaverbrook, and his former associates took control of his various companies. One of the most successful, Isaac Walton Killam, built the Killam group. Nesbitt, Thompson, and Co. organized the publicly traded Power Corporation to hold utilities in a pyramidal group. Other major new groups were Canadian Pulp and Power Investments and Hydro-Electric Bond and Share Corp. A very important pyramid builder of this period was the twice prime minister Arthur Meighen, who issued debt to acquire control blocks for his Canadian General Investment Trust group.

But despite these new groups, the late-1920s boom, unlike the Laurier years, saw a net erosion of pyramids. The 1920s boom, like the Laurier years, created new high-technology firms—this time in industries like automobiles, airplanes, metallurgy, motion pictures, office automation, and paper making. But now many were stock financed and widely held early on. Most disappeared in mergers, also financed with stock, eroding control blocks in the acquirer firms.

A global boom favored Canada, fueling demand for paper and minerals. MacMillan, founded by a forestry student who stayed in British Columbia after a summer job, soon dominated forestry. International Nickel developed new alloys that locked in its global dominance. Numerous other mining and minerals refining companies sprouted up. Thus, more new widely held firms joined the ranks of the top corporations.

The Great Depression hit Canada hard in the 1930s. Deflation reduced the cost of living by over 20 percent from 1929 to 1933, but wages fell much less. This, and moribund demand, depressed most industries—automobiles, base metals, oil, railroads, pulp and paper, and steel collapsed. Many old family firms failed in the 1930s, their assets bought up by others with money.

But mining prospered because investors viewed gold and silver as safe-haven assets. By refining these metals from composite ores, the widely held firms Noranda and Cominco grew, increasing the importance of the widely held sector.

New family fortunes also arose in the 1930s. Armand Bombardier's "snowmobiles" hit the market in the late 1930s. Kenneth Colin (K. C.) Irving built his family store into a new pyramidal group of gas stations, busing, trucking, auto sales, and bus making. Roy Jodrey, who first lost a considerable fortune, built his United Service bus line, as well as a chain of gas stations and auto dealerships, into a new pyramid. John and Alfred Billes built Canadian Tire into a large national retailer during the 1930s. Roy Thompson overcame a bad credit record to buy a radio station and then a newspaper. After paying back taxes, beverage exporters formalized their market shares in the post-Prohibition United States. Edward Plunkett (E. P.) Taylor built up a new major player, the Brewing Corporation of Canada. Charles Trudeau sold his chain of gasoline stations and Automobile Owners Association Service Clubs to buy stocks precisely at the 1932 low, greatly magnifying his already creditable fortune. This provided his son, Pierre, a life of great privilege.

Clarence Decateur (C. D.) Howe, an MIT graduate and professor at Dalhousie University, built a huge empire of grain elevators and then lost it. C. D. Howe was well disliked—the CPR president remarked, "He is not able to deal with ordinary individuals except on the basis of a superior dealing with inferiors" (qtd. in Bliss 1986, p. 443). However, as King's "minister of everything," Howe was the most powerful force in the economy through the middle of the century.

During World War II, Howe ran the centrally planned wartime economy as minister of munitions and supply. By 1945, with European and Asian factories in rubble, Canada was the world's third-largest economy by some measures. A wartime alliance with the Soviet Union, and memories of the Great Depression amid centrally planned prosperity, brought votes to the socialist Cooperative Commonwealth Federation (CCF), later renamed the New Democratic Party (NDP). The CCF outpolled both the Liberals and Tories in 1943 and took power in Saskatchewan in 1944. This, even more than the Progressives, deeply disturbed the country's polity. King countered by moving the Liberals leftward, absorbing moderate socialists to make the CCF disagreeably radical. In 1944, he let unions organize and compel collective bargaining, and made Howe minister of reconstruction and supply.

After the war, Howe liberalized the economy despite the objections of the CCF and business groups wanting state enforcement of their cartels. A mass privatization of wartime enterprises created yet more widely held firms.[28] The 1950s and 1960s in Canada were a near continual boom,

---

28. Howe retained state control in key industries, keeping Polymer, a plastics manufacturer, and El Dorado, a mining firm with uranium holdings he had nationalized in 1944.

though not as energetic as the Laurier years or late 1920s. After King retired, Howe served the new Liberal prime minister, Louis St. Laurent. His heavy-handed use of War Powers to organize a major pipeline project in 1956 cost the Liberals the 1957 election. But Howe's legacy was an economy mostly organized by market forces, save for a string of grand nation-building projects—a national airline, the trans-Canada highway, an aerospace program, a transcontinental oil pipeline, and the like.

The new Tory prime minister, John Diefenbaker, an upstart lawyer born in a shack in rural Saskatchewan, had little use for great nation-building schemes or business lobbyists. The decade and a half following the war was probably the apogee of free market philosophy in Canada. Growth slowed after 1957 but revived in 1961 and remained brisk through the sixties.

European and Japanese reconstruction fueled demand for metals and wood. Several new mining companies emerged during this era. The Iron Ore Company of Canada was organized by Hollinger, Timmins, and the Hannas family of Cleveland. Gunnar Gold Mines, run by Gilbert LaBline, whom Howe fired from El Dorado, developed a huge uranium mine. Joe Hirshhorn struck uranium and sold out to Rio Tinto and Rio Algom. A Czech migrant farm worker, Stephen Roman, bought claims near Hirshhorn's operations and found more uranium. His Consolidated Dennison Mines quickly became a major producer.

Many older companies also became widely held after the war. MacMillan took over Bloedel, Stuart, and Welch to form MacMillan-Bloedel, which became widely held. Alcan Aluminum became widely held after a U.S. court ordered its parent, Alcoa, to divest some assets. Hiram-Walker, Hydro-Electric, Fraser, Shawinigan Water & Power Co., and Great Lakes paper also passed from family control to become widely held.

But other pyramidal groups were on the rise. The Sobey and Steinberg families built groups from land development and food retailing. Simard, Demarais, and Basset built new corporate groups in Quebec. Older empires also flourished in the war's aftermath—the Irving group in New Brunswick, the Billes family's Canadian Tire, Roy Thompson's media group, and the Bronfman's distilleries.

The most important creation of this period, however, was the Argus Group, a vast pyramid run by E. P. Taylor, whose Canadian Breweries provided a bountiful cash flow. He expanded into food with Canadian Food Products and soft drinks with Orange Crush. He took control of Massey-Harris and, with auto glass heir Eric Phillips, took over Standard Chemicals. In 1945, he reorganized his holdings, plus William Horsey's Dominion Stores and other firms, into a classic pyramid. Argus Corporation, the apex firm, was 50 percent owned by Taylor, with Horsey, Phillips, and several others owning lesser stakes. Taylor believed all industries evolved toward monopoly, and he sought to position Argus to benefit from this.

George Black, a professional manager, helped Taylor grow Argus rapidly. Argus expanded into Europe, merging the British tractor firm Ferguson into Massey-Harris. The group acquired control of a posy of family forestry firms, consolidating them into British Columbia Forest Products, and entered broadcasting by taking control of Standard Broadcasting. Argus subsidiaries were also aggressive acquirers. Standard Chemicals took control of Dominion Tar and Chemical (Domtar) and of pulp and paper companies like St. Lawrence Corporation and Donnaconna Paper. British Columbia Forest Products took over a series of family-controlled firms. Like the Galts in the nineteenth century, Taylor got into the land business too, building the new city of Don Mills, Ontario, as a single project.

The period saw a changing of the guard in top corporate offices. Isaac Walton Killam and Sir James Dunn both died in the mid-1950s. Howe decided that Algoma should become widely held and sold Dunn's shares in several small blocks. Killam's heirs broke up that group and sold out. Widely held firms now dominated the large corporate sector—despite a series of nationalizations by the Quebec government and more foreign takeovers, like that of the widely held Algoma Steel by Mannesmann and of Westcoast Transmission by Philips Petroleum.

The Argus pyramid remained the largest, though Taylor had retired. A team of professional managers, led by Albert Thornborough, a Harvard M.B.A., ran Argus well, with Canadian breweries, Dominion Stores, and Massey Ferguson all growing at sustained double-digit rates. By the 1960s, Massey Ferguson was a major multinational in its own right.

Fueled by its oil and gas wealth, Alberta was now a major center of economic activity. New widely held companies, like Alberta Gas Trunk Lines, Dome Petroleum, Hudson's Bay Oil and Gas, and others rose to national prominence. Vancouver also became a major center to rival Toronto and Montreal.

However, Canada was changing. In a landmark 1965 book entitled *The Vertical Mosaic,* John Porter (1965) argued that an Anglo-Scots elite still held virtually all the levers of economic and political power in what was now a distinctly multicultural country. The need to dislodge this elite would become, in many guises, the central political issue of the next quarter century. Increasingly educated Quebecois demanded to be *maîtres chez nous*—"masters in our own house." Most immigrants populating the increasingly economically important western provinces (and Toronto) were neither British nor French, and many felt alienated from the whole national debate.

The Liberal Lester Pearson succeeded Diefenbaker in 1963 and launched a variety of social programs, including National Health Care. Pearson's economic philosophy was probably not greatly different from Diefenbaker's, but his minority government dependent on the socialist NDP. This began a new trend toward greater state intervention in the economy. Pearson stepped down in 1968, and the wealthy Université de Montréal law lecturer, Pierre Elliott Trudeau, won the Liberal leadership and took power. Trudeau saw himself as a scholar, interested in philosophy, social justice, and constitutional law. He was profoundly bored by economics, though he audited a Harvard class by John Kenneth Galbraith.

Figures 1.6 and 1.7 highlight an abrupt turning point at this time. The steady rise of widely held firms reverses. A few, like Hunter Douglas, failed. But the main reason for this reversal seems to be a flurry of control block acquisitions by new and old pyramidal groups.

In 1978, Conrad Black inherited a block of Argus, acquired control of the apex company in a series of complicated deals, and then dismantled the entire group.[29] Black sold control blocks into the rising merger wave of the 1980s—some to other wealthy families and others, like Massey Ferguson, to the public. Black retained yet others, including Dominion Stores, in his Hollinger group, which he built into an international newspaper group. Lord Black remained a power in the newspaper business until overwhelmed by allegations of scandal in the early 2000s.

Sam Bronfman passed control of his empire to his sons and grandsons, but his nephews had to be bought out. Sam's brother was a partner early on, and his nephews therefore had a legitimate claim.[30] Thus, Edward and Peter Bronfman obtained a cash hoard to establish a second, separate Edper Bronfman pyramid that would eventually overtake the first.

The Edper group grew rapidly through the 1970s and 1980s, acquiring control of several large previously widely held firms, including Brascan and Noranda. Noranda, in turn, took control of British Columbia Forest Products, a former Argus firm, and amalgamated it into Crown Forest Products to form Fletcher Challenge Canada. Noranda also took a 48 percent control block in the previously widely held MacMillan Bloedel. Meanwhile Brascan took a control block in Great Lakes Power, also formerly widely held.

Other widely held firms joined other great pyramidal groups during the Trudeau years. The Power group took a control block in Dominion Glass. The Reichmanns bought much of Taylor's Toronto real estate. Their flagship Olympia and York took control of Abitibi Paper, Abitibi-Price, and Gulf Canada—the last after its parent spun off its Canadian operations.

And family firms took over widely held firms too. Molson and Labatt's, together, took control of the formerly widely held Canada Malting. The

29. His motives are unclear, for diversification was not yet out of vogue. Newman (1998) notes that E. P. Taylor, the architect of Argus, fired Conrad's father, George Black. George invested successfully through the 1960s and put the money into Argus, perhaps contemplating a takeover.

30. The two Bronfman branches separated in 1952, establishing two trusts, Cemp and Edper. In the early 1960s, Sam purchased Seagram shares from Edper at lower-than-market prices, causing resentment. The final split occurred in 1968, when Edper tried to acquire Great-West, which was eventually taken over by the Desmarais Group.

Gordon family assembled a control block in Canadian Corporation Management.

The Trudeau Liberals sought a just society and distrusted markets. An alphabet soup of federal agencies began micromanaging "strategic industries," like energy and the media. Complicated systems of taxes and subsidies redistributed income across corporations and regions. By the mid-1980s, the economy was floundering, and anger in Quebec and the western provinces escalated.

In 1985, Brian Mulroney's Tories routed the Liberals and redirected the country back onto a free market path. In 1987, the Tories relaxed the rules forbidding banks from owning other companies, and they quickly acquired control of all the main trust companies, investment banks, and other financial services companies. And in 1989, Mulroney signed a free trade agreement with the United States, finally burying MacDonald's National Policy. But many Trudeau-era programs were entrenched. Cutting regional and industrial development funds, tax advantages, and business subsidy programs proved politically impossible. Dissention within Tory ranks over this issue fractured the party, and the Liberals, under Jean Chrétien and later Paul Martin, held power after 1993.

The Mulroney Tories ran Canada's second mass privatization, floating Air Canada, the CNR, PetroCanada, Polysar Chemical and Energy, Westcoast Energy, and other state-owned enterprises. Though often lengthy and multistage, all these privatizations eventually created freestanding widely held firms.

But the great family groups more than made up for this. The Reichmanns took control of Hiram Walker Resources. Interprovincial Pipe Lines took control of Consumer's Gas, and was then acquired by the Reichmann group. The Edper group took control of Falconbridge and Fraser and expanded its existing businesses with debt financing.

In the early 1990s, both the Reichman and Edper Bronfmann groups were overleveraged. The Richmanns lost some of their properties to creditors, and Edper divested John Labatt & Co. as a widely held firm, though it was later taken over by a Belgian conglomerate.

After the Tories enacted an unpopular consumption tax, the Liberal prime minister Jean Chretien took power in 1993. Chretien was a Trudeau liberal, but the party was now more moderate, and finished the incomplete privatizations of Canadian National and PetroCanada.

Newman (1998) makes much of a new elite taking charge of Canadian business in the 1990s, writing of the death of the "Jurassic Canadian Establishment." He correctly notes (p. 5) that the old elite

practiced insider trading with exuberance, feathered each others' nests with considerable grace, maintained their workers in patronizing insecurity, and, with the instincts of an unregulated oligarchy, gleefully

> forced competitors out of their misery [and] operated in what was a vir-
> tually risk free environment . . . nurtured by government subsidies hav-
> ing formed a cozy marriage with the political establishment.

Several grand old families, such as the Eatons and Woodwards, did indeed reap the fruits of long years of mismanagement in the 1990s and largely disappeared from the headlines. Newman may be right that the old establishment lost influence because of its British ideal of "lovable dimness" (p. 13).

But figures 1.6 and 1.7 attest that Canada at the end of the twentieth century looked much as it did at the beginning. Much of the domestic private sector consisted of large family-controlled pyramidal groups.

The lineal descendents of Sam Bronfman were humbled by their foray into Hollywood, but the Edper Bronfman group remains the largest in the country. The Reichmann group, after stumbling badly in British property investments, recovered and still ranks second. The Thomson group acquired control of the venerable Hudson's Bay Company. The venerable Power group is now controlled by the genuinely entrepreneurial Paul Desmarais.

New corporate groups have arisen. Jimmy Pattison built a used-car lot into a large business group. Peter Munk, a penniless Hungarian Jewish refugee, built a huge corporate empire. Tainted with insider trading allegations, he moved to the South Pacific to build a hotel empire. Plowing his hotel profits into the Canadian mining firm Barrick restored his standing, but his posting bail for the Arab arms dealer Adnan Kashoggi troubled some. Semour Schulich, another new baron of Canadian business, joked famously, "Reputation is character minus what you can get away with."

Thus, while merger activity corresponds to business-cycle peaks, no clear pattern emerges relating ownership structure changes to either. The boom of the 1920s and the prosperous mid-century decades correspond to a rising importance of freestanding widely held firms. Families cashed out into what were probably overvalued markets, and new widely held firms grew rapidly. Entrepreneurs tapped public equity to build new firms in industries like mining. Boom and bust alike increased the importance of widely held firms through the 1960s, and then boom and bust alike reversed this. Family pyramidal groups grew rapidly in the 1970s and early 1980s. A brief resurgence raised the profile of widely held firms in the late 1980s and early 1990s, but only slightly. This reflects a mass privatization that created new widely held firms, even as others were absorbed into pyramidal groups and a brief bout of financial problems that pruned back two large pyramidal groups.

Thus, although merger waves are unquestionably periods of more rapid change in ownership structure, as are business cycle troughs, no clear pattern emerges. The conditions under which booms and busts raised diffuse ownership do not seem systematically different from those under which diffuse ownership faded away. Understanding the historical determinants of corporate ownership structures therefore requires more nuanced considerations of the institutional changes affecting these periods.

We therefore put under the microscope changes in financial development, tax policy, competition policy, labor rights, shareholder rights, industrial policy, trade policy, and cultural policies. Our objective is to see if any of these track changes in ownership structure.

1.5.2 Financial Development

Rajan and Zingales (2003) describe a "Great Reversal," in which many countries' financial systems shrank over the first part of the twentieth century and then rose again in the century's last two or three decades. They report such an event for Canada, measuring financial development by the size of both the banking system and stock market. Figure 1.8 charts their measures of financial development for Canada and the United States through the century.

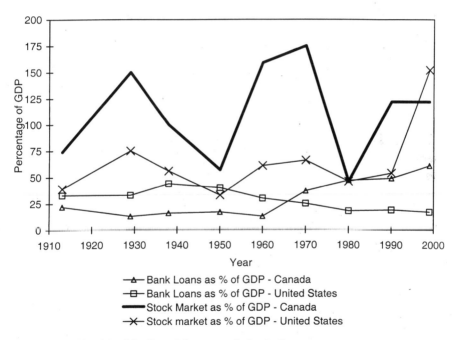

Fig. 1.8   The size of the financial system relative to the economy

Source: Rajan and Zingales (2003).

Notes: This figure illustrates the evolution of commercial and savings deposits (bank loans) and total market capitalization (stock markets), both as percentages of gross domestic product. Missing data on the size of the Canadian stock market in 1938 are estimated using the ratio of trading volume to market capitalization for other years.

Canada's banking system underwent a profound crisis in the 1920s and another in the 1930s. World War I inflation ushered in several years of deflation, bankruptcies, and bank failures. Much merger activity in the early and mid-1920s involves government-orchestrated consolidations of healthy banks with distressed ones in the early 1920s. By 1928, Canada had only ten chartered banks, down from thirty in 1910. The last narrowly held family bank, Molson's Bank, was taken over by the Bank of Montreal. The downturn wiped out several of the professional managers running former Aitkin group firms and several old family fortunes, contributing to the decline in importance of family groups.

In the late 1920s, the stock market was effervescent and clearly overvalued. For example, investors valued the troubled radio firm Canadian Marconi, with $5 million in assets, at over $130 million in 1928. Heirs to the family groups built by Massey, Dunsmuir, McLean, Simpson, and others sold out via public equity offerings. Again, this broadened the ranks of freestanding widely held firms.

Stocks collapsed in 1929, and unemployment rose. The new prime minister, R. B. Bennett, responded to the crisis by leaving the gold standard. The dollar immediately fell precipitously, and foreign lenders called in their loans. Major investment houses, like McDougall and Cowans, Greenshields and Co., and Watson and Chambers, failed. To avert a financial collapse, Bennett authorized banks and insurance companies, almost all now insolvent, to use "special valuation methods" to convince the public of their soundness.[31] Canada barely escaped a sovereign default through a National Service Loan, floated on wartime rhetoric in a huge advertising campaign. The top fifty stocks dropped an average of 85 percent from their October 1929 highs to their May 1932 lows.

For the next half century, the banking system was very stable. The 1967 revision to the Bank Act bestowed 10 percent voting caps on all chartered banks—making it illegal for any single shareholder to own a stake larger than this. The politics surrounding this seem to be public concern about foreign control of Canadian banks, or at least concern by important lobbying groups. The banking system remained highly regulated until the Mulroney Tories took power in the mid-1980s. They slowly unwound longstanding prohibitions on banks' owning other financial services businesses. Over the next decade, Canada's five major banks took over all the country's large brokerage houses, underwriters, and trust companies.

All this is reflected in figure 1.8, which shows bank loans declining as a fraction of GDP after the Laurier boom and not surpassing 1913 levels again until 1970. In contrast, the U.S. banking system actually expanded as a percentage of GDP until roughly 1938, and then slowly receded as the stock market grew more important. The economic importance of both

---

31. For details, see Kryzanowsky and Roberts (1993).

countries' stock markets peaked in 1929 and again at about 1970. The Canadian stock market was much more important economically than the U.S. market in the 1920s boom and again in the 1950s and 1960s.

Thus, large Canadian firms grew steadily more widely held when the stock market was large relative the economy and the banking system small. The shift back to more narrowly held ownership very roughly corresponds to a period when the stock market was less prominent and the banking system more important.

Beck and Levine (2002) show that both bank- and stock market–based financial systems can fuel growth. However, little is known about whether the distributions of wealth and corporate control that emerge from such growth differ. Banks are thought to depend more on relationships in making financing decisions, and stock markets are more impersonal. It is possible that family business groups have a greater advantage when banks are more important, since a single relationship covers many firms. Daniels, Morck, and Stangeland (1995) show that Edper Bronfman group firms were substantially more leveraged than otherwise similar freestanding firms, perhaps consistent with this hypothesis.

However, the size of the financial system is not God-given. It depends on other institutional features of the economy. Relating ownership structure to the structure of the financial system only pushes the question out one level. What determines this? And what other factors might be in play?

1.5.3 Taxes

Taxes changed substantially over the century. One major change that might have affected the relative attractiveness of stocks was the introduction of a capital gains tax by the Trudeau Liberals in 1972. This corresponds to the abrupt decline of the stock market relative to the economy's size. Since this also corresponded to the beginning of a prolonged high-inflation period, stocks were probably rendered especially unattractive, as the tax applied to inflationary as well as real gains. However, the stock market did not resume its prior importance in the 1980s, when inflation abated. Moreover, several other events also occurred at approximately this time, so causality is hard to infer.

One of these events, also involving the tax system, was clearly related to corporate ownership diffusion. Canada had very high succession taxes in the middle of the century, but virtually no succession taxes, at least on very large estates, at the century's beginning and end. Could this have affected the viability of large corporate groups at different times?

Prior to World War I, Canada's main source of tax revenue was the tariff and its main public expense was industrial subsidies. However, the incessantly rising subsidies that first Laurier and then Borden needed for what would become the CNR, plus an accumulating war debt, forced the government to devise additional revenue sources. In 1916, Parliament had passed an excess corporate profits tax to fund the war. When this lapsed, it enacted a permanent manufacturers' sales tax at 6 percent. Corporate and personal income taxes, enacted in 1917, rose sharply—top marginal rates for both soon surpassed 50 percent. To avoid double taxation, dividends and capital gains were exempt. In 1926, dividends became taxable personal income, but intercorporate dividends remained exempt, allowing pyramidal groups to continue.

Unemployment relief was constitutionally a provincial matter, and the provinces all needed tax revenues. Ontario introduced a "succession tax" in 1892, and by 1894 all the other provinces followed suit. Although England introduced death taxes in the eighteenth century, many American states levied them from the 1820s on. Thus, succession taxes were decried as Americanization of Canada.[32] Although the original rates were in the 5 to 10 percent range, by the 1930s top marginal rates were as high as 30 percent. Smith (1993) finds that succession duties accounted for a significant share of provincial revenues during the 1930s.

In 1941, the federal government enacted a federal succession tax to generate war revenue, but it was always envisioned as a permanent tax. Rates rose quickly and approached provincial levels by 1947. That year, the federal government doubled the rate to 54 percent and offered half its take to provinces that withdrew their taxes. Seven did. Ontario and Quebec retained their own succession taxes, which could be credited against federal tax.

These taxes took a substantial bite out of corporate groups as the business elite of the 1920s passed away. For example, both the Killam and Dunn estates were broken up to pay death taxes in the 1950s. The government's $100 million boon financed university expansions and established the Canada Council. To pay these tax bills, the heirs sold stock, and a new cadre of widely held firms came into being. These included Calgary Power, once part of the Killam group, the Algoma Central and Hudson Bay Railway, formerly controlled by James Dunn, and many other firms. Many large freestanding family firms—for example, Burns & Co.—also became widely held upon the death of their patriarchs.

As governments expanded, federal income taxes and taxes in most provinces rose to Scandinavian heights. However, Alberta began competing for wealthy family investments by promising to rebate its share of the succession taxes collected by the federal government. This tax competition threw the entire succession tax system into disarray, and Trudeau decided to abolish it entirely in 1972. Inheritances were now tax-free income. In place of the old estate tax, the Liberals now taxed capital gains, including capital gains upon death. However, a huge loophole allowed the transfer of

32. For example, Bliss (1986) writes that the "Ontario Act of 1892 was purely American in origin."

assets to a family trust, which deferred capital gains taxes for two generations. The Bronfman heirs escaped capital gains taxes entirely by moving
their wealth out of Canada before capital gain taxes fell due on their family trust.

Thus, succession taxes seem to have played an immediate role in the
breakup of several large pyramidal groups and the creation of widely held
firms of their remnants. However, this too is hardly a complete explanation. The Killam and Dunn heirs could have sold their shares to other controlling shareholders rather than the public. In the 1950s, public shareholders must have offered a better price. Succession taxes are probably part
of the story, but only part. It may be that the absence of capital gains taxes
caused small investors to be more generous before 1972, but this is far from
clear.

1.5.4   Competition Policy

Demsetz and Lehn (1985) argue that product and factor market competitive pressures weed out firms with suboptimal ownership structures. If,
for example, widely held firms have worse agency problems, as in Jensen
and Meckling (1976), they might be more commonplace when product and
factor market competition eases but less evident in periods of brisk competition. This suggests that we examine the strength of competitive pressures at different periods.

Canada had no real antimonopoly legislation through most of the century. MacDonald's Anti-Combines Law of 1889 legalized price fixing by
making restraints on trade actionable only if they "unduly" or "unreason-
ably" lessened competition. Thus, fairly overt cartels are a recurring feature of Canadian business history.

In particular, restraints on bank competition were acceptable. For example, the *Journal of the Canadian Banking Association* wrote in 1898 that

> [T]here should be certain things universally considered unprofessional
> within our ranks. Giving service without profit or at an actual loss
> should be unprofessional. Solicitation of business by offering to work
> more cheaply should be as unworthy of a banker as we consider it un-
> worthy a doctor. (qtd. in Bliss 1986, pp. 360–61)

The Canadian Bankers Association was formed in 1891 to fix interest rates
and other bank fees (Bliss 1986, p. 361). It was Canada's most important
industry association, for Parliament granted it the legal power to block
charters for new banks, to reduce deposit interest rates, and increase loan
rates. It lobbied successfully for an abolition of government savings accounts that "drained the lifeblood of the country."

The flawed Anti-Combines Law seemed a deliberate shot into its own net
by a government of vested interests. Yet it was not replaced until 1989,
when the Mulroney Tories brought in a new law. Canada thus had no real

antimonopoly law until 1989—long after the rise and fall of the widely held firm in figures 1.6 and 1.7. Competition policy per se is thus not responsible for changes in ownership structure.

However, the government affected the intensity of competition in other ways. In the 1930s, Canada was hit badly by the Great Depression and a sustained deflation, which the Retail Merchants Association of Canada loudly blamed on predatory pricing by "big business." The solution of Tory prime minister R. B. Bennett was the 1934 National Product Marketing Act, which enforced the cartelization, through marketing boards, of any industry whose producers so desired. Businesses from barbers to taxicabs were quickly cartelized under the direction of trade associations. Reynolds (1940) writes,

> The Canadian associations perform scarcely any of the service functions which characterize trade associations in the United States. General statistical services, institutional advertising, cooperative research, and the like are very rare. The Canadian associations center upon the maintenance of "fair prices" and it is judged largely by its success or failure in this field. One trade association secretary, indeed, remarked that "manufacturers up here wouldn't be bothered with an association that couldn't control prices. (qtd. in Bliss 1986, p. 427)

Although Bennett vigorously denounced laissez-faire in a cross-country radio address in 1935, he was no socialist. An enthusiastic imperialist and thoroughgoing Tory, he sought only to protect established business from instability, not unlike the Tories of the Family Compact a century earlier. Hankin summarizes the prevailing Canadian economic philosophy thus: "There must be planning, order, and cooperation in economic affairs between individuals, groups, and nations or disaster will overtake us all" (qtd. in Bliss 1986, p. 428).

The economy deteriorated further, and Bennett lost the 1935 election to Mackenzie King's Liberals. King repealed some of the cartel enforcement legislation, but similar provincial laws soon supplanted it in everything except agricultural products and banking. Federally enforced cartelization remained in place until the 1990s for most agricultural sectors, and it still endures for wheat, eggs, and dairy products. Provincial cartelization created trade barriers within Canada, some of which are still in place—for example, blocking interprovincial beer sales.

During World War II, King's "minister of everything," C. D. Howe, reorganized the economy for the war effort. To manage the private sector, he took key industrialists and representatives of wealthy families into the government as *dollar-a-year men* and assigned them production targets. The War Measures Act and Wartime Prices and Trade Board kept wages and prices low as production surged. The War Contracts Depreciation Board granted case-by-case accelerated depreciation tax deductions. If a contractor's profits seemed too high, Howe renegotiated the deductions down or levied an excess profits tax. If no private firm could deliver on Howe's terms, he established a state-owned enterprise. Both entrants and business failures were vanishingly rare.

After the war, Howe ended wage and price controls and curtailed officially sanctioned price fixing by most industry associations in 1951. The economy was probably soon as competitive as it was before the Great Depression. As various rounds of trade negotiations slowly lowered MacDonald's National Policy tariffs, imports further stimulated competition.

The Trudeau Liberals probably lessened competition in the 1970s and early 1980s through an extensive program of nationalization, aimed at restructuring the economy to limit foreign control and execute industrial policies of various sorts. The most invasive, and economically disastrous, of these was the National Economic Policy. This policy set all energy prices and subjected that industry to an intricate system of taxes and subsidies designed to shift oil and gas production onto federally owned land in the Arctic. The program devastated the existing oil and gas industry and ultimately led to no new production in the North. However, ordinary rules of competition clearly ceased for the duration of the program.

Finally responding to decades of complaints by economists and consumer groups, the Mulroney Tories proclaimed a new Anti-Combines Act in 1989. Less focused on concentration ratios and more on entry barriers than the comparable U.S. law, the new act is a more serious barrier to price fixing. The Mulroney Tories also ended most remaining Depression-era cartelization. Canada's corporations are thus probably subject to more competitive pressure now than at any other time in history.

Thus, enforced cartelization and war economy programs probably restrained competitive forces severely from the 1930s through the end of World War II. Competitive forces probably picked up after the war, died down in the 1970s and early 1980s, and picked up again thereafter. Supplementing the history of anticombines policies with that of cartelization policies still yields a pattern at odds with that of corporate ownership. Widely held ownership expanded as competition eased in the Depression and war economies, and then picked up through the 1950s and 1960s. Widely held ownership abated as the Trudeau Liberals reduced competitive pressures, and it continued to ebb after the Mulroney Tories brought in the first real antimonopoly laws. This does not disprove the theory of Demsetz and Lehn (1985), for subtler renditions of it are possible. But there is clearly no simple pattern linking ownership structure to the likely briskness of competition.

1.5.5   Labor Rights

Roe (2003) argues that, in countries that give workers extensive legal rights, companies need strong shareholders to balance this. He shows that developed countries with stronger employee protection laws have more concentrated corporate ownership structures, including pyramidal ones. How does this hypothesis fit Canadian historical data?

Billionaires of the Laurier era had little regard for their workers or public welfare in general. Although Canada's billionaires could relocate Scottish castles to Toronto and build Tudor palaces on Vancouver Island, the major charitable foundations in Canada were the Ford and Carnegie Foundations. Canadian tycoons and wealthy families funded local good works, but none remotely considered charitable giving on the scale of Bell, Carnegie, or Hershey. Instead, the new rich, like the old, planned family dynasties. Although sporadic strikes and occasional labor unrest affected nineteenth-century Canada, labor was generally accepting of its station. Labor unions were deeply antithetical to the traditional Catholic values of Quebecois habitants and the Tory traditions of United Empire Loyalists. Voices for both condemned unionization as lamentable Americanization of the country. Certainly, business saw no need to be generous. The British Columbia tycoon Robert Dunsmuir instantly fired any employee he thought was even contemplating any connection to organized labor, perhaps setting the stage for that province's union militancy.

But World War I inflation and the postwar recession, aided by the American Federation of Labor's expanding into Canada, raised a backlash against concentrated wealth. Wartime inflation roughly doubled the cost of living by 1920, and fixed wages could no longer be justified out of patriotism. Union membership grew by 50 percent in 1919, and strikes paralyzed Canada's major cities, with the bloody Winnipeg general strike attaining Bolshevik proportions.

Labor relations deteriorated in the 1920s, when Roy Wolvin and other former Beaverbrook associates created British Empire Steel (BESCO) from a merger of Nova Scotia Steel and Coal, Dominion Coal, Dominion Iron and Steel, Dominion Steel, a Halifax shipyard, and several other firms. Their timing could not have been worse, for steel prices collapsed and BESCO died, slowly. Wolvin slashed wages, and a genuine class war burst forth. By 1922, a full third of the Canadian Army guarded BESCO plants. One commanding officer even called in air strikes.[33] Nova Scotia labor was irredeemably radicalized, and this may have cost Atlantic Canada its industrial edge. And one of the great pyramidal groups from the Laurier era was in tatters.

The Liberal prime minister MacKenzie King dismissed talk of unemployment as subsidy seeking by provincial governments, and lost the 1930 election after quipping that he would not give a nickel to help a Tory provincial government alleviate "alleged" unemployment (Bliss 1986, p. 415). The new Tory prime minister, R. B. Bennett, was a corporate lawyer and longtime as-

---

33. See Bliss (1986, p. 389) for details.

sociate of Max Aitken. Married to the heiress to the E. B. Eddy Company, he was also a millionaire. Bennett also had little use for labor "agitators."

C. D. Howe, unlike his counterparts in the other Allied countries, did not invite labor representatives to participate in planning the wartime economy. Strikes grew more frequent as the war wound down, and public opinion shifted toward unions. The agrarian socialist CCF party, championing social security and labor rights, nearly won elections in Ontario and British Columbia in 1943 and won power in Saskatchewan in 1944.

King, having learned from his past mistake, issued an order in council (executive decree) in 1944 granting trade unions the right to organize and compelling collective bargaining. This was a sea change—from virtually no legal rights to substantial union powers. A wave of strikes engulfed the country as workers exercised their new rights.

In 1945, the courts found that all employees, even nonmembers, must pay union dues and that employers must collect them. This enabled unions to hire legal experts, lobbyists, and public relations experts. In 1961, organized labor took charge of the agrarian socialist CCF party and rechristened it the New Democratic Party (NDP). Labor now had a clear voice in Parliament, and soon it exercised power through its support of a Liberal minority government. In 1965, an illegal postal strike ushered in collective bargaining for civil servants, who unionized in record numbers. This too greatly expanded the financial resources of the union movement, and the influx of civil servants radicalized its political agenda.

The Quebec Federation of Labor became the most militant wing of the movement, its intellectual leaders informed by French political thinking. A new wave of strikes engulfed the public and private sectors in 1966. Especially in Quebec, strikes were violent and union leaders often flouted the law.

By the late 1970s, the rest of the public largely lost sympathy with unions, and union membership in the private sector plummeted in the 1980s. Unionized firms and industries downsized and failed, and new firms and industries took extraordinary measures to avoid unions. However, overall union membership remained much higher and union finances much stronger than in the United States because of public-sector unions.

However, NDP governments intermittently held power in British Columbia, Saskatchewan, Manitoba, and Ontario; and the separatist Parti Québécois, whose labor policies paralleled those of the NDP, won power in Quebec. Provincial labor legislation strengthened labor bargaining position further in these jurisdictions. Liberal governments in the Atlantic provinces have also become champions of labor rights.

In summary, labor rights remained very weak in Canada until 1945. They grew stronger in 1965. Unionization in the private sector fell from the 1980s on, but labor rights remained unchanged and even grew stronger in certain provinces. If strong labor rights necessitate strong controlling shareholders, we should see predominantly widely held firms until 1945 and then a steady increase in ownership concentration, especially after 1965. This is not observed. Roe's (2003) theory thus loosely explains the fall of the widely held firm after the 1960s but not its rise over the first half of the century.

1.5.6   Shareholder Rights

La Porta, López-de-Silanes, and Shleifer (1999) argue that large widely held firms currently dominate the ranks of large corporations in the United States and United Kingdom because those countries provide investors with better legal protection against pilfering by insiders and asset appropriation by corrupt officials. Small investors have limited resources for monitoring firms to detect such problems and intervening to correct them. Consequently, small investors only hold common shares in numbers sufficient to render most large firms widely held where they feel protected against such abuses. Also, corporate insiders get a higher price, all else being equal, for shares issued to small investors where public shareholders' legal rights are strong. Weak legal rights for small investors thus make them less interested in holding shares and corporate insiders less interested in selling shares to the public.

This line of reasoning, developed more formally by Burkart, Panunzi, and Shleifer (2002), suggests that widely held firms should become more commonplace as shareholders' legal rights grow stronger. Did shareholder rights grow stronger through the first half of the century and then somehow erode?

Armstrong (1986, 1997) traces the historical development of shareholders' rights. Canada's corporate governance laws early in the century were extraordinarily weak.[34] A 1906 Royal Commission on Life Insurance exposed extensive tunneling in the Mackenzie-Cox pyramid, with money flowing from insurance companies to power companies, as well as extensive insider trades by the pyramid companies in each other's stocks (Bliss 1986, p. 370). The result was a 1910 law tightening investment rules and reporting standards—for insurance firms only.

Corporate governance was essentially a matter of private reputation, constrained loosely by vague and often contradictory provincial statutes and common-law precedents. No federal corporation law existed until 1910, and that law required no annual general meetings. Until 1917 they needed only hold meetings every two years, and then only to elect the board. Only Ontario required annual shareholder meetings. The law mandated neither minority shareholder rights nor fiduciary duties by officers and directors to shareholders. Directors and officers had a "duty to the

---

34. See Armstrong (1997) for a detailed review. A good summary is also provided in Boothman (2000).

corporation" under common law, which was interpreted as trumping any duty to shareholders.[35] Conflicts of interest were of no concern to the courts. Shareholders had no rights in common law to inspect books or records unless they could persuade a judge of a definite legal objective and could identify the specific records that would certainly contain the information. Auditors had no duty to inform shareholders of potential or actual misconduct; their duty was purely arithmetical. One key precedent held that auditors were "justified in believing tried servants in whom confidence is placed by the company."[36] Another warned that an auditor who opines on governance "does so at his peril and runs a very serious risk of being held judicially to have failed to discharge his duty."[37]

Despite the absence of clear shareholder rights, stock ownership expanded rapidly during the 1920s. A. E. Ames and Co., Dominion Securities, Royal Securities, Nesbitt, Thompson, and Wood Gundy underwrote a boom of new issues. Ike Solloway and Harvey Mills established a chain of Solloway, Mills, and Co. offices across the country to handle the surging investor demand. By 1929, the Alberta-based firm had forty offices, fifteen hundred employees, and 13,500 miles of private wire. McDougall and Cowans, Greenshields and Co., and Watson and Chambers also became major players in the investment banking and retail brokerage businesses.

Following the crash of 1929, the *Financial Post* published exposés of the investment industry. As the government struggled with a huge foreign debt run up by the CNR and an expanding trade deficit, Ike Solloway was arrested and jailed.

The United States greatly expanded its public shareholders' rights in the 1930s, with the establishment of the Securities and Exchange Commission and other regulatory systems to clean up its stock markets after the abuses revealed by the 1929 crash. At the time, Canada was governed by William Lyon Mackenzie King's Liberals, and the influential senior cabinet minister, C. D. Howe, felt such regulation had no place in a capitalist country. Besides, stock market regulation was an area of provincial jurisdiction, and the provincial authorities condemned securities regulation as undue Americanization. Although provincial securities commissions were established in the 1930s, disclosure remained piecemeal and trading on insider information remained legal.[38] High-pressure "boiler

---

35. Technically, the Canadian courts held, and continue to hold, that officers and directors have a fiduciary duty to the *legal person of the corporation,* not to the shareholders. The courts are unclear about what exactly constitutes faithful service to this fictional person. However, the courts permit officers and directors to destroy shareholder value if this benefits the corporation's legal person. Shareholder derivative lawsuits, American public investors' primary weapon against self-serving or inept corporate insiders, are therefore seldom used.

36. Re Kingston Cotton Mills (1986) 2 ch. 279 at 688, 65 LJ ch 673.

37. Re London and General Bank (1895) 2 ch. 685, 64 LJ ch 866.

38. Bris (2003) argues that insider trading remains a greater problem in Canada than in other developed economies.

room" sales techniques remained an esteemed institution of Canadian finance.[39] Consequently, Canada's stock markets in the 1950s still resembled the New York Stock Exchange in the 1920s. Disclosure was often minimal, insider trading was a perk, and anything short of outright fraud was fair game.

Hearing of the vast riches in oil and minerals north of the 49th parallel, small U.S. investors responded in droves to telephone pitches from Canadian boiler rooms. The lucky widows and orphans across America found themselves the humiliated owners of worthless moose pasture. The unlucky ones lacked such title, for they had all bought the same patch.

Senators and congressmen in Washington, prodded by their outraged constituents, repeatedly demanded that Canada do something. The response was always that stock market regulation was not a federal matter in Canada. After a series of especially egregious swindles, the United States threatened an embargo on investment in Canada unless the Toronto market was cleaned up. Under heavy federal pressure, the Ontario government established the Ontario Securities Commission, mandated standardized disclosure, and moved to curtail insider trading in the mid-1960s.

Shareholder rights were further strengthened as the Canada Business Corporations Act came to include an Oppression Remedy, whereby small shareholders could sue large shareholders. The Oppression Remedy quickly became small shareholders' main weapon against corporate insiders. In many ways, oppression lawsuits are superior to shareholder derivative actions because the former target the ultimate controlling shareholder, not just his or her professional managers. Various exchange and securities commission reforms in the 1990s further expanded shareholders' legal rights. Although solid by international standards, Canadian securities laws are probably still substantially weaker than in the United States. For example, small block holdings, executive pay, research and development, and several other critical items need not be disclosed in the same detail as in the United States.

If widely held firms become more viable when shareholder rights are stronger, they should have been rare until circa 1960 and then more common. But Canadian shareholder rights were consistently weak up to the 1960s, while diffuse ownership inexorably expanded. Then, in the 1960s, shareholder rights were abruptly strengthened, and widely held firms began to fade away. Changing shareholder rights seem a poor candidate to explain the rise and fall of the widely held firm.

Of course, laws and statutes do not necessarily make or break shareholders' legal rights. Insider norms of behavior might have risen and fallen through the century, first encouraging diffuse ownership and then discouraging it. However, we have no evidence of such a pattern. Another possi-

39. See Armstrong (1997) for details regarding the lack of reform.

bility is that judicial inefficiency or official corruption, either of which can render legal rights dead letters, abated and then resurged.

1.5.7   Colonial Origins Revisited

Twentieth-century Canada is, by and large, not a terribly corrupt place.[40] Bribes to officials are not part of everyday life. However, Canada's deep colonial mercantilist heritage gives rise to situations that resemble corruption in many ways. These situations are encompassed by the term *political rent seeking,* wherein businesses invest in government connections to reap subsidies, monopolies, or favorable legislation. Political rent seeking is usually not illegal, though it can be embarrassing to politicians. It is a normal activity in virtually every developed and developing economy. But there are reasons to think that political rent seeking is more important in Canada than in many other developed countries.

As noted above, many authors argue that conditions far back in a country's history define its modern institutions and constrain its modern economy. The defining feature of Canada's colonial past is mercantilism. Canada, as a private domain of Jean Baptiste Colbert, was immersed more totally in French mercantilism than even France herself. The British who took charge retained French colonial institutions, realizing their benefit to the local elite—now themselves.[41] The Loyalist refugees from the United States, victims of liberal revolutionary excesses, sought stability in the Family Compact—an institution that brought business and government intimately together. The Liberals who displaced them in the mid-nineteenth century immediately used their offices to divert public moneys to their businesses, resurrecting the mercantilist philosophy of Colbert and Talon. Thus, mercantilism lived on in Canada long after it lost support elsewhere.

Close ties between politicians and businesses remain part of the Canadian economic landscape. These ties need not signify corruption. That Prime Minister Jean Chrétien's daughter wed the son of Paul Desmarais, whose Power Corporation controls one of Canada's largest pyramidal groups, is not associated with any improprieties. Nor is the fact that his successor, Prime Minister Paul Martin, ran Canada Steamship Lines, a former Power company. But business-government relations in Canada often parallel personal relationships. This always risks letting well-connected businesses capture public-spirited industrial policies.

If politicians are disposed to cut deals with certain businesses, they

---

40. Francis (1988), however, details a long series of swindles, stock market frauds, and money-laundering operations based in Canada and argues that the country is much more corrupt than is commonly believed. Cameron (1994) and Savoie (1990) present evidence that official corruption in Canada is worse than is commonly believed, and Swatsky (1987) presents indirect evidence of this in passing.

41. See Parkman (1867).

might find some better favor-trading partners than others. Landes (1949, p. 50) argues that family businesses are more willing partners, and he blames the weak nineteenth-century French economy on business families that regarded the state as "a sort of father in whose arms [they] could always find shelter and consolation." Morck and Yeung (2004) argue that family-controlled pyramidal groups are more reliable partners than free-standing widely held firms for politicians. They cite a variety of reasons why old, powerful families are more capable of cooperative behavior in repeated games of reciprocal favor trading. For example, old families have longer horizons, so they more dependably repay old debts. Pyramidal groups can repay favors for one firm with cash flow from another. And powerful families can better punish politicians who fail to deliver. Thus, pyramidal groups controlled by old families might have an edge in political rent-seeking competitions.

Canada's ubiquitous corporate subsidies were often controversial, and politicians were frequently lampooned for corruption. Van Horne, the CPR baron, well summarized the view of business leaders that "people who put pigs in office ought not to complain if they eat dirt and are bought and sold" (Bliss 1986, p. 368). But some governments were clearly more into subsidizing nation-building projects than others. We therefore see if family-controlled pyramidal groups grew more important in periods when superior rent-seeking ability was probably more valuable.

Wilfrid Laurier appears to have avoided most such dealings until his last term, when he took to subsidizing railways generously. His successor, Borden, broadened and deepened these subsidies, ultimately buying out the railway men with state funds to form the CNR.

A Progressive movement arose out of western Canada to combat concentrated economic and political power. Sensing mixed public feelings about mercantilist policies, Laurier made free trade *the* issue of the 1911 election, and lost when many Liberals defected to defend the National Policy. It soon became clear that the Progressives too sought to reform mercantilism, not bury it. A Progressive "people's power" campaign, aided by businesses lobbying for subsidized electricity, brought Ontario a provincially owned power company.[42] A similar campaign in Alberta led to the state-owned Alberta Government Telephones (Bliss 1986, p. 371). Ultimately, the Progressive Party and Tories would find sufficient common cause to merge into the Progressive Conservative Party.

Through the century, Canada's reaction to unfolding events always paralleled those of other English-speaking countries, but with a mercantilist twist. Tory prime minister Bennett's solution to the deflation of the Great Depression was industry-organized state-enforced cartels to raise prices, clearly a return to mercantilist basics. King embraced Keynesian fiscal

42. See McKay (1983).

policy in 1945 after intense industry lobbying, especially by construction firms, as a way to extend government subsidies to businesses. Even Canadian social programs often appear first through a mercantilist lens. For example, Canada established unemployment insurance in 1940 after a sustained lobbying campaign by Arthur Purvis, the president of Canadian Industries Limited. The government was to adopt a broader insurance role to free business of the burden of retaining workers during downturns.

Mercantilism changed its character in the series of wartime and post–World War II Liberal governments that centralized economic power in the hands of C. D. Howe. Howe believed fervently that Canada always needed a grand project, on part with the CPR, to spur development. In this, he was a traditional mercantilist.

His first grand project was a state-owned airline. In 1935, Howe became Transportation Minister, immediately squashed a nascent private-sector airline, organized Trans Canada Airlines (TCA, later renamed Air Canada) as a subsidiary of the state-owned CNR, and handpicked all its senior managers. He supervised the construction of the Trans-Canada Highway. A series of nation-building exercises ranged from massive construction projects to subsidies for "strategic industries" like jet fighter building. For example, in the 1950s, Howe subsidized aircraft manufacturers A. V. Roe (Avroe), Canadair, and De Havilland. Howe also used subsidies to prop up depressed regions. For example, he directed an increasing flow of subsidies to Dominion Steel and Coal in northern Nova Scotia.

But Howe also sought to control all business-government relations through his office, and this was new. After running the wartime planned economy, Howe held a rotating portfolio of cabinet positions, with economic power following him from office to office. Howe sought to steer the economy however he could. He granted or denied import permits on a case-by-case basis, favoring some firms over others. High taxes were now institutionalized, and Howe quickly realized that the tax system was now his major tool for micromanaging the economy.

Canadian business was still in the hands of a small network connected by ethnicity, school ties, and family connections; and by the war's end, Howe had a personal relationship with every member of that network. Corporate presidents routinely asked Howe to recommend bureaucrats for corporate management jobs. Years later, the top executives of the country's biggest firms owed their careers to Howe. Howe invested heavily in the stocks of such companies, and his policies often greatly affected their profits. For example, James Dunn, the CEO of Algoma Steel, called Howe, whose policies saved the company and who (through a trust) was a major investor, the "great white father in Ottawa" (qtd. in Bliss 1986, p. 472). The recipient of major government contracts, C. D. Howe and Co. was run by Howe's son and son-in-law.

In 1956, with subsidized construction of the St. Lawrence Seaway nearing completion, Howe chose a transcontinental oil pipeline as his next grand project. The "dictator" pushed enabling legislation through parliament, invoking closure from the outset to end debate, and then wielded his war powers to organize its construction by American oil companies. Howe won the pipeline debate, but the Liberals, since 1948 led by Louis St. Laurent, lost the 1957 election because of it. C. D. Howe lost his seat to a Socialist schoolteacher. Apart from his infatuation with grand nation-building projects and the contracts associated with them, Howe largely left the economy to the invisible hand. By concentrating business-government relationships in his office, Howe professionalized the civil service and forced other politicians to get by without wielding such influence.

The new Progressive Conservative prime minister, John Diefenbaker (1957–63), an upstart lawyer born in a shack in rural Saskatchewan, inherited Howe's nation-building schemes. The dearest was A. V. Roe Co., which now produced an ill-designed jet fighter called the Avro Arrow.[43] Roe allegedly used A. V. Roe's cost-plus government financing to build a pyramid of engine makers, steel firms, and railway car builders, and finally to acquire DOSCO, a pyramid of steel and coal companies.[44] Diefenbaker cut its subsidies in 1957, at the onset of the so-called Diefenbaker Recession.

With Howe gone, nation building seemed almost passé. However, Canada's mercantilist heritage could not long be suppressed. Its noisiest eruption was in Quebec. The Révolution Tranquille of the early 1960s marginalized the Roman Catholic hierarchy, opening the public mind to increasingly radical ideas—first secular education and divorce, then socialism, and finally separatism. Quebec subsidized a new steel industry, built vast hydroelectric projects, and supported gigantic aluminum smelting ventures. Its most intrepid venture was the Caisse de Dépôt et Placement du Québec, which began buying control blocks of listed firms in 1967. The Caisse was to be a government-controlled pyramidal group, a much cheaper way to take charge of the economy than outright nationalizations, and more effective than regulation. Many of the firms the Caisse took over were previously widely held.

Partly to deflect Quebec separatism, the Trudeau Liberals trumpeted Canadian nationalism. Trudeau disliked economics, and he delegated economic policy to his college chum Marc Lalonde, a committed nationalist who aspired to replace American dominance of the economy with links to Europe and Japan. This philosophy acquired more force between 1972 and 1974 when a Trudeau minority government depended on the Socialist, and now highly nationalist, New Democratic Party. Tories, especially those of Loyalist lineage, joined the anti-American cries.

---

43. The company also received subsidies from the U.S. Defense Department to produce the Avrocar, a small flying saucer.

44. See Bliss (1986, p. 475) for details.

Although patriotism, ideology, and history certainly kindled this wave of nationalism, it quickly acquired a mercantilist hue. Canadian executives feared U.S. takeovers as career disasters, and old families feared foreign competition. In this setting, successive Trudeau governments constructed an alphabet soup of government agencies to subsidize "Canadian" firms, vet foreign takeovers, and control ownership structures explicitly in "strategic" industries like culture and energy.

Publishing companies, like the Southam group and Maclean-Hunter, lobbied strenuously for foreign content rules to drive U.S. competitors, like *Time* and the *Wall Street Journal,* out of Canada. Canadian filmmakers lobbied successfully for generous tax subsidies in the name of Canadian culture. The Canadian Radio and Television Commission (CRTC) mandated that Canadian-made programs constitute set fractions of broadcasting schedules, and licensed entry into broadcasting to create profit cushions to finance this programming. The regulation, cartelization, subsidization, and protection of "cultural industries" became national policy.

Canadian content regulations did succeed in relocating substantial parts of U.S. program and film production to Canada, for "cultural products" are "Canadian" if they are partially produced in Canada. Thus, many U.S. network programs and films now count as "Canadian culture."[45] Television content regulations also made Canada a world leader in cable television technology, as Canadians subscribed in droves to receive foreign stations.

In 1971, the Liberals set up the Canada Development Corporation (CDC) as a white knight to block takeovers by foreign firms. In 1973, they established the Foreign Investment Review Agency (FIRA) to vet foreign takeovers. The FIRA took its work seriously, and began blocking foreign takeovers with considerable energy. A spike of takeover activity in the early 1970s corresponds to multinationals' exiting and selling their operations either to state organs or to private-sector Canadian firms.

The acme of Trudeau era mercantilism was the National Energy Policy, enacted in 1981. All current and future energy prices were legislatively set and were preannounced in 1981, cutting the profits of existing energy firms sharply. Up to 80 percent of drilling costs in Federal Territories (the Arctic) would be paid by the government, but only if the drilling company was at least 75 percent Canadian owned. Less than 50 percent Canadian ownership disqualified a company entirely from operating in Federal Territories. These provisions were designed to discriminate against foreign-controlled companies and to lessen Alberta's importance by damping its economy and developing oil and gas in the arctic, where the federal government owned the mineral rights. The most controversial element of the National Energy Policy (NEP) was the direct expropriation of 25 percent

---

45. See Acheson and Maule (1999).

of the properties of all foreign controlled companies already active in Federal Territories. These properties were reassigned either to PetroCanada, the new federally owned oil company, or to other government organs. PetroCanada was also to buy foreign-controlled oil companies with money from a new Canadian Ownership Account (COA), to be financed with a new federal tax.

The government began nationalizing industrial firms, including De Havilland Aircraft, Westcoast Energy, and many others. Air Canada acquired private airlines, and other state-owned enterprises expanded. State ownership, control, and regulation were dominating the land almost as they had during the war.

Businesses either learned to navigate the new environment or foundered. Swatsky (1987) writes that business leaders "yearned for the not so distant time when they could phone C. D. Howe and resolve their problems on the spot." Prior to Howe, self-interested politicians routinely and overtly undertook joint ventures with business leaders, and these "business government partnerships" enriched both. Howe professionalized the civil service and insulated it from political pressures—other than his own. With the economy liberalized and Howe gone, business leaders continued to lunch with politicians, but the urgency of such meetings faded as the government withdrew its hand from the economy.

Now, suddenly, the Trudeau government's hand was visible everywhere, and there was no longer a single point of contact for business. Numerous agencies, offices, and authorities now took part in regulating the economy. The Trudeau-era federal government was large and complicated, with interconnected lines of control that did justice to the most complicated corporate pyramids. Increasingly estranged from this new public sector, business leaders were repeatedly hit with regulations, laws, and decisions that seemed to come from out of the blue.

Swatsky (1987) describes how some of the most brilliant young Canadians of the 1970s came to realize that "business was fundamentally incompetent in dealing with government" and that the increasing complexity of government created golden business opportunities. These young entrepreneurs built a new industry of consulting firms to monitor government, alert clients about impending problems, coach them about how to deal with different government organs, and intervene on their clients' behalf. The value of these interlocutors became increasingly evident. Swatsky (p. 98) recounts how a multinational consortium invested $150 million dollars in an application to build a natural gas pipeline along the Mackenzie valley and then lost out to a hastily conceived, ill-prepared, and underfinanced rival through "bad lobbying." The business of helping business deal with government grew in leaps and bounds, creating a new troop of millionaires.

Companies that learned to build their strategies around government policies prospered. Nova, a new widely held pyramidal group, grew rapidly through a spate of takeovers, cheered on by the supervisors of the NEP as it "Canadianized" firm after firm. While most oil and gas companies railed against the NEP, Nova learned to love it. Of course, the firm was also buttressed by its legislatively protected cost-plus natural gas transmission monopoly. Dome Petroleum also earned laurels from the NEP for its purchase of Conoco in a complicated takeover deal involving Mesa and Occidental Petroleum.

Although most of the federal government's Trudeau-era corporate acquisitions were of formerly foreign-controlled firms, provincial governments—especially Quebec—were less fussy. The separatist Parti Québécois, now running the province, took its economic ideology from France and directed its vast state-controlled pyramidal group, the Caisse de Dépôt et Placement du Québec, to acquire control blocks in Dominion Textile, the former Argus company Domtar Inc., and many other firms.

In 1984, Brian Mulroney routed the Liberals, and his Progressive Conservative government quickly dismantled or defanged many Trudeau-era industrial policy agencies and ownership restrictions. Mulroney also embarked on a privatization program, floating Howe's Air Canada, Borden's Canadian National Railway, Trudeau's PetroCanada, and a host of other state-owned enterprises as freestanding widely held firms. Free trade with the United States, enacted in 1989, greatly reduced the returns to rent seeking for preferential tariffs. Exposés of improprieties in the Caisse undermined Quebec's industrial policy, and other provincial governments began selling off their state-owned enterprises too.[46] However, subsidies to politically powerful industries, like autos and aerospace, continued, as did funds for regional development, especially in Atlantic Canada. Corporate taxes remained a Byzantine maze of implicit subsidies, and regulatory bureaucracies remained powerful. Patronage appointments remained a staple in the political diet.

In 1993, Jean Chrétien led the Liberals back into power. More interventionist than the Mulroney Tories, they reinvigorated the rules and regulations protecting "cultural industries." Now the Liberals were divided between those of the Trudeau era and those who looked back to Laurier for inspiration, but continued subsidies, regulations, and industrial policies won the day. The Mulroney and Chrétien regimes were also both plagued by allegations of kickbacks, cronyism, and misappropriation of public funds.[47] However, in fairness, government was much more transparent, the press more aggressive, and the populace less accepting than in the past. The allegations against the Mulroney Tories are small change, and those against the Chrétien Liberals, though more substantial, remain unproved.

46. See Arbour (1993) for a detailed history of the Caisse.
47. See Cameron (1994) for allegations of corruption in the Mulroney governments, and the auditor general's 2004 Report to Parliament for evidence of corruption under Chrétien.

An explanation of ownership structure with differential success at rent seeking thus must go as follows. The first decade of the twentieth century was probably a period of rising mercantilist expectations, and family groups grew in importance in Laurier's last years. Influencing government was not terribly useful early in the Laurier years, but this apparently changed in his last term. The cartels of the 1930s, though state enforced, were administered by industry association, not the government. And though business government relations were close during the Second World War, political rent seeking was probably constrained by patriotism, or at least by the fear of being branded a profiteer. Family groups gave ground to widely held firms from the 1920s to the 1950s. In the 1950s, Howe continued to intervene in the economy but monopolized business-government relationships. Shleifer and Vishny (1993) argue that monopolistic corruption is much less expensive to firms than decentralized corruption. A similar argument may apply for legal political rent seeking. By centralizing political rent seeking in his office, Howe perhaps reduced the benefits of being a superior rent seeker. In the 1960s, Diefenbaker and then Pearson cut back on subsidies to industry, presumably keeping the benefits of superior rent-seeking ability low. Trudeau returned to large-scale intervention, and the benefits of superior rent seeking soared, giving pyramidal groups a decided advantage. This accounts for their upswing in the last third of the century.

1.5.8   Ethnic Divisions

Easterly and Levine (1997) show that greater ethnic divisions slow growth in modern African emerging economies. This reflects lower public expenditure on schools, worse political instability, larger government deficits, weaker financial systems, more distorted foreign exchange, and less infrastructure investment in general. They argue that all of these problems reflect different ethnic groups fighting to divert public revenues toward themselves and away from other groups.

There is no evidence that ethnic tensions cause problems of similar magnitudes in developed economies. However, Canada's French-English linguistic divide is an ongoing source of political and economic crises. Quebec's Révolution Tranquille of the 1960s brought long-dormant linguistic grievances to the surface, ultimately leading to Quebec separatism. Canadian politics focused on uniting Canada's linguistic solitudes thenceforth. One of Canada's greatest financial crises of the last half century occurred in 1976 when the separatist Parti Québécois won power. The Canadian dollar, previously trading above the U.S. dollar, plummeted and never recovered. The motive of the Quebec government in building up its own pyramidal group, the Caisse de Dépôt et Placement du Québec, was certainly to inject Francophone control into the corporate sector, though a European socialist perspective was clearly at work too. The motive of the Trudeau Liberals in building their vast system of subsidies, taxes, and regulations through the 1970s and 1980s was overtly nationalist—to forge a Canadian identity to supersede English or French Canadian identities, much as Bismarck did in nineteenth-century Germany. But again, a socialist economic philosophy may have been more important.

This line of reasoning is certainly the most speculative we advance, and we do so cautiously. Canadians are highly educated, and it seems unlikely that tribal loyalties could so unbalance the nation as to affect its institutions and the control of its great corporations. There is most likely a coincidence of timing, and at most a marginal effect worsening slightly a relapse into mercantilism.

1.5.9   Openness

Canada entered the twentieth century protected by the high tariffs of MacDonald's National Policy, in place since 1879. Wilfrid Laurier's Liberals, disposed to free trade, had to promise loudly and repeatedly not to touch the National Policy to gain business support in their campaigns. When they finally let principles prevail over prudence, in the 1911 election, they lost handily.

High tariffs remained in place through the 1920s, but Canadian exporters penetrated deeply into the U.S. market in certain sectors. Abe and Harry Bronfman, who ran hotels in western Canada, discovered the highly profitable mail-order liquor business. His attention to quality and cost soon made Harry the biggest liquor wholesaler in Saskatchewan, with most of his business in border towns. By 1927, having gained control of Seagram's, an old family distillery in Ontario, the Bronfmans were among the richest families in Canada. The Ontario hotelier Harry Hatch took over Gooderheim and Hiram Walker distilleries and set up a rival mail-order and wholesale liquor business. The stalwartly devout Labatt family turned over management of their breweries to Edmund Burke, an Irish Catholic who cheerfully maximized exports. By the mid-1920s, competition in beer and spirits exports was so intense that profits were dangerously thin and Canadian exporters organized to fix prices

All of these enterprises owed a deep debt to the Molson family, who vigorously worked their political connections to keep Canada, and especially Quebec, from succumbing to the hysteria of Prohibition—America's "War on Alcohol." Since American shippers, like Al Capone, handled customs formalities, tariffs were not an impediment to trade.

But other Canadian industries were in worse shape by the end of the 1920s. Worldwide overcapacity in minerals, paper, wheat, and manufactured goods depressed prices. In 1930, the United States enacted the Smoot Hawley Act, which implemented high tariffs that crippled Canada's exports. Industry after industry crumpled, hiring stopped, and layoffs started. Prime Minister Bennett's solution was to raise the tariff to protect industry association cartels committed to keeping prices high.

At the Ottawa Imperial Economic Conference of 1932, Bennett orchestrated an empirewide retaliation to U.S. tariffs. The new Imperial Preferences abruptly shut U.S. and Baltic lumber and paper out of imperial markets, resurrecting the British Columbia industry. Canada Packers could now undercut Danish pork producers, and U.S. firms had to establish branch plants in Canada to re-enter imperial markets.

In the late 1940s, Howe argued for a final elimination of the National Policy, and Prime Minister King negotiated a free trade treaty with the United States. But, apparently reflecting on Laurier's 1911 defeat, King quietly discarded the plan.

Trade barriers only started falling with the General Agreement on Tariffs and Trade—rounds of negotiation and multilateral treaties after World War II. However, multilateral negotiations were, from a pragmatic viewpoint, less important than regional trade barriers, especially those between Canada and the United States. Prime Minister Pearson ultimately negotiated an Auto Pact with the United States in 1965 that permitted free trade in automobiles and auto parts. The pact also contained useful market share provisions for Canadian manufacturers. The Auto Pact transformed a dying industry into an engine of the Ontario economy, and it would serve as a blueprint for subsequent negotiations to reduce trade barriers in other industries.

Further multilateral and industry arrangements steadily lowered trade barriers between Canada and the United States up to the 1980s, when the bureaucratic hassle at the border was often a larger cost than the actual remaining tariffs. The Mulroney Tories therefore negotiated a comprehensive Free Trade Agreement (FTA) with the United States to abolish all remaining trade barriers. After winning a majority government in a snap election called to gain a mandate for the agreement, the Tories enacted the FTA in 1989. The agreement removed remaining trade barriers, industry by industry, over a ten-year period. Tariffs on motorcycles and computers disappeared the first year, excluding only cultural industries (at the insistence of the Canadians), defense industries (at the insistence of the Americans), and agriculture and textiles (at the insistence of both).[48]

Thus, trade barriers were high and rising through the first half of the century, as widely held freestanding firms grew predominant, and then fell in the second half of the century as family groups reasserted their supremacy. Although the timing is not exact, figures 1.6 and 1.7 might be interpreted as suggesting that freestanding widely held firms do better in economies protected by trade barriers. However, other evidence makes this unlikely. Morck, Stangeland, and Yeung (2000) find that the stock prices of Canadian firms controlled by old-money families dropped relative to other firms

48. With no major changes as regards United States–Canada trade, the FTA was extended to Mexico and rechristened the North American Free Trade Area (NAFTA).

in their industries upon the surprise victory of the Mulroney Tories in the election called on free trade. Rajan and Zingales (2003) argue that many countries possessed better developed financial systems a century ago than now, and that unconstrained elites undermined these systems later in the century to deprive upstart competitors of capital. They find that this occurred less in countries more open to the global economy—suggesting that openness averts concentrated corporate control by a narrow elite. They emphasize openness in both goods and capital markets.

Openness to foreign capital need not always accompany trade openness, so before forsaking openness as an explanation of changes in ownership structure, we explore the history of openness to global capital markets.

Prior to World War I, Canada was on the gold standard and fully open to foreign capital. The Great War interrupted the flow of British capital, as well as most transatlantic shipping and immigration. Canada returned to the gold standard after the war, and foreign capital again flowed in during the 1920s, this time from New York more than London.

In the 1930s, Bennett abandoned the gold standard as he raised tariffs, but Canada remained open to foreign capital under the post–World War II Bretton Woods system and after it.

The substitution of American for British capital, first visible in the 1920s, was now complete. In the 1960s and especially the 1970s, American capital flowed into Alberta oil and gas firms, fueling the region's rapid growth. Although Safarian (1969) and others show that this capital flow was beneficial, high-profile takeovers, like Gulf's acquisition of British American Oil, irked nationalists and probably scared corporate insiders, who feared losing out in takeovers. American ownership became more controversial than the foreign capital inflows overseen by Laurier or King. Imperialists saw increasing U.S. influence undermining ties to Britain. Socialists, nationalists, and old-fashioned conservatives gained media attention condemning U.S. multinational corporations for any number of sins. Some top managers at widely held firms and old family patriarchs surprised the socialists by chiming in with unexpected support.

Diefenbaker, the prairie lawyer, was unimpressed by all of this. An outsider to the Anglo corporate elite, he was disinclined to interfere in the market for corporate control. The farthest he went was to permit defensive tactics like the mutualization of the largest insurance companies, including Canada Life, Confederation, Equitable Life, Manufacturers, and Sun. This allowed their delisting, thus blocking takeovers (not just foreign ones) and ensconcing their top managers.

Howe had angered nationalists by turning construction of his pipeline over to Americans. Then Diefenbaker infuriated them by canceling the Arvro Arrow. That fury contributed to his loss of the 1962 election, which returned the Liberals to power under Lester Pearson. An old guard rebellion within the Tory Party forced Diefenbaker out as opposition leader a few years later. However, the Pearson Liberals avoided protectionist policies for the most part. An early exception set this tone. In 1963, the Liberal finance minister, Walter Gordon, announced a 30 percent takeover tax on the sale of publicly traded companies to foreigners. Amid a storm of controversy, the tax was hurriedly withdrawn.

The Liberals sought to campaign from the left and rule from the center, but their explicit embrace of economic nationalism exposed them to charges of hypocrisy. When the takeover of a small bank by U.S. interests triggered more nationalist outcry, the Liberals responded in 1964 by legislating voting caps on the big banks. These forbade any single shareholder from holding more than a 10 percent stake and capped aggregate foreign ownership at 25 percent. Both restrictions were enshrined in the 1967 revision to the Bank Act. Garvey and Giammarino (1998) conclude that these restrictions "were put in place to prevent American ownership of Canadian banks and there is little indication that consideration of economic costs played a significant role in the decision."

The other major economic initiative of the Pearson Liberals was a half step in the opposite direction. The 1965 Auto Pact paved the way for vast U.S. investment in the Ontario auto sector and for the FTA in 1989.

Foreign direct investment from the United States became one of the highest-profile evils to be fought by successive Trudeau governments from the late 1960s to the mid-1980s. Their CDC was a white knight to block foreign takeovers, their FIRA had the legislative power to block foreign takeovers, and their NEP established unfavorable tax and subsidy rules for foreign controlled companies. The CRTC and other government organs blocked, taxed, and regulated foreign investment in "cultural" industries.

The inflow of foreign capital to Canada was thus unrestricted through most of the century, except for the abandonment of the gold standard during the First World War and the Great Depression. However, foreign capital inflow was highly regulated and discouraged with various tax and subsidy provisions under the Trudeau governments. The rise of widely held firms corresponds to capital account convertibility; their decline, to capital account restrictions. How the two might be connected is unclear, but there are several possibilities.

The Trudeau governments wielded greater and more wide-ranging economic power than any previous government, with the possible exception of King's wartime administration. They also sought to stop American takeovers of Canadian firms, but in this they were constrained by revenue shortfalls, which they could not relax much further through loose monetary policy because of growing public discontent with inflation. It is conceivable that Trudeau-era officials might have rewarded Canadian business families that took control blocks in widely held firms, and so saved them from possible foreign takeovers. Globerman (1984) argues that Trudeau-era restrictions on foreign takeovers created rents for Canadian families, as they were better able to disguise payoffs for running such nationalist errands than freestanding listed firms. However, no government records attest to such dealings, so this explanation remains highly hypothetical.

The FIRA publicized its high approval rates on FDI reviews, but Globerman (1984) correctly argues that foreign investors likely to be turned down did not apply. Moreover, the approvals were often contingent on agreements to source from Canadian firms, undertake other investments, and so on. Globerman argues that such restrictions are, in essence, transfers from foreign investors to favored Canadian firms. The government might have used such restrictions, among its other economic powers, to reward firms that helped advance its Canadian control agenda. The NEP formalized this, granting explicit tax breaks and subsidies to reward Canadian acquirers of control blocks in previously foreign-controlled energy. However, outside the energy and cultural industries, formal arrangements like this are not evident, and the hypothesis cannot be confirmed.

He also argues that the Trudeau-era barriers, discriminatory subsidies, and tax penalties against foreign investment may have had another unintended effect. Canadian entrepreneurs may build companies with a view to selling them eventually to larger concerns and retiring or starting other new ventures. These firms might be sold to public shareholders, thus becoming widely held, or sold to existing firms. By constricting the pool of potential buyers to Canadians and favored foreigners, the Trudeau governments probably reduced this ultimate payoff to entrepreneurship. This could have deterred new firms from forming. Not formed, they never became large freestanding widely held corporations.

1.6   Conclusions

Recent work, including La Porta, López-de-Silanes, and Shleifer (1999, 2000), La Porta et al. (1997a,b, 1998, 2000), Acemoglu and Robinson (2000), Acemoglu, Johnson, and Robinson (2001, 2002, 2003), and others, stresses the importance of legal system origins and distant colonial conditions in constraining the evolution of modern institutions. We provide a detailed case study of how this occurs. Canada's institutions of both government and business have deep mercantilist roots, stretching back to colonial times. Those roots nourish modern developments and ideologies, transforming them to direct institutional development down mercantilist paths.

Khanna and Palepu (1997, 2000b, 2001) argue that family-controlled business groups have a survival advantage over freestanding widely held firms in India and other developing countries because group firms can deal with each other, avoiding transactions in corrupt or otherwise flawed open markets. Consistent with newly industrialized Canada having weak institutions supporting its markets, most large Canadian companies belonged to business groups at the beginning of the century. Canada's early industrialization also provides insights into the general validity of many current theories of economic growth. This period of Canada's development is consistent with Acemoglu and Robinson (2000), Acemoglu, Johnson, and Robinson (2003), Murphy, Shleifer, and Vishny (1989), Sokoloff and Engerman (2000), and others.

The early and mid-twentieth century were periods of ascendant economic liberalism, featuring a well-developed stock market, solidified shareholder rights, increasing competition, and a shrinking role of government. These events all favored the profusion of large freestanding widely held firms, consistent with La Porta, López-de-Silanes, and Shleifer (1999) and Burkart, Panunzi, and Shleifer (2002).

Events in the latter decades of the century encouraged government intervention in the economy for laudable political reasons and high ideals. However, Canada's mercantilist roots, never fully eradicated but kept alive through successions of elites, found this expanded public sector fertile ground. Soon, socially progressive institutional innovation became a thicket of complicated subsidies, transfers, tax advantages, and regulation that stimulated vast corporate investments in political influence. Morck and Yeung (2004) argue that family-controlled corporate groups are more effective political rent seekers than freestanding widely held firms. Consistent with this, the final decades of the century saw a marked resurgence of corporate groups. Labor rights were also strengthened substantially later in the century, so Roe's (2003) theory that concentrated ownership arises to counter strong labor unions has some traction regarding the fall of the widely held firm after the 1960s, but not their rise over the first half of the century.

Our findings are consistent with previous work in this area, including Rajan and Zingales (2003), who argue that entrenched elites in many countries acquiesce to or promote policies that erode financial systems; Olson (1963, 1982), who describes the behavior of entrenched elites; and others, like Baumol (1990) and Krueger (1974), who advance theories of rent seeking.

References

Acemoglu, Daron, Simon Johnson, and James A. Robinson. 2001. The colonial origins of comparative development: An empirical investigation. *American Economics Review* 91 (5): 1369–1401.
———. 2002. Reversal of fortune: Geography and institutions in the making of the modern world income distribution. *Quarterly Journal of Economics* 117 (4): 1231–94.
———. 2003. Understanding prosperity and poverty: Geography, institutions and

the reversal of fortune. Massachusetts Institute of Technology, Department of Economics. Mimeograph, February.

Acemoglu, Daron, and James A. Robinson. 2000. Economic backwardness in historical perspective. NBER Working Paper no. 8831. Cambridge, MA: National Bureau of Economic Research.

Acheson, Keith, and Christopher Maule. 1999. *Much ado about culture: North American trade disputes.* Ann Arbor: University of Michigan Press.

Almeida, Heitor, and Daniel Wolfenzon. 2003. A theory of pyramidal ownership and family business groups. New York University, Leonard N. Stern School of Business. Working Paper.

Arbour, Pierre. 1993. *Québec Inc. and the temptation of state capitalism: Québec's caisse de dépôt et placement du Québec and state-owned corporations; What legacy for a new generation?* Montreal: Robert Davies.

Armstrong, Christopher. 1986. *Moose pastures and mergers: The Ontario Securities Commission and the regulation of share markets in Canada, 1940–1980.* Toronto: University of Toronto Press.

———. 1997. *Blue skies and boiler rooms: Buying and selling securities in Canada, 1870–1940.* University of Toronto Press.

Armstrong, Christopher, and H. V. Nelles. 1986. *Monopoly's moment: The organization and regulation of Canadian utilities, 1830–1930.* Philadelphia: Temple University Press.

Baskerville, Peter. 1987. *The bank of upper Canada.* Ottawa: Carleton University Press.

Baumol, William J. 1990. Entrepreneurship: Productive, unproductive, and destructive. *Journal of Political Economy* 98:893–921.

Beck, Thorsten, and Ross Levine. 2002. Industry growth and capital allocation: Does having a market- or bank-based system matter? *Journal of Financial Economics* 64 (2): 147–80.

Bliss, Michael. 1986. *Northern enterprise: Five centuries of Canadian business.* Toronto: McClelland and Stewart.

Boothman, Barry. 2000. High finance/low strategy: Corporate collapse in the Canadian pulp and paper industry, 1919 to 1932. *Business History Review* 74 (Winter): 611–56.

Bris, Arturo. 2003. Do insider trading laws work? Yale University School of Management. Working Paper.

Browde, Anatole. 2002. Settling the Canadian colonies: A comparison of two nineteenth-century land companies. *Business History Review* 76 (Summer): 299–335.

Burkart, Mike, Fausto Panunzi, and Andrei Shleifer. 2002. Family firms. NBER Working Paper no. 8776. Cambridge, MA: National Bureau of Economic Research.

Cameron, Steve. 1994. *On the take: Crime, corruption, and greed in the Mulroney years.* Toronto: Macfarlane, Walter, and Ross.

Daniels, Ron, Randall Morck, and David Stangeland. 1995. High gear: A case study of the Hees-Edper corporate group. In *Corporate decision making in Canada,* ed. R. Daniels and R. Morck, 223–41. Calgary: Industry Canada and the University of Calgary Press.

Demsetz, Harold, and Keneth Lehn. 1985. The structure of corporate ownership: Causes and consequences. *Journal of Political Economy* 93:1155–77.

Easterly, William, and Ross Levine. 1997. Africa's growth tragedy: Policies and ethnic divisions. *Quarterly Journal of Economics* 112 (4): 1203–51.

Engerman, Stanley, and Kenneth Sokoloff. 1997. Factor endowments, institutions, and differential paths of growth among New World economies: A view from economic historians of the United States. In *How Latin America Fell Behind,* ed. Stephen Haber, 260–306. Stanford, CA: Stanford University Press.

Fauteux, Joseph-Noël. 1927. Essai sur l'industrie au Canada sous le régime français. Quebec: LS-A Proulx.

Francis, Dianne. 1986. *Controlling interests: Who owns Canada?* Toronto: Macmillan Canada.

———. 1988. *Contrepreneurs.* Toronto: Macmillan Canada.

Garvey, Gerald, and Ron Giammarino. 1998. Ownership restrictions and the value of Canadian bank stocks. University of British Columbia research paper prepared for the Task Force on the Future of the Canadian Financial Services Sector.

Glaeser, Edward L., and Andrei Shleifer. 2002. Legal origins. *Quarterly Journal of Economics* 117 (4): 1193–1229.

Globerman, Steven. 1977. *Mergers and acquisitions in Canada: A background report for the Royal Commission on Corporate Concentration.* Ottawa: Government of Canada.

———. 1984. Canada's foreign investment review agency and the direct investment process in Canada. *Canadian Public Administration* 27 (3): 313–28.

Haber, Stephen. 2002. *Crony capitalism and economic growth in Latin America: Theory and evidence.* Stanford, CA: Hoover Press.

Hedley, James, ed. 1894. *Canada and her commerce: A souvenir of the Dominion Commercial Traveller's Association.* Montreal: Sabiston.

Henry, Peter Blair. 2000a. Do stock market liberalizations cause investment booms? *Journal of Financial Economics* 58 (1–2): 301–34.

———. 2000b. Stock market liberalization, economic reform, and emerging market equity prices. *Journal of Finance* 55 (2): 529–65.

Irwin, Douglas. 2002. Interpreting the tariff-growth correlation of the late 19th century. *American Economic Review* 92 (2): 165–69.

Jensen, Michael, and William Meckling. 1976. The theory of the firm: Managerial behavior, agency costs and ownership structure. *Journal of Financial Economics* 3:305–60.

Khanna, Tarun, and Krishna Palepu. 1997. Why focused strategies may be wrong for emerging markets. *Harvard Business Review* 75 (4): 41–51.

———. 2000a. The future of business groups in emerging markets: Long-run evidence from Chile. *Academy of Management Journal* 43 (3): 268–85.

———. 2000b. Is group affiliation profitable in emerging markets? An analysis of diversified Indian business groups. *Journal of Finance* 55 (2): 867–93.

———. 2001. Emerging market business groups, foreign investors, and corporate governance. In *Concentrated corporate ownership,* ed. Randall Morck, 265–92. Chicago: University of Chicago Press.

Khemani, R. S., D. M. Shapiro, and W. T. Stanbury. 1988. *Mergers, corporate concentration, and power in Canada.* Halifax: Institute for Research and Public Policy.

King, Robert, and Ross Levine. 1993. Finance and growth: Schumpeter might be right. *Quarterly Journal of Economics* 108 (3): 717–37.

Krueger, Anne. 1974. The political economy of the rent-seeking society. *American Economic Review* 64 (June): 291–303.

Kryzanowski, Lawrence, and Gordon Roberts. 1993. Canadian banking solvency, 1922–1940. *Journal of Money, Credit, and Banking* 25 (1): 361–77.

La Porta, Rafael, Florencio López-de-Silanes, and Andrei Shleifer. 1999. Corporate ownership around the world. *Journal of Finance* 54 (2): 471–517.

————. 2000. Investor protection and corporate governance. *Journal of Financial Economics* 59 (1–2): 3–27.

La Porta, Rafael, Florencio López-de-Silanes, Andrei Shleifer, and Robert Vishny. 1997a. Legal determinants of external finance. *Journal of Finance* 52 (3): 1131–50.

————. 1997b. Trust in large organizations. *American Economic Review* 87 (2): 333–39.

————. 1998. Law and finance. *Journal of Political Economy* 106 (6): 1113–57.

————. 2000. Agency problems and dividend policies around the world. *Journal of Finance* 55:1–33.

Lambton, John George, Earl of Durham. 1838. *Imperial blue books on affairs relating to Canada.* Repr. as Craig, Gerald M. 1963. *Lord Durham's report.* Ottawa: Carleton University Press.

Landes, David. 1949. French entrepreneurship and industrial growth in the nineteenth century. *Journal of Economic History* 9:45–61.

Lunn, Jean. 1942. Economic development in New France. PhD diss., McGill University.

Marchildon, Gregory. 1990. Promotion, finance, and mergers in Canadian manufacturing industry. PhD diss., London School of Economics.

Maule, Christopher J. 1966. Mergers in Canadian industry, 1900 to 1963. PhD diss., University of London.

Mauro, Paulo. 1995. Corruption and growth. *Quarterly Journal of Economics* 110 (3): 681–712.

McKay, Paul. 1983. *Electric empire: The inside story of Ontario Hydro.* Toronto: Between the Lines.

Mills, David M. P. 1872. Railway reform: The Canadian Pacific Railway. *Canadian Monthly and National Review,* November: 438–39.

Morck, Randall, David A. Stangeland, and Bernard Yeung. 2000. Inherited wealth, corporate control, and economic growth: The Canadian disease. In *Concentrated corporate ownership,* ed. Randall Morck, 319–69. Chicago: University of Chicago Press.

Morck, Randall, and Bernard Yeung. 2004. Family firms and the rent-seeking society. *Entrepreneurship: Theory and practice* 28 (4): 391–409.

Murphy, Kevin M., Andrei Shleifer, and Robert Vishny. 1989. Industrialization and the big push. *Journal of Political Economy* 97:1003–26.

————. 1991. The allocation of talent: Implications for growth. *Quarterly Journal of Economics* 2 (May): 503–30.

————. 1993. Why is rent-seeking costly to growth? *American Economic Review* 82 (2): 409–14.

Myers, Gustavus. 1914. *A history of Canadian wealth.* Chicago.

Naylor, R. Thomas. 1975. *History of Canadian business 1867–1914.* Toronto: James Lorimer.

Newman, Peter. 1975. *The Canadian establishment.* Toronto: McClelland and Stewart.

————. 1981. *The Canadian establishment: The acquisitors.* Toronto: McClelland and Stewart.

————. 1991. *Merchant princes.* Toronto: Penguin Viking.

————. 1998. *Titans: How the new Canadian establishment seized power.* Toronto: Viking.

Olson, Mancur, Jr. 1963. Rapid growth as a destabilizing force. *Journal of Economic History* 23 (4): 529–52.

————. 1982. *The rise and decline of nations.* New Haven, CT: Yale University Press.

Parkman, Francis. 1867. *Parkman's works.* Repr., Boston: Little Brown and Co., 1910.

Porter, John. 1965. *The vertical mosaic.* Toronto: University of Toronto Press.

Prebisch, Raoul. 1971. *Change and development: Latin America's great task.* Washington, DC: Praeger and the Inter-American Development Bank.

Rajan, Raghuram, and Luigi Zingales. 2003. The great reversals: The politics of financial development in the twentieth century. *Journal of Financial Economics* 69 (1): 5–50.

Reynolds, Lloyd. 1940. *The control of competition in Canada.* Cambridge, MA: Harvard University Press.

Roe, Mark. 2003. *Political determinants of corporate governance.* Oxford: Oxford University Press.

Safarian, A. E. 1969. *The performance of foreign-owned firms in Canada.* The Hague: Kluwer Nijhoff.

Savoie, Donald. 1990. *The politics of public spending in Canada.* Toronto: University of Toronto Press.

Shleifer, Andrei, and Robert Vishny. 1993. Corruption. *Quarterly Journal of Economics* 108 (3): 599–617.

Smith, Rogers. 1993. *Personal wealth taxation: Canadian tax policy in a historical and international setting.* Toronto: Canadian Tax Foundation.

Sokoloff, Kenneth L., and Stanley L. Engerman. 2000. Institutions, factor endowments, and paths of development in the New World. *Journal of Economic Perspectives* 14 (3): 217–32.

Swatsky, John. 1987. *The insiders: Government, business, and the lobbyists.* Toronto: McClelland and Stewart.

Taylor, Graham, and Peter Baskerville. 1994. *A concise history of Canadian business.* Oxford, UK: Oxford University Press.

Timothy, Hamilton. 1977. *The Galts: A Canadian odyssey.* Toronto: McClelland and Stuart.

Tulchinsky, Gerald. 1977. *The river barons: Montreal businessmen and the growth of industry and transportation 1837–53.* Toronto: University of Toronto Press.

Urquhart, M. C. 1993. *Gross national product, Canada 1870–1926: The derivation of the estimates.* Montreal: McGill-Queen's University Press.

Weber, Max. 1958. *The Protestant ethic and the spirit of capitalism.* New York: Scribner's.

Comment   Jordan Siegel

This chapter features an admirable effort by Morck, Percy, Tian, and Yeung to apply recent developments in law and finance theory to a longitudinal single-country case study. The authors closely examine nearly 500 years of Canadian corporate governance and analyze the numerous institutional changes that occurred, particularly over the past two centuries. The fruits

Jordan Siegel is an assistant professor at Harvard Business School.

of the authors' efforts are a series of questions that can be asked about the underlying theory itself. This longitudinal case study points the way forward for a more complete and nuanced corporate governance theory that does not seek to find the one "magic bullet" institution that leads to better governance, but instead looks for strong and positive interaction effects between mutually reinforcing sets of institutions.

The theory that Morck et al. test includes the following now well-accepted propositions in the law and finance literature. First, British common law is associated with greater controls on insider malfeasance and official corruption (La Porta et al. 1997, 1998, 2000). Second, large pyramidal corporate group controlled by wealthy families or individuals are often plagued by governance problems (Morck and Yeung 2003). These governance problems lead to underinvestment in worthy projects, and therefore large pyramidal corporate groups have a negative effect, ceteris paribus, on long-term economic growth. The negative effects of large pyramidal corporate groups controlled by concentrated groups of insiders is exacerbated when (a) the legal system is based on a system other than British common law; (b) corporate groups lack strong minority blockholders with the incentive to monitor insider actions; (c) there is automatic inheritance of corporate control by family heirs; and (d) succession taxes do not lead these heirs to have to sell off any significant portion of the corporate group to the investor public. Recent theory further states that large pyramidal corporate groups exist primarily because of their access to political rents. Politicians prefer to transact with family-controlled corporate groups because families can make multigenerational commitments of support (Morck and Yeung 2004).

Morck et al. take pains to reconcile the above corporate governance theory with the prior work by Khanna and Palepu (2000, 2001) on business groups. The law and finance literature argues that pyramidal corporate groups exist primarily to collect political rents and to funnel (or tunnel, as the case may be) liquid assets to the insiders who control these groups. Khanna and Palepu, in contrast, see the families controlling these large business groups as well-intentioned investors who are using networks of cross-ownership to amass economies of scale and scope necessary for rapid development in emerging economies. Similarly, Amsden (1989, 2001) treats these business groups as the agents of positive change building necessary technical and marketing capabilities essential for entering first-world industries. Morck et al. try to reconcile the prevailing law and finance theory with the "family business groups as value creators" perspective. They argue that

> [our] findings also give credence to the arguments of Morck and Yeung (2004) that family-controlled corporate groups have an advantage in weak institutional environments because of superior rent-seeking skills.

However, [our findings] in no way undermine the thesis of Khanna and Palepu (2000, 2001, 2002) that other institutional deficiencies can also confer advantages on groups.

While neither theory is undermined by the present analysis, follow-up work needs to be undertaken to test both competing theories, to understand their respective boundary conditions, and to perhaps craft a more contingent approach. Some business group owners may derive their competitive advantage from rent seeking, while others grow without any government support. Even among the business group owners who receive rents, some may use the rents to invest in capabilities, whereas others use the rents for solely nonproductive uses.

The question of what underlies the motives and behaviors of business group owners, and how their investments in either market capabilities or political rents impacts economical development and growth, should be at the center of this debate. With few exceptions, the literature has not included direct tests of these competing theories, and the Canadian case study shows that it is essential that further work be focused on these questions. The Canada chapter, for example, offers ample evidence for the fact that pyramidal corporate groups engage in large-scale investment that might not otherwise have been possible given the local institutional deficiencies. At the same time, this chapter also shows that at least some, if not many, of these pyramidal corporate groups are plagued by large-scale corruption and tunneling.

Authors working in the law and finance literature have made enormous progress in theory development over the past decade, but the current theory is clearly unable to explain much of the richness of the Canadian case study. Empirical results likely need to account for certain omitted variables, and the theory itself likely needs to take into account further interactions between included variables and omitted variables. Even in the present Canadian case, one wonders whether business groups can be separated into those whose competitive advantage derives primarily from political rent seeking and those whose advantage comes primarily from the development of technical, operational, and marketing capabilities. Furthermore, even among the firms that negotiate large-scale government subsidies, how did they use these subsidies? Amsden (1989, 2001) makes the argument that government preferential treatment can be positive for long-term economic growth as long as the firms are forced to actively invest all the rents in these technical, operational, and marketing capabilities. There is a strong need to test empirically the causal mechanisms that these theorists identify, whether from political ties to active investment in market-oriented capabilities or from business group formation to investment in scarce resources, or from political rent seeking to the growth of corporate groups to tunneling. Each of these causal pathways could be identified em-

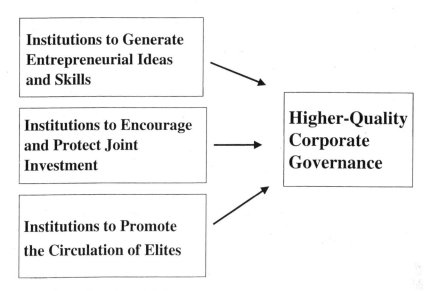

Fig. 1C.1   A life-cycle model of corporate governance

. pirically with the use of publicly available data on terms of finance, corporate structure, political ties, and use of company cash for productive investment. While there are inherent endogeneity problems in this literature, authors should better exploit the use of exogenous events that only affect certain classes of firms (e.g., Siegel 2004).

I here propose that further examination should be given to the attached life-cycle model of governance institutions. (See figure 1C.1.) A first set of institutions can be labeled in the diagram as institutions necessary to generate entrepreneurial ideas and skills. These include educational institutions that train enterprising young individuals in the arts and sciences. The greater the meritocratic access to these institutions, the more likely it is that the most qualified young entrepreneurs will gain access both to the ideas and the social networks necessary for building new ventures. More diffuse entrepreneurial networks should enable a larger number of independent start-up firms to be created. Next, a second set of institutions can be labeled in the diagram as those that encourage and protect joint investment. Without protection, outsiders will be reluctant to invest their scarce time, technology, and finance in new entrepreneurial ventures. Without these outside investments, most entrepreneurial ventures will fail to reach efficient size and scale. Protection may come from formal legal institutions, where outsiders can go to court to recover their investments from expropriators. It may also come from social networks, where information sharing and in-group enforcement leads to the ostracism of those who cheat their outside partners (Greif 1993; Siegel 2004). Finally, even with joint investment, there is the danger that successful incumbents will amass such high levels of market power that no future incumbent can challenge them. A third category of institutions that promotes the circulation of elites (Mosca 1939) is necessary to prevent ossification of the corporate elite. These institutions include public policy over inheritance and corporate succession, nondisclosure agreements, and antitrust policy. Without some policies designed to help challengers compete against incumbents, the corporate structure in any country can veer toward inefficiency and ossification.

These institutions work on their own, and through their interaction, to produce a competitive and dynamic corporate governance structure. The social scientist Gaetano Mosca wrote in his *The Ruling Class* (see, for example, 1939 translated edition) that each society had a minority of its citizens that enjoyed disproportionate economic and political power. He added that if this minority was chosen through meritocratic methods and was continually subject to new entry and competition, the society would be more efficient. Also, if every individual in the society believed in open potential for entry into the elite, every individual would be more likely to invest in her children's human capital and to participate in public and corporate governance. Both Pareto (1966 translated edition) and Mosca (1939 translated edition) discussed the benefits of having a circulation of elites and avoiding entrenchment. The present literature needs to take their cue and to use the more sophisticated econometric methods currently available to study each of these sets of circulation-generating institutions, not in isolation but in interaction with one another.

By focusing renewed attention on the interaction between governance institutions, we ought to be able to explain even more of the historical variation in corporate governance outcomes. We may find that having particularly strong institutions in some dimensions might counteract the effect of other weak institutions. We may also find that certain institutions like rule of law operate successfully only when combined with other reinforcing institutions. These reinforcing institutions serve to generate more diffuse entrepreneurial networks and/or to open up competitive challenges to industry incumbents.

The Canadian case study itself suggests that other institutions at least partially compensated for weak corporate governance. This could come from policies regarding foreign competition, privatization, inheritance taxation, and antitrust law. In the case of foreign competition, the authors describe how Canada had a protected market until 1989, when the Conservatives under Prime Minister Mulroney signed a free trade agreement (FTA) with the United States. The FTA, which was followed by the passage of the North American Free Trade Agreement (NAFTA) in 1993, has had an unclear effect on firm-level development. The authors place great importance, at least in terms of corporate governance, on the privatization enacted during this same period, which the authors argue led to the creation of numerous freestanding and widely held firms. In the case of inheritance taxation, there seems to be a clear causal link drawn between changes in tax rates and the preponderance of family-controlled business groups. By 1947, rates on inherited estates had doubled to 54 percent, and as a result numerous business groups were broken up. Conversely, the end of direct inheritance taxation in 1972 can be directly linked to the resurgence of family-controlled business groups. If the government makes it costless for families to hand down profits to their living progeny, and also to transfer outright ownership and control upon the death of the current generation, then it makes sense that families will see their corporate reach expand in terms of both scale and scope. That is indeed what the authors show to have occurred in the two decades after the inheritance policy change. The fact that the inheritance tax was replaced by a capital gains tax appears to have been counterproductive for corporate governance, according to the authors, perhaps because capital gains on highly inflationary gains over the following decade led many small investors to avoid equity investments. We cannot measure the effect of antitrust law from this case study because the authors describe how Canada never had a strongly enforced set of antitrust rules.

In summary, when one reviews the institutional changes made in Canada between 1800 and 2000, it appears that weak legal institutions were successfully counteracted at various times through heavy investment policies, inheritance taxation, and privatization. The legal institutions, while based in large part on British common law, do not appear to have ever functioned successfully in controlling official corruption and insider malfeasance. Even changes in shareholder rights, introduced in the 1960s, have had an uncertain effect. The authors believe that the creation of oppression lawsuits was helpful, but no direct evidence proves their effectiveness. Rather than the law leading to better corporate governance over time, it appears that other institutions were primarily responsible for growth and governance improvements. In terms of free trade, we just do not know from this case what role free trade played in improving government. Free trade may or may not have also played a counteracting role. Industrial policy, which may likely have been associated with corruption, was associated with one- to two-decade spurts of high growth. Krugman (1994) described for Asian countries how a high level of investment intensity can lead to high growth for at least several years, even if it is not sustainable over the long term. In this Canadian case, periods of high investment intensity led to growth booms that were followed by busts, which were in turn followed by booms. Some of these booms were the result of exogenous shocks, such as oil and gold discoveries, but others were stimulated by government policies supporting the concentrated and intense investment of public funds in industrial expansion. Whereas the authors correctly criticize the corruption and recurring ineffectiveness of these policies, it does appear that they often produced high growth rates for two or three decades at a time.

Beyond investment intensity, the most interesting lesson of this case study comes from the stories about inheritance taxation. When the median size of Canadian corporate groups is determined more by inheritance taxation than by market motives, we have reason to doubt whether family-dominated business groups are economically optimal or even second-best in the presence of weak legal institutions. Still, more analysis can be done to distinguish between family-dominated groups whose competitive advantage was based primarily on government support and those whose dominance was built primarily through reputation and market-based capabilities.

Another concluding lesson from this case study is that property rights can sometimes be too strongly protected and lead to an overly rigid and uncompetitive industrial structure. Policymakers want people incentivized to invest in property, but that sometimes requires giving new entrants help in challenging entrenched industry incumbents. Note the example of Silicon Valley cited in Licht and Siegel (2004). Saxenian (1996) identified how, even within the context of the United States—a country rated as having some of the best governance institutions in the world—there are vast regional differences in institutions between California's Silicon Valley and Massachusetts's Route 128 Corridor. Both regions have high-tech industry, but Gilson (1999) points out that differences in legal rules protecting incumbents have had a dramatic effect on both cultures and, in turn, on entrepreneurial behavior. The two states have vastly different rules concerning the enforceability of covenants not to compete. Therefore, Massachusetts incumbents can more easily defend themselves against upstart challenges from former employees, whereas in California the courts interpret the state's employment law as flatly banning all such covenants (Gilson 1999). The result is that, according to both Saxenian and Gilson, Silicon Valley has a much more open competitive structure in which upstarts find it easier to challenge industry incumbents. A final lesson from this Canadian case study is that we need to examine much more closely when too much property rights protection for certain groups (e.g., incumbents, but politically favored and heavily subsidized Canadian incumbents in particular) has negative consequences both for firm-level creation and for overall growth and development of the economy.

References

Amsden, Alice. 1989. *Asia's next giant: South Korea and late industrialization.* New York: Oxford University Press.
———. 2001. *The rise of "the rest": Challenges to the West from late-industrializing economies.* New York: Oxford University Press.

Gilson, R. J. 1999. The legal infrastructure of high technology industrial districts: Silicon Valley, Route 128, and covenants not to compete. *New York University Law Review* 74:575–629.

Greif, Avner. 1993. Contract enforceability and economic institutions in early trade: The Maghribi Traders' Coalition. *American Economic Review* 83:525–48.

Khanna, Tarun, and Krishna Palepu. 2000. Is group affiliation profitable in emerging markets? An analysis of diversified Indian business groups. *Journal of Finance* 55 (2): 867–93.

———. 2001. Emerging market business groups, foreign investors, and corporate governance. In *Concentrated corporate ownership,* ed. Randall Morck, 265–94. Chicago: University of Chicago Press.

Krugman, Paul. 1994. The myth of Asia's miracle. *Foreign Affairs* 73 (6): 62–78.

La Porta, Rafael, Florencio López-de-Silanes, Andrei Shleifer, and Robert Vishny. 1997. Legal determinants of external finance. *Journal of Finance* 52 (3): 1131–50.

———. 1998. Law and finance. *Journal of Political Economy* 106 (6): 1113–57.

———. 2000. Agency problems and dividend policies around the world. *Journal of Finance* 55:1–33.

Licht, Amir N., and Jordan I. Siegel. 2004. Social dimensions of entrepreneurship. Harvard Business School. Working Paper.

Morck, Randall, and Bernard Yeung. 2003. Agency problems in large family business groups. *Entrepreneurship Theory & Practice* 27 (4): 367–82.

———. 2004. Family control and the rent-seeking society. *Entrepreneurship Theory & Practice* 28 (4): 391–409.

Mosca, Gaetano. 1939. *Elimenti di scienza politica* [The ruling class]. Ed. Arthur Livingston. New York: McGraw-Hill.

Pareto, Vilfredo. 1966. *Sociological writings.* Ed. Derek Mirfin. New York: Praeger.

Saxenian, A. 1996. *Regional advantage: Culture and competition in Silicon Valley and Route 128.* Cambridge, MA: Harvard University Press.

Siegel, Jordan I. 2004. Is political connectedness a paramount investment after liberalization? Harvard Business School. Working Paper.

2

The History of Corporate Ownership in China
State Patronage, Company Legislation, and the Issue of Control

William Goetzmann and Elisabeth Köll

Introduction

In the last fifteen years, China's market liberalization and enterprise reforms have triggered stunning economic growth and privatization initiatives in all areas of Chinese society. After decades of socialist economic policies controlling the market through state-owned enterprises, China has begun to experiment with corporate enterprise—first through the issuance of minority ownership shares in state-owned enterprises and the creation of share markets—and more recently with the development of legal and regulatory frameworks that seek to protect shareholder rights and insure managerial responsibility. One feature that continues to distinguish modern Chinese corporations is that they typically preserve a joint public-private ownership structure that, in fact, also characterized some of China's first large-scale domestic companies. As Chinese enterprise moves toward more complete privatization, using and adapting foreign models to its purposes and taking what is generally characterized as a gradualist ap-

William Goetzmann is the Edwin J. Beinecke Professor of Finance and Management Studies at Yale University, director of the International Center for Finance at the Yale School of Management, and a research associate of the National Bureau of Economic Research. Elisabeth Köll is associate professor of Modern Chinese History at Case Western Reserve University.

We would like to thank the National Bureau of Economic Research and the organizer of the project and editor of this volume, Randall Morck. We benefited from discussions with all the participants of the three preparatory conference workshops in Cambridge in 2002, Lake Louise, Canada, in 2003, and INSEAD in 2004, as well as seminars at the Shanghai Center for Law and Economics in Beijing and Peking University's China Center for Economic Research. We are especially grateful to Dwight Perkins and two anonymous reviewers for the National Bureau of Economic Research and the University of Chicago Press for their insights. The usual disclaimers apply.

proach to nurturing a private business sector, there are few contemporaneous models it can turn to for study. Certainly the Russian experience with privatization and the adoption of corporate capitalism before the development of a legal system to maintain it must be taken as a cautionary tale in the problems of abrupt transition.

One potentially useful model for capitalism with Chinese characteristics is China's creation and adoption of its own code of corporate governance a century ago. Then, as today, some of China's most important enterprises were structured as public-private enterprises—financed in part by equity capital, but effectively governed under the auspices of official oversight. In this setting, China adopted a Western-style corporate code, which had limited but instructive effects. The analysis of this salient episode in the history of corporate ownership in China can help modern policymakers and market analysts understand not only the economic and political conditions in which the first models of the Chinese corporate firm originated, but how corporate governance and markets responded to regulatory innovation in a Chinese setting. This in turn may help us to understand whether China's corporate sector is likely to converge to Western models or whether instead the public-private structure of enterprise will remain dominant.

Almost exactly a century ago, in 1904, China's imperial government promulgated a set of laws that created a framework for modern, Western-style limited-liability corporations in China. Until the late nineteenth century, the private firm run as family business was the predominant form of business institution aside from a few state-controlled monopolies like salt production and imperial silk and porcelain manufacturers. Many of the family business institutions were substantial in scale and financially successful, operating throughout the local, regional, and interregional markets. In its effort to maintain the agrarian base of the state and to control the production and distribution of commercial goods, the imperial government did not allow private business enterprises to engage in large-scale industrial production. This attitude began to change at the turn of the century, and the introduction of the company law in 1904 should be interpreted as the government's belated response to the ever-increasing competition and stimulus from foreign business enterprises in China.

As one might expect, the newly introduced corporate structures based on Western business models contrasted with existing managerial and financial structures in the Chinese business environment influenced by kinship networks and state patronage. As our analysis shows, Chinese business institutions essentially imitated the form of Western corporate institutions without fully installing essential structures and features of the corporate system according to our Western interpretation. Although China's first corporate code contained many elements of the modern formula for privatization—including some requirements for transparency, separation of ownership and control, and annual auditing and reporting requirements—it ultimately failed to effectively transform Chinese business enterprises into full-blown corporate institutions. Why?

We argue that the code fell short on two counts. First, it did not sufficiently shift ownership and control from managers, previously empowered by government patronage, to shareholders—despite vigorous attempts by shareholders to assert their rights. Second, the company code was not effective in stimulating the emergence of an active share market that would induce family-owned firms and entrepreneurial managers to exchange control for access to shareholder capital and the liquidity of an active exchange. While a market for domestic Chinese companies began in Shanghai as early as the 1870s, it was subject to a series of booms and busts, preventing it from being an effective means to tap investor savings. In contrast, during this same period the Shanghai Stock Exchange for foreign-domiciled companies became one of the world's most active equity markets.

Without any doubt, the evolution of corporate structures in Western nations was slow, incomplete, and difficult. However, what we argue in this paper is that the historical development of the corporation in early twentieth-century China sets an immediate precedent for the revival of the corporate economy in contemporary China. Characteristics of the Chinese corporate company in 1904 with regard to ownership and control are useful for understanding corporate enterprises in 2004, from the different modes of capital access for Chinese and foreign investors to the influence of local governments and their officials then and now.

This paper is structured as follows. In the first part we discuss the general historical trajectory of business institutions in China and the changing role of government participation in companies in the nineteenth century in order to create a framework for our discussion of the 1904 Company Law. In the second part we explore the law's impact on the development of corporate business structures and use the Dasheng spinning mills, a major industrial conglomerate founded in 1895 in Shanghai's hinterland, as a case study to examine in detail the process of incorporation in terms of legal, managerial, and financial changes. Although our analysis of ownership structures is limited by the extremely complex nature of Chinese accounting material available in the archives and the absence of a strict regulatory institutional framework, in the third section we focus on the issue of control and ownership by exploring the role of shareholders, their rights and representation, investment patterns, and the development of capital markets. One of our major findings is that control in corporate enterprises in China, even if the founder and his family continued to play a major role, did not depend on establishing ownership through majority shareholding. The conclusion discusses the lessons that modern market reformers can learn from the historical Chinese experience. Considering the "top-down" approach of the current Chinese government and the hope of other nations

around the world to create effective capital markets, this paper has implications for the modern challenges of privatization and introduction of corporate capitalist structures in the twenty-first century.

2.1   Business Institutions in Nineteenth-Century China: State Governance through Patronage and Sponsorship

Before the introduction of the first Company Law in 1904 and the founding of the Republic in 1911, private household businesses, many of them
of substantial size and scope, were the central institutions for domestic
private economic activities in imperial China during the Ming (1368–1644)
and Qing (1644–1911) dynasties. Family businesses have a long tradition in
China and have been highly successful in the production and/or distribution of commercial goods, including long-distance trade.[1] The largest and
most successful of these enterprises also relied upon some form of state
sponsorship. For example, in the late seventeenth and eighteenth centuries
famous family firms such as those of the Tianjin salt merchants benefited
from nurturing policies of the Qing government such as deferment and ex-
tensions of tax payments, salt price adjustments responding to fluctuations
in the exchange rate between copper cash and silver, deposits and loans
with the Imperial Household Department, and administrative measures to
deter salt smuggling. However, as these merchant businesses were dependent upon government patronage, they were forced to stay in good favor by
contributing large sums to the state's military campaigns and making huge
donations to various public and imperial projects (Kwan 2001, pp. 37–45).

Large private enterprises for industrial production like the gas and brine
wells for salt production, operated by the merchants in Zigong, Sichuan
province, remained an exception among business institutions in nineteenth-century China. The state interacted with these contract-based unlimited liability shareholding companies only through taxation and market
regulation but did not interfere in their business organization and management structures (Zelin 2005, introduction). However, the absence of the
law of limited liability and the law of bankruptcy had an increasingly negative impact on the expansion of those businesses at the turn of the century.
Thus, only changes in business law, which came about first in the treaty
ports and then by 1904 in the rest of China, were conducive to the incorporation of those private business institutions.

By contrast, foreign corporate enterprise developed vigorously in Chinese treaty ports during the late nineteenth century. Shares of foreign-
registered corporations doing business in China began trading in Shanghai
in the 1860s, and the Shanghai Stock Exchange served as a conduit for domestic and foreign investment in China for the next seventy years. While

---

1. See, for example, Choi (1995) and Chan (1995).

Chinese domestic corporations did not trade on this colonial stock exchange, the evolution of a domestic Chinese corporate code and domestic capital markets must be studied against a backdrop of a colonial business that was regarded by the Chinese government both as a foreign competitor to domestic business and, eventually, as a useful structure for adaptation to China's own purposes.

The issue of Chinese "imitation" of Western practice in this period has been much discussed, and numerous authors have pointed out legitimate domestic precursors to nearly every kind of large-scale business enterprise in China before the appearance of foreign capitalism in the treaty ports. There is no doubt that China before Western influence possessed the seeds of a long-distance/interregional banking system, experience with large-scale business institutions, the capacity to plan and execute large-scale infrastructure improvements, and countless manufacturing and mercantile entrepreneurs whose firms employed numerous workers and whose business ventures extended great distances. Given the existence of large-scale domestic business ventures in China prior to the presence of Western enterprises, we suggest that the utilization of a Western-style corporate code in 1904 should be thought of as an adaptation of an international financial and managerial "technology" to Chinese business needs. The term *technology* is appropriate here because the early champions of Western-style finance in China regarded it as a tool to advance the goal of improvement to China's social, military, and economic well-being, rather than as a means to "Westernization" or acquiescence to foreign influence.

Indeed, the processes of adaptation began well before the formal introduction of the corporate code in 1904. These processes were largely motivated by a sense of competition with the West, rather than a sense of imitation. The first attempts to build large-scale industrial enterprises on the Western model were undertaken by concerned Chinese government officials after the end of the Taiping Rebellion in 1864. In the wake of this major political crisis, a fourteen-year-long civil war in southern China with catastrophic economic consequences, the Qing government experienced a substantial weakening of its central political authority and fiscal stability: political power shifted from court officials to governor-generals with strong regional military bases, who became instrumental in defeating the Taiping rebels and profited from the newly introduced commercial transit tax (*likin*) for the support of their troops (Feuerwerker 1980; Eastman 1989, pp. 1158–70; Wright 1957, pp. 167–74).

The next decade was characterized by political debates about the weak state of the national economy and sovereignty in the face of foreign economic and political aggression, which eventually led to moderate and rather haphazard attempts at reform. In the so-called Self-Strengthening Movement during the Tongzhi Restoration period between 1862 and 1874, reform-minded government officials—mostly politically powerful provincial governor-generals—attempted to revive the national economy and military after the devastating Taiping Rebellion. Therefore, whatever little industrialization resulted from China's Self-Strengthening Movement was characterized by a focus on heavy industries' serving the government's military and defense purposes (Wright 1957; Feuerwerker 1980).

When Li Hongzhang (1823–1901) was appointed governor-general of Zhili and imperial commissioner of the northern ports in 1870, he became the most ardent proponent of the Self-Strengthening Movement. One significant part of his plan was to acquire knowledge from the West—including knowledge of Western industrial and financial practices. He secured permission from the imperial government to send Chinese students to study in France in the 1870s. One of them, his protégé, reformer Ma Jianzhong, conducted a careful study of Western railroad finance in 1879 and proposed the adoption of public bond issues for infrastructure development in China (Bailey 1998, p. 14).

Together with moderately reform-minded officials and political authorities such as Zeng Guofan (1811–72) and Zuo Zongtang (1812–85), Li Hongzhang demanded that the Chinese government strive to improve its military equipment and technology in order to defend against the Western powers who had displayed their military superiority so forcefully at China's expense. However, these government officials were not proponents of launching an industrial revolution or a modern economy in China. On the contrary, they wanted to restore the traditional economy, including agriculture and commerce, and were not planning on "enhancing the strength and wealth of the country at the cost of its traditional institutions" (Wright 1957, p. 153).

Thus, the initial establishment of industrial enterprises has to be interpreted as a step toward regaining military strength and national pride without contesting the status quo of government and society, rather than as a step toward planned economic development. In order to secure control over this policy, any industrial enterprise founded before 1895 required not only sanction or permission but even active supervision and sponsorship from the government and its agents, the official bureaucrats. Notable examples of this promotion of industrial enterprises under government sponsorship in the 1860s and 1870s included the Jiangnan Arsenal (Jiangnan zhizao ju) and the China Merchants' Steamship Navigation Company (Lunchuan zhaoshang ju), both in Shanghai, as well as the Kaiping Coal Mines (Kaiping meikuang) near Tianjin.

Curiously, the China Merchants' Steamship Navigation Company evolved from a business proposal by Yung Wing, an 1857 Yale graduate, who like Ma Jianzhong drew upon his experience overseas to propose innovations in Chinese enterprises. Albert Feuerwerker notes that the idea of beating the West at its own game—that is, adopting Western-style corporate business practices to government-controlled enterprise—was present in Wing's initial conception. In the words of Yung Wing's auto-biography, "No foreigner was to be allowed to be a stockholder in the company. It was to be a purely Chinese Company, managed and worked by Chinese exclusively" (Feuerwerker 1958, p. 97). Once formed, the China Merchants' Steamship Navigation Company competed vigorously and effectively against Western shipping firms in Shanghai, fulfilling the original dreams of its founders, for whom the joint-stock enterprise form was simply a means to the end of reducing China's dependence upon foreigners.

In fact, all three enterprises self-evidently demonstrate the immediate goals of the Self-Strengthening Movement: the Jiangnan Arsenal was to improve China's military strength by manufacturing modern arms, and the steamship company was to facilitate the grain transport for the government as well as making China less dependent upon foreign-owned transportation companies, whereas the mines were supposed to provide the power for national transportation facilities and limited private consumption.[2] This strategy was certainly not an ambitious program aimed at nationwide industrialization through private initiatives. In order to stress their close relationship with the government's agenda, these new industrial enterprises carried the character *ju* for "governmental bureau" in their names instead of the characters for "factory" (*chang*) or "industrial company" (*gongsi*), which would have indicated a private business concern. While each of these firms was funded in part by the issuance of shares to Chinese merchants, they were not floated on a public capital market in the manner we understand today, nor indeed were they funded through a public issue in the manner used by foreign-registered companies in Shanghai at the time.

However, despite their public-private genesis, the shares of these first Chinese joint-stock companies did trade publicly in the first decade after their founding, and they seem to have been part of China's first stock market "bubble." In fact, whereas Chinese merchants invested heavily in Western enterprises in the treaty ports during the 1870s, as speculators they evidently also took a strong interest in the shares of these first domestic firms (Faure 1994, pp. 35–36). Trading in the 1880s was handled by at least one broker (the Pingzhun Stock Company) registered to trade and publish prices, and the prices appeared in local Chinese-language newspapers (McElderry 2001, pp. 5–6). A chart of these prices shows that they were trading at a 20 percent premium to par by 1882, only to drop to half of that by the middle of the 1880s (see figure 2.1). Speculations and price manipulations of some of the companies' major shareholders, who often were also the managers of the companies, contributed to the crisis (Faure 1994, pp. 38–40; McElderry 2001, p. 5). Thus it is curious that, at about the time

2. See Feuerwerker (1958), Lai (1992, pp. 139–55), and Carlson (1971).

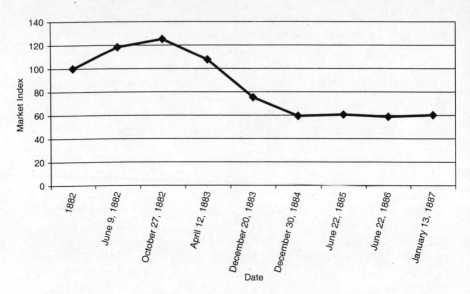

Fig. 2.1   Equal-weighted index of Chinese stocks in Shanghai, 1882–87

Source: Goetzmann, Ukhov, and Zhu 2001.

Note: The figure represents an equal-weighted index of the capital appreciation of thirty-five shares of companies listed in the Chinese-language newspaper *Shenbao,* published in Shanghai.

that the robber barons Gould and Fisk were manipulating prices of railroad securities on the New York Stock Exchange, the Shanghai market suffered from the same problems of insider trading.

This was thus not a failure of corporate law per se but rather a regulatory failure. While the New York Stock Exchange (NYSE) eventually managed to recover the trust of investors and serve as a conduit for investor capital, the domestic Shanghai market was not so lucky. After the crash of 1883, the Shanghai market for domestic shares did not recover for decades. Except for a flurry of speculative trading in domestic railroad companies' initial public offerings (IPOs) in the first decade of the twentieth century, public quotes for shares were few and far between. As David Faure notes, "tradition-bound attitudes were not replaced by share-holding in the modern companies. Rather, it was share-holding that was being absorbed into the Chinese business tradition" (Faure 1994, p. 39). Indeed, from 1887 to the 1920s, when a formal exchange was finally created for Chinese firms in Shanghai, the public market for shares was moribund.

This market failure was particularly unfortunate, for, as we will show later in the paper, it removed one of the major motivations for entrepreneurs and managers to cede control to outside shareholders. If the public would not willingly commit new capital to the enterprise, and if privately held shares were worth relatively little in the public market, why should owner-managers give up the private value of ownership and control?[3]

One way to overcome the predicament of the lack of public markets would have been to establish the new enterprises as government monopolies as in the economic strategy employed by the Meiji government in Japan during the 1870s and 1880s. However, given its strained financial situation, the Qing government did not have sufficient funds available for such investment. In addition, the machinery and the technological and managerial procedures of the new enterprises required expertise that Chinese government officials with their administrative background could not provide.[4]

It is important to point out that the financial problems China faced in the 1870s and 1880s were not unique. This was the era of a worldwide transportation revolution, and the challenge of financing the construction of large-scale transportation networks confronted virtually every sovereign nation in some form. Major infrastructure projects like rail, gas, and electrification required a quantum leap in financial technology. It was the fundamental nature of these projects that their benefits were experienced only after large up-front costs were incurred. Most nations, including China, turned to the foreign capital markets in London, Paris, and Brussels to fund construction through railroad bonds and deals with foreign railroad companies. However, these deals were conceptually at odds with the initial motivation for establishing domestic firms to compete against foreign businesses. China possessed considerable economic potential at the turn of the century; however, without a functioning domestic capital market, it was unable to tap these resources to retain control of its own technological development.

In order to address some of the failures of the domestic capital marketplace, new industrial enterprises established in the 1870s and 1880s took the form of government-sponsored enterprises, known as *guandu shangban* (government supervision and merchant management) enterprises. The bureaucratic term for this type of enterprise had its origin in the traditional setup of the government's salt monopoly, where merchants had provided capital and management while government officials maintained control of production and trade quotas.[5] Under the new scheme for large-scale industrial enterprises, private investors, mostly merchants, were expected to put up the capital and to manage their investment under the supervision of government officials. This arrangement meant that apart from some financial sponsorship through government loans, the merchants bore all the fi-

3. See Zhu (1998) and McElderry (2001). A time series comparison of prices of domestic and foreign shares can be found in Goetzmann, Ukhov, and Zhu (2001).
4. For a general introduction see Chan (1980). On Japan's industrial development see Hirschmeier (1964) and Smith (1968).
5. On the salt monopoly in the eighteenth and early nineteenth centuries see Metzger (1972).

nancial risks of the enterprises, which often became joint-stock operations. In addition, they were required to work under the thumb of supervising government officials who often followed their own, not necessarily government-directed business agendas and who introduced bribes, corruption, and inflexible management into these enterprises. Albert Feuerwerker (1958) and Guohui Zhang (1997) have shown in detail the manifold problems these industrial government enterprises encountered due to the peculiar financial and managerial arrangements. Not surprisingly, the financial profit for the private investors in these *guandu shangban* enterprises in the 1870s and 1880s was rather limited.

For example, the China Merchants' Steamship Navigation Company attempted for a short while to consolidate the government-business cooperation with its new joint-stock structure between 1872 and 1884, but continued under dominant government influence in the following years (Lai 1992). In the privatization process after 1895, the supervising director of the company appointed by the government, Sheng Xuanhuai (1844–1916), became an appointee of the board of directors, which was more a change in name than in fact, as Sheng, while supervising director, had already acquired substantial shares in the company.[6]

During this period of initial state-directed industrial efforts, Li Hongzhang, in his position as government official and personal supervisor/sponsor, became the most powerful patron of *guandu shangban* enterprises. The China Merchants' Steamship Navigation Company, the Kaiping Mines, and the Shanghai Cotton Cloth Mill were all under his official sponsorship, which actually translated his political power in the government into the opportunity to establish his own sphere of economic influence and to control these enterprises in a quasi-monopoly situation. This is not to say that Li Hongzhang's patronage had a completely negative impact on these enterprises. As Chi-kong Lai (1994) has shown for the China Merchants' Steamship Navigation Company, in the beginning Li's sponsorship in fact secured sufficient financial support and autonomy for the merchant managers (see especially p. 238). Only when Li Hongzhang was eventually unable to prevent the government from assuming more direct control of the management did the company encounter problems. Extraction, mismanagement, and misuse of funds accompanied the government's growing intervention in the enterprise, leading to decreasing merchant investment. In general, lack of auditing procedures and absence of distinction between private and company funds characterized these government-sponsored enterprises as much as any family business at the time.

In order to attract private investment from merchants who had become less and less willing to risk their money in government-sponsored enterprises in the 1880s, the government devised a compromise and promoted a

6. See Feuerwerker (1958), especially pp. 161–64, and Lai (1992).

more attractive kind of cooperation with merchants in the form of *guan-shang heban* (joint government-merchant management) enterprises. According to this new arrangement, merchants were to be more in control of the management and the allocation of the capital invested. However, this move by the government toward more flexibility and private financial as well as managerial involvement never really materialized and did not trigger the desired outpouring of investment funds. In fact, the dissatisfaction of the merchants grew during the early 1890s and was even acknowledged by government officials (Chan 1980, pp. 434–35).

Certainly, the now more restrained presence of the government in the *guanshang heban* enterprises still offered private investors some advantages with regard to official protection against inconvenient national and foreign competition. Nevertheless, creating a positive investment climate for private activity in the industrial sector would first require the more drastic step of abolishing the general protectionist mechanism against private enterprises in China, namely, the government policy that did not allow Chinese nationals to open private industrial enterprises independently anywhere in the empire. The turning point came in 1895 with a new phase of industrial entrepreneurship in China, initiated by a major political event (Quan 1991, p. 715). Indeed, the incentives for increased industrial activity and the changing ownership conditions did not originate in deliberate government reforms out of concern for a weak national economy; rather, they resulted from events in connection with China's foreign policy.

Having lost the first Sino-Japanese war of 1894–95, China was required by the Treaty of Shimonoseki to pay huge financial reparations to Japan and, most significantly, for the first time to grant foreigners permission to engage in manufacturing operations in Chinese treaty ports. Since permission had been given to foreigners for building factories in China, it was impossible for the government to prevent its own nationals from engaging in industry any longer. However, the fall of Li Hongzhang from power in 1895 was also a vital factor (Shao 1985, especially p. 369). Li Hongzhang's personal patronage of such enterprises as the Kaiping Mines, the Shanghai Arsenal, and the China Merchants' Steamship Navigation Company had been a crucial reason for their success. Li Hongzhang was powerful not only in Beijing near his power base in the Zhili province but also in Shanghai. There he exerted his influence in the appointment of the Shanghai circuit intendant, the most senior official in Shanghai's administration, and worked successfully for his operations by networking through fellow provincials, colleagues, and fellow examination graduates (Leung 1994). Through these formal and informal relationships Li Hongzhang was able to gain support from Shanghai and Jiangsu officials as well as from merchants and gentry members who were attracted either by Li's financial awards or by their own vested interests in the enterprises. As long as Li Hongzhang was in power, the operations under his supervision were protected through his patronage and thus also through their exceptional monopoly status. In short, the fall of Li Hongzhang and his monopolistic restrictions opened the industrial realm to private initiatives.

From 1895 on, enterprises in light industry and in the consumer goods industry were founded in greater numbers, with a significant shift from government-sponsored enterprises to enterprises with private involvement in ownership and management. For example, a boom in establishing cotton mills with full Chinese ownership took place after 1895. Between 1890 and 1894 only a total of five cotton-spinning mills had been successfully established (all but one with government involvement), while by 1916 thirty new mills were in operation, all of them under private merchant management (Du 1992, pp. 286–92).[7] The statistics for weaving mills are even more impressive. Whereas only one factory in private management was operating in 1897, by 1916 eighty-one private weaving mills were in business (Du, pp. 293–304).[8]

In another important sector, thirty-five mining enterprises were founded between 1895 and 1911 as private enterprises in contrast to nine mining enterprises in total government ownership, ten other enterprises under joint government-merchant management, and only two as government supervision-merchant management operations (Du 1992, pp. 460–70). As the government withdrew from direct involvement in the enterprises remaining under joint management, new forms of private business operations developed, now supported by structural aspects of incorporation, limited liability, and legal accreditation.

However, it needs to be said that it took more than a decade before China was to experience substantial industrialization in regard to the number of factories and their output, and it was not until the post-1900 Qing reforms that the imperial court openly encouraged private business and industrial enterprise.[9] Establishing factories for light industry production or transportation or banking businesses required considerable private capital investment from merchants or businessmen. Even without interference from the government and influential officials, the risk of investing private capital in major industrial operations such as cotton-spinning mills or silk filatures was still considerable in the early twentieth century. Without an open and accessible capital market for domestic shares, the raising of capital was still one of the major problems in founding private enterprises, with the exception of family businesses, which continued to recruit their capital from kinship and native-place networks.

There were, however, instances during this post-1900 period when the potential for full development of a Chinese share market appeared. Lee

7. All the mills included in this statistic have a starting capital of at least 10,000 yuan.
8. Only five of the eighty-six new weaving operations established between 1902 and 1916 were under government management (*guanban*).
9. See also Faure (1994), pp. 46–48.

En-han documents the evolution of the Chinese Railway Rights Recovery Movement from 1904 to 1911, a period in which a number of domestic Chinese railroad companies were chartered and capitalized in the wake of nationalistic efforts to recover the railroad concessions made to foreign development firms (Lee 1977). Nineteen major provincial railway companies were formed with Chinese capital raised through a combination of public share issuance, domestic and overseas Chinese merchant investment, and provincial government sponsorship. In some cases, these firms were given development rights that were stripped from foreign entities. However, virtually all of these ventures foundered in the late Qing or early Republican period: some for political reasons associated with the suspension of their charters by the imperial government, others from lack of capital and mismanagement.

So far we have addressed in our discussion some of the restrictive features of state interference in China's economic development in regard to corporate business and capital markets. However, the imperial bureaucracy's priority to maintain control over commercial production and distribution, prices, and markets was arguably based on a well-intentioned political philosophy and should not be simply interpreted as a governmental "grabbing hand." We also should not overestimate the state's impact on the formation of Chinese business structures. Religious trusts run by lineages managing land and other assets have operated for generations according to the most basic principle of a corporation in terms of property division and management based on the ownership of shares (Faure 1994, pp. 14–16). The introduction of the 1904 Company Law thus would not mean the introduction of the already familiar concept of shareholding to Chinese business institutions but rather the establishment of limited liability in legal terms with the goal of making companies more attractive to Chinese investors. Whereas the legal reforms initiated by the state were a step in the right direction, the following section will point out the serious caveats of the legislation that encouraged a hybrid development of the corporation in the Chinese context. The success and failure of newly founded corporate enterprises in early twentieth-century China, in particular the role of the shareholders, reflect this development. In the case of the reorganized railway companies mentioned above, aggressive proxy contests challenged managerial expropriation, some of which emerged in the evolution of one major Chinese industrial company, the Dasheng cotton mills, that we will examine in some detail in the following section.

2.2   The Power of the Law? Chinese Company Legislation in 1904

The late Qing reforms were a moderate attempt by the government to introduce legal, institutional, and educational reforms in order to satisfy popular demands for change and modernization while maintaining the political status quo of a conservative imperial monarchy. China's first Company Law (*gongsi lü*) was issued by the newly created Ministry of Commerce on January 21, 1904, based on Japanese and English company laws, but in much abbreviated form. The document was intended to define the terms of Chinese corporate enterprise and to create a better legal environment to encourage private investment, which would ultimately lead to greater national prosperity.

In the debate about the nature of business institutions and economic growth in China, the late appearance of business legislation has often been misinterpreted as a lack of clear definitions of property rights and their enforcement by the state. However, scholarship by China historians working on legal and economic issues has convincingly documented the widespread use of contracts in Chinese business culture for centuries and their role as primary instrument for the definition of property rights that were supported by the state.[10] At the same time, it is important to recognize that China did not lag too far behind Western legal corporate reform in the late nineteenth century. Britain, for example, only codified limited liability with its Companies Act of 1862, and from the mid-1860s through the 1880s British companies doing business in China experimented with adapting the Act and British law to the needs of overseas enterprise. Most major British firms in Shanghai only became limited-liability companies in the 1880s, and before 1907, most Shanghai-based British firms typically registered their official domicile in Hong Kong in order to avoid the ambiguities of a treaty port legal environment—governed as it was by a multitude of nationalities (Thomas 2001, p. 28*ff*).

In the 1870s and 1880s, the Western corporate model itself was evolving to address the challenges of international investment and business enterprise. The fact that shares of British firms traded as early as 1866 in Shanghai suggests that China was exposed quite early to the developing financial technology of British-style corporate capitalism. The creation of the China Merchants' Steamship Navigation Company as a Chinese corporate enterprise of sorts in 1872—ten years after the Companies Act—indicates that China, even at that time, chose to take its own financial course in the context of an evolving structure of capitalism in the late nineteenth century. Thus, the code of 1904 should not be viewed as a beginning of corporate capitalism in China in any sense, but rather a top-down "revision" of the course that large-scale Chinese business enterprise had taken over the previous three decades—a course that had already freely interacted with, and been adapted from, Western-style business models.

A new legal framework was certainly not inevitable, given the developments up to this time. The alternative to promulgating a code in 1904 was

10. The most recent contribution to the literature is Zelin, Ocko, and Gardella (2004). See especially part II on contracts and the practice of business.

the laissez-faire course of allowing the continuation of firm level adaptation and development under local official patronage. The code took an approach different from previous government forays into business enterprise. Rather than the "hands-on" inclusion of government officials in the governance structure, the code was "hands-off"—eliminating the direct participation of the government in the corporate entity, and instead replacing that presence with a set of external rules and structures designed to make the corporation responsive to shareholders. It thus sought to encourage the establishment of Chinese companies modeled on Western corporate structures that would be able to compete with foreign companies producing and selling goods in China. With regard to existing Chinese company structures, the company law was supposed "to overcome the constraints of the partnership," which, lacking the limited-liability concept, in the words of William Kirby (1995) "could be limiting, but not limited" (p. 47).

The 1904 Company Law, translated into English that same year by the Chinese secretary to the U.S. legation in Beijing (Williams 1904), contained 131 articles in eleven sections and stipulated issues such as company organizational forms, ways to report a company's founding, methods of business management, and shareholder rights (Zhu 1993). For example, it stipulated that the board of directors be elected at a general meeting of the shareholders, who also obtained the right to pass resolutions at those meetings. According to the code, businesses in the form of partnerships with unlimited or limited liability, joint-stock companies with unlimited or limited liability, and sole proprietorships with unlimited liability were allowed to register (Shangwu 1909, 2:a). Between 1904 and 1908, some 272 companies registered with the Chinese government, over half of them as joint-stock companies with limited liability (Chan 1977, pp. 180–82). Although these numbers are impressive, they represent only a fraction of the unlisted Chinese enterprises operating in China at the time.

Here are some examples of how existing Chinese businesses responded to the new Company Law. The Nanyang Brothers Tobacco Company was registered under English law in Hong Kong in 1905 and later as a joint-stock company with the Beijing government under Chinese law in 1918 (Cochran 1980, pp. 56 and 100–101). The management of the company, especially its debts and credit arrangements, had always been problematic because of the use of former compradors, because it was never clear whether they acted as agents or principals. With the new holding structure of the business company, Sherman Cochran documents a managerial innovation in the appointment of a financial controller in 1919 who was responsible for reorganizing the company's finances (Cochran, pp. 151–52).

Many families opted not to register their firms for fear of losing control over management and equity. Even those family firms that registered with the Chinese government (and most family firms in the treaty ports did not) did not necessarily give up their family business structure. The Yong'an

(Wing On) company, famous for its department stores in Shanghai and founded by the Guo family in Hong Kong in 1907, is an example of a large family business that was registered under English law and continued to exist as a joint-stock limited-liability company in 1912. However, the family continued to exert its strong financial control over the company's shareholding structure (Shanghai Shehui Kexueyuan Jingji Yanjiusuo 1981, p. 7). Despite taking the company public, the Guo brothers were able to achieve almost a consolidation between ownership and control through shareholdings from extended family, their overseas and native place networks, interlocking directorships, and intercompany loans (Chan 1995, especially p. 89).

Needless to say, the treaty ports, not rural areas, became preferred locations for Chinese to establish their new incorporated enterprises. Treaty ports were of course the places where foreign corporate capitalism presented the greatest competition to domestic enterprises—and also the places where new "financial technology" was first introduced to China. Compradors working for foreign firms quickly understood and mastered the structure of corporate capitalism, and they were among the first to introduce these methods to Chinese businesses. Chinese merchants and businessmen in turn valued the cooperation with compradors in the treaty ports in order to gain access to new financial sources and foreign products and technology. Finally, Chinese investors used the presence of foreign settlements and their special legal administration in order to register their companies under the protection of foreign legal statutes.[11]

The role of the imperial government in the registration process was remarkably restrained. According to the 1904 law, businessmen had to register their companies with the local chamber of commerce, not with the local government as one would expect. Then the registration was forwarded to the central government in Beijing. As a clear affirmation of the much more visible hand of the republican government coming to power in 1911, this practice was abolished in the law's 1914 revised and expanded form when registration now had to take place directly with the government.

In order to assess in detail the impact of the company law on the life cycle of a Chinese business from the late nineteenth to the early twentieth century, we shall now turn to the Dasheng cotton mills, by any measure a major business enterprise at the time. Its experience in many ways is typical of firms studied by economic historians interested in business history of the late Qing and republican periods. It reveals the strengths and weaknesses of industrial enterprises founded in the wake of 1895, and the transition that came about with the privatization process. Dasheng was originally conceived in a government initiative as a regional enterprise on the north-

11. Foreign registration of Chinese companies in Shanghai's foreign concessions became a particularly important device for Chinese businessmen to protect their assets during the Japanese occupation beginning in 1937. This option ceased in December of 1941 with Japan's occupation of the settlements. See Coble (2003), pp. 25–29.

ern bank of the Yangzi river in the Jiangsu province near the city of Nantong, northwest of Shanghai. Zhang Jian (1853–1926), a famous scholar with family ties to the region (but without business experience) who had left government service, was invited to found and manage the enterprise. Governor-general Zhang Zhidong lent his support as the patron in the beginning and officially initiated the Dasheng cotton mills as an operation under joint government-merchant management in 1895. However, in contrast to the previous patronage system under Li Hongzhang, Zhang Zhidong, who represented the *guan* or official side in the enterprise, did not represent the government as a corporate body but acted as an individual official. In this position he offered patronage and ineffective official protection for the enterprise, but not much else.[12]

One could say that the watering down of government patronage to individual official patronage eventually led to the complete disappearance of involvement by individual officials in the enterprise. Zhang Zhidong was unable to offer Dasheng crucial financial support, and without financial leverage his official influence faded from the picture. The originally government-sponsored enterprise thus soon became a privatized operation under the strong impact of the founder's (i.e., Zhang Jian's) family without ever developing into a family business with majority shareholding by kinship networks. A more detailed discussion of the company's shareholders and their investments can be found in the following section. Registered officially as a shareholding company with limited liability in 1907, Dasheng then grew into a major industrial complex with considerable financial success and a substantial life span that took the enterprise, even though with changing managerial and financial structures, into the early 1950s, when it became a state-owned enterprise in China's new socialist economy.

Despite required company registration it is difficult to establish the exact date when Chinese enterprises like Dasheng, or more precisely the Dasheng No. 1 Cotton Mill, acquired private, corporate status as a legal entity. After extensive search in various archives it is safe to say that no documents exist that formally dissolved the initial form of the enterprise at its foundation as a "joint government-merchant management" operation. The text printed on share certificates from 1897 and from 1903 still stated that the Dasheng spinning mills "were established in Tongzhou [i.e., Nantong] with approval granted by edict in response to a memorial from the Minister of the Southern Ports [i.e., Zhang Zhidong] . . . , by contract set up for perpetuity to be jointly managed by officials and gentry."[13]

---

12. For a detailed study of the development of Dasheng business and its role as a regional enterprise in northern Jiangsu from the late nineteenth century to the early 1950s see Köll (2003).

13. Nantong Textile Museum (Nantong fangzhi bowuguan), hereafter NFB; doc. 247, doc. 182. Share certificates from the years 1898 to 1903 with the same text are also kept in the Nantong Municipal Archives (Nantong shi dang'anguan), hereafter NSD: B 402-111-1.

In March 1905 the *Dagongbao* newspaper published an announcement that listed the Dasheng No. 1 Cotton Mill as approved and registered by the Ministry of Commerce (*shangbu*) together with ten other companies (*gongsi*) established by Dasheng's founder, Zhang Jian (*Dagongbao,* March 4, 2a–2b; March 6, 2a). This was the official recognition of the company registration required by the Company Law as promulgated in 1904 (Shangwu 1909, 10:3b). Finally, we know from the published report of the first shareholder meeting in 1907 that the Dasheng No. 1 Cotton Mill had now taken on the form of a stockholding company with limited liability (*gufen youxian gongsi*) (NSD B 402-111-445, 13b).

What did the shareholders of the newly incorporated companies say? We must not forget that although Dasheng had been operating with private share capital since its establishment in 1898, shareholders had no public forum within the enterprise to voice their suggestions or criticism regarding the company's policies. Thus, the new legal status of the company seems to have been met with great enthusiasm from the shareholders. Zheng Xiaoxu (1860–1938), one of the most prominent shareholders with an active career in business and national politics,[14] is quoted in the 1907 shareholder report, which documents the lively discussions at Dasheng's first-ever shareholder meeting:

> Formerly all the organization of this mill was unlimited and untouched by any law.[15] Now that we have shareholder meetings, the unlimited and without-law status should be changed into a company that is limited and with a complete law. We should first decide on its name as Dasheng Stockholding Company With Limited Liability (Dasheng gufen youxian gongsi). (NSD B 402-111-445, 12b)

One would expect that the new share certificates of the Dasheng No. 1 mill from 1907 onward would bear reference to the new legal status of the company—but they do not. The certificates refer only to the Dasheng Spinning and Weaving Company (Dasheng fangzhi gongsi) without indicating its new legal status. However, the text on share certificates from the years 1915 and 1919 at least no longer mentions the previous involvement of the government in the establishment of the company (NFB doc. 193, doc. 198).

While some companies like Dasheng, through incorporation, rid themselves of government patronage, some enterprises actively continued to seek and exploit government patronage during the republican period when

14. For the biography of Zheng Xiaoxu see Boorman (1967–1971), pp. 271–75. Zheng Xiaoxu is probably most famous for his Manchu loyalism and his refusal to recognize the Republic of China. Between 1925 and 1932 he served as assistant to the former Xuantong emperor Puyi.

15. To translate *wufa* as "illegal" would be beside the point, as there was no company law with required registration before 1904, and thus a company without official registration was not an illegal operation.

political power became even more fragmented. The Lanzhou Mining Company (Beiyang Lanzhou guankuang youxian gongsi) and the Qixin Cement Company (Qixin yanghui gongsi) are examples of such privatized enterprises under rejuvenated patterns of political patronage. Their founder, the government official Zhou Xuexi (1869–1947), enjoyed the political patronage of Yuan Shikai, who, first as governor-general of Zhili and later as president of the Republic, had great influence in the Beijing government. Yuan's support of the Qixin company through partial exemption from custom duties and its placement as major supplier of cement for the government-owned railways fortified the positive relationship between the most successful industrialist in northern China and the Beijing government. Although the establishment of the Nanjing government in 1927 meant a drastic change in the political scenario and thus a shift in the patronage advantages for Zhou Xuexi, his companies were already so well established that they continued their business with success in the 1930s (Feuerwerker 1995, especially pp. 287–302; Carlson 171, pp. 105–117).

In general, the change to limited liability did not evoke great changes in terms of the business organization of Chinese enterprises. The introduction of annual shareholder meetings appears as the most significant result of their legal transformation into private, incorporated companies. The new legal status did not affect the internal managerial structure or the overall structure of the business. The line of hierarchy remained basically unchanged, as the department heads were still appointed by the managing director, but now in consultation with the board of directors (NSD B 402-111-445, 17a-b).

In addition, according to the stipulations of the 1904 Company Law, two auditors were appointed to examine the company's finances. However, the law did not specify that these auditors had to be independent, only that company directors could not simultaneously serve as auditors for their own companies (Shangwu 1909, 10:7a–8b). This meant that legally auditors could still be selected from the remaining members of the board. For example, in the case of Dasheng, auditors were recruited from among the board members and thus from within the company management under Zhang Jian's immediate influence (NSD B 402-111-445, 4a). These auditors more or less rubber-stamped Dasheng's annual reports and signed the minutes of the shareholder meetings. We should not interpret their role as controllers who represented the interests of shareholders regarding financial clarity and critical examination. In fact, as part of the management, the auditors were there to defend the financial decisions they had approved on the board earlier on.

On the whole, it seems that the new legal status of incorporation, which we tend to associate with the form of a "modern" business enterprise in the Western sense, did not lead to significant improvements with regard to protecting shareholders' rights or curbing the power of the managing director.

In fact, judging from the complaints at shareholder meetings of Zhang Jian's enterprises, their complete ineffectiveness in every respect still placed shareholders at a disadvantage, despite all the potential prospects of openness and accountability through Dasheng's incorporation. The balance of power did not change in the company. Apparently the top-down approach encountered resistance at the managerial level, while the company founder stayed in control.

In line with common business practice used previously in government-sponsored enterprises, shareholders in companies that started after 1895 and incorporated relatively early received guaranteed interest payments at a fixed rate of 8 percent on their share investment. They collected their interest annually in person from the accounting office at the factories (Köll 2003, p. 130).[16] Thus, the common shares resembled what we now think of as preferred shares—at least insofar as the dividend payments were fixed and relatively high compared to the few existing investment options through financial instruments before the emergence of the modern banking system in China in the mid-1910s.[17] This practice clearly increased the risk of the enterprise: while reducing the fluctuation of income to shareholders, it also reduced the discretion of management to fund growth and investment from cash generated by operations. This would not be a major problem in a liquid capital market, in which managers could raise needed funds by issuing additional debt or equity. However, the domestic Chinese share market still suffered from the illiquidity of the 1880s crash—it did not provide the means to easily finance growth.

Why, then, were dividend payments comparatively high and fixed? It is tempting to consider a modern explanation founded in the limitations of corporate governance—the "free cash flow" hypothesis (Jensen 1986). In essence, Michael Jensen's free cash flow theory posits that cash from the operations of a company is a temptation to the manager, who seeks to use it to his own ends rather than returning it to shareholders. One way to prevent management from diverting corporate funds—or one way for the manager to prove to shareholders he is not diverting funds—is to set a high, fixed payout ratio. This could be achieved through a high debt-equity ratio or a mechanism like preferred shares. An alternative way to discipline the managers is to have a market for corporate control: that is, the ability to take over the company by buying all the shares and then replacing bad management with good. This, of course, necessitates an open and active public market for the shares—something largely lacking for domestic Chinese companies until roughly the third decade of the twentieth century. Given the documented concerns that Chinese shareholders might natu-

16. As Ellen Hertz (1998, p. 37) points out, even in China today dividends from Shanghai's stock market are distributed in person and not through the mail.

17. On the emergence of modern banking and expansion of investment options in China see, for example, Sheehan (2003) and Cheng (2003).

rally have about diversion of funds by managers and the lack of a market for corporate control, high fixed dividends might be expected to naturally arise as a means to assuage investor concerns.

The capital of the Dasheng No. 1 Cotton Mill remained unchanged at 1.13 million taels[18] between 1903 and 1914 (Nantong Shi Dang'an guan 1987, pp. 18–19, 93–103). The new legal status of limited liability did not attract tremendous interest or create greater trust among investors and did not prompt the management to seek a capital increase through the public offering of new share subscriptions. Shares of the Dasheng No. 1 mill were traded for the first time by the Shanghai Stock Merchants Association in 1917, but the trading volume of this trading association operating with government approval since late 1914 seems to have been rather limited.[19] When the Chinese Merchants Stock and Commodity Exchange opened in 1920, shares of the Dasheng No. 1 and No. 2 Cotton Mills were officially listed and their market prices regularly reported in the *Shenbao* newspaper published in Shanghai. Despite a new boom in domestic stock market speculation after 1920, it is unlikely that this public float of shares served in any meaningful way to discipline management. When the speculative bubble in the market burst at the beginning of 1922, public interest in shares again subsided to the point where, by 1931, virtually all the action on the domestic Shanghai exchanges was in government debt (McElderry 2001, p. 9).

In the context of financial transparency and control, the question arises whether the new company legislation of 1904 changed the process of creating and controlling accounts in Chinese enterprises. According to the stipulations in the 1904 Company Law, corporations were required to produce a detailed company report at least once every year. The annual report had to contain a profit and loss statement, a written statement on the company's commercial situation, the exact loss or profit figure, and the amount of money paid out as dividends and set aside for reserves, as well as a balance of the company's assets and liabilities (Shangwu 1909, 10:9a). Most of the companies complied with all these basic formal requirements in their annual company reports.

In fact, from existing published and unpublished company records it is clear that companies like Dasheng were fulfilling these basic publication requirements even before the 1904 legislation, and as a general trend accounting practices did not change significantly in the following decades.[20]

---

18. As a rough generalization, 1 tael, a silver unit of account, equaled 1.55 Chinese silver dollars or yuan. Rawski (1989, p. 162, footnote 94) calculates an annual inflation rate of 2.0 percent in China for the period between 1910 and 1936.

19. See McElderry (2001), in particular page 6 and footnote 1, which gives a partial list of the government securities and government shares traded in 1917.

20. See the annual company reports in Nantong Shi Dang'anguan covering the period between 1899 and 1930.

One would expect certain changes in the reporting style or at least a more detailed, lucid presentation of the accounts as a result of the introduction of new company legislation. However, a look into the Company Law from 1904 reveals that no regulations specified the way company accounts should be compiled and recorded, whereas the regulations for the annual financial statement were summarized in just two lines (Shangwu 1908, 10: 9a). Even the revised Company Law from 1914 under the section "company accounting" did not contain any further specifications for standardized bookkeeping (Zhongguo 1987, pp. 46–47).

In short, the law required an annual company report but no uniform system for company accounting. Modern, Western-style bookkeeping methods found their way into China only in the 1930s,[21] and to judge from archival evidence, most companies officially began to use a standardized, modernized accounting system only in the 1940s (Nantong museum [Nantong bowuyuan, hereafter NBY] E 123/1334, pp. 6–17, 19–20). Nevertheless, this is not to say that traditional forms of bookkeeping were inefficient or irrational; even in large-scale industrial enterprises they obviously served their purpose. Companies maintained, at least to the outsider, a complex bookkeeping system that provided some internal control within the branches, factories, and offices (Köll 1998).

All these observations confirm William Kirby's (1995) analysis of the 1904 Company Law in relation to its very limited impact on the development of Chinese enterprises and modern industries. Only a relatively small number of enterprises registered at all, and of those registered as stockholding companies with limited liability only a few were of substantial size and actually grew into sustainable enterprises (p. 48). Kirby also mentions the uncertainty of how commercial disputes of corporations would be settled by the imperial court system as a factor that might have deterred investors and discouraged seeking incorporation in the first place. Here we are reminded of the present situation in China where foreign investors are allowed to buy shares that are available to Chinese investors, and where legal disputes between domestic and foreign enterprises like the settlement of intellectual property rights are complicated by different legal frameworks and regimes. Due to the entrenchment of management and founder anchored in Dasheng's detailed corporate charter and a business legislation with many loopholes, disgruntled shareholders had no recourse with the government to protect their rights and interests through legal action. But then, judging from the interaction between founder-director, management, and investors, most shareholders seem to have willingly accepted their silent role as long as they received their annual dividend payments.

21. For the introduction of Western-style accounting to China see Gao Zhiyu (1985), pp. 84–91. From the 1920s onward the frequent advertising of bookkeeping manuals for industrial and commercial enterprises in newspapers and journals indicates the increasing demand for modern accounting expertise.

2.3   Corporate Ownership and Control in Early Twentieth-Century China

So why did people bother to register their companies at all? The fact that Zhang Jian registered the No. 2 branch mill in Chongming with the Ministry of Commerce as early as 1905, two years before this mill was even ready to go into operation, shows that he was actively interested in having his industrial companies registered with the government (*Dagong Bao*, 28 February 1905, 2b). Obviously the expectation that incorporation would make the company more attractive to potential investors must have played a role in his decision.

The issue of corporate ownership informs all the other contributions in this volume, yet in this paper so far we have mainly discussed structures and mechanisms of control in Chinese corporate enterprises emerging in the early twentieth century. Apart from the fact that it is extremely difficult to establish the identity of the investors and the exact amounts of their investments based on Chinese accounting records, the issue of control over the enterprise was not determined by ownership of shares in terms of majority shareholding as much as by means of establishing institutional structures of control in combination with social networks. For the purpose of clarifying this crucial point, let us now further investigate Dasheng's shareholding in the context of incorporation and the identity of the shareholders and their investments in 1907.

The regulations in the Company Law of 1904 required, on registration of any company, a statement of how many people were providing the capital, their names and addresses, and the overall amount of capital and number of shares (Shangwu 1909). These regulations concerned the initial setup and changes in the company's shareholding due to expansion and growth as would occur over time. Periodic shareholding inventories found in the Nantong archives are thus invaluable sources for the examination of shareholding structure and the practice of disguising personal accounts in the form of business accounts.

Holding capital under a business account was a common business practice in the late Qing dynasty. In fact, using a business name (*ji* or *hao*) for daily operations and holding property under another name in a family trust (*tang*) was a custom already adopted by merchants in the Ming dynasty (Faure 1994, p. 17). The use of front men, names of ancestral halls for individual families or associated groups, and assumed names was a frequent method to conceal ownership and true identity from the government, which imposed restrictions on the involvement of gentry members in business due to the official low esteem for merchants and their activities according to the rigid Confucian social hierarchy.[22] The practice of using these disguised accounts created problems in terms of establishing the

---

22. See Chan (1977), pp. 36–37.

identity of the owners as private persons and because of the ambiguous legal nature of these accounts in case of litigation. As Stephanie Chung (1999) points out in her analysis of a court case filed in Hong Kong in 1910, neither *tang* nor *hao* were recognized by the law as legal persons (*faren;* see especially, p. 60). Even if this decision was made in the context of a legal system under strong Western influence, it confirms the private nature of the *tang, hao,* and *ji* and the legal difficulties in case of legal action.

However, since the early twentieth century, gentry investment in industrial enterprises had become a legal and approved activity, and there existed no government taxation of income or capital gains, which holders of these business accounts would have preferred to avoid. Reasons for concealment of identity now lay in the inappropriate use and transfer of company funds to these disguised private accounts that were difficult to detect by auditors and other shareholders.[23] The Dasheng enterprise provides a model example for this peculiar shareholding practice.

The somewhat informative 1903 shareholding inventory shows that, first of all, most of the Dasheng shares were not held under the personal name of a shareholder but are recorded in the books under the business name of a *tang* (family trust) or *ji* (business; NSD B 402-111-1). For example, Zhang Jian's son, Zhang Xiaoruo, is recorded as holding shares under family-related account names of Zhang Xu, Zhang Liang, Zhang Wu, and Zhang Chen and under the family's ancestral trust name of Zunsu *tang,* but also under the business accounts of Ruo *ji,* Xiao *ji,* and Xuyin *ji.* Of course, if we take into consideration that the founder's son was only five years old in 1903, it is clear that these were in fact Zhang Jian's own personal accounts disguising his personal assets as company assets in the records.

One has to suspect that in reality Zhang Jian was the actual owner behind many more business accounts that cannot be clearly identified from the records, because in the majority of cases the entry under the personal name of the shareholder is left blank. For example, the account listed as holding shares under the business name Fengsi *tang* was in fact the account representing the charity land in possession of Zhang Jian's own family trust. Another family trust account, Zunsu *tang,* can be identified as an account associated with Zhang Jian's family residence in Haimen county. It is only possible to gain this type of information from Zhang Jian's obituary in 1926, where the distribution of his personal assets is described; the actual relationship between shareholding account and ownership identity is not clear from the company's shareholding register (*Nantong Bao tekan* [special edition of the *Nantong News*], 29 October 1926). Needless to say, investors from outside the family circle were also listed with their investments under the names of business accounts.

23. Dasheng's financial crisis due to this inappropriate transfer of funds in order to support ailing subsidiaries and affiliated companies is analyzed in detail in Köll (1998), pp. 158–208.

Even allowing for a considerable margin of error due to the fact that many of the family accounts may not have been identified, it is evident that control was not tied to majority shareholding in the Dasheng business complex. The 1907 shareholding inventory of the No. 1 mill supports this argument with straightforward numbers: the capital stock of 630,000 taels was subscribed by altogether 553 shareholders. The largest single shareholder was the Salt Bureau, with its investment of public funds (*gongkuan*) at a value of 23,000 taels or 4 percent of the total stock capital. Then follows a group of seventeen shareholders with investments between 15,000 and 8,000 taels each, which gave them ownership of 2.4 percent to 1.3 percent of the capital stock each (27 percent altogether). The remaining capital stock worth 435,000 taels (69 percent altogether) was subscribed by 535 shareholders, who individually owned less than 5,000 taels each in equity. The overwhelming majority of these shareholders owned between one and five shares at 100 taels each. Accounts that can be linked to Zhang Jian's family in one form or another reveal an ownership of 40,300 taels or altogether 6.4 percent of the total capital stock, a modest percentage even if it was higher than that of the largest single shareholder.[24] This shareholding pattern of a large number of minority shareholders, mostly cotton yarn traders and local businessmen from Nantong as well as members of the founder-director's kinship and social networks, was common among Chinese companies in the early twentieth century.

Another significant aspect of Chinese companies' incorporation is whether the new Company Law and its requirements like shareholder meetings really led to an empowerment of the shareholders with a simultaneous decrease in personal influence of the company founders and directors. The minutes of the meetings prove that Dasheng shareholders were only vaguely familiar with the stipulations of the new Company Law and the implications that limited liability brought for the enterprise and for their personal involvement with regard to rights and obligations. Nevertheless, it appears that there was a general consensus among those shareholders who voiced their opinion at the first meeting in 1907 that the law supported their claims as owners of the company and provided them with a tool to control the corporate management—or so they thought.

In this spirit, shareholders used their newly won influence to protest publicly for the first time against the reduction of the company's profit caused by Dasheng's generous donations to Zhang Jian's welfare and educational projects (NSD B 402-111-445, 20b). Again, Zheng Xiaoxu, as a concerned and critical shareholder but with no financial leverage in form of majority shareholding, expressed his opinion in an outspoken way:

Subsidies spent on the costs of the Normal School . . . are the virtues of the general manager [i.e., Zhang Jian] himself and have nothing to do

24. Numbers are extracted from NSD: B 402-111-2.

with the company. Now in accordance with the law, we have to discuss separately new regulations for the allocation of bonuses. (NSD B 402-111-445, 20b)

Obviously, Zheng Xiaoxu interpreted the law as a new protective mechanism for the benefit of shareholders against arbitrary bonus allocation to managers and fund distribution by the managing director. However, since Zhang Jian as the founder and managing director of the Dasheng mills had never been forced to seek appointment by a director's board but had automatically slipped into this position when transforming Dasheng from a government-sponsored into a private enterprise, Zheng Xiaoxu's criticism could not endanger Zhang Jian's position in any way.

In fact, the 1907 shareholder report is an excellent document, revealing Zhang Jian's authoritarian management of Dasheng and the simultaneous ineffectiveness of the shareholders' criticism and demands for change. The 1907 document, in recognition of the No. 1 mill's incorporation, contains eight clauses composed by Zhang Jian as the managing director for the regulation of issues such as managing working capital, reserves, and the election of members of the board (NSD B 402-111-445, 9a–12b). Interestingly enough, there is no regulation for the election of the managing director. Reading his response to shareholders' complaints in the context of the discussions at the meeting, his words are defensive, and instead of addressing some of the shareholders' complaints, he appeals to their integrity and moral conscience. Several other shareholders continued to voice questions in regard to bonus allocation and salaries for the managers; Zhang Jian never replied in person but had other members of the board explain Dasheng's—that is, his personal—position.

The founder/director's control over management, shareholders, and the flow of funds between company and personal accounts disguised as business accounts would not have been possible without certain institutional mechanisms. Dasheng's central accounts office (*zhangfang*) in Shanghai served as clearing house for the corporation, whose head accountant was accountable only to Zhang Jian and not to the shareholders. This central accounts office, originally an institution in the traditional silk industry and widely used in large family firms, was adopted by many of the new incorporated enterprises in early twentieth-century China. It conveniently concentrated managerial and financial power over the enterprise, including family and social networks, in one office under the ultimate control of the business founder-manager but still remained outside the formal structure of the corporation.[25]

A look into Dasheng's corporate charter, a lengthy document written by Zhang Jian in a highly autocratic and paternalistic fashion in 1897, shows how he designed the entrenched role of the managers, who were tied into a

25. On the role of the accounting office see Köll (1998), pp. 136–46.

strict company hierarchy confirming his own personal and absolute control. The lack of accountability and transparency facilitated Zhang Jian's transfer of company funds to his private accounts, risky intercompany loans to financially unstable subsidiaries in the form of deposits instead of equity without approval by the shareholders. These practices, together with problems following the WWI economic boom—such as rising raw cotton prices, decreasing cotton yarn prices, and a dangerous degree of debt due to expansion and business fragmentation—led Dasheng close to bankruptcy in 1922 (Köll 1998, pp. 158–208). Modern banks like the Shanghai Savings and Commercial Bank stepped in as major creditors and imposed various financial and managerial reforms, including the first external audit ever and Zhang Jian's removal as director, after taking over Dasheng in a bank consortium in 1924. However, these attempts at greater accountability and transparency reflected above all the financial interests of the banks and were not motivated by general concerns for the rights of Dasheng's shareholders and the protection of their investments in the company. In fact, as shareholders in an incorporated Chinese enterprise their level of power and control did not improve over the next decades.

2.4   Conclusion: Characteristics of Chinese Corporate Ownership Past and Present

In addition to exploring the incorporation process in late Qing China, we have tried, in this paper, to shed some light on the relationship between control and ownership in Chinese corporate enterprises. Historians have shown that in Chinese businesses under strong family influence the control of equity was rarely separated from the control of management, and that succession disputes were of great significance for the continuity of the company (Faure 1995; Choi 1995). We argue that the same characteristics apply to corporate enterprises: although the Dasheng No. 1 Cotton Mill had adopted the legal form of a limited-liability company as early as 1907, it was not managed in such a way as to allow the shareholders to curtail the power of the founder-director. Like the famous China Match Company, a large joint-stock limited-liability company founded and controlled by Liu Hongsheng and his family without majority shareholding, the newly incorporated companies combined traditional business practices and institutions rooted in Chinese family business with modern corporate structures to successfully gain and maintain control.[26] Paradoxically, even the issue of succession applies to some extent to Chinese corporations because members of the Zhang family continued to be involved in the financial and managerial organization of the company, even as a hierarchy of salaried executives came into existence to manage different parts of the business,

26. On the China Match Company see Cochran (2000), pp. 147–76.

which created an additional set of problems for Dasheng and its share-holders.

Nevertheless, the new code clearly brought Chinese business structures more in line with global corporate practice—from creation of limited liability to the attempted enactment of transparency and accounting requirements meant to protect the rights of shareholders. In many ways, it resembles corporate governance legislation that is being adopted today in the world's emerging markets. Then as now, the hope was to create a capital market to support the development of domestic business enterprise. In this respect the 1904 code was a visionary document. Why, then, was its effect so limited?

One explanation is cultural. Until recently, China business historians have tried to capture the essence of Chinese enterprises by focusing on personal relations, in particular in family businesses. Frequently, a business organization has been more or less reduced to the interpretation of being a network, often in the context of a search for the "spirit of Chinese capitalism."[27] Scholars have argued that "kinship and collegiality in China play roles analogous to those played by law and individuality in the West" (Hamilton 1996, p. 43), and the growth of the Chinese economy has been explained with increased economic opportunities and the simultaneous expansion of networks (pp. 53–54). Of course, business by its nature always involves networks. Considering the emergence of corporate ownership in Chinese companies in the early twentieth century, the real problem lies in the conflict of interest between the founder-director and his shareholders, and divided loyalties between people whose positions relied upon either the authority of the founder or the holding of shares.

Another explanation is institutional and to some extent historical. The top-down approach to creating a robust corporate sector in China around the turn of the last century overlooked the public capital markets as an important disciplinary and motivational institution for corporate managers. One cannot explore the development of early corporations in China without considering the serious effects of the boom and bust cycles in the Chinese capital markets over this same period. In some sense, they are two sides of the same coin: one cannot exist meaningfully without the other. Without an active market for corporate control—that is, a setting in which shareholders can fire the management—it is impossible to build public trust in equity investment. On the other hand, without the existence of a liquid capital market, managers have no motivation to relinquish control. Without a share market to provide new capital—or at least a market that would allow entrepreneurs to diversify their investment holdings—there is little to induce them to accept shareholder rule.

It is easy to argue in hindsight that the 1904 legislation was doomed from the start because it was not accompanied by a regulatory framework for

27. See, for example, Hamilton and Kao (1996).

the capital markets. Another possibility may exist, however. Perhaps the crashes of 1883 and 1922 were simply accidents of history. Perhaps corporate capitalism itself is a more fragile phenomenon than most believers in the invisible hand would like to believe. Some visionary thinkers in the 1870s set China on a vigorous course to development of share capitalism that involved its own blend of government patronage and state ownership. Might this new sector have matured and developed along its own course, had the share markets not collapsed? Why did American markets survive the era of crony capitalism and Chinese markets succumb? Perhaps the American markets were just lucky. American markets experienced another crisis in public confidence following the boom and crash of the 1920s. Had the Securities and Exchange Commission not taken steps to restore public confidence, might the U.S. markets have gone the same way as the Chinese exchanges in 1922?

The importance of history in the analysis of markets is that history contains the record of many alternative possible paths that today's markets might have taken. Specific historical circumstances and personalities rather than economic theory may at times better explain why some markets succeed while others—even those built from the same "genetic code"—ultimately fail. This is why China's first foray into capitalism a century ago is immediately relevant to the development of world capital markets today. Governments around the globe are currently eagerly adopting new codes of corporate governance. Russia and China are both engaged in pushing toward greater corporate transparency and shareholder accountability— both leading themes in the Chinese Company Act of 1904. This top-down approach is certainly laudable, for these are most likely necessary conditions for creating a well-functioning capital market. The early Chinese experience, however, suggests that they are not necessarily sufficient. The development of Chinese domestic stock markets suffered from a series of crashes that caused sustained mistrust in share trading. Whether these crashes and consequent shifts in investor opinion can be avoided through market regulation is an open but important question.

Finally, our historical analysis has serious implications for the transformation of property rights in the context of shareholding systems emerging in China today. This process is particularly significant for China's rural economy, where the state allows some collective and private (i.e., family or household) enterprises to turn into shareholding companies while maintaining their property rights in these companies. However, what to Western observers might look like solid incorporation with protected ownership of shares is called "property rights subversion" by scholars working on the transition process (Lin and Chen 1999, p. 168).[28] As Nan Lin and

---

28. See also the other chapters on enterprise reform and property rights in Oi and Walder (1999).

Chih-jou Chen document for the North China countryside, the local elites in control of these shareholding enterprises divert the power away from the state and local government but also from the worker stockholders and transfer the property rights into their own hands (pp. 146, 168–69). Similar to the trajectory of corporations founded at the turn of the twentieth century, we witness a "convergence of the corporate elite leaders and local elite family networks" (p. 169)—that is, the convergence of political power by party cadres or government officials and social power by influential families with no regard for shareholder rights at the turn of the twenty-first century.

For China today, on the course of vigorous economic development, shareholder rights and protections are of immediate importance. Poor disclosure and weak regulations are well-known and persistent problems of companies and the stock market in contemporary China, and new legislation with respect to corporate practice is a work in progress. Tumultuous shareholder meetings with protests by angry minority shareholders are not unheard of. The question is whether the visible hand of the state will succeed in creating structures of capitalist ownership with more success this time.

References

Bailey, Paul. 1998. *Strengthen the country and enrich the people: The reform writings of Ma Jianzhong (1845–1900)*. Surrey, UK: Curzon.

Boorman, Howard L. 1967–71. *Biographical dictionary of republican China*. 4 vols. New York: Columbia University Press.

Carlson, Ellsworth C. 1971. *The Kaiping mines* (1877–1912). Cambridge, MA: Harvard University East Asian Research Center.

Chan, Wellington K. K. 1977. *Merchants, mandarins and modern enterprise in late Ch'ing China*. Cambridge, MA: Harvard University Press.

———. 1980. Government, merchants and industry to 1911. In *The Cambridge history of China,* vol. 11, part 2, ed. Denis Twitchett and John K. Fairbank, 416–62. Cambridge: Cambridge University Press.

———. 1995. The origins and early years of the Wing On Company Group in Australia, Fiji, Hong Kong and Shanghai: Organisation and strategy of a new enterprise. In *Chinese business enterprise in Asia,* ed. Rajeswary A. Brown, 80–95. London and New York: Routledge.

Cheng, Linsun. 2003. *Banking in modern China: Entrepreneurs, professional managers, and the development of Chinese banks, 1807–1937.* Cambridge: Cambridge University Press.

Choi, Chi-cheung. 1995. Competition among brothers: The Kin Tye Lung Company and its associate companies. In *Chinese business enterprise in Asia,* ed. Rajeswary A. Brown, 98–114. London and New York: Routledge.

Chung, Stephanie Po-yin. 1999. Faren' gainian de yizhi: Xifang shangfa zai Zhongguo (The idea of 'legal person': The transplantation of Western company law to modern China). *The Hong Kong Baptist University Journal of Historical Studies* 1:49–69.

Coble, Parks. 2003. *Chinese capitalists in Japan's new order: The occupied Lower Yangzi, 1937–1945.* Berkeley: University of California Press.

Cochran, Sherman. 1980. *Big business in China: Sino-foreign rivalry in the cigarette industry, 1890–1930.* Cambridge, MA: Harvard University Press.

———. 2000. *Encountering Chinese networks: Western, Japanese, and Chinese corporations in China, 1880–1937.* Berkeley: University of California Press, 2000.

Dagongbao (L'Impartial). Tianjin, 1905.

Du, Xuncheng. 1992. *Minzu zibenzhuyi yu jiu Zhongguo zhengfu* (Native capitalism and the government of old China). Shanghai: Shanghai shehui kexueyuan chubanshe.

Eastman, Lloyd E. 1989. *Family, fields and ancestors: Constancy and change in China's social and economic history, 1550–1949.* Oxford: Oxford University Press.

Faure, David. 1994. *China and capitalism: Business enterprise in modern China.* Hong Kong: Hong Kong University of Science and Technology, Division of Humanities.

———. 1995. The control of equity in Chinese firms within the modern sector from the late Qing to the early Republic. In *Chinese business enterprise in Asia,* ed. Rajeswary A. Brown, 60–79. London and New York: Routledge.

Feuerwerker, Albert. 1958. *China's early industrialization: Sheng Hsuan-Huai (1844–1916) and mandarin enterprise.* Cambridge, MA: Harvard University Press.

———. 1980. Economic trends in the late Ch'ing Empire. In *The Cambridge history of China,* vol. 11, part 2, ed. Denis Twitchett and John K. Fairbank, 1–69. Cambridge: Cambridge University Press.

———. 1995. Industrial enterprise in twentieth-century China: The Chee Hsin Cement Co. In *Studies in the economic history of late imperial China: Handicraft, modern industry, and the state,* ed. Albert Feuerwerker, 273–308. Ann Arbor: University of Michigan Center for Chinese Studies.

Gao, Zhiyu. 1985. *Zhongguo kuaiji fazhan jianshi* (A brief history of the development of Chinese accounting). (Henan): Renmin chubanshe.

Goetzmann, William N., Audrey Ukhov, and Ning Zhu. 2001. China and the world financial markets 1870–1930: Modern lessons from historical globalization. Yale School of Management International Center for Finance. Working Paper.

Hamilton, Gary G. 1996. The organizational foundations of Western and Chinese commerce: A historical and comparative analysis. In *Asian business networks,* ed. Gary G. Hamilton, 43–57. Berlin and New York: Walter de Gruyter.

Hamilton, Gary G., and Cheng-shu Kao. 1996. The institutional foundations of Chinese business. In *Chinese business enterprise,* 4 vols., ed. Rajeswary A. Brown, vol. 1, 188–204. London: Routledge.

Hertz, Ellen. 1998. *The trading crowd: An ethnography of the Shanghai stock market.* Cambridge: Cambridge University Press.

Hirschmeier, Johannes. 1964. *The origins of entrepreneurship in Meiji Japan.* Cambridge, MA: Harvard University Press.

Jensen, Michael. 1986. Agency costs of free cash flow, corporate finance, and takeovers. *American Economic Review* 76 (2): 323–29.

Kirby, William C. 1995. China unincorporated: Company law and business enterprise in twentieth-century China. *Journal of Asian Studies* 54 (1): 43–63.

Köll, Elisabeth. 1998. Controlling modern business in China: The Da Sheng enterprise, 1895–1926. *Journal of Asian Business* 14 (1): 41–56.

———. 2003. *From cotton mill to business empire: The emergence of regional enter-*

prises in modern China. Cambridge, MA: Harvard University Asia Center, Harvard University Press.

Kwan, Man Bun. 2001. *The salt merchants of Tianjin: State making and civil society in late imperial China*. Honolulu: University of Hawai'i Press.

Lai, Chi-kong. 1992. The Qing state and merchant enterprise: The China Merchants' Company, 1872–1902. In *To achieve security and wealth: The Qing imperial state and the economy, 1644–1911*, ed. Jane Kate Leonard and John R. Watt, 139–55. Ithaca, NY: Cornell University Press.

———. 1994. Li Hung-Chang and modern enterprise: The China Merchants' Company, 1872–1885. In *Li Hung-chang and China's early modernization*, ed. Samuel C. Chu and Kwang Ching-Liu, 216–47. Armonk: M.E. Sharpe.

Lee, En-han. 1977. *China's quest for railway autonomy: 1904–1911*. Singapore: Singapore University Press.

Leung, Yuen-sang. 1994. The Shanghai-Tientsin connection: Li Hung-Chang's political control over Shanghai. In *Li Hung-chang and China's early modernization*, ed. Samuel C. Chu and Kwang Ching-Liu, 108–18. Armonk, NY: M. E. Sharpe.

Lin, Nan, and Chih-Jou Jay Chen. 1999. Local elites as officials and owners: Shareholding and property rights in Daquizhuang. In *Property rights and economic reform in China*, ed. Jean C. Oi and Andrew G. Walder, 145–70. Stanford, CA: Stanford University Press.

McElderry, Andrea. 2001. Shanghai securities exchanges: Past and present. Occasional Paper Series of the Asian Business History Centre no. 4. University of Queensland, History Department.

Metzger, Thomas A. 1972. The organizational capabilities of the Ch'ing state in the field of commerce: The Liang Huai salt monopoly, 1740–1840. In *Economic organization in Chinese society*, ed. W. E. Willmott, 9–45. Stanford, CA: Stanford University Press.

Nantong Shi Dang'an guan. 1987. *Dasheng qiye xitong dang'an xuanbian* (Selection of archival material of the Dasheng business complex). Nanjing: Nanjing daxue chubanshe.

Nantong Municipal Archives (Nantong shi dang'anguan. NSD). B 402-111-1: Dasheng diyi fangzhi gongsi laogu, guben dipu (copy of inventory of old shares, Dasheng No. 1 Textile Company), 1898–1903.

———. B 402-111-2: guben cunkuan (share capital), 1907.

———. B 402-111-445: tongzhou Dasheng shachang diyici gudong huiyi shilu (record of the first shareholder meeting of the Dasheng Cotton Mill), 1907.

Nantong Museum (Nantong bowuyuan, NBY). 1946. E 123/1334, Dasheng fangzhi gongsi kuaiji zhidu (Accounting system of the Dasheng Textile Company).

Nantong Textile Museum (Nantong fangzhi bowuguan, NFB). Doc. 182: share certificate from 1903.

———. Doc. 193: share certificate from 1915.

———. Doc. 198: share certificate from 1919.

———. Doc. 247: share certificate from 1897.

Oi, Jean C., and Andrew G. Walder, eds. 1999. *Property rights and economic reform in China*. Stanford, CA: Stanford University Press.

Quan, Hansheng. 1991. *Zhongguo jingjishi yanjiu* (Research in Chinese economic history). 2 vols. Taipei: Xinya yanjiusuo.

Rawski, Thomas G. 1989. *Economic growth in pre-war China*. Berkeley: University of California Press.

Shanghai Shehui Kexueyuan Jingji Yanjiusuo. 1981. *Shanghai Yong'an gongsi de chansheng, fazhan he gaizao* (The establishment, development, and transformation of the Shanghai Yong'an Company). Shanghai: Renmin chubanshe.

Shangwu, Yinshuguan Bianyisuo. 1909. *Da Qing Guangxu xin faling* (New legal regulations of the Guangxu period in the Qing dynasty). Vol. 20. Shanghai: Shangwu yinshuguan.

Shao, Xunzheng. 1985. Guanyu Yangwupai minyong qiye de xingzhi he daolu— lun guanliao shangban (The characteristics and ways of civil enterprises of the Yangwupai—discussion on officialdom and merchant management). In *Shao Xunzheng lishi lunwenji* (Collection of Shao Xunzheng's historical essays), ed. Li Kezhen, 349–71. Beijing: Beijing daxue chubanshe.

Sheehan, Brett. 2003. *Trust in troubled times: Money, banks, and state-society relations in republican Tianjin.* Cambridge, MA: Harvard University Press.

Smith, Thomas C. 1968. *Political change and industrial development in Japan: Government enterprises, 1868–1880.* Stanford, CA: Stanford University Press. Orig. pub. 1955.

Thomas, W. A. 2001. *Western capitalism in China: A history of the Shanghai Stock Exchange.* Ashgate.

Williams, E. T., trans. 1904. *Recent Chinese legislation relating to commercial, railway, and mining enterprises, with regulations for registration of trade marks, and for the registration of companies.* Shanghai.

Wright, Mary Clabaugh. 1957. *The last stand of Chinese conservatism: The T'ung-chih restoration, 1862–1874.* Stanford, CA: Stanford University Press.

Zelin, Madeleine. 2005. *The merchants of Zigong: Early modern industrial enterprise in China.* New York: Columbia University Press, forthcoming.

Zelin, Madeleine, Jonathan K. Ocko, and Robert Gardella, eds. 2004. *Contract and property in early modern China.* Stanford, CA: Stanford University Press.

Zhang, Guohui. 1997. The emergence and development of China's modern capitalist enterprises. In *China's quest for modernization: A historical perspective,* ed. Frederic Wakeman, Jr. and Wang Xi, 234–49. Berkeley: University of California, Institute of East Asian Studies.

Zhongguo, Di'er Lishi Dang'anguan (ed.). 1987. *Zhang Jian nongshang zongzhang renqi jingji ziliao xuanbian* (Selection of economic material from Zhang Jian's tenure as minister of agriculture and commerce). Nanjing: Nanjing daxue chubanshe.

Zhu, Ying. 1993. Lun Qing mo de jingji fagui (Economic legal regulations at the end of the Qing dynasty). *Lishi Yanjiu* (Historical Research) 5:92–109.

Zhu, Yingui. 1998. Three market crashes and the Shanghai securities market in the late 1880s and early 1900s. *China Economy History Research* 3:58–70.

Comment   Dwight H. Perkins

The authors of this paper have done an excellent job of presenting the early history of China's attempt to introduce limited liability corporations through passage of the 1904 Company Law. The central question they are concerned with is why this company law did not have a larger influence on the behavior of corporate management given that the law itself contained

Dwight H. Perkins is the Harold Hitchings Burbank Professor of Political Economy of Harvard University and director of the Harvard University Asia Center.

many of the modern features found in such laws in countries where corporate governance is largely carried out consistent with these laws. Their conclusion is that top-down legislative reforms of this type often do not work well because the supporting institutions for these laws are not strong enough to overcome business practices that are deeply rooted in historical and family-based ways of company management and control. They give special emphasis to the weakness of the Chinese stock market with its early boom and bust cycles, which made it a poor vehicle for the exercise of shareholder control over management, as they demonstrate most clearly with their case study of the Dasheng cotton mills. Zhang Jian, the head of the company both before and after the introduction of the 1904 law, operated as an autocratic manager who paid little heed to the interests of the many minority shareholders. Those minority shareholders in turn appear to have had little ability to enforce their rights as defined by law.

Protection of minority shareholder rights is a central concept in corporate finance and is an essential component of good corporate governance. Despite the existence of the 1904 law, there was little if any protection of minority shareholder rights in China and in much of the rest of Asia a century later. In China at the beginning of the twenty-first century there are two quite large stock markets and thousands of enterprises that have taken the limited-liability corporate form with large numbers of minority shareholders, but majority control still rests mainly with the government, and the government and Communist Party, not the shareholders, have the ultimate say in the selection of management. In Korea leading up to the 1997–98 financial crisis, interlocking directorates and other similar mechanisms ensured that control of the large firms rested firmly with family-dominated management and not with the shareholders.

The problem does not lie with the quality of the laws themselves. The 1904 Chinese law was based on Japanese and English company law. Nearly a century later the Harvard Institute for International Development together with others participated in major efforts to rewrite the financial laws of Indonesia and the commercial laws of Russia. These new laws drew on the best legal talent in the world, and the resulting legislation was probably more modern and less compromised by special interests than comparable laws of the United States or the European Union. And yet when the crisis came in 1997, Indonesia's laws provided little protection to creditors and minority shareholders alike. What was the nature of the problem? Was it primarily the weakness of the Chinese stock market, as Goetzmann and Köll suggest?

A weak stock market was no doubt part of the problem, but China's weak stock market rested on a weak foundation. There are primarily two ways of enforcing corporate governance laws. One way is to have a strong and independent regulatory body such as the Securities and Exchange Commission in the United States that oversees and enforces rules involving appropriate public reporting and accounting rules and much else. The other enforcement mechanism is a strong, competent, and independent legal system. With such a legal system, minority shareholders can go to court to enforce their rights. Neither of these institutions existed in the China of 1904.

China did have a legal system based fundamentally on a system developed over the centuries in which the county magistrate was both the representative of the central government and the judge in local disputes and criminal cases. No businesses involved in a commercial dispute went to this magistrate for decision—he did not have the competence to decide the case, nor was he likely to be impartial. Businesses developed their own mechanisms for dispute settlement through their guilds and other forms of association. This was the system as it existed in the nineteenth century and before, but by 1904 the government of the Qing dynasty was collapsing; it first was replaced by a military government and then further disintegrated into what we now refer to as the warlord period.

An independent regulatory agency in the context of the first decades of the twentieth century was inconceivable. Governments at that time had little capacity to do much of anything other than to mobilize an army to fight the government's political opponents. Judges, like everyone else, could be readily overruled by politicians and military figures, and that remains true to this day—not only in China but in many other parts of Asia as well. South Korea and Taiwan are finally (basically only since the late 1980s) creating legal systems that are truly independent and competent to deal with commercial disputes. China is moving in that direction, but politicians can still readily overrule judges.[1]

There is a further obstacle to establishing good corporate governance and protecting minority shareholder rights that existed in 1904 and to some degree still exists today, not only in China but in much of the rest of the region, with the notable exceptions of Hong Kong and Singapore. When China began its self-strengthening movement in the late nineteenth century, as Goetzmann and Köll point out, the main form of business organization was the government-supervised merchant-managed firm (*guandu shangban*). Patronage from high officials was essential for the success of the early firms. The 1904 law did represent a step away from this system toward more genuine private enterprises, but it was a modest step that got only so far.

If one jumps ahead to the second half of the twentieth century when most of Asia regained its independence, the preferred form of economic

1. For a more complete discussion of this argument and the argument that follows, see Dwight H. Perkins, "Corporate Governance, Industrial Policy, and the Rule of Law," chapter 7 in 2004's *Global Change and East Asia Policy Initiatives,* edited by Shahid Yusuf, M. Anjum Altaf, and Kaoru Nabeshima (New York and Washington: Oxford University Press and the World Bank).

development in much of the region was the Japanese model of government-led industrialization. This model was applied with varying degrees of success in Korea, Taiwan, Malaysia, and Indonesia, and, after 1978, in China as well. In recent years the term "crony capitalism" has been applied to describe this model, but this government-led approach did work fairly well in countries that were able to keep politics and rent seeking out of the industrial policy decisions, at least for a time. But one thing this approach did not and could not do was to protect minority shareholder rights. The essence of this approach to industrialization is for the government to promote certain industries and to work with private company management to carry out the government's goals. The implicit agreement is that management would do what the government wanted done, and government would help out if management got into trouble. In the absence of an independent regulatory or legal system, minority shareholders could only turn to the executive branch of government for help in settling a dispute with management, but that same government was already working hand in glove with management. The one economy in Asia where there is a strong legal system and some protection of minority shareholder rights is Hong Kong, but Hong Kong is also an economy where the government, at least until recently, has not had an industrial policy.

The Goetzmann-Köll study of corporate governance in China in the late nineteenth and early twentieth centuries, therefore, is more than just an interesting piece of history. It was the beginning of China's attempt to create a modern system of corporate governance, an effort that continues to this day and is still dealing with many of the same issues that existed in 1904.

3

Corporate Ownership in France
The Importance of History

Antoin E. Murphy

The French model of corporate ownership and control is quite distinct from the Anglo-American model. It has been described as an insider model because it contains a high degree of concentration of ownership, while the wider dispersion of ownership characterized by the U.K. and U.S. models has been termed an outsider model. Why are there such widely differing models between France, and, indeed, many Continental European countries, on the one hand, and the United States and the United Kingdom, on the other? La Porta, López-de-Silanes, and Shleifer (1998) have advanced the view that ownership in capital markets is concentrated where there is an absence of strong investor protection embodied in the legal system and regulatory arrangements. La Porta and coauthors highlight the role of contemporary institutions but downplay, aside from legal developments, the role of historical factors in shaping the structure of capital markets. More recently La Porta et al. (2000) asserted that "Common law countries have the strongest protection of outside investors—both shareholders and creditors—whereas French civil law countries have the weakest protection" (p. 8). Their explanation appears to be that the legal system and regulatory controls determine the structure of corporate ownership. The civil law system is perceived to be linked to a system of weaker control and protection for investors; ergo, it is natural to find a high degree of concentration of ownership in countries such as France because of investors' trepidation about investing in a relatively unprotected investment environment. In a post–Enron, Tyco, and WorldCom world, French jurists and finan-

Antoin E. Murphy is professor of economics and fellow of Trinity College Dublin.

My thanks to Michel Lutfalla, Roger Nougaret (Crédit Lyonnais), Cormac Ó Gráda (Department of Economics, University College Dublin), Daniel Raff (Wharton School), and two anonymous referees for their assistance with this paper. The usual disclaimer applies.

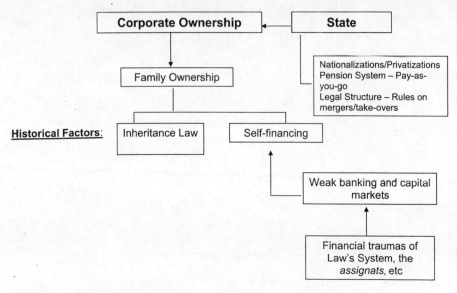

Fig. 3.1   Factors influencing France's corporate ownership structure

ciers might be permitted a wry smile at the implication that the common-law system is linked to a strong system of corporate control.[1]

This paper emphasizes the importance of history in the shaping of corporate ownership structures. The theme of this paper is that historical elements can produce profound shocks and deep afterwaves, the effects of which move through an economy for many generations, fashioning the collective psyche of people in such a way as to present barriers to innovation and change. The financing of a corporation may arise in three ways: bank borrowing, borrowing from the capital market, or self-financing through the use of retained profits. Borrowing from the banking sector and the capital markets dilutes the ownership of a corporation. Self-financing, on the other hand, strengthens the concentration of ownership. In France over the last three hundred years historical factors have produced a weak capital and banking structure. Because of these weaknesses there has been, until relatively recently, a significant reliance on self-financing. Self-financing in turn implies that ownership remains concentrated in the hands of individuals and families.

Figure 3.1 outlines some of the most significant historical factors that

1. By the end of December 2000 Enron had a market capitalization of over $60 billion and had been ranked by *Fortune* magazine as the most innovative large company in the United States. Its bankruptcy raises the issue of corporate governance in the United States. Healy and Palepu (2003) made the following observations: "Despite what they call an elaborate corporate governance network, Enron was able to attract large sums of capital to fund a questionable business model, conceal its true performance through a series of accounting and financial manoeuvres and hype its stock to unsustainable levels."

have influenced the structure of corporate ownership in France. The presentation starts with two major financial traumas in the eighteenth century. These were, first, the rise and collapse of John Law's Mississippi System and, second, the hyperinflationary experience generated by the *assignats* during the French Revolution. It is contended that these financial traumas, reinforced in the nineteenth century through the collapses of the Crédit Mobilier and the Union Générale, produced a weak banking and capital market structure in France. Deprived of access to banks and capital markets, entrepreneurs developed the tradition of reliance on self-financing. This self-financing led to high degrees of concentration of ownership in France. Figure 3.1 suggests that this self-financing tradition was reinforced by a further historical factor, namely the changes in the inheritance law introduced at the start of the nineteenth century by Napoleon. Primogeniture had been perceived by the revolutionaries as a system that had aided and abetted the survival and strength of the aristocracy. The new postrevolutionary regime, embodied in the Napoleonic code, destroyed the system of primogeniture and replaced it with one based on an equal allocation of property rights among all the children in the family. Younger children could no longer be disinherited. The property of the parents was deemed, in large part, to be the property of the children after the death of the former. Paradoxically, this element involves a legal dimension, but not the type of legal dimension that La Porta, López-de-Silanes, and Shleifer (1998) and La Porta et al. (2000) envisaged. In the French civil law it is practically impossible to disinherit one's offspring. Faced with the potential "idiot heir" problem, families have successfully used the *grandes écoles* system to provide educated new leaders of the next generation. Adept recourse to trusts (*les indivisions*) and insurance has enabled family wealth to be transferred from generation to generation, minimizing in the process the burden of inheritance taxes. Add to this legal change favoring the rights of all the children, a type of cultural *mentalité* that each generation is just the temporary custodian of the family's property (*patrimoine*) faced with the objective of passing it on in even better shape to the next generation, and one finds a different set of factors that helped shape the development of France's corporate ownership structure.

Figure 3.1 also incorporates a section dealing with state involvement in the economy. The state has always been a major player in the French economy since the days of Jean Baptiste Colbert (1619–83), who, during his period as controller general of finances, provided a template for sizable intervention by the state in the economy. Further manifestations in the form of nineteenth-century Saint-Simonianism and, later, socialism meant that France experienced bouts of nationalizations and privatizations that greatly influenced the balance between state and private-sector ownership of French companies. Finally, the state's approach to pension funding is believed to be an important recent contributory factor to the ownership mix in that the pay-as-you-go system in France has led to relatively small pension fund/insurance involvement in the equity market.

These factors emphasizing the historical factors that created the tradition of reliance on self-financing, the legal and cultural mix inherent in property ownership, and the state's involvement in the market are presented as helping to explain, at least in part, the current structure of family corporate ownership in France.

This paper starts with an overview of the current situation relating to corporate ownership in France. From there it moves back to the past to show how the failures of the banking system in 1720 and the *assignats* experiment in the 1790s, along with the collapse of the stock market in 1720, had deep effects on the emergence of an efficient banking and capital market structure in France. It will be contended that reliance on the self-financing of corporations was a natural outcome of the difficulties of both the banking system and the capital market. The change in the inheritance laws at the turn of the nineteenth century will be shown to have been a further contributory factor in the embedding of the family in French corporate life. The pension system in France will be presented to explain the sluggish growth of institutional investment in French companies relative to their counterparts in the United States and United Kingdom in the second half of the twentieth century.

Finally, three examples of the growth of family-controlled companies—car manufacturers Peugeot, cosmetic producer L'Oréal, and tire manufacturers Michelin—are presented to provide some support for the underlying themes of the paper. These companies also serve to counter Easterbrook's (1997) view that "a high concentration of ownership is associated with lesser efficiency."

3.1   The Current Corporate Ownership Structure in France

The ownership of companies in France has frequently been a very hot political issue. In the 1930s the prime minister, Edouard Daladier, vehemently criticized the two hundred "grandes familles" who, he contended, controlled all aspects of French business life as well as the Banque de France, the stock exchange, and the press. Daladier's two hundred big families have been shown to be a myth (Anderson 1965). Nevertheless, a wider range of families does exercise a highly significant part in the ownership of French companies.

Three salient features of France's current corporate ownership structure are concentration of ownership, extensive family ownership, and the role of holding companies. Bloch and Kremp (2001) in their recent study of French companies have shown that "concentration of direct ownership and voting power is very high in France." They found that "Around 40 percent of unlisted firms have, as first shareholder, individuals owning directly more than 50 percent of the capital. For the Cotation Assistée en Continu CAC 40 firms, individuals are not the largest blockholder, but when they effectively are present as blockholders, they hold around 30 percent of the voting rights and have the control in fact" (p. 123). A recent French study by Allouche and Amann (1995) showed that, in 1992, 28.3 percent of the top 1,000 industrial companies were controlled by families (foreigners 23.5 percent and state 28.2 percent). Furthermore, when excluding the state- and foreign-owned companies from the analysis, families controlled 59 percent of the top 500 industrial companies, an increase of 10 percent on the 1982 statistics. Blondel, Rowell, and Van der Heyden (2002) investigated the ownership structure of France's 250 largest publicly traded companies for both 1993 and 1998. They show that 57 percent of the listed Société de Bourse Française SBF 250 companies were patrimonial firms—that is, companies where individuals or families had an ownership stake exceeding 10 percent. Furthermore, confirming Allouche and Amann's results they noted that, rather than being on the wane, patrimonial firms grew from 48 percent to 57 percent of the SBF 250 over the period 1993–98. Taking all firms listed on the French stock exchanges between 1994 and 2000, Sraer and Thesmar (2004) observed that approximately a third of the firms were widely held, another third were founder controlled, and the remaining third were heir-controlled family firms. Their results show that both founder-controlled and heir-controlled family firms largely outperformed widely held corporations. In December 2002 the business magazine *Le Nouvel Economiste* estimated that the five hundred richest families in France had a fortune of 106 billion euro. Within this group the fifty richest families had assets of 72 billion euro, and the ten richest had assets of 43 billion euro.

Additionally, as distinct from the United States, where there has been a predominantly multidivisional corporate structure, there are many holding-company structures controlling large industrial groups in France. Lévy-Leboyer (1980) explained the development of these holding companies as arising from banking and capital market limitations: "financial constraints, particularly the inability of the banks and the capital markets to cope with businesses' new requirements, finally brought into being large industrial groups tied together by financial holding companies" (1980, p. 629).

3.2   History and Corporate Ownership: An Overview

History is revelatory in identifying many of the key factors that have produced the current corporate ownership structure in France. Analyzing this historical evolution and development is a complex task. Those looking for some type of linear progression with newer institutions building on and evolving from older institutions may be disappointed, for the last three hundred years embrace a wide range of diverging tendencies. There are many discontinuities. In this respect the history of corporate finance in France is quite distinct from that of the United Kingdom. In the latter country, political revolution, involving warring factions, had ended by the end of the seventeenth century, and a significant part of the financial revolution had taken place by the third decade of the eighteenth century. In Britain one can see a type of linear progress as institutions built on institutions. Through the eighteenth and nineteenth centuries British banks and insurance companies became increasingly adept at channelling savings to investors. The stock exchange efficiently raised finance to fund the borrowing requirements of the Exchequer and to provide capital to the trading companies that were extending Britain's imperial and colonial power. The political system hovered around the center, rarely oscillating excessively to the left. Additionally, and importantly, Britain was not invaded.

France was to have a more tumultuous three-hundred-year history. During the eighteenth century it was involved in a number of long and expensive wars (the War of the Spanish Succession, 1701–14; the War with Spain, 1718–20; the War of the Polish Succession, 1733–38; the War of the Austrian Succession, 1740–48; the Seven Years' War, 1756–63; the War for American Independence, 1778–83; the wars that emerged from the end of the Revolution in 1792 to the start of the Napoleonic Wars). It possessed a monarchy until the revolution of 1789, followed by a revolutionary government until the arrival of Napoleon. From there political life experienced the tumult of the restorations of the monarchy and of the Napoleonic dynasty. Add to these the siege of Paris by the Germans in 1870 and the commune in Paris when twenty to thirty thousand citizens were killed in a mini–civil war in 1871. The German invasion of 1870 was the prelude to two further invasions during the two World Wars of the twentieth century. These political developments frequently meant that industrial developments had to play second fiddle to the political orchestrations of wars, civil wars, and invasions. And yet, notwithstanding these developments on the home soil, France became one of the largest colonial powers of the last three centuries, ruling sizable tracts of land in Africa, North and South America, and Asia.

Because France was frequently at war, both internally and externally, the political instability of the country was accompanied by financial instability. Wars and revolutions require financing. This financing in turn created significant state borrowing and debt. Perforce the banking system and the capital market were heavily tapped to provide finance for these wars. As a corollary to this, the state's heavy recourse to borrowing left substantially less available for the banks and the capital markets to provide to the private sector. The next two sections show the development of (a) the banking sector and (b) the capital market against this background of long periods of warfare.

3.3   The Evolution of the French Banking System

This section highlights three elements in the early development of banking that cast a long shadow over France's financial history: John Law's Mississippi system, the surrogate banking system provided by the French *notaires,* and the *assignats* experience during the French Revolution. It will then show the knock-on effects that these developments had for the banking system in the nineteenth and twentieth centuries.

Renaissance Italy, seventeenth-century Holland and Sweden, and, belatedly, England, with the establishment of the Bank of England in 1694, grew through the establishment and development of their respective banking systems. While the English banking system evolved and helped to finance the war against Louis XIV, the French banking system remained underdeveloped to the point that Louis XIV had to rely on the protestant Genevan based bankers—many of whom he had persecuted and forced out of France through the revocation of the Edict of Nantes—to finance a large part of his budgetary deficit.

The death of Louis XIV essentially left France bankrupt, creating an environment in which the Scottish-born John Law (1671–1729) could present a new financial architecture aimed at (a) relieving the shortage of money through the establishment of a note-issuing bank and (b) reducing the state's indebtedness through the creation of a trading company that would have as one of its objectives the conversion of government securities into equity of the company. Both of these developments were to have a profound effect on banking and the capital markets in France. In the immediate short term, Law's System would make France the most innovative country with respect to corporate financing and banking in Europe. In the long term it would leave a deep hostility and mistrust toward banks and financial innovation.

The General Bank was established by Law in May 1716 (see Murphy 1997). It was modeled on the Bank of England in that it obtained its banking privileges from the state in return for taking up part of the national debt—part of the outstanding amount of short-term *billets d'état.* The early success of the General Bank enabled Law to embark on the second aspect of his macroeconomic strategy, namely the management of the national debt. To do so he needed to create a trading company modeled on the lines of the British trading companies such as the East India Company and the South Sea Company. In August 1717 he established the Company of the West (Compagnie d'Occident), which was given monopoly-trading rights over French Louisiana—an area representing half of the land mass of the United States today (excluding Alaska). It acquired these trading rights in return for restructuring, and accepting a lower interest rate on, part of the outstanding amount of *billets d'état.* The company benefited in that it acquired rights to exploit the agricultural and mineral potential of this huge area. The state benefited in that part of its floating short-term debt was converted into long-term debt, which bore a lower rate of interest. Shareholders in the new company, who swapped *billets d'état* in return for the company's shares, had the prospect of large capital gains if the wealth of Louisiana was properly exploited. The nominal value of each share, which came to be known as *mères,* issued by the Company of the West was 500 livres, but, as they were purchased with *billets d'état,* then standing at a discount of over 70 percent, it meant that the initial shareholders purchased their shares at a price of around 150 to 170 livres. It took nearly two years for the shares to reach their nominal issue price of 500 livres.

Initially there was little interest in the company, and Law had difficulty in selling its shares. A year after its establishment Law started to use the Company of the West to mount a series of spectacular takeovers and mergers. At the same time he developed the General Bank by ensuring that it was used as the government's bank for the receipt and disbursement of state funds.

In August 1718 the Company of the West acquired the lease of the tobacco farm, while in December it took over the Company of Senegal. In the same month the General Bank's operations were reorganized and it was renamed the Royal Bank. In May 1719 Law merged the enlarged Company of the West with the Company of the East Indies and China to form the Company of the Indies. Further acquisitions in the form of the Company of Africa and the lease of the Mint were made in June and July of that year. These acquisitions and mergers required financing. Law arranged this through the issue of two tranches of shares known as the *filles* and *petites filles.* It has already been shown that the *mères,* issued in 1717 on the establishment of the Company of the West, were subscribed for in *billets d'état,* which were standing at a very sizable discount, effectively costing the first shareholders only 150 livres. The second issue of shares, the *filles,* were issued in June 1719 at 550 livres. The share price jumped in July, enabling Law to issue a further batch of shares, the *petites filles,* this time at 1,000 livres each.

By the end of July 1719 Law's company had issued 300,000 shares with a nominal value of 150 million livres. As the share price had jumped from 150 livres in 1717 to over 1,000 in July 1719, the stage was set for further leverage of Europe's first major stock market boom. This boom was linked to Law's wish to take over France's national debt by swapping shares for government securities. The sheer magnitude of this operation proved to be breathtaking.

On August 26, 1719 the regent presented Law's proposal for the Mississippi Company, as it was popularly known, to take over the tax farms and the remainder of the national debt. Law's plan was to lend the king 1.2 billion livres at an interest rate of 3 percent so as to repay the national debt.

This money would be used to repay the long-term state debts, the annuities (*rentes*), the remaining short-term floating debt (*billets d'état*), the cost of offices (*charges*) that had been or would be suppressed, and the shares of the tax farms.

Under the plan holders of government securities were forced to give up government securities, bearing a 5 percent rate of interest, while at the same time they were offered the possibility of acquiring shares of the company yielding far less in terms of dividend but possessing the prospect of sizable capital gains. With the share price jumping from 2,250 on August 1 to 2,940 on August 14, to 5,000 and over in mid-September, capital gains rather than dividends occupied the minds of most transactors. By these measures Law proposed "the radical cure" for the French economy. He aimed to transform the company from a trading company to a trading-cum-financial conglomerate, controlling the state's finances, most notably tax collection and debt management.

The sharp price rose sharply during August. On August 1, 1719, the original shares, the *mères,* which, as has been shown, could have been bought for around 150 livres in 1717, stood at 2,750 livres. By August 30 they had risen to 4,100, and by September 4 they were at 5,000 livres, with the *filles* and *petites filles* rising *pari-passu.* The debt holders, recognizing the prospect of a capital gain, were quite happy to transfer their debt into shares rather than bonds. They needed the prospect of an expected capital gain to compensate for the interest reduction on their securities from 4 percent to 3 percent. Their difficulty in fact became one of converting quickly enough into the shares of the company, as the price of the shares rose very sharply during September.

Within a three-week period in September-October the company issued 324,000 shares, of which 300,000 were sold to the public at 5,000 livres a share, amounting in all to 1.5 billion livres. The company had now started to operate in a manner different from that characterizing its operations between August 1717 and August 1719, when it raised around 106 million through the first three share issues.

The shares reached a 1719 high of 10,000 on December 2. At this point the market valuation of the Mississippi Company was 6.24 billion livres. Concomitant with these developments the banknote issue of the Royal Bank had been increased from 160 million livres in June to 1 billion livres by the end of 1719 as money was lent to existing shareholders to purchase further shares. France was awash with liquidity, particularly after the company guaranteed a floor price of 9,000 livres a share in early 1720 through the establishment of a buying and selling agency known as the "*bureau d'achat et de vente.*" Effectively, the workings of this agency monetized shares.

In February 1720 the Royal Bank and the Company of the Indies were formally merged together. At this juncture, Law, who had been appointed controller general of finances in January 1720, wrote: "One sees here a sequence of ideas which are interlinked and which reveal more and more the principle on which they are based" (Law 1934, iii, 98–99). For a while Law's System, in all its unifying beauty, seemed to work. Economic activity boomed, the national debt appeared to be under control, money was plentiful, and the interest rate had been driven down to 2 percent.

Law had created a financial system the long-term viability of which was crucially dependent on the growth of the real economy. There had to be some equilibrium relationship between the financial system and the real economy. For a while a temporary equilibrium existed, as transactors seemed content to remain within the financial circuit trading money for shares, and shares for money. However, once money started spilling too quickly from the financial circuit into the real economy problems arose. The real economy proved to be incapable of generating a sufficient growth in commodities to match the monetary expansion so that the excess money created inflation and balance-of-payments problems. Law had always believed that the growth in the real economy, spurred on by monetary expansion, would be sufficient to mop up the newly created money. Indeed, in *Money and Trade* (1705) he went further and argued that monetary expansion would lead to a balance-of-payments surplus. For a period Law tried to lock transactors into the financial circuit by a series of measures ranging from prohibitions on the holding of more than 500 livres of specie or bullion, to the demonetization of gold and a phased monthly demonetization of silver. Temporarily these measures worked. But there was still too much liquidity in the Law System. On May 21, 1720, an *arrêt* was published stipulating that shares were to be reduced by four-ninths (from 9,000 to 5,000) and banknotes by half (e.g., banknotes worth 10,000 livres to be reduced to 5,000 livres) between May and December.

This was an attempt to reduce the liquidity of the system, thereby bringing the financial circuit back into line with the real economy. Despite the revocation of this May 21 *arrêt* a couple of days later—due to public pressure—the effect on confidence was so great that the system never recovered from it. The price of shares and banknotes fell continuously during the summer (ironically, at this point the shares in the South Sea were rising rapidly) and the autumn of 1720. Law was forced to flee the country, with the aid of the regent, in December.

Law had shown that he was able to conceptualize and establish, if only for a short period, a modern nonmetallic world at the start of the eighteenth century. He had shown, albeit for a brief three-year period, the massive potential of the capital market and the way in which positive wealth effects from this market could drive the economy to greater growth. It would take economists and financial leaders another couple of centuries to produce for the global economy what Law had briefly achieved in France during 1719–20. Du Tot (1935) realized the full extent of this achievement:

In this state, this construction was admired by everyone in France and was the envy of our neighbours who were really alarmed by it. Its beauty even surpassed all the hopes that had been placed in it since it made people despise and refuse gold and silver. It was a type of miracle which posterity will not believe. However, it is clear that there was a period, of many months, when no one wanted them [gold and silver]. (vol. I, p. 106)

The failure of Law's System produced a very strong reaction against banks, credit, and financial innovation. It also heralded a *retour en arrière* for the French financial system to the old one dominated by religious directives controlling the methods of borrowing and lending and the state constituting the main borrower of funds through the creation of *rentes* (annuities). In this strange financial no-man's-land where interest could not be explicitly charged, contracts had to be drawn up separating the ownership of savings from the streams of revenue it generated. The *notaires* (notaries) were at the center of this system. Indeed, their role was so central, in the absence of traditional-style bankers, that they became surrogate bankers.

3.4   The *Notaires* as Bankers

The credit market in eighteenth-century post-Lawian France cannot be interpreted as one in which there was a free flow of funds between surplus and deficit units with the rate of interest acting as an equilibrating factor in the allocation of funds.

The usury laws, allied with the failure of Law's Royal Bank, created an environment in which the standard evolution of banking from goldsmiths to credit-creating deposit banks did not take place in France in the eighteenth century. Between 1720 and the Revolution, aside from bankers who discounted bills of exchange—an important medium of exchange for merchants much neglected by historians—and one or two scattered sightings of banks such as the short-lived Caisse d'Escompte, eighteenth-century France existed without a formalized banking structure. While the Genevan-based Protestant bankers became major lenders to the government and big merchant companies, the question arises as to how the more mundane business of banking was carried out in the absence of clearly constituted banks in France during this century.

Recently Hoffman, Postel-Vinay, and Rosenthal (2001) have advanced the thesis that the French notarial system—in particular, the Parisian *notaires*—provided a sophisticated surrogate banking system. Because of the usury laws they were the intermediaries for every transaction embodying an implied rate of interest, as they were the only agents who could notarize financial instruments in the form of *obligations, rentes constituées,* and *rentes viagères.* The analysis of Hoffman et al. shows that the *notaires* acted as bankers by intermediating as agents between savers and borrowers.

However, notwithstanding the pervasiveness of their intermediating activities, the *notaires* were for the most part only demi-bankers acting as a conduit for savers with surplus funds to borrowers, most notably the state. The *notaires* were usually not principals in these transactions, nor did they act as bankers in the sense of lending credit to some multiple of the funds deposited with them. Furthermore, most of the lending activity that they arranged was of a long-term nature. Their banking role was narrowed down further in that most of the lending that they intermediated was to the government on a long-term basis through the acquisition of *rentes* or loans for the purchase of lands or property. Hoffman and his coauthors admit in a footnote that the development of long-term credit in both Britain and France was initially more beneficial for the public debt and the housing market than for industry and trade (p. 361). Whatever it says about the validity of their reflection on the British situation, it is revealing in that it shows that French lending activity was concentrated in two sectors, the state and real estate. The *rentier* mentality—a natural successor to the earlier financier mentality—has deep roots in French history.

The thesis of Hoffman, Postel-Vinay, and Rosenthal (2001) is that the *notaires* provided a type of golden age in banking, acting as highly efficient intermediaries between savers and borrowers. Their information base— they were able to pool and share information up to the early part of the nineteenth century—provided detailed knowledge on the assets of borrowers and whether they were encumbered or not. This information enabled them to provide high-quality borrowers for savers with surplus funds. The utilization of this information provided a stable background for lenders in which there was a low risk of default. This stability in turn generated confidence in the system and increased the number of lenders prepared to act through the notarial system.

An alternative interpretation is to view this surrogate banking system as costly, highly conservative, and inefficient because of the additional complication that the usury laws prevented the rate of interest from allocating credit between savers and borrowers. The *notaires* operated a highly effective cartel. In 1659 there were 113 *notaires* in Paris. Despite the growth of Paris, the number of *notaires* remained the same until it rose to 122 in 1859! The system was costly in that transactors were subject to notarial fees and excluded from the market if they did not have appropriate asset backing. The usury laws, which set a ceiling rate of interest of 5 percent, effectively ensured that the *notaires* faced with excess demand for credit could filter out borrowers by the value of their asset collateral rather than the quality of the intended investment project. The system was conservative in that the vast bulk of lending was to the government and property sectors. Incipient industrialists would have found it practically impossible to borrow through the *notaires.* Above all, it must be pointed out that the notarial system was not a banking system in the sense of providing a flexible structure for the expansion of credit. All the *notaires* did was to increase the velocity of circulation of money by making it easier for some borrowers to access savers. However, they were not principals in the financial transactions and were in no way capable of lending money against reserves deposited with them.

3.5   The *Assignats* Experiment

The revolutionaries were quick to recognize the straitjacket of the *ancien régime's* financial system. In October 1789 they repealed the legislation that criminalized the stipulation of a rate of interest on a contract. In July 1796 they abolished the ceiling rate of interest. Between these two dates they set up a paper money system. The revolutionaries, copying in many respects Law's earlier theoretical plans for a land bank in Scotland, financed the early stages of the Revolution through the issue of the *assignats,* a paper money initially assigned or collateralized by confiscated ecclesiastical property. When first issued through a decree of December 19, 1789, the *assignats* bore a rate of interest of 5 percent. The interest payments were quickly stopped, and the *assignats* were transformed into fiat money in 1790. The creation of the *assignats* produced heated debate in the French Assembly, with partisans of the Law System maintaining that they were not inflationary financial instruments because they were fully backed by the confiscated ecclesiastical property. Other parliamentarians tellingly reminded their listeners of Law and his system. Though seventy years had elapsed between the end of Law's System and the Revolution, the memories of Law's attempted financial revolution were still fresh in the minds of those sitting in the Assembly. Indeed, John Law was the most cited economist in the debates that took place in the Assembly on the *assignats.* In September 1790, the Abbé Maury held up a fistful of banknotes in the Assembly, remarking:

> Alas! At this moment I hold in my trembling hands many of Law's banknotes, these fictive pledges of an immense and illusory capital, which I drew from a huge depot where they have been held for the instruction of posterity. With sorrow I look at these paper instruments of so many crimes, I see them still covered with the tears and blood of our fathers and I offer them today to the representatives of the French nation as beacons placed on the reefs so as to perpetuate the memory of this massive shipwreck. (Archives Parlementaires, vol. 19, September 28, 1790, p. 300)

Maury's melodramatic warning words were not accepted. The *assignats* were much needed to finance the early stages of the Revolution, with Harris (1930) contending that they kept fourteen armies in the field (p. 53). They were first issued on April 1, 1790, for a total of 400 million. By September 1792 they had risen to 2.7 billion, and a year later they were over 5 billion. By March 1795 they had reached 8 billion, rising to 20 billion in the same year. When they were eventually taken out of circulation in 1796, 45.6 billion had been issued, of which 32.8 billion were still in circulation (Lafaurie 1981, p. 169). The overissue of *assignats* led to massive hyperinflation. Taking a price index of 100 in January 1791, White (1989) showed that it rose to 30,411 by March 1796! Kindleberger (1984) concluded that the assignats "embedded paranoia about paper money and banks more deeply in the French subconscious, and helped establish Napoleon successively as consul and emperor" (p. 99).

It was not until 1800 that a quasi-central bank, the Banque de France, was established, and even here the primary reason for its establishment was to lend money to Napoleon's government. Additionally, jealous of its monopoly issuing powers, the Banque de France spent its first fifty years trying to block the creation of other banks. The massive difference in progress between the British and French banking systems may be seen by reading Henry Thornton's *An Enquiry into the Nature and Effects of the Paper Credit of Great Britain* (1802) on the role of the paper credit system in Britain. Thornton, a professional banker, attacked Adam Smith for his lack of understanding of the extent to which banknotes and bank credit had become central to the financing of the British economy. He showed the sophisticated layers of different types of paper credit that had been introduced in Britain to finance economic activity and the central role of the Bank of England in the provision of credit. The London banks depended on the Bank of England, and the country banks in turn depended on the London banks. Furthermore, Thornton showed the ways in which the Bank of England could improve its function as a lender of last resort to the banking system. Thornton's analysis demonstrated that Great Britain had a far more sophisticated banking system than that of France, with the Bank of England acting as a quasi–Central Bank, all this at the very time that the Banque de France had just been established!

The hyperinflationary experience of the *assignats,* reinforcing the earlier collapse of Law's System, strengthened a strong antibanking and anti–financial innovation view in France. It intensified the French public's *bas de laine* mentality—that is, the hoarding of gold and silver in woollen socks underneath the mattress. Not only did the French hoard gold and silver, but they also used specie as the main medium of exchange for most of the nineteenth century. This strong preference for specie meant that it constituted 95 percent of the money supply in 1803, 82 percent in 1845, and 68 percent in 1870. By 1885 it still amounted to over 52 percent of the money supply (Cameron et al. 1967, p. 116). Flandreau (2004) has recently shown that, notwithstanding the growth of banking in the northeastern half of France in the 1850s, specie holding greatly increased across the country in that decade due to a combination of factors—the growth in farm incomes, the absence of a banking network in country areas, and the inflow of new supplies of gold from the Californian Gold Rush. The French love of gold continued through to recent times, as evidenced by the reporting of the daily price of small gold bars (*les lingots*) and gold coin (*le Napoleon*) alongside news of stock price movements on radio and television.

The vesting of significant monopoly powers in the Banque de France, along with the extensive use of specie as a circulating medium, meant that the banking system remained underdeveloped for the first half of the nineteenth century. This view runs counter to that developed by Lévy-Leboyer in *Les Banques européennes et l'industrialisation internationale dans la première moitié du XIX siècle* (1964). In this work Lévy-Leboyer concluded that, contrary to conventional opinion, the banking system was highly effective and that by 1843 "the financial market gave the impression of having become the living part of the economy" (p. 699). However, a couple of pages later, Lévy-Leboyer equivocated with respect to this strong conclusion, admitting that, aside from Paris, it was financial centers outside France, based in Geneva and Basle, that provided banking facilities for the merchants of Lyons and Mulhouse. Lévy-Leboyer equivocated further by admitting that

> It should not be forgotten that, in many regions, credit was unheard of: in the countryside, the usage of banknotes continued to be unknown; in the manufacturing towns bills of exchange were continually used for ordinary transactions, and in most cases, even in Alsace, those wishing to borrow money were obliged to go to the *notaires* (there were nearly 10,000 in France in 1840) or to less recommended business agents. (p. 705)

This latter description, showing the continued use of *notaires,* does not suggest that there was a highly effective banking system in France at the time.

There were still considerable constraints preventing the emergence of a proper credit-based banking system. How could a system based on a paper medium of exchange emerge when, up to 1847, the smallest denomination note of the Banque de France was 500 francs? This, as Cameron et al. (1967, p. 117) have pointed out, was greater than the annual per capita income in France at the time. How could a credit-creating banking system thrive when the ratio of currency (i.e., gold and silver coins) to deposits was so high? Furthermore, the Banque de France systematically blocked the emergence of other banks in order to maintain its monopoly banking powers. It was not until 1848 that legislation was introduced to charter joint-stock banks. The change in legislation enabled the Pereire brothers to establish the Crédit Mobilier in 1852, and in that same year the Crédit Foncier, which in turn established the Crédit Agricole and the Comptoir de l'Agriculture as subsidiaries, started business. In 1859 the Crédit Industriel et Commercial was created, while in 1863–64 the Crédit Lyonnais and the Société Générale were established. Notwithstanding the creation of these banks, checks were not legally recognized until 1865, and the public still had a strong bias in favour of specie. Cameron et al. concluded on the French banking system up to 1870:

> Comparisons with English and Scottish data reveal that the complaints of French businessmen were justified: bank facilities were too few, and bank resources pitifully inadequate. At the end of its "take-off" period the French economy had approximately the same bank density as Scotland had had in the middle of the eighteenth century. France had fewer bank assets per inhabitant in the mid-nineteenth century than England or Scotland had had in 1770 and in 1870 had not reached the position that they had held before the beginning of the nineteenth century. (1967, p. 110)

Furthermore, it continued like this with specie still constituting the preferred form of money up to World War I. By 1913, despite the expansion of bank deposits from 17.2 percent in 1880 to 44.3 percent of M1, defined as coin, banknotes, and bank deposits, they still constituted only a small part of the overall money supply. In the United States and United Kingdom, bank deposits represented about 88 percent of M1 at this point in time. This conservatism with respect to deposit creation had its counterpart in the area of credit expansion.

Gueslin (1992) observed that between the 1880s and 1930s companies had to rely on self-financing rather than bank credit: "banking credit remained more or less limited and the financing of the economy came about through the accumulation of savings: primarily as companies directly used parts of their cash flow, but also by the transfer of domestic savings via the financial market" (p. 63). This meant that the banking sector, despite its expansion in the middle part of the nineteenth century, continued to play a predominantly conservative role in the extension of credit to the industrial sector.

Between the two World Wars the relative imbalance between the development of banks in France and in Great Britain and the United States was very great. One indicator of this was the size of bank deposits per head of the population. Gueslin (1992) noted that in 1937 per capita bank deposits amounted to 1,700 francs in France as against 12,000 francs per inhabitant in the United States and 10,100 francs in the United Kingdom.

> The apparent backwardness of France can be explained by the lesser importance there of bank deposits, the existence of channels for financial savings, the competition of the savings banks . . . and by the probable existence of hoarding, reflecting the still essentially rural nature of the country. (p. 87)

In Gueslin's view, "It was only after 1966, and not without difficulty, that the commercial banks of France were really able to flourish" (p. 87). The road from John Law's Royal Bank in 1720 to an efficient commercial banking system in France in 1966 had been a long one.

3.6   Capital Market Developments

As has been shown, overborrowing by Louis XIV left France effectively bankrupt and created the conditions for John Law to embark on the most dramatic macroeconomic and corporate financing experiments of the eighteenth century. The apparent success of his Mississippi System showed the potential for an economy to operate without metallic money and to innovate with respect to restructuring the national debt. Fears that Law had discovered the Philosopher's Stone led the British to follow suit and use the South Sea Company to restructure the public debt. The strong antibanking mentality that arose from the collapse of the Royal Bank in 1720 was accompanied by a strong official reaction to joint stock companies. Again, the events of 1720 were central to this reaction. Ironically, in a bid to corner the market for loanable funds, the South Sea Company pressurized the British government to introduce the Bubble Act of 1720. The Act nullified bubble companies that had been established without joint stock charters from Parliament. It backfired in the face of the South Sea Company, for, in precipitating a collapse of the smaller bubble companies, it forced holders of such fallen stock to sell South Sea in order to pay for these losses. These sales in turn caused the price of the South Sea Company to collapse. The far greater consequence of the Bubble Act was that it effectively prevented most British companies from obtaining joint-stock charters for more than a century. This remained the situation in Britain until the repeal of the Bubble Act in 1825 and the introduction of the Companies Act—popularly known as the Limited Liability Acts—in 1862.

It was a similar, if not longer, story in France. From 1721 onward, due to the collapse of Law's Mississippi Company, it was particularly difficult for companies to obtain full limited-liability status. Investors wishing to form joint stock companies could only do so by acquiring permission from the government and undergoing a cumbersome process of establishing their charters through complicated legal procedures. Through the eighteenth and the first half of the nineteenth century French jurisprudence confined all but a restricted number of companies, in areas such as insurance and transportation, to two legal structures:

1. Simple partnerships (*sociétés en nom collectif*)
2. Limited partnerships (*sociétés en commandite*)

In the simple partnerships all partners were equally liable for the firm's debts. In the case of the limited partnerships the "sleeping partner" (the *commandite*) who subscribed the capital risked only the amount that he subscribed, whereas the active partner or partners assumed unlimited liability. For example, the Irish-born economist Richard Cantillon, who made a fortune out of the Mississippi System, ensured that he was the sleeping partner in his bank in 1718–20 so that his liability was limited to the capital that he subscribed (Murphy 1986).

The simple and limited partnerships were unsatisfactory corporate structures for the development of large-sized companies. Many owners and managers did not want to face the problem of unlimited liability. Additionally, there were very high transaction costs for partners wishing to withdraw their capital. Say and Chailley summarized the problems with this system:

> This was really a deplorable system because of the slowness that it entailed in the establishment of companies, because of its arbitrariness, and because, in the case of bankruptcy, shareholders blamed the government, and, believed themselves entitled to demand it to compensate them for their losses. (1891, vol. II, p. 887)

Lévy-Leboyer (1964) noted that the Council of State, to which companies had to submit their plans for going public, instead of helping the formation of share issuing companies "continually looked for ways of increasing its own powers without regard for the companies that it discredited nor for the economy the expansion of which it braked" (p. 702).

Cameron et al. contended that "the depression of 1857 revealed the undesirability of excessive reliance on the *commandite* form of organization for large-scale industry and commerce" (1967, p. 109). The Council of State started to liberalize its approach to company incorporation. The change in the British legislation in 1862, along with the incipient financing needs of the newly created railroads, further increased the pressure to change that started in 1863 and continued through the introduction of the Limited Liability Acts (Loi sur les sociétés) on July 24, 1867. This act ensured that companies could be established freely under a limited-liability charter without having to seek the formal and costly authorization of the Council of State. The new act encouraged the growth of limited-liability companies, but the ability of these companies to tap the capital market was constrained. Aside from the railway companies, domestic French companies had difficulties in initially attracting French investors. Lévy-Leboyer (1980) has focused attention on the relative immaturity of capital markets in France as against those of the United States and United Kingdom in the latter part of the nineteenth century and the first decades of the twentieth century. This lack of maturity prevented mergers from developing to produce growth in the industrial sector. He observed:

> Before 1913 and during World War I, the volume of security issues and the number of mergers remained rather low—probably because of a widespread prejudice against industrial shares and the lack of experience in marketing these securities on the part of banks and brokerage houses, which had previously dealt primarily in railroad bonds, public utilities and foreign securities. (p. 600)

In pre–World War I France there was a tendency on the part of French people to invest in government bonds or foreign securities rather than in equities. A German remarked at the time, "If they do not succeed in changing the attitudes of the higher classes of the population, then nothing will stop France from becoming a nation of *rentiers*. The organization of her banking system is well designed to produce such an outcome" (Gueslin 1992, p. 72). Pollard (1985) has shown that in 1870 over a third of French domestic savings were invested abroad, and by 1910 this figure had risen to over 50 percent. The oral tradition in France provides many stories of ancestors who lost fortunes in railway shares and loans to Russia and other eastern European countries. Trunks full of these useless shares and bonds are to be found in family attics and in junk shops.

Bonin (1988), writing of the Belle Epoque period from 1895 to 1914, noted that the majority of companies "remained hostile to external capital, to increases of capital, to borrowing and to the banks. Self-financing dominated (two thirds in 1913) due to profits, the quick amortization of capital expenditure, financial reserves and a treasury the abundance of which was revealed by the expansion of bank deposits" (p. 40). Using Teneul and Lévy-Leboyer's estimates, Gueslin (1992) concluded that "even if there were some exceptions, most investment on the eve of the First World War did come from undistributed profits" (p. 81). So self-financing was the norm for French companies. Notwithstanding Gueslin's conclusion, Rajan and Zingalese (2001) have recently presented statistics indicating that, on the eve of World War I, France had a relatively high stock market capitalization–GDP ratio of .78, double that of the United States (.39) and not too far from that of the United Kingdom (1.09). However, this statistic appears to be very much an outlier, as the stock market–GDP capitalization statistics for the rest of the twentieth century produced by Rajan and Zingalese (p. 61) show (see table 3.1).

So, while it appears that the French briefly flirted with the stock market in the first decade of the twentieth century, this flirtation, unlike the love affair in the United States and the United Kingdom, did not persist through the twentieth century. The statistics for 1999, most probably re-

Table 3.1	French stock market capitalization/gross domestic product (GDP)
Year	Ratio of French stock market capitalization to GDP
1939	0.19
1950	0.08
1960	0.28
1970	0.16
1980	0.09
1990	0.24
1999	1.17

flecting the privatizations of major French companies in the 1980s and the rise in their market value in the 1990s, show some revival of interest.

3.7   Conclusion on Historical Elements Influencing Corporate Ownership

By this stage some of the main themes of this paper have started to emerge. For a great part of its three-hundred-year history since the rise and fall of John Law's Mississippi System, France has been underbanked and has had a weak capital market. Unlike Great Britain, where the Bank of England was not brought down by the fall of the South Sea Company, the stock market crash of 1720 involved the complete destruction of the Royal Bank's banknotes and confidence in the banking system. The collapse of the fiat money system created considerable hostility to banks, credit, and financial innovation. This antibanking mentality was later exemplified in Turgot's magnum opus, *Réflexions sur la formation et la distribution de la richesse* (*Reflections on the Formation and the Distribution of Wealth*), first published in 1769–70. In the *Réflexions* Turgot introduced the concept of capital into economics for the first time and showed the link between savings and investment in the generation of economic growth. The work was to have a profound influence on the theory of capital formation in the nineteenth century. Yet, for all its brilliance, Turgot missed out because his analysis on the process of capital formation was confined to the time warp of eighteenth-century France, an economy in which banks did not exist and in which the capital market was the exclusive preserve of the government. Turgot maintained that savings financed investment and that savings were generated by abstention from consumption expenditure. He saw no role for the banking system in this process of capital formation. There is no mention of the words *bank* or *credit* in the *Réflexions!* Thus, we are left with the paradox that one of the outstanding economic works on capital formation has only a very elementary link with modern works on corporate finance because it is based exclusively on an internal financing model.

Turgot's strong antipathy toward banks, which started when, as a young seminarian at the Sorbonne, he pilloried John Law and his system (Turgot [1749] 1913), was symptomatic of eighteenth-century French attitudes toward money, banks, credit, and financial innovation. Add to this antipathy the hyperinflationary experience created by the *assignats,* and the French public's desire to use specie rather than money created by banks becomes clearer. The heavy reliance on specie as a medium of exchange made it difficult for banks to emerge. In turn, their ability to expand credit was limited by their difficulties in building up sufficient reserves of specie to create deposits. This view ties in with that of Kindleberger (1984), who maintained that "France lagged behind Britain in financial institutions and experience by a hundred years or so" (p. 113). This is not to say that there were no banks operating in France in the first half of the nineteenth century but that their influence was relatively weak. Even the *"haute banque"* that started to pioneer the art of merchant banking in the early part of the nineteenth century was so *"haute"* that it did not cater to most of the emerging industrial sectors. It concentrated on investments in the railways, real estate, public works (roads, bridges, canals), and insurance. The Crédit Mobilier, a bank established by the Pereire brothers in 1852, was an attempt to find more broadly based support from stock market investors. It competed with the *haute banque* by investing in public works and railways not only in France but across the European continent. Its collapse in 1867 along with the later collapse of the Union Générale, which lasted a mere four years from 1878 to 1882, reinforced French attitudes on the riskiness of banks.

Meanwhile the stock market, aside from financing the government, had difficulties in generating equity issues because of the legal restraints that prevented the creation of limited-liability companies up to 1867. Even after this, companies did not use the capital market intensively. A great deal of the later nineteenth-century French investment in the stock market was in railway stocks and foreign investments.

A second historical element that is important in the French case relates to the role of inheritance law. Napoleon, when he introduced the civil code, moved the inheritance system from one based on primogeniture to a new system based on equal rights for all the children in a family. This change is important to note in that, whereas in the United States and the United Kingdom a testator can leave his or her estate to a charitable foundation, this is not possible in France. The children are stakeholders in the parents' estate. So, almost by definition, the family, due to the inheritance laws, becomes a major player in the ownership of French corporations. The only way to keep the family out of the corporation is to sell the company prior to death and spend the proceeds. As the French have lived through three German invasions in the last 140 years, few of them are inclined to spend all of their wealth on current consumption because of the fear that they may face the days of the *"vaches maigres"* prior to death. Furthermore, in order to prevent the state from appropriating the family estate through death duties, parents frequently transfer assets from the older to the younger generation via trusts (*les indivisions*) that give the parents the usufructs of the assets while bestowing on the children the nominal ownership of these assets. Thus, at the death of the patriarch or matriarch, there is only a small part of the estate that may be subject to death duties. Additionally, a change in the inheritance laws in 1905 stipulated that estate duties would be payable on only the net rather than the gross estate. This sent out a clear signal to the owners of wealth to shift from equity financing to loan financing because the latter could be used to offset their gross wealth position whereas the former method would add to overall tax liabilities for their offspring. The French are also very adept at using insurance policies on the lives of the older generation to provide tax-free money to cover any death duties that may arise on the estate at inheritance. Combine these elements with a different cultural approach, which sees property as part of the *patrimoine* and holds that the perceived obligation of property holders is to pass on the *patrimoine* in a better state to future generations, and the reason why there is a high degree of concentration of ownership of corporations by families in the French model may be understood. Against such a background, it is not surprising to find family ownership, often concealed through a wide network of holding companies, exercising such a significant role in France's corporate ownership structure.

Finding companies that span the three hundred years that we are investigating and that might fit this particular historical template is a difficult task. It is the nature of companies to rise or fall, to be taken over or merged. Few remain in the same direct ownership over a prolonged period of time. One company that remained in the same family ownership for the period investigated was the printing and publishing company Didot, which later became Firmin-Didot. Founded in 1698, it remained in business for three hundred years. It was a major book publisher, it was the company that printed the *assignats* during the Revolution, and it was a publishing house always at the fore in the area of printing technology—it was the first to introduce, for example, the Stanhope press in France in 1818 (Jammes 1998). Throughout its long history the predominant form of financing for Didot was through the use of retained profits. Even when it issued shares it was only to family members for the purpose of facilitating the transfer of ownership from one generation to another. Blondel and Van der Heyden (1999) examined another family with a long history of corporate ownership, the Wendel family, which was involved in iron and steel production, a business founded in 1704.

Three companies with a strong family involvement and a corporate history spanning a hundred years or more have been selected to show the importance of self-financing in the evolution of their corporate histories. Each of these companies started with simple products: a rubber ball, a hair dye, and a pepper mill. From these simple origins they developed into global companies in which descendants of the founders still have very sizable holdings and representation in the management and direction of the companies. The companies are Michelin, L'Oréal, and Peugeot (PSA Peugeot Citroen). A sample of three does not prove the thesis of this paper. However, it is believed that these three companies are illustrative of a trend in French corporate life where family ownership is still so strongly embedded. They are also three of the most powerful and profitable French companies, employing a total of 370 thousand workers.

Because they have been family-owned and -controlled companies it is difficult to penetrate into the decision making of these companies. Families are discreet and, in many cases, reluctant to open their archives to the public. An alternative method is to side-tunnel into the activities of these companies by examining the archives maintained on them by one of their bankers, the Crédit Lyonnais. These archives show the assessments of this bank's financial analysts toward these companies over a long period of time. They constitute an invaluable, and much underutilized, source into decision making across all sectors of corporate France over the last 150 years. Loubet (1999) has edited a range of archival extracts specifically related to the links between the automobile industry and the bank.

3.8 Michelin

Michelin is Europe's biggest manufacturer of tires. It employs around 128,000 workers, who produced sales of 15.7 billion euro in 2002. The history of Michelin can be traced back to 1829, when a young Scotswoman, Elizabeth Pugh Barker, a niece of the Scottish scientist Charles Macintosh, married Edouard Daubrée. The new Madame Daubrée used the vulcanized rubber solution discovered by her uncle to make playing balls for her children. The use of rubber in this way attracted the attention of two of her husband's cousins, Aristide Barbier and Nicolas Edouard Daubrée. In 1832 they established a small factory using vulcanized rubber products for the manufacture of seals, belts, valves, and pipes that could be used in agricultural machinery. In 1889 André and Edouard Michelin took over their grandfather's (Aristide Barbier) agricultural equipment business. Edouard Michelin diversified the business into the manufacture of tires and managed the company for the next fifty years. He was assisted by his brother, André, a marketing genius, who promoted the company in its early days via schemes such as the sponsorship of motorcar races where the entrants were obliged to use Michelin tires; the identification of these tires with Monsieur Bibendum, a caricature of a rotund man made of tires; and the creation of the Michelin *Guide Rouge,* a publication that later developed into a gastronomic guide with its use of the star rating system for restaurants. The combination of Edouard's managerial and engineering skills along with André's marketing flair enabled Michelin to develop from a small-scale artisan enterprise to an international tire manufacturer. By the time of Edouard's death in 1940 he had built Michelin into a company employing 25,000 employees. Today the Michelin family is estimated to own 25 percent of the company, and its wealth in 2002 was estimated at 1.1 billion euro.

How has the Michelin family kept such a sizable amount of the ownership of the company? The first point to note about Michelin is its rather unusual corporate status in that it is still a partnership (*commandite*) but with the capacity to issue shares. Because of its partnership status the Michelin family members who are involved in this partnership are liable for the company's debts in the case of a bankruptcy. On the other hand, the partnership gives the family control over the company. The family has been able to maintain this position through reliance on self-financing. From its very inception self-financing appears to have been the *mot d'ordre* of the Michelin family. When Edouard assumed control of the company in 1886, he turned to the family rather than to the banks in order to provide the much-needed finance for new capital expenditure. He went to his aunt, Emilie Mage, and asked her if she could lend the company a sizable sum of money, the equivalent of 1.3 million euro. She asked Edouard to wait for a day. Then, having clarified with some nuns, the Petites Soeurs des Pauvres, that they would offer her a room in their convent if she became destitute due to the nonpayment of her loan, she lent Edouard Michelin the money, which helped turn the company around (Lottman 1998). Family ties can run deep at moments of crisis!

The nature of Michelin's business was transformed as it moved into the manufacture of tires for automobiles. Keeping up production with the growth of the automobile market meant that the company had considerable financing requirements. The family met these financing requirements by ploughing back retained profits into capital expenditure. When these profits were insufficient to meet their capital requirements they resorted to long-term bond issues. This in turn caused problems for their bankers because of their limited access to information on the company's balance sheet. In 1930 when Michelin was seeking a loan of 200 million francs the analysts of the Crédit Lyonnais attempted to uncover the financial situation of the company so as to determine whether the bank would provide some of the capital required. It is obvious from reading the analyst's report of May 1930 that it was difficult determining the profitability of the company, which, because of its partnership status, was not obliged to publish any public accounts. The analyst did provide the figures in table 3.2 for the period 1925–28.

Assuming that the banking analyst had access to part of the company's accounts—although he did state that he did not know how this "*réglement de l'exercise*" had been compiled—the statistics in table 3.2 show that Michelin appeared to have had a policy of retaining a very significant amount of its profits. The retention rate amounted to 50 percent of its profits in the years 1925, 1927, and 1929. In 1926, on the back of very signifi-

Table 3.2   Michelin's distributed profits and retained reserves, 1925–28

End year	Profits distributed	Amounts put aside in reserves (in millions of francs)
1925	29	29
1926	31	126
1927	58	58
1928	60	60

cant growth, it retained 126 million francs of its profits, over four times the amount it retained in 1925. The analyst concluded that "the development of the business has been made almost exclusively by recourse to retained profits and the management appears to be very prudent" (Archives du Crédit Lyonnais 4908/3, May 1930, p. 7).

By this stage Michelin, still a family business (*"une affaire de famille"*), had become the dominant manufacturer of tires in France—its main factory at Clermont-Ferrand was producing 4 to 5 million tires annually—and it was exporting more tires than its competitors in the United States.

In 1930 it was successful in borrowing 300 million francs at 4.5 percent repayable from 1931 to 1960. In 1946, with its main factory at Clermont-Ferrand badly damaged by Allied bombing, Michelin went back to the banks with a request to borrow 500 million francs. The banking analysts threw their hands in the air in trying to make sense of the accounts provided. The *"réglement de l'exercise"* that had shown results of as high as 126 million francs in 1927 had dropped to 6 million in 1934 and then risen to a high of 40 million in 1939! Because of the lack of knowledge on the distributions of profits to the shareholders and the management the balance sheet was impossible to decipher properly.

The extent of Michelin's recourse to self-financing may be seen from a further report by the Crédit Lyonnais in 1959 when Michelin was contemplating an issue of bonds to help finance its long-term investment. The investment program envisaged expenditure between 1958 and 1963 of 55.4 billion old francs. Of this sum 75 percent was to be met by self-financing.

Again, in 1972, when Michelin decided to expand its North American plants to produce radial tires, $250 million of the $400 million investment came from their reserves, while the other $150 million came from a group of New York–based banks (Lottman 1998, p. 403).

The second key factor in maintaining the Michelin family's control over the company was the use of dual-class shares. Control of the company was kept in the family through the use of the partnership's shares and strict rules as to who could hold these shares. In 1928 these rules stipulated how shares would be kept in the family:

> [Holders' shares] may be passed on to descendants or their relations up to the fourth degree [of consanguinity] or to someone who is already a shareholder. In all other cases the transfer is subordinate to the agreement of the Inspection Board and its managers, and, in default of this agreement, to the right of preemption that is formally reserved to the other shareholders. (Archives du Crédit Lyonnais 4908/3, May 1930)

With respect to the ordinary shares of the company the articles of association stipulate that shares held for more than four years by residents of a country within the European Union have double voting rights.

3.8   L'Oréal

L'Oréal, one of the leading fashion and cosmetics manufacturers in the world, was listed by the *Wall Street Journal* as the seventy-first largest global public company ranked by market value ($47 billion) at the end of August 2003. In 2002, with a labor force of nearly 50,000, it had sales of $15 billion. The origins of L'Oréal can be traced back to 1909, when a simple partnership trading as Schueller and Spery was established to sell a newly created synthetic product for dyeing hair. Eugène Schueller, a chemist by training, manufactured the hair dye in his home and sold it under the brand name Auréole. The name of the company summed up its activities, the French Company for the Harmless Dyeing of Hair (La Société Française de Teintures Inoffensives pour Cheveux). Starting with a capital of 135,000 francs it was transformed into a limited-liability company (*société anonyme*) in 1939 by a merger with Foncière Driant under the name Société l'Oréal. The new company had a capital of 7 million francs. In 1950 it merged with Monsavon, a company that it would later sell to Procter and Gamble. In 1953 its turnover was 60 million francs with net profits of 1.85 million. Over the next fifty years it grew at a very fast pace so that by 2002 it had net profits of 1.2 billion euros. This performance has made it one of the outstanding shares on the French stock exchange.

With such a sizable growth it might be natural to expect a wide diffusion of ownership of the shares of the company. This is not the case, with closely held shares accounting for 352 million of the 655 million shares outstanding. Its founder, Eugène Schueller, and more recently his daughter, Ms. Liliane Bettencourt, since the death of her father in 1957, have been the major shareholders. In 1967 analysts at the Crédit Lyonnais estimated that Madame Bettencourt owned over 50 percent of the capital of the company (Archives du Crédit Lyonnais Etude 9011/4, February 9, 1967) at a time when its turnover amounted to about 295 million francs and its market capitalization was 528 million francs. In 1974 she sold nearly half of her L'Oréal stock to the Swiss multinational Nestlé, combining with the latter to establish a French holding company, Gesparal, which owns 54 percent of L'Oréal. Madame Bettencourt and her family currently own 51 percent of Gesparal, with Nestlé controlling the other 49 percent. So although Madame Bettencourt's ownership of L'Oréal has been reduced, she still has over 25 percent of a far larger company. Effectively, through the link with Nestlé, Gesparal can ensure that no corporate predator takes over L'Oréal. The French business magazine *Le Nouvel Economiste* valued Madame Bettencourt's fortune at 13.7 billion euro in 2002, making her the richest person in France.

It was not always smooth sailing for L'Oréal. In the early 1950s it was regarded as a poor credit risk for long-term lending, and the difficulty the company had borrowing from the banking system at this stage in its development may be observed from the caution with which its bankers lent it money in 1951 shortly after its takeover of Monsavon. At that time the conclusion of the Crédit Lyonnais analyst was that

> A slowing down of its sales could quickly place the Company in difficulties: this slowdown has already manifested itself for some of the Oréal lines (permanent waves, hair dyes, Ambre Solaire, shampoos, etc.). The Company has announced some cutback measures: reductions in seasonal employments, and a cutback of 20% on the publicity budget but overhead costs have not been noticeably reduced, the Company contending that the two merged businesses cannot use the same sales representatives and that reductions in the advertising budget will take time. (CL, 5 July 1951)

The analyst was obviously intrigued as to how a company could boil and filter "tallow (60%), palm oil (20%), the residual elements of pork butcher's meat (10%) and horse grease (10%)" into soap and sell it as a quality product. He expressed misgivings as to the amount spent on advertising—a sine qua non of the cosmetics business—commenting on its "flashy publicity" (*"une publicité tapageuse"*). He recommended that the bank should be prudent and lend to L'Oréal on only a short-term rather than a long-term basis.

Faced with conservative bankers who found it difficult to detect the growth of a business in this dubiously perceived area of ladies' fashion (*"la mode féminine"*), the Schueller/Bettencourt family concentrated to a significant extent on self-financing to meet its capital expenditure requirements. In May 1971 another analyst emphasized the extent of this self-financing and the company's low level of indebtedness:

> For the period 1971–74 the group l'Oréal has an important investment programme amounting to a total of nearly 330 million francs. Its financing will be easily assured by the recent borrowing of 75 million francs and by self-financing (depreciation + retained profits 1970: about 81 million francs). No numerical increase in capital is expected, particularly because the level of indebtedness is only about 30 per cent of the group's permanent capital. (CL Etude 9011/8, 26 May 1971).

The reliance on self-financing provided L'Oréal with a strong balance sheet that enabled it to borrow long-term from the banking system to finance new acquisitions. By the 1970s ladies' fashion had become recognized as a very strong growth market, and L'Oréal was well positioned to become the global fashion leader that it has since become.

3.9   Peugeot

Peugeot is the leading French constructor of automobiles. It is the second largest automobile company in Europe. In 2002 it employed over

190,000 workers and produced sales of 54.4 billion euro. Peugeot, as a family-controlled company, has had a long and fascinating history. The origin of the Peugeot manufacturing dynasty stretches back to the water mill construction business of Jean Pequignot Peugeot in the eighteenth century. An ability to adapt to new trends and technologies has always been the hallmark of this family. In 1815 the brothers Jean-Pierre and Jean Frédéric Peugeot teamed up with Jacques Maillard-Salins to run a steelworks and a saw blade factory in the area of Montbéliard. The establishment of the saw blade factory was helped by loans from Swiss bankers in Basle; see Lévy-Leboyer (1964, p. 349). In 1842, Jean-Frédéric invented the pepper mill, still an essential element of the average kitchen. But this was only one of many ironmongery objects that the company specialized in. Saws, razors, sewing machines, clocks, stays, hoops for crinoline skirts, and so on were produced in the factory. Its ironmongery experience led to its producing the spokes of bicycle wheels, and this in turn led to its becoming the biggest bicycle manufacturer in France. Bicycle production in turn led to automobile production.

In 1896 Armand Peugeot established the Société Anonyme des Automobiles Peugeot despite the misgivings of some members of the family, who refused to allow him to use the Peugeot lion logo for a further fourteen years. The nominal capital of the company was 800,000 francs divided into 800 shares of 1,000 francs each. Armand Peugeot was granted 350 shares as a payment for "his contribution in bringing in the factory at Audincourt, the patents, cars in the process of production, leases, etc." (Archives du Crédit Lyonnais November 1908). In 1898 the nominal capital was increased to 2,400,000 francs through the creation of another 1,600 shares of 1,000 francs each.

This increase in capital was to help finance the establishment of a new factory at Lille. By 1900 Peugeot was producing the Peugeot Phaeton Type 28 with a speed of 35 kilometers an hour. Over its first ten years the company's balance sheet showed losses alternating with profits as the technology of the automobile industry underwent sizable transformations, as table 3.3, compiled by a Crédit Lyonnais analyst, shows.

The large losses experienced between 1900 and 1902 were due to expenditure incurred on outdated models and heavy depreciation of the stock of spare parts for these models, as well as losses on the hiring of commercial vehicles. Over the twelve-year period from 1896 to 1907 the company made profits of 3,547,000 francs, of which 2,104,000 francs (59 percent) were distributed as profits and 1,443,000 (41 percent) put into reserves. From this it may be seen that from the very start Peugeot had a policy of reinvesting a considerable part of its profits. Thus was Peugeot, at the turn of the twentieth century, a company that could be considered as a good lending opportunity for the bank. The analysts of the Crédit Lyonnais considered that the industrial and financial situation of the company was "good and

Table 3.3   **Peugot's profits and losses, 1896–1907**

Time period	Francs
1896–1897	–53,000
1897–1898	169,000
1898–1899	360,000
1899–1900	532,000
1900–1901	–345,000
1901–1902	–1,001,000
1902–1903	464,000
1903–1904	827,000
1904–1905	315,000
1905–1906	1,164,000
1906–1907	1,585,000

solid." They then qualified this by noting, "Nevertheless because of the risks inherent in the automobile industry arising from the intense competition both from French and international companies, the company is not guaranteed to produce regular profits in the future" (Archives du Crédit Lyonnais November 1908, p. 33). They were correct in this assessment because survival in the automobile industry at this time was difficult due to technological shocks ranging from changes in engine and chassis types to transformations in assembly line techniques.

The Peugeot family almost lost control of the company in the late 1920s due to financing problems. The Crédit Lyonnais blamed this policy on the arrival of three newcomers to the company between 1923 and 1929: Lucien Rosengart (1923–28) and Ricardo Gualino and Albert Oustric (1928–30). Rosengart was first employed by the Peugeot family to assist in the financing of the company. His financing technique was to set up a separate company and to use it to borrow against the inventories held by Peugeot. He drew bills of exchange against these inventories and discounted them at the Banque de France, an activity that split the management of Peugeot during Rosengart's five-year employment at Peugeot—see Loubet (1999, p. 179). He even briefly took over as managing director from Robert Peugeot as a result of the latter's long illness. Rosengart, described as someone who "*passait pour avoir des idées originales en matière de construction automobile*" (gave the appearance of someone who had original ideas for automobile construction), was criticized by the Crédit Lyonnais for changing the company's policy to one of expanding dividends at the expense of making sufficient provision for depreciation and increasing reserves. The analyst at the Crédit Lyonnais argued that rapid technological progress created the need for continuous retooling of factories, suggesting that annual depreciations of 20 million francs should have been made rather than the 12 to 13 million francs, as practiced between 1925–26 and 1928–29 at a time when dividend payments had been annually increased from 10 to 21 million francs. Rosengart was forced to resign in January 1929. Peugeot, in need of financial assistance, linked up with Gualino and Oustric. This was to be a very short arrangement for the bankruptcy of the latter's bank in 1930 led to considerable losses at Peugeot. The family took back control of the company, appointing three out of the five board directors—Robert Peugeot, Jean-Pierre Peugeot, and Jules Peugeot.

The brief association with financial controllers such as Rosengart and bankers such as Oustric, allied with the temporary move away from a policy of heavy reliance on self-financing, created a near-catastrophic result for the Peugeot family in the early 1930s. This experience appears to have hardened the family to returning to its tried and tested policy of investing through self-financing. Chadeau (1993) describing how Peugeot emerged as the market leader between 1932 and 1940 in France, focused on the self-financing strategy of the company: "Peugeot's leadership decreed that each model launched had to be profitable in its own right, rather than as apart of a range. Whatever the rationale, the strategy made self-financing feasible and left family ownership intact" (p. 195).

Loubet observed that up to 1963 it is clear that Peugeot gave priority to reducing indebtedness or not taking on debt, quite the contrary to the approach of state-owned companies Simca and Renault (Loubet [1995?], p. 81). By the 1970s Peugeot was sufficiently large for it to acquire 90 percent of Citroen's capital, and in 1977 it bought out Chrysler's European operations. Notwithstanding the acquisitions and mergers of Peugeot, and the use of dynamic outsiders such as Jacques Calvet and Jean-Pierre Folz as chief executive officers, the family's holding in Peugeot currently amounts to 27 percent. Even more significantly, the Peugeot family controls over 40 percent of the voting rights. The family's wealth was estimated at 2.67 billion euro in 2002 by *Le Nouvel Economiste*.

3.10   Conclusion

This paper has attempted to show that historical phenomena have had a major impact in the determination of France's corporate ownership structure. Corporate finance is generated from three sources—banks, the capital market, and self-financing. If we consider them as the three channels leading to corporate investment, then history shows that two of these channels, the banks and the capital market, were subject to considerable upheaval, rendering them inoperable as financing channels for a long period in France's corporate history. The major financial shocks arose as a result of the rise and collapse of John Law's Mississippi System and the hyperinflationary experience generated by the *assignats*. These events traumatized the generation that experienced them. Furthermore, the strong oral tradition that emphasized the failures of Law and the *assignats* soured further generations toward financial innovation. Kindleberger (1989) emphasized the extent that these episodes traumatized the French:

There [France] the trauma of the Mississippi Bubble and the collapse of John Law's System slowed down the development of banking and the expansion of industry. Together with the collapse of the Directorate in the 1790s, it made the French neurotic, or even paranoid, about banking for years. (p. 234)

The counterparts of this reaction against financial innovation were the continued recourse to *notaires* to fulfill a demi-banking role and the development of a strong specie-holding mentality among the French. This in turn made it difficult for banks to develop fully even after the establishment of the big multibranch banks, such as the Crédit Lyonnais and the Société Générale, in the 1860s. Faced with restricted access to the banks and capital markets, business entrepreneurs had to have recourse to a do-it-yourself approach, namely reliance on self-financing as a method of growing their business.[2] This restricted access, along with the banks' apparent willingness to invest outside France, may also have been responsible for having generated an antibanking sentiment on the part of French entrepreneurs. This antibanking sentiment was forcibly advanced by Louis Renault, the founder of Renault, when he stated: "Bankers are not philantrophists, they are money merchants and one should as often as possible not have any business with them" (Loubet n.d.). Self-financing in turn enabled these entrepreneurs and their descendants to retain sizable shareholdings in the family-controlled business. Hence, from an historical perspective, it is not surprising to see French families owning such a large proportion of French

---

2. The question may well be posed: if the thesis of a weak banking and capital market structure is accepted, what happened to the performance of the French economy? Initial economic research by scholars at the Research Center in Entrepreneurial History at Harvard, encapsulated in Landes (1969), suggested that the French economy had been backward relative to the British economy during the eighteenth and nineteenth centuries. Poor French entrepreneurship was put down as a causative factor of the inadequate performance. More recent quantitative research initiated by the Institut de Science Economique Appliquée, under the direction of Jean Marczewski, has challenged this retardationist approach and provided strong evidence that this was not the case; for a review of this literature see Cameron and Freedeman (1983). If this latter revionism is accepted then it may be argued that, because the French economy on average performed satisfactorily relative to its neighbours, the thesis that the banking and capital market structures were weak does not hold up. Two alternative interpretations may arise: (a) the French economy would have produced even greater economic growth if it had been underpinned by a strong financial sector. There is a growing literature showing the way in which the financial sector has assisted total factor productivity; see, for example, Levine (1997) and Beck, Levine, and Loayza (2000). This literature would imply that if France had possessed a more sophisticated financial sector between the eighteenth and twentieth centuries it would have achieved an even higher rate of growth than that ascribed to it by economic historians; (b) the reliance on self-financing enabled entrepreneurs to make long-term investment decisions free from the constraints of a capital market emphasizing short-term results.

corporations. Examples of this reliance on self-financing drawn from the experiences of the Michelin, Bettencourt/Schueller, and Peugeot families have been shown. Furthermore, this style of ownership ties in with the French mentality that asset ownership is an intergenerational phenomenon. The objective of holding wealth is to pass on to the next generation of the family assets that, hopefully, have risen in value.

Although this does not square with the Berle and Means (1932) approach as to the way corporations should be owned and controlled, it does not necessarily mean that the French-owned corporations are less efficient than their American counterparts. Family control can enable companies to take long-term investment decisions without all the emphasis of short-termism that widely diffused stock market ownership may necessitate. While Landes (1949, 1969) was of the view that France was hobbled by family control of companies, there is a strong counterargument to make that many of these family-owned companies provided France with dynamic leadership, promoting rather than retarding French economic activity.

This paper has emphasized the importance of history in the evolution of France's corporate ownership structure. There are of course other more recent elements that help explain the high degree of concentration of corporate ownership by families in France. The absence of funded pension schemes has led to a far lower profile by pension funds and assurance companies in the French stock market. In 1997 pension funds and assurance companies constituted 49 percent of household savings in the United Kingdom and 30 percent in the United States as against 18 percent in France. Recent industrial unrest in France has been exactly about this issue, with trade unions arguing that it is the state that should provide long and generous pensions on a pay-as-you-go basis. The continuation of this approach to pensions implies, given the demographic structure, that the percentage of gross domestic product (GDP) devoted to retirement payments will rise from 12 percent at present to 16 percent by 2040. The consequences of this for taxation are probably unsustainable in the long run. If so, there will be increasing emphasis on funded pension schemes that will produce greater investment by pension funds and assurance companies in the French stock market.

Changes in governments in France produced waves of nationalizations between 1945 and 1982. More recently this process has been reversed. The privatizations of the Chirac government in the 1980s increased the number of French shareholders from 1.7 million in 1982 to 6.2 million in 1987 (Goldstein, 1996, p. 463).

The different corporate ownership structure in France, and, indeed, in many continental European countries, from that of the Anglo-American model raises the issue as to why there has not been a universalist convergence to the latter. Has it been due to the inadequate corporate governance in the civil versus the common-law countries, as La Porta, López-de-

Silanes, and Shleifer (1998) and La Porta et al. (2000) have stressed? This paper has tried to show that there have been strong historical factors at work that help explain France's current corporate ownership structure. One of these factors has been the way financial collapses, such as the Mississippi System, and the *assignats* have fashioned attitudes toward money, banks, credit, and financial innovation—the major props of corporate finance. The Mississippi System—the biggest attempt at corporate restructuring in the eighteenth century—and the *assignats* both aimed to remove the Midas fixation on gold in France and replace specie with banknotes and credit. Ironically, their respective failures actually reinforced the Midas fixation. The result of this was that financial innovation was frowned upon and the banking sector, from 1720 until the 1930s, was only allowed to grow within the constraints of a specie-based monetary system. France's historical experience generated opposition to external finance that in turn led to internal finance and concentrated ownership. Another one of the historical factors highlighted in this paper is the different approach to inheritance. In France, even if one wanted to disinherit the "idiot heir" one could not do so. All one can do is to educate him or her. The French *"grandes écoles"* have been intensively used by the large corporate owning families to ensure that their successors are capable of handling the *patrimoine* in an appropriate manner. The continued participation of the Michelins and Peugeots in the management of the companies created by their ancestors in the nineteenth century shows the strength of the French family model.

Family control of companies is not necessarily the bad thing that some Anglo-American commentators make it out to be. Family ownership may prevent new blood coming into a company, but sometimes the old blood is able to take a longer-term perspective and to concentrate more resources on research and development than a young corporate raider whose leitmotif may be one of asset stripping at the expense of all that has been historically built up by a company. Evidence to support this view for France has recently emerged in Sraer and Thesmar's paper (2004). Furthermore, for the United States Anderson and Reeb (2003) have shown that family-owned companies in the S&P 500 had a 6.65 percent better return on assets and that their assets were valued 10 percent higher by the stock market in the United States. Keeping it in the family may be good for not just the insiders but also outsider shareholders.

References

Allouche, José, and Bruno Amann. 1995. Le retour triomphal du capitalisme familial. In *De Jacques Coeur à Renault: Gestionnaires et organisation.* Toulouse: Presses de l'Université des Sciences Sociales de Toulouse.

Anderson, Malcolm. 1965. The myth of the two hundred families. *Political Studies* 13 (June).

Anderson, Ronald, and David Reeb. 2003. Founding-family ownership and firm performance: Evidence from the S&P 500. *Journal of Finance* 58 (3).

Beck, Thorsten, Ross Levine, and Norman Loayza. 2000. Finance and the sources of growth. *Journal of Financial Economics* 58.

Berle, Adolf, and Gardiner Means. 1932. *The modern corporation and private property.* New York: Macmillan.

Bloch, Laurence, and Elizabeth Kremp. 2001. Ownership and voting power in France. In *The control of corporate Europe,* ed. Fabrizio Barca and Marco Becht. Oxford: Oxford University Press.

Blondel, Christine, and Ludo Van der Heyden. 1999. The Wendel family: "Affectio societatis"; The story of a French industrial dynasty (1704–1976). INSEAD Working paper. Fontainebleau: INSEAD.

Blondel, Christine, N. Rowell, and Ludo Van der Heyden. 2002. Prevalence of patrimonial firms on Paris stock exchange: Analysis of the top 250 companies in 1993 and 1998. INSEAD Working paper.

Bonin, Hubert. 1988. *Histoire économique de la France depuis 1880.* Paris: Masson.

Cassis, Youssef. 1992. *Finance and financiers in European history 1880–1960.* Cambridge: Cambridge University Press.

Cameron, Rondo, Olga Crisp, Hugh T. Patrick, and Richard Tilly. 1967. *Banking in the early stages of industrialization.* Oxford: Oxford University Press.

Cameron, Rondo, and Charles E. Freedeman. 1983. French economic growth: A radical revision. *Social Science History* 7 (1).

Chadeau, Emmanuel. 1993. The large family firm in twentieth-century France. *Business History* 35 (4).

Du Tot, [Nicolas]. 1935. *Réflexions politiques sur les finances et le commerce.* Ed. Paul Harsin. Paris: Droz. (Orig. pub. 1738.)

Flandreau, Marc. 2004. *The glitter of gold: France, bimetallism, and the emergence of the international gold standard, 1848–73.* Oxford: Oxford University Press.

Goldstein, Andrea. 1996. Privatizations and corporate governance in France. *Banca Nazionale del Lavoro Quarterly Review,* no. 196.

Gueslin, André. 1992. Banks and state in France from the 1880s to the 1930s: The impossible advance of the banks. In *Finance and financiers in European history 1880–1960,* ed. Youssef Cassis. Cambridge: Cambridge University Press.

Harris, S. E. 1930. *The assignats.* Cambridge, MA: Harvard University Press.

Healy, Paul M., and G. Krishna Palepu. 2003. The fall of Enron. *Journal of Economic Perspectives* 17 (2).

Hoffman, Philip T., Gilles Postel-Vinay, and Jean-Laurent Rosenthal. 2001. *Des Marchés sans prix.* Paris: Editions de l'Ecole des Hautes Etudes en Sciences Sociales.

Jammes, André. 1998. *Les Didot: Trois siècles de typographie et de bibliophilie 1698–1998.* Paris: Jammes.

Kindleberger, Charles. 1989. *Manias, panics and crashes.* London: Macmillan. (Orig. pub. 1978.)

Kindleberger, Charles. 1984. *A financial history of Western Europe.* London: Allen & Unwin.

Lafaurie, Jean. 1981. *Les Assignats et les papiers-monnaies émis par l'état au XVIIe siècle.* Paris: Le Léopard d'Or.

Landes, David S. 1949. French entrepreneurship and industrial growth in the nineteenth century. *Journal of Economic History* 9.

———. 1969. *The unbound Prometheus.* Cambridge: Cambridge University Press.

La Porta, Rafael, Florencio López-de-Silanes, and Andrei Shleifer. 1998. Corporate ownership around the world. *Journal of Finance* 54 (2).

La Porta, Rafael, Florencio López-de-Silanes, Andrei Shleifer, and Robert Vishny. 2000. Investor protection and corporate governance. *Journal of Financial Economics* 58.

Law, John. 1934. *Oeuvres complètes.* Ed. Paul Harsin. Paris: Librairie du Recueil Sirey.

Levine, Ross. 1997. Financial development and economic growth: Views and agenda. *Journal of Economic Literature* 35.

Lévy-Leboyer, Maurice. 1964. *Les Banques européennes et l'industrialisation internationale dans la première moitié du XIXe siècle.* Paris: Presses Universitaires de France.

———. 1980. The large corporation in modern France. In *Managerial hierarchies: Comparative perspectives on the rise of the modern industrial enterprise,* ed. A. Chandler and H. Daems. Cambridge, MA: Harvard University Press.

Lottman, Herbert. 1998. *Michelin: 100 ans d'aventures.* Paris: Flammarion.

Loubet, Jean-Louis, ed. [1995?] *Citroen, Peugeot, Renault: Histoire de stratégies d'enterprises.* N.p.: ETAI.

———. 1999. *L'Industrie automobile 1905–1971.* Geneva: Droz.

Murphy, Antoin E. 1986. *Richard Cantillon: Entrepreneur and economist.* Oxford: Oxford University Press.

———. 1997. *John Law: Economic theorist and policy-maker.* Oxford: Oxford University Press.

Pollard, Sidney. 1985. Capital exports, 1870–1914. *Economic History Review* 38 (4).

Rajan, Raghuram G., and Luigi Zingales. 2001. The great reversals: The politics of financial development in the 20th century. NBER Working Paper no. 8178. Cambridge, MA: National Bureau of Economic Research.

Say, Léon, and Joseph Chailley. 1891. *Nouveau dictionnaire d'économie politique.* Paris.

Sraer, David, and David Thesmar. 2004. Performance and behavior of family firms: Evidence from the French stock market. Malakoff, France: Centre de Recherche en Économie et Statistique–Institut National de la Statistique et des Études Économiques (CREST-INSEE). Unpublished manuscript.

Turgot, Anne Robert Jacques. [1749] 1913. *Oeuvres de Turgot.* Ed. Gustav Schelle. Paris: Alcan.

———. 1769–70. Réflexions sur la formation et la distribution de la richesse. In *Éphémérides du citoyen,* vols. 11–12 (1769) and vol. 1 (1770).

White, Eugene. 1989. Was there a solution to the Ancien Régime's financial dilemma? *Journal of Economic History* 49.

Comment   Daniel Raff

France is the locus classicus of a civil law country, the paradigm case of the civil law codes being the Napoleonic Code itself. A large and growing literature argues that weak investor protections characteristic of such sys-

Daniel Raff is an associate professor of management at the Wharton School, University of Pennsylvania, and a research associate of the National Bureau of Economic Research.

tems relative to common-law systems lead to relatively more concentrated ownership structures. This is an example of institutions—at least, certain sorts of institutions—mattering without history necessarily mattering. Antoin Murphy's paper argues that such an argument gets the behavior of the French economy, in the sweep of its development and at a series of moments in time—wrong.

The paper begins with some comparative quantitative evidence to suggest that the ownership structure of French companies is indeed strikingly concentrated. But the rest of the paper is devoted to laying out a different sort of case. Murphy ultimately believes that path dependency is important in understanding the French history. He argues, in particular, that the confluence of cultural influences (some resting ultimately, it seems, on the nation's long-dominant Catholicism) and a series of shocklike events put the French private sector onto a course in which concentrated ownership would, at least for a very extended period, have been a natural outcome holding constant the sort of legal institutions on which the recent literature has focused. The shocks are the collapse of John Law's Bank and Mississippi Company, the episode of the *assignats,* with its attendant hyperinflation, the crises of the Crédit Mobilier and the Union Générale, and repeated highly disruptive episodes of war (France having been invaded by Germany three times between 1870 and the 1940s). The cultural influences are long-enduring antiusury laws and a concern with family patrimony (the latter exacerbated by the Napoleonic change in the system of inheritance law). The argument is that these together undermined the otherwise normal development of bank and capital market sources of company finance and left firms far more inclined to rely upon retained earnings for investment funds.

Three capsule company histories illustrating the basic characterization of French firm behavior round out the body of the paper. There is a brief discussion at the end of the development of pensions and the relatively limited role this has offered to pension and insurance funds, which might have been a countervailing force, in France.

Evidence from a single country's (single) history is unlikely to be decisive in such an argument: the reader is inevitably far from the world of large samples and statistical hypothesis testing. It seems to me a reasonable first aspiration level for someone putting such an argument forth that the argument have some internal plausibility and the evidence be supportive, vivid, and thought provoking. I think the paper succeeds in this on all points. The one that will be of most interest to economists, but which they may need to take on faith, will be internal plausibility: might the French decision makers' values have been as Murphy described them? A long line of secondary literature suggests that this is so; and the claim is consistent with my own limited contact, through archival research and conversations with first-generation descendants, with the French *patronat.* I do indeed find Murphy's a plausible historical account as far as it goes.

The argument is thought provoking in the best way history can for economists: it leaves one full of questions about how other aspects of firms' operations and markets worked if these matters were as described and how one might know if hypotheses about these matters are true. My comment will focus on the thoughts—mainly though not entirely questions—the paper provoked in me.

Some of these fall under the heading of demand-side lacunae. The first concerns why (and how) founders and controlling families sold shares to outsiders. Was this entirely a matter of shares to long-term and highly trusted senior managers and issues in connection with late twentieth-century mergers? The statistics cited from Bloch and Kremp and from Sraer and Thesmar make one wonder. Presumably many of the shares held by outsiders were indeed originally sold to raise capital. One naturally wonders how such sale transactions were organized and carried out (and thus how concentrated the original incremental shareholdings were, how focused the monitoring incentives would have been, etc.), what sorts of information flows or other assurances potential holders would have had or sought, and how this sort of detail evolved, not just in the affairs of individual companies but in the French economy more broadly, as the economy developed and the scale of large firms grew. This amounts to testing Murphy's characterizations by probing, at least through examples, how the system responded to routine stresses and to secular change in operating environments. Such detail might tend to corroborate or to undermine the larger story.

The second concerns the other demands firms have for money. Day-to-day operations require finance. Well-known early stages of the development of the British banking system were all about institutions for the provision of trade credit. The paper is silent on French parallels. How was this managed, and how did the arrangements evolve over time? What did French business decision makers think about the possibilities? Murphy's comments on the notaries and the Crédit Lyonnais records suggest that light might be shed on these questions in both earlier and more recent times. As above, answers might help readers weigh the paper's argument.

Some other thoughts concern supply-side issues. What were, exactly, the institutions of capital supply in the period covered intensively in the paper? What controlled their growth? Answers to this are suggested, but the detail only whets this reader's appetite. It would also be very interesting to know what controlled the sources' investment patterns. Some companies' archives contain the background memos to key decision-making committees, but minutes of the meetings themselves that contain no more information than who was in attendance and what the motions and final votes were. If the Crédit Lyonnais records are more extensive, we could perhaps learn something about why the pressures on firms to change their behavior were not stronger.

In the context of the paper's main argument, the company vignettes raise in the economist's mind the question of how one might assess whether the paper's characterization of firm priorities in the period is true. Is it possible to explore this retaining the potential insights of detailed company-specific records but obtaining some of the virtues of a larger sample? One incremental approach might be to seek cross-national firm-level comparisons holding industry and period constant. This could offer the opportunity of comparing responses to common investment opportunities, new technologies, and changes in consumer tastes in the context of differing national institutions and extra-institutional influences on decision making. If there were essentially national differences, this could make them stand out boldly.

This approach suggests a deeper question. Is there some light to be shed by trying to reconstruct actual choice situations? To draw inferences, mechanically, only from situations in which companies had serious discussions with the Crédit Lyonnais would be to enact sample selection bias. But perhaps the bank's records, and the underlying surveillance and planning, are more extensive than that. Perhaps the bank's records could themselves give us some insight into who would come to them and when. This would be a step toward unambiguous information about what the French case tells us about the concerns of this volume. I found this paper memorable and stimulating, but (perhaps this is a compliment) I was left at the end of it wanting to know much more.

4

The History of Corporate Ownership and Control in Germany

Caroline Fohlin

4.1 Introduction

Since World War II, a general conception about German corporate governance has gradually emerged. This consensus view, founded largely on scant and unrepresentative evidence, contains a number of exaggerated claims about the German system of corporate ownership and control. The scholarly literature is replete with historical and theoretical arguments about the role—either beneficial or detrimental, but almost always significant—of Germany's system of close relationships among firms and similarly close relationships between firms and universal banks.[1] The common view holds that large and powerful universal banks dominate the financial landscape today as they have in the past. Early on, economic historians posited the universal bank as the central player in the industrialization of Germany, arguing that, from the mid-nineteenth century up to the start of World War I, these institutions mobilized and then efficiently utilized prodigious amounts of financial capital. In this traditional view the lynch-

Caroline Fohlin is research professor of economics and a fellow of the Institute for Applied Economics and the Study of Business Enterprise at Johns Hopkins University.

My gratitude goes to Thies Clausen, Julia Förster, Annette Lohmann, Steffen Reinhold, Julia Schneider, and Björn Sonnenberg for indefatigable research assistance and to Mary Davies for expert editorial assistance. Many thanks to Alexander Dyck, Sabine Klein, Randall Morck, and innumerable other commentators at the National Bureau of Economic Research (October 2002), Lake Louise (2003), INSEAD (2004), the University of California at Berkeley, the University of California at Davis, Stanford, and Columbia. This research, and past research on which this paper depends, has been funded generously by the U.S. National Science Foundation, for which I am very grateful. Finally, a special note of thanks goes to John Latting.

1. See the reviews in Calomiris (1995) and Fohlin (1999c). Wellhöner's (1989) detailed work on a few large companies turns up a wealth of evidence against the idea of bank domination during the pre-WWI period.

pin of the German universal banking system was direct bank involvement in the ownership and control of nonfinancial corporations. In the finance literature, such bank involvement in equity ownership and corporate governance has come to be known as relationship banking.

Despite the general enthusiasm—both popular and academic—for the German style of finance, and for relationship banking specifically, a smaller strand of the finance literature has always recognized potential hindrances inherent in that system. Even at the height of industrialization, critics lamented the excessive power of the largest banks and the national emphasis on heavy industry. Recent corporate finance literature on Germany, particularly since the postreunification downturn, has almost completely turned to exploring the problems of the German financial system: the failures of the universal banks and the underdevelopment of the securities markets. In the "law and finance" literature over the past several years, the questions have moved toward broader issues of governance: the concentration of ownership and control, the role of families in building up corporate dynasties or pyramids, the densely networked cross-ownership among firms, and the general lack of market mechanisms to efficiently distribute corporate control. In the 1990s, rather than viewing the relationship-oriented system as advantageous, many critics started to blame these institutional structures for the disappointing performance of the German economy.

This paper ties together these historical and contemporary concerns, examining both the overall evolution of ownership structures and the development of relationship banking practices within that framework. The paper also seeks to explain the patterns of involvement that emerge by looking to economic, political, legal, and even social factors. It aims to offer some balance between the two extreme views of German corporate governance and concludes that the German corporate economy has performed well. To be sure, Germany's corporate organizations differ in noteworthy ways from those of other countries, and these areas of divergence may have had an impact on firms or industries in specific instances. But the peculiarities of the German system have neither dramatically helped nor significantly hindered the corporate economy over the very long run.

4.2   Long-Run Patterns of Corporate Ownership and Control

4.2.1   General Patterns of Ownership: Families, Groups, and Pyramids

An ideal analysis would include the precise ownership patterns of German corporations dating back to the early industrialization period, but firm-level equity ownership data are virtually nonexistent for the pre–World War II era. As German share companies issued mainly bearer shares and considered the identity of shareholders to be private informa-

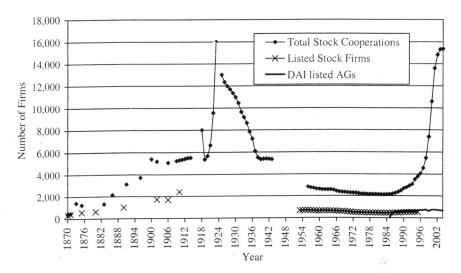

Fig. 4.1   Listed firms versus total stock corporations, 1870–2004

Sources: Deutsche Bundesbank (1976 and various years); Deutsche Börse (1992); Statistisches Bundesamt (1989–95); DAI Factbook (various issues). Data for earliest years come from multiple sources, described in text.

tion, it is not possible to determine the ownership structure of firms, much less to categorize the full population of firms by owner type or by levels of ownership dispersion.[2] Indeed, it is difficult even to provide comprehensive examples of individual firms' ownership structures—other than some famously family-dominated firms, such as Krupp.

The material that does exist suggests the existence of two principal lines in the evolution of corporate ownership and control. First, there is the emergence and expansion of the limited-liability share company (*Aktiengesellschaft* or AG) form with its accompanying managerial control (see figure 4.1 and table 4.1). Second, there is the increasing cooperation and integration between and among firms that led to cross-shareholding, communities of interest, corporate groups, and eventually pyramids (an ownership structure that can allow a firm to exert control over far more equity stakes than it directly owns). Patterns of the first type naturally facilitated trends of the second type.

Incorporation and the creation of the limited-liability company (GmbH) comprised the primary means of separating ownership from control. Not surprisingly, big enterprises took to the AG form of organization more quickly than average. Private, unincorporated enterprises fell to

---

2. For certain firms, it may be possible to use protocols from shareholder meetings to measure the dispersion of voting rights and the extent of proxy voting, and some efforts on that front are underway. Voting rights, however, may bear a highly variable relationship to ownership rights.

Table 4.1   **Number and share capital of joint-stock firms (AGs) and listings in Berlin, 1800–1914**

Year	Number of AGs	Share capital (millions of marks)	Officially listed in Berlin
1800[a]	4	387,000 Taler	
1830/35[b]	25		21
1850			63
1870[c]	200		325
1873/75	1,040		554
1880			612
1886/87[d]	2,143	4,876	
1890/91[e]	3,124	5,771	1,005
1896[f]	3,712	6,846	
1900[g]	5,400		
1902[h]	5,186	11,968	
1906[i]	5,060	13,848	1,113
1907[j]	5,157		
1908	5,194		
1909[k]	5,222	14,723	
1910[l]	5,295		2,400
1911	5,340		
1912	5,421		
1913[m]	5,486	17,357	
1914	5,505		

[a]Prussia only. Hans-Ulrich Wehler (1987, p. 103).

[b]1835: Manfred Pohl (1982, p. 171). Listed in Berlin, 1830 and 1850: Brockhage (1910, p. 170).

[c]Number of AGs: 1870 is an approximation for all AGs before 1870 in Prussia only, and 1873 is an approximate figure excluding non-Prussian issues before 1870. Both figures are from Horn (1979, p. 136). Officially listed in Berlin: 1870, 1875, 1880, and 1890 from Ernst Loeb (1896, p. 246–47; he estimates 395 listed in 1871). Loeb's figures are cited in Richard Tilly (1995).

[d]Number and share capital from Rainer Gömmel (1992, p. 152).

[e]Number and share capital for 1891 from Deutsche Bundesbank (1976, p. 294).

[f]Beckerath (1956, vol. 1, p. 153).

[g]Gebhard (1928, p. 103). Loeb (1902, p. 2) estimates 5,500 AGs in the same year.

[h]Deutsche Bundesbank (1976, p. 294).

[i]Number and share capital calculated from *Statistisches Jahrbuch fuer das Deutsche Reich,* 29 (1908, p. 328). Calculating from *Handbuch der Deutschen Aktiengesellschaften* (1907) yields an estimated number of AGs of 5,352. Berlin listings are estimated based on data from *Handbuch der deutschen Aktiengesellschaften* (1905–1906).

[j]Number of AGs for 1907–14 calculated from *Statistisches Jahrbuch* (1908–15).

[k]Share capital from Beckerath (1956, vol. 1, p. 153). Deutsche Bundesbank (1976, p. 294) estimates total share capital at 14,737 marks.

[l]Number of Berlin-listed firms from Stillich (1909), as cited in Tilly (1995).

[m]Total share capital from Deutsche Bundesbank (1976, p. 294).

minor importance compared to the largest firms well before the end of the nineteenth century. By 1887, four out of five of the largest companies were organized as AGs.[3] According to Pross (1965, p. 75), power struggles between capital lenders and capital administrators arose early on. The authority to dispose of management was in the hands of majority stockholders, their representatives, and managers further up the hierarchy. The record, such as it is, suggests that manager-controlled enterprises comprised a minority of firms throughout the nineteenth century. Thus, majority stockholders and their representatives retained primary control, and managers held the status of leading employees with important but limited authority. In this early phase of the history of German corporations, the generation of owners who had founded, enlarged, and made competitive the enterprises of the heavy industrialization period still held ultimate sway. The captains of industry of this era—the likes of Krupp, Thyssen, Stinnes, Wolff, Stumm, Klöckner, Siemens, and Bosch—possessed both the necessary equity and the personal authority to maintain solid control of their concerns. Professional managers outside the circle of major shareholders also arose, and a few of them clearly belonged among the economic elite. These employee managers, such as Emil Rathenau at AEG, Georg von Siemens, Emil Kirdorf at Gelsenkirchen, and others, wielded formidable influence despite their limited personal stock ownership.

The growing use of the corporate form, and the use of managers to run operations, led in turn to the second main phenomenon in the history of German corporate governance: cooperation and concentration among firms. The first buds of cooperation between enterprises emerged via the formation of trade and production cartels and the creation of concerns (Pohl and Treue 1978, p. 7). The process of concern building started quite late in the century: in 1887, fewer than 20 of the largest 100 industrial enterprises took on the form of a concern (Siegrist 1980, p. 86). Most cartels appeared in the economically prosperous years between 1888 and 1891, and the institution rose to great economic importance in the period between 1895 and 1900. Before 1865 there existed just four cartels, and a decade later that number was still only eight. By 1885, however, there were 90 cartels, and that number was more than doubled, at 210, in 1890. By 1905, a total of 366 industrial cartels had formed (Sombart 1954, p. 316).

Early Twentieth Century

After the turn of the century, the dual trends in ownership dispersion and interfirm cooperation continued with new vigor. Before World War I, the total number of AGs grew, while the share of AGs among the biggest German enterprises remained stable. In 1902, there were well over 5,000 AGs, with a total nominal capital of twelve billion marks. Those numbers

3. See Siegrist (1980), p. 88 and Wehler (1987), p. 627.

grew almost continuously in the prewar years (figure 4.2). In 1907, as in 1887, 80 percent of the biggest companies were organized as AGs (Henning 1992, p. 210). In 1907, the majority of enterprises remained entrepreneurial enterprises in the sense that small groups of owners, mostly families, owned the majority of the equity and controlled strategic decisions. Even if managers had begun to take over the more routine work of daily business, in Ziegler's (2000) view, the dynastic character of the economic elite was still "quite pronounced." Almost all industrial "big linkers"—more than fourteen mandates in supervisory boards of corporations—still held the role of owner-entrepreneurs with no manager and typically representing an industrial dynasty of sorts.

Still, the managerial enterprise, with widely dispersed ownership and salaried managers, had clearly gained importance and continued to do so in the prewar years (Siegrist 1980, p. 88). The trends toward concentration, cooperation, and increased size continued unabated, and the large AGs grew more and more dominant. In 1904, less than 1 percent of AGs held nearly a quarter of the corporate capital stock. Fewer than 10 percent (400 of 4,740) owned nearly two-thirds of the capital (Pross 1965).

As active as the concentration process was in the early twentieth century, World War I gave new impetus to these trends. Government incentives and intervention spurred the further creation and maintenance of cartels, with particular emphasis on vertical connections among suppliers and produc-

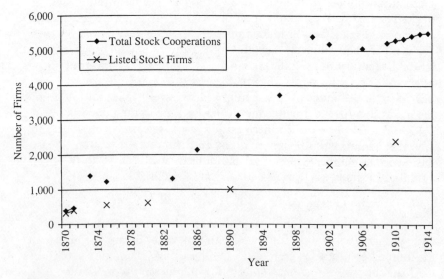

Fig. 4.2   Listed firms versus total stock corporations, 1870–1914

Sources: Deutsche Bundesbank (1976 and various years); Deutsche Börse Annual Report (1992); Statistisches Bundesamt (1989–95); DAI Factbook, May 2003. Data for earliest years come from multiple sources, described in text.

ers (Pohl and Treue 1978, p. 20). Meanwhile, smaller and smaller companies embraced the growing tendency toward incorporation. By 1919, just 6 percent of all German AGs (326 of 5,710) exceeded five million marks of share capital.

The Weimar Republic

After World War I, centrally managed concerns increased in importance and expanded their linkages via interfirm agreements. The tendency toward both concentration and oligarchy increased. During the inflation years between 1919 and 1923, AGs formed at breakneck speed: more than 16,000 AGs appeared by 1923, more than three times the number in existence in 1919. In 1925, over thirteen thousand AGs were registered with a total nominal capital of 19.1 billion marks. Nevertheless, many small family enterprises remained in the market, and small, unincorporated firms still accounted for 90 percent of all enterprises in 1925 (Gömmel 1992, p. 35). To some, managerial capitalism took over in this period, when large concerns often dominated both the markets and the cartels with rationally organized leadership structures, multiplant enterprises, coordinated management teams, and ambitious sales strategies (James 1986, p. 166). While managers clearly emerged as a major force, the underlying ownership structures remain somewhat mysterious. It is assumed, although it probably cannot be proven with the data that exist, that the big enterprises generally came more and more under the control of a small oligarchy of major stockholders and managers (Pross 1965, p. 76). Both types of control—that maintained by majority stockholders and that turned over to managers—could be found within the leading enterprises. While manager-controlled concerns likely remained a minority among the big enterprises, they emerged as a growing and important minority (Ziegler 2000, p. 42). Although the data are truly too sparse for certainty, Ziegler hypothesizes that the share of family dynasties in the German economic elite fell markedly in the early 1920s and was replaced by "new" families from the bourgeoisie (p. 42).

Patterns of corporate structure and control also varied with industry sector and business size. In the financial sector AGs clearly dominated, with ninety-three banking and insurance companies holding at least ten million marks of nominal capital each. The mining and steel industry had seventy-two AGs of this magnitude, and the electrical and machine industry together had fifty-five. Thirty AGs in transport and eighteen in the chemical industry held over ten million marks of nominal capital. Another seventy large-scale AGs were dispersed among different branches of industry. In some branches, many smaller firms incorporated and remained moderate in size. A large proportion of all AGs operated in the food and luxury food industry (in 1919 there were 905), but only seven of these firms held over ten million marks of share capital at that time.

In heavy industry as well as the chemical industry the trend toward horizontal integration quickened after World War I. Thyssen, Rheinische Stahlwerke, GHH, Krupp, and Hoesch, for example, represent the vanguard of the trend. In 1925, IG Farbenindustrie AG brought together major chemical firms to create the largest German enterprise in terms of stock capital. Of the 12,392 AGs existing in 1926 with a total nominal capital of 20.4 billion marks, nearly two thousand (1,967 AGs, with a total nominal capital of 13.3 billion marks) maintained membership in a concern. In other words, the stock capital bound up in concerns constituted 65 percent of the total at that time. That figure rose to 69 percent the next year and to almost three-quarters by 1930 (Laux 1998, p. 129). Overall, concentrated companies held 85 percent of the total nominal capital of all German AGs. It is claimed that by 1927 virtually all of the 100 largest industrial enterprises had become concerns—many in the form of holding companies (Siegrist 1980, p. 86). Independent, unlinked AGs had become the exception, while the concern had emerged as the norm (Pross 1965, p. 50).

Perhaps as a natural by-product of these changes in industrial organization, managerial enterprises became prevalent in the mining, iron, and metal industries and in the chemical industry. Managers dominated in the biggest industrial enterprises regardless of sector. Of the ten largest industrial enterprises with a nominal capital greater than 100 million marks—Deutsche Erdöl, Harpener, Vereinigte Stahlwerke, Mannesmann, Krupp, Siemens, AEG, I.G. Farben, Burbach, and Wintershall—only Krupp and Siemens remained entrepreneurial enterprises. The rest were already managerial enterprises (Siegrist 1980, p. 88).

During the 1930s, implementation of managerial capitalism continued. More and more, the leaders of enterprises were managers without a dynastical background, and the founders or controlling shareholders retreated into the oversight role of supervisory board membership (Ziegler 2000, p. 46). Meanwhile, capital became increasingly concentrated and the absolute number of AGs fell. In 1930 there were 10,970 AGs with a total nominal capital of 24.2 billion RM, and in 1932 there were 9,634 AGs with a total nominal capital of 22.3 billion RM. Fewer than 2 percent of these AGs held well over half of the total nominal capital.

The Nazi Regime

The Nazi regime reinforced power relationships within concerns. Nazis encouraged and assisted gentile founder families in retaining control over their firms (Joly 1998, p. 111). In 1932, on the eve of the Nazis' ascent to power, the number of stock corporations stood at 9,634 (see figure 4.1). With the government incentives instituted under the new regime, many AGs went private and their numbers quickly dropped to pre-WWI levels (about 5,500 in 1938) and dwindled slightly after that. By 1943, 5,359 stock corporations remained. For this period, data on ownership and control are

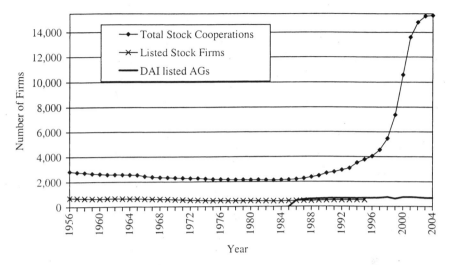

Fig. 4.3   Listed firms versus total stock corporations, 1956–2004

Sources: Deutsche Bundesbank (1976 and various years); Deutsche Börse Annual Report (1992); Statistisches Bundesamt (1989–95); DAI Factbook, May 2003 and June 2004.

still sorely lacking, and nothing very precise can be said as of yet.[4] One thing is clear: the Nazi regime brought great turmoil to the German corporate landscape and permanently altered the patterns of corporate ownership and governance. While they promoted private ownership, the Nazis simultaneously pushed centralization of control in crucial industries. As it was in so many other ways, the Nazi period was an exception to German economic, political, and legal traditions, and one that would have continued ramifications for decades to follow.

The Postwar Years (1945–2004)

After the war, the AG regained favor among large firms. In 1957, 87 of the 100 biggest companies in terms of business volume were AGs. Another nine took on the GmbH form, and the remaining four remained in other forms (Pross 1965, p. 52). More broadly, however, the effects of the war on incorporation persisted. Whereas in 1943 there were still more than 5,000 stock corporations, the number fell nearly 50 percent to 2,627 by 1960—approximately the level of the late 1880s.[5] Moreover, despite the rapid growth of the German economy, the number of stock corporations continued to fall until 1983. The decreasing importance of this company form can also be seen in the falling number of stock market listings over the same period (figure 4.3).

4. Research efforts with new archival materials are underway and seem promising.
5. See the Deutsches Aktien-Institut (DAI) *Factbook.*

Data on share ownership in the direct aftermath of World War II are scarce for West Germany, and the published figures from the Deutsches Aktieninstitut go back only to 1960. Still, some broad patterns emerge. Private households exited the stock markets: The percentage of households investing in the stock markets steadily declined. In 1950, over 46 percent of all households held shares, but the number declined steadily until quite recently. By 2000, just over 8 percent of the total German population held shares. With the mini-boom of 2001, the number had increased to 15 percent of all German households—a level still low compared to the more than a quarter of the U.S. population that held stocks. Strikingly, the proportion of shareholdings of private households declined by the same proportions: in 1950, private households held nearly half (48.6 percent) of all shares, but by 1996, the number dropped to only 17 percent. Similarly, the state decreased its holdings of corporate equity from 12 percent in 1960 to 3.9 percent in 1992.

As families and government decreased equity participation over the period, nonfinancial firms became the dominant shareholders in Germany. The proportion of shares held by nonfinancial firms increased from 18 percent in 1950 to more than 41 percent in 1996. At the same time, financial firms and foreigners, who held a total of 17 percent of shares in 1960, held a combined share of 37.1 percent in 1992 (table 4.2).

Similar trends also emerge for unified Germany in the 1990s. Notably, however, share ownership by nonfinancial firms dropped to 30 percent by 1998. Simultaneously, insurers and foreign shareholders increased their shareholdings, along with a new group of institutions, investment funds. Clearly, the importance of financial services firms versus all other types of shareholders has grown. While in 1990 banks, insurers, and investment funds held a combined share of 24.43 percent of all outstanding shares in Germany, by 1998 that group's share stood at 37 percent—an increase of more than 50 percent. A closer look, however, reveals that the direct influence of the financial services sector over the largest companies does not take the form of majority stakes.

Equity ownership in the 100 largest corporations in Germany has been remarkably stable and remarkably concentrated in the 1990s. Out of the 100 companies with the highest value added, slightly more than half are owned by one large shareholder. Another 16 to 21 percent of the sample has moderately concentrated ownership: that is, there is no majority owner, but less than half of the shares are dispersed. Less than one-third of the firms have widely dispersed ownership (table 4.3).[6] In all but four of the fifty-four firms with concentrated ownership, the majority stakeholders were foreign investors, public entities, or a private individual, a family, or an endowment.

6. See Brickwell (2001), p. 52, table 3.8.

Table 4.2   Share ownership in Germany, 1960–98 (%)

West Germany, 1960–92

Year	Banks	Insurers	Nonfinancial companies	Private households	Public	Foreign
1960	8.0	3.4	40.7	30.3	12.0	5.6
1965	7.5	3.7	39.3	30.6	10.0	8.9
1970	9.1	4.2	37.4	31.3	9.5	8.5
1975	9.7	4.2	42.1	25.1	8.9	9.9
1980	11.7	4.8	42.8	21.2	8.5	11.1
1985	11.0	5.8	38.8	22.5	7.5	14.4
1990	14.1	7.8	39.0	19.9	4.4	14.8
1992	14.9	9.0	41.4	17.6	3.9	13.2

Unified Germany, 1990–98

	Banks	Investment funds	Insurers	Nonfinancial companies	Private (including organizations)	Public	Foreign
1990	10.29	4.33	9.81	41.68	17.23	3.71	12.95
1991	10.27	4.84	10.32	41.36	16.65	3.67	12.89
1992	10.23	5.42	10.41	42.90	15.99	3.66	11.40
1993	9.78	7.27	12.22	38.72	16.66	3.17	12.18
1994	9.40	7.57	11.82	40.87	15.76	3.53	11.04
1995	10.12	7.45	10.93	41.46	15.35	4.39	10.30
1996	11.05	8.96	10.79	37.54	16.00	3.75	11.91
1997	10.93	11.28	14.50	30.46	16.61	2.86	13.35
1998	10.32	12.94	13.74	30.50	14.96	1.91	15.64

Source: Adapted from Ernst (2001, p. 18, table 2) and Ernst (2001, p. 19, table 3), citing Deutsches Aktieninstitut (1996, S. FB_08.1-2f), Deutsche Bundesbank (1976), and for 1990–98 (unified Germany) Deutsche Bundesbank (1999, S. 105).

This picture depends to some extent on the population of firms being examined, but the high concentration of ownership extends across a broad size range of companies. Between 1993 and 1997, the largest share block for large manufacturing firms averaged 81 percent. Even in the case of the listed AGs, the biggest shareholder held a 53 percent stake on average (Köke 2001, pp. 284–85). In stark contrast to the largest 100 firms, over 60 percent of manufacturing firms had another nonfinancial enterprise as their largest shareholder (Köke, p. 285). However, Köke still argues that cross-ownership is not widespread in the German manufacturing sector and seems to be of minor relevance in Germany (p. 285).

The continuous downward trend in the AG population is consistent with a fundamental economic force: the continued concentration of industrial power. The simultaneous divestment by households and increased investment by firms indicates that companies used stock markets to accumulate shares in other corporations in order to establish capital

Table 4.3   Ownership structure for the 100 largest German companies, 1988–98

Majority owner	1988	1990	1992	1994	1996	1998
Other top-100 company	1	2	0	0	1	0
Foreign investors	16	17	16	18	14	17
Public	13	8	11	13	13	13
Single investors, families, endowments	21	23	19	17	19	18
Other	3	4	5	5	5	9
Companies with majority ownership	54	54	51	53	52	57
More than 50% dispersed ownership	28	30	29	29	27	22
No majority	18	16	20	18	21	21
Companies without majority owner	46	46	49	47	48	43

Source: Adapted from Brickwell (2001, p. 52, table 3.8).

linkages.[7] This tendency then led to delistings and illiquid capital markets as companies held on to sizable equity stakes in order to establish long-term relationships. Attempts at revitalizing the stock markets in Germany began to some extent in the 1980s and seemed to have some success by the 1990s. But the bursting of the new economy bubble within a decade effectively reversed the positive trend, and the future prospects as of 2005 remain uncertain.

Clearly, the deconcentration efforts of the allies in the early aftermath of World War II—in terms both of equity ownership and of industrial organization—failed generally over the long run. The capital stock concentration of the AGs was higher than it had been before WWII, though other organizational forms, especially personal enterprises, retained their importance and position in the postwar economy. In 1950, the average AG was bigger (average nominal capital in 1925 was 1.5 million RM; in 1957 it was 10.3 million RM) and employed more people (1925: 307, 1950: 790) than in former times, but the share of AGs of all German companies stayed almost the same. For every thousand companies in 1950, just one took the AG form. In the same year, over 90 percent of all companies—including unincorporated firms—were owned by one or only a few owners (Pross 1965, p. 53).[8]

The ongoing concentration process in post–World War II Germany emerged most prominently among the large, listed AGs. Among these firms, concentration increased from the 1960s to the 1980s, and family domination simultaneously declined (Iber 1985). Despite their loosening

7. See also Iber (1985) and monthly reports by the Bundesbank over the period.
8. Unfortunately, Pross does not give exact numbers.

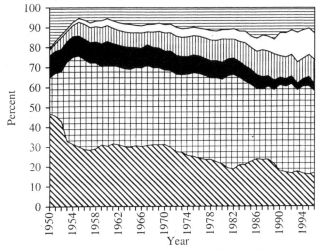

Fig. 4.4   **Ownership of German corporate equity**

of ties, families and individuals remained important shareholders. Between 1963 and 1983, the percentage as measured by number and nominal capital of corporations with majority shareholders increased at both the 50 percent and 75 percent thresholds. This concentration process slowed somewhat toward the end of the period and appears to have begun to move in the opposite direction at the end of the twentieth century.

Still, ownership remains relatively concentrated in Germany, and families take prominent roles, particularly for nonfinancial firms, unlisted companies, and smaller firms generally.[9] Nonfinancial firms also take a primary role as block holders, and one can see a shift in the importance from families as dominant shareholders to enterprises and banks starting by the '60s and '70s (figure 4.4). There is also strong evidence that controlling owners tend to be solitary.[10]

A look at today's firms shows the persistence of family ownership in Germany and the impact it has had on accumulated wealth. Seventeen of the twenty-one biggest German private fortunes (more than three billion DM in the 1990s) derive from family-founded enterprises (Joly 1998, p. 29).[11] Of the 274,139 enterprises with more than two million DM business volume

9. See Faccio and Lang (2002) for comparisons across countries and Klein and Blondel (2002) for in-depth evidence on Germany in particular (with comparisons to a parallel French study).
10. See Faccio and Lang (2002) or Becht and Boehmer (2003).
11. Joly unfortunately does not indicate whether these fortunes derive from family enterprise foundations of the pre- or post-WWII period.

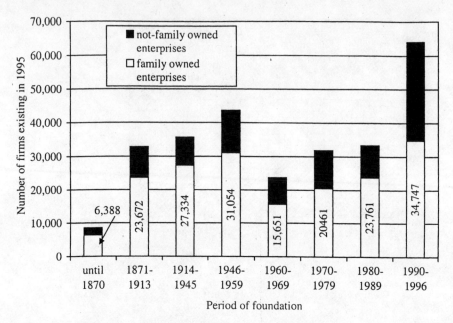

Fig. 4.5   Family and nonfamily firms by period of foundation
Source: Klein (2000).

in 1995, 3.1 percent were founded before 1870, and 12 percent between 1871 and 1913.[12] In the first group, 74.5 percent are still family enterprises, and in the second group, 72.1 percent are family owned. Thus, among pre-WWI survivors, family ownership is key. Families did lose some importance in corporate ownership after the Second World War, but they remain a significant force. Despite the decline in ownership by households generally, families or individuals are often dominant shareholders. That is, families are central to the ownership of many firms, but equity ownership is unusual among the population at large.

A large number of German corporations consistently have average ownership blocks well in excess of 50 percent, even in corporations listed on the stock exchange. Blocks tend to be higher in smaller and unlisted firms. But even in large and listed companies, large shareholdings are a common feature (see figure 4.5).[13] These stakes are probably held for control purposes, as stakes are clustered around important control thresholds of 25, 50, and 75 percent (Becht and Boehmer 2003). Because of the right to veto certain

12. It is assumed that during this period, apart from cooperatives (*Genossenschaften*), nearly all enterprises were founded as (potential) family enterprises. Evidence comes from the many personal enterprises cited in Klein (2000), p. 33.
13. See the evidence in Becht and Boehmer (2003), Faccio and Lang (2002), Iber (1985), Klein and Blondel (2002), Köke (2001, 2003), and Lehmann and Weigand (2000).

decisions, the 25 percent (blocking minority) and 75 percent thresholds are crucial. In more than 80 percent of sampled companies, at least one shareholder held a blocking minority in the years examined. Concentration also increased during that period—all the more striking given the sampling of large, listed firms, where one would expect greater ownership dispersion (Iber 1985).

The estimates of the prevalence of pyramids vary across studies: Köke (2002) finds that about half of the firms in his sample are controlled through pyramids, while, for example, Gorton and Schmid (2000) find much smaller numbers. Faccio and Lang (2002) also find that financial firms use pyramids to exert control much more often than did private households. These studies cover varying time periods and samples, making it difficult to draw conclusions about the trends in the use of pyramids in German corporate governance. It does appear, however, that the use of pyramids has been far more common and extensive in the last few decades of the twentieth century than it was before.

Overall, the patterns of corporate ownership suggest that, while ownership dispersion progressed as expected up to the Nazi era, the tendencies appeared to reverse from there up to the 1980s. Still, the most recent figures suggest a possible return to a pattern of gradual diffusion of ownership. Thus, it may turn out that future economists will look back at the mid-twentieth century as an aberration, rather than as a permanent trend away from the previous situation.

4.2.2   The Role of Banks in Corporate Ownership

It is difficult to talk about corporate ownership in Germany without dealing with the issue of control rights. Due to the phenomenon of proxy voting, the ability of those with ownership rights to cede their control rights to others, equity ownership is often separated from direct control; likewise, many institutions that exercise control over nonfinancial firms have no ownership rights over the resulting revenue streams. Owners of German corporations very often turn over control rights to financial institutions in the form of proxy voting rights. Such proxy control over voting rights grants banks direct participation in the selection of firm supervisory board members and therefore indirect control over the choice of top management. Banks may actively pursue close and long-term relationships with their client firms through direct connections with existing firm managers and supervisory board members. They forge these formal links with nonfinancial firms by gaining representation on firm supervisory boards (*Aufsichtsräte*) as well as through interlocking directorates more generally.

Historical Debates over the Role of Banks

Jeidels (1905) claims that "the power of the Great Banks is exercised via the legal institution of the supervisory board, rather than through direct influence of financial strength" (p. 145, my translation).[14] Gerschenkron (1962) echoes Jeidels, saying that "through development of the institution of the supervisory boards to the position of most powerful organs within corporate organizations, the banks acquired a formidable degree of ascendancy over industrial enterprises, which extended far beyond the sphere of financial control into that of entrepreneurial and managerial decisions."[15]

According to these standard accounts, bank seats on supervisory boards permit not just oversight, but also direct control over firms' strategic decisions. Such involvement arguably reduces uncertainty about borrowers, mitigates risks of moral hazard or simple bad judgment, and facilitates long-term lending through rolled-over current account credits.[16] From this perspective, formal relationships also make bankers willing to help firms solve idiosyncratic difficulties and ride out general downturns. Feldenkirchen (1991, p. 127) gives the example of Hoerder Bergwerks-und Hüttenverein, which, due to what Feldenkirchen argues was an exclusive relationship with the Schaaffhausen'schen Bankverein (and the private banker Deichmann & Co.), received crucial restructuring and survived a brush with bankruptcy. There are as well negative interpretations of bank control, in which the universal banks are seen to have exploited their positions of power to manipulate industrial firms to the banks' advantage.[17] At the same time, however, researchers have uncovered convincing firm-level evidence against the bank-power hypothesis for the prewar period.[18]

Evidence on Bank Ownership before World War I

While there is no definitive, general evidence on ownership structure for the pre–World War I period, ownership of nonfinancial firms by universal banks can be examined. A prevalent notion in the literature on German corporate finance is that universal banks hold significant equity stakes in

14. The Great Banks were the nine largest of the universal banks: Bank für Handel und Industrie, Berliner Handelsgesellschaft, Commerz- und Discontobank, Deutsche Bank, Discontogesellschaft, Dresdner Bank, Mitteldeutsche Creditbank, Nationalbank für Deutschland, and A. Schaaffhausen'scheur Bankverein.

15. Wallich (1905), Riesser (1910), Schumpeter (1930), Whale (1930), Chandler (1990), Tilly (1994), Calomiris (1995), and most others writing on the subject also emphasize this point.

16. See Lavington (1921), Schumpeter (1930), Gerschenkron (1962, 1968), Kennedy (1987), and, in the modern context, Mayer (1988). On current account lending, see the discussion in Pollard and Ziegler (1992), p. 21.

17. Hilferding (1910), a known socialist critic, energetically promoted such an idea. See also Tilly (1994), p. 4, citing also Cameron (1961), Levy-Leboyer (1964), Tilly (1966), März (1968), Kocka (1978), and Pohl (1982). See also Feldenkirchen (1979) and Kunze (1926).

18. See Wellhöner (1989), pp. 83–87, who, for example, shows that the bank representatives on Phoenix's board, yielding to pressure from other firms in the Steelworks Association, acted as a lever for Phoenix competitors with the powerful industrialist Thyssen in the lead. Wessel (1990) and Wengenroth (1992) also support the idea that bank power was waning (at least in the steel industry) and that large firms were mostly independent of the universal banks, well before 1900.

firms and use these positions to exert influence over the firms' decisions. This idea has persisted for at least a century, probably from the second half of the nineteenth century. The long-term holding of equities—indeed, anything held at the closing of a fiscal year—will appear in the balance sheets of banks. The size and variety of such holdings offer one way to assess their importance relative to the other activities of the banks and to the economy as a whole.

Although reporting laws were weak and vague in the pre–World War I era, banks did book their securities holdings if they existed. Naturally, there are reporting problems, and, according to such contemporaries as the banker Jacob Riesser, banks did undervalue their securities in their financial statements. Underreporting is most severe for industrial securities, since the banks feared that investors would view large holdings of nonfinancial shares as a signal of poor bank performance. Riesser (1911) explains that

> excessive holdings of securities will be interpreted to mean either that the times have not been propitious for the issue business of the bank, or that it maintains excessive speculative engagements, or that it is involved to an excessive extent in speculative transactions on its own account . . . or, finally, that it has been unable to find sufficiently profitable employment for its funds. It is for these reasons that a large proportion of the writing off done by the banks occurs under the head of securities account. (pp. 402–403)

Thus, bank-held equity stakes are probably undervalued relative to other financial assets in their balance sheets, and the extent of the misreporting is uncertain. The very fact that banks attempted to downplay their stock holdings, along with Riesser's contention that investors frowned upon significant stake holding, suggests that the banks did not pursue equity holdings as part of an active policy of direct control of nonfinancial enterprises. At least from the 1880s until World War I, banks seem to have avoided holding large proportions of nongovernment securities over the long term.

Corporate securities make up a small proportion of universal bank assets. For the great banks, the holdings varied between 7 and 8 percent of assets but did trend upward toward the end of the period.[19] For the whole period, the nongovernment equity holdings of the great banks never exceeded 11 percent (see figure 4.6). The denominators of these series are computed in real terms, since securities tended to be posted at book values. Loans and cash assets turn over frequently within any year and therefore

---

19. Banks often held significant amounts of government securities as reserves. Because these assets are unrelated to industrial finance, it is important to compare securities net of government issues. Data sources aggregate government and nongovernment securities until 1912, so the figures for the years before that are estimated. See Fohlin (2006) for details and additional results.

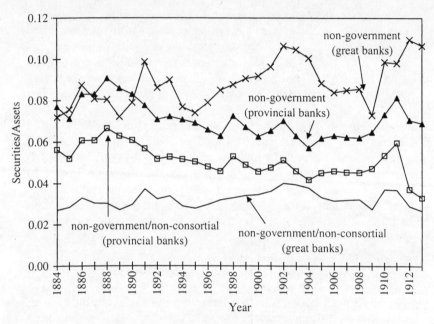

Fig. 4.6   Securities as a share of real total bank assets, 1884–1913
Source: Fohlin (2006).

increase or decrease in nominal value along with the general price level. Thus, as other assets inflate (deflate), the apparent proportion of securities to total assets would decline (increase). The low levels of equity holdings are surprising, especially considering the average contribution of the securities business to the overall revenues of the universal banks.

Because these figures aggregate all nongovernment securities holdings, they include many stakes that the banks did not intentionally take as part of their investment strategy. In fact, a significant portion of the total investments by universal banks arose out of their involvement in underwriting consortia (or syndicates). Therefore, some shares remained on the banks' books only because the banks did not place the shares or due to the fact that the underwriting process crossed into the next business year (see figures 4.7 and 4.8). The subset of nongovernment securities *not* held as a result of underwriting syndicates thus gives an approximation of the proportion of assets that universal banks may have held as nongovernment securities, had the universal banks been organized more like specialized commercial banks.[20]

---

20. Nonsyndicate securities were estimated using a method similar to that described for nongovernment securities. See Fohlin (2005) for further details.

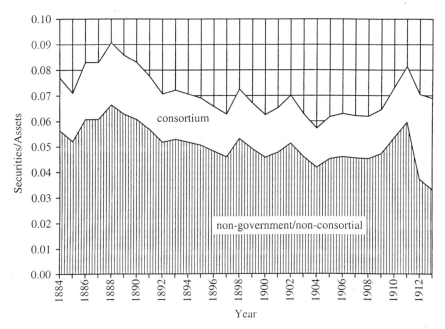

Fig. 4.7   **Securities as a share of real total bank assets, provincial banks, 1884–1913**

Source: Fohlin (2006).

Consortium-related holdings by the great banks increased steadily throughout the boom in joint-stock founding of the late 1890s and reached a prewar peak in the years just after the stock market crisis of 1900–1901.[21] Decline continued as the market improved, and holdings increased slightly after the 1907 stock market crisis. In 1909, syndicate securities holdings reached their lowest point in the twenty-five years of available data.[22] Smaller banks and provincial banks held even fewer total equity stakes than their Berlin-based counterparts throughout the period, and the provincial banks steadily lowered those holdings, relative to their other assets, from the early 1890s until sometime around 1905. Relative to other assets, the provincial banks also held far smaller proportions of syndicate

21. The rapid increase in joint-stock share capital following 1901 stemmed from an increase in the average nominal share capital of firms, while the upward trend of the 1890s related primarily to a rising number of companies.

22. In the run-up to World War I, universal banks markedly increased their holdings of syndicate securities. After the onset of the war, the great banks' syndicate holdings declined dramatically as a share of bank assets—from 8 percent in 1914 to 3 percent in 1919. Perhaps contrary to intuition, the decline is not primarily accounted for by crowding out by government securities. Government securities holdings did increase in the early years of the war, but all securities holdings declined steadily after the war.

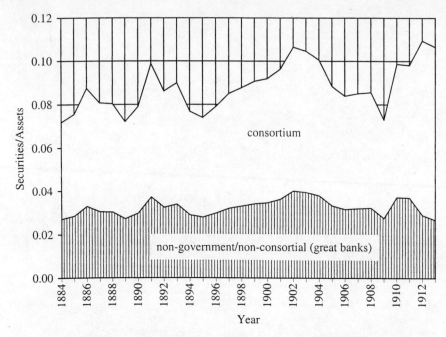

Fig. 4.8 Securities as a share of real total bank assets, great banks, 1884–1913
Source: Fohlin (2006).

securities than did the great banks. Only in the couple of years before World War I did the smaller banks substantially raise their syndicate holdings, though it is impossible to say from aggregate data whether the increase stemmed from greater participation in underwriting or simply less success in placing underwritten securities. Much of the difference likely stems from the proximity of the largest universal banks to the major securities markets (particularly Berlin) and the relatively stronger involvement of the great banks in large, more diffusely held firms. The fact that syndicate holdings crowded out other types of equity holdings suggests that the corporate relationships of the great banks via equity stakes were often nonexclusive. By definition, the consortium holdings represented participation within a larger group of banks. So, while the great banks likely engaged in long-term relationships with many of the firms whose shares they helped issue through syndicate participations, those relationships were clearly multilateral.

The data so far also do not reveal anything about the magnitude or duration of individual relationships, since aggregate figures provide no clue to the identity of the firms, the value of shares, or the length of their inclusion in a bank portfolio. To gain this sort of insight, we would need to look at the portfolios of individual banks, and those data are sparse and incomplete. When we patch together the available data on two of the largest Berlin banks, interesting patterns emerge. Between 1852 and 1900, Discontogesellschaft (DG) reported total equity holdings of between zero and 35 percent of assets. While the bank's holdings fluctuated markedly throughout the last half of the nineteenth century, the proportion of securities followed a generally downward trend toward the end of the period. From its founding in 1852 through 1855, DG held no securities among its assets. Thereafter, the bank acquired substantial interest in securities, but a quantitative breakdown of securities 1856 to 1865 indicates that two mining companies accounted for the major share of DG's industrial holdings. Shares in the two firms, Heinrichshütte and Bleialf, amounted to around 11 percent of assets for most of the period in which the bank held the shares.

Däbritz (1931) provides an account of the bank's involvement with these firms and indicates that such direct participation arose out of the bank's abortive plan to convert the firms into joint-stock companies. In one case, the bank bought an iron mining company in 1857 and invested heavily in the expansion of production capacity, but the firm immediately faced rapidly falling iron prices and profits. During the several years of low returns the bank's shareholders constantly criticized management for the misstep (Däbritz, p. 105). The other two firms presented similar problems for DG, and the bank was forced to hold their shares until they could extricate themselves in the more favorable market of the late 1860s and early 1870s. Other than these three companies, the bank's holdings of industry stocks amounted to between zero and 3 percent of its assets for the years in which disaggregated data are available (1852–65). Thus, it can hardly be argued that even the early activities of the great banks involved extensive, direct involvement in industrial companies.

Although the disaggregated data for DG run out before the second wave of the German industrialization hit its peak, the story can be picked up in the 1880s using evidence from another of the great banks. Darmstädter Bank (BHI) published unusually detailed accounts of its securities holdings, and *Saling's* reproduced the information in its series on Berlin-listed companies.[23] It is clear from the available data that holdings of industrial shares amounted to less than 1 percent of BHI's assets for most of the 1880s and '90s and that, even at its peak, the ratio of industrial shares to assets only reached 1.3 percent, in 1882. Including railway and real estate shares, the total of nonbank equity shares probably reached only 4 percent

23. Unfortunately, *Saling's* only began publishing in 1876, and the volumes before 1882 are scarce. Also unfortunate for this analysis, they stopped publishing details of securities holdings in 1899.

of assets. When bank shares are included, the total rises to no more than 6.5 percent. It should be underscored that the earlier numbers are estimated based on the ratio of industrial shares to total securities for the period in which both types of data are reported (1896 and 1897). The proportion of assets held in industrial, railway, or bank shares for those years peaked at 3.7 percent. Thus, only if BHI held a significantly greater part of its securities in the form of bank shares in the 1880s than in the 1890s (unlikely, given that the concentration of banking accelerated in the 1890s) would 6.5 percent be an underestimate. These data provide further support for the notion that the great banks invested a relatively small portion of their portfolios in the equity of industrial firms.

Bank Stake Holding in the Postwar Era

Given the often heated discussion about bank power and influence in Germany, the available evidence on banks' equity stakes is surprising: along with the state, financial enterprises hold the fewest large shareblocks in manufacturing firms.[24] Franks and Mayer (2001) report similar results for a sample of 171 large industrial companies in 1990—neither banks nor insurance companies held a stake of 50 percent or more in any of these companies. Moreover, only in 5.8 percent of all cases did a bank hold a stake that was both larger than 25 percent and at the same time the largest stake in the respective companies. For insurance companies, this figure drops to 1.8 percent, compared with 20.5 percent for family groups and 27.5 percent for domestic (German) companies.[25]

According to Brickwell (2001), in the 1980s and '90s, banks and insurance companies only owned stakes larger than 5 percent in those companies from the "Top 100" that did not have a majority stakeholder. There were forty-three companies that fell into this category in 1998 (table 4.3), and banks and insurance companies held stakes in twenty-eight of those (65 percent). In 1980, banks and insurance companies held stakes in 23 of the 100 major companies. This figure rose to 35 in 1996, before falling back to 25 in 2000. Nearly 90 percent of those investments in equity stakes are made for the long run, with one-third being older than twenty years. Finally, approximately 85 percent of all investments in the "Top 100" are stakes between 5 and 25 percent, and holdings larger than 25 percent have been scaled back since the mid-1980s (table 4.4). In 1990, the thirty main banking institutions—the ten largest private banks, the public banks, and credit cooperatives—held a total of 202 direct stakes (172 firms) and 276 indirect stakes (236 firms) among all capital companies (AG and GmbH

24. Data are from Köke (2001). See Adams (1994, 1999), Baums and Fraune (1995), and Kaserer and Wenger (1998) on the power of banks.
25. Yet Santucci (2002, p. 513) asserts: "In sum, due to their unique position as equity holders, banks and financial institutions are in a position to substantially control German companies."

Table 4.4   Shareholder structure by type and legal form: Largest share block (%)

	GmbH	Nonlisted AG	Listed AG	Weighted average[a]
1 Dispersed shares (%)	14.75	19.21	37.70	20.65
2 Individuals (%)	2.83	11.78	10.60	6.39
3 Nonfinancial firms (%)	67.92	58.81	41.18	60.25
4 State (%)	2.80	1.59	0.83	2.13
5 Financial enterprises (%)	0.18	0.42	3.81	0.98
6 Foreigners (%)	11.53	8.19	5.88	9.61
Total	100.00	100.00	100.00	100.00
No. of observations[b]	3,357	1,197	1,207	5,788

Source: Köke (2001, p. 276 table).

Notes: Type refers to the largest shareholder that is classified as having voting power using the Cubbin and Leech index. All firms with no large shareholder (just dispersed shares) or those having no large shareholder with voting power using the Cubbin and Leech index are classified as dispersed.

[a]Including KGaA.

[b]The KGaA is not reported here as a separate category because the number of observations is only 27.

form; Haas 1994, pp. 32–33). Averaged over the thirty banks, this sum amounts to fewer than sixteen stakes (fourteen firms) per bank. Moreover, the affected firms represent a small portion of the overall population of firms, since there were 2,682 AGs and 433,731 GmbHs in Germany at the time (Haas, p. 38).[26] From this study, one can also see that banks have held a handful of majority stakes, but only in smaller companies: 21.1 percent of all stakes of these thirty banks were larger than 50 percent, while nearly 13 percent were higher than 75 percent, but the target companies were not the large, listed share corporations (Haas, pp. 32–33).

The current level of bank shareholdings in nonfinancial firms remains comparatively low. In 2002, the German government abolished capital gains taxes in a widely publicized effort to encourage banks to divest themselves of equity stakes. Given the lack of major holdings, it should come as no surprise that banks have not sold large amounts of shares. More broadly, the trend toward disentangling the dense business webs in Germany began before the tax changes took effect. Wójcik (2001), for example, finds that ownership became more dispersed between 1997 and 2001. At the same time, firms started to dissolve cross-holdings, and financial institutions reduced their block holdings. The decline of bank involvement appears particularly pronounced compared to that of individuals and families as well as nonfinancial corporations (Wójcik, p. 15).[27]

26. The affected firms represent 3.62 percent of all AGs and KGaAs and 0.06 percent of all GmbHs. Since there are other banks not considered in the sample, the total proportion of companies with bank-held stakes is likely somewhat higher.
27. See also Beyer (2002), who finds similar patterns.

A look at the latest annual reports of the leading German banks confirms this general notion: even though all banks have myriad stakes in other, often unrelated companies, these are rarely significant, and overall the participation makes up much less than 5 percent of respective assets. In 1998, the ratios of stakes (market value) to total assets were 4.20 percent for Dresdner Bank, 3.92 percent for Deutsche Bank, 2.65 percent for Hypo-Vereinsbank, and 0.49 percent for Commerzbank (Brickwell 2001, table 3.9).[28] The figures on equity shareholding for the last few decades mirror those of the largest banks a century ago. Taken together, the empirical evidence seriously undermines the claim that big finance currently runs Germany's economy via its equity stakes. Contrary to commonly held beliefs, and excepting an active presence in a few firms, banks tend not to hold dominant stakes. Thus, the domination of corporate ownership by banks is just as much a myth for present-day Germany as it was for the industrialization period.[29]

4.2.3 Patterns of Corporate Control

The available evidence on corporate ownership suggests that bank stakes in German firms are generally small and have been significant only during unusual episodes. The scant evidence available for the pre–World War I period indicates that firms did not own large stakes in other firms, but such stakes are quite common in recent experience. With or without ownership stakes, banks and firms may still wield substantial control over corporations, either through proxy voting of shares or through seats on supervisory boards (*Aufsichtrat*).

Interlocking Directorates

Evidence on Interlocking Directorates before World War I. As with the idea of bank equity stakes, the practice of interlocking directorates—the placement of individuals on multiple boards of directors—has always played a prominent role in the historical accounts of the German industrialization. The institution arose to a substantial extent in the last quarter of the nineteenth century. Before mid-century, when few share companies existed, there were too few firms with formal boards of directors to permit substantial interlocking. As restrictions on chartering stock companies relaxed around 1870, however, and after the 1884 promulgation of regulations requiring stock companies to form supervisory boards, the

28. These are the four leading banks in Germany.
29. There is some evidence, however, that banks largely control themselves through cross-shareholdings and have thus effectively managed to shield themselves from outside influences. See Brickwell (2001), pp. 60–65 and Adams (1994), p. 151. See also Boehmer (2000), p. 117 for a critical view on the role of banks in corporate takeovers; Jenkinson and Ljungqvist (2001), pp. 430–31, for a more favorable view of banks aiding nonfinancial firms in equity stakebuilding; and Köke (2002) for related arguments and a more extensive discussion of block trading in Germany.

foundation was set for formalized relations among firms and between banks and firms.

Using data on share companies listed on the Berlin stock exchange, Fohlin (1999b) shows that German corporate governance forms changed considerably during the German industrialization period—particularly during the last twenty years of the nineteenth century. The data demonstrate marked growth in the formalized interaction between banks and industrial firms between 1882 and 1898, indicating that interlocking directorates grew along with industrial enterprises and became widespread among Berlin-listed companies only during the last stages of industrialization. These interactions involved many third-party relationships, in which one individual sat on the supervisory board of both a bank and a firm. The placement of bank directors on industrial firm supervisory boards was considerably less common and likely did not grow substantially over the period.

The historical evidence shows that some of the apparent relationships between banks and firms may have been merely coincidental, suggesting the importance of interlocking directorates between and among nonfinancial firms. Indeed, over half of joint-stock firms in existence in 1904 had at least one board member (either supervisory or executive) in common with a Berlin-listed nonfinancial firm.[30] Nearly 22 percent of these firm-linked companies had no board interlocks, either direct or indirect, with a bank, and one-third had no banker sitting on their supervisory boards. Of those with bankers on their boards, almost half had only a private banker—not one of the joint-stock universal banks. In other words, the practice of interlocking directorates extended well beyond the placement of bank directors on company supervisory boards. Many firms intertwined their governance structures with one another, making the involvement of the universal banks just one part of an overall system of shared corporate governance.

Table 4.5 gives a breakdown of the various types of board relationships in a group of nonfinancial share companies from 1895 to 1912, the subset of the industrialization period in which formal banking relationships were most widespread. Even in this later part of industrialization, only two-thirds of the sampled firms fall into the attached category, combining all types of bank relationships.[31] Closer to half of the firms had a bank director sitting on their supervisory boards, and 40 percent of these positions

---

30. See Fohlin (1997). The firms were randomly sampled from all joint-stock firms in existence in 1904, and their supervisory board members were compared with a list of all board members of all Berlin-listed corporations (*Adressbuch der Direktoren und Aufsichtsratmitglieder*).

31. The three main types are bank director on firm supervisory board, firm director on bank supervisory board, and concurrent membership of one person in both a bank and firm supervisory board. Occasionally, we see a fourth type, in which one individual sits concurrently in the directorates of a bank and a firm.

Table 4.5   Interlocking directorates by type, 1895–1912

Variable	Definition	Number	Mean (%)
ATT	Any type of attachment	3,347	67.07
V2AR	Bank director sits on firm supervisory board	2,684	52.56
GBV2AR	Great bank director sits on firm supervisory board	612	11.98
ARAR	Joint member of bank and firm supervisory boards	2,268	44.41
ARARonly	Joint supervisory board member; no V2AR	584	11.40
AR2V	Firm director sits on a bank supervisory board	265	5.19
V2V	Firm director is also bank director	107	2.10

Source: Fohlin (2005).
Note: There are 5,107 observations (firm-years).

Table 4.6   Firms with bank directors as supervisory board chair or vice-chair

	Chair		Vice-chair		Chair or vice-chair		Bank chair or vice-chair (% of firms with V2AR)
	Frequency	Percent	Frequency	Percent	Frequency	Percent	
No bank	5,050	86.31	5,258	89.86	4,582	78.31	
Private bank	253	4.32	178	3.04	410	7.01	36.5
Provincial bank	414	7.08	264	4.51	603	10.31	48.3
Great bank	48	0.82	54	0.92	100	1.71	25.9
Provincial and great bank	86	1.47	97	1.66	156	2.67	49.6
Total	5,851	100	5,851	100	5,851	100	

Source: Fohlin (2005).

(19 percent of the sample overall) were held solely by private bankers. A similar number of firms had provincial bank directors, and no other bankers, on their supervisory boards. Only 12 percent of joint-stock firms received representation from a great bank—one of the top nine banks—and that number is even smaller among the top four banks, the so-called D-banks: Deutsche, Dresdner, Darmstädter, and Disconto. In his 1911 treatise on the German universal banks, Jacob Riesser gave a list of all joint-stock companies with great bank directors on their boards. That list contained 171 industrial firms (that is, not counting railroads and commerce), which would have amounted to less than 5 percent of all joint stock firms in the relevant sectors.

The numbers decline further when considering bank control of the leading positions in nonfinancial firm supervisory boards. The chair (*Vorsitzender*) and vice-chair (*stellvertretender Vorsitzender*) of the supervisory board typically maintained the most control over the policy agenda of a firm. Thus, a banker in such a post might have wielded more power than he could as an ordinary member. Table 4.6 tabulates the frequency of such positions in the current sample and indicates that less than 22 percent of firms had a bank director as chair or vice-chair of their supervisory boards. That figure drops to less than 14 percent of firms when considering only chairmanships. In other words, in fewer than half of the cases in which a banker sat on a firm supervisory board was the banker in one of the top two posts. The provincial banks naturally held the most chair- or vice-chairmanships (10 percent of the sample), but the private bankers were close behind (7 percent of the sample). The great banks held relatively few chair or vice-chair positions, amounting to less than 5 percent of the full sample and less than 2.5 percent when considering only chairmanships. Compared to the smaller banks, the great banks were also less likely to hold the top positions among the firms on whose boards they sat: 26 percent of board seats for the great banks, compared with 48 and 37 percent of board seats for provincial and private bankers, respectively. In the cases of dual provincial and great bank directors, the figures fall in line with the provincial banks (50 percent of such board members were chairs or vice-chairs). Extrapolating to the full population of German industrial firms, these figures indicate that directors of the nine great banks chaired the supervisory boards of fewer than 100 German nonfinancial firms in the last two decades before World War I.

Although historians and contemporaries clearly underscore the pervasiveness of bank-firm relationships through interlocking directorates, the older literature does not explicitly reveal how or why these relationships emerged. Still, several hypotheses can and have been used to explain the development of formalized banking relationships and how these links may have benefited the German economy during the later stages of industrialization. Most of these hypotheses emphasize the amelioration of information problems for banks by screening firms before providing finance (ex ante monitoring), keeping watch over the firm's activities and results (interim and ex post monitoring), or affixing a seal of approval to signal investment-worthiness. Positions on firm supervisory boards are thought to have allowed banks access to and influence over strategic planning and investment decision making, thus facilitating the transfer of entrepreneurial expertise to firms. Theoretically, then, the intervention of bankers leads to better decisions by firms and outside investors, less incentive for credit rationing, and larger potential markets for new securities, especially equity, issues.[32]

The evidence on bank board seats clearly shows that firm characteristics

32. See Aoki (1988) on various types of monitoring and Diamond (1984) for a theoretical model of delegated monitoring. On credit rationing, see Stiglitz and Weiss (1981). In the framework of asymmetric information theory, all bank relationships are essentially the same; there is no a priori reason to assume that smaller, provincial universal banks resolve information problems better or worse than their Berlin counterparts. But since the data allow differentiation among the types of banks represented on firm boards, Fohlin (2006) uses a categorical variable to investigate possible systematic differences among private bank, provincial bank, great bank, and joint provincial and great bank attachments.

vary markedly depending on the type of bank considered.[33] This finding, in itself, indicates a lack of generality of the hypotheses laid out. Differences in bank size and location help determine relationships with industrial firms. Even within specific bank categories, the results demonstrate little support for the traditional hypotheses: investment, profits, and income growth should all positively predict bank board memberships, but in fact they do not. Among listed firms, dividend-adjusted stock returns are also statistically insignificant.[34] The insignificance of investment and income growth casts doubt on all three hypotheses, while the results for profitability undermine the consultancy hypotheses most specifically. At least, it is safe to conclude that, if universal banks were providing advising, their impact in the areas one would consider most important (such as profits) was small. Certain other variables are significant in some cases but not others. For example, financial asset level (normalized by total assets) negatively predicts board participation by private banks and provincial banks as anticipated but provides no statistical power for great bank or combined attachment. Age, also expected to relate negatively to attachment, is only significant and negative for provincial banks.

Debt-equity ratios are more difficult to forecast due to conflicting implications of the hypotheses. Curiously, high levels of debt finance positively predict supervisory board membership by a provincial bank or a great bank, but not for private banks alone. The coefficient of debt-equity ratio is positive for combined bank affiliation, and the level of significance only falls slightly short of 10 percent. Thus, while it is not a strong predictor of combined attachment, debt finance is clearly at least a weak factor. Size is included as a control variable, and it strongly predicts board membership by all but the provincial banks. Even for provincial bank affiliation, size obtains a positive coefficient—but it is statistically weak. It is not surprising that the largest banks should attract the largest customers, so one would expect that among attached firms, the largest ones would affiliate with the great banks and the smaller ones with the provincial banks. It is less clear, however, that size should be closely tied to attachment in general or attachment to the private banks (in most cases much smaller than their joint-stock counterparts) in particular.

This finding does point up the connection between many of the private bankers appearing on corporate boards and the great banks. As the forerunners and often founders of the universal banks, an important subset of private banks was intimately tied to various joint-stock universal banks. Some clearly maintained those links, often sitting on incorporated bank supervisory boards for many years. The most powerful of the private

---

33. Fohlin (2006) reports multinomial logit coefficient estimates, where the dependent variable is V2AR—the direct measure of bank attachment.

34. The inclusion of stock returns obviously limits the sample to listed firms and therefore reduces the number of observations by about two-thirds to three-quarters.

bankers were likely those associated with the largest banks, primarily the Berlin-centered great banks. Such an explanation for the connection between size and private bank board memberships therefore hints at the importance of location and prestige, in addition to bank size, in determining board memberships. So, for example, though private banks on their own were too small to fully underwrite securities issues for the largest firms, they participated in underwriting syndicates with other banks and gained access to corporate boards in this manner. The findings on size therefore lead naturally to the question of stock market listings and the role of universal banks in the securities markets.

Stock market listing is the only variable that provides consistent and significant prediction of board membership for all types of bank affiliations, though the magnitude of the effect varies depending on the type of bank involved. The probability of the various sorts of bank board membership differs markedly depending on whether or not a firm is listed on a stock exchange, even controlling for all the other factors that relate to bank relationships. For example, unattached firms comprise nearly half (48 percent) of the overall sample of firms, but among unlisted firms that share is 61 percent. After controlling for the other relevant factors, however, the adjusted probability of being independent given that the firm is unlisted is 53 percent. In contrast, listed firms have a 30 percent adjusted probability of being unattached, compared to a 26 percent unadjusted probability. These figures mean that, even when controlling for other firm characteristics, the chance of being unattached is 23 percentage points lower assuming a stock market listing than not (about a 75 percent reduction in the likelihood of independent status). In contrast, the probability of attachment rises between 3 and 9 percentage points, depending on bank type, when a hypothetical firm changes from unlisted to listed. Given the relatively low likelihood of having a great bank on an unlisted firm's board (about 9 percent, controlling for other factors and including those with combined attachment), the increase due to stock market listing represents a doubling of the probability. In comparison, the adjusted probabilities of private bank or provincial bank board membership rise less with listing status, but still increase by over one-third (17 to 25 percent for private bank attachment and 20 to 27 percent for provincial bank attachment).

The strong significance of listing suggests that bank board memberships were at least partly related to securities issues and trading. Such an explanation is very plausible for a number of reasons. By the end of the nineteenth century, companies wishing to gain admission to a German stock market were subject to several preliminary requirements, not least of which was the stipulation that the firm's share capital be fully paid up.[35] This reg-

---

35. See chapter 8 in Fohlin (2006) on the stock markets and their place in the overall corporate financial system in Germany.

ulation alone likely necessitated the engagement of a universal bank, and, having underwritten the new securities, that bank would have acquired some portion of the issued shares, and sometimes more than the bank could place with investors. Banks often joined forces to underwrite large issues, and larger firms naturally would have required a greater number of banks in order to keep each individual stake constant. Under such circumstances, the firms with the highest share capitals would be the most likely to end up with supervisory board representation from multiple banks.

In addition to their underwriting and placement activities, universal banks were actively engaged in the brokerage business. The extensive trading of securities through the banking system likely provided further opportunities for banks to hold firm shares. Furthermore, since the universal banks maintained extensive networks of commercial clients, retaining a universal bank may have allowed firms to reap the benefits of network externalities. Bankers not only created their own secondary markets in listed shares, but they also became fully ensconced in the governing bodies of the stock exchanges. As the gatekeepers of the German capital market, therefore, the universal banks gained easy access to a broad range of securities—particularly those that were listed.

Finally, it is also possible that firms made their way into bank networks because they were already listed or about to become so. Since the Reichsbank accepted as collateral only securities listed at a German bourse, such issues may have been in turn more likely to be accepted as collateral by universal banks.[36] A bank may have then exercised influence in the choice of supervisory board members of the firms whose shares the bank held as collateral, particularly when shares were owned by small, outside stakeholders.

Modern Patterns of Interlocking Directorates. In the past few decades, debates have continued over the placement of bank employees in the supervisory boards of nonfinancial firms. Some argue that bank employees were considered able monitors and that it was merely coincidental that bank employees were appointed to supervisory boards; others claim that banks sent employees to supervisory boards in order to better monitor their credit engagements and to position themselves to sell additional financial services and perhaps to influence corporate policy in favor of other companies in which the bank held a stake.[37] Contradicting the more activist theories of board membership, Hopt (1996a) argues that banks already had any necessary access to customer financial information by virtue of disclosure requirements stemming from the credit relationship itself, as well as from participation in the firms. A similar perspective sees these personal linkages as

36. See Engberg (1981).
37. See Böhm (1992), p. 186.

ways to build cooperation among firms in order to minimize risk and uncertainty (Schreyögg and Papenheim-Tockhorn 1995, p. 205).[38]

Twenty years ago, the view predominated that banks actively pursued board seats in an effort to exert control over corporations in which they were interested. One study, covering the 1960s and '70s, found that the banks held seats (mandates) in all branches of industry and had gradually shifted focus to mandates in larger corporations by 1978 (Albach and Kless 1982, p. 977). This move arguably demonstrated a new strategy of quality over quantity: gaining power in the most important firms rather than via a large number of mandates with smaller industry players (Albach and Kless, p. 977).

More generally, board members usually hold only one mandate at a time, at least among the relatively large German firms. In a 1989 sample of 492 such companies, having a total of 7,778 members in their management (2,061) and supervisory (5,717) boards, the vast majority of representatives (86 percent) had only one mandate.[39] Still, there was a substantial share of representatives who did hold multiple seats and therefore created interlocking directorates. Indeed, in this particular sample, 14 percent of the people holding seats in these firms accounted for one-third of all mandates in the companies, and a small handful held upward of ten to twelve seats apiece (Pfannschmidt 1995).

It also appears that bank relationships last, or they did at least in the 1970s and '80s. Banks at that time seem to have maintained purposeful and stable linkages with firms. For example, out of a sample of 56 of the largest 500 *Kapitalgesellschaften* in 1987, almost all of the bank board positions between 1969 and 1988 exceeded personal ties held by one individual bank employee and appeared to represent intentional moves to build lasting relationships (Schreyögg and Papenheim-Tockhorn 1995, p. 223).[40] Once again, though, the big-three banks were the main participants in these partnerships, holding forty-nine out of sixty-six stable linkages maintained by the top fifteen banks (Schreyögg and Papenheim-Tockhorn, p. 223).

Even among the largest 100 firms, the proportion of mandates held by bankers has fallen gradually since the late seventies—from 8.6 percent in 1978 to 6.4 percent in 1996 (Bokelmann 2000). Still, even among these large companies, the banks held relatively few board seats—never more than 15 percent of any board (Böhm 1992, pp. 194–95).[41] And most banks do not engage actively in these relationships. Half of the bank-held posi-

---

38. Tradition might also explain the reappointment of the same bank to a vacated seat.

39. Pfannschmidt (1995), whose sample includes 492 big German companies as of December 31, 1989 (consisting of the FAZ-list of the hundred biggest companies and companies out of the Bonner Stichprobe database).

40. Intent is evidenced by the new appointment of individuals from a given bank when a previous representative from that bank left a firm's supervisory board.

41. Size is measured by revenue as of 1986. Half of the mandates are elected by labor, which automatically halves the number of seats available to bankers. At the same time, this power-sharing arrangement may lessen the banks' influence via the supervisory board seats.

tions traced back to just two banks—Deutsche and Dresdner—with Deutsche holding twice as many as Dresdner.

Banks have also decreased the number of firms on whose supervisory boards they sit. In 1986, over two-thirds of the top 100 firms, and 43 of the top 50, had bankers on their boards. The Deutsche Bank alone sent representatives to 40 of the top 100 (in 1980). By 1990, that figure was down to 35 firms, while in 1998, it had dropped to 17 of the top 100 firms. Deutsche Bank and Allianz, two of the primary participants in board representation, have enacted clear plans to dissolve their formerly strong and thick ties with German companies—Deutsche, in particular, announced in March 2001 that members of the bank would no longer take up supervisory board chairmanships (*Aufsichtsratsvorsitze;* Beyer 2002).

If we constrain the pre–World War I sample to the largest firms—taking the top 10 percent by total assets, for example—the results are quite similar to those for the 1990s: approximately one-third to one-half of these large and mostly listed firms had one or more of the great banks represented on their supervisory boards, depending on the year in question. Thus, it is clear that banks, most noticeably the largest ones, have always taken an active interest in corporate control, especially of the largest firms. The latest swing away from board representation can also be placed in this much longer perspective and thereby be seen as a historical low point.

Proxy Voting

Direct ownership of shares accounts for only part of the networking between universal banks and industrial firms. As the first part of this chapter indicates, universal banks owned significant stakes in relatively few firms—quite clearly a smaller set of firms than those on whose supervisory boards they held seats. Bankers must have entered boards by other means, and one important avenue for such bank access is proxy votes—votes entrusted to the bank by the actual owner of the share.

Proxy Voting before WWI. Given their involvement with the placement of new issues, their provision of safe deposit services, and their lending secured by stocks, the universal banks would have been the logical parties to take an investor's proxy votes. Indeed, many investors would have seen proxy voting by banks as a valuable service. Having acquired voting power in the general assembly (*Generalversammlung*), the bank could directly influence the selection of supervisory board members and thereby indirectly influence firm management and strategy.

Unfortunately, it is difficult to test this hypothesis. As with direct ownership data, hardly any data exist on proxy voting in Germany before 1913, though qualitative evidence and descriptive accounts suggest that it was common.[42] It may be possible to provide additional insight into the matter

---

42. Some new efforts are underway and could clarify some of these issues.

with the current data, but several assumptions must be made. For example, if small stakeholders felt less compelled to vote their own shares than did those with large stakes, then small shareholders would have been more likely to deposit their shares and turn over their voting rights to a universal bank. According to this reasoning, closely held firms—firms whose capital was held by a small number of large shareholders—would experience less proxy voting than would widely held firms. As a result, the dispersion of capital ownership would increase the likelihood of accumulation of board seats by universal bankers.[43] The same customers who facilitated securities issues by a firm, therefore, may have been the main suppliers of proxy votes to universal banks.

Based on this reasoning and on data availability, figures on the number of shares issued substitute for dispersion of ownership. While it is hardly a perfect measure of dispersion, the number of shares outstanding does offer valuable information. For a given share, as the number of shares declines, the value of each share relative to total capital increases. If shares are indivisible, the number of shares outstanding represents the maximum number of shareholders in a firm.[44] Clearly, it is possible that firms with large numbers of shares were closely held, yet firms with relatively few shares outstanding are more likely to have been closely held. In the sample assembled by Fohlin (2006), share prices fall in a narrow range, regardless of attachment status, and therefore the number of shares issued is highly correlated with total assets, share capital, and net worth (96 to 98 percent). The stock of fixed assets is slightly less highly correlated with the number of shares (90 percent), making it the best available control for firm size.

The number of shares outstanding is the only variable that strongly predicts broadly defined bank affiliations of all types.[45] Several other variables (size, stock market listing, debt-equity ratio, age, and financial assets) also help explain multiple broad attachments. Beyond the industry sector, however, only number of shares helps predict broad attachment with a single category of bank (either a provincial or a great bank). The strong, positive relationship between the number of shares in circulation and broadly defined bank affiliation suggests that ownership dispersion is positively associated with at least loose involvement in a joint-stock bank network. Given the limitations on the data, this is the most compelling evidence available that proxy voting was an important factor in the involvement of firms in interlocking directorates with banks.

In contrast, the number of shares outstanding provides no strong pre-

---

43. See Chirinko and Elston (1998), in which the authors show that bank-influenced firms tend to have a more dispersed ownership structure than independent firms.

44. It may have been possible for several people to own a single share, but I have no evidence for or against such a practice.

45. The models repeat the multinomial logit model of narrow attachment (Fohlin 2005). Private bankers are considered unattached, since private banks do not generally have supervisory boards whose members can concurrently sit on firms' supervisory boards.

dictive power of narrowly defined bank attachment.[46] To the extent that the number of shares captures the dispersion of capital ownership, the change in the coefficients from those in the models using the broad definition of attachment suggests that proxy voting was relatively unimportant for the direct involvement of bank directors in supervisory boards. A hypothesis that can explain why the number of firm shares is a strong, positive indicator of broadly defined affiliation but is of no predictive value for narrowly defined attachment runs as follows. Bankers would have sought the closest oversight of firms in which the bank invested directly. Membership by bank directors on firm supervisory boards therefore may have stemmed from bank holding of a firm's securities or debt. Given the physical limits on a bank director's ability to monitor them, firms in which a bank held proxy votes but minimal securities or debt may have reasonably fallen to a lower priority for bank oversight. Proxy votes, therefore, may have simply represented a means by which banks could vote into office bank-friendly supervisory board members—in particular, individuals who already sat on their own supervisory boards or whom they might know from other business dealings. Clearly, these arguments about proxy voting and ownership structure are largely hypothetical. All that can be said from the analysis is that the importance of proxy voting cannot be rejected on the basis of the currently available data. It is unlikely that we will definitively resolve the uncertainty about the historical importance of proxy voting.[47]

Modern Patterns of Proxy Voting. The representation of banks on supervisory boards relates closely to the voting of ownership shares in these firms. Available figures on the voters present at annual shareholder meetings suggest that shareholders do not exercise the right to vote their shares. The attendance of small shareholders is extremely low, and rates decreased, at least at the largest German firms, from the mid-1970s to the early 1990s.[48] As they were in the pre–World War I era, these small share owners are still often represented via proxy votes turned over to institutions, largely banks. Data on proxy voting by banks continue to elude researchers, since there is no central database about general annual meetings. The list of participants (*Teilnehmerverzeichnisse*) is required to be recorded only in the commercial

46. Number of shares is significant in the narrow attachment logit model only when sector controls are excluded, clustering is not assumed, and normal (as opposed to robust) standard errors are used. Number of shares is also positive and significant in a panel probit model comparing all attached firms to independents, but the estimation technique appears to be rather unstable. In particular, different assumptions on the model provide significantly different results. Thus, the coefficients of such a model should be viewed with caution.

47. Despite some new efforts to gather proxy voting data, I remain pessimistic about the possibility of finding *sufficient* data to statistically test the proxy voting hypothesis in any direct or conclusive manner for the prewar period.

48. Adams (1994, p. 156) reports data for five of the largest German companies for 1975 and 1992, while Brickwell (2001, p. 62) provides an overview of turnout at the general meeting of shareholders of four financial services companies in 1998 and 1999.

registers of the city where the company has its seat. Moreover, banks may remain silent on whether or not they cast instructed proxy votes. These data limitations hamper the investigation of proxy voting, and past studies have often exacerbated the interpretation problems by constraining their samples to firms with dispersed ownership, in which proxy voting by banks is particularly important.

In one such study, for 1986, financial institutions, particularly the big-three universal banks, proxy votes played a decisive role in the representation of shares at annual general meetings of shareholders. In the thirty-two largest corporate firms with dispersed ownership, on average, 64.5 percent of shares received representation at the annual general meeting of shareholders.[49] While it was very rare that one bank alone dominated the general annual meeting, taken together, the big-three banks often held a majority of votes cast (45 percent share on average), and, with the notable exception of the meetings held by Volkswagen, banks as a group always held a majority of represented votes (83 percent share on average; Gottschalk 1988).[50] The big-three banks also held one-third to one-half of the votes present at their own general annual meeting (Deutsche Bank: 47.17 percent, Dresdner Bank: 47.08 percent, Commerzbank: 34.58 percent). Although it is unwise to infer any kind of trend, the data for 1990 show a slight reduction (to 72 percent) in the average share of votes held by the banks in the top 100 firms (Baums and Fraune 1995).[51] The big-three banks continued to hold substantial voting percentages at their own meetings.

A finer breakdown indicates that only ten of these firms had truly highly dispersed share ownership (less than 25 percent of shares held in blocks), whereas seventeen had some bank-held stake and thirteen had significant (nonbank) block holders (Böhm 1992).[52] Proxy voting by banks was greatest among the first group, giving the big-three banks 44 percent of votes cast at the annual meeting (versus 25 percent of all possible votes). Interestingly, when banks owned their own stakes in firms, they also held proxy votes, but they averaged lower total vote percentages (for the big-three alone, 25 percent of the total or 33 percent of votes present at the meeting)

---

49. See Gottschalk (1988). He started with the 100 biggest companies (as measured by value added in 1984) and selected those firms whose shares were more than half controlled by dispersed owners or by banks. He based his calculations on the index of participants (*Teilnehmerverzeichnisse*) of the general annual meetings of these companies in 1986 (1987 for some companies).

50. The big-three banks are Deutsche, Dresdner, and Commerzbank; he also included the Bayrische Vereinsbank, Bayrische Hypo, the state banks (*Landesbanken*) and savings banks (*Sparkassen*), the credit cooperatives (*Genossenschaftsbanken*), and other financial institutions.

51. Their sample contains only twenty-four companies, so it's possible that fewer firms had dispersed ownership, though data availability could also explain part of the difference in sample sizes.

52. Only thirty-two of forty attendance lists for annual meetings (*Hauptversammlungspräsenzlisten*) were available.

compared to widely held firms. Not surprisingly, the banks held the fewest proxy votes in firms with dominating block holders: the big three held only 6 percent of votes (7 percent present at the annual meeting), and all banks together held 13 percent (15 percent of those cast at the meeting).

Broadening the sample to include smaller firms, those with more concentrated share ownership, and unlisted companies, the findings show significantly less bank control, especially when instructed proxy votes are excluded.[53] For the Edwards and Nibler (2000) sample from 1992, proxy votes accounted for a greater share of total bank votes than did actual equity ownership, and the figures are far lower than for the more restricted samples used in other studies: banks as a group averaged an 8.5 percent share of firm voting rights in the form of proxy votes, compared to 6.7 percent from equity ownership.[54] The banks rarely held any proxy votes in unlisted firms but held at least some in the majority of the listed firms. As with previous studies, the big-three banks played the dominant role in proxy voting.[55]

Given the paucity of proxy voting data before the 1980s, it is difficult to compare these more recent patterns with those of previous periods. It is safe to say, however, that proxy voting by banks, especially by the largest banks, has been a key feature of the connection of banks to corporate ownership in Germany since the industrialization period. Moreover, that link has apparently always been the tightest among large firms with stock market listings and dispersed ownership structures.

4.3   The Underlying Political and Legal Factors

4.3.1   Roots in the Industrialization Period, 1870–1913

Incorporating Firms and Issuing Equity Shares

The majority of German corporations are organized as *Aktiengesellschaften* (AG), literally "share companies."[56] Share companies are required

53. While customers turning over voting rights are explicitly offered the chance to instruct banks on their voting, only about 2–3 percent of them take this opportunity (Baums 1996).

54. Their sample is based on 156 of the 200 largest nonfinancial firms as measured by in terms of turnover as of 1992.

55. See also Perlitz and Seger (1994), whose sample consists of 110 (large, listed) industrial companies of which only 57 could be evaluated for proxy voting and only for 1990. They found total proxy voting by banks of less than 10 percent in over one-third of the firms, but also found 30 percent of firms (17/57) had at least a majority of represented votes held in proxy by banks. Also, 83 percent of the 110 firms had at least one banker on its supervisory board. Böhm (1992) has similar findings. See also the earlier study by Cable (1985) on bank involvement through proxy voting in the 1970s.

56. See Whale (1930), pp. 331–33, for a discussion of different company forms in Germany up to that point (which remain essentially unchanged). But regulations and de facto rights of shareholders in AGs are very similar to those of the other major type of corporation, the *Kommanditgesellschaften (auf Aktien)*.

to have a general meeting of shareholders (*Generalversammlung*) and a supervisory board (*Aufsichtsrat*) to represent shareholders.[57] The supervisory board of an AG selects the executive board, a group composed of high-level firm managers.

Although the AG form predates the industrialization period, it took hold only after the liberalization of incorporation laws around 1870. These legal changes coincided with a rapid development of large-scale industry. Certain types of industries—particularly the railroads in the late 1830s and 1840s and then the banks in the late 1840s and 1850s—did avail themselves of the AG form. But the numbers remained low until 1870, when amendments to the 1861 company code (*Handelsgestzbuch*) replaced state concessions with objective criteria.

In the early years, the importance of the AG grew slowly in comparison with the personal enterprise. Very few AGs appeared before 1850: estimates put the numbers at only 16 in Prussia between 1800 and 1825, and 112 between 1825 and 1850. In the Bavarian Kingdom, just 6 existed between 1838 and 1848, and 44 more came in the following decade. The ranks of AGs expanded faster after 1850, with 336 AGs founded in Prussia up to 1870 and 57 in Saxony, where just 10 existed in the year 1850.[58] The real boom in formation came between 1870 and 1873, with the liberalization of company laws and the establishment of the German Empire: 928 new AGs were founded, with a total nominal capital of 2.81 billion marks (Henning 1992, p. 210). Yet, even by 1882, private firms still accounted for nearly 95 percent of all enterprises in Germany (table 4.1; Gömmel 1992, p. 35). The numbers exceeded 3,000 by 1890 and stayed well over 5,000 from the late 1890s until at least World War I.

The boom of the early 1870s ended in a prolonged crisis from 1873 to 1879, the effects of which prompted immediate political pressure for restructuring the economy and particularly for addressing the state of shareholder laws. The ensuing ups and downs in the markets and the broader economy spurred periodic revisions to the law, most of which had relatively minor impact in an era of overall prosperity and, given the context, liberal political thinking.[59]

The first of these efforts resulted in the company law of 1884—a revision to the unified national regulation of share companies of 1870. The new law added two important provisions: first, it required new corporations to create a prospectus, specifying a time period within which the subscriptions would take place, and, second, it stipulated that the opening general meet-

---

57. Most other types of companies, and particularly small ones, are not required to have a supervisory board.

58. Laux (1998) mentions 454 AGs for Prussia up to 1870. See Pross (1965).

59. See Fohlin (2002b, 2006) for a review of the pre-WWI laws and regulations concerning the stock exchanges and corporations as well as the imposition of taxes on exchange listing and transactions starting in 1882.

ing of shareholders must attract a minimum percentage attendance.[60] Underwriting issues on the basis of subscriptions could cause long delays and put new issues at risk for failure to meet regulations and deadlines. To insure success, companies therefore turned to informed intermediaries—the universal banks—who would purchase the new capital and subsequently sell individual equity shares to the public.

A second round of political and legal debates followed the financial crisis of the early 1890s (Wiener 1905; Buss 1913; Meier 1993; Schulz 1994). The resulting stock exchange law in 1896 contained a number of provisions regarding the issuing and listing of securities, and the revised company law of 1897 added further stipulations.[61] The new regulations—mostly making it more difficult to issue and list stock shares—added to the difficulties in attracting outside investors for firms and, it is commonly believed, created a need for greater bank credit, while pushing more securities trading from the exchanges to the banks. The new law may well have solidified simultaneous founding, and the central position of the universal banks, for stock issuance. Indeed, Robert Liefmann (1921, p. 476) attributed the form of the German universal banks partly to the regulations imposed on company promotions (cited in Whale 1930, p. 40).

The Supervisory Board and Corporate Control

In the first half of the nineteenth century, while the government still maintained tight control over incorporation, it imposed little regulation on corporate governance. The voting rights of shareholders and their representation by supervisory boards evolved over time. In the 1840s and '50s, scholars wrote on the distribution of voting rights according to share ownership.[62] Many were concerned about the ability of the smallest shareholders to be heard and the potential for excessive control by a small number of large shareholders. As the regulatory stance on incorporation liberalized, and as vast numbers of firms began to take advantage of limited liability, the clear need arose for legal guidelines for corporate control. Of particular concern were the smallest shareholders, who were often disenfranchised and also unable to access information about the firms in which they invested. Thus, in promulgating the 1870 company law, the government demanded, in return for free incorporation, greater uniformity and consistency in corporate accounting, reporting, and governance (Hopt 1998). In

60. Text of share company law of 1884 (*Gesetz, betreffend die Kommanditgesellschaft auf Aktien und die Aktiengesellschaften*), articles 209e and 210. The 1870 company code had already required the full amount of an issue to be subscribed and at least 25 percent to be paid up before a new joint-stock company could be founded; for shares issued at higher than nominal value, 50 percent payment was required.

61. See Nussbaum (1910).

62. See Dunlavy (1998).

particular, the law stipulated the creation of the dual board structure, in part as a means of protecting shareholder and public interest, independent of the management of the company.

The 1884 law added new regulations on corporate governance; among other stipulations, it prohibited simultaneous positions on the supervisory and executive boards of any one firm. Former company directors could, and often did, take seats on the supervisory board, as long as they had been officially discharged from the executive board (*Handelsgesetzbuch* art. 225a). The 1884 law also explicitly raised the level of responsibility inherent in supervisory board positions. Whereas the 1870 law granted supervisory board members the right to obtain information about the company, the 1884 law made such oversight a duty. At the same time, though the 1870 law stipulated that supervisory board members must own shares of the firm on whose board they sat, the 1884 law made such equity stakes optional.

Shareholder representation also grew more democratic as the nineteenth century wore on. The use of proxy voting may have partially alleviated the disenfranchisement problem, since small shareholders—or large ones—could deposit their shares with a bank and protect their stakes both literally and figuratively. That is, they found safe storage of easily lost or stolen bearer shares along with representation of their votes in the general meetings of shareholders. Bankers could hypothetically build up significant stakes from many disparate small shareholders and thereby attain far greater standing at the general meeting than could any one small stakeholder could. As long as the banker could be trusted to vote in the interest of the small shareholders, the system improved their position. This point leads naturally to questions of corporate control: Who really controlled or controls German corporations—the owners or their proxy holders?

4.3.2   Postindustrialization Developments

The early post–World War I period brought a wave of company foundations, and the hyperinflation of the early 1920s brought an even larger swelling of the corporate ranks. Financial crisis in 1931 and the ensuing depression of that decade reversed the trend. The Great Depression of the 1930s hit German corporations hard and sent large numbers of them into insolvency. The wave of corporate failures prompted new calls for reform to the corporation laws (*Handelsgesetzbuch* or HGB) as well as the desire to create a code (*Aktiengesetz*) specifically addressing shareholding and attendant rights and restrictions. Ultimately, the debates led to an "emergency order" (*Notverordnung* or NotVO) on stock companies. The act, set into force by the Nazi regime, without parliamentary action, included a tax credit, stronger regulation of banks, stronger disclosure rules, and several

other stipulations. The legal changes, and their underlying political motivations, played a major role in the patterns of corporate control that
evolved over the rest of the twentieth century.[63]

The Relationship Between Share Ownership and Voting Rights

Democratic intuition, liberal traditions, and today's market-orientation
trends suggest that one share should be associated with one vote. Deviations from a one-share-one-vote system, the most important of which appeared in the interwar years, greatly affected patterns of ownership and
control in Germany. Because the disassociation of ownership and control
allowed founders to control their firms longer than they would have otherwise, these legal changes altered the fates of families and their firms.

Multiple-Vote Shares (Mehrstimmrechtsaktien). Mehrstimmrechtsaktien
are quite literally shares that are associated with multiple votes. This means
that a few shares and little capital investment can lead to a lot of voting
power. In the interwar years, this instrument was used extensively and was
usually justified as means of fighting dilution of family control. Multiple
voting rights helped solve the need for capital after WWI, while allowing
founding families to keep their grip on their firms (Pross 1965, p. 84).
Based on a large sample of AGs studied by the national statistics office
(Statistisches Reichsamt), 842 out of 1,595 AGs in 1925, and close to 40
percent out of 913 in 1934, used shares with multiple voting rights. The
votes per share ranged between 20 and 250 times higher than the normal
voting right. These shares, usually associated with just a small fraction of
the overall capital, were loaded with as many votes as necessary for the
domination of the general meeting of shareholders. Usually, these privi-
leged shares were given to members of the *Aufsichtsrat* or to banks that
committed themselves to vote according to the controlling group. The remaining shareholders and any future shareholders effectively lost all
power. According to the Statistisches Reichsamt study, ownership of 10
percent of the shares was sufficient to control more than 40 percent of the
votes in 388 companies in 1925. Due to the generally poor attendance at the
general meetings of shareholders, 40 percent of the available votes usually
meant the majority of the votes present (Pross 1965, p. 86).

Multiple-vote shares were prohibited by the reform in 1937; however, the
Nazis apparently made exceptions favoring family enterprises—a topic
that appears again in the next section. The new AktG of 1965 allows
Mehrfachstimmrechte, but only after a special concession to be issued by a

---

63. The discussion here sticks to the primary focus of political and legal influences on corporate governance institutions. That approach is not intended to minimize the human tragedy
of the Nazi regime.

federal minister (AktG para. 12).[64] Today they are of little importance, and, in fact, the new law on control and transparency in the business sphere (KonTraG 1998) explicitly prohibits the issuing of *Mehrstimmrechtsaktien.*

Vorratsaktien and Vorzugsaktien. Vorratsaktien ("depot shares") were another instrument heavily used in the time of the Weimar Republic. According to Menke (1988), these shares were issued without granting stockholders a right to buy them. Officially, they were created to help the company react quickly when needed for mergers or acquisitions, and, pending their use, were not eligible for trade. Their actual purpose was different, though: Menke argues that the shares were loaded with multiple voting rights in order to keep the control over the company in the hands of the controlling group or an associated shareholder without having to invest huge amounts of capital.[65] This misuse led to legal changes in 1937, and they vanished thereafter.

Vorzugsaktien ("preferential shares") were created for the purpose of financing corporations in trouble. These shares granted holders preferential rights to dividend payments. This right was offered as an additional incentive for investors to buy into a poorly performing company. The shares came without voting rights, so as to raise substantial infusions of capital without diluting control of the firm. The 1937 reform of the AktG strengthened the right of holders of *Vorzugsaktien:* not more than 50 percent of the capital could be issued in these preferred shares, they had to have all other rights associated with shares except for voting, and they regained their voting right if the corporation was one year late with the payment of the preferential dividend.

Höchststimmrechte and Other Restrictions. Höchststimmrechte (maximum-voting rights) were rules that prescribed a limit to the number of votes a shareholder might hold. This could be achieved either directly by allowing fewer votes than the number of shares of an important shareholder or indirectly by prohibiting the purchase of more than a certain fraction of the shares.[66] While voting limitations have a long tradition in Germany— many of the corporations of the early nineteenth century had them—the rules proved generally ineffective, since it was not difficult for a determined investor to have someone else own the stocks and for that investor to still control their votes. This instrument could be used to limit the power of ma-

---

64. It would also be interesting to examine the cases in which *Mehrstimmrechtsaktien* were used after the war: with the influx of "oil dollars" from Near Eastern countries in the 1970s, these shares may have been used to prevent control losses to governmental investors from Near Eastern countries.

65. See Menke (1988), p. 98.

66. This section is based on Emmerich (2000) and Fey (2000).

jority shareholders, but it also worked as an effective threat against hostile takeovers. Heavy criticism of this restriction of the market for corporate control led to legal changes, and in the 1998 reforms *Höchststimmrechte* were phased out. The capital market actually rewarded this change: the prices for stocks from companies with *Höchsstimmrechts* clauses jumped when the legal changes were announced. The AktG 1965 had still allowed them, and even today corporations whose shares are not traded at stock exchanges are not subject to the prohibition of *Höchststimmrechten*. The rationale is to preserve control of founders—in many cases families—who are still involved, albeit with reduced ownership stakes, in smaller AGs. Of course, there are other related restrictions on voting shares, such as minimum stake requirements, and even on attending the general meeting of shareholders.[67]

Codetermination. The idea that the management of a stock corporation should be responsible not only to the shareholders but also to other stakeholders can also be seen in the codetermination laws. Employees send representatives to the supervisory boards in stock corporations. By giving employees voice without actual ownership, these rules cause a major deviation from the one-share-one-vote rule. Of course, codetermination was introduced in order to represent employee interests in the supervisory boards, regardless of the implications for shareholder rights. Codetermination may have limited ownership dispersion, because shareholders attempt to counterbalance the power of the employees and prevent the damages that could occur if management and employees collude.[68] Roe argues that, due to codetermination, managers and large block holders circumvented the supervisory board by making decisions outside the boardroom—largely obviating the supervisory board as a governance device. In addition, he argues that codetermination and block holding are complementary. That is, dispersed ownership fits poorly with codetermination, because it prevents block holders from selling their blocks to the public and also scares off potential minority investors. Codetermination evolved over two postwar regulatory episodes in 1951 and 1952 and then in 1972 and 1976. While theoretically appealing, studies that examine the effect on the shareholders of employees in the supervisory board find little or no effect of codetermination.[69]

Block Holding and Other Forms of Monitoring. Given this background, shareholders are left with only one possibility to effectively control management: block holding as a monitoring device. Dispersed ownership cre-

67. See Emmerich (2000) and Pross (1965).
68. See Roe (2003).
69. See Becht, Bolton, and Roëll (2003) for a review, including Svejnar (1981, 1982), Benelli, Loderer, and Lys (1987), and Baums and Frick (1999).

ates managerial agency problems, such as conflicts of interest between investors and managers.[70] There are several mechanisms that can mitigate these costs. Roe (1999) argues that there are four main monitoring mechanisms: market competition, takeovers, good boards of directors, and block holding. In his view, Germany has few takeovers, is weak at competition, and does not have strong boards. Hence, he argues, large block holders are the only control device for monitoring managers. If there is diffusion of ownership, no internal or external control device for the management will exist. When taken into account with the agency costs in corporate governance, the different mechanisms of monitoring are plausible. As effective as block holding may be, it is far from clear that it remains the only way of monitoring in Germany. Based on his empirical study, for example, Köke (2002, p. 128) argues that lenders use financial pressure to exert influence on management decisions and thereby positively impact productivity growth.

Legal Influences on Bank Control

The Shareholder Law of 1937. Legitimized by an overriding principle of acting for the good of the whole (known as the *Führerprinzip*), the 1937 shareholder law weakened the position of the shareholders—in particular, the general assembly—in favor of the management board (*Vorstand*). The management was no longer responsible specifically for shareholder interests but for all groups having a stake—figuratively—in the company, including the *Reich* (AktG para. 70I, p. 37).[71] The new laws eased the process of transforming stock corporations into partnerships (*Umwandlungsgesetz*), while a higher minimum share capital of 500,000 RM impeded the founding of new stock corporations. While the law did tend to undermine the use of the AG form, it also simultaneously provided for greater disclosure of information to the public.[72]

Although both the HGB and the AktG saw registered shares (*Namensaktien*) as the norm, in practice the market was dominated by bearer shares, because they allowed shareholders to stay anonymous.[73] Under the shareholder law of 1937, votes could not be cast by mail, making it even more likely that shareholders, especially small stakeholders, would be unable or unwilling to exercise their ownership rights directly. As an accommodation, the law provided two ways for shareholders to cast their votes by proxy. First, a shareholder could give his bank a *Stimmrechtsvollmacht,* al-

---

70. Again, see Becht, Bolton, and Roëll (2003) for a more thorough review.

71. It is easy to assume that the law represented standard Nazi thinking, given the date of its promulgation. Yet the president of the commission for preparing the new *Aktiengesetz* in 1965, Wilhelmini (1965, p. 153), argued that the 1937 law was not a piece of Nazi work. It seems that the main components of the law were actually articulated under the previous administration, the Weimar Republic.

72. See Kübler (1994), p. 12.

73. See von Falkenhausen (1967), p. 69.

lowing the bank to cast the votes in the shareholder's name but also forcing shareholders to reveal their identity. Second, and more important in practice, the *Stimmrechtsermächtigung* ceded the shareholder's voting rights to the bank.[74] A *Stimmrechtsermächtigung* had to be given in written form and, while valid for up to fifteen months, could be revoked at any time. This form of proxy voting was later called *Bankenstimmrecht* or *Depotstimmrecht,* due to the heavy use of banks as the proxy holder.[75] Interestingly, this new regulation actually weakened the banks' position, since some banks had required customers to turn over *Stimmrechtsermächtigungen* automatically upon opening securities accounts. Even with the new regulations, banks could still do more or less whatever they wished with the voting rights that continued to be ceded to them.[76]

Reforms of 1965. After World War II, American overseers, wanting to introduce shareholder democracy and to limit excessive concentration of power, began to initiate reforms in the German corporate sector.[77] These reforms, directed largely at the mining industry, included returning to registered shares, restricting proxy voting by banks to *Stimmrechtsvollmachten* (the weaker form) for every individual general assembly of shareholders, and outlawing all anonymous voting. The law enacted specifically for the privatization of Volkswagen in 1960 (*Gesetz zur Privatisierung des Volkswagenwerkes vom* 22.7.1960) contained similar provisions, and the Schuman plan likewise imposed restrictions on proxy voting by banks involved with mining firms. Along the way, smaller reforms, called *"kleine Aktienrechtsreform,"* tightened accounting standards and rules for building reserves.

The *Aktiengesetz* of 1937 was not seen as a major problem by many politicians in Germany after World War II, and even modern scholars suggest that arguments for reform stemmed from a desire to improve the lot of small shareholders and to promote a society based on democracy and capitalism, rather than to somehow right a wrong that was imposed under the Nazi regime.[78] The general atmosphere of reform that emerged during the reconstruction period favored a number of alterations to the status quo. Significantly, the 1965 reform bill abolished the *Führerprinzip* and, while retaining important powers for the management board, imposed a norm of majority rule for that body. Other elements of this new law included attempts to eliminate the practice of "silent reserves" that allowed corpora-

---

74. See Hüffer (2002), p. 694. Though similar, the *Stimmrechtsermächtigung* gave banks much more power. See also von Falkenhausen (1967), p. 69.

75. Hopt (1996a) calls the *Depotstimmrecht* a misnomer for that reason. The correct word is *Vollmachtsstimmrecht,* but at the moment these words are used synonymously.

76. See von Falkenhausen (1966), p. 71.

77. See von Falkenhausen (1966), p. 70.

78. See Kübler (1994), p. 13 and Gessler (1965), p. 344.

tions to hide their true returns, strengthen the general assembly of share-holders vis-à-vis the management board—especially its director. The law also mandated greater oversight and control of management by the supervisory board, greater dispersion of share ownership, improved access to company information for small shareholders, and even regulation of industrial groups (Konzern).[79]

One of the major changes of the 1965 law (AktG 65) concerned the process of proxy voting via banks. Under the new law, banks were allowed to cast votes as a proxy only when they received a written authorization (*schriftliche Vollmacht*) (§ 135 I AktG 65). Valid for up to fifteen months, the authorization could be given for all or only part of a customer's portfolio and could be revoked anytime (§ 135 II AktG 65). The shareholder could now stay anonymous, and banks offering to perform proxy voting had to offer customers the opportunity to provide specific instructions on how to vote (§ 128 II AktG). Likewise, the banks also had to inform their customers how the bank intended to vote. In the absence of customer instructions, the bank could vote according to its own plan (§ 135 V AktG, § 128 II AktG).

Recent Reforms. As important as the 1965 reform was, it left the banks with widespread and easy access to corporate control rights. Pressure for reform began to build anew as Germany's postwar economic miracle waned. By the 1990s, not long after reunification with the East, Germany slid into recession, and political debates focused once again on the power of banks in Germany's corporations. As a result, the government enacted three new laws to modify the existing shareholder law (AktG): specifically, the 1998 law on control and transparency in corporations (KonTraG 98), the law on registered shares and facilitation of voting rights (NaStraG 01), and the law on transparency and publicity (TransPubG 02). Political and public debates continue over further legislative changes in these areas.

The new laws stipulated some important alterations of corporate ownership and control, especially regarding the use of registered shares and the exercising of proxy voting rights. In the latter case, current law allows banks to take proxy voting authorization for an unlimited time but requires the proxy holder to inform shareholders yearly both of their option to revoke the authorization and of the opportunity for alternative representation. In an effort to avoid conflicts of interests, banks now also must create an organizational division of managers who prepare voting plans separate from other divisions of the bank—in particular, lending divisions. As further safeguards against conflicts of interest, banks must also inform their customers about personal linkages, such as bank employee membership on supervisory boards or major equity holdings in pertinent companies.

79. See Hopt (1996b), p. 210.

Furthermore, banks must also inform shareholders if the bank is a member of a consortium that prepared an initial public offering (IPO) or any issue of shares for a company in question. Notably, banks are not obliged to provide these services at all—but if they offer to cast votes in general, they are now required to offer the services to all customers (*Kontrahierungszwang*). This last provision aims to prevent banks from avoiding instructed votes in favor of only unrestricted voting rights.

The most recent regulations to be set in place (TransPubG 02) require corporations to declare whether they comply with the so-called "Corporate Governance Codex." They strengthen the supervisory board by increasing the information provision to that body; strengthen the general assembly of shareholders, among other things, by granting greater control over the distribution of profits; and specifically identify new ways for companies to communicate with shareholders and the market, for example, by broadcasting major meetings on television or via the internet. The underlying intent of this law was to bring the German corporate system into line with international standards and thereby increase the attractiveness of German firms in world markets. As further recommendations of the commission on corporate governance (chaired by T. Baums) remain under discussion, the situation bears continued monitoring.[80] Whether Germany will retain a relationship-oriented system of corporate ownership and governance remains to be seen. Whether such a system is desirable, or has in fact been widespread in Germany, is another question.

4.4 Consequences of German Patterns of Corporate Ownership and Control

Many have argued that poor legal protection of minority stockholders has led to the concentrated ownership found in Germany. Such concentration can affect firms in a variety of ways, though the theoretical issues are less than clear-cut. One possible benefit from concentrated ownership is better monitoring of management and improved performance. But ownership concentration could also permit block holders to reap private benefits at the costs of minority shareholders. Private benefits of control, as noted by Leuz, Nanda, and Wyoscki (2003), range from perquisite consumption to the transfer of firm assets to other firms owned by insiders or their families. Block holders seek to protect their private benefits, benefits that appear to be enjoyed only by insiders.

The available empirical evidence casts some doubt on these interpreta-

---

80. Proposals include measures to increase supervisory and management board liability and more generally to strengthen disclosure rules and informational rights of shareholders. Other possible adjustments include restricting supervisory board members to a maximum of five supervisory board positions and establishing a central database of information on all corporations (see Bundesregierung 2001).

tions. Dyck and Zingales (2002) find a relatively small private benefit in Germany as compared to other countries. And, while there does seem to have been an ongoing concentration process from the end of World War II until the 1980s, but for the codetermination laws, there was no weakening in minority shareholder protection. Thus, the German pattern is not explained well by changes in shareholder protection. The civil law tradition also provides a weak explanation at best because the German legal tradition remains fundamentally one of civil law throughout. History suggests a wide range of political movements that seem to go much farther in explaining the German case.

Despite the obvious pattern of ownership concentration in Germany, it is difficult to conclude much about the effects of this structure on corporate performance. Köke (2002) finds that ownership concentration in combination with fierce product market competition increases productivity growth. Other authors, including Cable (1985), find a clear relationship between ownership concentration and corporate performance. Lehmann and Weigand (2000) argue that the relationship depends on the type of owner. Gorton and Schmid (2000) also find a clear relationship. Edwards and Nibler (2000) argue that minority shareholders gain benefits from an increase in ownership concentration, though this, however, does not hold for nonbank firms and public-sector bodies. They also find that the presence of second and third large shareholders is generally beneficial, except, again, for nonbank firms. This could point to a conflict of interests that Iber (1985) also describes.

Another question is of a more dynamic nature: Audretsch and Elston (1997) pose the question as to whether the German system is capable of financing new and innovative firms. The question remains—is there truly a negative impact on the firm or economy level, even though the stock markets have clearly lost considerable ground since the interwar years? Franks and Mayer hold that while patterns of ownership do differ markedly between German companies on the one hand and U.K. and U.S. firms on the other, corporate control is similar. They also find little relation between concentration of ownership and the disciplining of management in poorly performing firms, and between the type of concentrated owner and board turnover (Franks and Mayer 2001, p. 974).

These findings for the recent period echo the historical findings for Germany overall: in the two decades before World War I, when the German economy combined large-scale, universal banking with active markets, managerial turnover was highly sensitive to the performance of firms.[81]

---

81. See Fohlin (2006). These findings stem from the regression of managerial board turnover on various indicators of firm performance (return on assets [ROA], dividends, and dividend-adjusted stock returns) plus a series of control variables and indicator variables for various subpopulations, such as firms with and without stock market listings and firms with and without bank directors on their boards.

Moreover, firms with listings on the Berlin stock exchange—that is, those that were most likely to be owned by external shareholders rather than founding families or other block holders—changed management even more in response to poor performance. In general, listed firms performed better, earning higher ROA and paying far higher dividends.

4.5   Concluding Remarks

This paper patches together the sometimes-spotty evidence on the structure of corporate ownership and control in Germany since the beginning of free incorporation (1870) and demonstrates several ups and downs that correspond largely to manifold political, legal, and economic events and crises. The discussion raises several particularly important points, summarized here.

4.5.1   Historical Patterns

- Corporate governance institutions—executive and supervisory boards—remained quite underdeveloped in Germany until the last quarter of the nineteenth century. Boards were generally small and grew little over the pre–World War I period.
- Universal banks had significant but not overwhelming presence in the governance of German corporations during this period of rapid heavy industrialization and economic expansion (roughly 1895–1912). Similarly, industrial firms played only a small role in the ownership and governance of other nonfinancial firms. Notably, financial firms, especially the large banks, did own shares in other banks and subsidiaries and did sit on the boards of those banks.
- Bank involvement in corporate ownership appears to have arisen largely out of active bank involvement with securities issues, particularly of listed firms. Substantial holdings were rare, though earlier universal banks (e.g., Discontogesellschaft in the 1850s) did sometimes unwillingly hold large stakes that could not be sold off for a period of time.
- Bank involvement in corporate control through interlocking directorates is closely related to firm size, sector, securities issue, and stock market listing. Control rights appear to have been granted largely via proxy voting for customers who deposited bearer shares with the bank.
- The combination of commercial, investment, and brokerage services within individual banking institutions may have facilitated the networking of bank and firm supervisory boards.
- Traditional explanations of German bank-firm relationships that focus on bank intervention in investment decisions and direct monitoring of debt contracts find little support in the available empirical analysis.

4.5.2 Comparisons with Modern Germany

- German corporate ownership continues to be often very concentrated, but nonfinancial firms appear to be more heavily involved in ownership of other nonfinancial firms than they were before WWI.
- Modern patterns of bank involvement in corporate ownership and control are remarkably similar to those of the late industrialization period. The war period, roughly 1915–1945, was probably an aberration from long-run patterns. Contrary to popular myth, banks do not—and never did—control most of the corporate economy. But they do participate actively—as they always have—in the ownership and control of a notable minority of corporations. Bank involvement continues to relate significantly to dispersion of corporate ownership, firm size, securities issue, and stock market listing—all pointing at proxy voting for customers depositing shares with the bank.

In light of these patterns, I argue that political, social, and economic factors constitute the proximate causes of change. Moreover, combining recent evidence offered in the corporate control literature with my own study of an extensive range of German corporations from the pre-WWI period, I argue that German ownership structures have not, in times of stability, produced the negative consequences predicted in much of the "law and finance" literature.[82] Indeed, the long-run perspective on Germany—particularly the wide swings in corporate and industrial concentration, along with positive findings on corporate performance in the pre-WWI and post-WWII eras—casts doubt on the notion that civil law traditions per se consistently undermine market functioning. In the German case, the string of disastrous political institutions and movements in the aftermath of World War I, culminating in the Nazi regime, dismantled the rich, highly functioning, hybrid financial system of the Second Empire. The postwar political and legal climate, one that continues to suppress the liberal tradition of the pre–World War I era, seemingly prevents the old dual system from reemerging.

References

Adams, Michael. 1994. Die Usurpation von Aktionärsbefugnissen mittels Ringverflechtung in der "Deutschland AG." *Die Aktiengesellschaft* 39 (4): 148–58.
———. 1999. Cross holdings in Germany. *Journal of Institutional and Theoretical Economics* 155:80–109.

---

82. Evidence on the period between 1918 and 1970 or so is sorely lacking, though new efforts are underway to fill this major gap.

Albach, Horst, and Heinz-Peter Kless. 1982. Personelle Verflechtungen bei deutschen Industrieaktiengesellschaften. *Zeitschrift für Betriebswirtschaft* 52 (10): 959–77.

Aoki, Masahiko. 1988. *Information, incentives, and bargaining in the Japanese economy.* New York: Cambridge University Press.

Audretsch, David, and Julie Ann Elston. 1997. Financing the German Mittelstand. *Small Business Economics* 9:97–110.

Baums, Theodor. 1996. Vollmachtstimmrecht der Banken Ja oder Nein? *Die Aktiengesellschaft* 41 (1): 11–26.

Baums, Theodor, and Christian Fraune. 1995. Institutionelle Anleger und Publikumsgesellschaft: Eine empirische Untersuchung. *Die Aktiengesellschaft* 40 (3): 97–112.

Baums, Theodor, and B. Frick. 1999. The market value of the codetermined firm. In *Employees and corporate governance,* ed. M. M. Balir and M. J. Roe, 206–35. Washington, DC: Brookings Institution Press.

Becht, Marco, and Ekkehard Boehmer. 2003. Voting control in German corporations. *International Review of Law and Economics* 23:1–29.

Becht, Marco, Patrick Bolton, and Ailsa Röell. 2002. Corporate governance and control. In *Handbook of the economics of finance,* Volume 1A, *Corporate finance,* ed. G. M. Constantinides, M. Harris, and R. M. Stulz, 1–109. Amsterdam: North-Holland.

Beckerath, Erwin von, ed. 1956. *Handwörterbuch der Sozialwissenschaften.* Stuttgart: Gustav Fisher Verlag.

Benelli, Guiseppe, Claudio Loderer, and Thomas Lys. 1987. Labor participation in corporate policy making decisions: West Germany's experience with codetermination. *Journal of Business* 60:553–75.

Beyer, Jürgen. 2002. Deutschland AG a.D.: Deutsche Bank, Allianz und das Verflechtungszentrum großer deutscher Unternehmen. MPIfG Working Paper no. 02/4. Cologne, Germany: Max Planck Institute für Gesellschaftsforschung, March.

Boehmer, Ekkehart. 2000. Business groups, bank control, and large shareholders: An analysis of German takeovers. *Journal of Financial Intermediation* 9:117–48.

Böhm, Jürgen. 1992. *Der Einfluß der Banken auf Großunternehmen.* Hamburg: Steuern und Wirtschaftsverlag.

Bokelmann, Bettina. 2000. *Personelle Verflechtungen über Aufsichtsräte: Aufsichtsratsmitglieder mit hauptberuflicher Vorstandsfunktion.* Frankfurt: Lang.

Brickwell, Daniel M. 2001. Zu den Einflusspotenzialen der Großbanken. PhD diss., Freie Universität Berlin.

Brockhage, B. 1910. Zur Entwicklung des Preuss-Deutschen Kapitalexports. *Schmollers Jahrbuch,* Heft 148.

Bundesregierung. 2001. Kurzfassung des Berichts der Regierungskommission "Corporate governance." http://www.bundesregierung.de

Buss, Georg. 1913. *Die Berliner Börse von 1685–1913.* Berlin: Gedenktage der ersten Versammlung im neuen Hause.

Cable, John. 1985. Capital market information and industrial performance: The role of West German banks. *Economic Journal* 95:118–32.

Calomiris, Charles. 1995. The costs of rejecting universal banking: American finance in the German mirror, 1870–1914. In *Coordination and information,* ed. N. Lamoreaux and D. Raff, 257–315. Chicago: University of Chicago Press.

Cameron, Rondo E. 1961. *France and the economic development of Europe.* Princeton: Princeton University Press.

Chandler, Alfred D. 1990. *Scale and scope: The dynamics of industrial capitalism.* Cambridge, MA: The Belknap Press of Harvard University Press.

Chirinko, Robert, and Julie Ann Elston. 1998. Finance, control, and profitability: An evaluation of German bank influence. Economics working paper no. 28. Washington, DC: American Institute for Contemporary German Studies.

Däbritz, Walther. 1931. *Gründung und Anfänge der Disconto-Gesellschaft Berlin.* Leipzig: Duncker und Humblot.

Deutsche Börse. 1992. Annual report. Deutsche Börse AG.

Deutsche Bundesbank. Various years. Capital market statistics (statistical supplement to monthly report 2). Frankfurt: Knapp.

Deutsche Bundesbank. 1976. *Deutsches Geld- und Bankwesen in Zahlen, 1876–1975.* Frankfurt: Knapp.

Deutsches Aktien-Institut (DAI). Various years. *Factbook.* Frankfort on the Main: DAI.

Diamond, Douglas. 1984. Financial intermediation and delegated monitoring. *Review of Economic Studies* 51:393–414.

Dunlavy, Colleen. 1998. Corporate governance in late 19th-century Europe and the U.S.: The case of shareholder voting rights. In *Comparative corporate governance: The state of the art and emerging research,* ed. Klaus J. Hopt, Hideki Kanda, Mark J. Roe, Eddy Wymeersch, and Stefan Prigge. Oxford: Clarendon Press.

Dyck, Alexander, and Luigi Zingales. 2002. Private benefits of control: An international comparison. Center for Economic Policy Research Discussion Paper no. 3177, Center for Research in Securities Prices Working Paper no. 535, and Harvard Program on Negotiation Working Paper.

Edwards, Jeremy, and Nibler, Marcus. 2000. Corporate governance in Germany: The role of banks and ownership concentration. *Economic Policy* 32:239–68.

Emmerich, Markus. 2000. *Die historische Entwicklung von Beschlussverfahren und Beschlusskontrolle im Gesellschaftsrecht der Neuzeit unter besonderer Berücksichtigung des Aktienrechts.* Berlin: Duncker and Humblot.

Engberg, Holger L. 1981. *Mixed banking and economic growth in Germany, 1850–1931.* New York: Arno Press.

Ernst, Christian. 2001. *Die Aktionärsstruktur deutscher und amerikanischer Unternehmen. Ein internationaler Vergleich.* Ulm: Verlag Ulmer Manuskripte.

Faccio, Mara, and Larry H. P. Lang. 2002. The ultimate ownership of Western European corporations. *Journal of Financial Economics* 65:365–95.

Falkenhausen, Bernhard Freiherr von. 1966. Das Bankenstimmrecht im neuen Aktienrecht. *Die Aktiengesellschaft* 11 (3): 69–79.

———. 1967. *Verfassungsrechtliche Grenzen der Mehrheitsherrschaft nach dem Recht der Kapitalgesellshaften (AG und GmbH).* Karlsruhe, Germany: C. F. Müller.

Feldenkirchen, Wilfred. 1979. Banken und stahlindusrie im Ruhrgebiet: Zur Entwicklun ihrer Beziehungen 1873–1914. In *Bankhistoriches Archiv* 2:27–52.

———. 1991. Banking and economic growth: Banks and industry in the nineteenth century and their changing relationship during industrialization. In *German industry and German industrialisation,* ed. W. R. Lee, 116–47. London: Routledge.

Fey, Gerrit. 2000. *Unternehmenskontrolle und Kapitalmarkt: Die Aktienrechtsreformen von 1965 und 1998 im Vergleich.* Stuttgart: Lucius and Lucius.

Fohlin, Caroline. 1997. Universal banking networks in pre-war Germany: New evidence from company financial data. *Research in Economics* 51:201–25.

———. 1998. Relationship banking, liquidity, and investment in the German industrialization. *Journal of Finance* 53:1737–58.

———. 1999a. Capital mobilization and utilisation in latecomer economies: Germany and Italy compared. *European Review of Economic History* 2:139–74.

———. 1999b. The rise of interlocking directorates in imperial Germany. *Economic History Review* 52 (2): 307–33.

―――. 1999c. Universal banking in pre–World War I Germany: Model or myth? *Explorations in Economic History* 36:305–43.

―――. 2002a. Corporate capital structure and the influence of universal banks in pre–World War I Germany. *Jahrbuch für Wirtschaftsgeschichte* 2:113–34.

―――. 2002b. Regulation, taxation, and the development of the German universal banking system. *European Review of Economic History* 6:221–54.

―――. 2006. *Financial empire: New perspectives on finance, governance, and performance in the German industrialization.* New York: Cambridge University Press, forthcoming.

Franks, Julian, and Colin Mayer. 2001. Ownership and control of German corporations. *Review of Financial Studies* 14 (4): 943–77.

Gebhard, H. 1928. Die Berliner Börse von den Anfängen bis zum Jahre 1896. PhD diss., University of Erlangen.

Gerschenkron, Alexander. 1962. *Economic backwardness in historical perspective.* Cambridge, MA: Harvard University Press. Quoted in Fohlin 2005.

―――. 1968. *Continuity in history and other essays.* Cambridge: Belknap Press of Harvard University Press.

Gessler, Ernst. 1965. *Aktiengesetz: Kommentar.* Munich: F. Vahlen.

Gömmel, Rainer. 1992. Entstehung und Entwicklung der Effektenbörse im 19. Jahrhundert bis 1914. In ed. H. Pohl, *Deutsche Börsengeschichte,* 133–207. Frankfurt: Knapp.

Gorton, Gary, and Frank A. Schmid. 2000. Universal banking and the performance of German firms. *Journal of Financial Economics* 58:29–80.

Gottschalk, Arno. 1988. Der Stimmrechtseinfluß der Banken in den Aktionärsversammlungen von Großunternehmen. *WSI-Mitteilungen* 5:294–304.

Haas, Wolfgang. 1994. *Die Auswirkungen des Betriebsübergangs insbesondere bei der Fusion von Kapitalgesellschaften auf Betriebsvereinbarungen.* Mainz: Dissertations Druck.

Handbuch der deutschen Aktiengesellschaften. Various years. Berlin: Verlag für Börsen- und Finanzliteratur.

Henning, Friedrich-Wilhelm. 1992. Börsenkrisen und Börsengesetzgebung von 1914 bis 1945 in Deutschland. In *Deutsche Börsengeschichte,* ed. H. Pohl, 211–90. Frankfurt: Knapp.

Hilferding, Rudolph. 1910. *Das Finanzkapital.* Vienna: Wiener Volksbuchhandlung. Translated by T. Bottomore in 1981 as *Finance capital.* Boston: Routledge and Kegan Paul.

Hopt, Klaus J. 1996a. Corporate governance und deutsche Universalbanken. In *Corporate governance: Optimierung der Unternehmensführung und der Unternehmenskontrolle im deutschen und amerikanischen Aktienrecht,* ed. D. Feddersen. Cologne: Otto Schmidt.

―――. 1996b. *Gesellschaftsrecht.* 4th ed. Munich: C. H. Beck.

―――. 1998. The German two-tier board: Experience, theories, reforms. In *Comparative corporate governance: The state of the art and emerging research,* ed. K. J. Hopt, H. Kanda, M. J. Roe, E. Wymeersch, and S. Prigge, 227–58. Oxford: Clarendon Press.

Horn, N. 1979. Aktienrechtliche Unternehmensorganisation in der Hochindustrialisierung (1860–1920): Deutschland, England, Frankreich und die USA im Vergleich. In *Recht und Entwicking der Großunternehmen im 19. und frühen 20. Jahrhunder,* ed. N. Horn and J. Kocka. Göttingen: Vandenhoeck und Ruprecht.

Hüffer, Wilhelm. 2002. *Theodizee der Freiheit: Hegels Philosophie des Geschichtlichen Denkens.* Hamburg: Felix Meiner.

Iber, Bernhard. 1985. Zur Entwicklung der Aktionärsstruktur in der Bundesrepublik Deutschland (1963–1983). *Zeitschrift fuer Betriebswirtschaft* 55 (11): 1101–19.

James, Harold. 1986. *The German slump: Politics and economics, 1924–1936.* Oxford: Oxford University Press.

Jeidels, Otto. 1905. Das Verhältnis der Deutschen Großbanken zur Industrie. Leipzig: Duncker und Humblot.

Jenkinson, Tim, and Alexander Ljungqvist. 2001. The role of hostile stakes in German corporate governance. *Journal of Corporate Finance* 7:397–446.

Joly, Hervé. 1998. *Großunternehmer in Deutschland: Soziologie einer industriellen Elite 1933–1989.* Leipzig: Leipziger Universitätsverlag.

Kaserer, Christoph, and Ekkehard Wenger. 1997. *The German system of corporate governance: A model which should not be imitated.* Washington, DC: American Institute for Contemporary German Studies.

Kennedy, William P. 1987. *Industrial structure, capital markets and the origins of British economic decline.* London: Cambridge University Press.

Klein, Sabine. 2000. *Familienunternehmen: Theoretische und empirische Grundlagen.* Wiesbaden: Gabler.

Klein, Sabine, and Christine Blondel. 2002. Ownership structure of the 250 largest listed companies in Germany. Working Paper. Paris: INSEAD.

Kocka, Jürgen. 1978. Entrepreneurs and managers in German industrialisation. In *The Cambridge economic history of Europe, the industrial economies: Capital labor and enterprise. Part one: Britain, France, Germany, and Scandinavia,* ed. P. Mathias and M. M. Postan, 492–589. Cambridge, MA: Cambridge University Press.

Köke, Jens. 2001. New evidence on ownership structures in Germany. *Kredit und Kapital* 2:257–92.

———. 2002. Determinants of acquisition and failure: Evidence from corporate Germany. *Structural Change and Economic Dynamics* 13:457–84.

———. 2003. The market for corporate control in bank-based economy: A governance device. *Journal of Corporate Finance* 10 (1): 53–80.

Kübler, Friedrich. 1994. *Gesellschaftsrecht.* 4th ed. Heidelberg: C. F. Müller Juristischer Verlag.

Kunze, W. 1926. *Der Aufbau des Phoenix-Konzerns.* Frankfurt.

Laux, Frank. 1998. *Die Lehre vom Unternehmen an sich: Walther Rathenau und die aktienrechtliche Diskussion in der Weimarer Republik.* Berlin: Duncker und Humblot.

Lavington, F. E. 1921. *The English capital market.* London: Methuen.

Lehmann, Erik, and Jürgen Weigand. 2000. Does the governed corporation perform better? Governance structures and corporate performance in Germany. *European Finance Review* 4:157–95.

Leuz, Christian, Dhananjay Nanda, and Peter D. Wyoscki. 2003. Earnings management and investor protection: An international comparison. *Journal of Financial Economics* 69:505–27.

Levy-Leboyer, M. 1964. *Les banques europeennes et l'industrialisation internationale dans la premiere moitié du XIX siecle.* Paris: Presses Universitaires de France.

Liefmann, Robert. 1921. *Beteiligungs und Finanzierungsgesellschaften.* Jena: Gustav Fisher Verlag.

Loeb, Ernst. 1896. Kursfeststellung und Maklerwesen an der Berliner Effektenbörse. In *Jahrbücher für Nationalökonomie und Statistik,* vol. 11.

———. 1902. Das Institut des Aufsichtsrat. *Jahrbuch für National-Ökonomie* 2 (23).

März, E. 1968. *Österreichische Industrie und bankpolitik in der Zeit Franz Josephs I.* Frankfurt: Europa Verlag.

Mayer, Colin. 1988. New issues in corporate finance. *European Economic Review* 32:1167–88.

Meier, Johann Christian. 1993. *Die Entstehung des Börsengesetzes vom. 22, Juni 1896.* Studien zur Wirtschafts und Sozialgeschichte, Vol. 9. St. Katharinen, Germany: Scripta Mereaturae Verlag.

Menke, Joachim. 1988. Die Kapitalbasis deutscher Aktiengesellschaften vom Beginn der Reformdiskussion im Jahre 1924 bis zum Erlass des Aktiengesetzes von 1937. PhD diss., University of Kiel, Germany.

Nussbaum, Arthur. 1910. *Kommentar zum Boersengesetz fuer das Deutsche Reich.* Munich.

Perlitz, Manfred, and Frank Seger. 1994. The role of universal banks in German corporate governance. *Business and the Contemporary World* 6 (4): 49–67.

Pfannschmidt, Arno. 1995. Mehrfachmandate in deutschen Unternehmen. *Zeitschrift für Betriebswirtschaft* 65 (2): 177–203.

Pohl, Manfred. 1982. *Konzentration in deutschen bankwesen, 1848–1980.* Frankfurt: Knapp.

Pohl, Hans, and Wilhelm Treue, eds. 1978. Die Konzentration in der deutschen Wirtschaft seit dem 19. Jahrhundert. Zeitschrift für Unternehmensgeschichte. Suppl. no. 11.

Pollard, Sidney, and Dieter Ziegler. 1992. Banking and industrialization: Rondo Cameron twenty years on. In *Finance and financiers in European history, 1880–1960,* ed. Y. Cassis, 17–38. New York: Cambridge University Press.

Pross, Helge. 1965. *Manager und Aktionäre in Deutschland: Untersuchungen zum Verhältnis von Eigentum und Verfügungsmacht.* Frankfurter Beiträge zur Soziologie 15. Frankfurt: Europäische Verlagsanstait.

Riesser, Jakob. 1911. *Die deutschen Großbanken und ihre Konzentration [The German great banks and their concentration].* Washington, DC: National Monetary Commission. (Orig. pub. 1910)

Roe, Mark J. 1999. German codetermination and German securities markets. *Columbia Journal of European Law* 5:199–211.

———. 2003. German codetermination and German securities markets. Harvard Law School. Working paper.

Santucci, Tanja. 2002. Extending fair disclosure to foreign issuers: Corporate governance and finance implications for German companies. *Columbia Business Law Review* 2002:499–539.

Schreyögg, Georg, and Papenheim-Tockhorn, Heike. 1995. Dient der Aufsichtsrat dem Aufbau zwischenbetrieblicher Kooperationsbeziehungen? *Zeitschrift für Betriebswirtschaft* 65 (2): 205–30.

Schulz, W. 1994. *Das deutsche Börsengesetz: Die Entstehungsgeschichte und wirtschaftlichen Auswirkungen des Börsengesetzes von 1896.* Frankfurt: Peter Lang.

Schumpeter, Joseph. 1930. *Theory of economic development.* Cambridge: Harvard University Press.

Siegrist, Hans. 1980. Deutsche Großunternehmen vom späten 19: Jahrhundert bis zur Weimarer Republik. *Geschichte und Gesellschaft* 6:60–102.

Sombart, Werner. 1954. *Die deutsche Volkswirtschaft im neunzehnten Jahrhundert.* Berlin: Georg Bondi.

Statistisches Jahrbuch für das deutsche Reich. 1908–15. Berlin: Statistisches Bundesamt.

Stiglitz, Joseph E., and A. Weiss. 1981. Credit rationing in markets with imperfect information. American Economic Review 71:393–410.

Stillich, O. 1909. *Die Börse und ihre Geschäfte.* Berlin.
———. 1924. *Die Banken, ihre Arten und ihre Beziehung zur Gesellschaft.* Berlin.
Svejnar, Jan. 1981. Relative wage effects of unions, dictatorship and codetermina-
    tion: Econometric evidence from Germany. *Review of Economics and Statistics*
    63:188–97.
Svejnar, Jan. 1982. Codetermination and productivity: Evidence from the federal
    republic of Germany. In *Participatory and self-managed firms,* ed. D. Jones, and
    Jan Svejnar. Lexington, MA: Heath.
Tilly, Richard. 1966. *Financial institutions and industrialization in the Rhineland,
    1815–1870.* Madison: University of Wisconsin Press.
———. 1994. Banks and industry: Lessons from history. University of Münster,
    Germany. Working Paper.
Wallich, Paul. 1905. *Die Konzentration im deutschen Bankwesen.* Stuttgart: Union
    deutsche Verlagsgesellschaft.
Wehler, Hans Ulrich. 1987. *Deutsche Gesellschaftsgeschichte.* Munich: C. H. Beck.
Wellhöner, Volker. 1989. *Großbanken und Großindustrie im Kaiserreich.* Göttingen:
    Vandenhoek-Ruprecht.
Wengenroth, Ulrich. 1992. Iron and steel. In *International banking, 1870–1914,* ed.
    V. I. Bovykin and R. Cameron. New York: Oxford University Press.
Wessel, Horst A. 1990. Finanzierungsprobleme in der Gründungs und Aus-
    bauphase der Deutsch-Österreichischen Mannesmannröhrenwerke A.G. 1890–
    1907. In *Zur Geschichte der Unternehmensfinanzierung,* ed. D. Petzina, 119–71.
    Berlin: Schriften des Vereins für Sozialpolitik, Vol. 196.
Whale, P. Barrett. 1930. *Joint-stock banking in Germany.* London: MacMillan.
Wiener, Fritz A. 1905. *Die Börse.* Berlin: Puttkammer und Mühlbrecht.
Wilhelmini, Hans. 1965. Das neue Aktiengesetz. *Die Aktiengesellschaft* 10 (6): 153–
    55.
Wójcik, Dariusz. 2001. Change in the German model of corporate governance: Ev-
    idence from block-holdings, 1997–2001. University of Oxford, School of Geo-
    graphy and the Environment. Working paper.
Ziegler, Dieter. 2000. Die wirtschaftsbürgerliche Elite im 20. Jahrhundert: Eine
    Bilanz. In *Großbürger und Unternehmer: Die deutsche Wirtschaftselite im 20.
    Jahrhundert,* ed. D. Ziegler, 7–29. Göttingen: Vandenhoeck und Ruprecht.

Comment   Alexander Dyck

The German economic system has performed remarkably well since industrialization. Firms and entrepreneurs have benefited from access to
deep financial markets. Combining together the private sector's borrowing
from banks and the capitalization in equity markets, Rajan and Zingales
(1998) estimate that Germany has the second-deepest market for providing external finance to firms among forty-one countries in the world. Apparently, these financial resources have been deployed efficiently. Wurgler
(2000) estimates that Germany has the highest efficiency of investment in

Alexander Dyck is an associate professor of finance at the Rotman School of Management,
the University of Toronto.

the world (proxied by sensitivity of industry investment to value added). And such efficiency is reflected in high rates of per capita GDP growth and the maintenance of a high level of income per capita since the 1870s (e.g., Maddison 1991).

It is worthwhile repeating these numbers, because if we were told just about the features of the German corporate sector, such outcomes are not what most of us would predict. Here, the traditional characterization goes, is a country dominated by very concentrated ownership structures, with weak protections for investors (one out of six, according to LaPorta et al. 1998), very limited equity markets, an almost complete absence of takeovers, and an overwhelming influence of the banking sector, among both listed and unlisted firms. Is this traditional characterization accurate, and, if so, why didn't this change over time, as it did in countries like the United States and Britain, and how could such corporate structures not lead to significant inefficiency rather than the positive indicators described above?

Caroline Fohlin, in this chapter on the history of corporate ownership and control in Germany, provides some new evidence and a new perspective on some of these questions. Fohlin sidesteps questions of economic performance and links between ownership and performance to focus on the evolution of corporate ownership and the role of relationship banking. She concentrates, in particular, on increasing our understanding of the growth of the corporate sector prior to World War I. And she brings to bear a wealth of data and a determination to rely on data-led conclusions.

The paper's first contribution is to provide some additional information on the origin and evolution of concentrated ownership structures in Germany. Fohlin reports that the entrepreneurs who founded many German corporations in the latter half of the nineteenth century retained significant corporate stakes for themselves and families. The story, interestingly, is then one of gradual dispersion of ownership and professionalization of management. But this dispersion halts rather abruptly at a high level of concentrated ownership in the interwar period. Perhaps more surprising is that in the postwar period, including when the Allies were in control, concentration persists and is stable until the most recent years.

Fohlin provides some evidence as to the driving forces behind these changes, for example, pointing to the emergence and wholesale endorsement of shares with multiple voting rights—whereby more than 50 percent of AGs in 1925 and 40 percent in 1934 had such voting rights—as an ingredient in maintaining concentrated control, as well as political changes in the Nazi era. But, unfortunately, other factors escape examination. Why didn't the founding families sell out? Why didn't those with significant minority stakeholders (like banks) sell out? Was it fear of tax implications of sales, or was it something else? These questions remain for the future.

The real heart of the paper, though, is not about concentrated ownership but about banks. Here Fohlin, step by step, asks the reader to reevaluate the notion that German banks controlled German corporations, through their direct equity stakes, their seats on supervisory boards, or the additional voting power arising from their holding of proxy voting rights for small shareholders. The target in this discussion is clearly a view in some of the literature that suggests overwhelming power of the great banks in corporate decision making.

Fohlin correctly asks us to center our attention on the voting power of banks. This is important, as certain major decisions are put to a vote at the general assembly as well as being the forum to appoint members of the managing board and the supervisory board. On the basis of extensive data collection efforts in the pre–World War I period she concludes that the great banks had 7–11 percent of their assets in the form of corporate equities, with provincial banks having slightly lower levels. And she points to more detailed studies of specific great banks to show that these levels likely are based on more significant stakes in a small number of firms. Fohlin incidentally tells a fascinating story of how in the latter half of the nineteenth century banks acquired equity stakes, almost incidentally, as a result of their investment banking arms and their lending operations. Here underwriting operations led firms to accumulate stakes, and these stakes multiplied in times of crisis when debt was exchanged for equity.

But her analysis does little to convince those without any vested interest in the debate about the power of banks to change their prior estimate that banks play an important role in corporate decision making. Focusing on equity stakes is likely to dramatically understate voting power. The most important reason for this is the traditional story of the free-rider problem faced by small shareholders. They cannot get sufficient reward, given their small stakes, to go through the effort to get informed and vote on corporate decisions, so anyone with a larger stake with a lower cost of getting informed (e.g., banks) is more likely to vote and have more effective voting power than is suggested by their stakes. In addition, in Germany there is the important fact that shareholders held bearer shares and that overtime banks offered services of holding those shares, and when they did so they held the proxy voting rights attached to these shares. This dramatically increased their voting power both in firms where they held equity stakes and in firms where they held no stakes.

The evidence on the composition of supervisory boards, which is where Fohlin directs our attention next, is a well-chosen sample to use to test for the power of banks, for it is a decision where votes will matter, and it is a decision where it is possible with effort to see whether banks get what they want, as measured by the identity of the board members. Again, Fohlin does an impressive job of accumulating and organizing data on board memberships in the pre–World War I period. And again, Fohlin's characterization of the data as revealing the weakness of the banks doesn't fit with my reading of the evidence.

To her, it is a reflection of weakness that "only two-thirds of the sampled firms fall into the attached category," meaning that in two-thirds of firms there is a board representative who shares a position on a firm and representation in a bank, that "half of the firms had a bank director sitting on their supervisory boards" and that "less than 22 percent of firms had a bank director as chair or vice chair." I guess my prior is just different from hers, as two-thirds with a connection, half with a direct member, and one-fifth with a commanding position suggests that the banks could use their voting power to protect their interests. This is significant bank involvement, and one suspects that if firms were ranked based on economic importance (e.g., just the top 100 companies) these percentages would increase, as the numbers do in the post–World War II period when Fohlin focuses on larger firms.

Also somewhat surprising since the discussion is of bank power is the lack of attention played to banks as providers of external finance to companies, and the relative importance of the vast stable of middle-sized companies, collectively called the *mittelstand*. Of course, through the provision of working capital and longer-term loans, banks have influence over companies. And this is only enhanced by the stable banking relationships where firms often established a near exclusive relationship with a specific bank, often called a *hausbank*. This influence of banks through their provision of external finance will of course be more important for the *mittelstand*, who lack the ability to raise finance through issuing equity, as well as finding it challenging to raise any bond financing.

So, to summarize, Fohlin successfully dislodges an extreme view of a domination of the corporate sector by the great banks, but based on this evidence a careful reader should do little to update prior estimates of the important role played by German banks in corporate life. While clearly not in absolute control, the evidence suggests a significant role indeed.

To finish, it is useful to return once again to the question of performance. While the evidence in this paper enriches our understanding, it also essentially confirms the traditional wisdom of the importance of concentrated ownership and banks in the German corporate sector. We are left with Fohlin's conclusion that "German ownership structures have not, in times of stability, produced the negative consequences predicted in much of the 'law and finance' literature." But we do not know why these structures weren't associated with worse performance. What, if anything, reduced the extent of pyramid structures that we associated with the worst corporate abuses? Did firms avoid the "stupid heir" problem of an incompetent next generation, and how did they do so? Why didn't banks use their dominant position on boards to protect their interests as debt holders or use this position to loot firms? What role has extensive product market competition (and an export orientation) played in limiting the potential extent of private benefits and agency costs for firms? And what role has bank competition played in avoiding the development of bad incentives in firms?

There is clearly room for more research here, to enrich our understanding and to alert us to gaps in our models and in our thinking. And good, careful historical research like this will be an important complement to the cross-sectional evidence that is the focus of much research today.

References

La Porta, Rafael, Florencio López-de-Silanes, Andrei Shleifer, and Robert Vishny. 1998. Law and finance. *Journal of Political Economy* 106 (6): 1113–55.

Maddison, Angus. 1991. *Dynamic forces in capitalist development.* New York: Oxford University Press.

Rajan, Raghuram G., and Luigi Zingales. 1998. Financial dependence and growth. *American Economic Review* 88 (3): 559–86.

Wurgler, Jeffrey. 2000. Financial markets and the allocation of capital. *Journal of Financial Economics* 58 (1–2): 187–214.

The Evolution of Concentrated Ownership in India
Broad Patterns and a History of the Indian Software Industry

Tarun Khanna and Krishna G. Palepu

5.1 Introduction

Concentrated ownership has been an important feature of the Indian private sector for the past seven decades. In this respect, India is no different from several other countries, including Canada, France, Germany, Japan, Italy, and Sweden. However, we show that, unlike in these countries, the identity of the primary families responsible for the concentrated ownership changes dramatically over time. In fact, by some measures the changes are even more dramatic than in a comparable set of U.S. data.

Concentrated ownership exists at any point in time because of institutional voids, the absence of specialized intermediaries in capital markets (Khanna and Palepu 1997, 2000c). However, if these concentrated owners are not exclusively, or even primarily, engaged in rent-seeking and entry-deterring behavior, there is no intrinsic reason why concentrated ownership is inimical to competition. Indeed, as a response to competition, we argue that at least some Indian families—the concentrated owners in question—have consistently tried to use their business group structures to launch new ventures. In the process they have either failed—hence the turnover in identity—or reinvented themselves.

Tarun Khanna is the Jorge Paulo Lemann Professor at the Harvard Business School. Krishna G. Palepu is the Ross Graham Walker Professor and senior associate dean, director of research, at the Harvard Business School.

We are grateful to Randall Morck for coordinating and spearheading the project on the history of concentrated ownership at the National Bureau of Economic Research and for seminar audiences who commented on earlier drafts of this paper in Cambridge and Fontainebleau. The Division of Research at the Harvard Business School financed this work. All errors remain our own.

Further, family-owned business groups, typically diversified over several industries, can coexist with specialist firms focused on a particular industry. We demonstrate this through an examination of the history of India's globally competitive software industry. This is an intriguing setting in which to explore the role of concentrated ownership since it is the setting least hospitable to the advantages that groups might have. We argue that groups' generally advantageous access to capital and talent through internal markets—when external markets do not work as well—offers less of an advantage, if any, in this setting. Here groups are also least able to influence regulations, since the sector is one of the few left untouched by vestiges of India's famed regulatory miasma, the License Raj. Yet it turns out that concentrated ownership, in the guise of business groups, plays a defining and prominent role even in this inhospitable setting, and does so in a way that is not inimical to entry from de novo entrepreneurs. We interpret the privately successful and socially useful persistence of groups in the software industry as a lower bound on the persistence of concentrated ownership in the economy writ large.

The rest of the paper is organized as follows. Section 5.2 begins with a sweeping overview of dominant business groups in India over the past century. We show that, while particular families have acted as concentrated owners at each of three points in time in the past seven decades, the identity of these families has changed drastically over this time period. We then consider two, not mutually exclusive, explanations for the persistence of concentrated ownership. The first (section 5.3) is political relationships between dominant families and the power structure. The second (section 5.4) is a process of entrepreneurship by the dominant families. From these sections we conclude that it is difficult to tell a story of concentrated ownership resulting purely in stasis and rent seeking. Section 5.5 characterizes changes in India during the last decade as moving toward less regulation and government intervention and toward freer markets. Even in this setting, we point out that family-based business groups continue to thrive. Finally, in section 5.6, we study the software industry.

5.2   A Brief History of Corporate Ownership in India

While there has been organized economic activity in India for hundreds of years, it was relatively fragmented until the advent of the British Raj. Under the Mughals, from approximately 1100 AD to 1650 AD, there was only a semblance of a "national market." The Mughals were content with tax revenues and tributes that they received as a result of their power and therefore did not rely on the merchant classes. The fragmentation and demise of the Mughal empire marked the advent and coexistence of dozens of smaller principalities, each of whom came to rely on local merchants

Table 5.1	**Origin of concentrated ownership over the years**			
	1900s	1950s	1960s	1990s
Period	Preindependence	Postindependence	License Raj	Liberalization
Representative business group	Tata, Birla	Goenka, Khaitan	Ambani	Wipro/Infosys Ranbaxy/DRL
Factor underlying rise	Ethnic community	Transfer of assets	Playing the license game	Advent of markets

and local financiers to sustain their princely states. Thus were created the nuclei of several prominent family businesses.

The British empire gradually filled the void left by the Mughals. And British merchants set up trading businesses in India after the East India Company lost its monopoly on trade with India, giving rise to the creation of several large trading houses.

Table 5.1 offers a bird's-eye view of the different factors underlying the emergence of family-based business groups over the past century. We list representative business groups that arose in each of four different time periods (though the Tata and Birla groups predate 1900), as well as a generic factor that described the rise of that type of group at that time.

By the early 1900s, in addition to the British trading houses, a number of indigenous business groups had come into prominence. Whether this happened in an atmosphere inimical to the rise of indigenous enterprise (Swamy 1979), indifferent to it (Das 2000, chap. 5), or supportive of it (Ferguson 2002) is a matter of continuing controversy.

Subsequently, the Indian economy underwent several phases of major structural changes after India achieved independence from Britain in 1947. In the first phase, in the 1950s, the assets controlled by the British trading houses were transferred to Indian owners. In the second phase, from the late 1950s through the 1970s, the Indian government intervened in the economy through a variety of measures, which collectively came to be known as the "Licence Raj." Finally, there was an economic reform era, which began with small steps of deregulation in the 1980s and picked up speed in the 1990s following a major economic crisis in 1991.

The next two subsections show that concentrated ownership persisted in India over several decades but that the identity of the concentrated owners changed over time quite drastically.

5.2.1   The Persistence of Concentrated Ownership

Remarkably, while the economy was governed by these significantly different regimes over time, family business groups continued to dominate the Indian corporate landscape. Table 5.2 shows comparative statistics on the Indian state-owned enterprises (SOEs, or public-sector companies)

Table 5.2   Comparison of Indian public sector, private sector, and multinational
                   corporations, 1993

Expressed in ratio	Private sector vs. public sector[a]	Indian private sector vs. all foreign companies[b]
No. of corporations	16.92	17.18
Sales	1.53	4.32
Profits	2.22	3.87
Assets	1.21	9.07
Equity	0.51	6.71

Source: Author's calculations from a database maintained by the Center for Monitoring the Indian Economy (CMIE), Bombay, India. Found in Tarun Khanna, "Modern India," HBS Case No. 979-108 (Boston: Harvard Business School Publishing, 1997, p. 7).

[a]The private sector is composed of Indian group-affiliated firms (IG) and Indian nongroup affiliated firms (IN). The public sector is composed of central and state government owned firms (P). This column depicts, for each category, the ratio (IG + IN)/P (i.e., there are 16.92 times as many companies in the private sector as there are in the public sector, but total sector sales are only 1.53 times greater than total public-sector sales).

[b]This column depicts the Indian private sector relative to foreign firms (F), i.e., the ratio (IG + IN)/F.

and exchange-listed private-sector companies, and multinational companies (MNCs) operating in India, as of 1993.[1] The ratio of number of traded private-sector companies to state-owned companies was approximately seventeen to one. Thus, there were far more traded private-sector companies than public-sector companies. However, public-sector companies were on average significantly larger than traded private-sector companies. Revenues of all traded private-sector companies were only 1.5 times the revenues of state-owned companies; similarly, assets of traded private-sector companies were only 1.2 times the assets held by the public-sector companies. More strikingly, the total amount of equity capital in traded private-sector companies was only 0.51 times the equity in public-sector companies. Thus, private-sector companies, while large in number, were more fragmented and relied on far less equity investment relative to the public-sector companies.

Table 5.2 also compares the traded Indian private-sector companies with multinational companies operating in India as of 1993. For each MNC operating in India, there were approximately seventeen exchange-listed private-sector companies. Domestic private companies were 4.3 times larger than MNCs in sales, 9 times in terms of assets, and 6.7 times in terms of equity. Thus, MNCs played a relatively minor role in the Indian corporate sector as of 1993.

Within the indigenous private sector, a distinction should be drawn between group-affiliated companies and unaffiliated companies. The term

1. This date is drawn from Khanna (1997).

group deserves discussion. Hazari (1966), in a classic study of Indian business groups, defined a group as the "area over which a decision-making authority holds sway" (p. 7). The decision-making authority in question was almost always a family, though it could be a close-knit ethnic community as well. The area of control in effect was almost always a very diversified range of businesses. Hazari started his work by saying that it was "based on the proposition that the business group, not the individual joint stock company, is the unit of decision and, therefore, of economic power" (see his preface). Earlier work concurred. For example, another influential study opined that the study of concentration of economy power is "unreal if divorced from a study of communities" (Gadgil 1951, p. 29; the reference is to ethnic communities).[2] Hazari's study provided an influential evaluation of the extent to which business groups had exercised monopoly power (he concluded that they had). Subsequent regulators and policymakers (e.g., Dutt Report 1969) built on this work to demonstrate that the control that Hazari used as the defining feature of groups was often exercised through nonequity channels—for example, through family ties or through manipulation of the boards of directors.

In 1993, a total of 1,113 group companies were publicly listed on one of India's several stock exchanges. Postindependent India also gave birth to a large number of new companies that went on to become publicly listed on the country's stock exchanges. In 1993, there were 1,539 publicly listed nongroup companies. These companies were in part a result of the government's policy of restricting existing companies from expanding their capacity. Promoters of these companies were also able to launch these businesses with relatively small amounts of own equity, thanks to the access to capital from state-owned financial institutions and public capital markets.

Table 5.3 compares group and nongroup companies listed on the Bombay Stock Exchange (BSE) as of 1993.[3] The sample consists of 567 group firms and 437 nongroup firms for which the necessary data were available. The group affiliates are members of 252 different groups. Ninety-five percent of the groups have five or fewer affiliates traded on the BSE, and the largest group (the Tata group) has twenty-one affiliated companies traded on the BSE. The mean (median) sales of group affiliates is 1,411 (666) million Indian rupees. This is significantly larger than the mean (median) sales of unaffiliated firms, which is 366 (217) million rupees. The mean (median) age of group firms, which is 28.3 (22) years, is also significantly larger than mean (median) age of unaffiliated firms. The mean (median) Tobin's q for

2. In recent work, Khanna and Rivkin (2002) have demonstrated econometrically that business groups in Chile can, at best, be identified only partially on the basis of equity interlocks. Director ties and common owner ties play an important role in delineating what Chileans (regulators and participants in financial markets) deem to meaningfully be part of a business group. Thus control is exercised, de facto, in ways very similar to India.

3. These data are from Khanna and Palepu (2000).

Table 5.3   Comparison of group and nongroup firms listed on the Bombay Stock
                   Exchange in 1993

Variable	Group firms		Nongroup firms	
	Mean	Median	Mean	Median
Sales (millions of rupees)	1,411	666	366	217
Age (years)	28.3	22	19.8	14
Tobin's q	1.39	1.14	1.37	1.06
Ownership by foreign institutional investors (%)	10.1	2.3	7.4	0.9
Ownership by Indian institutional investors (%)	15.6	13.3	11.3	6.5
Ownership by insiders (%)	31.9	31.3	20.8	17.1
Directors' ownership (%)	5.7	1.1	14.2	10.7
Top fifty owners excluding the above categories (%)	4.9	3.2	7.6	5
No. of firms	567	567	437	437

Source: Khanna and Palepu 2000a, p. 276. Data obtained from the Center for Monitoring the Indian Economy (CMIE) for 567 affiliates of 252 different groups and for 437 unaffiliated firms traded on the BSE.

Notes: The summary statistics in this table are based on 1993 values. Tobin's q is defined as (market value of equity + book value of preferred stock + book value of debt)/(book value of assets). Sales are measured in millions of rupees, with an approximate exchange rate at this time of U.S. $1.00 = Rs 30.00. Age measures number of years since incorporation. Foreign institutional ownership aggregates ownership of foreign corporations as well as that of foreign financial intermediaries. Domestic institutional ownership aggregates ownership in the hands of all state-run financial intermediaries. Insider ownership includes the stakes held by group family members and by other group firms and measures stakes held by insiders for nongroup firms. Directors' ownership captures the ownership of nonfamily directors. Top fifty ownership captures the largest shareholders not included in the aforementioned categories. Group membership is based on definitions of groups from CMIE (see text of paper for comments). The mean and median values for all the variables except for the mean value of Tobin's q and change in Tobin's q are significantly different between the group and nongroup firms at the 5 percent significance level.

group firms was 1.39 (1.14), insignificantly different from the mean (median) value of 1.37 (1.06) for the nongroup firms.

The total sample has the following mean (median) ownership structure: foreign institutions, 8.9 (1.6) percent; domestic institutions, 13.9 (10.2) percent; insiders, 27.1 (26.5) percent; directors, 9.4 (3.4) percent; top fifty owners excluding the above categories, 6.21 (4.0) percent. The remainder is held by dispersed shareholders. Relative to unaffiliated firms, group firms, on average, have significantly higher percentages of foreign and domestic institutional ownership, and higher insider ownership.

In summary, the Indian corporate sector as of the early 1990s had the following profile: a little more than 100 relatively large state-owned enterprises and more than 2,500 smaller publicly traded private-sector companies, roughly equally split between group affiliated and nongroup companies. In the private sector, companies affiliated with business groups, with concentrated family ownership, accounted for a substantial proportion of assets.

5.2.2   The Lack of Persistence of the Identity of Concentrated Owners

While there has been a significant persistence in the phenomenon of concentrated family ownership in India over much of the twentieth century, there was less persistence in the actual composition of the top business groups themselves. The Tata group remained the largest Indian group during the entire sixty-year period on which we present data below. But other leading groups from the pre-Independence era (e.g., British groups such as Martin Burn, Andrew Yule, Inchcape) did not persist in the form they then had. Several new business houses rose to prominence during this period, including the Thapar group in the 1950s and 1960s, the Ambani group in the 1970s and 1980s, and the Wipro and Munjal groups in the 1980s and 1990s. Thus, the history of the modern Indian corporate sector is characterized by both a persistence of concentrated ownership at the aggregate level and a significant lack of persistence of dominance at the individual business group level.

To demonstrate this point more formally, we analyzed the persistence of dominance for Indian business groups over the past sixty years. This is based on size rankings (assets) for the fifty largest business groups compiled by Dr. Gita Piramal of Mumbai, India, for the years 1939, 1969, and 1999 (table 5.4). Her rankings have themselves been compiled from miscellaneous historical sources, including, but not limited to, various government reports commissioned by the government of India at various points in time. Note that the rankings are not of firms but of groups. That is, all firms controlled by a single entity, typically a family, are treated as a single economic unit. As a benchmark against which to compare our analysis of the persistence of Indian groups, we also amass market value–based rankings of the fifty largest U.S. firms at identical time periods. These data are compiled from Compustat and are provided in table 5.5.

Consult table 5.6 for some summary statistics. Our first observation is that the Indian data show considerable turnover in ranks. Thirty-two out of fifty of the top groups in 1969 were not in the top-fifty list in 1939. Forty-three of the top groups in 1999 were not in the top-fifty list in 1969. This flux in the list of largest entities is greater than that in the United States in comparable time periods, where twenty-eight and thirty-seven firms enter the top-fifty U.S. list in 1969 and 1999, respectively. The comparison is all the more dramatic because the Indian data measure groups, which are collections of firms, while the U.S. data measure firms. (In other words, individual firms within Indian groups almost certainly would have greater turnover than that suggested by the data on groups.)

Of the eighteen groups that remain in the top-fifty list in the 1939–69

Table 5.4   **Top 50 Indian business groups over the years**

Ranking	1939 Group	Assets	1969 Group	Assets	1997 Group	Assets
1	Tata	62.42	Tata	505.36	Tata	37,510.80
2	Martin Burn	18.02	Birla	456.40	B.K.-K.M. Birla	19,497.94
3	Bird	12.40	Martin Burn	153.06	Reliance	19,345.59
4	Andrew Yule	12.38	Bangur	104.31	RPG	9,664.12
5	Inchcape	10.70	Thapar	98.80	Essar	9,593.78
6	E.D. Sassoon	9.56	S. Nagarmull	95.61	O.P. Jindal	5,456.10
7	ACC	8.68	Mafatlal	92.70	MAC	4,782.10
8	Begg	5.75	ACC	89.80	L.M. Thapar	4,434.09
9	Oriental Tel. & Elec.	5.60	Walchand	81.11	Ispat	4,425.35
10	Dalmia	5.51	Shriram	74.13	Group USHA	4,210.87
11	Jardine	5.33	Bird Heilgers	68.62	Lalbhai	4,112.44
12	Wallace Bros.	5.33	J.K. Singhania	66.84	Videocon	3,737.87
13	Birla	4.85	Goenka	65.34	Lloyd Steel	3,705.27
14	Wadia	4.70	Sahu Jain	58.75	Bajaj Group	3,415.87
15	Duncan	4.54	Macneill & Barry	57.28	Williamson Magor	3,351.62
16	Finlay	3.84	Sarabhai	56.72	Hari S. Singhania	3,275.80
17	Scindia	3.66	Scindia	55.99	K.K. Birla	3,094.90
18	Killick	3.51	Lalbhai	51.20	Torrent	3,077.23
19	Kilburn	3.23	Killick	51.08	Hinduja	2,967.20
20	Sarabhai	3.00	ICI	50.06	Arvind Mafatlal	2,862.94
21	Brady	2.82	Andrew Yule	46.75	Murugappa Chettiar	2,840.62
22	Rajputana Textiles	2.80	TVS	43.83	Escorts	2,642.22
23	Steel Bros.	2.77	Kirloskar	43.02	Mahindra	2,633.70
24	MacLeod	2.67	Parry	41.93	G.P. Goenka	2,630.43
25	Walchand	2.61	Jardine Hend.	40.19	C.K. Birla	2,530.32
26	Lawrie	2.55	Mahindra	38.58	Kirloskar	2,622.61
27	Thackersey	2.56	Bajaj	35.28	Nagarjuna	2,511.54
28	Mafatlal	2.45	Simpson	32.92	Jaiprakash Group	2,442.48
29	BIC	2.38	Seshasayee	32.72	Indo Rama	2,440.88
30	Lalbhai	2.33	Gill Arbuthnot	29.02	U.B. Group	2,414.65
31	Kettlewell	2.23	Kilachand	27.22	Kalyani	2,395.29
32	Gillanders	2.16	Dalmia J.	26.72	G.E. Shipping	2,357.59
33	Shri Ram	2.16	Naidu G.V.	26.41	Oswal Agro	2,342.36
34	Swedish Match	2.05	Shapoor Pallonji	26.36	Wadia	2,334.97
35	Octavious Steel	2.00	Turner Morrison	23.15	Manu Chhabria	2,286.02
36	Shaw	1.95	Ruia[a]	22.40	T.S. Santhanam	2,214.06
37	C.V. Mehta	1.90	Naidu V.R.	21.55	S.K. Birla	2,080.11
38	Mangaldas	1.80	A&F Harvey	21.33	Vijaypat Singhania	1,979.88
39	Daga	1.67	Wadia	20.56	Modern	1,967.85
40	Forbes	1.59	Shaw Wallace	20.14	M.M. Thapar	1,963.47
41	Harvey	1.50	Murugappa	20.07	Ranbaxy	1,875.71
42	Dunlop	1.42	Modi	19.38	SRF/A. Bharat Ram	1,863.26
43	Spencer	1.38	RamaKrishna	18.79	Finolex	1,712.73
44	Williamson	1.23	Chinai	18.36	Godrej	1,695.97
45	Harrisons	0.89	Jaipuria	18.24	BPL	1,691.57
46	Henderson	0.63	Kamani	18.05	Vinod Doshi	1,519.89
47	C. Jehangir	0.42	Rallis	17.94	Usha Martin	1,514.06

Table 5.4   (continued)

Ranking	1939 Group	Assets	1969 Group	Assets	1997 Group	Assets
48	Turner	0.39	Thackersey	17.19	OWM	1,412.76
49	Provident	0.34	Thiagaraja	16.55	Amalgamation	1,353.47
50	J. Warren	0.22	Swedish Match	15.70	Vardhman	1,282.40

Sources: 1939 data compiled from Markovits (1985), pp. 192–93. Significant exclusions (for miscellaneous reasons) from the list are BAT, Thomas Duff, J. Taylor, Assam Company, Burmah Oil, E. Peek, and Hukumchand. As we are concerned only with Indian groups and as rankings are not relevant for the purpose of this article, we can safely assume that all the key Indian business houses have been accounted for in the preindependence period in the table. 1969 data compiled from Report of the Industrial Licensing Policy Inquiry Committee, 1969. 1997 data compiled from *Business Today.*

Notes: Assets in RsCr. Normally sales or market cap are the accepted international criteria for ranking business performance. However, assets have been taken in this case for the sake of uniformity. Accurate, reliable, and complete data for Indian business houses by sales are not available pre-1984.
[a]Ruia in 1969 list should not be confused with Essar Ruia of the 1997 list.

period (fifty less thirty-two), sixteen change ranks, while only two have ranks that remain unchanged. Further, ten of the eighteen groups whose ranks change do so dramatically (that is, by more than ten ranks in either direction). In contrast, a smaller proportion of the firms whose ranks change in the U.S. top-fifty list in 1939–69 do so dramatically (five out of twenty-two). The proportion of radical rank changers is also higher in India during the 1969–99 period (three out of seven) than in the United States in the same period (five out of thirteen).

Note also that the turnover in the ranks of Indian groups is greater in the second thirty-year window than in the first. This is important because part of the turnover in the 1939–69 period was due to transfer of assets from British ownership to Indian ownership at the end of the British colonial rule of India. The turnover in the 1969–99 period reflects less unusual circumstances.

Finally, an analysis of the groups or firms that are born in any period suggests that they do not generally leapfrog to the top of the rankings, nor do the top groups or firms in any period dramatically fall off the rankings. A regression of ranks on "births" and on a variable that measures whether the group or firm is going to "die" (that is, exit the top rankings) the following period reveals positive and significant coefficients on both variables. That is, firms born in a particular period have higher ranks (are smaller), and firms that are about to die in the next period have higher ranks (are smaller). The regression reveals point estimates that are quite similar for both the Indian top-fifty group and U.S. top-fifty firm rankings, hinting at some underlying similarity in the competitive processes underlying such turnover.

This pattern of corporate ownership in India is inconsistent with a pure

Table 5.5   Top U.S. firms over the years

Ranking	1939	1969	1999
1	AT&T	International Business Machs	Microsoft
2	General Motors	AT&T	General Electric
3	DuPont	General Motors	Cisco Systems
4	Standard Oil (New Jersey)	Eastman Kodak	Wal Mart Stores
5	General Electric	Standard Oil (New Jersey)	Exxon Mobil
6	Union Carbide	Sears Roebuck	Intel
7	U.S. Steel	Texaco	Lucent Technologies
8	International Nickel (Canada)	Xerox	International Business Machs
9	Texas Co.	General Electric	Citigroup
10	Sears Roebuck	Gulf Oil	America Online
11	Coca Cola	Minnesota Mining & Mfg	American International Group
12	SH Kress & Co.	DuPont	SBC Communications
13	Allied Chemical & Dye	Avon Products	AT&T
14	Procter & Gamble	Coca Cola	Oracle
15	Eastman Kodak	Mobil Oil	Home Depot
16	Kennecott Copper	Procter & Gamble	Merck
17	Standard Oil (Indiana)	Standard Oil (California)	MCI WorldCom
18	Chrysler	Polaroid	Procter & Gamble
19	Socony-Vacuum Oil	Merck	Coca Cola
20	FW Woolworth Co.	Atlantic Richfield	Nortel Networks
21	RJ Reynolds	American Home Products	Dell Computer
22	Consolidated Edison (New York)	International Telephone & Telegraph	Johnson & Johnson
23	Commonwealth Edison	Standard Oil (Indiana)	Bristol Myers Squibb
24	United Gas Improvement	Johnson & Johnson	Pfizer
25	Standard Oil (California)	International Nickel (Canada)	Sun Microsystems

#			
26	Chesapeake & Ohio Railway	GTE	QualComm
27	Pennsylvania Railroad	Shell Oil	Hewlett Packard
28	Norfolk & Western Railway	Ford Motor	Yahoo
29	Westinghouse Electric & Mfg	Burroughs Corp.	EMC
30	Montgomery Ward	JC Penney	Bell Atlantic
31	American Can	Pacific Telephone & Telegraph	Motorola
32	International Harvester	Caterpillar Tractor	BellSouth
33	Bethlehem Steel	Weyerhaeuser	Bank of America
34	Anaconda Copper Mng	Westinghouse Electric	TimeWarner
35	American Tobacco	Georgia Pacific	Morgan Stanley Dean Witter
36	General Foods	Union Carbide	Daimlerchrysler AG Stuttgart
37	Roan Antelope Copper Mines	Goodyear	Texas Instruments
38	United Fruit	Chas. Pfizer & Co.	Berkshire Hathaway
39	JC Penney	Bristol Myers	American Express
40	Pacific Telephone & Teleg	Honeywell	BP Amoco PLC
41	Liggett & Myers Tobacco	RCA	Eli Lilly
42	Parke-Davis	Warner-Lambert Pharmaceutical	Warner-Lambert
43	Pacific Gas & Electric	Dow Chemical	DuPont
44	Union Pacific Railroad	General Foods	GTE
45	Phelps Dodge	Imperial Oil	Wells Fargo
46	North American	Creole Petroleum	Tyco International
47	Phillips Petroleum	Pacific Gas & Electric	AT&T
48	Commercial Investment Trust	SS Kresge	Chase Manhattan
49	Public Svc	RJ Reynolds	Federal National Mortgage
50	William Wrigley Jr.	U.S. Steel	Schering Plough

Source: Compustat, based on market values.

Table 5.6   Persistence of dominance of Indian groups and U.S. firms over sixty years

	Indian groups		U.S. firms	
	1939–69	1969–99	1939–69	1969–99
Birth	32	43	28	37
RankUp	6	3	7	5
RankDown	10	3	15	6
RankUp10	5	2	1	2
RankDown10	5	1	4	3
RankSame	2	1	0	2

Notes: Birth refers to the number of groups or firms that are "born" in the thirty-year window in question—that is, that enter the top 50 list for that country in that time window, given that they were not part of the list in the previous thirty-year window (there are no groups or firms that exit and then re-enter the top 50 list in either country). RankUp refers to the number of groups or firms that rise in the asset-based size rankings. A smaller rank measures a larger group or firm, with rank = 1 and rank = 50 being the largest and the smallest of the top-50 groups or firms in each country in each time period. RankUp10 counts the groups or firms whose rank rises by more than 10. RankDown and RankDown10 are defined analogously. RankSame counts the number of groups or firms whose rank remains unchanged during that thirty-year period.

corporate ownership entrenchment story. We will turn, in each of the next two sections, to considering two potential explanations for concentrated ownership in an emerging economy like India (Ghemawat and Khanna 1998; Khanna 2000). The first explanation has to do with rent-seeking behavior by prominent business families with strong political connections. Under this hypothesis, business families control business groups to extract personal gains, and they attain their position through directly unproductive economic activities and through their influence over government policies and actions. The second hypothesis is that family business groups arise as a result of their entrepreneurial activity, which is in short supply in emerging economies such as India with significant market failures and institutional voids (Khanna and Palepu 1997, 1999, 2000b,c).

5.3   Political Connections and Rent-Seeking Behavior

In this section, we first describe how business-government relationships evolved over the relevant time frame for this paper, and then we consider particular groups' relationships with the government, with a view to uncovering whether or not there is systematic evidence to support the political connections story for persistence of concentrated ownership.

5.3.1   Shifting Contours of Business-Government Relations

A close relationship between business and government had existed for quite some time in India. During the British colonial rule, the interest of British companies was naturally favored over the interest of Indian business houses (Piramal 1998, pp. 162, 230). As the movement for freedom from the British Raj gathered momentum in the 1920s and 1930s, close relationships developed between Indian businesses and leaders of the political movement for India's independence. Underscoring their symbiotic relationship in a letter, as he was building steam for India's independence movement in 1927, Mohandas Gandhi told G. D. Birla, a prominent Indian businessman, "I am ever hungry for money" (cited in Piramal 1991).

The pragmatic collaboration between the new Indian government and the business community to build modern India continued in the immediate aftermath of independence (1947 to 1960). For example, Hindalco and Telco collaborated with the government of India to set up Hindustan Aeronautics Limited to develop the aviation sector in India. However, the relationship soured in the 1960s as Indian government, under the leadership of Prime Minister Jawarharlal Nehru, moved the country's economic policies toward socialism. This period, often characterized as the License Raj, began with the government's desire to curb big business houses and to directly intervene in economic activities through public-sector corporations.

Several prominent government commissions, including the Mahalanobis Committee of 1964, the Monopolies Inquiry Commission of 1965, the R. K. Hazari Committee of 1966, and the Industrial Licensing Policy Committee of 1969, were established during this period. These commissions documented evidence that big business houses were exerting significant influence on Indian economy and that they were exploiting growth opportunities through favorable access to finance and government permits. These commissions were followed by the creation of the Monopolies and Restrictive Trade Practices Act (MRTP) and the Foreign Exchange Regulation Act (FERA), and the nationalization of the largest private-sector banks. These policy changes, spearheaded by the government of Prime Minister Indira Gandhi, imposed strict government controls on the private sector's ability to pursue growth opportunities, access domestic finance, or collaborate with foreign technology or business partners. The FERA also required that multinational companies operating in India divest their ownership so that a majority of the ownership in the Indian operations was held by Indian shareholders.

In the mid-1980s, under the government of Prime Minister Rajiv Gandhi, a gradual move toward deregulation began. These reforms relaxed some of the MRTP and import restrictions and freed up some of the economy from licensing requirements. Despite these changes, the Indian economy grew at a fairly modest rate during this entire period, culminating in a foreign exchange payment crisis in the early 1990s. This crisis led to a dramatic deregulation and liberalization of the Indian economy. Under the Congress Party government of Prime Minister Narasimha Rao, and then subsequently under the Bhartiya Janata Party government of Prime Minister Atal Behari Vajpayee, the MRTP and FERA Acts were repealed, several sectors of the economy, including telecommunications, commercial aviation, and banking—previously reserved for the public sector—were opened to the private sector, and import duties were dramatically reduced.

5.3.2 Business Groups and Government

As the contours of business-government relations shifted in India during the past half century, there were complex shifts in relationships between individual business groups and the government in power. Different groups occupied different positions of favoritism at different times. There is evidence that these political connections played an important role in the rise and fall of different business houses. But it is interesting that the groups that remained dominant throughout did so despite ebbs and flows in their relationship with the government. Clearly proximity to government was not the only cause of their success.

Consider the House of Tata. J. R. D. Tata, in the preindependence period, presided over a group that was, in fact, quite reliant on government contracts. Before World War I, Tata Steel would not have started without a guarantee from the British government for Indian Railways, nor would Tata Steel have grown into the largest integrated steel factory in the British Commonwealth without such government contracts. And Tata Steel was protected by tariffs against German and Japanese, if not British, steel (Hazari 1986). The Tatas adopted a neutral stance in the Independence movement. As Piramal (1998, p. 481) puts it, in the British Raj, the Tata Group "bristled" with knights.

But by 1960, the group remained India's largest even though it had fallen out of favor, as it was opposed to the socialist philosophy of Prime Minister Nehru. Reacting to the various government commissions suggesting that large business houses manipulated and abused the licensing system, J. R. D. Tata is reported to have cynically said, "Yesterday in Parliament, they called me a monopolist with 'great concentration of power.' I wake up every morning and I am supposed to say, 'I have great concentration of power. Whom shall I crush today? A competitor or a worker in my factory or the consumer?' . . . No dear boy I am powerless. . . . I cannot decide how much to borrow, what shares to issue, at what price, what wages or bonus to pay, and what dividend to give. I even need the government's permission for the salary I pay to a senior executive" (quoted in Das 2000, pp. 168–69). Indeed, far from manipulating the licensing system to its advantage, the Tata group reportedly made 119 new proposals for expansions in (existing or de novo) businesses between 1960 and 1989, and every one of them was rejected (Das, p. 93). Further, some of the Tatas' assets were nationalized, most famously Tata's airline. And J. R. D. Tata contributed to the Swatantara Party's coffers to create an alternative to Nehru's Congress since the former stood for less regulation than that espoused by the latter.

Let us turn to the Birlas next. Under G. D. Birla, the group supported the Independence movement financially. Sarojini Naidu, herself a prominent figure in the India of that era, famously said, "it took all Birla's millions to enable Gandhi to live in poverty. And he gave for free" (Piramal 1998). The group rose to prominence in the postindependence period and by 1969 became the second-largest Indian business group. However, under the government of Prime Minister Indira Gandhi, the Birla group became the target of criticism for its manipulation of the licensing system, as it was targeted by the Hazari reports and criticized for preempting licenses—that is, for applying for licenses that it then failed to use. Indeed G. D. Birla's successor, Aditya Birla, was allegedly sufficiently disappointed by being, in his view, unfairly tarnished by the government's allegations, that he simply shifted his expansion plans overseas. So much so that, between 1970 and 1995, the Birlas had established plants in Egypt, Indonesia, Malaysia, the Philippines, and Thailand, with overseas activity accounting for a third of their overall business, and the world's leading position in viscose staple fiber, palm oil, and insulators, and the world's sixth-largest position in the manufacture of carbon black (Das 2000, p. 176). The implication is that the size and prominence of the group is due to the Birlas' entrepreneurial tendencies' finding expression around the licensing restrictions at least in part, rather than by embracing them and engaging purely in rent-seeking activities.

All this is not to deny that rent seeking existed. Clearly there were abuses in the system; far too many indicators are consistent with this. See recently Bertrand, Mehta, and Mullainathan (2002), for example, and our own earlier work (Khanna 2000; Khanna and Palepu 2000a) on the dark side of business groups.[4] But it is a mistake to tar the entire corporate sector with the same broad brush. As the caselets above suggest, some of the groups remained dominant despite sustained periods of falling out of favor. Others directed their energies to expansion outside India rather than manipulating the licensing system.

Further, note the following possibility of possibly misplaced emphasis and incorrect inference. We do not contest that the License Raj was bad for economic development. As Hazari (1986, p. xxiv) put it, "the abuses and failures are no longer, as the Italians say, mere *apertura;* they are wide-open doors." But whether concentrated ownership was the cause of this miasma is less clear. The "Kafkaesque maze of controls" (Bhagwati 1993) had more to do with a heady fascination with the intellectual cuisine of the London School of Economics and Cambridge (Hazari 1986), and the wonder of the then-ascendant Soviet planning machine, than with the actions of India's

---

4. De Long (2001) suggests, based on an analysis of growth rates of several countries, that the effects of the License Raj might have been overstated (or, at least, the negative effects were offset by other positive factors).

dominant family businesses. Business groups had to either manipulate it, as some did, or invent themselves around it, as did others.

5.4 Entrepreneurship in the Context of Institutional Voids

In an emerging economy, many institutions necessary for the functioning of product markets, labor markets, and financial markets are typically missing or underdeveloped. In India, this was certainly true under colonial rule. Indeed, the heavy state intervention in the economy in the first few decades of independence was justified by successive governments as a way to deal with these market failures.

As Khanna and Palepu (1997, 1999, 2000b,c) and others (Leff 1976, 1978; Strachan 1976) argue, business groups could be seen as a private-sector response to the institutional voids in the economy. Groups often perform functions traditionally performed by market institutions in more mature markets. One such important function is the provision of something akin to venture capital, consisting of identifying promising new business opportunities in the economy and exploiting them with in-house risk capital and managerial talent, which are traditionally in short supply in the economy at large. This, in turn, leads to the observed predominance of the business group type of organizational form in emerging economies.

It is important to note that this hypothesis only implies that economies such as India will have a preponderance of business group–type organizations. It does not necessarily imply that the same set of business groups will continue to be prominent in the economy over time. This continued success of a business group under this explanation depends on its ability to sustain its entrepreneurial nature over a long period of time. While some groups may succeed in this endeavor, others may fail. In this sense, the rise and fall of business groups over time in emerging economies is akin to the rise and fall of businesses in advanced economies.

The history of the Tata group provides a classic example of how some Indian business groups pursued new business opportunities successfully over time. Figure 5.1 shows the time line of the entry of the Tata group into various new businesses, from 1870 to 2001—textiles in 1874, the hospitality industry in 1902, steel in 1907, power in 1910, cement in 1912, soaps and toiletries in 1917, printing and publishing in 1931, aviation in 1932, chemicals in 1939, consumer electronics in 1940, commercial vehicles and locomotives in 1945, cosmetics in 1952, air-conditioning in 1954, pharmaceuticals in 1958, tea and coffee in 1962, information technology in 1968 (see section 5.6), watches and financial services in 1984, auto components in 1993, telecom services in 1994, passenger cars in 1998, retail in 1999, and insurance in 2001. Despite the remarkable diversity of these businesses, the group has been able to maintain a leading position in many, if not most, of the businesses it entered over time. It had to exit only a small handful of businesses

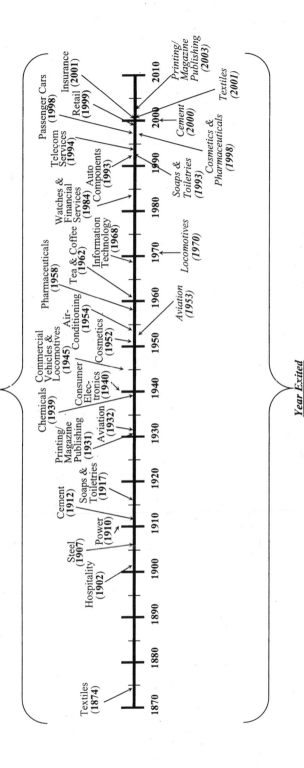

Fig. 5.1 Evolution of the Tata group, 1900–2003

Source: Tata Sons Private Limited, Mumbai, India.

in its history—aviation in 1953 (due to government nationalization), loco-motives in 1970, soaps and toiletries in 1993, cosmetics and pharmaceuti-cals in 1998, cement in 2000, textiles in 2001, and printing and publishing in 2003.[5]

The role played by the Tatas is exactly to fill the institutional void of ven-ture capital in these instances as well as to provide an exit mechanism to as-piring entrepreneurs in the absence of well-functioning public markets. For example, Tata Chemicals supported its engineers' efforts to innovate. In some instances, these engineers left to start up their own companies, and the Tatas had been known to buy out the results of these efforts subse-quently (see example in Piramal 1998, p. 473).

It is interesting that this process of entrepreneurship is often criticized in the media as being undisciplined and characterized by a failure to adhere to core competencies. This reflects a mistaken notion of what constitutes the "core competence," as it were. Here it is at least as much an ability to cir-cumvent institutional voids as it is some industry-specific knowledge. As N. A. Soonawala, a board member of Tata Sons, the main holding company of the Tatas, said to us in 1998 in response to criticisms by leading multi-national consulting firms at the time, "If everyone is told not to go into un-related businesses, how will the airlines, oil, and telecommunications in-dustries develop? The government has said that they can't do it. So there's a social benefit to all this diversification" (Khanna, Palepu, and Wu 1998).

An important feature of entrepreneurship in India is the reliance on the ethnic group to supplement family networks (Lamb 1976). The Marwari, Gujerati, and Parsi communities are, by far, the dominant business com-munities in India in recent decades, and even today. For example, these communities collectively controlled 62 of the 100 largest companies in 1989 (Piramal 1989). Other active communities include the Punjabis, Chet-tiars, and Maharashtrians.

These communities share their distinctive tenors. For example, Gujeratis were traditionally traders with countries in the Middle East and East Africa. Parsis, from the small minority Zoroastrian community in India, were most "Westernized" in their business outlook, and traditionally played the role of intermediaries with Europe. Marwaris, a demographically small segment originally from the state of Rajasthan in western India, have been the most geographically spread business community, pursuing businesses all over the country. By 2000, Das (2000, p. 174) quotes an estimate that says that the Marwaris controlled half the industrial assets of India.

Timberg (1978) chronicled the modus operandi of Marwari businesses. Traditionally, the great Marwari firms had networks spreading all over

5. There appears to have been a short-lived and aborted entry into shipping in the late 1890s. This effort, along with those of a number of other Indian entrepreneurs until the es-tablishment of Walhand Hirachand's Scindia shipping company, foundered when faced with the British-controlled shipping "conference" controlled by Inchcape and others.

Asia and deep into China. They relied on their own kin for information and for effective contractual enforcement. In our terminology, these ethnic networks were substitutes for institutional voids, and shared features with the networks used by the Genoese and Maghribi traders studied by Greif (1994) and by the Rothschilds. Famously, the Marwaris' simple and rigorous, if manual, cost-accounting systems provided a cost-effective means of financing that allowed them to stomach risks in a time of capital scarcity.

In pre-British and British India, the history of prominent business groups is characterized by the willingness of the successful members of each ethnic community to help spawn new members, sometimes even to compete with their existing businesses. For example, several prominent Marwari groups in existence today are spun off from the Birla group. Birlas have been known to actively encourage talented employees to pursue their own business opportunities, and sometimes even finance these new ventures. Several groups spun off the Birla group (e.g., Khaitan and Kejriwal, to cite just a couple) and continue to exist today (Piramal 1998, pp. 142–43). Kasturbhai Lalbhai, a prominent textile businessman, helped his ethnic group members with the technology of setting up textile mills. Walchand Hirachand Doshi actively promoted shipping companies, including direct competitors of his own, as part of the struggle against the British Raj (Piramal, pp. 162, 230). As Lamb (1976) puts it, the acts of entrepreneurship in British India were heroic, especially in view of the powerful interests arrayed against the entrepreneurs.

The entrepreneurship has continued in modern times and extends beyond expansion of product lines to institutional innovation. A good example is that of the Ambanis. A relatively recent entrant into the leading business groups, the flagship company, Reliance, is India's only entry into the Global Fortune 500. While many point to a close relationship with the government of Mrs. Indira Gandhi as being part of the reason for the company's initial success—founder Dhirubhai Ambani famously said he would "salaam" (salute) anyone to sell his ideas[6]—the fact remains that the group has developed world-class capabilities in managing large-scale capital intensive projects and is an innovative financier. Its most notable contribution to institutional innovation in India is perhaps the creation of an equity cult. As Das (2000, chap. 13) chronicles, Dhirubhai Ambani single-handedly mobilized small investors around the country in 1977 and listed on the Bombay and Ahmedabad stock exchanges when the dominant public financial institutions would not lend him capital. Between 1980 and 1985, the number of Indian shareholders went from one to four million, and fully 25 percent of these shareholders owned shares in Reliance, the Ambani company.

To recapitulate, we have considered two classes of explanations—rent-

6. The quotation is from *India Today,* 30 June 1985 (cited in Piramal 1991).

seeking behavior and entrepreneurial activity—to explain the dual phenomena of persistence of concentrated ownership but turnover in the identity of the concentrated owners. Both explanations have circumstantial evidence in favor of them. Superficial attempts to attribute data to one or the other of these explanations should be met with disdain. It is hard to believe, in particular, that rent seeking can provide a full explanation, especially of the shifting identity of concentrated ownership.

5.5   The Recent Evolution of Groups and Markets

The evidence presented to this point is consistent with the idea that Indian business groups with family and community ties arose historically, in part, due to the absence of well-developed financial markets. During the past three decades, financial markets in India have developed significantly, in part due to paradoxical consequences of policies aimed at other ends during the era of socialism, and in part due to direct attempts by the government aimed at market development during the more recent reform era.

Under the Foreign Exchange Regulation Act passed during the socialist era of the 1960s and 1970s, multinationals operating in India were required to reduce their ownership to below 40 percent and divest the rest to Indian investors. To comply with this requirement, many multinationals offered their shares to public investors through public offerings on the BSE. The issue prices were set by the Controller of Capital Issues, a government body, at book values that were often dramatically below economic values. As a result, individual investors were able to buy shares at very attractive prices in very good companies. These public offerings had a number of spillover effects. First, they created a culture of equity ownership in India on a large scale, because many retail investors were attracted to the opportunity of earning significant returns that were almost assured. Second, the process of listing these companies on the BSE resulted in the creation of an intermediation and market infrastructure—accounting and auditing professionals, financial analysts, investment bankers, and stockbrokers.

When India began to liberalize its economy in the 1990s, one of the key objectives of the government policy was to attract foreign institutional investors. To accomplish this, the government established the Securities and Exchange Board of India (SEBI), modeled closely after the U.S. Securities Exchange Commission. Following the establishment of SEBI, a number of significant capital market reforms were put in place: new regulations strengthening corporate disclosure and governance standards, new regulations and enforcement mechanisms to ensure orderly and fair trading practices on the country's stock exchanges, and the opening of the market to international financial intermediaries. Companies were allowed to float shares at market prices, rather than at the artificially low prices dictated by the Controller of Capital Issues. Finally, Indian companies were also allowed for the first time to list on international stock exchanges. All these changes resulted in significantly improved financial markets in India and enhanced the ability of entrepreneurs and established businesses to access domestic and international equity capital.

These changes, coupled with a significant deregulation of product markets, led to new opportunities and challenges for business groups. A number of first-generation entrepreneurs were able to tap into the capital markets to exploit new business opportunities. Prominent among them was the Reliance group, which raised vast sums of money on the BSE to finance its petrochemical ventures to become one of the largest enterprises in India. Reliance went on to become a diversified business group when it began to exploit new business opportunities thrown open with the deregulation of power and telecommunication sectors. This era also gave rise to a number of prominent companies in the software and pharmaceutical sectors—Infosys, Wipro, and Satyam Computer Services in software, and Ranbaxy and Dr. Reddy's in pharmaceuticals. Some of these companies are family controlled but professionally managed (Wipro, Satyam, Ranbaxy, and Dr. Reddy's); some are diversified (Wipro operating in consumer products and information technology); while others are focused in one sector (Infosys, Satyam, Ranbaxy, and Dr. Reddy's).

While the development of capital markets and the deregulation and globalization of the Indian economy have given rise to the birth of these new entrepreneurial firms, some of the old family business groups have also adapted and grown during this era. The most prominent among them is the Tata group, which continues to be the largest business group in India. The Tata group has been able to exploit many of the new business opportunities in software and telecom. Today, Tata Consultancy Services, one of the Tata group companies, is the country's largest information technology services company, and Tata Telecom is one of the largest telecommunication companies in India.

5.6 The Indian Software Industry

5.6.1 Why study the software industry?

The software services industry provides a lower bound on the relative advantage of family business groups over independent entrepreneurs in exploiting new opportunities for a number of reasons. First, the industry was very conducive to de novo entry because of low capital requirements, little government regulation on entry, and a relatively low level of minimum economic scale to achieve profitability. Further, the Indian government invested in elite technical institutions, such as the Indian Institutes of Technology and Indian Institutes of Management, and a large number of other engineering colleges. These institutions produced abundant talent, a critical input for the software services industry. Graduates of these institutions, relying on a recognized education brand, were more willing to work for de novo startups than for incumbent business groups. Finally, government policies restricting operations of multinationals such as IBM left plenty of opportunities for domestic entrepreneurs. Given all these factors, software services is one industry where individual entrepreneurs could compete effectively with the established family business houses of India. Further, business houses could not rely on any ability they might have had to exercise regulatory muscle, since there were no regulations to muscle into. Thus, the history of software industry, and the role of business groups in this industry, provide further evidence on why business groups play such an important role in India even today.

5.6.2   Origins of the Indian Software Industry

Until the mid-1960s, there was virtually no software development going on in India. Whatever software sold was bundled with computers sold by multinational companies like IBM. The early software development efforts focused on producing in-house applications for efficient use of these computers. Government policies attempted to encourage the growth of a domestic hardware industry through high import tariffs on hardware. State-owned hardware companies, such as the Electronic Corporation of India Limited, attempted to produce computers for domestic (academic and commercial) use, and these efforts included development of operating systems, compilers, and application packages. Most of these efforts, however, were not very successful.

Of course, many of the reasons to which modern observers attribute the success of today's Indian software industry—for example, low-cost talent, English language, and a tradition of entrepreneurship—did in fact exist prior to the 1960s. The fact that the industry did not, however, and the fact that the industry continues not to have made a mark in other low-cost, English-speaking countries suggests that these are certainly not sufficient conditions for the success of the Indian software industry.

It is instructive that the industry really got its start with the establishment in 1968 of Tata Consultancy Services (TCS), a wholly owned subsidiary of Tata Sons, itself the holding company of the Tata Group, a diversified business group and the epitome of concentrated ownership. According to Heeks (1996), TCS was the first commercial organization to subscribe to the export commitment–related terms under which the Indian government allowed the import of hardware. Tata's ostensible purpose was to allow its diverse companies to use computers in their operations. Toward this end, the company formed an alliance with Burroughs Corporation. Under this alliance, Burroughs would help secure U.S. clients for TCS; in return, TCS would act as an exclusive sales agent for Burroughs hardware in India. Based on this alliance, TCS secured its first U.S. client—the Detroit police department. Today TCS is the largest software services company in India, employing more than 19,000 software engineers. The company is privately held, fully owned by Tata Sons Limited, the apex of the Tata group companies.

But it was a serendipitous event that triggered the rise of TCS, having to do with the withdrawal of the incumbent, IBM, in 1978. IBM took this step in response to the FERA, which limited MNCs to a maximum of 40 percent ownership stake in their Indian subsidiaries and specified policies for access to foreign exchange for imports and for the use of foreign exchange earned through exports. Multinational companies had to choose between reducing their stake to this level by selling their shares to the Indian public and leaving the country. Several MNCs chose to dilute their stakes through public offerings on the BSE, but IBM and Coca-Cola were two prominent exceptions. The decision of IBM to leave India meant that 1,200 employees of the company had to look for other alternatives to exploit their skills. Many of these employees set up small software consulting companies that would offer software development and maintenance services to former IBM customers, leading to the beginnings of the Indian software industry. The departure of IBM also allowed many smaller hardware companies to expand into India, exposing Indian software programmers to a variety of software platforms.

Other unintended consequences of Indian government policy also played a role in shaping the nascent industry. For example, the severe import restrictions on hardware—requirements of government permits, high customs duties, and control of foreign currency availability—gave a fillip to the industry practice that received the derogatory title of "bodyshopping," whereby programmers were shipped off to the client site and worked on the client's computers. This in turn led to some companies' building relationships with their clients that were then to play a major role in shaping the industry.

The outward-looking nature of the industry from the outset was also influenced by the unattractiveness of the domestic market. This, in turn, had several causes. First, fearing unemployment from automation, the government did not encourage the adoption of computerization in government and state-owned enterprises. Second, its interest in developing a domestic hardware industry led the government to impose extremely high tariffs (350 percent in much of the 1970s and early 1980s). Third, Indian private-sector companies had little incentive to adopt information technology to improve operations and productivity, given the highly protected nature of the economy. As a result, Indian software firms found it difficult to generate much demand for their services in the domestic market. This outward orientation stood in significant contrast to the orientation of much of the Indian private sector, which was focused on the Indian domestic market rather than the export market.

More broadly than these specific serendipitous events, software slipped under the discerning bureaucrat's otherwise omnipresent proverbial radar screen, so to speak. The origin of India's socialist policies and heavy-handed micromanagement of enterprise lay in Oxford- and Cambridge-indoctrinated Fabian socialism, which sought to regulate the "commanding heights" of the economy. But this required physical assets to control. Software, with its characteristic intangibles, was too ephemeral to be included in the purview of these regulations.

Other than the intangible nature of the assets in question in the software industry, another reason why the industry escaped some of the pernicious effects of Indian socialism had to do with its non-capital-intensive nature. The state's stranglehold on the financial sector did not matter as much. Several of the last decade's changes have helped move an already existing industry along. For example, far-ranging deregulation initiated following an exchange rate crisis in 1990 generically improved the outlook for business. The delicensing of hardware imports and the greatly falling hardware prices internationally meant that entry barriers into the Indian domestic software industry fell drastically. Software firms were allowed to set up private telecommunications networks to promote remote software services (often to clients in the west). The party in power until early 2004, the Bhartiya Janata Party (BJP), was generally pro-business and the first to explicitly support the software industry in its election manifesto.

But our general point is that these recent changes do not shed much light on the origins of the industry. It is interesting to ask how a low-cost, talent-intensive environment could become a world player in a knowledge-intensive industry. Clearly serendipity, as opposed to explicit design, played a role. More interesting for our purposes, concentrated ownership, in the garb of TCS, was the best positioned to capitalize on the opportunities revealed by serendipity. Indeed, the ownership links among the Tata companies were among the ties that cemented them (along with director interlocks, a shared if informal access to the Tata brand, and shared senior-level talent) and permitted TCS to leverage the Tata group's reputation. It is doubtful that an entity could have arisen in a vacuum, unaffiliated with an existing reputable private-sector entity, to capitalize on the software industry opportunity. In a subsequent subsection, we will show how TCS's approach differed from that of other firms in India and that not only did TCS not deter the entry of de novo aspirants, but it actually facilitated entry.

5.6.3   The Modern Industrial Organization of the Indian Software Industry

Table 5.7 shows the distribution of the companies in the industry by revenues. Table 5.8 shows a list of top-twenty companies and their revenues. The top five firms in the industry, with sales greater than 10 billion Indian

Table 5.7   **Structure of Indian software exports industry**

	No. of companies	
Annual turnover	2000–2001	2001–2002
Above Rs. 1,000 crore	5	5
Rs. 500–1,000 crore	7	5
Rs. 250–500 crore	14	15
Rs. 100–250 crore	28	27
Rs. 50–100 crore	25	55
Rs. 10–50 crore	193	220
Below Rs. 10 crore	544	2,483

Source: Adapted from NASSCOM (2003).
Note: In 2001–2, companies with under Rs. 10 crore in revenues included non-NASSCOM member companies.

Table 5.8   **Top 20 IT software and services exporters from India**

Ranking	Company	Rs. crore	US$ million
1	Tata Consultancy Services	3,882	813
2	Infosys Technologies Ltd.	2,553	535
3	Wipro Technologies	2,256	481
4	Satyam Computer Services Ltd.	1,703	357
5	HCL Technologies Ltd.	1,319	277
6	IBM Global Services India Pvt. Ltd.	764	160
7	Patni Computer Services	732	153
8	Silverline Technologies	603	126
9	Mahindra-British Telecom Ltd.	541	113
10	Pentasoft Technologies Ltd.	459	96
11	HCL Perot Systems Ltd.	449	94
12	Pentamedia Graphics Ltd.	431	90
13	NIIT Ltd.	400	84
14	Mascot Systems Ltd.	399	84
15	i-Flex Solutions Ltd.	392	82
16	Digital Globalsoft Ltd.	331	69
17	Mphasis BFL Group (consolidated)	313	66
18	Mascon Global Ltd.	307	64
19	Orbitech	264	55
20	Mastek Ltd.	259	54

Source: Adapted from NASSCOM (2003).

rupees, account for 32 percent of the total revenues of the industry. These five firms are TCS, Infosys Technologies, Wipro Technologies, Satyam Computer Services, and HCL Technologies. Wipro, TCS, and Satyam are affiliated with family-owned business groups, which entered the software industry as part of a diversification move by their parent groups. Within these three, TCS is privately owned; Wipro is publicly traded, but approximately 84 percent of the shares are held by the founder; Satyam is publicly traded, with only 11 percent of the shares held by the founding family. Infosys and HCL were started by computer professionals and are publicly listed companies. There are also several large Indian software companies that are affiliates of multinational companies. These include Indian arms of overseas software services firms such as IBM Global Services. Also, there are arms of multinational operating companies that use India as a base for their internal software development needs. Examples include Siemens Information Systems Limited and Motorola. Affiliates of multinational companies together account for 22 percent of the industry's total revenues. There are twenty-four large software companies that are publicly traded on the Indian stock exchanges.[7] Three of these—Infosys, Satyam, and Wipro—are also listed on the U.S. stock exchanges.

Compare the industrial organization of the software industry to that of the Indian economy as a whole reported in tables 5.2 and 5.3. The role of the private sector looms much larger than that of the (absent) public sector in the software industry than it does in the economy at large. There are large, dominant software firms that have emerged—separating the wheat from the chaff, as it were—and this has happened through the normal forces of global competition. Three of the five most successful companies in the software industry—TCS, Wipro, and Satyam—were launched by business groups and remain affiliated to these groups.[8] Whereas the absence of capital barriers to entry characterizes the industry, reputation, the forte of those groups that have succeeded, poses a formidable barrier to entry. Further, from the fact that multinationals have not been able to displace the domestic group companies, we can conjecture that the reputation of the former is probably based at least in part on some hard-to-replicate ability to run a software company in India.

5.6.4 The Success of the Indian Software Industry

The case of the Indian software industry provides a contrasting picture to the received wisdom that primarily emphasizes the ills of concentrated ownership.[9] Here, we provide some broad data to support the claim that the software industry is, in fact, a success story despite the ubiquity of con-

---

7. There were also other software companies that are publicly listed, but these have very small amounts of sales.
8. A fourth company, Infosys, has a very high level of insider ownership even though it is not affiliated with a business group.
9. Morck, Shleifer, and Vishny (1988) used U.S. data to argue that the monitoring benefits of concentrated ownership declined beyond a certain threshold level of concentrated ownership. A more recent literature on corporate governance around the world points to the exploitation of minority shareholders by controlling concentrated owners as being a prevalent problem (La Porta et al. 2000; Shleifer and Wolfenzon 2002). Morck, Shleifer, and Vishny have argued that concentrated ownership has resulted in the onset of "Canadian disease," which they associate with slower growth, lower innovation, and other forms of noncompetitive malaise.

centrated ownership. Why do we think of this as a success? In contrast to the lackluster performance of the Indian economy as a whole, the performance of the Indian software industry has been impressive.[10] The industry's total revenues in 2002 stood at $10.2 billion, and it grew at more than 40 percent per year during the 1990s. The industry accounted for $7.7 billion in exports in 2002, which was a significant portion of the approximately $73.3 billion total exports of goods and services from India in that year. One indication of technical prowess is that five of the nine software development centers in the world with capability maturity model (CMM) level 5 ratings, the highest ratings on the predominant quality scale developed for software at Carnegie-Mellon University, were located in India. Companies like General Electric, Citicorp, and IBM had their only CMM-certified operations in India rather than in the United States.[11] According to a report prepared by the international consulting firm McKinsey for the National Association of Software and Service Companies (NASSCOM), an industry trade association, the industry is expected to grow to $77 billion by 2008, accounting for 7 percent of India's gross domestic product (GDP), 33 percent of its foreign exchange inflows, and four million jobs. By all these measures, software industry is the crown jewel of India's postindependence economy.

While this establishes that the Indian software industry has done well relative to any sensible domestic benchmark, two other benchmarks are worth considering. Consider, first, comparisons with U.S. software companies, and then comparisons of the Indian industry with itself, as it were, over time.

10. This history relies on the following sources: De Long and Nanda (2002), Heeks (1996), Ghemawat (1999), NASSCOM (2002, 2003), Kennedy (2001), and Kuemmerle (2003).

Some aggregate performance indices for the country are worth keeping in mind to interpret the software industry numbers. At the macro level, India's overall economic performance during the postindependence years can only be characterized as relatively poor. For example, the United Nations' Human Development Report of 2002 ranks India 124 among the 173 countries. According to the statistics reported by the Planning Commission of the Government of India, the country's gross national product (GNP) grew at annual average rate of approximately 4 percent between 1951 and 1990. This rate increased to approximately 6 percent in the postreform years of 1990 to 2002. India's population grew significantly to 1.05 billion by 2002. While government spending on public education was more around 3 percent of GNP, a disproportionate amount of this went to supporting higher education. According to the Indian government's 2001 Census of India, the adult illiteracy rate stood at 34.6 percent in 2001. Agriculture still remained the dominant source of income for a very significant portion of the population, and there were significant levels of unemployment and underemployment. Per capita GNP in 2001 stood at approximately $450. A caveat to this interpretation is that, in the two decades leading to 2000, India's cumulative average growth rate was second only to China's in this time period. Our reading is that it was a good performance, but not stellar enough to alleviate the suffering of the Indian masses. In a recent analysis, De Long (2001) argues that India was in the middle of the pack of countries that he analyzes over longer time periods.

11. It may be that quality concerns are greater when a firm is located in an environment with a reputation for poor governance and poor quality products. Perhaps U.S. firms do not find it necessary to seek certification of this sort.

Table 5.9   A comparison of the large U.S. and Indian software companies

	Revenues (June 2002, $ million)	Operating margin (June 2002, %)	No. of employees (June 2002)	Market capitalization (October 2002, $ million)
U.S. companies				
Accenture	11,600	3.9	75,000	12,400
CSC	11,500	4.7	67,000	4,800
EDS	22,300	10.3	143,000	6,370
KPMG Consulting	2,368	5.6	9,300	1,240
Sapient	217	n.a.	2,427	123
Indian companies				
HCL Tech	340	28.1	5,587	1,209
Infosys	571	32.1	10,470	7,140
Satyam	421	26.7	9,532	1,370
TCS	810	25	19,000	8,100
Wipro	734	24.5	13,800	6,340

Source: Adapted from NASSCOM Newsline, November 2002.
Note: n.a. = not available.

Table 5.9 compares the largest Indian software companies with some of the largest U.S. software companies in terms of revenues, employees, profitability, and market capitalization, all as of 2002. Indian companies are clearly not as large as some of the largest U.S. software firms, such as CSC, Accenture, and EDS, in terms of revenues or manpower. However, in terms of profitability, Indian firms are significantly better than their U.S. counterparts. The stock market valuations of Indian companies, despite their smaller size, are often larger than the market capital of the U.S. firms.[12]

Consider, now, the industry's evolution over time. Table 5.10 shows the time series of the total activity of the Indian software industry from 1988 to 2002. The industry had a total revenue of 0.7 billion Indian rupees in 1988, and the proportion of exports to domestic sales was 41 percent. By 2002, the industry grew to a size of 365 billion rupees, with exports accounting for 76 percent. This is driven by the rising importance of off-shore services (51 percent of export revenues in 2002 from 5 percent in 1991), the value-added part of the Indian software firms' offerings. This, in turn, is a reflection of gradually developed reputations for reliability and high quality of services, starting from a base of primarily bodyshopping (Banerjee and Duflo 2000). By 2000, the United States accounted for 66 percent of the total exports of the industry, and the United Kingdom

---

12. Software industry market capitalization on Indian stock exchanges rose from $4 billion in January 1999 to a high of $90 billion and then, following the NASDAQ crash and its ripple effect in India, settled at $55 billion by mid-2000.

Table 5.10   **India's software exports, domestic sales, and imports (Rs. billion/U.S. $ million)**

Time period	Exports		Domestic sales	Exports/total sales (%)
	Rs.	US$		
1987–88	0.70	52	1.00	41
1990–91	2.50	128	2.25	52
1991–92	4.30	164	3.20	57
1992–93	6.70	225	4.90	57
1993–94	10.20	330	6.95	59
1994–95	15.30	485	10.70	59
1995–96	25.20	735	16.70	60
1996–97	39.00	1,110	25.00	61
1997–98	65.30	1,790	35.80	64
1998–99	109.00	2,650	49.50	68
1999–2000	171.50	4,000	94.10	70
2000–2001	283.50	6,230	98.90	74
2001–2	365.00	7,680	115.00	76

Source: Adapted from Ghemawat (1999), p. 20. Data from Heeks (1996) and NASSCOM.
Note: The figures for the domestic software activity do not include in-house development of software by end users, which is presumed to be a considerable amount.

accounted for the second-largest share of exports, at 14 percent. Of the Fortune 500 U.S. companies, 185 were customers of the Indian software services industry.

This smorgasbord of data leaves us relatively convinced that, despite the ubiquity of concentrated ownership, it is hard to tell a story of a sclerotic industry, engulfed with rent-seeking behavior and in its death throes. Quite the contrary. It is also instructive to note that direct measures of corporate governance, which we turn to below, also do not yield predictions consistent with the predicted dismal effects of concentrated ownership.

The Indian software industry, on average, appears to follow better corporate governance practices relative to the rest of the Indian industry, consistent with the hypothesis that globalization puts pressure on companies to improve their governance to global standards. Some data from Credit Lyonnais Securities Analysis (CLSA; 2001) supports this assessment of the current state of Indian corporate governance. The data are from a set of questions regarding corporate governance administered to 482 companies in twenty-four emerging markets in 2001. The companies are generally the ones of greater interest to foreign investors, typically characterized by some subset of the following characteristics: large size, greater equity float, and foreign listings. When we ranked countries by the mean corporate governance score constructed by CLSA, we found that India ranked in about the middle. Since most countries in these data have poor average corporate governance (with some exceptions like Hong Kong and Singapore), and since the selected companies are generally the better governed ones, this confirms the characterization offered above.

The same CLSA data, however, also point out that the corporate governance ratings of the software firms are higher than those of other Indian firms. The mean ratings for software firms (of which there are eight in the CLSA data) and for nonsoftware firms (of which there are seventy-two) are, respectively, 64.3 and 54.7 (minimum of 0 and maximum of 100), with the difference statistically significant with a p-value of 0.02. The medians are, similarly, 62.9 and 53.8, with the difference statistically significant with a p-value of 0.2.

The data also confirm that software firms are, on average, more exposed to global competition than other Indian firms. To ratify this assertion, we supplemented CLSA data with a variety of indicators of global competition. Software firms are more likely to be traded on a U.S. stock exchange (p-value 0.02) and on the London Stock Exchange (p-value 0.08) and more likely to be listed on the New York Stock Exchange (p-value 0.01). Software firms garner a higher percentage of their revenues through exports (p-value 0.01), are more likely to employ foreign talent in senior managerial positions (p-value 0.01), and are somewhat more likely to employ a Big 5 accounting firm (p-value 0.12).[13]

Finally, having established that the Indian software industry outperforms domestic benchmarks (in terms of profitability, market capitalization, and corporate governance), outperforms U.S. benchmarks, and is improving over time, consider some evidence that, while least precise, is perhaps farthest reaching. The social transformation brought about by the rise of the software industry is difficult to exaggerate. Most compellingly, Indian talents have role models of entrepreneurship—from both de novo bootstrapped firms and from business group offshoots—to spur them forward (Khanna and Palepu 2004). Individuals, in both rural and urban settings, are much closer to having the information they need to be "empowered" (Das 2000). Indeed, rural India is being transformed by the roadside availability of computing power (in much the same way that a previous dissemination of franchised telephone kiosk services around the country revolutionized telecommunication service provision). It is thus difficult to escape the conclusion that the positive spillovers from the Indian software industry exceed, perhaps vastly, the direct benefits internalized by stakeholders of the industry.

5.6.5   A Tale of Two Software Firms

In this section, we provide a more detailed description of two very successful firms in the Indian software industry: TCS, affiliated with the Tata

---

13. However, there is no statistically significant difference between software and nonsoftware firms in the proportion of equity held by institutional investors.

group, and Infosys, a new entrepreneurial venture arising out of the opportunities provided by the new economic environment. Elsewhere, we have argued that there are two qualitatively different "solutions" to the institutional voids that hamper entrepreneurship in emerging markets. The first is for incumbent groups to leverage their internal access to capital and talent to start new ventures—this is the TCS story—and the second is for aspirants to tap into external institutions outside the country—this is the Infosys story (Khanna and Palepu 2004).

The stories of these two firms show how group-affiliated firms coexist successfully with independent entrepreneurial firms in this industry. It also demonstrates that the success of group-affiliated firms is attributable not to their ability to exploit government connections but to their ability to successfully exploit entrepreneurial opportunities in the economy. Finally, not only is it not the case that the group, the embodiment of concentrated ownership, deterred the entry of the unaffiliated firm, but it actually laid the groundwork for a vast array of subsequent entrants.

The founding of TCS in 1968 marks the birth of the first Indian domestic software firm at a time when IBM was riding herd in India.[14] Tata Consultancy Services was set up by India's oldest business group, the house of Tata, by pooling together management talent from existing Tata companies to create a new entity to act as an information technology bureau for various members of the Tata group. In two senses, it is the prototypical example of the filling of institutional voids (Khanna and Palepu 1997, 1999, 2000b,c), that is, of the creation by diversified business groups of internal solutions to compensate for the absence of external specialized intermediaries (institutional voids). The voids in question here refer to the absence of intermediaries facilitating the pooling of talent to launch such a company and the absence of an entity to provide information technology services to service the corporate demands of the time.

Armed with the reputation of the Tata group and its track record in India, TCS sought business overseas, turning successfully to secure an alliance with Burroughs Corporation in the United States, whereby Burroughs would secure programming contacts and TCS would execute them. Under newly appointed chief executive officer (CEO) F. C. Kohli, TCS built up a credible list of major Indian customers between 1969 and 1973.[15]

It is important to realize that India's distortionary foreign exchange regulations played a key role in prompting TCS to solicit business overseas. Foreign exchange was needed to pay for importing the hardware on which TCS performed its software programming services. It is also worth noting

14. The data, though not the interpretation, for the few paragraphs on the founding of TCS are from Kennedy (2001).

15. It is true that the MIT-trained Kohli's own contacts in the United States, as part of the IEEE association, no doubt played a facilitating role in securing contacts. But of course the Tatas had the reputation to attract someone of Kohli's stature in the first instance.

that such cross-border arrangements have been common in the history of the Tata group. For example, its ventures in the late 1990s included joint venture agreements with the likes of AT&T, NTT, Honeywell, Jardine Matheson, (the then) Daimler Benz, and numerous others. Elsewhere we have argued that the network of joint venture agreements represent credible commitments not to engage in short-term opportunistic behavior toward the marginal joint venture partner, and that the network itself is facilitated by the diverse (cross-industry) scope of the Tata group (Khanna and Palepu 1997).

Experience gained domestically and through Burroughs meant that TCS was well positioned when another distortionary Indian regulation—the requirement of divesting sufficient equity to local partners—forced IBM (and several other multinationals) out of India in 1977. A separate entity—Tata Burroughs (later Tata Infotech)—was created to focus on business based on the Burroughs platform, while TCS decided to focus on the rising IBM platform in its outside-India work. A U.S. office was opened in 1979 to solicit business, and, with successful projects for various banks, American Express, IBM, and others under its proverbial belt, TCS had established the industry, and its position, by the mid-1980s.

In contrast to TCS, Infosys Technologies, another of India's software success stories, is the prototypical example of building a business by leveraging external (i.e., non-India-specific) institutions to compensate for domestic (India-specific) institutional voids. Narayan Murthy, the individual most associated with Infosys today, mused that the biggest challenge facing Infosys was "running a first-world firm in a third world country" (De Long and Nanda 2002, p. 9). Infosys was founded in 1981 by seven entrepreneurs, all ex-employees of Patni Computer Systems (itself one of the entrants into the post-IBM-withdrawal vacuum). Its initial capital consisted of approximately $1,000 of personal savings and no Tata-like reputation to leverage. However, at least one of the founders, Murthy, had his professional outlook sensitized to the importance of personal incentives by his own stint working outside India (in Paris).

Infosys struggled, teetering on the precipice of bankruptcy in 1989, until a foreign exchange crisis forced India to "open up." Reasons cited for Infosys's early difficulties can reasonably be traced to pre-1991 institutional voids in product markets (lack of availability of quality hardware), capital markets (limited availability of financing for de novo entrepreneurs), and labor markets (visa restrictions preventing cross-border talent mobility). A lot of these constraints were removed when barriers to the flow of people, capital, and ideas were relaxed so that Infosys software engineers could be relocated relatively easily to their customer sites, Infosys management did not have to spend excessive time circumventing regulations in New Delhi, foreign know-how regarding the industry was accessible, and equity capital could be accessed locally through listings (which Infosys did in 1993).

While the post-1991 liberalization eliminated some institutional voids, more fundamental ones remained. A *Forbes* article commented that there was a "perception that a smart, honest, reputable company could never come out of a country where cows still run in the street" (Pfeiffer 1999, quoted in De Long and Nanda 2002, p. 13). A 1999 NASDAQ listing was designed to ameliorate informational problems that hampered Infosys from reaching blue-chip companies in the global market. Several executives at Infosys and its competitors, and several regulators at SEBI (India's SEC equivalent), commented to us, for example, that the NASDAQ listing was designed primarily to gain credibility with customers and to permit the issuance of dollar-denominated stock options to compete in global markets for talent.[16] For a company that, by this time, was not liquidity constrained, as we have demonstrated elsewhere (Khanna and Palepu 2004), raising capital was not the reason to list overseas. Securities and Exchange Board of India member Jayanth Verma's comment to us regarding the spate of software listings overseas that followed is instructive: "The industry that probably needs capital the least, went after the international capital markets most aggressively. . . . In fact many of these companies don't know what to do with the capital they raised. . . . The pressures that the capital markets can put on a company that doesn't need to raise capital are next to nothing."

A few final points are worth noting. First, TCS's moves arguably laid the foundation for the industry's development. Azim Premji, founder of Wipro, India's second largest software company and an NYSE-listed company, commented, "The legacy of the early pioneers—Tata Consultancy Services—was a growing number of foreign companies favorably impressed about what Indian companies could do in software" (Ramamurti 2001). Thus, TCS, launched by the Tata group, far from deterring entry, appears to have facilitated it.

5.7   Discussion: The (Socially Useful) Persistence of Concentrated Ownership

In this section, we argue that the persistence of concentrated ownership is, in fact, a robust feature of many, if not most, emerging markets. The story of the Indian software industry, and the (socially) useful role that business groups with concentrated ownership play in it, is not an artifact of serendipitous outcomes but has generalizable aspects to it. In contrast, the literature's current focus on the dark side of concentrated ownership,

---

16. Note, however, that the international listing was not feasible until Infosys had a stable track record. As Azim Premji, CEO of rival Wipro, commented, "It is also important to remember that Indian companies built their expertise serving domestic customers before venturing abroad" (Ramamurti 2001). Even TCS ventured overseas after it had a strong domestic track record.

to the virtually complete exclusion of the positive aspects, has the potential to understate the beneficial aspects of such ownership, especially in emerging markets.

Consider other instances in space and time that are consistent with this idea of the socially productive longevity of concentrated ownership. We have focused on Chile in earlier work on the sustainability of business groups (Khanna and Palepu 2000b) because Chile is the one country in modern economic history that has arguably undergone one of the most rapid movements toward a market economy, starting from the socialist society left behind by Salvador Allende in 1973 (following his overthrow by the right-wing general Augusto Pinochet). In particular, Chilean markets are widely celebrated as being the best in Latin America, especially since 1990. Thus, if one were to see business groups atrophy as external markets develop, this is where one ought to find the effect most glaringly. Our study confirmed that the value of business group affiliation fell during the ten years between 1987 and 1997. But business group affiliation, even in the relatively developed markets of the late 1990s, continued to be valuable. Our interpretation was that group capabilities, under attack in this instance since 1973 and especially since 1990, fall slowly.

We supplemented this by detailed fieldwork in nine of Chile's largest groups over the same time period (Khanna and Palepu 1999). It is important to note that these were not the ten best-performing groups. Here we found that these groups bucked the trend, so to speak, not only by improving their performance over this time period but also by increasing the trend toward greater concentration in ownership, greater family control, and greater diversification, all allegedly correlates of the deleterious effects of concentrated ownership. Similar field evidence was obtained and reported from India in the 1990–97 time period.

The parallels with business groups in history are uncanny and relatively unexplored (Jones and Khanna 2003). Here we draw largely on the work on multinational trading companies in the 1800s and 1900s by Geoffrey Jones (2000). Primarily around the mid-1800s, British trading houses in particular (and trading houses originating elsewhere in Europe to a lesser extent) were cross-border structural analogs of the sorts of contemporary business groups that one observes in Chile, India, and elsewhere (Khanna 2000). In these trading companies, which Jones describes as business groups, the merchant house was the "core" and was tied through a medley of contracts, informal and formal, to a series of separately publicly quoted (traded) affiliates around the world, which operated in very diverse industries.

Examples of such British trading companies included the Inchcape/Mackinnon group, a shipping enterprise spread over Asia and Australia, with a trading business in the Gulf, India, and Africa, and plantations in India. Another was Jardine Matheson, which originated as an opium trader between China and India and, drawing extensively on its Scottish heritage to source talent, evolved into a multinational business group with operations in China and outposts in Japan, the United States, South Africa, and Peru in diverse services and manufacturing businesses, as well as an active venture capital business in mining worldwide.

Some funds were drawn from British (and other) expatriate savings in the colonies and from the London capital markets, and a lot of funds were sourced locally. That is, there was the structural issue of controlling and minority shareholders that we have already discussed as a hallmark of contemporary groups. Yet, as Jones points out, while the potential for minority shareholder exploitation existed in spades, there were very few such cases. Why? His answer is that reputation mattered, and these business groups sought to build trust by doing things like forgoing commissions (owed to the core firm by the affiliates as compensation for management services rendered) when times were bad. The groups referred to a "moral responsibility" toward their affiliates. Thus we have an instance where concentrated ownership appears to have exercised self-restraint, even amid a weak corporate control environment, a factor that was probably associated with its longevity.

Consider also the adaptability of this historical business group, another reason why the concentrated ownership has persisted. Continuing the examples above, the Inchcape group gradually divested from India in the late 1960s and 1970s as that country became less attractive, and also withdrew from the Middle East and Africa, ultimately reconfiguring itself as a group invested in Southeast Asia, Hong Kong, and Australia. Jardines and Swires recovered from rather drastic business setbacks, including the Communist revolution in China, reconfigured themselves as Hong Kong–based groups, and entered numerous new businesses. Such reconfigurations can be observed even in contemporary groups. The Tata group started, for example, with steel and airlines and insurance in the 1800s, had to undergo nationalization and confiscation of several of its major businesses (including airlines and insurance), built up and eventually divested major businesses in consumer products, and most recently successfully entered automobiles and software. Thus, TCS, discussed above, is a recent diversification of the Tata group. Similarly, the roughly $4 billion Ayala group in the Philippines started with distilleries, evolved into a real estate and financial services group as of the 1990s, and most recently emerged as a major and very successful player in mobile telephony (Khanna, Palepu, and Vargas 2004).

Groups, and the concentrated ownership that they represent, whether in history or in contemporary emerging markets, are robust forms of business organizations. They potentially last centuries, changing their footprint and functional form, and weathering severe shocks. Whereas egregious violations and crony capitalism by groups are often reported (e.g., Fisman's

2001 study of groups in Suharto's Indonesia), the constructive stories are actually far more numerous, even though lacking the drama of exploitation.

As a coda, it is worth commenting on the implicit counterfactual that underpins our assertion that groups are socially productive organizational forms. One should ask, what would happen if there were no groups? Would organized commerce happen in quite the way that it does in emerging markets, when the specialized intermediation needed to facilitate arm's-length transactions between buyers and sellers in all manner of markets are missing? We think not. Such a world would be closer to first-best, but is also patently unrealistic. Then, a critic of groups might say, groups are sensible responses to the absence of specialized intermediation at a point in time, but their very presence deters the emergence of intermediaries. Therefore groups are self-perpetuating. There is some truth to this (Khanna 2000), but it is a characterization that rings more true for extreme concentration of groups as in South Korea or South Africa, than for the "median" emerging market.

References

Banerjee, Abhijit V., and Esther Duflo. 2000. Reputation effects and the limits of contracting: A study of the Indian software industry. *Quarterly Journal of Economics* 115 (August): 989–1017.
Bertrand, Marianne, Paras Mehta, and Sendhil Mullainathan. 2002. Ferreting out tunneling: An application to Indian business groups. *Quarterly Journal of Economics* 117 (1): 121–48.
Bhagwati, Jagdish. 1993. *India in transition: Freeing the economy*. Oxford, UK: Clarendon Press.
Credit Lyonnais Securities Analysis (CLSA). 2001. Saints and sinners: Who's got religion? Credit Lyonnais Securities Asia, Research Report. Hong Kong: CLSA.
Das, Gurcharan. 2000. *India unbound: From independence to the global information age*. New Delhi, India: Penguin Books.
De Long, J. Bradford. 2001. India since independence: An analytic growth narrative. University of California, Berkeley, Department of Economics. Working paper, July.
De Long, Thomas, and Ashish Nanda. 2002. *Infosys technologies.* HBS Case no. 801-445. Boston: Harvard Business School Publishing.
Dutt Report. 1969. Report of the industrial licensing policy enquiry committee: Main Report. New Delhi: Government of India.
Ferguson, Niall. 2002. *Empire: The Rise and Demise of the British World Order and the Lessons for Global Power.* London: Penguin Books.
Fisman, Raymond. 2001. Estimating the value of political connections. *American Economic Review* 91 (4): 1095–1102.
Gadgil, D. R., with staff of Gokhale Institute of Politics and Economics, Poona, India. 1951. Notes on the rise of the business communities in India. New York: International Secretariat, Institute of Pacific Relations. Mimeograph, April.

Ghemawat, Pankaj. 1999. *The Indian software industry in 2002.* HBS Case no. 700-036. Boston: Harvard Business School Publishing.

Ghemawat, Pankaj, and Tarun Khanna. 1998. The nature of diversified business groups: A research design and two case studies. *Journal of Industrial Economics* 46 (1): 35–62.

Greif, A. 1994. Cultural beliefs and the organization of society: A historical and theoretical reflection on collectivist and individualist societies. *Journal of Political Economy* 102 (5): 912–50.

Hazari, R. K. 1966. *The structure of the corporate private sector: A study of concentration, ownership and control.* Bombay: Asia Publishing House.

———. 1986. Industrial policy in perspective. In *Essays on industrial policy.* New Delhi: Naurang Rai Concept Publishing.

Heeks, Richard. 1996. *India's software industry: State policy, liberalisation and industrial development.* New Delhi: Sage.

Jones, G. 2000. *Merchants to multinationals.* Oxford: Oxford University Press.

Jones, G., and Tarun Khanna. 2003. Bringing history into international business. Harvard Business School. Mimeograph.

Kennedy, Robert E. 2001. Tata consultancy services: High technology in a low-income country. HBS Case no. 9-700-092. Boston: Harvard Business School Publishing.

Khanna, Tarun. 1997. *Modern India.* HBS Case no. 797-108. Boston: Harvard Business School Publishing.

———. 2000. Business groups and social welfare in emerging markets: Existing evidence and unanswered questions. *European Economic Review* 44 (4–6): 748.

Khanna, Tarun, and Krishna Palepu. 1997. Why focused strategies may be wrong for emerging markets. *Harvard Business Review* 75 (4): 41–49.

———. 1999. Policy shocks, market intermediaries, and corporate strategy: Evidence from Chile and India. *Journal of Economics and Management Strategy* 8 (2): 271–310.

———. 2000a. Emerging market business groups, foreign intermediaries, and corporate governance. In *Concentrated corporate ownership,* ed. Randall Morck, 265–94. Chicago: University of Chicago Press.

———. 2000b. The future of business groups in emerging markets: Long-run evidence from Chile. *Academy of Management Journal* 43 (3): 268–85.

———. 2000c. Is group affiliation profitable in emerging markets? An analysis of diversified Indian business groups. *Journal of Finance* 55 (2): 867–91.

———. 2004. Globalization and convergence in corporate governance: Evidence from Infosys and the Indian software industry. *Journal of International Business Studies,* forthcoming.

Khanna, Tarun, Krishna Palepu, and Danielle Melito Wu. 1998. *House of Tata 1995: The next generation (A).* HBS Case no. 798-037. Boston: Harvard Business School Publishing.

Khanna, Tarun, Krishna Palepu, and Ingrid Vargas. 2004. *Globe Telecom.* HBS Case no. 704-505. Boston: Harvard Business School Publishing.

Khanna, Tarun, and Jan Rivkin. 2002. Ties that bind business groups: Evidence from an emerging economy. HBS Working Paper no. 00-068. Boston: Harvard Business School Publishing.

Kuemmerle, Walter. 2003. *Infosys: Financing an Indian software start-up.* HBS Case no. 800-103. Boston: Harvard Business School Publishing.

Lamb, Helen B. 1976. *Studies on India and Vietnam.* New York: Monthly Review Press.

La Porta, Rafael, Florencio López-de-Silanes, Andrei Shleifer, and Robert Vishny.

2000. Investor protection and corporate governance. *Journal of Financial Economics* 58 (1–2): 3–27.

Leff, N. 1976. Capital markets in the less developed countries: The group principal. In *Money and finance in economic growth and development,* ed. R. McKinnon. New York: Marcel Dekker.

———. 1978. Industrial organization and entrepreneurship in the developing countries: The economic groups. *Economic Development and Cultural Change* 26:661–75.

Markovits, Claude. 1985. Indian business and nationalist politics 1931–39. Cambridge: Cambridge University Press.

Morck, Randall, Andrei Shleifer, and Robert W. Vishny. 1988. Management ownership and market valuation: An empirical analysis. *Journal of Financial Economics* 20 (1–2): 293–315.

National Association of Software and Service Companies (NASSCOM). 2002. *NASSCOM-McKinsey report 2002: Strategies to achieve Indian IT industry's aspiration.* New Delhi, India: NASSCOM, June.

———. 2003. *Strategic review: The IT industry in India.* New Delhi, India: NASSCOM, February.

Pfeiffer, Eric. 1999. From India to America. *Forbes.* August 23, 19–24.

Piramal, Gita. 1989. Long shadows of the past. Corporate dossier, *The Economic Times* (India). August 18.

———. 1991. The politics of business. *Perspectives: The Independent Journal of Politics and Business* (India). March 28.

———. 1998. *Business legends.* New Delhi, India: Viking Penguin India.

Ramamurti, Ravi. 2001. Wipro's CEO Azim Premji on building a world-class Indian company. *Academy of Management Executive* 15 (2): 13–19.

Shleifer, Andrei, and Daniel Wolfenzon. 2002. Investor protection and equity markets. *Journal of Financial Economics* 66 (1): 3–27.

Strachan, H. 1976. *Family and other business groups in economic development: The case of Nicaragua.* New York: Praeger.

Swamy, Subramanian. 1979. The response to economic challenge: A comparative economic history of China and India; 1870–1952. *Quarterly Journal of Economics* 93 (1): 25–46.

Timberg, Tom. 1978. *The Marwaris.* New Delhi, India: Vikas.

Comment   Ashoka Mody

In this paper, the authors offer a panoramic view of Indian business over the past century. They reach three conclusions. First, at any point in time, a small number of family-based business groups, spanning a number of lines of activity, have typically dominated the Indian (nonagricultural) private sector. Second, this dominance has not necessarily meant the persistence of particular groups: there has been significant turnover in the identity of the major groups. And, finally, more recently, professionally

Ashoka Mody is assistant director in the European department at the International Monetary Fund (IMF). The views expressed here are those of the author and should not be attributed to the IMF.

managed "specialist" firms have coexisted in socially beneficial competitive relationships with family-owned firms.

The main analytical theme underlying these important observations is the value of family-based business groups in emerging markets. The authors caution against the tendency to focus on the "dark side" of concentration of economic resources and power. Instead, they argue that "institutional voids" in emerging markets render family ownership of groups of firms an important mechanism for mobilizing necessary resources for growth.

In this comment, I focus my discussion on two themes. First, owing to the ubiquity of family-owned business groups in emerging markets, a deeper understanding requires scholarship to move to the differentiation of such groups across countries and over time. Group characteristics and country conditions determine the value of family-owned businesses in delivering economic growth and aiding the transformation of the economy. Second, applying this approach of differentiating both group and country features, I review the role of business communities in India and reach a more pessimistic conclusion on their transformational role during the past century.

Consider, first, the interaction between business groups and the state of a country's development. In a comparison of South Korea and Taiwan, I have argued that South Korea deliberately fostered the formation of business groups to acquire new capabilities and thus dynamically change its "factor" endowments to transition to a higher growth path (Mody 1990). The business groups were new—largely a post–World War II phenomenon—and were a calculated effort to break out of a low-growth trajectory. Even in the late 1980s, when this research was originally conducted, some of the Korean business groups were already among the world's largest firms (placing them in *Fortune* magazine's list of the fifty biggest international firms). Since then they have grown further to establish valuable international brand names and occupy prominent positions in several key industrial activities.

Thus, in the Korean context, business conglomerates performed the function of substituting for missing capital and information markets, as emphasized especially by Oliver Williamson in his many writings, and the internal resource-allocation mechanisms generated growth that might otherwise not have occurred. The result was that Korea, which lagged behind Taiwan by most development indicators, progressed rapidly to catch up and even move ahead of Taiwan in certain dimensions.

The comparison of Korea with Taiwan is interesting precisely because Taiwan has itself been such a dynamic economy over the same period. Taiwan was not without its own conglomerates but relied during the 1970s and 1980s primarily on entrepreneurship fostered in relatively small firms. These smaller firms delivered impressive growth, drawing on the economy's superior human capital and infrastructure. Over time, some of the Taiwanese firms have themselves grown to be large conglomerates, also with their own international brand names.

The Korea-Taiwan comparison offers many lessons and is also subject to important caveats. The structure of business enterprise can have a significant bearing on aggregate growth—micro structures can have macro implications. But there is no simple formula that relates business organization to macroeconomic performance. Thus, as Khanna and Palepu argue, concentrated ownership can be "socially useful" and the persistence of such concentration can be valuable, but both theory and practice suggest more nuanced messages of country and time variation in their performance. Even in the context of Korea, the economic crisis in 1997 and 1998 revealed substantial inefficiencies in the operation of the *chaebol* conglomerates, forcing changes in both private and regulatory approaches to their management.[1]

Thus, under the premise that business groups respond to the context of the country's economic conditions, the performance of Indian business can be viewed broadly over three time periods. The first of these periods commences some time in the late nineteenth century and runs through to India's independence in 1947. The Parsi business houses were pioneers in the textile industry. India's first cotton textile mill, the Bombay Spinning and Weaving Company, was established in 1851 (Gadgil 1944) by Cowasji Nanabhoy Daver, who, Desai (1968) notes, had been active in cotton export and also established three banks between 1845 and 1861. Thus, the concept—and practice—of business conglomerates with internal capital markets goes back a long way.

The question of interest, then, is how well these early business conglomerates performed and what their legacy was for the further evolution of Indian industry. In describing the contributions of the Parsis, Desai (1968) notes that Parsi entrepreneurship was based in Surat and Bombay. He concludes (p. 314) that "Wherever we look among pioneers, they are found to come from or be related to a small circle of shippers, shipbuilders, traders and financiers in Bombay; the landlords and manufacturers of Surat-Navsari do not figure among them." Desai attributes the success of the Bombay Parsis to "their close connections with the British" (p. 315), which allowed them to share in British-controlled foreign trade and to form links to British cotton textile manufacturing in India. Thus, early Indian efforts at factory-based manufacturing, while pioneering, were made in the space provided by British entrepreneurs.

Fast-forwarding, Gadgil (1944, p. 198) concludes that industrial pro-

---

1. At the same time, continued robust performance of the Korean economy has depended on a high-quality and industrially literate workforce combined with internationally sophisticated infrastructure.

gress in India up until the start of the First World War in 1914 must be judged to have been "very small," especially if the decline in traditional industries is taken into account. Taking stock of progress made in the early 1920s, Gadgil once again states: "Yet the main features of the situation are not substantially changed. Organized industries as yet play too small a part in the national economy, and even in the industrial population a very large proportion is engaged in the simpler seasonal, miscellaneous or repair industries" (p. 294). He then goes on to note: "Indian public opinion had always clamoured for active assistance to industries being given and at last Government appointed in 1916 an Industrial Commission, specifically to inquire as to how direction encouragement to the development of industries could be given by the Government" (p. 323).

Thus, a reading of the preindependence history of industrial development points to some significant achievements, including the establishment of the Tata Iron and Steel Company in 1907 and its initial output of steel in 1913, but the overall picture is one of limited progress, with the domestic business community dependent on its relationship with British business and increasingly calling for active government support. It is not surprising, therefore, that a remarkable document, popularly known as the "Bombay Plan," was written just before independence in 1944 and 1945 by a group of Indian industrialists, among them J. R. D. Tata and G. D. Birla, who went on to lead the two biggest Indian business groups in the first few decades after independence in 1947 (Thakurdas et al. 1944). The Bombay Plan called on government support for industrialization, including a direct role for the government in the production of capital goods, foreshadowing postindependence Indian planning, typically considered an outgrowth of socialist ideas drawn either from the Soviet Union or the so-called Fabian socialists.

Khanna and Palepu go on to recount the story of the second important period, from 1947 to the early 1990s. Scholars continue to debate the end point of this period, but its crucial feature is the collaboration of the big business houses with the government in sustaining an enervating environment. The government chose to control industrial growth in onerous ways, and big business readily acquiesced in this relationship, choosing to make money through its control over scarce licenses to operate. Those that played this game well prospered. It is the case, as Khanna and Palepu document, that new houses emerged during this period, but whether such emergence can be regarded as an entrepreneurial success in any true sense of the term is open to question.

The final period, that of economic liberalization, which continues to the present, is the most interesting. Here, as Khanna and Palepu highlight, a new generation of entrepreneurs emerged. They were not tied to traditional business groups and, rather than originating from shipbuilders, traders, and financiers, they were often the children of public-sector officials; they were trained in highly subsidized engineering colleges and were ready to exploit the lack of government regulation of a new "software" industry. The Tatas also saw early opportunities in software and developed a successful business, but the sprouting of entrepreneurs from middle-class families with salaried parents is a noteworthy development in the evolution of Indian entrepreneurship. A similar phenomenon has since occurred in the pharmaceutical industry.

This is a moment of high expectation for India, one that poses several questions for students of business. Will some of the successful businesses evolve into conglomerates in the style of Korean conglomerates and use internal capital markets to force the pace of growth? Or is that an antiquated model, given Indian firms' access to world capital markets, as demonstrated by the ability of several to list on international stock exchanges? Of course, the challenge to growth may come from internal infrastructure, human capital, and regulatory bottlenecks, which may imply surrendering the independence that the most innovative firms have enjoyed and which may generate a war of attrition of the type that has stymied Indian business in the past. Or the Indian lead in the knowledge of English and skilled engineers may be tested by China. Another stocktaking, another paper!

References

Desai, A. 1968. The origins of Parsi enterprise. *Indian Economic and Social History Review* 5:307–17.
Gadgil, D. R. 1944. *The industrial evolution of India.* London: Oxford University Press. (Orig. pub. 1924)
Mody, A. 1990. Institutions and dynamic comparative advantage: The electronics industry in South Korea and Taiwan. *Cambridge Journal of Economics* 14:291–314.
Thakurdas, P., J. R. D. Tata, G. Birla, A. Dalal, S. Ram, K. Lalbhai, A. Shroff, and J. Mattha. 1944. *A plan of economic development for India.* London: Penguin Books.

The History of Corporate Ownership in Italy

Alexander Aganin and Paolo Volpin

6.1 Introduction

Recent contributions show that the Italian corporate governance regime exhibits low legal protection for investors and poor legal enforcement (La Porta et al. 1998), underdeveloped equity markets (La Porta et al. 1997), pyramidal groups, and very high ownership concentration (Barca 1994). Arguably, due to these institutional characteristics, private benefits of control are high (Zingales 1994), and minority shareholders are often expropriated (Bragantini 1996). How did this corporate governance system emerge over time?

In this paper we use a unique data set with information on the control of all companies traded on the Milan Stock Exchange (MSE) in the twentieth century to study the evolution of the stock market, the dynamics of the ownership structure of traded firms, the birth of pyramidal groups, and the growth and decline of ownership by families.

We find that all our indicators (stock market development, ownership concentration, separation of ownership and control, and the power of families) followed a nonmonotonic pattern. The MSE showed more signs of development at the beginning and at the end of the century than in the middle of the century. Widely held pyramids were more common in 1947 and in 2000 than in 1987. Pyramidal groups and the separation of owner-

Alexander Aganin is manager at Cornerstone Research. Paolo Volpin is an assistant professor of finance at the London Business School.

We thank Daniel Wolfenzon (the discussant), Marco Becht, Luca Enriques, Andrea Goldstein, Ross Levine, Randall Morck, and participants at the Conference on the History of Corporate Ownership organized by the National Bureau of Economic Research and the European Corporate Governance Institute at Lake Louise (Canada) and at INSEAD. The views expressed in this paper do not represent in any way the views of Cornerstone Research.

ship from control were more widespread in the 1980s than in either the 1940s or in 2000. Family-controlled groups were more powerful in the middle of the century than at the beginning or at the end of it.

The results of our analysis can be explained as the joint effect of laws and politics on the Italian financial market. During the beginning of the century, Italian capitalism was characterized by a limited and indirect intervention of the government in the economy and in the stock market. The Great Depression forced the government to intervene on a much larger scale because the crisis led to the collapse of Italy's three main investment banks. Since then, the government has maintained a direct role in the economy by bailing out companies in trouble, as well as by controlling companies, especially in capital-intensive sectors.

Direct intervention by the state as an entrepreneur partially replaced and crowded out the role of the private sector in the accumulation of capital. Since the state took a direct and massive role in allocating capital, Italian legislators did not consider the improvement of investor protection important for Italy. This is at odds with the experience of countries such as the United States, where the government faced similar challenges to those of Italy but chose to intervene as a regulator of capital markets rather than as a substitute. In an environment with no regulatory reforms, and frequent direct intervention by the state, Italian stock market activity declined in the 1950s and 1960s to a level lower than that of the early twentieth century.

With low investor protection and underdeveloped capital markets, new entrepreneurs found it very expensive to go public. Conversely, incumbent groups thrived in the market by allying themselves with politicians. During the fascist regime, autarchy protected them from foreign imports. By the postwar period, family capitalism firmly controlled the Italian economy. Important families enjoyed both economic and political power, which was transmitted from generation to generation. New publicly traded family groups seldom emerged. When they did, it was always due to strong political connections.

In this environment the majority of Italian firms stayed away from the stock market, were closely held by the founders' families, and operated on a relatively small scale in niche markets. Family-controlled pyramidal groups and state-controlled conglomerates dominated the stock market. Because poor investor protection made Italian stock market unattractive, investors preferred to invest in government bonds rather than in equities.

To finance the costs of its active role in the economy, the government increased taxation and public debt. Eventually, public debt soared out of control, and in the 1990s the government engaged in a sweeping privatization program in an effort to reduce this debt. The government coupled the sale of assets with substantial improvement of the legal protection for minority shareholders. These changes made going public more appealing for private companies and benefited the stock market. With a more developed stock market came a greater demand for good corporate governance by investors, which imposed tighter constraints on family groups.

Currently, Italian capitalism is going through a very difficult transition period. Family groups, who were initially caught unprepared for the increased demand for good corporate governance, are slowly adapting to the rules of the international capital markets.

The structure of this paper is as follows. Section 6.2 briefly describes the institutional framework of Italian capitalism, focusing specifically on its legal and political environment. Section 6.3 focuses on the evolution of the stock market. Section 6.4 studies the dynamics of the ownership structure of traded firms. Family capitalism and the growth and decline of ownership by families are discussed in section 6.5. Section 6.6 concludes.

6.1.1 Related Literature

The paradigm in the literature on comparative corporate governance is the law and finance view, as developed by La Porta et al. (1998). This approach emphasizes that the protection of minority investors provided by the law is the key determinant of the corporate governance regime within a country. The argument is that investors will not provide equity to finance a firm unless they are confident of receiving a fair return from their investment. If shareholder protection is low, minority shareholders require a high return from their investment to compensate them for the high risk of expropriation by the management or by the controlling shareholder. Because external finance is more costly, ownership will be more concentrated and fewer companies will go public.

Several cross-country studies show that better legal protection of minority shareholders is associated with more developed stock markets (La Porta et al. 1997), higher valuation (La Porta et al. 2002), greater dividend payouts (La Porta et al. 2000), lower concentration of ownership and control (La Porta, López-de-Silanes, and Shleifer 1999), lower private benefits of control (Dyck and Zingales 2004; Nenova 2003), lower earnings management (Leuz, Nanda, and Wysocki 2003), lower cash balances (Dittmar, Mahrt-Smith, and Servaes 2003), higher correlation between investment opportunities and actual investments (Wurgler 2000), and a more active market for mergers and acquisitions (Rossi and Volpin 2004).

This paper builds on this literature but looks at the time series implication by focusing on one country (Italy) over one century of history.

6.2 Institutional Framework

Over the century, several important political decisions affected the stock market and the regulatory environment. In this section, we briefly review the main political interventions in the economy, distinguishing between economic policy and legislation.[1]

6.2.1 Economic Policy

At the end of the nineteenth century, Italy was still lagging behind in the industrialization process. The absence of spontaneous industrialization led to the creation of substitute factors (Gerschenkron 1962) and specifically to the development of universal banks. Banca Commerciale Italiana and Credito Italiano were both established in 1894 with the backing of German capital and management.

The period from 1896 to 1914 was the first phase of intense industrialization in the country. The two banks provided financial resources and managerial skills to the most important entrepreneurial initiatives, including Breda (train engines), FIAT (automobiles), and Montecatini (mining), and facilitated the birth of essential electrical and steel sectors.

However, universal banks were not able to bear the entire weight of the industrialization process. Already in 1887, government intervention was needed to rescue a large steel company, Terni, and its lenders from bankruptcy. In 1911, the government and the largest banks rescued the entire steel sector. In 1923 the Bank of Italy bailed out the largest company of the time, Ansaldo, and its two major creditors, Banca Italiana di Sconto and Banco di Roma.

These events indicate that Italian capitalism required the continuous assistance and involvement of the government from the start. The Great Depression forced the government to intervene on a much larger scale. The financial crisis led to the collapse of Italy's three main investment banks: Banca Commerciale, Credito Italiano, and Banco di Roma. As a result, in 1933 the government created a new agency, the Instituto per la Ricostruzione Industriale (IRI), to manage the large portfolio of companies previously controlled by the three banks.

Since that time, the Italian state has maintained a direct presence in the economy as the controlling shareholder of profit-oriented firms. The role of the state in the economy grew larger with the advent of the Republic. Instead of limiting its interventions to bailing out troubled companies, the state began acquiring sound companies and directly investing in all sectors of the economy. Due to its increased involvement in the Italian economy, the government created a second agency, named the Ente Nazionale Idrocarburi (ENI), in 1952. The ENI coordinated state-owned companies operating in the chemical, oil, and mining sectors. The government formed other institutions in 1962 (Efim) and in 1972 (Gepi) to direct state economic intervention in Southern Italy. All of these agencies were indepen-

---

1. The focus here is on policymaking rather than political regimes, which also changed dramatically during the twentieth century. Until 1923, Italy was a constitutional monarchy; from 1923 to 1945, it was a dictatorship. Since the end of the Second World War, Italy has been a democracy.

dent of one another. In principle, they were managed as profit-oriented corporations, though they could rely on financial assistance from the Treasury if they ran into deficits. Their presidents had very strong personalities and ample opportunities to take advantage of their power.[2] Over its life from 1933 to 2000 (IRI was liquidated in June 2000), IRI acquired forty-two traded companies, did twenty-six carve-outs of subsidiaries, delisted forty, and sold twenty-eight companies. ENI acquired eight companies, did six carve-outs of subsidiaries, delisted five, and sold six companies.

The government's decision to nationalize the electrical industry in early 1960s proved to be an important event for the Italian stock market. Political goals determined such a decision. The Christian Democrats, in power since the end of the war, had seen their share of electoral consensus steadily decrease from 49 percent in 1948 to around 38 percent by 1958. After failing to co-opt parties that were ideologically closer, to retain power, the Christian Democrats resorted to attracting the Socialist Party, which controlled about 8 percent of the seats in Parliament. As a condition of their support, the socialists required the nationalization of the electric industry.[3]

The fate of the electric sector had been set since the end of the 1950s. The political debate concerned whether to acquire only the assets from the electric companies, or to acquire the companies themselves. The decision to pay companies for their assets was made on June 17, 1962, and became law on December 12, 1962. The government left other decisions about the future of the companies to their shareholders.[4]

The 1962 nationalization had important implications for the stock market and the entire economy. The electrical groups played a crucial role in the stock market: not only did they represent approximately one-third of the total market capitalization, but they also functioned as a nucleus of economic and political power to a large extent free of government control. The first effect of the nationalization was a sequence of mergers inside these groups, later followed by mergers among these groups. Rather than paying out the proceeds to shareholders, the groups invested the payments obtained from the nationalization. Incompetent or dishonest managers[5]

---

2. The second president of ENI, Eugenio Cefis, serves as one extreme example. At the beginning of the seventies, he used his power to push ENI through an intense period of acquisitions and suspicious financial operations. Some years later he was found guilty of corruption. For a detailed discussion see Barca and Trento (1997).

3. Like Labour in the United Kingdom and Socialists in France, who implemented similar projects just after the war, Italian Socialists wanted to reduce the rents enjoyed by the companies operating in that industry.

4. The railways' nationalization at the beginning of the century served as a model for this plan. The compensation paid to railway companies on that occasion provided them with the resources to invest in and give birth to the electric industry.

5. A good example is the merger in 1964 between SADE, a former electric company, and Montecatini, a chemical company. As reported by Scalfari and Turani (1974), Vittorio Cini, the CEO of SADE, negotiated a very poor deal for SADE's shareholders in exchange for a seat on the board of directors of Montecatini for himself.

channeled most of the resources toward the chemical industry, giving birth to Montedison, which soon also came under government control (ENI). However, investing in the chemical industry proved unprofitable in a country with limited natural resources. As a result, the financial resources provided by the government as a compensation for the forced nationalization ended up almost entirely wasted.

State-owned enterprises contributed significantly to the growth of the country in the 1950s and 1960s (Barca and Trento 1997). However, over time they became a burden for economic growth because of weak managerial incentives, soft-budget constraints, inefficient production technologies, and misallocation of resources. The government financed these losses mainly with public debt. At the beginning of the 1990s, public debt soared out of control. Under pressure from the European Union, Italy's high level of debt forced the government to engage in a sweeping privatization program (see Goldstein 2003).

The extent of product market competition in Italy also changed throughout the century. The absence of antitrust legislation until 1991 implied that large companies enjoyed unlimited market power until that time. Most families whose companies traded on the stock market financed the expansion of their empires with the large profits achieved from monopolistic rents in their core sector (the cases of Agnellis, Pesentis, and Pirellis are discussed in section 6.5).

Because of the government's direct intervention the extent of international competition followed a nonmonotonic pattern. The beginning of the twentieth century saw a trend of increasing market integration across European economies. By 1930 European economies were effectively truly interdependent. The trend waned after the Great Depression with the reemergence of nationalist isolationism, the introduction of foreign exchange controls, and the abolition of external convertibility.

Effectively, Italy remained in an autarkic regime until 1958, when it joined the European Economic Community (EEC). Since then, product markets and capital markets have slowly liberalized, allowing foreign competition. The EEC directives first imposed a liberalization of product markets, and later a liberalization of the capital markets as well (see Battilossi 2000). Not until 1990 had all constraints on cross-border transactions effectively been lifted.

6.2.2   Legal and Regulatory Environment

Over the sample period analyzed in this paper, the legal environment in Italy and, consequently, the degree of investor protection afforded by the law has also changed considerably. Table 6.1 lists in chronological order the major regulatory events affecting traded companies and financial markets. All events listed in the table occurred either before the Second World War or after 1974. This suggests us to divide the century into three subperiods,

Table 6.1	Evolution of investor protection in Italy

Stock Exchange

Aug. 4, 1913	Regulation of stockbrokers: banks cannot engage in trading on the stock market.
Apr. 8, 1974	Creation of CONSOB, agency in charge of the supervision over the stock markets.
Mar. 31, 1975	Definition of CONSOB's powers.
May 17, 1991	Insider trading law.
Nov. 14, 1991	Regulation of disclosure requirements by companies offering securities to the public.
Feb. 12, 1992	Takeover law: mandatory bid rule.
Feb. 24, 1998	Passivity rule: managers cannot fight against a takeover without shareholder approval (*legge Draghi*).

Bankruptcy code

Mar. 16, 1942	Bankruptcy Law. The main procedures for non-state-owned firms are: liquidation (*fallimento*) or reorganization (*amministrazione controllata* or *concordato preventivo*). State-owned companies are subject to a third procedure called *liquidazione coatta amministrativa*.
Jan. 30, 1979	Special procedure (*amministrazione straordinaria*) for large firms (*legge Prodi*).
June 5, 1986	Simplification of the procedure for state-owned companies.

Banking

Mar. 12, 1936	Delegation to the Bank of Italy of the supervision over the banking sector. Separation between commercial and investment banks: only the second group can engage in long-term lending and can own equity stakes in nonfinancial companies.
Sept. 1, 1993	New law on banking and lending. Universal banking is allowed.

Information disclosure by traded companies

Mar. 16, 1942	New commercial code: Shares with multiple votes are prohibited and cross-shareholdings are limited.
June 7, 1974	New disclosure requirements. New limits to cross-shareholdings. Listed companies can issue nonvoting shares ("savings shares").
Mar. 31, 1975	External auditing required for the annual report.
June 4, 1985	Removal of a restriction to the ability to trade shares (*clausola di gradimento*).
Apr. 9, 1991	Consolidated balance sheet required for groups.
Feb. 24, 1998	Strengthening of minority shareholders' rights (*legge Draghi*).

Institutional investors

Mar. 23, 1983	Open-end mutual funds are allowed to operate and are subject to CONSOB's supervision.
Jan. 2, 1991	Regulation of institutional investors.
Jan. 27, 1992	Definition of disclosure and accounting requirements for mutual funds.
Aug. 14, 1993	Authorization to the creation of close-end funds.
July 23, 1996	Regulation of mutual funds and financial intermediaries.
Feb. 24, 1998	New law on financial intermediation.

Notes: This table lists the most important regulatory acts affecting investor protection in Italy. The events are classified into five categories depending on whether they are mostly relevant for the stock exchange, the bankruptcy procedure, the banking sector, information disclosure by traded companies, or institutional investors. The main feature of each regulatory act is briefly described.

1900–1941, 1942–1973, and 1974–2000, each characterized by an increasing degree of investor protection.

In the first subsample, the stock market was virtually self-regulated. Firms could issue shares with multiple votes and use cross-shareholdings without limitation. Until the Bank Law of 1936 no limitations existed on banks' abilities to own industrial companies, lend money for both short- and long-term periods, underwrite security issues, and hold deposits. Effectively, banks served the role of today's venture capitalists, investment banks, and commercial banks. There was only one bankruptcy procedure, which consisted of a straight liquidation. Though legally allowed to incorporate as joint-stock companies—*società anonime*—since 1865, only few large firms took advantage of limited liability. The Commercial Code of 1882 required the approval of an annual report by shareholders but not the extent of information disclosure.

During the entire second period (1942–1973), laws introduced at the beginning of the period under the fascist regime regulated traded companies and financial markets. The laws included the Bank Law (1936), the Civil and Commercial Code (1942), and the Bankruptcy Law (1942). These laws improved shareholder protection in limited-liability companies. Companies were required to provide some minimal amount of information on their performance in annual reports for shareholders. In an attempt to curb cross-shareholdings, controlled companies could no longer exercise the voting rights of shares owned in the holding company. The Bankruptcy Law allowed creditors to opt for a form of reorganization as an alternative to straight liquidation. The Bank Law prohibited universal banking and prevented banks from holding equity stakes in nonfinancial firms. Commercial banks could engage mainly in short-term lending.

This set of laws, designed for a small economy in which the capital markets had a marginal role (as they did in Italy in the 1930s), gradually became obsolete and unable to address the needs of a developed country competing in international markets. For instance, the company law did not draw any distinction between traded and nontraded companies, imposing the same set of rules on both. No specific rules existed regarding information disclosure by a traded company, and no specific agency was in charge of stock market supervision. As a result, in the 1960s the balance sheets of large companies like Edison, Pirelli, and Snia Viscosa did not disclose basic items such as sales (Amatori and Brioschi 1997). In theory the stock market was free to set its own rules, but without any enforcement power, it was effectively unregulated.

In 1974, the legislature finally broke its thirty-year-long neglect of the stock market by creating CONSOB, the agency in charge of supervising the stock market, and by drafting a set of disclosure requirements explicitly created for traded companies. The Italian government modeled CONSOB on the Securities Exchange Commission in the United States. It took the government a year to define CONSOB's powers and another year for CONSOB to become operational. It took much more time for the power and relevance of CONSOB to become real.

At the same time, the legislators drafted specific requirements for traded companies to stimulate investment in the stock market by the general public. To this end, disclosure requirements were introduced in 1974 and traded companies were allowed to issue nonvoting shares ("savings shares"). Although these shares did not provide any voting rights, they entitled the owner to a higher dividend than ordinary shares. As suggested by their name, savings shares were deemed appropriate for unsophisticated investors. In 1975, the government imposed external auditing of the balances of traded companies as a requirement and also introduced new accounting rules for statements of financial companies, banks, and insurance companies. Since 1974, the acquisition of more than 2 percent of the voting rights of a traded company must be reported to CONSOB within forty-eight hours (since 1992, this information must be disclosed to the public).

The 1990s proved a period of very intense legislation, largely due to the European Community's pressure to harmonize stock market regulation within Europe. In 1991 came the requirement of consolidated balances for groups; in 1992 came the takeover law. At the same time, regulations by CONSOB in 1991 and 1992 imposed information disclosure on mutual funds.[6] These requirements increased the transparency of the ownership structure of traded companies. In 1991, the Italian government enacted its first antitrust law.

Even with these important improvements, in 1994 Italy still ranked among the lowest of the industrial countries in legal protection for investors among the industrialized countries (La Porta et al. 1998). Antidirector rights, their index of shareholder protection, equaled one out of six for Italy.[7] Despite all of the protections put into place, the legislation did not sufficiently protect small shareholders from expropriation by controlling blockholders. In fact, the regulation of groups of companies and the takeover law both contained loopholes, such as the limited protection offered to the owners of nonvoting shares. Moreover, minority shareholders had too little power to protect themselves. For example, 20 percent of the capital was needed to call a shareholder meeting, a very high threshold to meet. Shares had to be deposited in a bank in order to be voted, and

6. Mutual funds were allowed to operate since 1983.

7. The index is formed by adding one when (a) the country allows shareholders to mail their proxy vote to the firm, (b) shareholders are not required to deposit their shares prior to the general shareholders' meeting, (c) cumulative voting or proportional representation of minorities in the board of directors is allowed, (d) an oppressed-minorities mechanism is in place, (e) the minimum percentage of share capital that entitles a shareholder to call for an extraordinary shareholders' meeting is less than or equal to 10 percent (the sample median), or (f) shareholders have preemptive rights that can be waived only by a shareholders' vote. According to La Porta et al. (1998), in 1994 Italian shareholders had only preemptive rights.

there was no vote by mail. These and other rules made it costly for small shareholders to vote.

In 1998, important steps were taken toward better legal protection for investors with the so-called Legge Draghi (Draghi's Law), named for its leading drafter. The law prohibited managerial opposition to takeovers without shareholder approval. If evaluated in terms of the index of shareholder protection developed by La Porta et al. (1998), the impact of this law was an improvement in shareholder protection from one to five. Specifically, the law reduced the threshold to call a shareholder meeting to 10 percent, it also corrected the loopholes in the takeover law, and it gave minority shareholders more rights to voice their opinions.[8]

6.3   The Stock Market

In 1808, the Napoleonic government established the Milan Stock Exchange as a market for securities and commodities. As noticed by Baia Curioni (1995) and De Luca (2002), unlike the markets in London and Amsterdam, the MSE was not created spontaneously by the financial operators of the time but was created by the government. Possibly for this reason, the market did not start to serve as the main financial center in Milan until the 1850s. At that time, the only traded securities were government bonds. In 1859, the first shares (of a railway company, Societa' delle Strade Ferrate Lombardo Veneto) were listed. This first traded company was followed by many banks and a few industrial companies. In 1873, shares of twenty-five companies were traded on the MSE.

At that time, the MSE was a local exchange. Stock exchanges of similar size were set up in several other Italian cities. In 1873, the MSE ranked second for trade volume after Genoa, but before Turin, Florence, Rome, and Naples.

The absence of regulation offered speculators wide opportunities to profit and kept uninformed investors (and liquidity) away. The turning point for the MSE came with the intense industrialization push between 1895 and 1907. In twelve years, the number of traded companies jumped from 27 to 171. The intense activity of the universal banks, Banca Commerciale and Credito Italiano, caused the boom of the stock market. The two banks helped many entrepreneurs raise capital for their projects by setting up limited-liability companies and selling shares on the stock market. According to Bonelli (1971), in 1907 72 percent of the equity of all limited-liability firms was traded on stock markets.

The stock market boom lasted only for a few years. According to Sicil-

---

8. According to Enriques (2003), for the period 1942–93 the correct score on antidirector rights for Italy is 2 rather than 1 because proportional representation on the board was an option available to any firms since 1942.

iano (2001), Banca Commerciale, Credito Italiano, and the other banks probably inflated stock prices by purchasing shares while borrowing against their equity stakes in traded firms. An increase in the short-term interest rates in 1907 increased the banks' costs of sustaining prices. The resulting liquidity crisis forced the banks first to stop buying shares and then to sell their stakes in the traded firms. In turn, the sale of their stakes put downward pressure on prices, thereby exacerbating the crisis. This major financial crisis lasted until 1914.

The crisis of 1907 spurred a regulatory intervention by the government. After years of debates, in 1913 a new law prohibited banks from trading shares of companies listed on the stock exchanges. According to Baia Curioni (1995), this regulatory intervention proved the major cause of the underdevelopment of the Italian stock market. Siciliano (2001) disagrees, however, because France, the United Kingdom, and the United States introduced similar laws without damaging effects on the stock market.

With no doubts, the crisis of 1907 profoundly impacted small investors. A good example is FIAT, the automotive company at the core of the Agnellis' empire, which was then traded on the Turin stock exchange. The company operated in a glamorous (for the time) sector, which had tremendous growth opportunities and had generated a lot of excitement in the investing public. In 1906, FIAT's stock traded at Lit 2,000 per share (a price-earnings ratio of twenty-eight). The collapse of the stock market brought the share price down to Lit 17 in just a few months. The creditors stepped in to rescue the company from the brink of liquidation. A pool of banks, led by Banca Commerciale, cancelled existing shares, approved a new share issue, and gave back the control of the company to Giovanni Agnelli, the chief executive officer (CEO) before the crisis.

A thousand small shareholders, who had seen the value of their shares disappear, sued the managers of FIAT for accounting irregularities and price manipulation. The trial received significant attention because of Giovanni Agnelli's close friendship with Prime Minister Giovanni Giolitti. The trial lasted five years and concluded with the declaration that Agnelli was not guilty of any wrongdoing.

By 1918, the MSE became Italy's main stock exchange, although by then the phase of strong development had ended. Figure 6.1 plots the number of companies traded on the MSE over the twentieth century as a raw number and as a fraction of the population (in millions). La Porta et al. (1997) suggest that the latter measure is a good indicator of stock market development. The figure shows a highly nonmonotonic pattern of development. The strong growth of the beginning of the century lasted until 1914, and a period of limited growth followed until 1930.

Figure 6.1 shows that the Great Depression brought about a drastic reduction in the number of traded companies. With the nationalization of the

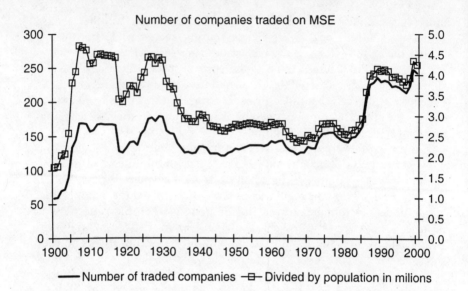

Fig. 6.1   Evolution over time of the number of companies traded on the MSE

Notes: The continuous line represents the raw number and is measured against the axis on the left. The dotted line, whose values are shown on the right axis, represents the number of firms divided by the population in millions. The time series of the population is obtained from Rey (1991) and Datastream.

universal banks and the creation of IRI, the stock market became secondary in the process of allocation of capital toward investment.

One important cause of the end of the period of growth for the stock market was the lack of protection for minority shareholders. There was a general market perception that universal banks and managers like Agnelli used the investment boom early in the century to pump and dump their shares. Further, the drastic increase of dividend taxation at company and personal level introduced by the fascist government made investment in the stock market even less attractive (Aleotti 1990).

The situation improved marginally after the Second World War. In this period, a total of ten local stock markets existed in Italy. In 1962, the nationalization of the electric industry caused a pronounced reduction in the total market capitalization as shown in figure 6.2, which plots the total market capitalization as a percentage of the gross national products over time. It is interesting to note that the nationalization itself was not associated with a decrease in market capitalization. To the contrary, total market capitalization increased considerably while the politicians debated the new law. It was the subsequent wasting of resources in negative net present value (NPV) projects brought the market down.

The slow decline of investment in the stock market continued until the middle of the seventies, when the government established CONSOB (in

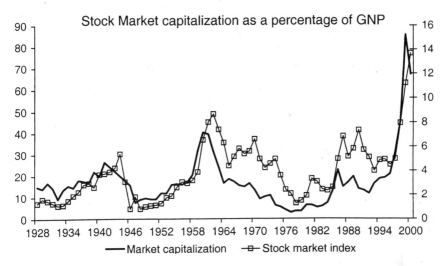

Fig. 6.2   Evolution over time of the market capitalization of the MSE

Notes: The continuous line is the total market capitalization as a percentage of the gross national product (GNP) and is measured against the axis on the left. The time series of the GNP is obtained from Rey (1991) and Datastream. The dotted line, whose values are shown on the right axis, is the index of stock prices on the MSE. The index is from Dimson, Marsh, and Staunton (2001); it measures the evolution of stock prices in real terms and is normalized so that it takes the value 1 in 1900.

1974). Substantial growth of the stock market began with the introduction of the mutual funds in 1983. In the three years between 1983 and 1986, mutual funds raised and invested about $6 billion in the stock market (De Luca 2002). These new available resources induced many companies to go public. Between 1983 and 1989, the number of companies traded on the stock market jumped up more than 50 percent. However, most of the new listings were subsidiaries of traded companies going public to take advantage of the stock market boom (Pagano, Panetta, and Zingales 1998).

    The real push in stock market development came after the start of the recent privatization program. In 1995 the stock market capitalization was only 20 percent of the gross national product (GNP). In 2000 it had grown to 70 percent. The increase in market capitalization was due to the listing of huge government-controlled companies, such as ENI (chemicals), INA (insurance), IMI (banking), and ENEL (energy), and the sale of the government-owned control stakes in already-listed banks, such as Comit, Credit, and BNL. These privatizations went hand in hand with regulatory reforms, such as the law on insider trading in 1991, the takeover law in 1992, and Draghi's Law in 1998.

    With a total market capitalization in 2000 of 70 percent of GNP, the MSE is comparable to stock markets in other developed countries. However, the Italian stock market does not mirror the Italian economy. Large corporations and financial institutions dominate the stock market, while the greatest majority of firms shy away from the stock market.

6.3.1   Investor Protection and Stock Market Development

According to La Porta et al. (1998), stock market development should be positively correlated with shareholder protection. The intuition is that investors will not provide equity to finance a firm unless they are confident of receiving a fair return from their investment. If shareholder protection is low, minority shareholders require a high return from their investment to compensate them for the high risk of expropriation by the management or controlling shareholder. The high required rate of return makes external finance costly and leads fewer companies to go public. Consistent with this prediction, La Porta et al. (1997) find that in the 1990s countries with stronger shareholder protection were characterized by larger stock markets.[9] This finding results from a cross section of countries, but it should also hold with time series data for a single country.

To test this prediction we compare the stock market development across the three subsamples identified in section 6.2.2, which display significant differences in investor protection. As discussed before, the period 1900–41 had the lowest level of investor protection; 1974–2000 exhibited the highest investor protection of the periods; an intermediate level of investor protection characterized the years between 1942 and 1973. As alternative measures of stock market development, we use the ratio of the number of traded companies to population (in millions) and market capitalization as a percentage of GNP.

As shown in column (1) of table 6.2, the indicators for the periods with the lowest and the highest investor protection are both positive and statistically significant in the regression explaining the variation of the number of traded companies scaled by population during the century. This implies that the subsample 1942–73 is characterized by higher investor protection but lower stock market development than the subsample 1900–41. The comparison between the second (1942–73) and third (1974–2000) subsamples is instead fully consistent with the theory: higher investor protection accompanies more financial development. The results do not change in column (2), where we add the stock market index to control for firms' opportunism in their decision to go public.[10]

In column (3), we use the index of antidirector rights proposed by La Porta et al. (1998). We follow Enriques (2003) and compute the evolution of this index from 1900 to 2000. As discussed in footnote 8, the index takes a value of 1 before 1942, equals 2 for the 1942–93 period, increases to 3 in

9. Shleifer and Wolfenzon (2002) formally model this theory.
10. Pagano, Panetta, and Zingales (1998) find that market timing is an important determinant of the going-public decision by Italian companies.

Table 6.2	**Investor protection and stock market development**					
	No. of traded companies scaled by population			Market capitalization divided by GNP		
Dependent variable	(1)	(2)	(3)	(4)	(5)	(6)
Constant	2.68***	2.34***	4.80***	17.15***	−0.47	26.06***
	(0.11)	(0.17)	(0.34)	(1.67)	(3.42)	(3.20)
Dummy 1900–1941 = lower	0.98***	1.18***		−0.49	7.83***	
investor protection	(0.15)	(0.17)		(1.99)	(2.19)	
Dummy 1974–2000 = higher	0.75***	0.69***		0.96	−2.57	
investor protection	(0.17)	(0.16)		(4.12)	(2.31)	
Stock market index		0.08***	0.03		4.44***	2.54***
		(0.03)	(0.03)		(0.80)	(0.49)
Antidirector rights			−1.50***			−19.61***
			(0.26)			(3.20)
(Antidirector rights)^2			0.27***			4.44***
			(0.04)			(0.83)
R^2	0.31	0.36	0.23	0.01	0.61	0.76
No. of observations	101	101	101	69	69	69

Notes: Stock market development (the dependent variable) is measured alternatively as the number of traded companies divided by population in millions (in columns [1] and [2]) or market capitalization as a percentage of GNP (in columns [3] and [4]). Independent variables are: a dummy variable that takes value 1 in the years from 1900 to 1941 and 0 otherwise to represent the period with relatively lower investor protection; a dummy variable that takes value 1 in the years from 1974 to 2000 and 0 otherwise to represent the period with relatively higher investor protection; and the stock market index. The latter is obtained from Dimson, Marsh, and Staunton (2001), is measured in real terms, and is normalized so that it takes value 1 in 1900. Antidirector rights measure the degree of shareholder protection. It is produced by La Porta et al. (1998) and extended over time for Italy by Enriques (2003). OLS regressions: robust standard errors are in parentheses.
***Significant at the 1 percent level.

1994, and jumps to 5 from 1998. The results in column (3) confirm a strong nonlinear relation between stock market development and investor protection. Starting from a low level of investor protection (below 2), an increase in investor protection reduces stock market development. The opposite happens if we start from a high level of investor protection (above 3).

In columns (4) to (6), we use the market capitalization as a percentage of GNP as an alternative measure of stock market development. The results in column (4) indicate that there is no significant difference in stock market development across the three subsamples. When we add the stock market index, in column (5), we find that the period 1900–41 (the period with the lowest investor protection) is characterized by higher stock market development than the later periods. The results in column (6) confirm the U-shaped relation between stock market development and investor protection. Overall, the findings in table 6.2 suggest that there is no monotonic relationship between investor protection and stock market development, which is difficult to reconcile with the law and finance view.

6.3.2   Discussion

An important missing variable in the regressions reported in table 6.2 is enforcement. La Porta et al. (1998) and Bhattacharya and Daouk (2002) show that enforcement is a crucial explanatory variable in a cross-country setting. To evaluate the effect of enforcement, Enriques (2003) analyzes the quality of Italian corporate judges' decisions in 123 cases between 1986 and 2000. He finds that judges tend to be biased in favor of corporate insiders and very formalistic in their arguments. Moreover, he finds no evidence that judges take into account the impact of their decisions on the incentives and the behavior of corporations and managers. These findings confirm the evidence in La Porta et al. that the quality of legal enforcement in Italy is very low, as measured by rule of law and judicial efficiency. Unfortunately, we do not have a time series measure of enforcement that we can use in our study.

A second variable missing from the regressions in table 6.2 is politics. A growing academic literature argues that a country's financial development is the outcome of ideology and the economic interests of voters and pressure groups. Rajan and Zingales (2003) argue that the stock market can be either fostered or hampered by government action, depending on the balance of powers between pressure groups. Pagano and Volpin (2001) and Biais and Perotti (2002) argue that state intervention in the economy should be negatively correlated with financial development, because the state acts as a substitute for financial markets. One proxy for the government's intervention in the economy is the number of government-controlled companies on the stock market as a percentage of the total number of traded companies.

Figure 6.3 plots the evolution of stock market development and public ownership of traded companies over time. The initial period of growth ended with the Great Depression and was followed by a long period of stagnation, which lasted until the 1980s. Only in 1985 did the number of companies on the stock market exceed the level it had reached in 1930. When combined with the observation that gross domestic product increased by 200 percent in real terms between 1950 and 1980, these data emphasize what little relevance to the Italian economy the stock market has had since the Great Depression. While the stock market stagnated, the role of the government increased. From 1950 to 1980, between 15 and 20 percent of traded companies in Italy were controlled by the government. The correlation between the two series is –70 percent.

According to Rajan and Zingales (2003), another important variable to explain stock market development is openness, defined as the ratio of the sum of imports and exports to GNP. Their argument is that a country opens to trade to take advantage of growth opportunities. To finance these investment opportunities, incumbents needs to raise capital and therefore

Stock market development and State ownership

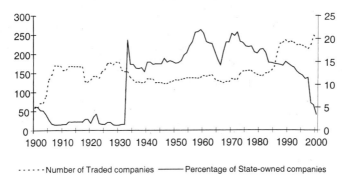

Fig. 6.3   **Evolution of the presence of the government on the stock market**

Notes: The variable called government-controlled traded firms is the percentage of traded companies under government control. It is plotted as a continuous line, and its value is shown on the right axis. The dotted line (measured against the left axis) is the number of companies traded on the MSE.

demand more financial development. As discussed in section 6.2.2, Italy was relatively open to trade at the beginning of the century, became an autarchy in the 1930s, and opened up to trade again in the late 1950s.

In table 6.3, we add the measures of government intervention and openness to the legal variables. In column (1), we use the number of traded companies as a fraction of population as the dependent variable. We find that only the political variable is significant and has the predicted negative sign. This result is also robust across specifications. We obtain the same result in column (2), where financial development is measured as market capitalization over GNP. In this specification, the index of antidirector rights is also statistically significant and positive. This result suggests that once we control for government intervention investor protection has the predicted positive impact on stock market development.[11] Contrary to Rajan and Zingales (2003), openness is negatively correlated with financial development. A possible reason is that openness is positively correlated with GNP, which is at the denominator in this measure of financial development.

In column (3), we look at the number of independent public offerings (IPOs) as an alternative measure of financial development. The fraction of government-controlled traded firms is negatively correlated with the number of IPOs. Also, as in column (2), an increase in investor protection is associated with an increase in the number of IPOs. Consistent with Rajan and Zingales (2003), openness is positively correlated with the number of IPOs. The evidence in column (3) is consistent with all three channels dis-

---

11. When we estimate the specification in column (1) on the smaller sample of sixty-nine observations used in column (2), not reported, we obtain the same results as in column (1).

Table 6.3   Investor protection, openness and politics

Dependent variable	No. of traded companies scaled by population (1)	Market capitalization divided by GNP (2)	No. of IPOs (3)
Constant	3.78***	17.41***	2.62
	(0.17)	(2.65)	(2.19)
Antidirector rights	−0.04	8.50***	2.46**
	(0.07)	(2.07)	(1.10)
Government-controlled traded firms (%)	−0.08***	−0.70***	−0.46***
	(0.01)	(0.17)	(0.12)
Openness	0.54	−60.23***	11.87*
	(0.35)	(8.71)	(6.21)
Stock market index	0.09***	3.41***	0.49
	(0.02)	(0.42)	(0.36)
R^2	0.49	0.78	0.24
No. of observations	97	69	97

Notes: The dependent variable is the number of traded companies divided by population in millions (in column 1), the stock market capitalization as a percentage of GNP (in column 2), and the number of IPOs (in column 3). Independent variables include the index of antidirector rights, as produced by LLSV (1998) and extended over time for Italy by Enriques (2003); the number of government-controlled companies as a percentage of all traded companies; openness, which is the sum of exports and imports of goods divided by GNP; and the stock market index. The latter is obtained from Dimson, Marsh, and Staunton (2001), is measured in real term, and is normalized so that it takes value 1 in 1900. OLS regressions: robust standard errors are in parentheses.
***Significant at the 1 percent level.
**Significant at the 5 percent level.
*Significant at the 10 percent level.

cussed above. Once we control for the other channels, stock market development increases with investor protection and openness and decreases with government intervention.

One concern with the results on the political variable is about its interpretation. We argue that state intervention in the economy should be negatively correlated with financial development because the state acts as a substitute for financial markets. However, the negative impact of government intervention on the number of traded companies could be more direct and less interesting. If the government fully nationalizes one traded company, the number of traded companies mechanically decreases by one unit. If this is the case, we expect to see delisting following an increase in the fraction of government-owned companies. We did not find such a relationship in the data (not reported).

The results in this section leave a key question unanswered: How did Italian companies finance the extraordinary economic growth of 1950s and 1960s if the stock market was stagnant? Figure 6.4 suggests that the growth

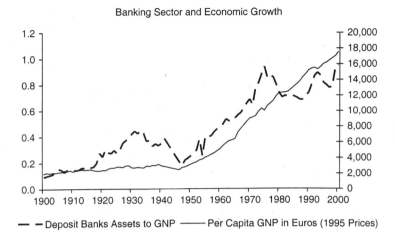

Banking Sector and Economic Growth

— — Deposit Banks Assets to GNP ——— Per Capita GNP in Euros (1995 Prices)

Fig. 6.4   Evolution of the ratio of deposit banks' assets to GNP and evolution of per capita GNP

Sources: Ciocca and Biscaini Cotula (1982), Rey (1991), and International Financial Statistics.

of the banking sector may be the answer. The growth in per capita GNP occurred at the same time as a similar expansion of the banking sector. The correlation of 91 percent exists between the ratio of deposit banks' assets to GNP and per capita GNP. The correlation of the growth in per capita GNP with stock market development is much lower: 3 percent if stock market development is measured as the number of traded companies to population and 22 percent if measured as the stock market capitalization to GNP.

6.4   The Ownership Structure of Firms

As shown by Barca (1994) and La Porta et al. (2000), high ownership concentration and pyramids characterize Italian corporate governance. Shleifer and Wolfenzon (2002) argue that high ownership concentration should be more common in countries with lower shareholder protection because of the inability of companies to sell equity to small shareholders when investors are not sufficiently protected by the law. Bebchuk (1999) points to the fact that control proves valuable in countries with low investor protection and therefore companies are closely held to ensure that control is not contestable.[12] Wolfenzon (1998) argues that pyramidal

12. Within this second interpretation, countries with low shareholder protection should exhibit controlling shareholders. This, however, does not necessarily imply that there will be concentrated ownership. Indeed, there can be a lock on control even without a large owner. This can happen through cross-participation, shareholders' agreements, and powerful political connections.

groups are created in order to expropriate shareholders, and this should occur more often in countries with lower investor protection. Bebchuk, Kraakman, and Triantis (1999) suggest the same empirical prediction by highlighting that pyramidal groups allow the separation between owner-ship and control without giving up control, which is a very important feature in a country in which control is very valuable.

6.4.1   Investor Protection and Ownership Concentration

Detailed data on ownership structure is available only from 1987 onward. Before 1987, only information on control can be found.[13] The only exception is a booklet produced in 1948 by the trade union of the Communist Party, the CGIL, which documents the ownership structure of all Italian firms at the end of the Second World War.

Because of this data limitation, in this section, we compare the ownership structure of all companies traded on the MSE in three years: 1947, 1987, and 2000. These years can be sorted by investor protection. According to our classification in three subperiods, investor protection was lowest in 1947, intermediate in 1987, and highest in 2000. Using the index of antidirector rights instead, antidirector rights equaled 2 in 1947 and 1987, and 5 in 2000. Table 6.4 compares six different measures of ownership concentration across these three samples.

The first measure is the fraction of voting rights owned by the largest shareholder. On average, the largest shareholder directly controlled about 45 percent of the votes in 1947, 55 percent in 1987, and 48 percent in 2000. According to this measure ownership concentration was higher in 1987 than in 1947 and 2000, while there was no difference between 1947 and 2000. This result suggests that ownership concentration has changed in a nonmonotonic fashion, first increasing and then decreasing.

The second measure is an indicator variable that takes a value of 1 if the company did not have a controlling shareholder (that is, if there was no shareholder with more than 20 percent of voting rights) and 0 otherwise. Excluding banks and insurance companies, no difference in this measure of ownership concentration existed over time. Only between 3.5 and 7.8 percent of the companies had no controlling shareholder. This result suggests that control was very valuable in all three years.

In companies with a controlling shareholder, one can reconstruct the chain of control and find the identity of the ultimate owner. The remaining four other indicators in table 6.4 characterize ownership concentration in companies with a controlling shareholder, that is, with a shareholder controlling at least 20 percent of the voting rights.

The number of voting rights controlled by the ultimate owner is the sum of all votes controlled both directly and indirectly by the ultimate owner in

13. See the appendix for a detailed description of this issue.

Table 6.4   **Evolution of the ownership structure: Summary statistics**

	1947	1987	2000	1947 vs. 1987	1947 vs. 2000	1987 vs. 2000
				Tests (significant percentage level)		
No. of observations	120	207	231			
Voting rights owned by largest shareholder (%) [538 observations]						
Mean	44.58	55.46	48.00	1	0	1
Median	48.65	54.14	52.11	1	5	1
Fraction of firms with no controlling shareholder (%) [558 observations]						
All companies	10.00	4.35	12.99	5	0	1
Excluding banks and insurance companies	7.76	3.53	5.62	0	0	0
Voting rights controlled by ultimate owner (%) [494 observations]						
Mean ·	48.98	59.87	57.73	1	1	0
Median	50.10	58.69	55.23	1	1	0
Cash-flow rights owned by ultimate owner (%) [494 observations]						
Mean	40.38	42.11	51.31	0	1	1
Median	44.10	47.00	52.92	0	1	1
Separation between ownership and control (voting rights/cash-flow rights) [494 observations]						
Mean	1.90	3.16	1.41	5	5	1
Pyramidal level [494 observations]						
Mean	1.43	1.86	1.31	1	0	1

Notes: This table compares the mean and median ownership structure in traded companies across the three subsamples: 1947, 1987, and 2000. Six measures are used to characterize the ownership structure of a firm: the percentage of voting rights owned by the largest shareholders, the percentage of firms with no controlling shareholder (no shareholder controlling more than 20 percent of the votes), the percentage of voting rights controlled (directly or indirectly) by the ultimate owner, the percentage of cash-flow rights owned by the ultimate owner, the ratio of voting rights and cash-flow rights controlled by the ultimate owner, and the pyramidal level, that is, the number of traded companies along the chain of control, including the company itself. The last four variables are computed only for firms with a controlling shareholder. For each of these measures, the sub-sample means (medians) are compared across years using pair-wise tests of equality of means (medians). 0 denotes no significant difference. 1 denotes significance at the 1 percent level. 5 denotes significance at the 5 percent level.

a given company. This measure is significantly higher in 1987 and 2000 than in 1947. On average, the ultimate owner owned approximately 60 percent of the voting rights in 1987 and 2000 compared to approximately 50 percent in 1947.

The total sum of cash-flow rights owned by the ultimate owner is the product of the fractions of cash-flow rights along the control chain: it represents the exposure of the ultimate owner to the cash flows produced by the company. On average, cash-flow exposure increased over time: the ultimate owner owned about 40 percent of the cash flow rights in 1947, 42 in 1987, and 51 percent in 2000.

Separation between ownership and control is the ratio of voting rights controlled by the ultimate owner to his cash-flow rights. This variable also followed a nonmonotonic pattern. First it increased from 1947 to 1987, and then it decreased from 1987 to 2000.

Pyramidal level is the number of traded companies along the chain of control, including the company itself. This variable followed a nonmonotonic pattern as well. The degree of pyramiding was significantly higher in 1987 than in 1947, as many subsidiaries of traded companies went public during the stock market boom. The degree of pyramiding decreases in 2000 as many subsidiaries were taken private.

6.4.2   Discussion

Overall, there are three main conclusions from table (4): (a) between 1947 and 1987, ownership became more concentrated and there was an increase in pyramiding; (b) between 1987 and 2000, there was a reduction in ownership concentration and in pyramiding; and (c) across all samples there was no significant change in the fraction of widely held companies, which remained very rare.

Result (a) seems in contrast with the law and finance view. Indeed, an improvement in shareholder protection should decrease ownership concentration (Shleifer and Wolfenzon 2002) and pyramiding (Wolfenzon 1998). One obvious objection is that possibly there was no real change in investor protection between 1947 and 1987. Although several reforms were introduced in the 1970s, the index of antidirector rights did not change and so, probably, did enforcement. This argument does not explain why there was no pyramiding in 1947.

Result (b) is in favor of the law and finance view. Between 1987 and 2000, investor protection certainly improved. The 1990s were characterized by intensive regulation of traded companies and the stock market. The index of antidirector rights increased from 2 to 5. Consistent with Shleifer and Wolfenzon (2002) and Wolfenzon (1998), between 1987 and 2000 there was a significant decrease in ownership concentration and less pyramiding.

Result (c) is difficult to reconcile with law and finance. Indeed, the improvement in investor protection was not associated with any change in the fraction of MSE companies that are widely held. One obvious explanation is that enforcement has always been very poor and has not changed over time. If so, control remained equally valuable across time because the improvement of investor protection did not affect the value of control. But if there is no significant difference in effective investor protection across the three years, then how do we explain result (b)?

A possible concern with the methodology used in table 6.4 is that the results may be due to a composition effect. For instance, since the optimal ownership concentration may vary across industries, the variation observed in the data may be simply due to changing industry composition over time. In table 6.5 we evaluate the impact of the legal indicators after controlling for industry effects. The three main findings are substantially

Table 6.5   **Evolution of ownership structure: Regressions**

	Constant	Dummy for 1947	Dummy for 1987	Fixed effect	Adjusted R^2	No. of observations
	Dependent variable: Voting rights owned by largest shareholder (%)					
(1)	48.25***	−5.74**	8.00***	Industry	0.06	538
	(1.37)	(2.63)	(2.00)			
(2)	48.50***	−2.84	5.82*	Group	0.12	538
	(2.06)	(5.03)	(3.10)			
	Dependent variable: Fraction of firms with no controlling shareholder (%)					
(3)	0.11***	0.05	−0.08***	Industry	0.12	558
	(0.02)	(0.03)	(0.03)			
(4)	0.09***	−0.00	0.01	Group	0.29	558
	(0.03)	(0.06)	(0.04)			
	Dependent variable: Voting rights controlled by ultimate owner (%)					
(5)	57.74***	−9.25***	2.33	Industry	0.08	494
	(1.12)	(2.16)	(1.59)			
(6)	56.53***	−6.12***	3.85	Group	0.06	494
	(1.80)	(4.36)	(2.62)			
	Dependent variable: Cash-flow rights owned by ultimate owner (%)					
(7)	51.26***	−11.40***	−8.68***	Industry	0.07	494
	(1.51)	(2.91)	(2.15)			
(8)	43.49***	−0.83	5.45*	Group	0.36	494
	(2.00)	(4.90)	(2.89)			
	Dependent variable: Separation between ownership and control (voting/cash-flow rights)					
(9)	1.41***	0.55	1.67***	Industry	0.09	494
	(0.23)	(0.44)	(0.32)			
(10)	2.05***	0.02	0.37	Group	−0.05	494
	(0.39)	(0.96)	(0.56)			
	Dependent variable: Pyramidal level					
(11)	1.29***	0.02	0.55***	Industry	0.12	558
	(0.06)	(0.11)	(0.08)			
(12)	1.53***	−0.22	0.04	Group	0.26	558
	(0.08)	(0.20)	(0.12)			

Notes: This table compares the ownership structure in traded companies across the three sub-samples (1947, 1987 and 2000) while controlling for industry and groups fixed effects. Ownership structure is characterized by the six measures described in table 6.4. Regressions with fixed effects: robust standard errors are in parentheses.

***Significant at the 1 percent level.

**Significant at the 5 percent level.

*Significant at the 10 percent level.

confirmed. We also control for fixed effects at the group level, because different groups may have idiosyncratic reasons for choosing a specific ownership structure. For instance, pyramiding is likely to be more common in larger groups. In table 6.5, we find that the group fixed effects eliminate the differences in pyramiding.

Figure 6.5 describes the evolution of the control of traded companies

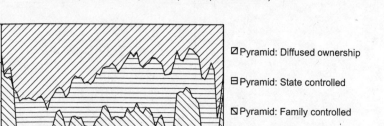

Control Composition of Traded Companies (Market Value)

☑ Pyramid: Diffused ownership

🖶 Pyramid: State controlled

◨ Pyramid: Family controlled

☐ Stand alone company: Diffused ownership

■ Stand alone company: State controlled

⊞ Stand alone company: Family controlled

Fig. 6.5   Distribution of different types of control over time

Notes: The size of each class is based on its relative market value. First, we distinguish between stand-alone companies and members of pyramidal groups. Then, within each category, we separate state-controlled, family-controlled, and widely held companies depending on whether the ultimate owner is the government, a family, or dispersed shareholders, respectively.

over time. Firms are classified into six classes of control: first, we distinguish whether the firm is a stand-alone or belongs to a pyramidal group. Second, we differentiate between family, widely held, and state-controlled firms. The figure shows that stand-alone companies rarely counted for more than 30 percent of the market value of all traded companies. It is interesting to observe that from the Great Depression on, the importance of widely held pyramids steadily declined. This trend has been reversed only recently with the government's program of privatization. State- and family-controlled pyramids were the groups whose shares increased the most. Family-controlled pyramids represented 30 percent of market capitalization of MSE in 1950 and increased steadily to 40 percent in the middle 1980s. More recently, they declined to about 20 percent at the end of the 1990s. Government-controlled pyramids went from 0 to 20 percent of market capitalization of MSE during the 1930s and increased steadily to 40 percent by the end of the 1970s. By 2000, after the recent sweeping program of privatizations, they had almost disappeared.

The extent of pyramiding may be affected by the tax treatment of intercompany dividends (Morck 2003). The data on Italy do not support this explanation. Before 1955, dividend income was not taxable in Italy (with the exception of a few years during the fascist regime when dividend income was subject to taxes). Hence, no double taxation of intercompany

Average Pyramidal Level

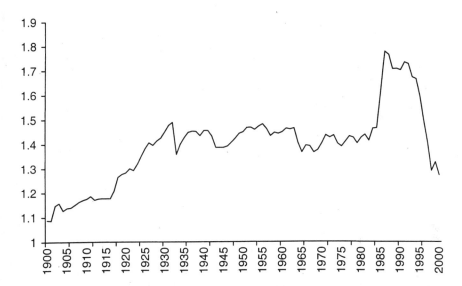

Fig. 6.6   Evolution over time of the average pyramidal level
Notes: All government-controlled firms are excluded. Pyramidal level is defined as the number of traded companies along the chain of control, including the company itself.

dividends existed. In 1955, Italy introduced a new tax on corporate income at an average rate of 18 percent, including surcharges. This additional tax was not deductible in the hands of recipient corporations and therefore discriminated against vertical groups.[14] Under the general income tax reform of 1974, the additional tax burden on vertical groups further increased as intercompany dividend income became taxable at a 25 percent rate in the hands of a recipient company. However, pure holding companies became eligible for taxation of dividend income at a 7.5 percent rate.[15] This tax regime changed in 1977, when the law introduced a tax credit for dividends that removed double taxation.

Since the treatment of intercompany dividends is the same in the three years (1947, 1987, and 2000), taxes cannot explain the difference of pyramiding shown in table 6.4. More generally, the evidence is weak. Figure 6.6 shows that the introduction of double taxation in 1955 was not followed by any significant changes in pyramiding.[16] Because there was no concurrent

14. Dividends were taxed both as corporate income of subsidiary and as dividend income of its parent.
15. Such favorable taxation of pure holding companies may explain why many Italian traded companies chose to present themselves as pure holdings on the stock market.
16. The steep drop in the average pyramidal level after 1962 was the result of rapid consolidation of former electrical companies after nationalization of electrical assets.

change in shareholder protection or other aspects of the institutional environment, any changes in the degree of pyramiding can be largely attributed to the tax effect, which turns out to be very small. At the same time, the elimination of double taxation in 1977 was not followed by any significant increase in the number of subsidiaries traded on the Italian stock market. The steep increase in pyramids came only ten years later and can hardly (if at all) be attributed to the change in the tax regime.

So what caused the increase in pyramids in the 1980s? A tentative explanation to be addressed more carefully in future research is that the financial reforms of the second half of the 1970s and the beginning of the 1980s channeled new liquidity to the stock market. Because of the reforms, investors had found new faith in equity investment (for instance, via the newly established mutual funds). Companies took advantage of this liquidity to raise money via IPOs and carve-outs and grow. Very soon, this stock market boom came to a stop, and what was left was several pyramidal groups.

6.5   Family Capitalism

The three major family-owned companies in 1928 were Italcementi, a producer of cement owned by the Pesentis; Pirelli, a producer of rubber cables and tires owned by the Pirelli family; and FIAT, a car company owned by the Agnelli family. Their growth largely benefited from the market power enjoyed in their industries and protection from foreign competition. The insulation from foreign competition in their core sector partly continued after the war. Hence, these three major families diverted some resources to invest outside their core sectors, acquiring electric companies, real estate firms, banks, and insurance companies.

The history of these three family groups is remarkably similar. Italcementi was set up in 1865 by Carlo Pesenti I, Pirelli was founded in 1872 by Giambattista Pirelli, and FIAT was founded in 1899 by Giovanni Agnelli I. The first went public on the MSE in 1874, the second in 1922, and the third in 1924. Each of them soon acquired control of their product market with between 60 and 80 percent market share of the domestic market and then expanded outside their industry. The Pesentis invested in banks and insurance companies; the Pirellis expanded in the electric sector and abroad; the Agnellis mostly invested in the mechanical and electrical components sectors and in real estate.

In what follows we present in detail the evolution of the Pesenti group and discuss more generally the fortunes of the other families.

6.5.1   Evolution of the Pesenti Group

In 1865 Carlo Pesenti I established the first company of the Pesenti group, Italcementi, which went public on the MSE in 1874. The group began to expand outside the cement industry in 1945, when Carlo II, grandson of the founder, took over what had become a very profitable and powerful cement group. According to Confederazione Italiana del Lavoro (CGIL; 1948), at the time Italcementi produced 60 percent of the cement in Italy. In the following decade, Italcementi made several diversifying acquisitions through a nontraded subsidiary, Italmobiliare. Turani (1980) and Galli (1984) argue that monopolistic profits enjoyed by the group in the cement industry partially financed the acquisitions, as well as the unlimited credit obtained through strong political connections with the ruling Christian Democratic party and the Vatican. By 1953, Italmobiliare had gained control of an important stake in a traded company producing machinery, Franco Tosi; after subscribing to its major capital increase, it had acquired a 38 percent controlling stake in a traded insurance company, RAS; and it had obtained indirect control of its traded subsidiary, l'Assicuratrice Italiana. In this early period, the group also owned several nontraded banks, including Banca Provinciale Lombarda and Credito Commerciale (a third bank, Ibi, was acquired in 1967).

In 1967, at the apex of its expansion, the Pesenti group's involvement spanned the cement industry, construction and real estate, the mechanical and automotive sector, banking, and insurance. At that time the Pesenti group was second in wealth only to the owners of FIAT group, the Agnellis. The expansion into such diverse industries, financed with high leverage, proved a very risky strategy. The first difficulty came in 1968, when Carlo II had to sell the control of a troubled car company, Lancia, acquired in 1960, to the Agnellis, at a considerable loss. A second problem arose in 1972 when Michele Sindona, a Sicilian banker, acquired control of 36.5 percent of Italcementi. This acquisition threatened the Pesentis' control of their empire and forced Carlo II to buy out Sindona. The leverage of the group further increased as a result of financing the buyout with loans from Banca Provinciale Lombarda, which was still controlled by Italcementi through the nontraded subsidiary Italmobiliare. In 1979, Carlo II had to fend off another takeover attempt, this time by the Agnelli group, which acquired control of 10 percent of Italcementi and also threatened the Pesentis' market power in the cement industry through the expansion of Agnelli's cement company Unicem. In order to strengthen control over the group, the Pesenti group decided to change its organizational structure. In 1979 Italcementi distributed its stake in Italmobiliare to its shareholders on the basis of one Italmobiliare share for every two Italcementi shares held. The operation led to a listing of Italmobiliare on the MSE in 1980. In the same year Italmobiliare acquired 50.22 percent of Italcementi's capital from the Pesentis and became the holding company for the newly formed group.

The huge amount of debt incurred during the previous three decades of expansion led to the group's implosion in the early eighties. In 1981 l'Assicuratrice Italiana was delisted from the MSE after having been acquired by RAS in 1980; in 1984 the German group Allianz purchased a controlling stake in RAS. Credito Commerciale was sold to Monte dei Paschi di Siena in 1982, Ibi was sold to CARIPLO in 1983, and the group's last bank, Banca Provinciale Lombarda, was sold to San Paolo Group in 1984. Adding to its financial problems, Italmobiliare was also heavily involved in the notorious bankruptcy of Banco Ambrosiano, being its largest minority shareholder at the time of its collapse in 1982. Carlo Pesenti II died in 1984 during court proceedings against him and other executives of Italmobiliare for alleged fraud related to Banco Ambrosiano.

Carlo's son, Giampiero, who took control of the family business after Carlo's death, shaped the present of the Pesenti group. Under Giampiero, the group returned to its roots by refocusing on the cement industry. In 1987 Italcementi began trading publicly with two subsidiaries, Cementerie Siciliane and Cementerie di Sardegna, on a wave of investor optimism. By 1995, a year of investor pessimism, both cementeries and the manufacturing company Franco Tosi were losing money. They were delisted from the MSE after merging with their respective holding companies in 1996 and 1997. Capital increases as well as a subsequent swap of shares of holding companies and subsidiaries financed their three buybacks. In 1997 Italcementi increased its presence in the cement industry by purchasing a controlling stake in cement company Calcemento, a former member of the bankrupt Ferruzzi group. This subsidiary merged with Italcementi two years later. Franco Tosi was taken private through a share exchange with its parent Italmobiliare the same year. The evolution of the group is summarized in table 6.6 and figure 6.7.

Table 6.6   Evolution of the Pesentis' group

Event	Company	Year
IPO	Italcementi	1874
	Italmobiliare	1979
	Cementerie Siciliane	1986
	Cementerie di Sardegna	1986
Acquisition	RAS	1952
	Franco Tosi	1953
	Calcecemento	1997
Sale	RAS	1985
Going private (delisting)	L'Assicuratrice Italiana	1980
	Cementerie Siciliane	1996
	Cementerie di Sardegna	1996
	Franco Tosi	1997
	Calcecemento	1999

Note: This table summarizes the corporate events affecting the structure of the group, distinguishing among IPOs, acquisitions, sales, and delistings.

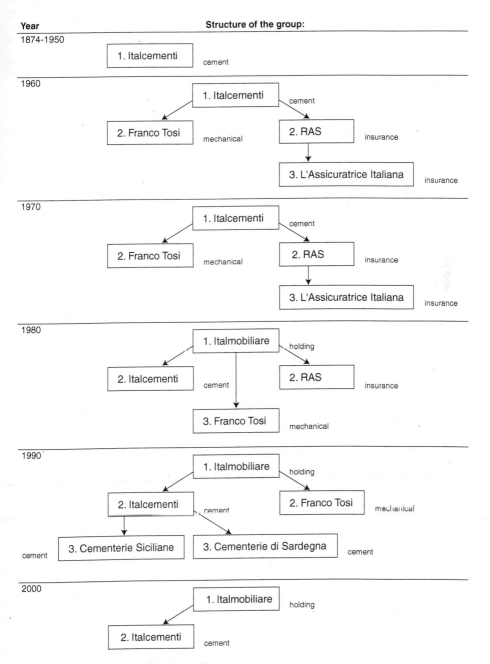

Year   **Structure of the group:**

1874-1950
1. Italcementi — cement

1960
1. Italcementi — cement
2. Franco Tosi — mechanical
2. RAS — insurance
3. L'Assicuratrice Italiana — insurance

1970
1. Italcementi — cement
2. Franco Tosi — mechanical
2. RAS — insurance
3. L'Assicuratrice Italiana — insurance

1980
1. Italmobiliare — holding
2. Italcementi — cement
2. RAS — insurance
3. Franco Tosi — mechanical

1990
1. Italmobiliare — holding
2. Italcementi — cement
2. Franco Tosi — mechanical
3. Cementerie Siciliane — cement
3. Cementerie di Sardegna — cement

2000
1. Italmobiliare — holding
2. Italcementi — cement

Fig. 6.7   Evolution of the Pesenti group

Notes: This figure shows the traded members of the Pesenti group and the structure of the group at ten-year intervals. Each box represents a traded company. An arrow denotes the chain of control. The number in the box denotes the pyramidal level.

6.5.2 General Findings

In table 6.7, we show the ten largest groups as measured by market capitalization at the end of 1930 and at ten-year intervals until 2000. The names of groups controlled by families are designated with a superscript b. The names of government-controlled groups are designated with a superscript a. As one can immediately see, in 1930, only one family-controlled group appeared in the top ten: the Agnelli group. A large widely held investment bank, Banca Commerciale, headed up the largest group on the stock market. Several management-controlled public conglomerates also topped the chart. Among those, Edison was the largest holding company in the electricity sector and Montecatini controlled mining and steel. In 1940 after the collapse of Banca Commerciale, IRI, the government-controlled agency created in 1933, was the largest group by market capitalization because it had taken over all companies previously controlled by Banca Commerciale. One new family made its appearance in the top ten, the Pirellis.

The presence of family groups in the top ten increased steadily, reaching four in 1960: together with Agnellis and Pirellis, we find Pesentis and Olivettis. Family-controlled groups controlled five of the top ten spots from 1970 to 1990. A change in trend is evident in 2000, when only two family-controlled groups remained in the top ten: the Agnellis and the group controlled by Silvio Berlusconi.

A similar trend characterizes the evolution of the group controlled by Mediobanca, a secretive investment bank chaired by Enrico Cuccia that dominated Italian corporate finance through the second half of the century. Table 6.7 measures very ineffectively the power of Mediobanca in 1970s and 1980s. Because Mediobanca typically held minority stakes in traded companies and exercised significant influence through board seats and close relationships with creditor banks, it is difficult to quantify its influence.

Throughout the twentieth century, the Italian corporate governance system always had a reference point, a person or institution able to balance the interests of banks, families, and government. At the beginning of the century, Bonaldo Stringher and the Bank of Italy served as a reference point. From 1929 to the Second World War, the reference point was Alberto Beneduce and IRI. In the second half of the century, it was Enrico Cuccia and Mediobanca.

Table 6.7 confirms the view that family capitalism became important in the fifties and sixties and seems to have lost some ground since 1990. By contrast, widely held groups decreased in importance after the Great Depression and decreased in importance even more after the nationalization of the electricity industry when widely held conglomerates merged together and were taken over by the government. This trend reversed in the

Table 6.7   **The evolution of groups**

Group name	No. of companies	MV (%)	Group name	No. of companies	MV (%)
	1930			**1970**	
Banca Commerciale	21	30.68	IRI[a]	18	29.30
Edison	16	13.82	Agnelli[b]	8	16.33
Montecatini	5	4.46	Montedison[a]	3	8.57
SADE	6	4.34	Generali	1	5.92
Banca Italia[a]	2	4.19	Pesenti[b]	4	4.60
La Centrale	3	3.96	Bastogi	7	3.19
Snia Viscosa	8	3.75	Pirelli[b]	2	2.61
Ligure Lombarda	4	3.34	ENI[a]	4	2.03
Sme	1	3.13	Sindona[b]	5	1.96
Agnelli[b]	3	2.10	Olivetti[b]	1	1.94
C4 (%)	27.12	53.29	C4 (%)	22.56	60.12
C10 (%)	38.98	73.77	C10 (%)	39.85	76.45
	1940			**1980**	
IRI[a]	19	23.26	IRI[a]	18	25.20
Edison	17	16.45	Generali	2	12.73
Montecatini	5	9.09	Agnelli[b]	8	8.14
La Centrale	4	7.26	Montedison	10	7.84
SADE	5	5.65	Pesenti[b]	6	7.68
Bastogi	6	4.46	Ambrosiano	5	5.55
Agnelli[b]	2	3.46	Olivetti[b]	1	3.99
Snia Viscosa	1	3.44	Bonomi[b]	7	3.59
Pirelli[b]	3	2.96	Mediobanca	1	2.93
Ligure Lombarda	5	2.66	Ferruzzi[b]	3	2.87
C4 (%)	33.58	56.07	C4 (%)	26.76	53.92
C10 (%)	50.00	78.69	C10 (%)	42.96	80.52
	1950			**1990**	
IRI[a]	16	17.37	IRI[a]	17	18.54
Edison	11	15.04	Agnelli[b]	22	15.00
Montecatini	3	8.48	Generali	2	11.44
La Centrale	6	5.70	Ferruzzi[b]	13	10.02
Snia Viscosa	1	5.47	ENI[a]	9	5.99
Bastogi	4	4.84	De Benedetti[b]	10	3.55
SADE	6	4.72	Ministero Tesoro[a]	3	3.11
Agnelli[b]	3	4.12	Mediobanca	2	2.82
Pirelli[b]	4	3.34	Pesenti[b]	5	2.39
Riva[b]	2	3.00	Ligresti[b]	4	2.07
C4 (%)	27.69	46.59	C4 (%)	23.68	55.00
C10 (%)	43.08	72.08	C10 (%)	38.16	74.93

(*continued*)

Table 6.7   (continued)

Group name	No. of companies	MV (%)	Group name	No. of companies	MV (%)
1960			2000		
IRI[a]	25	22.07	Olivetti	6	24.07
Edison	12	14.28	Generali	3	10.20
Montecatini	2	7.83	ENI[a]	3	7.59
Agnelli[b]	3	7.33	ENEL[a]	1	6.55
La Centrale	6	5.25	Intesa	4	5.48
Pirelli[b]	3	3.97	San Paolo	4	5.46
SADE	7	3.53	Unicredito	3	4.89
Pesenti[b]	3	3.42	Berlusconi[b]	3	3.61
Bastogi	4	3.42	Agnelli[b]	5	2.70
Olivetti[b]	1	3.29	Montedison	7	2.28
C4 (%)	29.58	51.51	C4 (%)	5.53	48.41
C10 (%)	46.48	74.39	C10 (%)	16.60	72.83

Notes: This table reports the name and the size (as measured by the number of traded companies and the market capitalization as a percentage of the stock market capitalization) of the ten largest groups present on the MSE at ten-year intervals from 1930 to 2000. For every year and each measure of size, two indices of stock market concentration are provided: C4 and C10 are respectively the size of the four and ten largest groups relative to the total market.
[a]Government-controlled groups.
[b]Family-controlled groups.

1980s and 1990s because of the government's massive privatization program. In 2000, large financial groups (Generali, Intesa, San Paolo, and Unicredito) and large conglomerates (Olivetti, ENI, ENEL, and Montedison) occupied the top positions.

The current crisis at FIAT symbolizes this revolution. But the transformation goes beyond the events in the Agnelli group. Interestingly, all three major family groups of the past have experienced significant changes in recent years. Pirelli came close to a financial collapse in the 1990s and was rescued by a manager, Marco Tronchetti Provera. Tronchetti Provera, who married into the Pirelli family and steered the group away from tires toward telecoms, is now the company's largest shareholder. The Pesenti group experienced financial distress in the 1980s and had to refocus on the cement sector by selling its controlling stakes in banks and insurance companies. The family still controls the group, although it has lost most of its economic influence. Finally, the Agnelli group might not survive the current crisis.

6.5.3   Discussion

So why did family capitalism persist for so long in Italy? Most likely the absence of regulatory intervention and the abundance of government corruption preserved the right conditions for family capitalism over time.

During the entire twentieth century, there was virtually no change in the inheritance tax in Italy. Therefore, taxation did not change a family's incentives to sell controlling stakes. In contrast, the top rate of the inheritance duties in Britain increased to 80 percent in 1949. Colli, Fernandez Perez, and Rose (2003) argue that inheritance duties profoundly affected family firm behavior in Britain, causing a large increase in the number of companies going public. Similarly, no major external institutional shocks existed. Unlike in Japan at the end of the Second World War, the Americans did not engage in a reform of Italian capitalism. As discussed by Amatori (1997), the "Americanization" process in Japan led to the improvement of regulation and the dismantling of the *zaibatsu,* the large family groups. In Italy, due to a lack of regulatory changes, both family- and state-controlled groups survived after the war.

In addition to a lack of regulatory changes, little change occurred in legal enforcement. Enriques (2003) shows that enforcement of the law has always been extremely poor in Italy. With poor enforcement, changes in investor protection impacted companies little. With low effective investor protection, controlling shareholders continued to enjoy large private benefits of control from generation to generation.

6.6   Conclusion

In recent years, Italian capitalism has shown signs of a historical transformation.

Since the 1980s the stock market has grown in significance for the Italian economy. Many important private companies, including Benetton, Luxottica, Campari, and De Longhi, now trade publicly. Many more are considering public listings. Furthermore, recent governments have been committed to a program of privatization and have engaged in a stream of reforms to improve investor protection.

At the same time, the control of the largest traded companies has become relatively more contestable. Currently, out of the top ten groups in terms of market capitalization, only the group led by Prime Minister Silvio Berlusconi is controlled with more than 30 percent of votes. The market for corporate control has become more active with the first successful hostile takeover in Italy occurring in 1999 (the takeover of Telecom Italia by Olivetti).

The banking sector is also undergoing a sensational transformation. Mediobanca no longer predominates as an underwriter and investment bank. A process of consolidation has created an oligopoly of universal banks.

Finally, investors have become more aware of corporate governance issues. As a consequence, several groups have begun simplifying their control structure by taking the holding companies in the intermediate layers of their pyramidal groups private.

Appendix

Description of the data

This paper uses a unique set of yearly data on valuation, financials, and control structure of all companies traded on the MSE from 1900 to 2000. The data have been hand-collected from several sources.

The investment guide *Indici e dati* (Mediobanca, various years–b) serves as the main source of financial data and year-end market capitalization. *Indici e dati* covers most companies traded on the MSE and selected companies traded on small exchanges. Another investment guide, *Guida dell'azionista* (Credito Italiano, various years), was useful for this purpose because it reports some financial indicators for all companies traded on all Italian stock exchanges. Unfortunately, this source provides less information than Indici e dati on many key variables, most importantly, describing valuation of the companies: unlike *Indici e dati, Guida dell'azionista* shows only maximum and minimum yearly price instead of market values of the companies. In most cases we are able to correct this problem by calculating market value using share prices on the last day of December published in a Milan newspaper, *Corriere della Sera,* and the number of outstanding shares from *Guida dell'azionista.* Since *Indici e dati* does not have balance data after 1977, *Guida dell'azionista* and *Calepino dell'azionista* (Mediobanca, various years–a) serve as the source of financial data for the second half of the sample.

Taccuino dell'Azionista (SASIB, various years) is the primary source of information for control over the companies in the sample. This publication gives brief histories of the companies listed on the MSE every year. Most recent volumes (since 1987) also present data on exact shareholding breakdowns. Most traded Italian companies have majority shareholders controlling more than 20 percent of votes in recent years. This concentration of voting power makes our definition of control unambiguous in most cases. Before 1987, we have precise information on ownership of all traded companies only for 1947, from CGIL (1948). For all other years, we have reconstructed the chain of control that ends with the ultimate owner (a family, the state, or a widely held company), where we have used all available sources to track all transfers of controls however defined. One limitation of this approach is that the definition of control may vary across sources. However, the information for 1947 suggests that ownership has always been quite concentrated. Hence, we find it likely that the definition of control is consistent across sources for most firms. Since we prefer to be conservative in defining control, we assume that control rests in the hands of the most recent controlling shareholder unless we have explicit information otherwise. In some cases our sources describe the control structure as a coalition control or as a widely held company. The first usually corresponds to an agreement by a group of shareholders to exercise relative majority control through coordinated voting of stakes with combined share of votes less than 20 percent. No controlling shareholders or controlling coalitions exist in the second case. We do not distinguish the cases of coalition control from the cases of widely held companies in the analysis. An incomplete list of our sources on control is the following: Amatori and Brioschi (1997), Amatori and Colli (1999), Barca et al. (1997), Brioschi, Buzzacchi, and Colombo (1990), Chandler, Amatori, and Hikino (1997), Ciofi (1962), Colajanni (1991), De Luca (2002), Grifone (1945), Scalfari (1961, 1963), Scalfari and Turani (1974), and Turani (1980).

Companies are classified into sixteen industrial sectors: (a) food and agriculture; (b) banks; (c) cement, glass, and ceramics; (d) chemicals and pharmaceuticals; (e) communications; (f) construction and real estate; (g) editorial and paper; (h) electric; (i) electronics; (j) financial; (k) insurance; (l) mechanical; (m) metals; (n) textiles; (o) transportation, and (p) other industries.

References

Aleotti, Aldo. 1990. *Borsa e industria, 1861–1989: Cento anni di rapporti difficili.* Milan: Comunità.

Amatori, Franco. 1997. Growth via politics: Business groups Italian Style. In *Beyond the firm: Business groups in international and historical perspective,* ed. Takao Shiba and Masahiro Shimotani. Oxford: Oxford University Press.

Amatori, Franco, and Francesco Brioschi. 1997. Le grandi imprese private: Famiglie e coalizioni. In *Storia del capitalismo italiano dal dopoguerra ad oggi,* ed. Fabrizio Barca, 118–53. Rome: Donzelli Editore.

Amatori, Franco, and Andrea Colli. 1999. *Impresa e industria in Italia.* Venice, Italy: Marsilio Editori.

Baia Curioni, Stefano. 1995. *Regolazione e competizione: Storia del mercato azionario in Italia (1808–1938).* Bologna, Italy: Il Mulino.

Barca, Fabrizio. 1994. *Assetti proprietari e mercato delle imprese.* Vols. I and II. Bologna, Italy: Il Mulino.

Barca, Fabrizio, Francesca Bertucci, Graziella Capello, and Paola Casavola. 1997. La trasformazione proprietaria di FIAT, Pirelli e Falck dal 1947 ad oggi. In *Storia del capitalismo italiano dal dopoguerra ad oggi,* ed. Fabrizio Barca, 155–84. Rome: Donzelli Editore.

Barca, Fabrizio, and Sandro Trento. 1997. La parabola delle partecipazioni statali: Una missione tradita. In *Storia del capitalismo italiano dal dopoguerra ad oggi,* ed. Fabrizio Barca, 186–236. Rome: Donzelli Editore.

Battilossi, Stefano. 2000. Financial innovation and the golden ages of international banking: 1890–1931 and 1958–81. *Financial History Review* 7:141–75.

Bebchuk, Lucian. 1999. A rent-protection theory of corporate ownership and control. NBER Working Paper no. 7203. Cambridge, MA: National Bureau of Economic Research.

Bebchuk, Lucian, Reinier Kraakman, and George Triantis. 1999. Stock pyramids, cross-ownership and dual class equity: The creation and agency costs of separating control from cash flow rights. NBER Working Paper no. 6951. Cambridge, MA: National Bureau of Economic Research.

Bhattacharya, Utpal, and Hazeem Daouk. 2002. The world price of insider trading. *Journal of Finance* 57:75–108.

Biais, Bruno, and Enrico Perotti. 2002. Machiavellian privatization. *American Economic Review* 92:240–58.

Bonelli, Franco. 1971. *La crisi del 1907: Una tappa nello sviluppo industriale in Italia.* Turin, Italy: Fondazione Luigi Einaudi.

Bragantini, Salvatore. 1996. *Capitalismo all'italiana.* Milan: Baldini & Castoldi.

Brioschi, Francesco, Luigi Buzzacchi, and Massimo G. Colombo. 1990. *Gruppi di imprese e mercato finanziario: La struttura del potere nell'industria italiana.* Rome: Nuova Italia Scientifica.

Chandler, Alfred D., Franco Amatori, and Takashi Hikino, eds. 1997. *Big business and the wealth of nations.* Cambridge, UK: Cambridge University Press.

Ciocca, Pierluigi, and A. M. Biscaini Cotula. 1982. *Interesse e Profitto.* Bologna, Italy: Il Mulino.

Ciofi, Paolo. 1962. *I monopoli italiani negli anni cinquanta.* Rome: Editori Riuniti.

Colajanni, Napoleone. 1991. *Il capitalismo senza capitale.* Milan: Sperling & Kupfer.

Colli, Andrea, Paloma Fernandez Perez, and Mary Rose. 2003. National determinants of family firm development? Family firms in Britain, Spain, and Italy in the nineteenth and twentieth centuries. *Enterprise and Society* 4:28–64.

Confederazione Italiana del Lavoro (CGIL). 1948. *Struttura dei monopoli industriali in Italia.* Rome: Ufficio Statistica, Casa editrice Progresso.

Credito Italiano. Various years. *Guida dell'azionista: Ragguagli su tutte le azioni quotate in borsa e sulle societa emittenti.* Genova, Italy: Credito Italiano.

De Luca, Giuseppe. 2002. *Le società quotate alla borsa valori di Milano dal 1861 al 2000: Profili storici e titoli azionari.* Milan: Libri Scheiwiller.

Dimson, Elroy, Paul Marsh, and Mike Staunton. 2001. *Millennium book II: 101 years of investment returns.* London: ABN-AMRO and London Business School.

Dittmar, Amy, Jan Mahrt-Smith, and Henry Servaes. 2003. International corporate governance and corporate cash holdings. *Journal of Financial and Quantitative Analysis* 38:111–33.

Dyck, Alexander, and Luigi Zingales. 2004. Private benefits of control: An international comparison. *Journal of Finance* 59:537–600.

Enriques, Luca. 2003. Off the books, but on the record: Evidence from Italy on the relevance of judges to the quality of corporate law. In *Global markets, domestic institutions: Corporate law and governance in a new era of cross-border deals,* ed. Curtis J. Milhaupt, 257–94. New York: Columbia University Press.

Galli, Giancarlo. 1984. *Il romanzo degli gnomi.* Milan: Rusconi.

Gerschenkron, Alexander. 1962. *Economic backwardness in historical perspective.* Cambridge, MA: Harvard University Press.

Goldstein, Andrea. 2003. Privatization in Italy 1993–2002: Goals, institutions, outcomes, and outstanding issues. CESifo Working Paper no. 912. Munich: CESifo.

Grifone, Pietro. 1945. *Il capitale finanziario in Italia.* Rome: Einaudi.

La Porta, Rafael, Florencio López-de-Silanes, and Andrei Shleifer. 1999. Corporate ownership around the world. *Journal of Finance* 54:471–517.

La Porta, Rafael, Florencio López-de-Silanes, Andrei Shleifer, and Robert Vishny. 1997. Legal determinants of external finance. *Journal of Finance* 52:1131–50.

———. 1998. Law and finance. *Journal of Political Economy* 101:678–709.

———. 2000. Agency problems and dividend policies around the world. *Journal of Finance* 55:1–33.

———. 2002. Investor protection and corporate valuation. *Journal of Finance* 57: 1147–70.

Leuz, Christian, Dhananjay Nanda, and Peter D. Wysocki. 2003. Earnings management and investor protection. *Journal of Financial Economics* 69:505–27.

Mediobanca. Various years–a. *Calepino dell'azionista.* Milan: Mediobanca.

———. Various years–b. *Indici e dati relativi ad investimenti in titoli quotati nelle borse italiane.* Milan: Mediobanca.

Morck, Randall. 2003. Why some double taxation might make sense: The special case of inter-company dividends. NBER Working Paper no. 9651. Cambridge, MA: National Bureau of Economic Research.

Nenova, Tatiana. 2003. The value of corporate voting rights and control: A cross-country analysis. *Journal of Financial Economics* 68:325–51.

Pagano, Marco, Fabio Panetta, and Luigi Zingales. 1998. Why do companies go public? An empirical analysis. *Journal of Finance* 53:27–64.

Pagano, Marco, and Paolo Volpin. 2001. The political economy of finance. *Oxford Review of Economic Policy* 17:502–19.

Rajan, Raghuram, and Luigi Zingales. 2003. The great reversals: The politics of financial development in the 20th century. *Journal of Financial Economics* 69: 5–50.

Rey, Guido. 1991. *I conti economici dell'Italia, 1: Una sintesi delle fonti ufficiali 1890–1970.* Rome: Edizione Laterza.

Rossi, Stefano, and Paolo Volpin. 2004. Cross-country determinants of mergers and acquisitions. *Journal of Financial Economics* 74:277–304.

SASIB. Various years. *Taccuino dell'azionista: Annuario di documentazione finanziaria industriale e di borsa.* Milan: Solé 24 Ore.

Scalfari, Eugenio. 1961. *Rapporto sul Neocapitalismo in Italia.* Bari, Italy: Editori Laterza.

———. 1963. *Storia segreta dell'industria elettrica.* Bari, Italy: Editori Laterza.

Scalfari, Eugenio, and Giuseppe Turani. 1974. *Razza padrona: Storia della borghesia di stato.* Milan: Feltrinelli Editore.

Shleifer, Andrei, and Daniel Wolfenzon. 2002. Investor protection and equity markets. *Journal of Financial Economics* 66:3–27.

Siciliano, Giovanni. 2001. *Cento anni di borsa in Italia.* Bologna, Italy: Societa' Editrice Il Mulino.

Turani, Giuseppe. 1980. *Padroni senza cuore.* Milan: Rizzoli.

Wolfenzon, Daniel. 1998. A theory of pyramidal ownership. Harvard University, Department of Economics. Mimeograph.

Wurgler, Jeffrey. 2000. Financial markets and the allocation of capital. *Journal of Financial Economics* 58:187–214.

Zingales, Luigi. 1994. The value of the voting right: A study of the Milan stock exchange experience. *Review of Financial Studies* 7:125–48.

Comment   Daniel Wolfenzon

Italy is one of the best-known examples of a country in which pyramidal business groups dominate the corporate landscape. Aganin and Volpin's

Daniel Wolfenzon is assistant professor of finance at the Stern School of Business, New York University.

paper tracks down the origin and evolution of these groups. They also document the history of financial development and ownership concentration in Italy in the twentieth century. In addition, the authors provide an interesting case study of the evolution of the Pesenti group.

The paper finds that the number of firms in the Milan Stock Exchange (MSE) has not been increasing monotonically. Instead, the number of publicly traded firms per inhabitant was higher in the beginning of the century than in the middle. This number starts increasing around the early 1980s and today is above the level it had in the beginning of the century. Other variables followed an inverted U-shaped pattern. Ownership was more concentrated in the middle part of the century than it was both in the beginning and in the end. Also, there were more pyramids between 1930 and 1980 than there were in the periods 1900–1930 and 1980–2000.

Aganin and Volpin explain these patterns using the effect of laws and the level of government intervention in the stock market. The law and finance view states that the number of listed firms is a positive function of the level of investor protection (La Porta et al. 1997) and that the opposite relation holds for ownership concentration and the level of pyramiding (Shleifer and Wolfenzon 2002; Almeida and Wolfenzon 2004). Because in Italy the level of protection afforded by the law has been increasing over the century but the actual patterns of the financial variables are U-shaped, it appears as if the law and finance view does not provide a full explanation for ownership and financial development patterns.

The paper proposes that the missing force shaping these patterns is government intervention in the stock market. The Great Depression caused a large number of listed firms to fail. This prompted the Italian government to intervene in the economy by bailing them out. The upshot was that the government kept a controlling stake in most of these failing firms. The paper argues that this massive government intervention in the stock market was the cause of the decrease in the number of listed firms. The role of the government started to decline in the 1990s due to the large privatization plan. In line with the political view, as the government withdrew from the stock market, the number of listed firms started to increase again.

Aganin and Volpin have done a fantastic job of putting together the facts with the potential explanations. Despite the fact that they analyze a single country and that there are essentially only two changes (one from the beginning of the century to the middle of the century and the other from the middle to the end of the century), they have done a careful job at looking at all other potential explanations.

I have two comments. First, I will argue that the law and finance view and the political view are not mutually exclusive theories but can be seen as two elements of a single mechanism. In my second comment I highlight what I believe are the most important aspects of the case study of the Pesenti group. I think we can draw many lessons from this case study to help us understand why business groups are formed and why they frequently adopt a pyramidal ownership structure.

My first comment relates to a unifying framework to think about the two views (law and finance and politics). In this framework politics shapes the government's incentives to improve or worsen investor protection, and the laws and regulations are just some of the tools that the government has at its disposal to achieve these changes. Thus, laws do affect investor protection (law and finance view), but the reason why these laws are in place can be traced back to the government's incentives (political view).

But how can it be that the incentives of the government do not always point to increasing the level of investor protection? Among other reasons, it could be that, with low levels of investor protection and the resulting poorly developed financial markets, talented potential entrants might not be able to set up firms due to lack of finance. Therefore, incumbents benefit from a low level of investor protection since it effectively acts as a barrier to entry. If incumbents have sufficient influence over policy decisions, investor protection will remain low. If, for some reason, incumbents lose their influence, investor protection has the potential to improve.

This is not a new idea. In a study of more than twenty countries over the twentieth century, Rajan and Zingales (2003) find a similar U-shaped pattern in financial development. They explain these patterns with the different incentives that incumbent industrialists and financiers faced throughout the century to either retard or accelerate the level of financial development (see also Morck, Yeung, and Wolfenzon 2004). Moreover, in a recent paper, Braun and Raddatz (2004) find that, following a shock to the political equilibrium, financial development improves only in countries in which the strength of the group of incumbents that benefit from financial development is higher than the strength of the group that is negatively affected by it. Interestingly, and confirming the unified theory of politics and law and finance, Braun and Raddatz point to specific policy reforms that caused the higher levels of financial development.

However, aren't these results inconsistent with the law and finance view that proposes an immutable link between investor protection and legal origin? I do not think so. In my opinion, the law and finance view (La Porta et al. 1998) makes three important contributions. The first one is that the rights of investors are not protected equally across jurisdictions and that differences in this protection influences corporate decisions, financial development, and a number of real variables. In fact, theoretical models in the law and finance tradition (e.g., Shleifer and Wolfenzon 2002; Burkart, Shleifer, and Panunzi 2003; Almeida and Wolfenzon 2004) simply require that there be differences in investor protection and are agnostic about the source of variation. These models are consistent with differences in investor protection arising from differences in the laws, but they are also consistent with differences arising from enforcement, quality of accounting, efficiency of the judiciary, and so on. The second contribution of the law and finance view is that differences in laws can explain a large fraction of the variation in investor protection. Finally, the third component is that these laws are highly correlated with the legal origin of the country. The combined law and finance and politics view I described is perfectly consistent with contributions one and two.

Going back to the case of Italy, how can we explain the U-shaped pattern in the level of financial development when the level of investor protection afforded by the laws was monotonically increasing throughout the century? After all, a strict reading of the framework I described suggests that the effects of government incentives to alter the level of investor protection should be summarized in the laws and then only these laws should affect the level of investor protection.

One potential answer is that the level investor protection afforded by the laws as *measured* in the paper does not capture all the relevant aspects of investor protection. This could be due to either one of the following possibilities: (a) that the authors, despite their formidable effort, might not be capturing all the relevant laws, or (b) that, in addition to the laws, there are other factors, like the level of enforcement, that determine investor protection. If the investor protection afforded by the laws as measured in the paper is not a sufficient statistic for the actual level of investor protection, then it is possible that other proxies of investor protection show up significantly in the regressions. One such proxy could be a measure of the government's incentives to maintain a low level of investor protection. It turns out that government involvement in the stock market is a good measure of these incentives. As the authors explain, during the period in which the Italian government had a significant presence in the stock market, it had no incentives to improve the level of investor protection. However, when the time came to privatize the state-owned enterprises, the government had strong incentives to provide the highest level of investor protection possible. As Aganin and Volpin find, including both the level of protection afforded by the laws and the level of government intervention in the stock market in the regressions leads to the right sign on the coefficient of investor protection.

My second comment relates to the case study of the Pesenti group. The paper documents how the group grew from a single firm to a very large organization composed of many independent firms in a period of roughly 130 years. Most of the time, new firms were added to the group as partial subsidiaries of existing firms, thereby creating a pyramid. The case study also documents the enormous financing needs of the Pesenti group.

There is an emerging literature trying to explain the existence of business groups and their ownership structure. We can draw a couple of lessons from this case study. First, groups are not formed instantly; rather, they grow over time, starting from a single firm. As a result, a theory of business groups and pyramids should incorporate these dynamic aspects. Thinking about business groups as the optimal organization form chosen at a single point in time is perhaps less realistic. Second, the Pesenti group needed a great deal of external finance to set up or buy new firms. Members of the Pesenti family could have avoided creating a pyramid by setting up these new firms and holding shares directly in them. However, this would have required raising even more external finance. Setting the firm up as a partial subsidiary (pyramid) allowed the family to tap the internal resources of the existing firms. Thus, pyramids emerge as a result of large financing needs and poorly developed capital markets. In a recent paper Almeida and Wolfenzon (2004) explain the creation of groups and the use of pyramidal ownership using these two elements: a dynamic framework and poor financial development.

References

Almeida, Heitor, and Daniel Wolfenzon. 2004. A theory of family business groups and pyramidal ownership. New York University, Stern School of Business. Working paper.

Braun, Matias, and Claudio Raddatz. 2004. Trade liberalization and the politics of financial development. University of California at Los Angeles and World Bank. Working paper.

Burkart, Mike, Andrei Shleifer, and Fausto Panunzi. 2003. Family firms. *Journal of Finance* 58:2167–2202.

La Porta, Rafael, Florencio López-de-Silanes, Andrei Shleifer, and Robert Vishny. 1997. Legal determinants of external finance. *Journal of Finance* 52:1131–50.

———. 1998. Law and finance. *Journal of Political Economy* 106:1113–55.

Morck, Randall, Bernard Yeung, and Daniel Wolfenzon. 2004. Corporate governance, economic entrenchment and growth. NBER Working Paper no. 10692. Cambridge, MA: National Bureau of Economic Research.

Rajan, Raghuram, and Luigi Zingales. 2003. The great reversals: The politics of financial development in the twentieth century. *Journal of Financial Economics* 69:5–50.

Shleifer, Andrei, and Daniel Wolfenzon. 2002. Investor protection and equity markets. *Journal of Financial Economics* 66:3–27.

A Frog in a Well Knows
Nothing of the Ocean
A History of Corporate
Ownership in Japan

Randall K. Morck and Masao Nakamura

7.1 Introduction

An ancient Japanese proverb speaks of a frog prideful of the beauty at the bottom of his well and ignorant of the world beyond. The history of Japanese corporate governance is especially interesting because the Japanese literally searched the world for the best institutions of capitalism, and changed their institutions more radically and more often than in any other major industrial economy. These changes, and the associated successes and failures associated, illuminate fundamental issues of corporate governance, corporate control, and the economics of institutions.

Historical and contemporary research into corporate ownership in Japan both focus on intercorporate networks. In the last third of the twentieth century, the interfirm networks of interest are horizontal and vertical *keiretsu* groups. Horizontal *keiretsu*, like the Mitsui group, are interindus-

Randall K. Morck is the Stephen A. Jarislowsky Distinguished Professor of Finance in the School of Business, University of Alberta, and a research associate of the National Bureau of Economic Research (NBER). Masao Nakamura is Konwakai Japan Research Chair and professor at the Sauder School of Business and the Institute of Asian Research, University of British Columbia.

We are grateful for comments by Sheldon Garon, Akiyoshi Horiuchi, Yishay Yafeh, and two anonymous reviewers on an earlier version of this paper, entitled "Been There, Done That: The History of Corporate Ownership in Japan." We are also indebted for useful suggestions to Barry Eichengreen, Masaharu Hanazaki, Katsuyuki Kubo, Richard Sylla, Seki Obata, Dwight Perkins, Juro Teranishi, Yupana Wiwattakantang, and participants in the NBER History of Corporate Ownership conference. The Rise and Fall of Great Business Families at Lake Louise in 2003, the European Corporate Governance Network (ECGN)–NBER–University of Alberta–INSEAD conference of the same name at Fontainebleau in 2004, the Strategy and Business Economics seminar at the University of British Columbia, and the Hitotsubashi University Workshop on Corporate Governance in East Asia. This research was done while Randall K. Morck was visiting Hitotsubashi University in Tokyo.

try networks of firms whose small individual equity stakes in each other collectively sum to control blocks. Vertical *keiretsu* encompass the suppliers and customers of a single large firm, such as Toyota Motors. In both variants, public shareholders only have access to minority interests, rendering them essentially irrelevant to corporate governance. Adjunct to the *keiretsu* networks, most Japanese firms have strong ties to their lead lenders, or *main banks*.

However, *keiretsu* are a relatively recent development. During the feudal Takagawa period (1603–1868), Japanese firms were owned entirely by families—or, perhaps more properly, by clans. The Mitsui and Sumitomo family businesses both emerged during this era. In both cases, extensive sets of family rules and traditions determined corporate governance issues.

Following the Meiji Restoration of 1868, the new government promoted rapid industrialization. The Mitsuis, Sumitomos, and other new family businesses like Mitsubishi (run by the Iwasakis) needed capital vastly in excess of their own wealth, and they turned to public equity markets. The families organized a new firm to float equity for each new venture and organized them into pyramidal groups. At the apex of each was a family partnership (later a family corporation), which controlled several public corporations, each of which controlled other public corporations, each of which controlled yet other public companies, and so on. These structures, called *zaibatsu,* resembled modern Korean *chaebol* and similar pyramidal groups elsewhere.[1] Despite much research, the contributions of *zaibatsu* to the rapid development of the prewar period remain unclear. The *zaibatsu* were clearly key players in this development. But questions remain about whether powerful *zaibatsu* families grew overly concerned about preserving their wealth and control, and avoided high-risk projects in new industries that might have further accelerated Japan's modernization. Also, *zaibatsu*-controlled banks that lent solely to other firms in their *zaibatsu* failed during the interwar depressions, exposing problems inherent in related lending.

During World War II, Japan de facto nationalized many major corporations, subordinating them to central planners.[2] The Temporary Funds Adjustments of Law of 1937 created the Kikakuin, or Planning Agency, to centralize economic planning and administration. This required corporate boards to obtain government approval for most important decisions, such

1. The Kanji characters for zaibatsu are pronounced *chaebol* in Korean. One sees a stricter adherence to blood kinship in the governance of *chaebol*. Confucianism, influential in Korean cultures, extols respect for family, while Japanese Buddhism allows more leeway for sidelining inept blood kin.
2. Central planning in Japan involved rigid central plans, state command and control over all aspects of the economy, and the de facto abolition of ownership rights for capital. However, de jure private ownership of land was retained, as in communist Poland, as was de jure private ownership of zaibatsu and many other private-sector corporations. Japanese central planning was corporatist, rather than socialist, though much rhetoric of the period obscures this.

as changing their articles of incorporation and issuing equity or debt. Further government decrees abolished boards' rights to set dividends in 1939 and to appoint managers in 1943, reassigning these powers to Kikakuin. Although established by an extreme right-wing government, the Kikakuin consciously imitated many of the planning methods the Soviet Union used for its heavy industrialization in the 1930s.[3] As in Nazi Germany, this was accomplished amid much condemnation of "shareholders" (meaning the controlling shareholders, or *zaibatsu* families) for their self-interest, risk aversion, and unpatriotic myopia. This rhetoric would resurface later as a justification for depriving small shareholders, rather than controlling shareholders, of governance input.

Following the war, Japan was governed by the United States military from 1945 to 1952. General MacArthur broke up the *zaibatsu*. Consequently, Japan was briefly a widely held economy, like the United States and United Kingdom, in which most large public companies had no controlling shareholders. Japanese firms undertook hostile takeovers of each other, and raiders extracted greenmail from unwilling target firms.

Following the end of the U.S. occupation in 1952, Japanese firms began preempting takeovers by acquiring *white squire* positions in each other.[4] The major banks were often key in organizing these intercorporate equity placements. These holdings grew into the *keiretsu* system in the 1950s and developed more fully in the 1960s. That system, which still characterizes Japanese big business, is now under growing stress. At the beginning of the current century, Japan is once again bracing for major institutional changes.

Throughout all of these changes, the principals of Japan's great businesses actively pursued their own interests, balancing profit and control. In general, they shaped and reshaped organizational forms to accommodate this balance as new legal and other constraints emerged. This paper examines the emergence and evolution of these different organizational structures as responses to changing political and institutional circumstances.

Of course, institutional changes also reflected lobbying by big business. However, critical points in Japan's business history seem to involve exogenous events that clearly required adaptation by the business sector. The abrupt opening of Japan to world trade and the decision of the Meiji government to embark on a crash program of modernization are examples. The generally negative attitudes of both the Japanese military government and the Allied occupation force in the mid-twentieth century to the great *zaibatsu* families are two others.

Many factors underlie the rise of *zaibatsu* and the organization of *keiretsu*—economies of scope and scale, reputation, the circumvention of

---

3. See Okazaki (1994) for details.
4. A *white squire* is a friendly firm that buys a block of stock in a target firm to protect it from a raider. If the friendly firm takes the target over entirely, it is called a *white knight*.

flawed markets and institutions, and numerous other factors. However, we argue that the primary purpose of both *zaibatsu* and *keiretsu* was to protect the control rights of the great *zaibatsu* families and of professional managers, respectively. The *zaibatsu* families and *keiretsu* managers, especially main bank managers, also apparently benefited from political ties at certain times. This allowed both to become entrenched, and sometimes to retain governance powers they might otherwise have forfeited.

This paper is organized as follows. Section 7.2 describes the initial state of ownership of Japan's largest businesses immediately prior to the country's industrialization. Section 7.3 describes the formation and development of Japan's great *zaibatsu* in the late nineteenth and early twentieth centuries. Section 7.4 details the culling of Japan's corporate sector that took place in the 1920s and 1930s, as the country endured tandem depressions. Section 7.5 describes the imposition of a centrally planned economy by the military in the late 1930s and 1940s. Section 7.6 describes the U.S. occupation and the reconstruction of Japan as a widely held economy with Anglo-American corporate governance. Section 7.7 describes the modification of this system into the present *keiretsu* ownership structures. Section 7.8 reflects on the economics underlying the *zaibatsu* and *keiretsu,* and attempts to distill lessons from Japan's corporate governance history. Section 7.9 concludes.

Finally, we acknowledge a pervasive debt throughout this chapter to Hirschmeier (1964), Hirschmeier and Yui (1981), McMillan (1984), Nakamura and Odaka (2003), and Yafeh (2004) for general background information. We are also grateful to Teranishi (2003), who made an English draft of his volume available to us, also as general background information. To avoid repetition, these sources are not cited except where we specifically stress particular points they highlight.

7.2 Initial Conditions: The Tokugawa Economy

Acemoglu, Johnson, and Robinson (2001), Glaeser and Shleifer (2002), and other students of institutional economics stress the importance of very early historical events. We therefore begin with an overview of the economy of preindustrial Japan.

Japan's first contact with the Western world was a 1542 Portuguese trading expedition. At the time, Japan was divided into warring principalities. By 1590, General Hideyoshi Toyotomi had united the country by force. To pacify it, he demanded absolute submission from every part of society. Foreign merchants and missionaries interfered with this submission, so Hideyoshi persecuted and expelled foreigners.[5]

Hideyoshi died in 1598 after a failed invasion of Korea, and his comrade

---

5. Japanese shoguns and warlords are often cited by their first names.

General Ieyasu Tokugawa quickly took charge. By 1603, Ieyasu had defeated rival warlords, many backed by foreigners, and was appointed shogun by the emperor in Kyoto. He established a government in Edo (renamed Tokyo in 1868 when the emperor moved there from Kyoto), and his line would govern Japan as shoguns for over 250 years. Tokugawa froze an already rigid caste system,[6] with *samurai* warriors at the top, peasants in a second tier, craftsmen below them, and merchants in the bottom stratum.[7] Unsurprisingly, this moral inversion resulted in a prolonged economic stagnation, exacerbated by a code of chivalry, called *bushido,* that glorified honor above all else, entrusted all *samurai* with the power of life and death over the lower castes, forbade the higher castes from transacting business, and disparaged the pursuit of wealth as dishonorable.

Nonetheless, Ieyasu promoted foreign trade as he suppressed Christianity. But the third Tokugawa shogun, his grandson Iemitsu, concluded that trade and ideas were inseparable. Consequently, in 1633 he forbade traveling abroad, banned foreign books, and proclaimed a death sentence on foreigners found outside a small enclave in Nagasaki. Although some foreign books seeped in again after 1720, this early antiglobalization backlash continued to hermetically isolate Japan.

Although foreign trade was prohibited, domestic trade continued, and many merchant families grew wealthy. The Mitsui dynasty was founded by Hachirobei Takatoshi Mitsui (1622–94), a silk merchant who expanded into other commodities because of his extensive use of barter. The Sumitomos, who grew wealthy mining and smelting copper, apparently started in Kyoto and then moved to Osaka in the early Edo period. Both families established complicated *house rules*—constitutions governing all aspects of business. Power was divided between a patriarch and a *family council,* which served a quasi-parliamentary function.

For example, the Mitsui family consisted of eleven founding clans and devised elaborate rules for maintaining a balance of power among them. Representatives from each clan participated in management. The Mitsui house rules prohibited the founding clans from withdrawing their ownership shares and prohibited other branches of the family from gaining ownership rights. Voting power in the family council passed to the eldest sons of each founding clan. Younger sons could serve as managers or could be given start-up funding. The Mitsui family was known for adopting com-

---

6. The basis for this system dates to Hideyoshi Toyotomi (1536–98), a shogun who was born as a peasant, became an adopted *samurai* soldier, and conquered Japan after confiscating the weapons of peasants and religious institutions in 1588. Worrying that social mobility might produce another Hideyoshi, he made castes permanent and hereditary in 1590. None but *samurai* could carry weapons or wear armor. Despite this, some fluidity reappeared—for example, some feudal lords in the Edo era sponsored sumo wrestlers to become *samurai* and carry two swords. Because of this, contemporary historians typically use the more ambiguous term *status group,* rather than *caste.*

7. Only *eta,* outcasts with unclean professions, were lower.

petent hired managers through marriage to Mitsui daughters.[8] Additional house rules governed the disposition of property, marriage, divorce, adoption, and inheritance, and were strictly enforced at family councils to avoid intrafamily feuds. House rules forbade any Mitsui from bringing any family dispute to the public courts, becoming involved in politics publicly, creating debts, and guaranteeing debts. Involvement or investment in any nonfamily business and serving in public office were proscribed unless the Mitsui council granted an exception.[9]

Mitsui assets were divided into three classes. *Business assets* belonged to the entire Mitsui family, and the house rules permitted no division of them among the clans. *Common assets* were used for disasters and emergencies, and so served as a sort of insurance fund. Each clan managed its common assets as it chose, and the principal passed from generation to generation, but accumulated returns did not. When a clan patriarch died, the family council redistributed these gains among the eleven clans to preserve the rankings of the eleven founding clans. *Clan assets* were the undisputed property of the individual clans and could not be redistributed by the family council under normal circumstances.

The Sumitomo *zaibatsu* began when Tomomochi Soga, who married into the Sumitomo family and adopted its name, successfully reproduced a copper-smelting method he had learned of from a Western merchant in Osaka. The method, which uses lead to extract silver and other impurities from copper ore, increases the efficiency of copper smelting drastically and remained in use in Japan until the late nineteenth century. Soga built a copper refinery in Kyoto in 1590 and then (with his father) opened a business in Osaka to license the new copper-smelting method to competitors. This concentrated virtually all Japan's copper smelting in Osaka and earned Soga as much respect as a merchant might gain. He marketed his copper products using the trade name Sumitomo Izumiya. In 1691 the family began mining copper at Besshi for the Shogunate.[10] This proved extraordinarily lucrative, and financed virtually all subsequent Sumitomo businesses—including textiles, clothing, sugar, and medicines. Subsequently, one Sumitomo clan began a money exchange firm.

The Sumitomo family code resembled the Mitsui code in many ways.

---

8. Adoptions, like marriages, had to be approved by the Mitsui family council. An important example of this is Rizaemon Minomura (1821–77). Born to an unemployed *samurai* in Nagano, he migrated to Edo. While working for a merchant, he negotiated with Mitsui. Mitsui hired him in 1866 and ultimately adopted him into the family as head of the Minomura clan, one of the eleven at the Mitsui family council. (He adopted the Minomura name.) He subsequently held various key positions with Mitsui companies. In 1876 he reorganized the family money exchange operation into the Mitsui Bank and became its president. Rizaemon Minomura later adopted a merchant's son, Risuke Minomura (1843–1901).

9. See Yasuoka (1984) for details.

10. The Besshi copper mine remained in operation until 1973 and produced 700,000 tons of copper during its lifetime.

However, a few differences are worth noting. The Sumitomo code provided for its own revision, declaring a consensus of the council sufficient to change the code.[11] Perhaps more important, the Sumitomo code had no provision governing inheritance or requiring continued family dominance. Nonetheless, family control was preserved, probably because of two other differences. First, the Sumitomo patriarch led a symbolic existence. He gave formal approval to matters set before him, but the council actually made all significant decisions. This prevented one clan from dominating and creating a situation in which other clans might want out. Second, all family disputes, even ones within a single Sumitomo clan, had to be referred to the council. This made the council aware of discontent within clans at early stages. It also created a much more centralized management structure than in the Mitsui group. Very detailed reporting of anything extraordinary to the upper ranks was required.[12]

Famines, riots, and especially a growing financial dependence of *samurai* on merchants slowly weakened Tokugawa rule. The Mitsui and Sumitomo families served the government in all manner of commercial and financial dealings. This "corruption" (by the standards of *bushido*) undermined Tokugawa legitimacy, as did incompetence and declining morality among the Tokugawa leadership. From the late eighteenth century on, Russia and other European nations tried to force Japan's market open. In 1853 and 1854, the American commodore Perry bombarded Edo until the Tokugawa government agreed to open a few ports to foreign trade.

However, foreign trade remained very limited until the Meiji Restoration in 1868. Contemptuous of the Tokugawas' increasingly craven attitude toward foreigners, a group of *samurai* captured the emperor and seized power, claiming legitimacy by restoring his rightful rule. In fact, the imperial family, which provided titular emperors in Kyoto throughout the Edo period, had been symbolic throughout Japanese history. Real power remained with these *samurai* now as well. Nonetheless, this era is called the Meiji Period, in honor of the emperor who reigned from 1868 to 1912.

7.3   Early Industrialization Following the Meiji Restoration

The new Meiji rulers quickly realized that, to gain freedom from foreign pressure, Japan needed Western technology and therefore Western ideas. They dispatched a cadre of Japan's brightest students to study abroad and return with descriptions of foreign institutions. The government then launched a two-decade program of modernization, copying what they perceived to be best practice abroad. This period in Japan's history closely resembles some of the "shock therapy" reforms of the 1990s in post-Socialist

11. See Yasuoka (1984) for details.
12. See Asajima (1984).

states. In rapid fire, the new government introduced democracy modeled on the German Diet, compulsory education modeled on the French and German school systems, universities and an army modeled after those of Prussia, and a navy modeled after the British Royal Navy. Religious freedom, social mobility, and land reform quickly undermined both *bushido* and the caste system.

But most important, the Meiji government introduced the institution of capitalism. During its crash modernization, Japan adopted a legal system largely based on German civil law. Public bond trading began in the 1870s, and in 1878 the Tokyo and Osaka Stock Exchanges were formed and subjected to regulation under the Stock Exchange Ordinance. Leading merchant families issued stock to finance industrialization, and the great pyramidal *zaibatsu* groups that came to dominate Japan formed.

A central problem Meiji governments confronted was the distaste of the great mercantile families for pooling their capital with that of outsiders. On the one hand, the government wanted Japan's existing large businesses to grow, and this required respecting the sensibilities of their principals. On the other hand, the Meiji leaders knew that economic growth required strangers to pool capital. Apparently with government prodding, the Mitsuis, the Onos, and several other families formed the First National Bank. Yet the Mitsui and Ono families could not get along. Dissatisfied, the Mitsuis founded the Mitsui Bank in 1876. Similarly, after the Yasudas and Kawasakis set up the Third National Bank, the Yasudas set up their own Yasuda Bank in 1880.

This tension created apparent inconsistency in Meiji legal codes. For example, the 1896 civil code stipulates that "joint owners of property can demand their due shares of the property at any time." Yet the same code grants the head of a family control of family property, including that of subfamilies, "to provide for their future support." The same tension affected the evolution of the *zaibatsu*.

7.3.1   Defining a *Zaibatsu*

Before proceeding further, it is useful to define *zaibatsu,* a term replete with the ambiguity Japanese so admire. Many academics and others, both inside and outside Japan, use the term to refer to all the large business groups in the country prior to World War II. However, beyond that, there is no clear-cut unified definition of a *zaibatsu.* Several ambiguities are noteworthy.

First, the Japanese business and economic history literature generally holds that the *zaibatsu* developed in the Taisho period (1912–26) after World War I.[13] This seems to be because the term *zaibatsu* came into use in

13. Historians assign periods corresponding to the reigns of emperors. The Meiji period is from 1868 to 1912, the Taisho period is from 1912 to 1926, and the Showa period is from 1926 to 1989. Note that emperors choose official names upon their ascension. Thus in 1926, Hirohito chose the official name *Showa,* meaning enlightened peace.

discussions of income distribution and monopoly capital (and Marxism) in the Taisho period. However, both the Mitsui and Sumitomo groups, always listed among the *zaibatsu,* formed long before this. Other major groups, like the Mitsubishi and Yasuda *zaibatsu,* became important in the Meiji period (1868–1912). Yet other *zaibatsu* clearly formed after World War I.

Second, even though *zaibatsu* typically implies family control, the often-cited list of the ten main *zaibatsu* (table 7.1) includes Nissan. As we show below, no family voted a majority of Nissan's stock through most of its existence. Nevertheless, Yoshisuke Aikawa and his family successfully maintained control until the end of World War II.

Third, *zaibatsu* were often thought to have substantial monopoly power in many, not just a few, industries. Indeed, the U.S. military government used industry market shares to ascertain whether or not a group was a *zaibatsu* and thus to be broken up. Fourth, *zaibatsu* are often thought to have been relatively independent of bank financing. Fifth, *zaibatsu* were business groups with vast land holdings, under which lay great mineral wealth. Sixth, a *zaibatsu* was sometimes defined as a group of firms connected with, and dependent on, a general trading firm, or *sogo shosha.* Seventh, the term *zaibatsu* is now sometimes extended to cover family-controlled groups of listed companies in developing economies in general.

Table 7.1	Ten *zaibatsu* combines designated by the Holding Companies Liquidation Commission (HCLC) for dissolution		
Zaibatsu	Number of subsidiaries in 1937	Number of subsidiaries in 1946	Paid-in capital as % of Japan's 1946 total[a]
Mitsui	101	294	9.4
Mitsubishi	73	241	8.3
Sumitomo	34	166	5.2
Yasuda	44	60	1.6
Total	252	761	24.5
Nissan	77	179	5.3
Asano	50	59	1.8
Furukawa	19	53	1.5
Okura	51	58	1.0
Nakajima	—	68	0.6
Nomura	—	19	0.5
Total	197	439	10.7
Top ten *zaibatsu* total	449	1,200	35.2

Sources: HCLC volumes as cited in Hadley (1970), Takahashi and Aoyama (1938, pp. 151–52).

[a]Japanese government estimates for Japan's paid-in capital in 1946 are 32 billion yen (Ministry of Commerce and Industry), 43 billion yen (Ministry of Finance), and 48 billion yen (Bank of Japan). The HCLC used the Ministry of Commerce and Industry estimate without any explanation in deriving these figures.

Finally, *zaibatsu* had pyramidal structures. A family holding company or partnership controlled a set of directly owned subsidiaries, which then controlled other firms, which then controlled yet other firms, and so on. The family usually had an operating decision rule for determining which firms to own directly versus indirectly. Figure 7.1 illustrates the stylized structure of a pyramidal corporate group. As we show below, the vague definition of *zaibatsu* in the minds of the Japanese and foreign architects of the postwar system may be, at least in part, responsible for their less-than-complete dissolution after the war.

We use the term *zaibatsu* to denote any large pyramidal group of listed firms. This distances the term from both origin and control, from contentious issues like monopoly power or land rents, and from difficult-to-

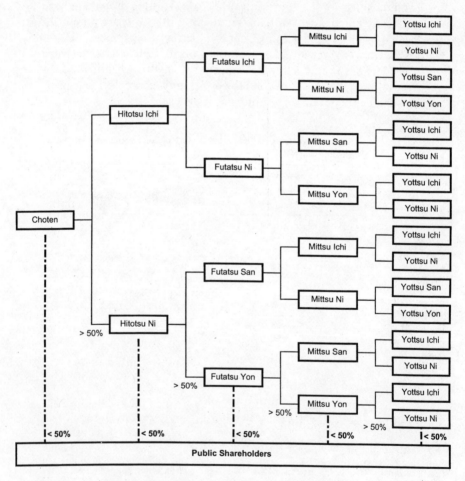

Fig. 7.1   A stylized representation of a *zaibatsu* control pyramid

measure concepts like the importance of bank financing or general trading firms. It also distinguishes the pyramidal *zaibatsu* from the *keiretsu* groups of postwar Japan, whose structure of intercorporate ownership is not pyramidal.

We use the term *apex firm* to denote the family-controlled entity at the top of the pyramid. Firms whose shares it holds we refer to as *directly controlled subsidiaries.* Firms it controls but whose shares it does not hold we call *indirectly controlled subsidiaries.* Indirectly controlled subsidiaries can be controlled by either directly controlled subsidiaries or other indirectly controlled subsidiaries. These terms are illustrated in figure 7.1.

7.3.2   *Zaibatsu* Formation

The development of *zaibatsu* (and other firms) was relatively unhindered by government intervention until the 1930s. Few regulations existed in financial markets, yet capital markets provided 87 percent of the new capital required by Japanese corporations in 1931. Rajan and Zingales (2003) describe a substantial stock market in early twentieth-century Japan, despite the absence of statutory shareholder rights. Corporate governance was generally in the hands of controlling shareholders—usually wealthy families. Banks had little or no corporate governance role. Public shareholders bet on the honesty of insiders.

The main *zaibatsu* families first expanded beyond their traditional businesses when the Meiji government undertook a mass privatization in 1880. The state had established industries it deemed essential to modernization but had accumulated a huge public debt doing so. To solve this fiscal problem, the government implemented a mass sell-off of state-owned enterprises in all areas except munitions. Included were factories producing virtually all important manufactured goods—steel, cement, coal, metals, machines, ships, textiles, and so on.

The main buyers, Mitsui, Mitsubishi, Sumitomo, and a few other *zaibatsu,* thus entered new lines of business.[14] Although there was no clear-cut method of allocating state-owned factories, each of the three main *zaibatsu* ended up with some assets in each key industry: mining, shipbuilding, machinery, textiles, and so on.

7.3.3   *Zaibatsu* Expansion and the Problem
of Preserving Insider Control

One of the most important corporate governance considerations for business families during this period was preserving family control while satisfying an ever-growing need for capital. Families that kept their firms unlisted found this growing need for capital a serious problem.

Such problems were not new. As the number of relatives grew with each

---

14. Some historians consider this the beginning of Japan's *zaibatsu.*

generation, preserving meaningful control for the patriarch had always presented problems. As mentioned above, and illustrated in table 7.2, the Mitsui family redistributed assets to the different clans of the Mitsui family continuously since its foundation in 1694. The stakes are remarkably stable.

Nonetheless, the Mitsui patriarch dictated most family businesses decisions. This system, divided ownership with an imposed centralized control that largely negated the rights of individual owners, grew increasingly difficult to maintain. The problem grew even worse when the Meiji government

Table 7.2   **Ownership shares of the Mitsui families**

Mitsui family member in 1694	1694 Takatoshi's will[a]	1722 Takahira's will[b]	1867–1873 End of Edo/Meiji Rest.	1909 Mitsui partnership established[c]
Mitsui, Takatoshi's sons				
Oldest son	29 (41.5)	62 (28.2)	62 (28.2)	230 (23.0)
Second oldest son (Takahira)	13 (18.6)	30 (13.6)	30 (13.6)	115 (11.5)
Third oldest son	9 (12.9)	27 (12.3)	27 (12.3)	115 (11.5)
Fourth oldest son	7.5 (10.7)	25 (11.4)	25 (11.4)	115 (11.5)
Sixth oldest son	4.5 (6.4)	22.5 (10.2)		
Ninth oldest son	1.5 (2.1)	22.5 (10.2)	22.5 (10.2)	115 (11.5)
Tenth oldest son (merged with sixth)	1.2 (2.1)		22.5 (10.2)	115 (11.5)
Other relatives and wife				
1 Takatoshi's wife	100 kanme[d] of silver			
2	2 (2.9)	8 (3.6)	8 (3.6)	39 (3.9)
3	1.5 (2.1)			
4	0.8 (1.1)	6 (2.7)	6 (2.7)	39 (3.9)
5		7 (3.2)	7 (3.2)	39 (3.9)
6			2.5 (1.2)	39 (3.9)
7			3 (1.4)	39 (3.9)
Remainder		10 (4.5)	4.5 (2.0)	
Total	70 (100)	220 (100)	220 (100)	1,000 (100)

Note: Numbers in parentheses are percentages.

[a]The founder of the Mitsui family enterprise, Hachirobei-Takatoshi Mitsui (1622–94), began co-ownership of their family business. His 1694 will states that total family business annual profits be divided into 70 units for an annual distribution among his wife and sons.

[b]Takahira, the second-generation head of the Mitsui family business, revised the profit distribution method in his 1722 will. The will states that total annual profits be divided into 220 units for an annual distribution among the family owners of the business. In this revision the ownership shares of the first and second sons' families were decreased, while the ownership shares of other family members and relatives were increased. These revised ownership shares remained unchanged for the following 150 years.

[c]After the revision of the Mitsui family constitution was worked out during the first 20 years of the Meiji period, the Mitsui family partnership was created, and its ownership shares remained unchanged into the 1940s.

[d]1 kanme is about 3.75 kg.

instituted new laws affirming individual ownership rights. Although these rights could be relaxed in family firms to preserve the power of the patriarch, this exemption did not extend beyond blood kin—for example, to share-owning employees.

This presented problems, for shareholders who were not blood kin had become common. It made sense to reward competent hired managers with shares. And sometimes competent hired managers, rewarded in other ways, grew wealthy and demanded the right to buy stock.

When the Meiji government established the civil code, large family businesses were usually recognized as general partnerships. As more outsiders supplied capital, and as each new generation created more insiders, these businesses found the legal status of a limited partnership advantageous. In 1893, when Japan enacted a commercial code, many *zaibatsu* holding company partnerships incorporated, though most remained unlisted. More new laws on ownership granted hired managers who had become shareholders a legal status equal to that of family members. This was difficult for the great families to accept, but the concept of random members of society buying and selling such a status was intolerable.

Even letting skilled managers and distant relatives hold shares often proved unbearable, and controlling families often went to considerable lengths to repair such perceived errors. For example, the Mitsui Bank, founded in 1876, soon had more than four hundred manager-shareholders. When the Mitsui group reorganized it as a general partnership in 1893, they bought up all of these shares. When the Kamoike *zaibatsu* family established the Thirteenth National Bank, forty distant relatives were shareholders. In 1897, the family's main branch bought them out and reestablished the bank as the Kamoike Bank, privately owned by the Kamoike patriarch.[15]

This sort of response is perhaps understandable, for successful family businesses operated with a common objective imposed by a core of family values, traditions, and history. Outsiders, even very competent ones, could not share fully in this, and their input would surely appear to the family as interference. Nevertheless, family firms closed to outsiders risked alienating their best managers and being shut out of the top end of the managerial labor market. Family businesses lacking management skill among blood kin, and unable to hire it, risked degeneration.

Some *zaibatsu,* most notably the Mitsui and Sumitomo *zaibatsu,* were particularly successful in growing rapidly without outside equity financing. Their success has been attributed to a series of highly competent hired managers, but their connections with important political leaders were certainly at least as important as their raw competence.

15. The Kamoike Bank subsequently became the Sanwa Bank, which evolved into the current UFJ Bank.

The Sumitomo family owned a lucrative cash cow, the Besshi copper mines they obtained from the shogunate, and so could afford to keep more distant from the Meiji government—at least initially. The Mitsui group, however, needed the Meiji government's gratitude. They gained this by financing the struggling new government in its critical first years. In return, Mitsui was appointed government treasury agent, a duty that provided many opportunities.

To fulfill their treasury duties, the Mitsuis established a national network of branch offices. These generated cash flows from treasury business and served as bases for other trading. Business grew so fast that the Mitsui group had to set up the Kokusangata Karihonten, or Temporary Head Office for Domestic Trade, in Tokyo in 1874. Learning of the Meiji government's aim of promoting foreign trade, the Mitsui group began selling silk yarn and tea to Western merchants for commissions, and shipping imports between Tokyo and Yokohama.[16] The Mitsui group's trading business, handled by employees steeped in Tokugawa traditions, lost money. In 1876, the Mitsui group was about to close its trading ventures when Kaoru Inoue (1835–1915), a leading Meiji politician, offered his Senshusha company to the Mitsui group to raise political funds.[17] The Mitsui group jumped at this, for Senshusha came not only with government contracts but also with its top manager, Takashi Masuda, who trained at the largest American merchant house in Japan. The Mitsui group established Mitsui Bussan (Mitsui and Co.) in July 1876 by merging Senshusha and the Temporary Head Office for Domestic Trade, and appointed Masuda manager.

Mitsui Bussan's first government business was a monopoly selling coal from the state-owned Miike mine. Exporting Miike coal on commission to China through Shanghai was highly profitable, and Mitsui Bussan established its first foreign office in there late in 1876. This let Mitsui Bussan acquire international trade experience. Since Mitsui Bussan traded coal, like all other items, entirely on commission, its capital requirements were minimal. The only financing the Mitsui group provided was a ¥50,000 overdraft allowance from the Mitsui Bank. In 1877, Mitsui Bussan made ¥200,000—a fortune at the time—supplying 60 percent of the military procurements for the Seinan War, a large operation to put down rebellion in Kyushu in 1877.

The Sumitomo and Mitsui houses were not the only great Takagawa merchant houses. But they were the only ones to expand their capital bases as the economy grew, and they were clearly the most adept at positioning

16. See Yamamura (1976).
17. Inoue subsequently served as minister of foreign affairs, the interior, and finance, and also as privy councilor. Senshusha, established in 1872 by Inoue and others, was a moderately successful trading business, mostly due to Inoue's political influence. Its primary business was executing government procurement orders for imports for Inoue's powerful political associates. Senshusha imported wool, guns, and fertilizer, and exported rice, tea, and silk.

themselves to assist the government in implementing its economic policies. Other great business families of the Tokugawa era, such as the Kamoike *zaibatsu,* were less nimble, grew too slowly, and were gradually eclipsed.

Expanding the capital base by bringing in outsiders held a different danger. New investors could seize control, reducing the family to a limited partner. Both the Shimomura and Ohmura *zaibatsu* brought in outside investors who took control. Even worse from the perspective of the old families, the new controlling shareholders shifted the business out of their (money-losing) traditional Japanese clothing businesses and into department store–based retailing.

Despite its freedom from outside shareholders, the Mitsui group faced legal problems when different branches of the family began exerting their new rights as investors. Preserving control while accessing ever greater capital, whether from more distant relatives or strangers, became increasingly difficult.

7.3.4 Pyramids as a Solution

In his memoirs, Yoshisuke Aikawa (1934), the founder of the Nissan *zaibatsu,* describes pyramidal groups as an elegant solution to all of these problems—they preserve total control by insiders while permitting access to limitless capital. To see this, consider a family with a fortune of ¥1 billion invested in a family business, Choten Corp.[18] The family sees a multitude of profitable business opportunities and feels it could profitably invest many billions of yen. To see how the family can undertake all of these investments yet retain control of Choten and all these new ventures by constructing a pyramidal group, return to figure 7.1.

First, the family expands Choten Corp. by issuing new public shares worth almost ¥1 billion. Public shareholders end up owning almost 50 percent of Choten, which is now worth almost ¥2 billion. This gives the family almost ¥1 billion in cash yet preserves its complete control of the family business. The latter is because its 50 percent–plus stake lets it appoint the board of directors. Choten is now set to become the apex firm of the pyramidal group.

Next, the family organizes two new firms, Hitotsu-Ichi Corp. and Hitotsu-Ni Corp.[19] Each is financed with a ¥500 million equity investment from Choten and a public offering to raise almost ¥500 million by selling outside shareholders almost 50 percent. Hitotsu-Ichi and Hitotsu-Ni now each have ¥1 billion. The family now fully controls three firms, with unconsolidated balance sheets totaling ¥4 billion, and ¥3 billion in consolidated assets. The family's control is complete because it fully controls

18. *Choten* is Japanese for *apex.*
19. In one Japanese counting system, *hitotsu* is one, *futatsu* is two, *mittsu* is three, and *yottsu* is four. In another, *ichi* is one, *ni* is two, *san* is three, and *yon* is four. The appropriate use of the two systems is a matter of grammar.

Choten, and Choten's board votes a 50 percent–plus stake in both Hitotsu-Ichi Corp. and Hitotsu-Ni Corp., and thus controls their boards.

To expand further, the family has Hitotsu-Ichi and Hitotsu-Ni set up four new firms. Hitotsu-Ichi organizes Futatsu-Ichi and Futatsu-Ni, financing each with a ¥500 million equity investment and a public offering to raise almost ¥500 million by selling outside shareholders almost 50 percent. Hitotsu-Ni Corp. organizes Futatsu-San and Futatsu-Yon similarly. The family now fully controls seven firms, with unconsolidated values totaling ¥8 billion and ¥5 billion in consolidated assets.

In the next step, each Futatsu-level firm organizes two new companies. The family now fully controls fifteen firms, with unconsolidated balance sheets totaling ¥16 billion and ¥9 billion in consolidated assets. Each Mittsu-level firm can then similarly organize two Yottsu-level firms, resulting in a pyramid of thirty-one firms worth ¥32 billion on paper and holding ¥17 billion in consolidated assets. This process can be repeated until the family runs out of attractive investment opportunities. A pyramid with n tiers contains $2^n - 1$ firms, with unconsolidated book values totaling 2^n billion yen and consolidated assets worth $1/2(3 + \Sigma_{v=1}^{n} v)$ yen.

Thus, a five-tier pyramid lets the family raise ¥14 billion in public equity but retain complete control. Had the family instead merely expanded their first company by issuing ¥14 billion in additional Choten shares, their stake would have been diluted to one-fifteenth or 6.67 percent, and they would have lost control.

The elegance and simplicity of this solution, later extolled by Aikawa (1934), the founder of the Nissan *zaibatsu,* appealed to the great mercantile families, for they enthusiastically embraced this model to build the vast prewar *zaibatsu.* Both public investors and querulous relatives could be tapped for capital *and* excluded from corporate governance.

Of course, variations from this formula were possible. For instance, the controlling families often kept the apex firm of the pyramid unlisted. They thus used only family money to establish the first tier of subsidiaries. Since the Mitsui and Sumitomo families had both run highly profitable businesses for generations, their accumulated retained earnings easily let them skip the first step in the above recipe. In contrast, later groups, like Nissan, had public shareholders in their apex firms. Nonvoting or supervoting shares permitted much more leverage at each tier. Firms at different levels could also have real assets and engage in real business while serving as holding companies for firms in lower tiers. Actual pyramids were much messier than shown in figure 7.1, in that different levels of firms sometimes cooperated to control firms in all levels, including higher tiers of the pyramid. Nonetheless, figure 7.1 captures the essential logic of a pyramidal group.

Figures 7.2 and 7.3 illustrate the actual structure of the Mitsui group at its greatest extent.

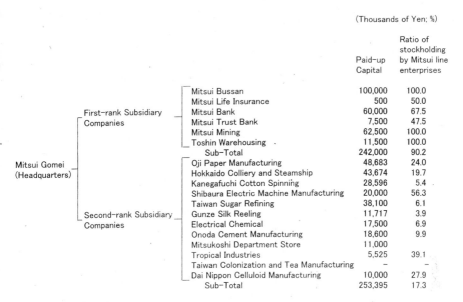

(Thousands of Yen; %)

		Paid-up Capital	Ratio of stockholding by Mitsui line enterprises
Mitsui Gomei (Headquarters)	**First-rank Subsidiary Companies**		
	Mitsui Bussan	100,000	100.0
	Mitsui Life Insurance	500	50.0
	Mitsui Bank	60,000	67.5
	Mitsui Trust Bank	7,500	47.5
	Mitsui Mining	62,500	100.0
	Toshin Warehouse	11,500	100.0
	Sub-Total	242,000	90.2
	Second-rank Subsidiary Companies		
	Oji Paper Manufacturing	48,683	24.0
	Hokkaido Colliery and Steamship	43,674	19.7
	Kanegafuchi Cotton Spinning	28,596	5.4
	Shibaura Electric Machine Manufacturing	20,000	56.3
	Taiwan Sugar Refining	38,100	6.1
	Gunze Silk Reeling	11,717	3.9
	Electrical Chemical	17,500	6.9
	Onoda Cement Manufacturing	18,600	9.9
	Mitsukoshi Department Store	11,000	
	Tropical Industries	5,525	39.1
	Taiwan Colonization and Tea Manufacturing	–	–
	Dai Nippon Celluloid Manufacturing	10,000	27.9
	Sub-Total	253,395	17.3

Fig. 7.2   The structure of the Mitsui *zaibatsu* in 1928

Japan, of course, was not the only country whose business tycoons came to appreciate pyramidal groups as a solution to the quandary of tapping public equity financing without risking the loss of corporate governance power. As the other chapters of this book show, *zaibatsu* were commonplace in Canada, the United States, and Europe during this period as well. And as La Porta et al. (1999) show, *zaibatsu* remain the most commonplace ownership structure everywhere except Japan, the United States, and the United Kingdom at the end of the twentieth century too, though the term *pyramidal group* is used outside Japan.

7.3.5   The Big Four *Zaibatsu*

While the Mitsui and Sumitomo *zaibatsu* may be said to have formed in the late nineteenth century in the sense that their pyramidal structures arose at that time, both have their true origins in the Tokugawa period. However, other *zaibatsu* were genuinely new. The largest were Mitsubishi and Yasuda. These four were the largest *zaibatsu,* so their development merits close inspection.

The founding of the Tokyo and Osaka Stock Exchanges in 1877 allowed Japanese companies to tap capital from individual investors. Mitsui and Sumitomo both began expanding by constructing pyramids. However, their first investments outside their primary lines of business were relatively small, experimental, and limited.

Thus, the Mitsui family, having begun as silk merchants, expanded into

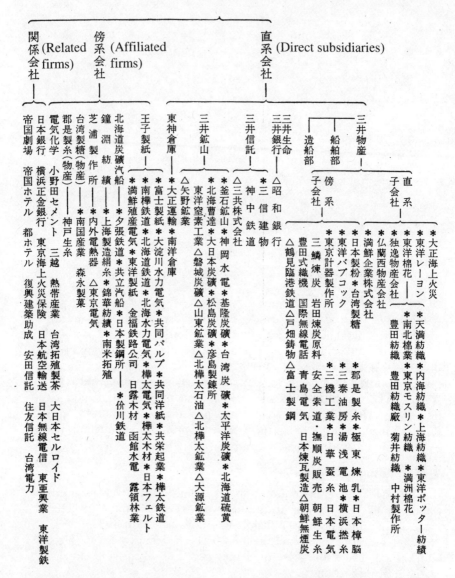

Fig. 7.3　Record of the structure of the Mitsui _zaibatsu_ in 1930

Source: Takahashi (1930b, p. 50).

Notes: Mitsui's first-tier direct subsidiaries were Mitsui Bussan, Mitsui Life Insurance, Mitsui Bank, Mitsui Trust Bank, Mitsui Mining, and Toshin Warehousing (see also table 7.2). Mitsui Partnership owned and controlled fully its first-tier direct subsidiaries but did not necessarily fully control or own affiliated or related firms. More specifically, Mitsui Partnership controlled the firms with asterisks fully and the firms with no asterisks or triangles predominantly but not fully. Mitsui Partnership's control was weakest over the firms with triangles.

areas related to clothing manufacture and sale. The family established trading operations in other commodities to facilitate barter transactions for silk, and a currency exchange operation to deal with foreign companies. However, the Mitsuis did invest significant capital more broadly from time to time. During the first twenty years of the Meiji era, the government established state-owned enterprises to develop strategically important industries. The Mitsui group often cooperated in these projects, and became the government's favored partner in many such ventures.

Toward the end of the nineteenth century, the government's fiscal problems necessitated a mass privatization of all state-owned enterprises, save armament factories, postal and telegraph systems, mints, and railroads. The magnitude of this mass divestiture was unprecedented. Between 1874 and 1896 alone, twenty-six major government projects—including coal, copper, silver, and gold mines; cotton- and silk-spinning mills; shipyards; cement factory; ironworks; sugar refinery; and glass factory—were transferred to private owners, usually the large *zaibatsu*.

However, except for these privatized enterprises, the great *zaibatsu* remained commerce based. Only at the century's end did they diversify further, and this was often at the prodding of hired managers, not family members. Extensive diversification would wait until after the First World War. Morikawa (1992, p. 27) argues that it took time for people knowledgeable of the possibilities opened by limited liability and stock markets to attain positions of influence.

Economic historians' assessment of the mass privatization is mixed.

The limited number of bidders, their political acuity, and the government's financial exigency perhaps made for bargain prices. The great *zaibatsu* families were well connected, and though some sales were auctions, others were negotiated privately. The great *zaibatsu* families were also virtually the only entities with pockets deep enough to participate extensively.

Certainly, most privatization prices were far lower than the Meiji government's capital outlays in establishing these enterprises.[20] However, many state owned enterprises were in dismal shape, and although many privatized enterprises subsequently encountered serious difficulties, the

---

20. For example, Takashima Coal Mine (government outlay by 1885, ¥393,848) fetched ¥550,000 in 1874 from Shoraisha, owned by Shojiro Goto, who resold it to Mitsubishi's Iwasaki family in 1881. Other examples include the Shinmachi Silk Spinning Mill (setup cost ¥138,984), sold to Mitsui in 1887 for ¥141,000; the Nagasaki Shipyard (¥1,130,949), sold to Mitsubishi for ¥459,000; Tomioka Filature (¥310,000), sold to Mitsui in 1893 for ¥121,460; the Sado Gold Mine (¥1,419,244) and the Ikuno Silver Mine (¥1,760,866), sold together to Mitsubishi in 1896 for ¥2,560,926; and Kamaishi Ironworks (¥2,376,625), sold to Chobei Tanaka, an iron merchant and supplier for the Japanese army and navy, in 1887 for ¥12,600. Tanaka subsequently sold Kamaishi Ironworks to his company, Kamaishi Mining, in 1924, and then divested it to Nippon Steel. Tanaka and the Kamaishi Mining succeeded spectacularly, gaining a 72 percent market share in pig iron by 1900. The rarity of exceptions, such as the sale of the Miike Coal Mine (setup cost ¥757,060), sold to Mitsui in 1888 for ¥4,590,439, only accentuates the low privatization prices. For further details, see Kobayashi (1985), pp. 64–65.

Japanese government rarely provided direct subsidies. When an 1889 earthquake destroyed the Kattate shaft of the Mitsui Miike coal mine, Finance Minister Matsukata refused Mitsui pleas, supported by cabinet ministers, for subsidies and a debt rescheduling. The Mitsuis completed their payments in 1902, as per the original agreement. Of course, the state did provide generous tariff protection and other indirect assistance to insure the success of the privatized enterprises.

Regardless of the government's intentions, many privatizations turned out to be plums. At the time, mining was highly profitable because of the expense of importing. Privatized mining companies, acquired by the Mitsui and Mitsubishi companies at this time, served as core cash cows until the mid-1950s, when major veins were exhausted. Most *zaibatsu* electric equipment manufacturers also developed by supplying equipment to their affiliated mining companies.

The positions of different firms within the *zaibatsu* pyramids were apparently of great concern. From time to time, weaker businesses were moved to lower tiers and stronger businesses to higher tiers.

For example, the Mitsui group's primary lines of business were still Japanese clothing and money exchange when the family diversified into banking in 1876. When Japanese clothing sales became shaky around 1873, the family restructured the pyramid, moving that business to a lower tier and delegating its management to distant relatives. The Mitsui Bank became increasingly profitable and served as the apex firm of the Mitsui *zaibatsu* until 1893.

Again, in 1909, the Mitsui council restructured the pyramid, creating a holding company at the apex to control the Mitsui Bank, Mitsui Mining, and the trading firm Mitsui Bussan. This was accompanied by a major rearrangement of firms throughout the pyramid, with good performers moving closer to the apex and weak firms moving deeper into the pyramid. Morikawa (1980, pp. 46–57) and others argue that greater direct ownership by the Mitsui family indicates a greater family "concern" for a firm. The placement of undoubtedly key companies in deep levels of the Mitsui pyramid confutes this. For example, the Mitsuis moved Mitsukoshi, the direct descendent of their original silk business, to a low tier after its conversion into a Western-style department store chain in 1904. Oji Paper and Kanebo, firms of considerable national importance, were also low in the pyramid. Shibura Engineering Works, which merged with Tokyo Electric to form Tokyo Shibura (Toshiba) Electric in 1939, was also not a core Mitsui firm.[21] General Electric had obtained 25 to 30 percent of Shibura in 1904 for technology licenses.[22]

---

21. Morikawa (1980) proposes that some Mitsui top managers and partners recognized the importance of Shibaura's operations but could not understand them. The Mitsui considered divesting Shibaura in 1902, but opposition from Mitsui Mining and others forestalled this. Shibaura went public as a Mitsui-group company in 1904.

22. Zaibatsu were often important technology importers; see Goto (1982).

Table 7.3   Amounts of shares held

Company	Date	Shares held (paid-in book value, ¥1,000)
Mitsui Bussan	April 1910	1,699
Mitsui Bank	December 1909	4,893
Mitsui Partnership	January 1910	42,420

It seems likely that firms' positions in the pyramids were also selected to facilitate tunneling—self-dealing to concentrate profits in firms owned directly by the Mitsuis and losses in firms merely controlled by them. This readily explains the better apparent performance of firms higher in the pyramids, and the location of many clearly important firms in lower tiers.[23] Certainly, Shibura's performance in the early 1900s lagged behind that of other major Mitsui firms.

Records attest that the Mitsui head office carefully considered which companies to place where in the pyramid, and what stakes each company should hold in other group firms. As the *zaibatsu* grew ever more complex from 1912 to 1930, the lower tiers were periodically drastically restructured, but the apex tiers changed little. The Mitsui Bank, Mitsui Bussan, Mitsui Mining, and Toshin Warehousing remained direct subsidiaries of the Mitsui partnership. The only significant change was the addition of the Mitsui Life Insurance and Mitsui Trust Bank as direct subsidiaries after 1912.[24]

Table 7.3 shows that the amounts of other companies' shares held by these three Mitsui firms were already significant by the early 1900s, though Mitsui Bussan's holding was relatively minor compared to the other two Mitsui family firms.

The Mitsui group's most intensive diversification began with Mitsui Mining's entry into chemicals in the early 1910s. Mitsui Bussan founded a shipbuilding company in 1917, purchased an iron and steel firm in 1924, and established Toyo Rayon to enter chemical textiles. This wave of diversification was undertaken exclusively through new subsidiaries of Mitsui Mining, the Mitsui Bank, and Mitsui Bussan, or through new subsidiaries of their subsidiaries. Table 7.4 shows the extent of this expansion, and figures 7.2 and 7.3 illustrate the structure of the *zaibatsu* at this point.

23. See, e.g., Claessens, Djankov, and Lang (2000), Claessens et al. (2002), Faccio and Lang (2003), Bertrand, Mehra, and Mullainathan (2002), and Johnson et al. (2000). Recent work suggests that tunneling is more common in countries whose minority shareholders are poorly protected, like Japan throughout its history. Shareholder rights were poorly protected before the war, and La Porta et al. (1999) assign Japan one out of six in an international comparison of shareholder rights. Porter (1990) argues that weak shareholder rights advantaged Japanese companies by freeing their managers from myopic shareholders, but Morck and Nakamura (1999) dispute this. At present, shareholder rights remain a controversial issue in Japan.

24. See Tamaki (1976, pp. 84–86). Fruin (1992, pp. 100–102) describes how the Mitsubishi pyramid was reorganized several times between 1916 and 1926 and argues that this reflected evolving strategic considerations such as economies of scope and scale.

Table 7.4   The Mitsui *zaibatsu* companies in 1930

	Authorized capital (millions of yen)	Paid-in capital (millions of yen)	Mitsui Gomei percent stake
Mitsui family holding company,			
Mitsui Gomei	300	300	n.a.
Mitsui's designated subsidiaries			
Mitsui Bank	100	60	100
Mitsui Bussan	100	100	100
Mitsui Mining	100	62.5	100
Toshin Warehousing	15	12.5	100
Mitsui Trust	30	7.5	100
Mitsui Life Insurance	2	0.5	100
Subsidiaries of Mitsui's designated subsidiaries			
Taiheiyo Colliery	11	5.5	
Kamaishi Mining	20	20	
Claude-Process Nitrogen Industries	10	10	
Toyo Cotton Trading	25	15	
Toyo Rayon	10	10	
Mitsui's ordinary subsidiaries			
Ojo Paper	65.91	48.68	24
Shibaura Engineering Works	20	20	56.4
Hokkaido Colliery & Steamship	70	43.68	19.7[a]
Nippon Steel Works	30	30	12.5
Dai Nippon Celluloid	10	10	27.9
Kanegahuchi Cotton Spinning	60	28.6	5.3
Onoda Cement	31	21.82	9.6
Denki Kagaku Kogyo	18	17.5	6.9
Mitsukoshi Department Store	15	15	0

Sources: Shogyo Koshinsho (1930), Morikawa (1992)

Note: n.a. = not applicable.

[a]Also 20.7 percent owned by Mitsui Mining.

Figure 7.4 shows the Sumitomo pyramid with a structure quite similar to the Mitsui pyramid. Financial institutions sit near the apex, and industrial firms fill lower tiers. Direct Sumitomo subsidiaries include a bank, *sogo shosha,* trust bank, insurance firm, mining company, and warehousing operation. Relatively fewer Sumitomo companies had publicly traded shares. The Sumitomo Bank went public in 1917, Sumitomo Trust in 1925, Sumitomo Chemical in 1934, Sumitomo Metal Industrials in 1935, and Sumitomo Electric Wire and Cable Works in 1937. Other Sumitomo firms remained unlisted until relatively late.

The Yasuda *zaibatsu,* whose structure also follows this pattern, is new compared to Mitsui and Sumitomo. The Yasuda *zaibatsu* began at the end of the Tokogawa era, when Zenjiro Yasuda (1838–1922), the son of a poor samurai in Toyama, moved to Edo and obtained work in a money-changing house. In 1863 he began providing tax-farming services to the

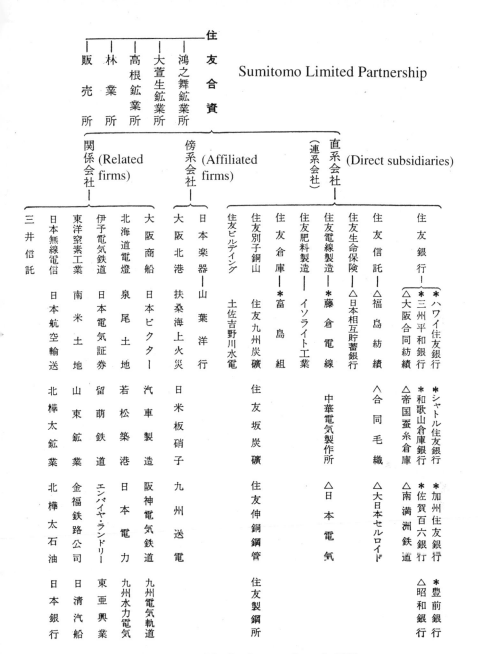

Fig. 7.4 Record of the structure of the Sumitomo *zaibatsu* in 1930

Source: Takahashi (1930b, p. 161).

Notes: Sumitomo's first-tier direct subsidiaries were Sumitomo Bank, Sumitomo Trust Bank, Sumitomo Life Insurance, Sumitomo Electric Wire and Cable Works, Sumitomo Fertilizer Manufacturing, Sumitomo Warehousing, Sumitomo Besshi Copper Mines, and Sumitomo Building. Sumitomo Limited Partnership owned and controlled fully its first-tier direct subsidiaries but did not necessarily fully control or own affiliated or related firms. More specifically, Sumitomo Limited Partnership controlled the firms with asterisks fully and the firms with no asterisks or triangles predominantly but not fully. Sumitomo Limited Partnership's control was weakest over the firms with triangles.

shogunate, overseeing the collection and transport of silver and gold. After the restoration, he provided the same services to the Meiji. Yasuda profited from the delay between the collection of taxes and their forwarding to
the government. He greatly magnified his wealth by buying up depreciated
Meiji paper money that the government subsequently exchanged for gold.

Yasuda and Kawasaki established the Third National Bank in 1876, and
then the Yasudas set up their own Yasuda Bank in 1880. Although the Yasuda Bank's investors consisted of several members of the Yasuda family,
it seems likely that Zenjiro provided all its initial ¥200,000 capitalization.
Zenjiro needed several family members to satisfy the Meiji government's
dictate that no single investor establish a bank.

In 1887 Zenjiro capitalized his family company, Hozensha, with an initial one million yen, designated as the paid-in capital of the Yasuda Bank.
Zenjiro assigned half to Hozansha and the other half to ten of his relatives:
six Yasuda families given ¥360,000, two branch clans given ¥80,000, and
two other relations given ¥60,000. Hozensha's ¥500,000 of stocks were
designated the common property of the six Yasuda families. The charter
Zenjiro established forbade the transfer of Yasuda Bank, even within the
family. No certificates were issued, and ownership was recorded in a registration book in Hozensha's safe. Yasuda Bank shareholders also relinquished the right to embark on commercial activities of their own.

After observing the 1909 reorganization of the Mitsui group as a general
partnership, Yasuda reorganized Hozensha similarly in 1912. The partnership served as a holding company for Yasuda securities, properties, and
business operations. By this time, the Yasuda *zaibatsu* already contained
seventeen banks and sixteen other business operations. New biological
and adopted sons boosted the number of Yasuda family investors from ten
to thirteen. In 1919 the Yasuda group established its house constitution,
freezing the number of Yasuda investors at thirteen. The Yasuda *zaibatsu*
remained focused on financial businesses. By not expanding into capital-
hungry heavy industries as aggressively as the other great *zaibatsu,* the Yasuda group limited public shareholders' participation.[25] Table 7.5, which
summarizes the industrial diversification of the ten major prewar *zaibatsu,*
illustrates this focus.

The Yasuda focus on banking was narrowed by the folding of eleven
Yasuda-controlled banks into the Yasuda Bank in 1913. The new bank was
the greatest of all the *zaibatsu* banks, with a 1913 paid-in capital of ¥150
million—compared to ¥600 thousand, ¥500 thousand, ¥430 thousand, and
¥300 thousand for the Mitsui, Sumitomo, Daiichi, and Mitsubishi banks,
respectively. The Yasuda Bank continued expanding via mergers with
other banks, and rapidly developed strong relationships with the smaller

25. A reorganization as a joint-stock company was discussed during World War II but never
implemented.

Table 7.5   Industrial diversification of the ten major *zaibatsu* in 1945, in millions of yen

Zaibatsu	Finance	Heavy industry	Light industry	Other	Zaibatsu Total	Zaibatsu (% of economy)
Mitsui	169	2,214	274	404	3,061	9.4
Mitsubishi	160	1,866	73	605	2,704	8.3
Sumitomo	65	1,469	29	102	1,667	5.2
Yasuda	209	119	117	64	510	1.6
Nissan (Aikawa)	5	1,558	103	38	1,703	5.3
Asano	0	419	89	76	594	1.8
Furukawa	4	479	3	4	490	1.5
Okura	6	218	34	56	314	1.0
Nakajima	0	188	24	0.768	213	0.6
Nomura	26	50	27	62	165	0.5
Top ten *zaibatsu* total	644	8,582	773	1,412	11,420	35.0
Economy total	1,215	17,513	4,600	9,108	32,437	100.0
Top ten *zaibatsu* (% of economy)	53	49	17	16	35	

Source: Holding Company Liquidation Committee (HCLC), *Japanese* zaibatsu *and Its Dissolution,* as cited in Yasuoka (1976, pp. 34–35).

Azano and Mori *zaibatsu.* These ties gave the Yasuda Bank an industrially diversified loan portfolio, but the Yasuda core businesses remained financial—encompassing banking, insurance, and other financial services. As table 7.5 shows, the house of Yasuda limited its entry into heavy industries even during World War II.

The Mitsubishi *zaibatsu* began as Tsukumo Co. and was renamed Mitsukawa Company in 1872 because it had three (*mittsu*) owners—S. Ishikawa (1828–82), S. Kawada (1836–96), and K. Nakagawa.[26] In 1873 Mitsukawa Co. was renamed Mitsubishi Co., which appears to have been a limited partnership between the three original owners and Yataro Iwasaki (1834–85). After Yataro's death, his son Hisaya (1865–1955) and Hisaya's younger brother Yanosuke (1851–1904) joined the partnership. The Mitsubishi partnership was dissolved around 1891, and Hisaya and Yanosuke Iwasaki each invested ¥250 million in 1893 to set up a new limited partnership—also called the Mitsubishi Company.

The Mitsubishi Company's direct subsidiaries included Mitsubishi Shipbuilding and Mitsubishi Mining, which both extensively developed the privatized state-owned enterprises the *zaibatsu* purchased. Unlike the Mitsui, Sumitomo, and Yasuda charters, the Mitsubishi charter allowed

26. Nakagawa's birth and death dates are unknown. One variant of the number three in Japanese is *mittsu*. The precise origin of the Mitsubishi group is a somewhat contentious issue among Japanese historians; see Mishima (1981).

each Iwasaki clan to retain its income and start up its own businesses. This flexibility let individual Iwasaki clans enthusiastically capture business opportunities that the Mitsubishi Company itself could not. For example, Horaisha bought the privatized Takashima Coal Mine, whose continuing government subsidies prevented direct Mitsubishi ownership.[27] Other important de facto Mitsubishi firms, like Asahi Glass, Meiji Life Insurance, and Kirin Beer, were de jure separate from the Mitsubishi *zaibatsu*. This was clearly a bureaucratic slight of hand, for these companies had extensive financing and other relationships with formal members of the Mitsubishi *zaibatsu* and were controlled by the Iwasaki family. These firms also all became Mitsubishi *keiretsu* companies after World War II.

Mitsubishi Company, the pyramid's apex, was reorganized as a joint-stock company in 1937, and shares were distributed to Iwasaki relatives and seven unrelated executives, all of whom were forbidden to transfer their shares without permission from the company. In 1940 the company raised its paid-in capital from ¥120 million to ¥240 million, and the original two Iwasaki families together retained a 47.5 percent stake.

Although Mitsubishi, like Mitsui and Sumitomo, remained family controlled, the Iwasaki used marriage extensively to bring talented men into the family. Thus, unusually in a family enterprise, marriageable daughters were valued as highly as sons, if not more highly (Morikawa 1992, p. 53).

Mitsubishi Company's stakes in direct subsidiaries, like the Mitsubishi Bank and Mitsubishi Corporation, were small, averaging around 30 percent, versus 66 percent for Mitsui. Similarly, Mitsubishi's average ownership in direct subsidiaries of direct subsidiaries was only 18 percent, versus 9 percent for Mitsui. The Mitsubishi *zaibatsu* was less averse to issuing public equity, and so expanded further into capital-intensive industries like machinery, mining, finance, and shipping. This made Mitsubishi firms market leaders in these rising sectors, yet the Iwasakis retained full control, for their stakes were always sufficient to dominate shareholder meetings.[28]

Figure 7.5 illustrates the structure of the Mitsubishi *zaibatsu* as it later developed.

7.3.6   Industrial *Zaibatsu*

The Mitsui, Sumitomo, Mitsubishi, and Yasuda *zaibatsu* are generally ranked as the major family-controlled pyramidal groups of prewar Japan. Three other *zaibatsu* were also important, but their influence extended along specific product chains and did not include banks or financial firms.

These so-called *industrial zaibatsu* included the Asano group, built by Soichiro Asano (1848–1930) around the Asano Cement Company; the

27. The Iwasaki family was only allowed to purchase it from Horaisha when Takashima experienced financial distress. See Yasuoka (1976, p. 64) for details.
28. For details, see Mishima (1981, pp. 340–41).

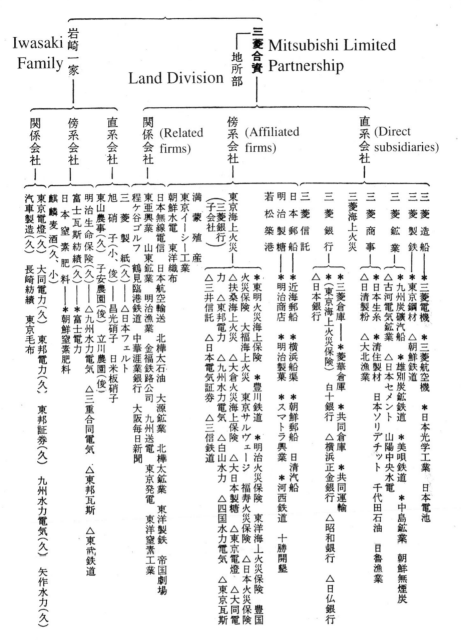

Fig. 7.5 Record of the structure of the Mitsubishi *zaibatsu* in 1930

Source: Takahashi (1930b, pp. 108–9).

Notes: Mitsubishi Limited Partnership's first-tier direct subsidiaries were Mitsubishi Shipbuilding, Mitsubishi Steel, Mitsubishi Mining, Mitsubishi Corporation, Mitsubishi Marine and Fire Insurance, Mitsubishi Bank, and Mitsubishi Trust Bank. Mitsubishi Limited Partnership owned and controlled fully its first-tier direct subsidiaries but did not necessarily fully control or own affiliated or related firms. More specifically, Mitsubishi Limited Partnership controlled the firms with asterisks fully and the firms with no asterisks or triangles predominantly but not fully. Mitsubishi Limited Partnership's control was weakest over the firms with triangles. The same ownership and control relationships apply to the firms under the Iwasaki family's control.

Kawasaki group, built around Kawasaki Shipbuilding Co. by Shozo Kawasaki (1837–1911); and the Furukawa group, built by Ichibei Furukawa (1832–1903) around his Ashio Copper Mines Co.

7.3.7   Widely Held *Zaibatsu*

In addition to the four major family *zaibatsu* and the three industrial *zaibatsu,* five other pyramidal groups emerged in the early 1900s—Nissan, Nichitsu, Mori, Nisso, and Riken. These structures grew with the stock market, which became much more active in the 1900s. Share prices rose rapidly from 1917 to 1919, and individual investors, like landlords and other property owners, bought increasingly into equity (Hashimoto 1997, p. 101). This augmented flow of capital into the market allowed, and perhaps arose from, the construction of pyramids financed with public equity throughout.

While the Mitsui, Mitsubishi, and Sumitomo apex firms were family owned, these new *widely held zaibatsu* had widely held apex firms. Although their founders often held quite small equity stakes in the apex firms, they had little fear of losing control because they were usually highly skilled engineers, whose expertise was essential to critical company operations. The chemistry experts Shitagu Noguchi, Tomonori Nakano, and Nobuteru Mori built the new Nichitsu, Nisso, and Mori *zaibatsu,* respectively. Masatoshi Okochi, an expert in machinery manufacture, built the new Riken *zaibatsu,* and the all-around genius Yoshisuke Aikawa built Nissan into a large, diversified *zaibatsu,* although machinery remained its most important business.

This technical expertise factor kept these new *zaibatsu* focused on heavy industry, chemicals, and electric power. However, as they grew, they also diversified to compete directly with family *zaibatsu.* Widely held *zaibatsu,* like industrial *zaibatsu,* did not control financial institutions and relied heavily on outside finance.

The development of the widely held *zaibatsu* can best be illustrated by the history of the largest such group—Nissan. The Nissan group was founded by Yoshisuke Aikawa (1880–1967) in a rather roundabout way.

By 1919, Aikawa's brother-in-law, Husanosuke Kuhara (1869–1965), had acquired 30 percent of Japan's domestic copper mines, 40 percent of its gold mines, and 50 percent of its silver mines. He accomplished this by floating ¥2.4 million in an initial public offering of his Kuhara Mining Company. After the First World War, Japan experienced a series of depressions, and Kuhara Mining was badly hurt. When its subsidiary, Kuhara Trading, failed, Kuhara was forced to retire on a sick leave. He delegated the rebuilding of his company to his brother-in-law, Yoshisuke Aikawa, whose own much smaller firm, Tobata Cast Iron, had survived the depressions. Aikawa was an engineer and had studied state-of-the-art iron

Table 7.6   Kuhara Mining Company: The composition of shareholders, 1918–27

	June 1918	June 1920	May 1927
Total number of outstanding shares	1,500,000	1,500,000	1,500,000
Total number of shareholders	9,761	13,842	14,858
Average number of shares held per shareholder	153.7	108.0	100.9
Shareholders with 5,000 or more shares			
Total number of shareholders	31	20	18
Share ownership (%)	67.3	51.4	44.3
Average number of shares held per shareholder	32,566.5	38,550.0	36,916.7
Shareholders with fewer than 500 shares			
Total number of shareholders	9,544	13,649	14,739
Share ownership (%)	28.5	35.8	39.6
Average number of shares held per shareholder	44.7	40.0	40.3
Kuhara family and relatives (%)	45.6	45.1	37.3

Source: Udagawa (1976).

casting in the United States. To save Kuhara Mining, he pooled his own money with funds from relatives, managers, and outsiders to inject more than ¥25 million into the company.[29]

Having dealt successfully with Kuhara Mining's debt crisis, Aikawa joined its board in 1926 and quickly replaced Kuhara as president. To put the firm on a solid long-term financial course, Aikawa needed to raise more capital without losing control. In December 1928 he listed a new holding company, Nippon Sangyo (Nissan). Simultaneously he also organized Nippon Mining, into which he merged Kuhara Mining. Since table 7.6 shows that Kuhara Mining had many public shareholders, this merger left Nippon Mining publicly held but controlled through a majority stake by Nissan.

Aikawa understood that Nissan, or any other new *zaibatsu,* would need substantial capital very quickly to achieve economies of scale comparable to those of the existing *zaibatsu.* The funds needed were far beyond his family assets, so bringing public shareholders in was unavoidable. Aikawa clearly understood the efficacy of pyramidal groups for tapping unlimited outside capital while retaining full corporate governance control. Figure 7.6 is Aikawa's (1934) vision of how a pyramid of listed subsidiaries, subsidiaries of subsidiaries, and so on, can put an unlimited amount of public stockholders' capital under his control.

Aikawa (1934) recognized that, since the apex firm of his pyramid was widely held, it was his responsibility to make sure the company always

29. He was widely expected to fail. Kuhara was compared at the time to Suzuki, described below. That Kuhara ultimately prospered and formed the basis of a new zaibatsu, while Suzuki failed and brought down an entire zaibatsu, greatly enhanced Aikawa's standing.

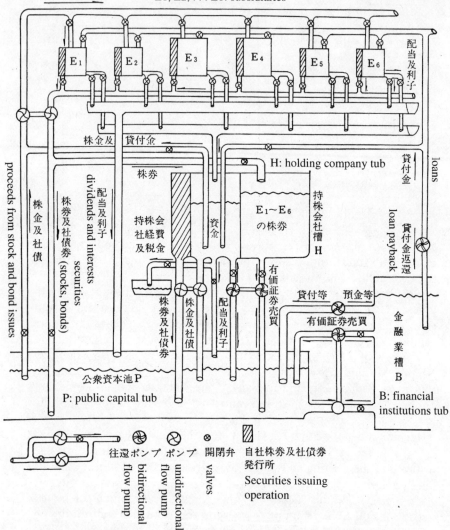

Fig. 7.6 Aikawa's vision for using capital markets to finance Nippon Sangyo (Nissan)

Source: Aikawa (1934).

Notes: Unidirectional flow pumps set the one-way flows of funds corresponding to, for example, payments of interest and dividends, and the proceeds from new issues of securities such as bonds and shares. Bidirectional flow pumps set the two-way flows of funds corresponding to, for example, the proceeds from and the repayments of loans, and the purchasing and selling transactions of securities. Aikawa's vision was that a holding company (H) and its subsidiary firms (E1, E2, . . . , E6) could grow using primarily public capital (P) and financial institutions (B) while enriching the capital base of the holding company, represented by B, the holding company tub.

made acceptable profits and that its shareholders received a stable payment of dividends.[30] Some 70 percent of Nissan's assets were shares in Nippon Mining, so Nissan was still dangerously exposed to that sector, which remained chronically weak until the Japanese government began accumulating gold in 1932. Using this business upturn, Aikawa sold Nippon Mining shares and used the funds raised to diversify Nissan's holdings extensively.

Aikawa's main strategy was to purchase promising firms, develop them as fully owned subsidiaries, and then take them public through initial public offerings (IPOs). In creating these spin-offs, or *bunshin kaisha,* Nissan's role in Japan's development resembled that of the 1990s venture capital firms in the United States (see, e.g., Gompers and Lerner 2002). However, while venture capitalists seek to sell their start-ups completely to the public to raise funds for the next venture, Nissan always retained a control block, using further IPOs to extend the pyramid. This appears to reflect Aikawa's desire to retain a final say in important decisions.

Nissan's partially spun-off subsidiaries usually prospered, further enriching both Nissan's shareholders and their own. Subsidiaries acquired or spun off their own subsidiaries, and the pyramidal structure expanded. Nissan's own paid-in capital increased from ¥5.25 million in 1933 to ¥198.37 million in 1937. During the same period, its total assets increased from ¥91.08 million to ¥383.10 million, and its securities held increased from ¥53.38 million to ¥269.92 million. Table 7.6 shows Nissan's share price for the period 1930–37.

All the while, Nissan itself became ever more widely held. By May 1937, Nissan had 51,804 shareholders, 50,783 of whom owned fewer than 500 shares. The fraction of shares Aikawa and his relatives held continued to fall—from 19.2 percent in 1929 to only 4.5 percent in 1937. By 1937, only four shareholders, including Aikawa, held more than 10,000 Nissan shares.

By this time, table 7.7 shows Nissan at the apex of a pyramid exceeded in scale only by the Mitsui and Mitsubishi groups. The Nissan group now included Nippon Mining, Hitachi Ltd., Hitachi Power, Nissan Motor, and many other large manufacturers and utilities.[31]

---

30. However, Aikawa (1934) also justifies "management nationalism" as a legitimate reason for having invested in "a few new business lines" that he thought were promising for the future but would currently generate no returns in the near term.

31. Unlike Mitsui and Mitsubishi, which kept full family control of their holding companies (first as partnerships and then as joint stock companies) until the end of World War II, Nissan's equity ownership was more widely held and became more so toward World War II. Nevertheless, Yoshisuke Aikawa and his relatives managed to keep the Nissan pyramid under their full control all the way through the end of World War II. Judging from his survey on budgeting practices of many Japanese firms in the 1930s, Hasegawa (1938) concludes that Nissan as a holding company uses the budgeting process of its more than thirty surveyed subsidiaries in various industries in a centralized totalitarian way.

Table 7.7   **Rankings of the top *zaibatsu* as of midyear 1937 by number of firms and paid-in capital**

Zaibatsu	Number of group firms	Total paid-in capital
1. Mitsui	101	¥1,177,200,000
2. Mitsubishi	73	¥848,204,000
3. Nissan	77	¥473,632,000
4. Sumitomo	34	¥383,800,000
5. Yasuda	44	¥263,866,000
6. Asano	50	¥236,261,000
7. Nichitsu	26	¥197,100,000
8. Mori	20	¥141,996,000
9. Okura	51	¥133,845,000
10. Furukawa	19	¥101,994,000

Source: Yasuoka (1976).

7.3.8 Local *Zaibatsu*

There were many locally important business families in Japan at this time, whose operations were limited to specific geographical areas (e.g., prefectures) and usually also specific lines of business. These families accumulated wealth in closely held family firms and then used this wealth to expand into new businesses, sometimes bringing in other local investors. Mostly, these pyramidal structures remained small, but a few acquired national scope—though they kept their head offices in the original localities. In general, these local *zaibatsu* did not develop into highly industrialized operations. It is possible that their limited access to capital explains this. Indeed, their dominance in certain regions may explain why industrialization favored some regions over others.

The role of local *zaibatsu* in regional development remains poorly understood. Important local *zaibatsu* include the Nakano group (based in Niigata), the Itaya group of Hokkaido, the Ito group based in Nagoya, another Ito group in Hyogo, the Yasukawa group of Fukuoka, the Kaishima group of Fukuoka, and the Katakura of Nagano. Figure 7.7 describes some of these groups.

Fig. 7.7 **(facing page) Representative local *zaibatsu* families**
Source: Morikawa (1976).
Notes: There were many family-based *zaibatsu* groups in many localities in Japan before World War II. The scale of their business operations and geographic coverage was much smaller than that of the major *zaibatsu* groups such as Mitsui, Sumitomo, and Mitsubishi. Nevertheless, these local *zaibatsu* groups often organized their companies in pyramidal structures as the major *zaibatsu* groups did. Some of these local *zaibatsu* companies survived World War II and still exist today. For example, Kikkoman (Mogi *zaibatsu* in Chiba), Matsuzakaya Department Store (Ito *zaibatsu* in Nagoya), Kurashiki Textile (Ohara *zaibatsu* in Okayama), and Yasukawa Electric (Yasukawa *zaibatsu* in Fukuoka) are shown here.

Name	Location	Holding Co. (capital in 10,000 yen)	Familiy members/relatives	Business	Where they invested
地方資産家（代表名）	住所	本社（資本金）	家族・同族	家業	投資先
板谷　宮吉	北海道小樽		宮吉、順助（宮吉養子）	醸造 雑穀肥料問屋 板谷商船 北門貯蓄銀行	南洋郵船 北海水力電気 洞爺湖電鉄 樺太銀行
相馬　哲平	北海道函館	相馬合名（400万円）	哲平、堅弥（同長男）、市作（同長女の夫）、省三（同次男）、廉平（同次女の子）	相馬商店（株）（問屋、金融、漁業、鉱業） 相馬銀行	百十三銀行 函館貯蓄銀行
茂木　七左衛門	千葉野田	千秋社（名）	七左衛門、高梨兵左衛門（七左衛門の妹の夫）	醤油醸造	野田醤油 野田商誘銀行 野田運輸
中野　忠太郎（寛一長男）	新潟金津	中野興業（2,500万円）	忠太郎、信吾（寛一次男）、孝次（忠太郎次男）、冬松（寛一次女の夫）	中野興業（原油採掘販売） 中野殖産興業	日本石油 新潟港湾倉庫 蒲原鉄道
西脇　済三郎	新潟小千谷	西脇合名	済三郎、健次（同弟）、新次郎（同姉の夫）	西脇銀行 西脇商店	小千谷銀行 北越水力電気 三光紡績
片倉　謙太郎（三代目）	長野諏訪	片倉合名	兼太郎（二代長男・初代甥）、勝衛（初代いとこの長男）、武雄（初代長男）、今井五介（初代弟）等21名	片倉製糸 日東紡績 片倉生命 片倉殖産 片倉米穀肥料	信州電気 昭和絹靴下
鈴木　与平（六代目）	静岡清水			鈴与商店（回漕、米穀肥料・塩・石灰問屋、運送） 鈴与倉庫	清水銀行 三十五銀行 清水運送 清水食品
中埜　半左衛門	愛知半田		半左衛門、又左衛門、半六、良吉、盛田善平	中埜酢店 中埜醤油店 中埜酒店 中埜銀行 中埜貯蓄銀行 半田倉庫 敷島屋製粉所	日本麦酒鉱泉 知多鉄道
伊藤　次郎左衛門	名古屋	伊藤総本店 伊藤産業合名（1,000万円）	次郎左衛門、松之助（同長男）、銃次郎（同次男）、鈴三郎（同二男）	松坂屋 伊藤銀行 山東煙草 山東窯業 三綿商店	愛知銀行 日本貯蓄銀行 中央信託 名古屋製陶 愛知時計電機
辰馬　吉左衛門	兵庫西宮		吉左衛門	辰馬本家酒造（白鹿醸造元） 辰馬汽船 辰馬海上火災保険 夙川土地	三十四銀行 神戸瓦斯 神戸海上運送火災保険 兵庫大岡信託
八馬　謙介	兵庫西宮	多聞合資（200万円）	謙介、安二郎（同弟）、駒雄（同上）	西宮酒造 多聞興業 八馬汽船	武庫銀行 西宮銀行 神戸海上運送火災保険 兵庫大岡信託

Name 地方資産家 (代表名)	Location 住所	Holding Co. (capital in 10,000 yen) 本社 (資本金)	Familiy members/relatives 家族・同族	Business 家業	Where they invested 投資先
伊藤 長次郎	兵庫印南	静得社(資) (170万円)	長次郎、熊三(同長男)、勇次郎	酒造業 伊藤土地合名	三十八銀行 神栄生糸 昭和毛糸紡績 山陽中央水電
大原 孫三郎	岡山倉敷		孫三郎	倉敷紡績 倉敷紡織	中国銀行 岡山合同貯蓄銀行 中国信託
安川 敬一郎	福岡戸畑	安川松本合名	敬一郎、松本健次郎(敬一郎次男)、安川清三郎(同三男)、安川兼五郎(同五男)	明治鉱業 九州製鋼 明治紡績 安川電機 黒崎窯業	若松築港 嘉穂鉱業
貝島 太市	福岡直方	貝島合名 (2,000万円)	太市(太助三男)、栄一(太助孫・宗家)、健次(栄一叔父)、栄四郎(栄一叔父)	貝島鉱業 貝島商事 貝島乾溜 貝島木材防腐	中央火災傷害 若松築港
麻生 太吉	福岡飯塚		太吉、太七(同弟)、義之介(同養子)	麻生商店 嘉穂銀行 嘉穂貯蓄銀行 嘉穂電燈	九州水力電気 若松築港 幸袋工作所

Fig. 7.7   (cont.)

7.3.9   The *Zaibatsu* and Independent Companies

Numerous independent entrepreneurs also shaped the economy in this era. Sakichi Toyoda patented the Toyoda wooden hand loom in 1891 and an innovative automatic loom in 1924.[32] Platt Brothers and Co. of England, a world leader in looms, paid the 1929 equivalent of one million yen for the rights, and Toyoda later used these funds to found Toyota Motors. Another important entrepreneur, Konosuke Matsushita, founded Matsushita Electric Industries in Osaka in 1918 and developed it into one of the world's largest electronics manufacturers. Many of these new ventures were affiliated with established *zaibatsu* to varying degrees.

Toyota was loosely affiliated with the Mitsui *zaibatsu* until the end of World War II and the Mitsui *keiretsu* after the war.[33] In 1898, Mitsui Bussan agreed to market Toyoda's products. When Toyoda set up his own textiles firm, Toyoda Shokai, Mitsui Bussan provided capital. When he established Toyoda Style Textile Machines, a predecessor to Toyoda Boshokuki,

32. During his lifetime Sakichi Toyoda made 119 inventions, of which 13 were awarded U.S. and other foreign patents.

33. As of 1930, figure 7.3 lists Toyoda Boshokuki (Toyoda Textile Machines) and another Toyoda company as controlled by Toyo Menka Trading Firm, which was owned by Mitsui Bussan.

in 1906, Mitsui Bussan again provided capital. The Toyoda and Mitsui continued to have close business and family ties. For example, Sakichi Toyoda adopted his son-in-law, Risaburo Toyoda (formerly Risaburo Kogama), the second son of the Kogama family, which ran Mitsui's Toyo Menka. Risaburo subsequently became the first president of Toyota Motor.[34]

Matsushita did business with the Jugo Bank, but Sumitomo opened a branch near his factory in 1925 and approached him about doing business. Matsushita asked Sumitomo for a ¥20,000 line of credit, an unusual arrangement at the time, and Sumitomo agreed. Although Matsushita had never used the line of credit, when Jugo Bank failed in a depression shortly thereafter, Sumitomo honored the agreement and extended credit. Matsushita accordingly began a long-term relationship with the Sumitomo Bank in 1927. Matsushita was never listed as a Sumitomo company, since the group has as its own electronics firm, NEC. However, its close relationship with the Sumitomo Bank continued for decades. Matsushita expanded, building its own pyramidal group, and was numbered among the great *zaibatsu* by the Allied forces charged with rebuilding Japan's postwar economy. Following World War II the Sumitomo Bank became the largest bank block holder of Matsushita shares and its main bank. At the end of World War II Matsushita was not formally owned by the Sumitomo family. Yet it was designated as a *zaibatsu* group by the Allied forces in June 1946, and Konosuke Matsushita and all other top executives with ranks above managing directors were purged from all public offices in November 1946. Konosuke Matsushita was apparently respected by the Matsushita employees, and the purge generated sympathy among Matsushita's labor unions. The union leaders presented 15,000 signatures from their members and families to the general headquarters of the Allied forces and the Japanese government. Because of this unusual support, Konosuke Matsushita's and other Matsushita executives' purge was downgraded and then was dropped entirely in May 1947. Matsushita companies were able to resume operation.

Table 7.5 shows *zaibatsu* firms owning about 35 percent of corporate assets in 1946, with the remainder held by independent firms. Many independent firms, like Toyota and Matsushita, were actually bound, more or less tightly, to an established *zaibatsu*. Many that would become important decades later were not key players in the prewar corporate sector. But *zaibatsu* firms' dominance of key industries like natural resources, chemicals, manufacturing, and trade, and of the associated distribution channels, was overwhelming by the start of World War II. Thus, despite their number and

---

34. Kiichiro Toyoda, Sakichi's son with his first wife, spent most of his life developing automobiles, but he got along poorly with Risaburo and died without taking charge of Toyota Motors.

collective economic importance, independent firms were unquestionably less politically influential during this period.

7.4   Ownership Changes during the Depressions

In the 1920s and early 1930s, Japan endured a series of depressions, culminating in the Great Depression. The Great Kanto Earthquake of 1923 so disrupted the economy that the Roaring Twenties were essentially mute in Japan. Several major *zaibatsu* collapsed. Studying which *zaibatsu* failed and which survived is highly instructive.

Key factors explaining survival appear to be the existence of a bank in the *zaibatsu,* its position in the pyramid, and its role in the business dealings of the group. The Mitsubishi, Mitsui, and Sumitomo *zaibatsu* all had banks very near the apexes of their pyramids. Consequently, their banks' health was a primary concern of the controlling families. Moreover, any tunneling that occurred would tend to increase the assets and incomes of these banks.

The Mitsubishi, Mitsui, and Sumitomo banks also had well-diversified loan portfolios, with only 10 to 20 percent of outstanding loans to other firms in their own *zaibatsu*.[35] Moreover, these banks held equity in many firms spanning many industries. Indeed, the reticence of the Mitsubishi Bank to lend to related companies during the depressions forced many, though not the mining and shipbuilding concerns, to issue public shares. The average stake of the Mitsubishi apex partnership in its first tier subsidiaries fell from 83.5 percent in 1921 to 69.0 percent in 1928.

Other *zaibatsu* families used their banks primarily to raise money for their *zaibatsu* firms. These so-called *organ banks* were thus poorly diversified. For example, 94 percent of the Nakazawa Bank's loans were to insiders, as were 75 percent of the Watanabe Bank's loans. Likewise, 75 percent of the loans held by the Matsukata *zaibatsu*'s Jugo Bank were to Matsukata firms. Prior to their collapses in 1927, 72 percent of the loans of the Suzuki's captive bank, the Taiwan Bank, were to Suzuki companies.

7.4.1   The Rise and Fall of the Suzuki *Zaibatsu*[36]

The Suzuki family, like many other Tokugawa-era mercantile families, participated actively in Japan's foreign trade after the restoration. Even though they began as specialists in silk, copper, clothing, or sugar, they eventually required a general trading firm, or *sogo shosha,* to transact barter business domestically and to handle transactions with foreigners. A

---

35. Such diversification is clearly sound banking practice to reduce risk. This may have been the banks' deliberate objective, but this is not entirely clear.

36. Kato (1957) details the use and structure of organ banks, including that of the Suzuki group, and is the source of much of this section. See also Okazaki and Yokoyama (2001) for empirical evidence and a summary of other work.

sogo shosha was a general entity that could deal with all types of profit opportunities in both domestic and foreign markets. The first and largest was Mitsui Bussan, which served as a model for many others.[37]

One imitator was Suzuki Shoten, the Suzuki Merchant Company. The Suzukis began as sugar traders and organized a *sogo shosha* to handle miscellaneous transactions related to that business. Suzuki Shoten quickly grew to become the second largest *sogo shosha*. Suzuki's rapid expansion took place in two stages.

The first was during Japan's intensive drive to develop its new colony in Taiwan, acquired during the Sino-Japanese War of 1894 to 1895. Taiwan's climate was ideal for sugar cane, and the Suzukis were the logical point men to handle Japanese investment in that industry. To transport sugar to Japan, the Suzukis needed ships, so it expanded into shipping and shipbuilding. At this point, the apex firm of the *zaibatsu* remained a single proprietorship run by the family patriarch, soon one of Japan's richest merchants.

The second stage occurred in the period immediately after World War I. During a sustained boom from 1914 to 1919, Japan's gross national product (GNP) grew fivefold, and the Suzuki *zaibatsu* expanded aggressively, proliferating new firms into many industries. In 1903, the apex firm became a general partnership capitalized at ¥500,000. By 1920, this had increased one hundredfold to ¥50 million yen. Already in 1915, the Suzukis' annual business in foreign trade reached ¥1.54 billion, exceeding that of Mitsui Bussan. By the end of the boom, the Suzuki group looked comparable in many ways to the Mitsui and Mitsubishi *zaibatsu*.

One of the Suzukis' critical successes occurred in November 1914, three months after the beginning of the First World War. Although Japan was mired in a deep recession, Naokichi Kaneko (1868–1944), the manager of Suzuki Shoten, and Seiichi Takahata, the company's London branch manager, foresaw that German U-boats would raise ship and commodity prices sharply. Kaneko ordered Takahata to buy everything available, including raw materials aboard any transport ship. Suzuki's purchases of ships, iron, steel, sugar, wheat, and other commodities wrought an immediate profit of over ¥100 million. This move, more than anything else, make Suzuki a global player in trade.

Takahata was also skillful in dealing with Great Britain and the other allied countries, procuring for them raw materials, iron and steel products, food supplies, ships, and the like. With 50,000 tons of ships sunk on an average day, Britain suffered a severe shortage of transport capacity, and was directly in the business of buying ships. At one point, the British government advanced Suzuki an unprecedented £500,000 deposit toward the purchase of ships. Suzuki was also flooded with orders for food from the

---

37. Others were organized by the Mitsubishi, Masuda, Abe, Mogi, Takada, Iwai, Ataka, and Yuasa groups.

British and allied governments. Takahata responded, for example, by selling them entire cargos of beans, grain, and other food items from Hokkaido together with the ships themselves.

These developments caused Suzuki to enter a long-term relationship
with the Taiwan Bank. Suzuki's foreign trade transactions were now so
enormous that Japan's only government-authorized foreign exchange
bank, Yokohama Shokin Bank,[38] was incapable of handling them all, forcing Suzuki to rely on more expensive merchant bankers.[39] The Japanese
government had granted the Taiwan Bank special privileges to deal in foreign exchange, and Takahata seized upon this to unplug Suzuki's foreign
exchange bottlenecks. The Taiwan Bank welcomed Suzuki's overtures because its extensive nonperforming loans in China had discouraged other
zaibatsu companies from doing business with it.

A brief but severe recession followed the November 1918 armistice, and
several small *zaibatsu,* including Mogi, Kuhara, Masuda, and Abe, failed.
The Suzuki group survived, and when the economy recovered in September 1919, Takahata foresaw another boom. The pace of the Suzukis' global
expansion was unprecedented. The Suzuki group gleaned huge profits in
everything from Java sugar to wheat and soybeans from Siberia, Manchuria, and Qingdao. In one transaction, the Suzukis shipped 360,000 tons
of wheat from Manchuria to Great Britain using 10,000 boxcars of the Manchurian Railway and forty-five 8,000- to 10,000-ton freighters. In 1919 and
1920, Takahata sold fifty shiploads of Java sugar and earned 65 million
guilders on the 1920 transactions alone.

In 1923, Kaneko restructured the Suzuki pyramid, floating the trade
division of Suzuki Shoten as the Suzuki Stock Company, or Kabushiki
Suzuki, capitalized at ¥80 million and with a paid-in capital of ¥50 million.
Suzuki Shoten's remaining operations were reorganized into a holding
company, Suzuki General Partnership or Suzuki Gomei, capitalized at ¥50
million. Suzuki General Partnership became the new apex firm, controlling seventy-eight listed firms. Of these, ten were in food industries, twenty-
four in chemicals, four in textiles, two in tobacco, five in mining, five in iron
and steel, three in electric machinery, three in electric power, three in railways, two in shipping, two in fishing, two in real estate and warehousing,
three in development, two in the banking and trust business, four in insurance, and three in commerce.

The sixty-five of these that were integral parts of the Suzuki *zaibatsu* had
a capitalization of ¥560 million. The apex firm employed 3,000 people, and
the pyramid firms had 25,000 employees in total. Figure 7.8 diagrams the
Suzuki pyramid at its greatest extent.

38. Yokohama Shokin Bank became the Bank of Tokyo after World War II, which more recently merged with the Mitsubishi Bank to form the Bank of Tokyo-Mitsubishi.
39. The only other Japanese trading firm that had enough foreign business to warrant using merchant bankers was Mitsui Bussan.

	Company name 会社(株)別	Paid-in capital (million yen) 資本金(払込み)	Date of establishment 設立年月	Location 所在地	A	B	C	D	E	F	G	H	I	J	K
1	第六十五銀行	10(6.25)	明治 11.11(1878)	神戸		X						△		△	△
2	天満織物	7(5.243)	20. 3	大阪		X	○	○	○	△		+	○	△	X
3	日本セメント	5(5)	21. 3	東京			△		△			+	△		
4	日本教育生命保険	0.3(0.075)	29. 9(10)	東京	○	◎	△	△	△	△		+	△	△	◎
5	日本製粉	12.3(12.3)	29.10(9)	東京		X	○	○	○	△		+	○	△	X
6	大日本塩業	4(3.802)	36. 9	東京	○	◎	○	○	○	△		+	○	△	◎
7	神戸製鋼所	20(20)	38. 9(44.6)	神戸	○	✪	○	○	○				○	○	●
8	東亜製粉	2.5(1.25)	39. 10	東京		X									
9	東亜煙草	10(5.8)	39.11(10)	東京`		X	△	△	△	△		+	△	△	
10	東京毛織	16(16)	39.11	東京		□	△	△	△	△				△	□
11	日本酒類醸造	5(2.15)	39.12	大里	○										◎
12	東工業	0.5(0.5)	40. 1	大阪		✪	○	△	○	○		-	○	○	○
13	東洋製糖	36.25(22.03)	40. 2	台湾		X	○	○	○	△		+	△	△	X
14	塩水港製糖	25(21.563)	40. 3(2)	台湾		X	△	△						△	
15	東洋海上火災保険	3(0.75)	41. 6	東京			△	△	△	△		+	△		
16	日本商業	5(5)	42. 2	大阪	○	✪	○	○	○	○	●		○	○	●
17	帝国麦酒	10(5.5)	45. 5(6)	大里		□	△	△	△	△		+	△	△	□
18	南満州物産	1(1)	大正 2. 1	大連	○	✪	○	○		○	●		○	○	●
19	大正生命保険	0.5(0.125)	2. 4	東京	○	◎	○	○	○	△		+	△	△	◎
20	宜蘭殖産	0.475(0.475)	4. 3(4)	台湾	○	◎	○	○	△	○		-	△	△	◎
21	山陽製鉄	0.5(0.5)	4.12	大阪			△		△			-		△	
22	沖見初炭坑	2(2)	5. 3(9)	下関	○	◎	○	○	△	○		-	○	○	◎
23	朝鮮鉄道	54.5(17.65)	5. 4	朝鮮			△		△			+	△		
24	日本金属	1(1)	5. 5	神戸		✪	○	○	△	○	●	-	○	○	●
25	日本火薬製造	2.5(1.375)	5. 6	東京			△		△				△		
26	八重山産業	0.3(0.1125)	5. 8	神戸		◎									
27	東洋燐寸	2.8(2.8)	5. 9(7)	神戸	○	◎	△	△	△	△		+	△	△	◎
28	帝国汽船	1(1)	5. 10	神戸	○	✪	△	△	△	△	●	-	△	△	●
29	帝国染料製造	0.555(0.555)	5.11	福山		◎	△	△	△	△		-	△	△	◎
30	福島炭坑	2(1.2)	5.12	東京			△		△				△		
31	佐賀紡績	5(3.5)	5.12	佐賀			△	△		△		-	△	△	□
32	浪華倉庫	5(5)	6. 6	大阪	○	✪	○	○	○	○	●	+	○	○	●
33	東海製油所	0.5(0.125)	6. 6	名古屋			△								
34	関門窯業	0.19(0.19)	6. 8	彦島			△	△	△			-	△	△	
35	南洋製糖	1.25(1.25)	6.11	東京		□	○	○	○	△		+	△	△	□
36	日沙商会	3(2)	6.12	兵庫	○	✪	○	○	△	○	●	+	○	○	●
37	帝国燐寸	0.2(0.2)	7. 1	神戸			△						△		
38	彦島坩堝	0.3(0.3)	7. 2(3)	彦島		◎	○	○	○			-	○	○	
39	日本樟脳	9(6.75)	7. 2	神戸	○	X	△	△	△					△	X
40	帝国人造絹糸	12.5(8.75)	7. 2(6)	神戸	○	✪	○	○	△	○			○	○	●
41	山陽水力電気	6(4.5)	7. 9	神戸			△								
42	千代田信託	10(2.5)	7.10	東京			△	△	△				△	△	
43	日本冶金	0.35(0.35)	8. 3(7.11)	大阪		□	△	△	△			-	○	△	□
44	信越電力	32(32)	8. 5	東京			△		△			+	△		
45	帝国炭業	10(10)	8. 5	下関	○	◎	○	○	○	○			○	△	◎
46	国際汽船	80(77.148)	8. 7	神戸			△	△	△	△		-	△	△	X
47	大日本セルロイド	10(10)	8. 9	堺		X	△	△	△	△		+	△	△	X
48	大成化学工業	1(0.5)	8.10	東京		X									
49	内国食品	0.08(0.06)	8.10	神戸			○		○	○		-	○	○	◎
50	太陽曹達	1(0.5)	8.10	神戸	○	✪	○	○	○	○			○	○	●
51	三国紡績	5(2.5)	8.10	大阪											X
52	日本拓殖	10(3)	8.11	台湾			△		△	△			△		

Fig. 7.8   The Suzuki *zaibatsu*: Affiliated firms, 1923–27

Source: Katsura (1976).

Notes: The 76 firms listed here were established between 1878 and 1926 and were generally considered members of the Suzuki *zaibatsu*. Analysts before and after World War II differ on the precise control relationships the Suzuki Shoten had with these Suzuki companies. Columns (A)–(G) and (I)–(K) compare the estimated control relationships published by ten different analysts and securities firms between 1923 and 1928. ○ = directly owned by Suzuki; ◎ = majority-controlled; ✪ = minority-controlled; O = fully controlled; ● = spin-offs; △ = affiliated (mostly for investment purposes); × = closely related with little control. Column (H) compares estimates of the chances of independent survival for former Suzuki companies, published in a business magazine after the Suzuki *zaibatsu*'s collapse in April 1927. + = very good prospect, no impact from the collapse; – = no possibility for survival; | = survival possible depending on restructuring efforts.

	Company name	Paid-in capital (million yen)	Date of establishment	Location	Notes										
	会社(株)別	資本金(払込み)	設立年月	所在地	A	B	C	D	E	F	G	H	I	J	K
53	再製樟脳	2(1.7)	大正 8.12	神戸	○	◎	○	○	○	○		+	○	△	◎
54	新日本火災海上	5(1.25)	9.8	東京	○	◎	△	△	△	△		+	△	△	◎
55	大源鉱業	2(1.36)	9.9	東京		X									
56	支那樟脳	2(2)	9.12	上海	○	◎	○	○	○	○	●	+	○	△	□
57	樺太漁業	0.75(0.6)	9.12	函館	X	△	△	△	○		-	△	△		
58	旭石油	9.6(9.3)	10. 2(11.3)	東京	□	△	△	△	△		-	△	△	□	
59	合同油脂グリセリン	5(5)	10. 4	東京	○	◎	○	○	○	○		+	○	△	◎
60	太田川水電	3(0.75)	10. 10	神戸			○		○	○		-	○		
61	日本トロール	2(1)	10. 10	東京			△	△	△			+	△		
62	米星煙草	1(0.5)	10.12	青島	○	✿	△	△	△	○	●	+	○	○	●
63	豊年製油	10(10)	11. 4	東京	○	✿	○	○	○	○	●	+	○	○	●
64	クロード式窯業工業	10(10)	11. 4	神戸	○	✿	○	○	○	○	●	I	○	○	●
65	南朝鮮製紙	1(1)	11. 5	朝鮮	○	✿	○	○	○	○	●	I	○	○	●
66	大陸木材工業	0.75(0.75)	11. 6	神戸	○	◎	○	○	○		○	I	○	○	◎
67	東京無線電機	1(0.25)	11. 10	東京			△	△	△			-	○		
68	帝国樟脳	1(1)	11.12	神戸	○	✿	○	○	○	○	●	I	○	○	●
69	株式鈴木	80(50)	12. 3	神戸							●				
70	日本輪業	1(0.6)	12. 3	兵庫		✿	○	○	○	○	●	I	○	○	
71	山陽電気軌道	4.5(0.45)	13. 3	下関			△	△	△			I			
72	大日本酒類醸造	2.865(2.865)	13. 7	下関		◎	△	△	△	○		I	○	△	
73	日本エヤーブレーキ	0.6(0.45)	14. 3	神戸			○	○	○			I	○	○	
74	紡機製造	0.2(0.2)	14. 5	神戸			△	△	○			I	○		
75	長府土地	1.5(0.375)	14.12	長府			△				●	I	○		
76	第一窒素工業	5(1.5)	15. 6(5)	神戸			○	○	○	○	●	I	○	○	

Fig. 7.8   (cont.)

Kaneko apparently created some of these manufacturing companies out of a sense of nationalism. He shared with many Japanese managers of the era a belief that import substitution would free Japan of its ignominious dependence on foreigners.

The 1923 restructuring caused the Suzuki *zaibatsu* to take on a structure superficially resembling those of the other large *zaibatsu*. A holding company stood at the apex, major Suzuki powerhouse companies filled the first tier of subsidiaries, their spin-offs filled the second tier, and various acquired companies filled out the lower tiers. Many of these companies continued on with their original names.

However, two key differences figured in the Suzuki group's demise.

First, while Suzuki Shoten's trading division was separate from the apex holding company, there was no corresponding separation in personnel. In fact, figure 7.9 shows that numerous Suzuki family members and managers held cross-appointments in Suzuki companies. And though the Suzuki family held control rights, a hired manager, Kaneko, was actually making all the management decisions. The Suzuki group's rapid expansion of its business activities was not accompanied by a corresponding expansion of its management personnel.

Second, the Suzuki companies were financed differently. Suzuki firms borrowed much more than other *zaibatsu* firms, both to finance expansion

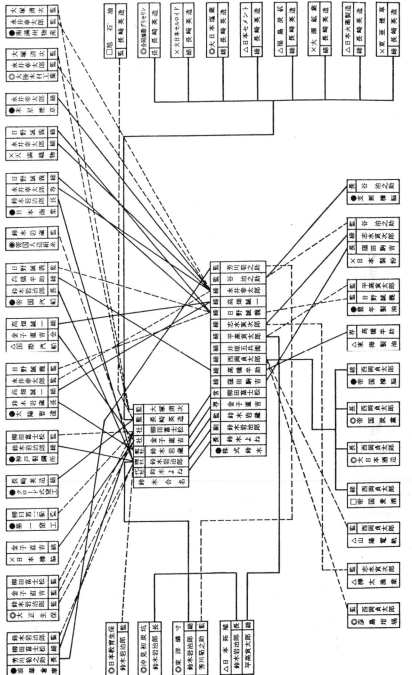

Fig. 7.9 Board interlocks in the Suzuki zaibatsu in 1926

Source: Katsura (1976).

Note: Key family members and managers served many Suzuki companies as CEOs and directors.

Table 7.8   Suzuki Trading Company debt to the Bank of Taiwan (yen)

Year	New debt	Total debt
1920		80,811,300
1921	42,907,587	123,718,887
1922	55,317,426	179,036,313
1923	47,869,445	226,905,758
1924	49,145,662	276,051,420
1925	37,223,293	313,274,713
1926	43,581,754	356,856,470
1927	22,002,099	378,858,569

Source: Fouraker (2002, p. 8).

and to finance day-to-day business dealings. This debt generally took the form of loans from the Taiwan Bank, the Suzuki group's de facto group bank. This seems to have reflected Kaneko's desire to maintain undisputed control throughout the pyramid. Equity financing risked empowering outside shareholders, and even invited takeovers, jeopardizing Kaneko's absolute control. Debt from sources other than the Taiwan Bank risked interference from outside creditors. This aversion led to a rapid buildup of Suzuki companies' debts to the Taiwan Bank, shown in table 7.8, and a similarly rapidly increasing exposure of the Taiwan Bank to the Suzuki companies' fortunes.

Soon, the bulk of the Taiwan Bank's loan portfolio was tied up in other Suzuki companies. However, the integration of the Taiwan Bank into the Suzuki group was via a "long-term relationship." Kaneko only controlled the Taiwan Bank because of its financial dependence on business with Suzuki companies. And the Suzuki group's financial position was weakened in the early 1920s because of a costly failed effort to merge two large flour companies, Nisshin and Nihon Flour Companies. Finally, most of Suzuki General Partnership's capital was tied up in Kabushiki Suzuki, the trading company.

The collapse of the Suzuki *zaibatsu* was spectacular.[40]

The September 1919 boom that Kaneko gambled on turned out to be short lived. The Japanese economy stumbled in 1920, and again in 1922, and then collapsed with the Great Kanto Earthquake depression of 1924, and the Showa finance depression of 1927. The latter two events kept Japan's economy from realizing the growth that seemed likely in 1919 and exposed the weakness of the Suzuki *zaibatsu* and other similar pyramids.

The Great Kanto Earthquake of September 1, 1923, was one of the worst

40. The collapse of Suzuki zaibatsu compares in scale with the collapses of Ivar Kreuger's STAB in Sweden in 1932 and that of the Stinnes concerns in Germany in the 1920s (Kato 1957).

in world history. It destroyed Tokyo, Yokohama, and the surrounding area, killing 140,000 people either directly, in the ensuing fires, or in mob violence against Koreans in the quake's aftermath. Business offices and records were destroyed, and much of Japan's most modern infrastructure was ruined.

But another effect of the earthquake was purely financial—the Showa depression. The earthquake seriously damaged numerous businesses, many of which had issued bills prior to the quake that they were now unable to pay. This, in turn, created cash flow problems for the banks holding those bills. The government therefore developed a program under which the Bank of Japan would rediscount bills listing the disaster area as place of payment or listing a merchant with offices in the disaster area as the debtor. These *earthquake bills,* or *tegata,* provided a two-year grace period for collection, subsequently twice extended, adding two more years of grace. The government promised compensation to the Bank of Japan for any losses due to the program. At the end of 1926, more than ¥200 million in unsettled earthquake bills remained, of which ¥160 million had been rediscounted by the Bank of Japan.[41]

Suzuki companies used more debt financing than Mitsui, Sumitomo, or Mitsubishi firms. The Suzuki group's total debt at the end of 1926 was ¥500 million, of which ¥379 million was owed to the Taiwan Bank. Kaneko had accumulated this amount of debt through adept financial maneuvers mixing and counterbalancing credit created by the Taiwan Bank, Suzuki firms, other firms, and the Bank of Japan. Thus, a disproportionate fraction of these unpaid earthquake bills were for debts owed by Suzuki companies, and the Suzuki *zaibatsu*'s bank, the Taiwan Bank, accounted for fully 58 percent.[42]

When the Japanese Diet debated how to absorb these unpaid promissory notes, Suzuki hired heavy-handed lobbyists to sway votes. The campaign backfired, and Suzuki's financial problems were exposed. Suzuki companies found themselves unable to float debt. The final law the Diet passed on March 23, 1927, was accompanied by a resolution to rescue the Taiwan Bank. On March 24, the Taiwan Bank announced that it was severing its ties with the Suzuki group entirely. The sudden abandonment of Suzuki companies by the Taiwan Bank forced them to default on payments due the Mitsui Bank and other banks. Angered by the Taiwan Bank's move, the other banks called in their Taiwan Bank loans, putting the Taiwan Bank (once again) on the verge of bankruptcy.

Suzuki collapsed on April 2, 1927. On April 13, the Bank of Japan, despite the above resolution, refused to mount a second rescue of the Taiwan

41. See, for example, Ito (2001) for the role of the Bank of Japan in the depression periods in the 1920s and 1930s.

42. Both Taiwan and Korea Banks were given special status by the Japanese government.

Bank. Cha (2001) argues that a determination by the central bank to end the gold embargo figured largely in this decision, but the politics of the situation surely also played a role. The Upper House of Parliament voted down a special provision to rescue Taiwan Bank, arguing that the measure was unconstitutional, and the Japanese cabinet fell on April 17. The Taiwan Bank closed temporarily on April 18. This resulted in an immediate nationwide financial panic.

7.4.2   The Disposition of the Remains

Although the Suzuki group failed because of its inability to pay its promissory notes, it never actually went into bankruptcy. The Suzuki group moved all its business to another company, Nissho, reorganized as a stock company in 1928.[43] The original Suzuki company undertook all repayment and restructuring activities and was dissolved in 1933 after repaying all of its debts. During this six-year restructuring, no creditors' meeting took place, and the Japanese courts never declared Suzuki bankrupt. In their investigations, the Suzuki group's creditors found no book fudging whatsoever, and accepted that the collapse was an honest financial and management failure. They unanimously agreed to settle all remaining accounts privately. In this process no overseas clients of the Suzukis' were adversely affected either.

Because the failure was purely financial and managerial, the Suzuki pyramid still contained viable firms with significant assets. These, realizing Kaneko's worst nightmares, fell to the other major *zaibatsu* as Suzuki debts were settled. The primary buyers were Mitsui and Mitsubishi, which accumulated all of the Suzuki group's most promising business units plus the Taiwan Bank. This consolidation significantly raised concentration ratios in certain industries. For example, 84 percent of Taiwan's sugar production was now under the control of three *zaibatsu:* Mitsui, Mitsubishi, and Fujiyama. Intangible assets, notably the many exclusive distribution rights the Suzuki group owned, were transferred to Mitsui Bussan (Mitsui and Co.) and Mitsubishi Shoji (Mitsubishi Corp.), the general trading firms of those groups.

Suzuki had been willing to take risks. The established *zaibatsu* groups, such as Mitsui, Mitsubishi, and Sumitomo, had been much more cautious. After acquiring Suzuki's chemical companies—including plants, patents, engineers, and scientists—Mitsui established a major ammonia production facility. Mitsui clearly used research conducted by the former Suzuki companies, whereas Mitsui itself would never have paid for such research—at least without large government subsidies. Thus, although the

---

43. Nissho Company continued as a general trading firm and merged with Iwai Trading Company in 1968 to form the present Nissho Iwai Corporation. Their web site (http://www.nisshoiwai.co.jp/in/e/index2.html) presents their corporate history involving the Suzuki Shoten.

Suzuki group ultimately failed, it still probably made a major contribution to Japan's subsequent development.[44]

7.4.3 Post Mortem

Kaneko (1928) himself reflected on the collapse of the Suzuki *zaibatsu* and summarized the reasons for its collapse. In Kaneko's opinion, a highly centralized management system imposed on widely disparate firms prevented proper monitoring and was the most important reason for Suzuki's ruin. Second, Kaneko reflects that Suzuki companies had too much debt capital requiring too high interest payments given the recessionary environment, noting that the "high cost of debt capital subsequently killed us."

The two reasons Kaneko lists correspond precisely to the differences noted above between the Suzuki pyramid and the *zaibatsu* that survived, such as Mitsui, Sumitomo, and Mitsubishi. The Suzuki group's organizational weakness, as pointed out by Kaneko himself, was its overly centralized management. The Suzuki group's financial weakness stemmed from its extensive use of debt financing from a single bank. Kaneko, quoted by Nissho (1968), explains that "the profits earned by Suzuki Shoten's hard work should be monopolized by the Suzuki family. I would rather borrow money from banks than pay profits out as dividends." The two reasons were not unrelated, for this statement is often interpreted to mean that Kaneko wanted to maintain Suzuki family control in order to preserve his own control. This left Taiwan Bank's loan portfolio highly concentrated in Suzuki companies—and essentially an organ bank for the group. In contrast, by 1912 most Mitsui companies were already able to grow on retained earnings and equity issues. The Mitsui Bank was not needed as an organ bank, and lent extensively to companies outside the Mitsui group. Table 7.9 shows quite stable relationships between deposits and loan balances for the six largest *zaibatsu* banks for the early 1930s.

A third reason, which Kaneko does not mention, for the Suzuki group's collapse is that he expanded the Suzuki group too fast and in the wrong directions. He certainly failed to foresee the chronic weakness of the Japanese economy through the 1920s. Had the 1920s economy in Japan resembled that in the United States, Suzuki might well have prospered. However, in retrospect, the more risk-averse strategies of the Mitsui, Mitsubishi, and Sumitomo groups proved superior. Moreover, Suzuki missed some of the most profitable new industries of the 1920s, such as electrical machinery. The Suzuki group was vulnerable to a downturn because, unlike Mitsui, Mitsubishi, and Sumitomo, it lacked a reliably highly profitable mining op-

---

44. After the collapse of Suzuki, Kaneko set up a holding company, Taiyo Soda, in 1931, with which he began another business career. He died in Borneo in 1944, while engaged in aluminum processing. Takahata was at his deathbed. Kaneko, with help from Nissho, developed Taiyo Soda (renamed Taiyo Sangyo in 1939) into a holding firm controlling twenty-five companies, including Kobe Steel Works.

Table 7.9   Six largest *zaibatsu* banks' deposits and loans, 1931–37 (in millions of yen)

Date	Mitsui	Mitsubishi	Daiichi	Sumitomo	Yasuda	Sanwa
June 1931	710 (413)	647 (313)	659 (371)	684 (402)	610 (438)	
June 1932	620 (441)	616 (344)	648 (394)	679 (423)	607 (460)	
December 1932	687 (429)	640 (317)	703 (399)	735 (447)	664 (479)	
June 1933	696 (386)	705 (324)	769 (406)	815 (472)	730 (507)	
December 1933	715 (409)	661 (274)	787 (418)	798 (461)	740 (511)	1,025 (519)
June 1934	759 (366)	696 (259)	816 (409)	827 (426)	800 (519)	1,063 (489)
December 1934	748 (383)	722 (265)	852 (422)	872 (466)	807 (548)	1,077 (496)
June 1935	759 (380)	752 (265)	868 (432)	886 (471)	818 (571)	1,080 (494)
December 1935	796 (451)	730 (294)	913 (448)	952 (522)	832 (578)	1,114 (494)
June 1936	824 (437)	805 (341)	940 (450)	970 (543)	891 (616)	1,151 (526)
December 1936	856 (518)	810 (370)	972 (545)	1,017 (618)	928 (679)	1,197 (532)
June 1937	904 (531)	903 (441)	1,054 (657)	1,093 (691)	1,023 (744)	1,263 (577)

Source: Mitsubishi Bank (1954).
Note: Loans in parentheses.

eration to serve as a cash cow for the entire groups during downturns. It is also sometimes argued that the lack of mining in its industrial portfolio prevented Suzuki from vertically integrating into electrical machinery, which provided an additional financial cushion for the Mitsui, Mitsubishi, and Sumitomo *zaibatsu.*

A fourth reason, which Kaneko also fails to note, is that he was quite ham-fisted at lobbying. An interesting aspect of Kaneko's personality was that he apparently had no interest in personal wealth. He did not benefit personally in any way from his business dealings. He likewise could not comprehend that politicians might value money, and he refused to make any payments to bureaucrats or politicians. During the Meiji period, rent-seeking investments seem to have been important aspects of the business strategies of the other *zaibatsu,* and they probably played some role in Mitsui and Mitsubishi taking over state mining operations. Tou-suke Fukuzawa (1868–1938), a successful entrepreneur and well-known industrialist responsible for much of the development of Japan's electric power industry in the early decades of the twentieth century, argues that this was the biggest reason for the Suzuki group's collapse and that Japan should thank Kaneko deeply for not contributing to political corruption.[45] A less laudatory interpretation is that Kaneko relished power rather than wealth and failed to understand that others viewed life differently. In any event, Kaneko's lack of preexisting political connections certainly hurt him, and his last-minute attempts to manipulate the Diet backfired badly.

45. Fukuzawa (1930) regards Kaneko more highly than Iwasaki, the Mitsubishi zaibatsu's founder.

7.4.4   The Culling of the *Zaibatsu* and Their Banks

Although the fall of the Suzuki *zaibatsu* was the most spectacular, it was not an isolated event. The 1920s depressions felled many other pyramidal groups. The Nakazawa, Watanabe, and Matsusaka *zaibatsu* also collapsed about the same time as the Suzuki *zaibatsu*.

Like the Suzuki group, these families preserved control by using loans from their group banks to finance group companies. Thus, like the Taiwan Bank, the Nakazawa, Watanabe, and Matsusaka banks were organ banks of their *zaibatsu*—heavily dependent on interest payments from their respective group companies. When key nonfinancial companies in each of these *zaibatsu* encountered financial difficulty, the group bank failed and the rest of the *zaibatsu* then collapsed.

Moreover, these organ banks were located deep in their pyramids. Consequently, tunneling would have concentrated losses and debts in the banks, with income and assets rising toward the apex firms. In contrast, the banks of the Mitsui, Sumitomo, and Mitsubishi *zaibatsu* were near the apexes of those pyramids. Consequently, tunneling would have concentrated income and assets in the banks, with losses and debts sinking toward the lower-tier firms.

Noting this pattern, Kato (1957) proposes the so-called *organ bank hypothesis*. This hypothesis holds that certain banks were excessively tightly connected to their *zaibatsu* industrial companies, made easy loans to those companies, failed, and caused the Showa financial crisis in 1927. Okazaki and Yokoyama (2001) present empirical evidence supporting this hypothesis.

Since the stability of a country's banking system has positive externalities, there may be a public policy lesson here. Countries whose major banks are parts of pyramidal groups should encourage the positioning of banks near the apexes of those groups.

7.5   The Centrally Planned Economy under the Military Government

As the economy staggered, an anti-Westernization backlash grew. In part, this was a result of Japan's successful adoption of many Western ideas. Japanese, now educated and middle class, chafed at Western arrogance when the Americans and British rejected Japan's proposal for a racial equality clause in the League of Nations Covenant. A revival of conservative and nationalistic feelings renewed interest in *bushido*.

Japan had taken Taiwan from China in 1895, gained a foothold in Manchuria by defeating Russia in 1905, annexed Korea in 1910, and installed the emperor of China in a puppet government in Manchuria in 1931. These victories amid economic stagnation elevated the prestige of the military and weakened that of the political and business elite.

Emboldened, the military slowly seized power by assassinating civilian politicians. Navy and army officers soon held most important public offices, including that of prime minister. Japan attacked China in 1937, and by 1942 it had conquered Hong Kong, Indochina, Singapore, Indonesia, and Burma, proclaiming a Greater East Asian Co-Prosperity Sphere.

To support the war effort and further consolidate its power, the military government enacted laws that stripped shareholders of their corporate governance powers. Japan was soon a rigidly centrally planned economy. Although *zaibatsu* families retained titular ownership of control blocks, they had little say in management, and dividends were restricted so that earnings could be reinvested patriotically. The military government denigrated the families' objections as unpatriotic shareholder fixation on current dividends. Thus, by 1945, Japan had an economy little different from that of Russia in the 1920s.[46]

7.5.1   The Military Buildup

By the mid-1930s, Japan was recovering from its prolonged bout of depressions. In part, this was because the yen depreciated sharply after Japan left the gold standard, triggering a surge in textile exports.[47] This depreciation also gave domestic heavy industry and chemical industry firms an advantage over imports, allowing them to expand (Teranishi 2000).

In part, the recovery also probably stemmed from Finance Minister Korekiyo Takahashi's adoption of Keynesian policies at the end of 1931, when the government issued deficit-covering bonds underwritten by the Bank of Japan that were then sold to city banks. The government spent the proceeds on public works and military industries, which further increased demand for heavy and chemical industry products.

And in part, the recovery was due to the Manchurian Incident of September 1931, when a bomb ripped through a Japanese-built railway near Mukden (Shenyang). The Japanese Kwantung army, or Kantogun, which planted the bomb while guarding the railway, used the incident as a pretext to occupy Southern Manchuria despite the government's direct order to withdraw. A subsequent military buildup elevated demand for chemicals and heavy industry products.

Rising military spending seemed increasingly linked to economic prosperity in the minds of business leaders, politicians, and ordinary Japanese.

---

46. See Okazaki (1994) for details. Wartime Japan was, of course, not a communist country. However, the economic structure imposed by its extreme right military government was surprisingly similar to that of Russia in the 1920's, as described by Hoskins (1992).

47. Japan abandoned the gold standard in September 1917, along with many other countries. After World War I, many other countries promptly returned to the gold standard, but Japan delayed doing so until January 1930. It then abandoned the gold standard again in December 1931. For details, see Ogura (2002).

Table 7.10	Japanese production output by industry, 1929 and 1942 (in 1,000 yen)			
	1929		1942	
Rank	Industry	Output	Industry	Output
1	Raw silk	795,599	Iron and steel	2,626,512
2	Cotton yarn	678,466	Navy and army arsenals	2,294,100
3	Electric power	658,316	Aircraft	1,930,400
4	Broad cotton fabrics	526,096	Guns, bullets, and weapons	1,915,242
5	National railways	517,795	National railways	1,441,921
6	Japanese sake	302,120	Electric power	1,375,943
7	Coal mining	245,762	Coal mining	1,077,769
8	Private railways	232,254	Shipbuilding	858,377
9	Military ordinance	208,537	Industrial chemicals	785,169
10	State-run steel mills	189,551	Special steel	753,170
11	Printing	186,304	Electrical machinery	633,292
12	Wool fabrics	176,896	Medicine	630,800
13	Steel products	173,833	Private railways	560,337
14	Sugar	158,125	Lumber	551,600
15	Flour milling	134,895	Pig iron	502,631
16	Chemical fertilizers	132,711	Raw silk	463,098
17	Broad silk fabrics	129,516	Metal machine tools	449,442
18	Lumber	112,170	Coke	421,210
19	Nonferrous metal mining	108,204	Cotton yarn	327,520
20	Copper	108,166	Tools	323,895

Source: Yamazaki (1988, p. 13).

When the Second Sino-Japanese War broke out in 1937, the Japanese government mobilized the economy, emphasizing military-related industries and shifting production away from light industries, like textiles. Table 7.10 illustrates. This rapid change in Japan's industrial structure, in turn, had a major impact on the corporate sector.

The older *zaibatsu*—Mitsui, Sumitomo, and Mitsubishi—had expanded aggressively into heavy industries and chemicals from the early 1930s on, financing this expansion with equity issues. Table 7.11 shows that these became their most profitable operations in the 1940s, accounting for about 30 percent of the fifty most profitable firms. Thus, while the number of established *zaibatsu* firms in the top fifty did not change greatly, their industrial composition did.

Until the early 1930s the first-tier subsidiaries in the *zaibatsu* pyramids, except Mitsubishi, were almost wholly owned by members of the *zaibatsu* family and the apex firms collectively, as shown in table 7.12. In the 1930s, however, the *zaibatsu* listed these first-tier subsidiaries. This was because the families saw immense profit opportunities in rapidly growing military-related industries if they moved quickly, as illustrated in table 7.13. Superfluous stakes in control chains throughout the established pyramids were

Table 7.11   **Group affiliations of the fifty firms with highest net profits**

	1929	1943	1955	1973	1984
State-controlled firms[a]	9	20	2	2	3
Firms	5	14			
Banks	4	6			
Foreign-controlled firms	0	0	0	1	1
Zaibatsu total	16	25	23	23	19
"Old" *zaibatsu* total	16	17			
Mitsui	7	7	3	4	3
Mitsubishi	5	6	6	7	6
Sumitomo,	2	1	2	3	2
Yasuda	1	1			
Furukawa		1			
Asano	1	1			
"New" *zaibatsu* total		8			
Nissan		5			
Nichitsu		2			
Nisso		1			
Keiretsu total[b]			23	23	19
"Old" *keiretsu* total			11	14	11
"New" *keiretsu* total			12	9	8
Fuji			4	5	3
Sanwa			5	2	3
Daiichi-Kangyo			3	2	2
Independent	29	14	25	24	27

Source: Yamazaki (1988, p. 17).

[a]In 1943 three Manchurian firms are double-counted to be affiliated with both the government and the Nissan *zaibatsu*.

[b]For the post-WWII years, firms with two *keiretsu* affiliations, such as Hitachi, Ltd., and Nippon Express, are counted as independent.

Table 7.12   **Number of first-tier subsidiaries and stockholding ratios (1928)**

	Number	Stockholding ratio	
Zaibatsu	of first-tier subsidiaries	Shares held by family and headquarters (%)	Shares held by all members of the same *zaibatsu* (%)
Mitsui	6	90.2	90.6
Mitsubishi	10	69.4	77.6
Sumitomo	13	79.1	80.5
Yasuda	12	31.7	48.1
Furukawa	4	72.8	89.4
Asano	6	50.8	
Okura	20	84.7	92.7

Source: Takahashi (1930b).

Table 7.13   **Shareholding by large block holders**

	1919	1936
No. of sample firms	379	477
Holdings by large shareholders		
No. of large shareholders (%)	0.59	0.36
Shares held by large shareholders (%)	21.0	37.4
Shares held by other types of shareholders		
Individuals (%)	15.5	5.9
Banks (%)	0.8	2.1
Insurance/securities/trust firms (%)[a]	0.5	4.8
Corporations (%)	3.1	20.7[b]
Average number of shareholders per firm	2,040	3,589
Average number of shares held per shareholder		
12 largest shareholders	4,644	17,434
Other	103	95

Source: Takeda (1995).
[a]Insurance firms, securities firms, trust banks, and firms.
[b]Holding firms owned 53.8 percent of these shares owned by corporations.

sold to the public to raise capital for expansion. Thus, the stakes of *zaibatsu* companies in their subsidiaries declined significantly between 1929 and 1943 (table 7.14).

Table 7.11 shows that the newer *zaibatsu* were also present in these profitable sectors, with eight of their affiliates among the most profitable firms of 1943. Most notably, Japan Industries represents Nissan, Japan Nitrogenous Fertilizer represents Nichitsu, Nippon Soda represents Nisso, Mori Industrial Enterprises represents Mori, and the Physical and Chemical Research Institute represents Riken. Recall that many of these newer *zaibatsu* groups were developed by single entrepreneur chemists or engineers.

The number of independents among the most profitable firms fell from twenty-nine to fourteen, perhaps in part because of the state's increased control over the *zaibatsu*. Table 7.15 reveals the decreasing controlling family stakes in independent enterprises, as these firms issued ever more equity to finance expansion. By 1943, family holding company stakes were less than the stakes of state-controlled banks, like the Industrial Bank of Japan, which were now the most significant shareholders in many independent firms.[48]

48. The Industrial Bank of Japan was created in 1900 under the Industrial Bank of Japan (IBJ) Act, which provided ¥10 million in government money as initial capital and granted it the privilege of issuing IBJ long-term debentures to raise further funds. The IBJ began operating as an investment bank in 1902. A 1918 revision of the IBJ Act let it underwrite securities. The IBJ Act was nullified in 1950, and the IBJ became an ordinary bank. Also in 1950, the government passed the Bank Debentures Issuance Act, which let ordinary banks issue long-term bonds to raise capital. In 1952, after the Allied occupation ended, the Japanese government abolished the BDI Act and passed the new Long-Term Credit Bank Act. This

Table 7.14   Changes in *zaibatsu* structure, 1929–43

	No. of shareholders		Combined stake of other *zaibatsu* companies (%)	
Subsidiary	1929	1943	1929	1943
A. First-tier subsidiaries' ownership structure				
Mitsui Bussan	31	15,155	100	75.8
Mitsui Mining	26	6,912	100	84.8
Mitsubishi Shipbuilding	23	6,912	100	40.9
Mitsubishi Shoji	20	5,940	100	47.2
Sumitomo Steel	14	7,557	100	41.4
B. First-tier subsidiaries that experienced mergers				
Oji Paper Co.	6,000	23,516	25.2	3.5
Toshiba Electric	211	5,885	58.4	15.1
			1929	1943
C. Average percentage ownership of group companies by other zaibatsu companies				
Mitsui			51	31.7
Mitsubishi			52.5	35.2
Sumitomo			52.9	32.8
Yasuda			46.4	58.3
Furukawa			65.2	44.5
Asano			19.8	21.5

Source: Yamazaki (1988).

7.5.2   The March to Serfdom

The military assumed dictatorial powers over the economy in stages. Thus, the latter part of the 1930s is called the *creeping war economy.*

This development was possible because the weak economy convinced many in Japan, as elsewhere, that democracy and free-market capitalism had failed. Indeed, this view was widespread among business leaders themselves. In response to the Suzuki failure, the government organized the Council on Commerce and Industry in 1927. The council recommended a thorough cartelization of the economy to allow "cooperation" and government educational measures to induce "patriotic economic behavior" by consumers.

The Ottawa Imperial Conference erected tariffs around the British Commonwealth, shutting Japan out of her best markets, and the ensuing breakdown of trade allowed the council's recommendations to move forward.

---

designated long-term credit banks and granted them the privilege of issuing long-term bonds to finance corporate investment. The IBJ, along with the Long-Term Credit Bank, the Japan Credit Bank, and the Bank of Tokyo, became a long-term credit bank. For further details, see, e.g., Patrick (1967) and Tamaki (1995). We are grateful to Richard Sylla for pointing this out.

Table 7.15   **Composition of 10 largest stockholders of independent enterprises: 1929 and 1943**

	Corporations (%)	Financial institutions (%)	Family holding companies (%)	Individuals (%)
1929				
Toyo Spinning	3.1	0.8	1.1	8.0
Osaka Godo Spinning	6.2	2.3	1.9	7.1
Dai Nippon Spinning	5.5		1.1	7.0
Sanjushi Bank	4.6	0.9	2.4	6.9
Yamaguchi Bank	36.2	1.0	33.3	10.7
Kamoike Bank	85.6		82.9	13.3
Dai Nippon Sugar Mfg.	6.9	2.8	2.9	6.0
Dai Nippon Breweries	10.8	2.1	8.7	3.0
Nippon Oil	9.1	1.9	7.2	7.4
Kobe Steel Works				
Kawasaki Shipbuilding	17.0		15.9	15.2
Osaka Mercantile Steamship	3.1		1.5	4.4
Meguro-Kamata Electric Railway	28.1	23.5	4.5	30.4
1943				
Toyo Spinning (merged)	8.2	2.8	1.1	3.5
Dai Nippon Spinning	7.6	1.8	1.0	3.1
Sanwa Bank (merged)	19.2	4.9	14.2	4.7
Dai Nippon Sugar Mfg.	22.1	17.4	4.7	1.6
Dai Nippon Breweries	13.8	10.8	1.2	
Nippon Oil	9.4	2.9	5.6	9.5
Kobe Steel Works	38.7	27.2		
Kawasaki Heavy Ind.	29.5	4.2	2.5	
Osaka Mercantile Steamship	5.8	1.5	0.4	1.2
Meguro-Kamata Electric Railway	25.5	13.8	2.9	2.2

Source: Yamazaki (1988, p. 38).

The 1931 Important Industries Law sanctioned cartels run by "control committees" of officials, and executives would designate crucial industries in which cartels should regulate production and prices. Cartels could be formed in any industry where at least half of the firms requested it. If two-thirds of the firms requested cartelization, the remaining firms could be forced into the cartel. The minister could rescind cartel actions only with the approval of the control committee.[49] The control committees, of course, would end up staffed by military personnel.

The mood of the times is well captured by Takahashi (1930a), who blames shortsighted shareholders who care only for high dividends and neglect the long-term future of the firm. He declares that

The primary manifestations of "the degeneration of firm management" were the short-sighted attitude towards business management and the

49. See Fletcher (1989) for details.

inability of management to aim at so-called "business prosperity for 100 years." . . . [D]egeneration of company management was largely caused by the "high handed and short sighted selfishness of large stockholders" and the corruption of the board of directors. (quoted in Okazaki, 1994, pp. 4–5)

He also asserts that corrupt, inept directors preoccupied with big bonuses and stock manipulation governed Japan's large companies and that

It is uncommon to find members of the board of directors who acquired their status and position by virtue of their management ability. A large number of directors get their position on the board only because of being large stockholders of the firm or having special relations in government circles. (quoted in Okazaki 1994, p. 233)

Takahashi thus blamed Japan's economic malaise on corrupt, inept, and entrenched directors placed in charge of large companies by dint of family history or political rent seeking. The military largely accepted (or at least exploited) these views, and concluded not only that it should take over the task of corporate governance but also that there would be broad public support for this. They were correct.

Thus followed a creeping nationalization of the banking system and the *zaibatsu*. Ironically, Okazaki (1994) argues that *zaibatsu* firms were actually the better performers because their dominant shareholders were more likely to entrust governance to professional managers. Thus, they ought to have been less vulnerable to such attacks. This was not the case.

The attack was three-pronged. First, the banking sector was placed under state control. Second, the *zaibatsu* families were isolated and their control rights negated. Third, a full-fledged central planning system was erected. It is still a matter of debate whether this strategy was planned from the beginning or whether the military government simply acted as opportunities presented themselves.

State control encompassed the banking sector in two ways. First, the government proposed to stabilize the sector by implementing a one-local-bank-per-prefecture policy.[50] Still traumatized by the recent depressions, the bankers gratefully accepted this largesse. This objective was achieved by the end of World War II, reducing the number of banks from 1,402 in 1926 to 377 in 1937 to only 61 in 1945. While this policy did stabilize the banking sector, it also erected an insurmountable barrier to entry. Bank fi-

---

50. The Bank Law of 1927 let the government restructure the banking industry, and the number of banks fell sharply. This law, which was not substantially revised until 1981, gave the government considerable flexibility in regulating bank competition. For example, the Ministry of Finance used it to announce its one-bank-per-prefecture policy in 1933, giving these banks a degree of monopoly power according to Horiuchi (1999). The policy was implemented fully in the 1940s but temporarily relaxed in the early 1950s when the Ministry of Finance allowed twelve new small banks. The policy was subsequently tightened again.

nancing was now in the hands of a relatively small cadre of people, whom the military government could either control or replace.

At the same time, the Japanese government increased the amount of funds supplied by the state-owned long-term credit banks, such as the Industrial Bank of Japan. This made the state a major creditor to many industrial companies. State banks also increasingly took equity positions, explaining the observation in table 7.11 that these organizations had become the most significant shareholders in many independent companies. Thus, when the cabinet decided in November 1938 to regulate loans, the number of banks to be controlled was small and their dependence on state power was evident to all bankers. By then, most senior economic planners under Japan's right-wing military government were Soviet trained.

The military government pried corporate control away from the *zaibatsu* families in two steps. Again, it is not clear that this was fully premeditated, though it might have been.

The first step was the conversion of the apex holding companies from limited partnerships into joint-stock companies. This was done through inheritance and dividend income tax reforms in 1937 and 1938 that made partnerships unviable. Dividend income was subjected to double taxation—once as corporate income of the partnership and again as personal dividend income of the family. The latter was at an especially high rate.[51] However, if the holding company was a joint-stock company rather than a partnership, double taxation could be avoided.[52] By 1940, the holding companies at the apexes of all Japan's *major zaibatsu* had been transformed from partnerships into joint stock companies.

At this point, Nissan was favored over other *zaibatsu* groups such as Mitsui, Mitsubishi, and Sumitomo by the military government because its apex firm, unlike those of the other major *zaibatsu*, was not family controlled.[53] This favored status led to a drastic change in the organization of the Nissan *zaibatsu* when Nissan was renamed the Manchurian Heavy Industry Company and recapitalized as a fifty-fifty joint venture with the Japanese and Manchurian governments. The Manchurian Heavy Industry

51. The partnership was subject to an income tax of between 18 and 28 percent, depending on the location of business, plus a capital tax. The same income was then subject to a personal income tax with a top marginal rate of 65 percent.

52. For details, see Morikawa (1992, p. 213). Corporate income tax was only introduced in Japan in a 1940 reform, which also increased tax burdens across the board. See Shiomi (1957) for general information on these changes. Miyamoto (1984) describes the previous tax regime in detail.

53. Reischauer (1988, p. 305) writes that "by the 1920s and 1920s there was widespread condemnation of the zaibatsu, particularly by the supporters of the military, as elements of Western decadence in Japanese society, corrupters of the parliamentary system, and money grubbing betrayers of Japan's imperial destiny." The lives of many *zaibatsu* leaders were threatened. For example, Ikuma Dan (1858–1932), a former civil servant and chairman of Mitsui Gomei (Mitsui Partnership), was assassinated by young naval officers in front of the Mitsui Bank in Tokyo in 1932.

Company was granted a monopoly on all development projects in Manchuria.

The government also acquired controlling interests in a variety of previously independent firms. However, other *zaibatsu* firms remained under the control of their family shareholders.

The military government's second step was to cut off the income of the *zaibatsu* families. The same November 1938 cabinet decision that regulated loans also placed dividends under state control. This was justified as a patriotic measure to build up Japan's industries by raising retained earnings. Since the apex companies of the *zaibatsu* were now joint-stock companies, the *zaibatsu* families were entirely dependent on dividends for their income. These were apparently now sharply curtailed. Thus, Asajima (1984), noting that the Sumitomo group expanded dramatically from 1937 to 1945 using retained earnings, remarks that "if all the income from dividends is channeled into paid-up capital, the question arises as to what the Sumitomo family relied on for income. This is also unclear at present" (p. 110).

On September 13, 1940, the State Planning Ministry, the Kikakuin, announced its new Outline of the Establishment of a New Economic System, under which firms were "set free from the control of shareholders" and subjected to a system of quantitative production orders. Thus, the Kikakuin set up full-fledged central planning system, in which it assumed the role of Gosplan.[54] Under this system, the Kikakuin issued production orders to industry control boards, or *toseikai,* which in turn issued orders to individual firms. The cabinet explicitly commissioned the Kikakuin to investigate and imitate Soviet best practice. In all of this restructuring, firms were seen as consisting of workers and manager/bureaucrats. There was no mention of shareholders, for they were by now effectively irrelevant.

The Kikakuin also took control of the banking system, directing banks to transfer capital to firms in accordance with the central plan.[55] The Mitsubishi apex company began issuing bonds to obtain the needed funds, while the Mitsubishi Bank and Mitsubishi Trust Co.—deviating from their prior practice—began large-scale lending to other Mitsubishi companies.

The planners who set quantitative targets for output also controlled the prices of goods and services throughout the economy. By early 1945 (the war ended in August 1945), the state was setting about ten thousand prices.

By 1942, the economy was in a state of crisis because many firms failed to meet production quotas. Okazaki (1994) writes that the officials at the Kikakuin now realized that firms were still thinking about production in terms of making profits, and were not willing to "bear sacrifices" despite the removal of stockholder influence.

---

54. Gosplan (Госплан) was the command and control section of the Soviet government. Okazaki (1994) states that Kikakuin was explicitly modeled on Gosplan and staffed by Soviet-trained personnel.

55. See Horiuchi (1999) for details.

The government responded in two ways. First, the February 1943 Outline of Emergency Measures for Price Controls organized a system whereby the government would raise producer prices through subsidized spending. Thus, market forces were allowed back into the system, though in a very restricted way. Second, the Munitions Corporation Law of 1943 required each company to have one "responsible person" who was to be "accountable" for the company's achieving its production quota. All workers had an unconditional duty to obey all orders of the responsible person. Thus, rather tougher corporate governance standards were established.

When the U.S. occupation force entered Japan in 1945, they thus entered a country that, though a former right-wing dictatorship, was nonetheless virtually as centrally planned as many Eastern European countries were in 1989. While economic historians sometimes write that the *zaibatsu* were dismantled and the banking system was reorganized under the U.S. occupation, this is perhaps an overstatement. The *zaibatsu* families had already lost control, and the banking system was already changed beyond recognition from its prewar structure. The issue of whether or not to destroy the prewar system was moot. The real question was whether to rebuild it as it had been or as something different.

7.6 MacArthur Brings Anglo-American Capitalism to Japan

General Douglas MacArthur, the supreme commander of the Allied powers (SCAP) and military governor of Japan under the U.S. occupation from 1945 to 1952, apparently shared his predecessors' suspicion of powerful business families. Certainly, *zaibatsu* companies increased their market power during the war and played important roles in providing military equipment and supplies to the Imperial Army.[56] However, the *zaibatsu* families' involvement in these activities remains unclear. Although no fan of socialism, MacArthur let a cadre of New Dealers introduce SCAP economic policies aimed at dismantling the *zaibatsu*.[57] Prominent among these efforts were the reorganization of the banking industry and the restructuring of former *zaibatsu* member firms as freestanding widely held firms of the sort that had recently replaced pyramidal groups under the new Deal in the United States.[58] Hostile takeovers and greenmail ensued under Japan's brief, but action-packed, adventure in Anglo-American corporate governance.

56. See Yafeh (2000).

57. Dower (2000) describes MacArthur's orchestration of anti-Communist purges, his vast antired censorship system, and his distinctly right-wing approach to dealing with unions.

58. The New Deal broke up pyramidal groups in the United States by subjecting intercorporate dividends to taxes and by proscribing intercorporate ownership in public utilities. See Becht and DeLong (chap. 11 in this volume) and Morck (2005) for details.

7.6.1   The Agenda of the Supreme Commander of the Allied Powers

Following World War II, the U.S. occupation oversaw a full-scale revamping of Japan's corporate and financial systems along the lines of the U.S. systems. This revamping, while immensely complicated, has two key elements that relate to the topic at hand. Both were copies of reforms enacted in the United States under Roosevelt's New Deal.

First, banks could no longer underwrite securities, as in the United States under the Glass Steagall Act of 1933, a key plank of the New Deal. Although the U.S. government exerted considerable pressure for a complete ban on bank ownership of nonfinancial firms' stock, along the lines of U.S. practice, the Allied forces ultimately decided against this. Banks' share ownership in other companies was limited to 5 percent stakes. This effectively prevented banks from being situated near the apex of a pyramid. Nevertheless, banks remained equity blockholders in their clients and other firms.[59]

Second, MacArthur permanently broke up large pyramidal groups, as Roosevelt did in the United States via the New Deal. Despite the military's usurpation of corporate governance power, the *zaibatsu* families' shareholdings remained on the books. In 1950, MacArthur ordered their shares confiscated, all intercorporate blockholdings unwound, and the senior executives of *zaibatsu* firms purged.

The primary reasons the SCAP used to justify the breakup of the *zaibatsu* was their alleged market power. Thus, the Department of State and the War Department jointly reported in 1946 that

> The almost complete *zaibatsu* control of banks and financial institutions prevented independent businesses from getting needed financing; *zaibatsu*-controlled distribution systems could cut off the supply of raw materials and supplies needed by independent businesses entirely; similarly, selling independent business's [sic] finished products outside strictly local markets required the cooperation of the *zaibatsu* trading houses, which largely controlled Japan's distribution systems; and *zaibatsu* firms were able to cripple small firms by pirating their key employees and skilled workmen. These practices, and the independents' respect for not violating *zaibatsu*'s territories, prevented meaningful competition from existing in Japanese markets.

The SCAP seemed intent on removing barriers to entry for political as well as economic reasons. The revamping it supervised was clearly intended to democratize the economy and encourage a new cadre of entrepreneurs. Hadley (1970, p. 19) writes that

---

59. This let banks become major players in the postwar horizontal *keiretsu*, a unique Japanese form of industrial organization that emerged after the U.S. withdrawal.

the aim of the Allied economic deconcentration program was to give all Japanese businessmen the opportunity to engage in the modern sector of the economy, that is, to remove those conditions which preserved this sector for chosen few, those conditions which in fact made it a private collectivism.

Whether *zaibatsu* would have exercised an unhealthy degree of market power in a free-market postwar economy is academic. Certainly, their market shares had grown substantially in the 1930s and 1940s under the controlled economy. Historically, Japan always had some sectors in which competition was keen and entry open. However, especially after the demise of the Suzuki *zaibatsu,* the remaining large pyramidal groups came to hold substantial market shares in many key industries, as shown in table 7.5. The central planners of the military government had little interest in entrants and preferred directing the affairs of large companies. Dealing with many companies instead of a few simply made the transmission of orders more complicated.

7.6.2   The Incomplete Process of *Zaibatsu* Dissolution

To implement MacArthur's order to "dissolve large industrial and banking combines," the Japanese government established the Holding Company Liquidation Commission (HCLC). The HCLC designated ten combines and eighty-three holding companies for dissolution. The *zaibatsu* core families and their relatives were ordered to surrender their shares in exchange for ten-year nonnegotiable government bonds.[60] Thus, no property was formally confiscated without compensation. Indeed, the old shareholders initially appeared generously compensated for their property. However, the subsequent inflation made the government bonds almost valueless.

The hired managers of *zaibatsu* companies, many of whom were competent, were purged by the SCAP. This probably created a shortage of able managers that persisted at least through the early 1950s. More extensive purges in *zaibatsu* than in other firms might explain Yafeh's (1995) finding of poorer accounting performance by former *zaibatsu* firms in 1953. This could also explain depressed values for these same firms, as reported by Miyajima (1994, table 10). After the occupation ended in 1952, many purged managers returned in various capacities.

In contrast to the purgings of corporate executives, Noguchi (1998) reports that Japanese bureaucrats were, to a large extent, untouched. While

---

60. Tamaki (1976, p. 453) records that the HCLC redistributed about 166 million shares, nominally worth ¥7.6 billion in paid-in capital, from these holding companies and fifty-six zaibatsu family individuals. The firms designated for dissolution constituted about 42 percent of the paid-in capital of the corporate sector, or about ¥18.4 billion.

21,000 managers were purged from other sectors of Japanese society, only 2,000 bureaucrats, mostly from the Ministry of the Interior, were chucked. Most notably, only nine bureaucrats of the Ministry of Finance were purged. This was important, for the Ministry of Finance worked to alter or circumvent SCAP orders regarding many policy matters, often aggressively. Indeed, Hadley (1970, p. 15) mentions the deep puzzlement the U.S. personnel involved in this policy felt at the support business groups, individuals, and Japanese government officials provided for this interference. Overall, the implemented *zaibatsu* dissolution policies left considerable wiggle room for the Japanese government to permit business interests to organize new business groups along the lines of former *zaibatsu* groups.

For example, we noted above that several alternative definitions of *zaibatsu* are advanced by Japanese and foreign students of the Japanese economy. This ambiguity also affected the non-Japanese personnel supervising the postwar revamping of the economy, and may have been in part responsible for the less than complete implementation of the original dissolution plan. Thus, the HCLC decided not to disassemble the small group built around Japan Nitrogenous Fertilizer Company, the Nippon Chisso Hiryo *zaibatsu*, because its founder died in 1944 and it was therefore not really a *zaibatsu* (Hadley 1970, p. 21).

The SCAP used market share as the primary determinant of whether a *zaibatsu* was in need of dissolution. This had several odd effects. For example, the banking sector, in which no single bank held a clearly dominant market share, was left relatively untouched throughout the occupation, save that banks had to disgorge their shares in nonfinancial companies in excess of 5 percent stakes. Many pyramidal structures in nonfinancial sectors also remained in place and were carried over to the postwar era in the formation of *vertical keiretsu*, also called *capital keiretsu*.

Confronted with a deepening cold war and the rising influence of the Soviet Union in the Pacific, policymakers in Washington deemphasized MacArthur's restructuring plans and sought to reconstruct Japan as rapidly as possible to defend the region jointly with the United States.[61] The HCLC was thus left to its own interpretation of its orders.

7.6.3   The Subsequent Stock Market Collapse

The SCAP closed Japan's stock exchanges in September 1945 and reopened them on May 16, 1949. Table 7.16 shows the de jure shareholdings of the Mitsui, Mitsubishi, Sumitomo, and Yasuda *zaibatsu* in 1945. The SCAP transferred these shares, and most other intercorporate block holdings, to employees and other assigned investors. Employees and other se-

---

61. This policy shift actually became evident when Ridgeway succeeded MacArthur in mid-1950, well before the end of the occupation of Japan in April 1952.

Table 7.16   **Ownership structures of top four *zaibatsu* in 1945**

			Percent stakes of *zaibatsu* parties			
Zaibatsu	Firms	Shares	Family	Apex firm	First-tier firms	Total
Mitsui	1	10,000	63.6		0.9	64.5
First-tier firms	10	17,979	9.5	53.9	11.9	75.3
Second-tier firms	13	9,038	0.0	35.9	17.2	53.1
Mitsubishi	1	4,800	47.8		10.8	58.6
First-tier firms	11	41,234	1.4	28.9	15.3	47.5
Second-tier firms	16	8,053	0.2	18.2	40.3	58.7
Sumitomo	1	600	83.3		16.7	100.0
First-tier firms	17	34,312	8.4	19:5	16.6	44.5
Second-tier firms	6	5,325	0.5	12.7	30.7	43.9
Yasuda	1	300	100.0			100.0
First-tier firms	20	9,469	3.5	24.3	17.8	45.6
Second-tier firms	12	3,860	0.1	16.9	15.3	32.3

Sources: HCLC (1950), Ministry of Finance (1983)

lect groups could buy these shares at very low prices, and in many cases the shares were virtually or actually given away.[62] This greatly diluted the equity of many of the companies involved and sharply reduced their share prices. Because the larger *zaibatsu* contained the most extensive cross-holdings, instances where subsidiaries also hold stock in their parent companies or in which subsidiaries hold stock in each other, the impact of this dilution was especially severe in those firms.

Figure 7.10 explains the dilution effect and assumes for simplicity that the intercorporate equity blocks were simply given to employees or other favored investors. The upper panel shows a cross-holding arrangement, common within pyramids. The family-controlled Firm A owns one million shares in its subsidiary, Firm B, but B in turn owns one million shares in the parent Firm A. Each lists its shares in the other as assets and its div-

62. Tamaki (1976, p. 454) records that the HCLC sold about 23 percent of holding companies' and zaibatsu families' former shares to employees. The rest were sold through a variety of general, special, and regional auctions, via underwriters or to trust accounts. Employees could each buy up to ¥30,000 of shares at deeply reduced prices, and each manager could buy up to 1 percent. Employees and executives typically cashed out when the stock markets reopened in 1949. For example, Mitsui Bussan, prior to its dissolution, had 7,050 employees. Many of these workers, who lost their jobs after the dissolution, used the cash so raised to set up new companies to take over their former employers' business. The SCAP prohibited any new company from employing more than 100 workers, not including executives, who formerly worked for either Mitsui Bussan or Mitsubishi Corporation, and prohibited any new company from involving in any way more than one person who was a manager of any rank, consultant, or executive of either Mitsui Bussan or Mitsubishi Corporation. Former employees of Mitsui Bussan are thought to have set up as many as 220 small companies to take over former Mitsui Bussan business while satisfying the legal requirement. The corresponding figure for the Mitsubishi Corporation was 140.

Panel A. Prior to Dissolution

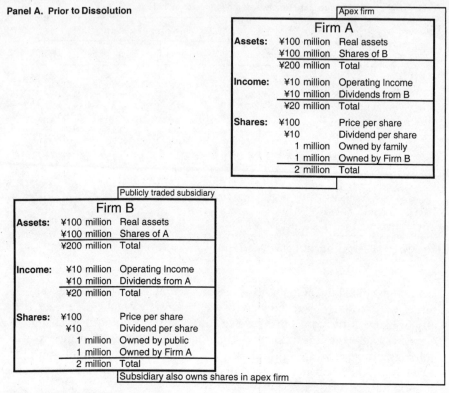

Apex firm

Firm A

Assets:	¥100 million	Real assets
	¥100 million	Shares of B
	¥200 million	Total

Income:	¥10 million	Operating Income
	¥10 million	Dividends from B
	¥20 million	Total

Shares:	¥100	Price per share
	¥10	Dividend per share
	1 million	Owned by family
	1 million	Owned by Firm B
	2 million	Total

Publicly traded subsidiary

Firm B

Assets:	¥100 million	Real assets
	¥100 million	Shares of A
	¥200 million	Total

Income:	¥10 million	Operating Income
	¥10 million	Dividends from A
	¥20 million	Total

Shares:	¥100	Price per share
	¥10	Dividend per share
	1 million	Owned by public
	1 million	Owned by Firm A
	2 million	Total

Subsidiary also owns shares in apex firm

Panel B. After Dissolution

Firm A

| Assets: | ¥100 million | Real assets |
| | ¥100 million | Total |

| Income: | ¥10 million | Operating Income |
| | ¥10 million | Total |

Shares:	¥50	Price per share
	¥5	Dividend per share
	2 million	Owned by public

Firm B

| Assets: | ¥100 million | Real assets |
| | ¥100 million | Total |

| Income: | ¥10 million | Operating Income |
| | ¥10 million | Total |

Shares:	¥50	Price per share
	¥5	Dividend per share
	2 million	Owned by public

Fig. 7.10   How cross-holdings affect the value of shares upon *zaibatsu* dissolution

idends from the other as income, so each has assets and income twice what would be the case were they freestanding firms. Since each has ¥200 million in assets and two million shares outstanding, both firms' shares are worth ¥100.

The lower panel shows what happens after dissolution of the sort implemented in Japan by the HCLC. The shares previously held by the *zaibatsu* family and the cross-holdings are appropriated by the HCLC and sold to

Table 7.17   New share issues, 1948–53

	1948	1949	1950	1951	1952	1953
(A) Number of new shares issued	50,094	78,718	39,192	83,644	123,336	91,569
(B) Percent of (A) issued to finance restructuring	30.5	17.0	5.6	0.3		
(C) No. of shares released by HCLC for *zaibatsu* dissolution purposes	40,317	39,711	854	996		
(D) Average price per share		128.85	74.00	93.8	124.06	156.05
(E) Stock return (%)	4.02	4.65	6.61	7.99	8.02	7.96
(F) Excess return above interest rate	−4.80	−4.96	−2.47	−1.22	−1.03	−0.85

Source: Miyajima (1994).
Notes: Figures in rows (A), (C), and (D) are for 1,000 shares.

other shareholders.[63] The funds so raised are kept by the government. None of the proceeds go to either Firm A or Firm B. Thus, the only assets in both are now their physical assets, and their only incomes are now their operating incomes. Yet the number of shares outstanding has not declined proportionately. Consequently, share prices of both firms fall by 50 percent.

Cross-holdings of this sort were commonplace. For example, 64 percent and 59 percent of the outstanding shares of the apex companies of the Mitsui and Mitsubishi *zaibatsu,* respectively, were owned by Mitsui and Mitsubishi subsidiaries. The holding companies of both the Sumitomo and Yasuda *zaibatsu* were actually entirely owned by their respective *zaibatsu* subsidiaries. Thus, stock prices plunged as the dissolution was announced and as the value of the bonds issued as compensation dropped.

Share prices in the immediate postwar period were also depressed because of the extensive damage the war had inflicted on the physical assets of industrial firms. To begin rebuilding, firms issued more new shares, adding these to the former *zaibatsu* control block shares flooding the market. The SCAP also ordered the government to suspend the promised payments to munitions suppliers to prevent these firms from profiting off their wartime activities. The Corporation Reconstruction and Reorganization Act of 1946 allowed firms bankrupted by the nonpayment of wartime indemnities to resume operations as "special account companies" and also allowed firms' net losses due to official nonpayment to be written off (Hoshi 1995). Average paid-in ratios of capital to total assets fell to 10 percent by 1950 (Ministry of Finance 1983). Finally, Yafeh (2004) argues that the population of potential investors was impoverished and probably highly risk averse. They consequently rapidly sold the shares the SCAP assigned them to finance consumption and low-risk savings. Table 7.17

63. See footnote 62.

shows the numbers of new shares issued, as well as the shares brought to the stock market by the HCLC for sale. The shares HCLC brought to the market amounted to 30 percent of the newly issued shares in 1948, 17 percent in 1949, 5.6 percent in 1950, and 0.3 percent in 1951.

It is clear that the shares freed by the *zaibatsu* dissolution order had a major impact on the overall stock market. Although non-*zaibatsu* firms suffered smaller stock price declines because their shares were not diluted, their stocks nonetheless fell as the total amount of equity available to the public rose. Thus, new shares issued by firms like Toshiba and Hitachi fetched low prices.

Several economic measures were introduced in 1949 to stabilize the Japanese economy. These included fixing the exchange rate and suspending new loans from the Reconstruction Financing Bank. The latter policy reduced the supply of funds available to Japanese industry, increased interest rates, and induced even more firms to issue equity. This, on top of the other factors listed above, triggered a collapse of the Japanese stock market. Table 7.18 shows the drop in stock prices from 1949 to 1950. These stock price fluctuations are also evident in the ratios of price to capital stock and market to book, shown in table 7.19.

Over the next few years, firms shied away from further diluting their equity by issuing shares at the prices prevailing. During the period 1950–54, new issues accounted for less than 20 percent of Japanese industrial firms'

Table 7.18   Tokyo Stock Exchange price index

	1949	1950	1951	1952
Low	98.50 (December)	85.25 (July)	102.20 (January)	167.80 (January)
High	176.88 (September)	114.99 (August)	170.20 (October)	370.56 (December)

Table 7.19   Price-capital stock and price-equity ratios for Mitsui, Mitsubishi, and Sumitomo *zaibatsu* firms, 1949–53

Zaibatsu	Ratio	1949	1950	1951	1952	1953
Mitsubishi	W/K	1.61	0.46	0.39	0.72	1.00
	W/E	2.43	0.68	0.45	0.75	0.97
Sumitomo	W/K	1.96	0.34	0.35	0.78	0.86
	W/E	3.22	0.34	0.31	0.68	0.77
Mitsui	W/K	0.91	0.27	0.27	0.45	0.57
	W/E	1.71	0.34	0.44	0.75	0.80

Source: Miyajima (1994).

Notes: W = average share price; K = fixed capital stock (book value); E = stockholders' equity set equal to (total assets [book value] – total debt [book value]). The numbers of firms included for Mitsubishi, Sumitomo, and Mitsui groups are 15, 8, and 12, respectively.

external financing. Short-term bank debt was now becoming the main source of corporate financing.

By the end of the occupation, Japan was an Anglo-Saxon economy, in that its major firms were freestanding and widely held. The number of shareholders rose from 1.7 million in 1945 to 4.2 million in 1950. The *zaibatsu* dissolution by SCAP massively redistributed the stocks of Japanese corporations.[64] The shares transferred from the *zaibatsu* families to the public by the HCLC amounted to over 40 percent of all corporate assets in Japan. The consequence was a widely diffused ownership of much of the Japanese corporate sector, with individual shareholders holding 70 percent of the outstanding shares of typical Japanese corporations in 1949 and 1950 (Bisson 1954).

7.6.4   The New Legal Framework for Shareholders

The SCAP also supervised the enactment of new laws that would shape Japan's future business activities.

The Anti-Monopoly Law of 1947 was actually also an antipyramid law. It prohibited the establishment of holding companies, 25 percent or more of whose asset base consists of the stock of other firms; manufacturing firms' owning the stock of other firms; and financial institutions' owning more than 5 percent of other firms. Subsequently, this law was frequently amended in response to corporate lobbying.

An amendment in 1949 allowed manufacturing firms to own other firms, permitting the formation of vertical (capital) *keiretsu,* in which large manufacturers partly own other manufacturers. A 1953 amendment increased the limit of banks' ownership of industrial firms from the original 5 percent to 10 percent. This 10 percent limit was reduced to 5 percent again in 1987. For most practical purposes these limits had never been a barrier for Japanese banks intent upon exercising corporate governance power over their client firms, particularly those under financial distress. Banks often voted additional shares through controlled financial subsidiaries, like insurance and trust companies.

The Securities Trading Act of 1948 was designed to protect small shareholders. An auditor system was also established in 1948, followed by a set of corporate accounting principles in 1950. In 1951, new depreciation rules ended firms' freedom to determine their own depreciation rates and methods. These initiatives were significant, for prewar Japan had no serious shareholder rights, accounting standards, auditing procedure rules, public disclosure rules, or depreciation rules.[65]

---

64. Some authors have found some analogy between this historical event and more contemporary privatization of government-owned corporations. See, e.g., Yafeh (1995).

65. See Miyajima (2000).

The Japanese commercial code was also revised in 1950 to give small shareholders rights to access company books and records and to establish fiduciary duties of directors to shareholders. However, the government defined a small shareholder as one with at least 5 percent equity ownership. In subsequent years, Japanese banks intervening in their client firms' management often used this rule.

7.6.5   The *Keiretsu* Defense

An active market for corporate control developed quickly. Hostile takeover bids became high-profile events, and several were launched against former *zaibatsu* firms—including Taisho Marine and Mitsui Real Estate.[66] As in the United States and Britain, the possibility of a hostile takeover appears to have a governance impact greatly out of proportion to the actual frequency of these events.[67] In response to this threat, the managers of firms from each former *zaibatsu* began to act as a group—coordinating white knight and white squire defensive arrangements to protect their former affiliated companies from hostile takeovers.

In the white knight defense, the target of a hostile bid arranges to be taken over instead by a friendly company that safeguards the positions of the target's top executives. In the white squire defense, the target arranges for a friendly company to purchase temporarily a large enough block of target stock to prevent the hostile takeover from succeeding.

These coordinated actions were possible because top managers constructed postwar analogs to the family councils that coordinated *zaibatsu* affairs prior to the war. Thus, former Mitsubishi firms' presidents began having regular Friday luncheon meetings in June 1946, immediately after the Mitsubishi family council was formally abolished. The Sumitomo group began their presidents' council in 1949, and the presidents of the former Mitsui companies formed their presidents' club around 1950. Subsequently, these regular meetings of the presidents of former *zaibatsu* companies all came to be called *presidents' clubs*.

Hideki Yokoi was one of the best-known corporate raiders in postwar Japan. Yokoi became wealthy from dealings with MacArthur's general headquarters (GHQ) and, allegedly, in the black market created by prewar and wartime price controls. With a huge cash hoard, Yokoi launched takeovers of company after company.

In 1953 he purchased more than 40 percent of the outstanding shares of Shirokiya, a department store company.[68] Yokoi then organized a general

---

66. For details of some notable Japanese takeovers and takeover defenses at this time, see Sheard (1991) and Miyajima (1994).

67. See Morck, Shleifer, and Vishny (1988a,b, 1989) regarding hostile takeovers in the United States and Franks, Mayer, and Rossi (chap. 10 in this volume) regarding the United Kingdom.

68. Its major property is now a part of the Tokyu department store in Nihonbashi.

stockholders' meeting, at which he won control of the board. Shirokiya sued Yokoi, and four days later Yokoi lost control of the company. Yokoi had to ask Keita Goto, then the chief executive officer (CEO) of Tokyu, for mediation. Yokoi (1960) reflected on the benefit of his takeover to Shirokiya, noting that

> I sacrificed myself to do the best for Shirokiya which now is in such great shape; without my takeover and the following business intervention by Keita Goto of the Tokyu group, Shirokiya would have been unable to increase its capacity and would have either become a third-rate department store or an office building, closing its 300-year history. (quoted in Sataka 1994, p. 35)

Yokoi continued launching corporate takeovers over the following two decades. After Shirokiya, he mounted raids on Toa Oil, Daikyo Oil, Imperial Hotels, Tokai Shipping Line, Toyo Sugar, Shibaura Sugar, Taito Sugar, Dainippon Sugar, and many other companies. He died in 1998 at the age of eighty-five.

A pivotal event in the development of the Anglo-American system in Japan was the raid by Kyujiro Fujinami against Youwa Properties. By 1952 Fujinami, by then a well-known corporate raider, had purchased 250,000 of the 720,000 outstanding shares of Youwa Properties, a company that had managed landholdings and other properties for the Mitsubishi group. Fujinami, a former security guard at the Tokyo Stock Exchange, demanded seats on the board of Youwa. The Mitsubishi Bank, together with the companies run by other members of the Mitsubishi Presidents' Council, offered to pay greenmail and buy back all the shares Fujinami had acquired at a price of ¥1600 per share, well above the market price of ¥240. This coordinated action was necessary because Japanese law prohibited firms from repurchasing their own stock. Youwa thus could not pay its own greenmail. Mitsubishi group firms each bought a small block of shares from Fujinami to avoid contravening the Anti-Monopoly Law of 1947.[69]

This event is thought to have triggered the realization by top executives that corporate raids could be blocked by establishing sufficiently large crossholdings among former *zaibatsu* firms. If each former Mitsubishi *zaibatsu* firm owned a little stock in every other former Mitsubishi *zaibatsu* firm, the members of the Mitsubishi presidents' club could collectively vote control blocks in every former Mitsubishi firm. These firms would then all be safe from hostile takeovers, the need to pay greenmail would disappear, and the company presidents would have secure tenure in their jobs.

This *keiretsu defense* is a variant of the white knight or white squire defense. In the *keiretsu* defense, a cadre of friendly companies each take a small position in the target such that these positions, taken together, add

---

69. Subsequently, in 1953 Mitsubishi Estates, Mitsubishi's main land development company, absorbed both Youwa and another Mitsubishi realtor, Kantou Properties.

up to a control block sufficient to deter a hostile takeover. Evidence from the United States suggests that modest white squire positions can deter raiders. Morck, Shleifer, and Vishny (1988b) argue that management-affiliated blocks as small as 5 percent can deflect raids because they give insiders a head start in any race to accumulate shares. La Porta et al. (1999) show that intercorporate stakes of 10 percent confer control rights in *zaibatsu*-like pyramidal groups in many countries. Yafeh (2004) summarizes data on such intercorporate holdings in postwar Japan and shows them to be in this range or higher.

7.7 Self-Assembling *Keiretsu*

Japan's postwar *keiretsu* formed in two waves. In both, defenses against corporate takeovers appear to have been the primary motive.[70] The first wave, discussed above, took place in the 1950s and involved the self-organization of *keiretsu* comprising the former member firms of the old Mitsui, Mitsubishi, and Sumitomo *zaibatsu*. The second wave, in the 1960s, saw the self-organization of three new horizontal *keiretsu*. The Fuji Bank helped organize the Fuyo *keiretsu* by orchestrating a network of intercorporate share placements. Simultaneously, the Sanwa Bank helped construct the Sanwa *keiretsu*, and the Daiichi Kangyo Bank (DKB) helped assemble the Dai Ichi Bank *keiretsu*. In both cases, the banks apparently sought to insulate the managers of their client firms from hostile takeovers.

Each *keiretsu* firm has a "main securities firm" or *kanji gaisha*, with which it has a long-term relationship. These *kanji gaisha* usually hold the group's cross-holdings equity certificates in their vaults. Thus, one firm cannot sell its cross-holdings in another without notifying the *kanji gaisha*, which then notifies the other firm. Hence, there is a credible promise to be a "stable shareholder."[71]

Recent work by Miwa and Ramseyer (2002) contests much of the praise for Japan's *keiretsu* by students of corporate strategy, such as Porter (1990). While we concur that much laudatory discussion of the "Japanese Model" in the 1980s is problematic, we do not agree with the contention of Miwa and Ramseyer that *keiretsu* are fables.[72] Morck and Nakamura (1999) doc-

---

70. Yafeh (1995, 2000, 2004) argues more generally that poor performance caused firms to reconfigure their ownership structure. Since takeovers and the *keiretsu* takeover defense are both instances of ownership structure reconfiguration and Morck, Shleifer, and Vishny (1988a,b, 1989) argue that poor performance invites hostile takeovers, this argument is not inconsistent with ours.

71. See Sheard (1994).

72. Note also that Gerlach (1992), Lincoln, Gerlach, and Takahashi (1992), Lincoln, Gerlach, and Ahmadjian (1996), and other quantitative sociologists typically find that *keiretsu* connections are important in unconditional multivariate data analysis. See Aoki (1988) and Kojima (1997) for a detailed analysis of how Japanese corporate governance was thought to differ fundamentally from that elsewhere. Many of Aoki's points have not been refuted.

ument a clear pattern of repeated bailouts of weak *keiretsu* firms, but not of otherwise similarly troubled independent firms. *Keiretsu* firms—and especially *keiretsu* main banks—were remarkably successful at shaping Japanese institutions to their advantage. *Keiretsu* are a genuinely important feature of postwar Japan, but their role is primarily to entrench top corporate management and to safeguard a monotonous stability in Japan's list of leading corporations.[73]

Modern Japanese *keiretsu* divide into two genres: horizontal *keiretsu* and vertical *keiretsu*.

7.7.1   Horizontal *Keiretsu*

As noted above, takeover defense arrangements led to groups wherein member firms were controlled collectively by all the other firms in the group through a multitude of small equity stakes. These groups, called horizontal *keiretsu*, recreated for their member firms' top managers the freedom from outside shareholder pressure the *zaibatsu* had provided. Moreover, since no family holding company exercised control, horizontal *keiretsu* also freed top managers from oversight by a controlling shareholder. Thus, member firms of the *keiretsu* of postwar Japan were similar to the widely held firms described by Beale and Means (1932), for their top managers were accountable only to themselves.

But horizontal *keiretsu* took the Beale and Means firm a step further. Because a majority of their companies' stock was in the hands of white squires, or stable investors, the managers of *keiretsu* member firms had no need to fear corporate raiders, proxy contests at shareholder meetings, or institutional investor pressure. They were truly free to run their firms as they saw fit, without regard for share value, profits, or dividends. *Keiretsu* top managers were thus more insulated from shareholder pressure that was possible in even the most widely held firm.

Figure 7.11 illustrates a stylized horizontal *keiretsu*. The intercorporate stakes involved are each individually quite small, so that each firm looks superficially as if it were widely held. However, only a minority of the stock in each of the companies is left available to public shareholders and thus to potential raiders.

As rules against pyramids were relaxed after the U.S. withdrawal, core *keiretsu* member firms began establishing new pyramids, with themselves at the apex. Thus, horizontal *keiretsu* in contemporary Japan are best thought of as clusters of core firms, each of which controls its own pyramid of publicly traded subsidiaries in a substructure akin to a prewar widely held *zaibatsu*. It is only the core firms that collectively control a majority of each other's shares through a dense network of individually tiny intercorporate equity blocks.

---

73. See He, Morck, and Yeung (2004).

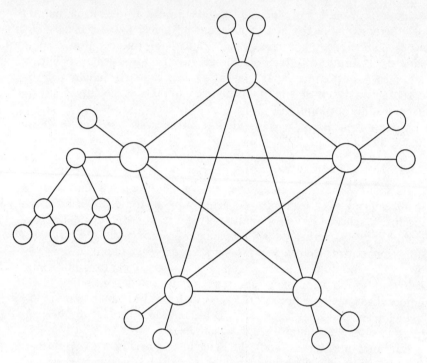

Fig. 7.11   A stylized diagram of a post–World War II horizontal *keiretsu*

Notes: Large circles represent core member firms of the *keiretsu,* which hold small blocks of stock in each other that collectively sum to control blocks. Each core *keiretsu* firm holds control blocks of lesser *keiretsu* member firms, indicated by small circles, and many of these sit at the apex of their own pyramid of such firms. For simplicity, only one such nested pyramid is shown.

7.7.2   Vertical *Keiretsu*

A second genre of *keiretsu,* called vertical *keiretsu,* exhibits a more classically pyramidal structure. Some are simply industrial *zaibatsu* that escaped dissolution. These include Shibaura Manufacturing Works (now Toshiba) and Hitachi, Ltd. Shibaura was a second-tier member of the Mitsui *zaibatsu* and the most important prewar electric appliances manufacturer. In 1939, it spun off twelve supplier firms and acquired control blocks in eight other companies with which it had close customer-supplier relationships. Toshiba executives also served as directors of these companies.[74] Hitachi was part of the Nissan *zaibatsu.* By 1937 it had set up its own vertically integrated group with nine supplier companies within the Nissan group.[75] Many of these

74. Tamaki (1976, pp. 154–55) describes Toshiba's relationships with these firms in more detail.
75. See Tamaki (1976, p. 399).

Toshiba and Hitachi suppliers still exist and are now members of their respective vertical *keiretsu.*

However, the ranks of vertical *keiretsu* also contain new groups. These arose after the war in certain manufacturing industries, like automobiles and electric appliances, where product assembly was divisible into discrete steps, each to be carried out by a separate firm. Again, white squire takeover defenses were probably key to their original formation.

Vertical *keiretsu* are more pyramidal than horizontal *keiretsu.* An apex firm holds control blocks in a first tier of key suppliers. Each holds control blocks in its suppliers, which hold control blocks in yet another tier of suppliers, and so on.

Despite their similarity to prewar industrial *zaibatsu,* some differences justify a new term. Unlike industrial *zaibatsu,* vertical *keiretsu* also feature dense fogs of small intercorporate equity stakes of any number of member firms in each other, much as in horizontal *keiretsu.* For example, Toyota Motors owns controlling blocks in the range of 15 to 30 percent in each of its main parts suppliers. Nonetheless, only a minority of the stock in these suppliers is available to public investors, for holdings by other members of the Toyota *keiretsu* raise the total stakes of stable shareholders above 50 percent in each case. Still, as in a prewar *zaibatsu,* the Toyoda family has substantial control over Toyota Motors itself.[76] Some of the Toyota *keiretsu* firms are spin-offs from Toyota Motors or from other older *keiretsu* member firms. Others are independent firms that find it advantageous to cement their alliances to Toyota by selling control blocks to Toyota firms, and so joining the Toyota *keiretsu.*

Another important difference is that the apex firm in an industrial *zaibatsu* clearly directed activities in all the member firms of the pyramid. In contrast, vertical *keiretsu* firms are alleged only to coordinate decision making with the firms directly above and directly below them in the pyramid. This decentralized planning is said to be possible because the integration in vertical *keiretsu* is much tighter, with no superfluous firms that are not direct parts of the production chain leading to the final products of the apex firm. Industrial *zaibatsu,* in contrast, often contained firms whose activities were disjoint from their main production chains, and even firms in entirely unrelated industries.

7.7.3   Other Firms

Some prewar local *zaibatsu* survive in various forms, having escaped the notice of the SCAP and the HCLC. Some are even controlled by their prewar controlling families. One example is the Ito group of Nagoya, which continues to run Matsuzakaya department stores. Others are the Katakura

---

76. As discussed above, Toyota Motors was itself spun off from Toyota Jido Shokki, a loom maker.

group of Nagano, whose Katakura Industries remains important in textiles; the Yasukawa group of Fukuoka, whose Yasuoka Electric remains a major electric appliance maker; and the Mogi group, based in Chiba prefecture, which controls Kikkoman, the soy sauce maker, and other firms.[77]

Finally, just as some firms in prewar Japan were not parts of *zaibatsu,* some firms in postwar Japan belong to no *keiretsu.* Some of these independents have prewar roots. For example, Masatoshi Ito built a small family clothing business founded in 1920 into Ito Yokado, the largest retail chain in Japan and owner of Seven-Eleven. Other essentially independent firms are entirely postwar phenomena. Prominent examples include Honda and Sony.

Firms represented in the presidents' clubs of the six major horizontal *keiretsu*—Mitsui, Mitsubishi, Sumitomo, Fuyo (formerly Yasuda), Sanwa, and Daiichi-Kangyo—employed only 4 percent of the total workforce of all nonfinancial listed firms in 1986–90 but owned in 1990 15 percent of their total assets (14 percent in 1986) and 17 percent of their total paid-in capital (14 percent in 1986). Also, in 1990, they owned 26 percent of the outstanding shares of all listed firms (24 percent in 1986), provided 37 percent of corporate debt of all listed firms (39 percent in 1986), and provided 45 percent of the directors of the boards of all listed firms throughout the period 1986–90 (Toyo Keizai 1991).

Independent Japanese firms are either private or narrowly held, usually with a founding family as the dominant shareholder. At present, Japan has no large widely held firms in the Anglo-American sense.

7.7.4   More Definitional Ambiguities

Like the term *zaibatsu,* the word *keiretsu* is deeply flavored with the characteristic Japanese taste for ambiguity. Deciding which, if any, *keiretsu* a firm belongs to is usually straightforward. However, there are cases where things become somewhat convoluted. For example, in addition to having its own vertical *keiretsu,* Toyota also belongs to the Mitsui *keiretsu.* Toyota's president attends meetings of the Mitsui presidents' club, and Toyota considers the Mitsui Bank its main bank, even though Toyota has no bank debt. Toyota participates in Mitsui-wide activities with other Mitsui firms, like Toshiba.

If one stretches the definition of a *keiretsu* somewhat, even independent firms like Sony and Honda have group ties. Thus, Sony is sometimes listed as a member of a "quasi-Mitsui group," as in Okumura (1976, p. 183), because of its ties and historical dealings with the Mitsui bank. The primary reason Sony is not explicitly a member of the Mitsui presidents' club seems to be that Toshiba is already a member, and each horizontal *keiretsu* contains only one company from each industry. This may be a holdover from the SCAP's concerns about high market shares. Likewise, Honda has extensive financial ties to the Tokyo-Mitsubishi Bank but does not belong to

77. See, e.g., Fruin (1983).

Mitsubishi's presidents' club. Again, since Mitsubishi Motors belongs to the Mitsubishi presidents' club, there may be no room for Honda. Nevertheless, Honda is sometimes listed as a member of a "quasi-Mitsubishi" group, as in Okumura (p. 171).

By the end of the 1960s, the widely held firm had disappeared from the Japanese economic landscape. Japan's brief acquaintance with Anglo-American corporate governance was over, and its current patterns of corporate ownership were essentially in place.

7.7.5   The Former *Zaibatsu* Banks

Banks were exempt from the SCAP's *zaibatsu* dissolution program because it deemed their market shares all acceptably low. However, the former *zaibatsu* families lost ownership of their *zaibatsu* banks—Teikoku Bank (a merger of the former Mitsui and Daiichi Banks), Tokyo-Mitsubishi Bank, Sumitomo Bank, and Yasuda Bank.

The SCAP continued using the banks much as the military government had—assigning specific banks to "rubber-stamp" loans to selected strategically important firms. Thus, firms' "main banks" in the 1950s tended to be their "assigned banks" from the 1940s. Banks also won influence restructuring firms damaged by wartime losses.[78] The shareholding culture of prewar Japan faded from collective memory, and banks assumed a leading role in the economy.[79]

The continuity of this role, and banks' ties to state planners, give rise to the so-called 1940s theory. This theory, due to Okazaki and Okuno-Fujiwara (1993) and Noguchi (1998), proposes that the current managed market economy originated in wartime Japan.[80]

Regardless, the SCAP's attitude toward long-term financial institutions was generally negative, and banks were proscribed from issuing bonds. In response to a perceived capital shortage in 1952, the year of the U.S. withdrawal, the government passed the Long-Term Credit Law, which permitted a new type of bank, the *long-term credit bank,* that could issue bonds but not take deposits. Other banks, thenceforth known as *ordinary banks,* could take deposits but not issue bonds.[81] Three major new long-term credit banks formed: the Industrial Bank of Japan, the Japan Long-Term Credit Bank, and the Nippon Credit Bank.[82]

---

78. See Hoshi and Kashyap (2001) on the postwar continuation of the wartime system and on the banks' roles in postwar restructuring.

79. See Hoshi and Kashyap (2001).

80. See Hamada (1998) for a critique of this view.

81. At present, this structure of the Japanese banking system is the subject of considerable debate. There has already been a degree of reform, and further reforms would appear likely.

82. The IBJ, which practiced investment banking since 1900 under the Industrial Bank of Japan Act, became an ordinary bank in 1950 when the IBJ Act was repealed. The IBJ resumed its special status as an investment bank in 1952 when the new Long-Term Credit Bank Act was created. For details, see footnote 48.

Most extant banks, including all the former *zaibatsu* banks, chose to be ordinary banks. This was because they had large established deposit and short-term lending businesses that generated significant profits before the war and looked set to do so again. By remaining ordinary banks, they could tap Japan's high household savings rate and lend to large corporations on a year-to-year basis. Despite their formal short-term structure, these loans were often really long term, in that they were rolled over indefinitely.

The former *zaibatsu* banks retained most of their prewar business relationships with their fellow former *zaibatsu* member firms and were referred to as the main banks of these client firms (Teranishi 1999). These networks of relationships were critical in the formation of the *keiretsu* in the 1950s and 1960s, for the former *zaibatsu* banks often organized the white squire equity placements that constitute the *keiretsu*.

This regulatory fragmentation of the Japanese banking system meant that main banks sometimes had inadequate capital to accommodate their largest clients' borrowing needs. In response, the Bank of Japan permitted syndicated loans.

Under the syndicated bank loan system, a large borrower's main bank took charge of organizing a syndicate of banks that could collectively meet the borrower's financing needs. The main bank apparently was expected to take a lead role in monitoring the borrower, to take charge of correcting any impending problems, and to take a disproportionately large hit in the event of a default.[83] This pattern continues in recent cases of defaulting firms, where the main bank becomes the "special manager" of a firm under reorganization.

Banks were thought to collect substantial private information about each other and about Japanese firms in general via syndicated lending, and to utilize this information to promulgate good corporate governance. However, Morck and Nakamura (1999), while documenting increased banker representation on the boards of troubled client firms, find no evidence consistent with corporate governance improvement. They argue that banks use their influence on boards primarily to maximize the value of their loan portfolios, and that this can deviate substantially from firm value maximization and economic efficiency. Hanazaki and Horiuchi (2004) go further, arguing that lax bank governance contributed to governance problems in other industries.

Japan's large banks also greatly affected the postwar development of the financial system. Bank lobbying is widely believed to underlie the Japanese government's ongoing and virtually complete suppression of the corporate

---

83. In contrast, Japanese banks did not usually get involved with rescue operations of distressed client firms prior to the early 1950s. Failing firms were simply liquidated. See Miyajima (1999).

debt market until the 1990s. Corporate debt issues were forbidden unless fully backed by real property or explicitly approved by the government. Thus, what corporate bonds existed were little more than alienable mortgages. Debentures and other corporate debt securities were outlawed entirely.

The reason the banks took this route is fairly clear. They saw bonds as competition both for their depositors' money and their client firms' loans. Why the government accommodated their lobbying is less clear. The SCAP had promoted the stock market but largely ignored the corporate bond market. This may have reflected a lack of investor interest, for bondholders were badly hurt by the high postwar inflation. Also, the military government had used the banking system to carry out centrally planned capital allocation, so corporate bonds played little role in the wartime economy. Managers were not used to issuing debt. Still, the continued interdiction of corporate debt issues decades later raises puzzling political economy issues.

It is hard to escape the conclusion that the government and the banks worked to preserve market power for the country's major banks. Market power certainly derived from the barriers to competition the prewar and wartime regulators erected. Banks probably also held an informational advantage giving them a degree of market power over their clients, as in Rajan (1992). Whatever the precise nature of this market power, it corresponds to a period of great stability for the Japanese banking system. From the end of the war to 1997, no major bank failed and there were few bank mergers. While the strong regulatory hand of the Ministry of Finance may be partially responsible, such stability is certainly also consistent with prolonged bank market power.

Indeed, the two explanations are often intertwined in discussions of postwar Japanese banking. Thus, Hanazaki and Horiuchi (2003) write that

> the primary purpose of the MOF's [Ministry of Finance's] administrative guidance was to suppress full-scale competition in each of the compartmentalized financial businesses. . . . The government was able to utilize the rents accumulated in the banking sector as a means of dealing with banks in financial distress. Specifically, regulators relied on the cooperation of private banks in implementing the blanket guarantee, and major banks faithfully bore a disproportionate share of the costs involved. . . . [B]y manipulating regulatory measures the MOF could do favors to those banks that towed [*sic*] the line and penalize those that failed to heed its guidance.

They argue that the Mitsubishi Bank, for example, got permission to pursue trust banking as a reward for rescuing Nippon Trust. Moreover, the view that banks transferred the financial value of *keiretsu* to themselves through such practices is consistent with the finding of Caves and Uekusa (1976) that group membership does not benefit industrial firms, and that any benefits must therefore be captured by nonindustrial firms—that is, banks.

Aoki (1994) argues that rents are necessary to motivate proper monitoring by banks. Hellman, Murdock, and Stiglitz (2000) argue that restricted competition is beneficial in that it reduces banks' incentives to maximize shareholder value by taking excessive risks in near-default situations. In contrast, Allen and Gale (2000) argue that competition is necessary to reveal which managers know what they're doing. Hanazaki and Horiuchi (2000, 2001) argue that such competition is responsible for the success of independent Japanese manufacturing firms and that its absence explains the weakness of *keiretsu* firms and the failure of its banks.

They argue that the international success of Japan's best firms undid this market power. By the 1980s, the country's most successful multinationals routinely issued debt abroad through their foreign subsidiaries. In response, the government relaxed the rules (somewhat) in the 1990s to allow firms whose financial ratios exceeded predetermined criteria to issue certain debt securities.[84] This partial deregulation may have let Japan's best firms abandon bank loans and may have concentrated low-quality debt in the banking system.[85] This argument, while probably true, does not explain the alacrity with which the more profitable firms abandoned bank loans as a source of capital. That the banks were extracting market power rents in the provision of capital would explain this rush for the exits.

7.8   Lessons from the Well-Traveled Frog

Japan's wide-ranging corporate governance history provides some insights into the value of corporate groups under different economic circumstances. Except under the military government, entrepreneurs (and querulous relatives) were free to start new firms. Since both *zaibatsu* and *keiretsu* formed spontaneously, survived, and prospered, they must have had some competitive advantage over new freestanding firms. There are several candidate explanations for this advantage.[86]

7.8.1   Economies of Scope and Scale

Corporate groups might exist because they are superior modes of corporate organization and so are good for the economy. *Zaibatsu* and *keiretsu* are clearly large enough corporate structures to capture a variety

---

84. See Morck and Nakamura (2001).

85. Aoki and Sheard (1992) and Hoshi, Kashyap, and Schaftstein (1993) show that the most financially sound firms switched to bond financing very quickly. Hellman, Murdock, and Stiglitz (2000) argue that this undermined the banking system. Boot and Thakor (2000) and Fraser, Ghon Rhee, and Shin (2002) both describe the importance of regulatory restraints on competition to relationship banking.

86. See also Yafeh (2003).

of economies of scope and scale. However, the expansions of both did not seem driven by such economies. *Zaibatsu* remained tightly focused and of limited size until the mass privatizations at the turn of the twentieth century. Antitakeover defenses seem historically more important than economies of scale and scope in the formation of the *keiretsu*, especially the horizontal *keiretsu*. Despite their historical pedigrees, both might still have ended up capturing such economies. However, the usefulness of corporate groups is also limited in several ways.[87]

A major limitation on scale and scope economies in large firms is the agency problem described by Jensen and Meckling (1976). Aoki (1988, 1994) and others argue that Japanese corporate groups limit such problems. However, Morck, Stangeland, and Yeung (2000) and others show that the presence of a controlling shareholder in a pyramidal group is no delivery from agency problems; rather, it provides a different form of separation of ownership from control and new agency problems, such as entrenchment and tunneling.

Caves (1982) argues that important returns to scale involve innovation, and Goto (1982) finds that *zaibatsu* were big technology importers.[88] Diversified groups of firms, importing technology and expanding rapidly in concert, might have allowed a "big push" growth strategy, as in Murphy, Shleifer, and Vishny (1989). However, a literature survey by Yafeh (2004) reports no similar finding for postwar *keiretsu*. Economies of scope in vertically integrated *keiretsu* are perhaps more plausible than in horizontal *keiretsu*, from, for example, just-in-time inventory management. This gave Japanese firms a worldwide reputation for efficiency in the 1980s. Huson and Nanda (1995) confirm that just-in-time inventory management adds value in U.S. firms if inventories are a large fraction of assets, but not otherwise. But little is actually known about the impact of just-in-time methods on the bottom line of the typical Japanese firm. Vertical *keiretsu* also shield corporate managers from takeovers, however. This became overtly evident in the failed 1989 hostile takeover by T. Boone Pickens of Koito Manufacturing, a first-tier supplier in the Toyota vertical *keiretsu*. Even after he became the largest single shareholder of Koito, Pickens could not put himself on Koito's board. This was because other members of the Toyota *keiretsu* collectively controlled more of Koito's shares than Pickens and acted in concert to block him. *Keiretsu* also appear vulnerable to tunneling, for the findings of Morck and Nakamura (1999) are certainly consistent with this. However, we are unaware of direct tests for tunneling in *keiretsu*.

Other economies of scale and scope can arise from superior managers

---

87. See Yafeh (2004) for a more detailed survey.

88. See, for example, Aoki (1988, chap. 6) and Blinder (1991) for a detailed presentation of this view regarding vertical keiretsu. See Morck, Shleifer, and Vishny (1990), Lang and Stulz (1994), and many others for evidence of agency problems associated with large, diversified firms.

and workers. Morikawa (1980, pp. 16–19) reports that *zaibatsu* recruited top managers and technicians and argues this was a decided advantage. However, the collapse of the Suzuki *zaibatsu* was due to the concentration of corporate control in the hands of one exceptional manager—Naokichi Kaneko. Kaneko made few errors, but a single major mistake destroyed the entire *zaibatsu.*

The postwar *keiretsu* promised lifetime employment, so they were also preferred career paths for Japan's best university graduates. After the war, many older managers were tainted by wartime associations, engendering a renewed scarcity of talent at that time.[89] Perhaps scarce superior management gave *keiretsu* an edge at critical points in Japanese history too. However, Morck and Nakamura (1999) find evidence of poor governance in *keiretsu* firms.

Yet another possible source of group economies of scale and scope is centralized capital allocation.[90] Since external funds cost more than internal funds, a freestanding undiversified company is subject to the vagaries of cost and demand in a single industry. A group bank, or an apex firm that acts as a de facto bank, can move funds from member firms where they accumulate to where they are needed. Since the group bank has better information about the investment opportunities available to each firm, it can do this at much lower cost than could outside banks or financial markets. Miyajima (2000) finds little evidence of this in 1930s *zaibatsu,* but some in *keiretsu.* See also Weinstein and Yafeh (1998).

The depression-era failures of many *zaibatsu* cast further doubt on the merits of groups as capital allocators. The Mitsui, Mitsubishi, and Sumitomo banks, which avoided lending to their own group companies, survived the depressions. In contrast, *zaibatsu,* like Suzuki, that used their banks to allocate their capital to their own firms, failed. One possible reason is moral hazard—managers were more reckless if they had guaranteed financing from so-called organ banks. Another is diversification in management strategy—all the Suzuki firms followed the same strategy, whereas the Mitsui, Mitsubishi, and Sumitomo banks lent to firms with diverse strategies.

Hoshi, Kashyap, and Scharfstein (1990a,b, 1991, 1993) argue that such financial transfers reduce the cost of financial distress in *keiretsu.*[91] Yafeh (2004) summarizes a literature showing depressed performance in *keiretsu* firms *and* less variation in their performance. This suggests a co-insurance,

89. Aoki (1988, 1994) proposes that *keiretsu* main banks were special repositories of managerial talent and lent their expertise to troubled *keiretsu* member firms. Corporate groups could allocate talent to where it was needed and so make efficient use of scarce governance expertise. Kaplan and Minton (1992), Morck and Nakamura (1999), and others show that bank executives were routinely transferred to the boards of financially troubled client firms later in the postwar period.

90. See Asashima (1982), Okazaki (1999), and others regarding *zaibatsu,* and Hoshi, Kashyap, and Scharfstein (1990a,b, 1991, 1993) and others regarding *keiretsu.*

91. But see Hayashi (2000).

rather than banking, role—*keiretsu* banks rescue distressed member firms rather than funding the best firms. Morck and Nakamura (1999) argue that this perpetuated poor governance. Evidence in Hanazaki and Horiuchi (2000, 2001) and Bremer and Pettway (2002) suggests that it also promoted poor governance in the banks themselves and set the stage for Japan's 1990s financial crisis, which undermined the credibility of *keiretsu* main banks' commitments in any case.

Japanese corporate history tells against using a group bank as a financial clearinghouse or provider of financial insurance. Despite short-run advantages, it carries longer-term dangers. The Suzuki *zaibatsu,* and other groups with organ banks, prospered in the short run but failed when the economy as a whole took a downturn. The *keiretsu* main banks prospered during Japan's long postwar boom but are clearly having serious problems riding out the current prolonged downturn.

Thus, arguments for scale and scope economies in corporate groups must be balanced against a series of costs these structures impose.

7.8.2   Institutional Asthenia

If groups do not provide an advantage in general, they may do so under circumstances particular to Japan at critical points in its history. Corporate groups might then persist because of the path dependence of institutional development.

Khanna and Palepu (chap. 5 in this volume and elsewhere) argue that the economies of scale and scope from corporate groups are more likely to dominate these countervailing costs in economies with weaker institutions. *Zaibatsu*-like groups in modern India survive and prosper because they are an adaptation to market transactions made prohibitively costly by endemic fraud and corruption. Since group firms are all controlled by the same principal, they have greatly reduced incentives to cheat each other. This lets them do business more efficiently than freestanding firms, which depend on dysfunctional markets for capital, managers, labor, suppliers, and customers. Khanna and Palepu (2000) also argue that investments in reputation might have large returns to scale. The Tata family of India invested heavily in acquiring a reputation for fair dealing, sometimes at great financial cost. However, once it established a nationwide reputation for honesty in an otherwise highly corrupt economy, all manner of firms, banks, and individuals were willing to pay a premium to do business with Tata firms rather than risk being cheated. It seems plausible that similar conditions prevailed in Meiji and Taisho Japan.

This view is closely related to the idea that coordination across group companies reduces costs, as in Fruin (1992, p. 101) and others. Some popular accounts of *keiretsu* go further, arguing that group firms pool information from across a wide range of industries, unavailable to freestanding companies, to foresee critical events, react appropriately, and develop flexibility strategically. This seems implausible, for government planners seem chronically unable to reproduce this feat despite using the whole apparatus of the state to collect information for them.

However, such explanations take a weak institutional environment as given. This seems a strong assumption over the 135 years surveyed in this chapter. Haber (1989) argues that oligarchic families in Mexico, who controlled corporate pyramids much like *zaibatsu,* deliberately weakened institutions to benefit themselves and block the entry of competitors. The *zaibatsu* families are thought to have generally supported modernization programs and institutional development such as legal reforms. However, the *zaibatsu* families also clearly had close ties to the premilitary state and may have shaped institutions to benefit themselves. In postoccupation Japan, there is more discussion of *keiretsu* managers' lobbying for institutional weaknesses. It seems likely that *keiretsu* undermined the market for corporate control, thus short circuiting other corporate governance mechanisms, like proxy fights and institutional investor activism. The large banks and the keystone firms of the great horizontal *keiretsu* almost certainly lobbied for the suppression of the corporate bond market in postwar Japan. Thus, weak institutions may well have been a consequence, as well as a cause, of corporate groups.

7.8.3   Private Benefits of Control

This leads to another possibility—groups might benefit those who control them, rather than the economy as a whole. *Zaibatsu* families may have been willing to pay more for control blocks because they valued control per se more than other shareholders did. This might be because members of these families had utility functions that assigned greater weight to power. If the families were not the most able managers, this could have depressed publicly traded shares while raising the family's private valuation of its shares. Or private benefits of control might have existed because these families were more proficient than other shareholders at using control over corporate assets to enrich themselves. Likewise, the managers of postwar *keiretsu* firms organized those structures to stymie corporate takeover threats. If they garnered utility from their control of great corporations, these actions follow logically.[92]

92. It is theoretically possible that these managers were blocking takeovers out of beneficence. For example, their goal might have been to protect myopic shareholders from selling at a large premium to the raider because even larger run-ups in their share prices were likely in the future. However, the repeated empirical rejection of shareholder myopia models (e.g., Chan, Martin, and Kensinger 1990) undermines such arguments. Also, the top managers of many Japanese corporations receive fringe benefits including expensive housing, golf club membership, chauffeured automobile, and access to special restaurants. Even though their market value is quite high, none of these fringe benefits appear in the executives' income figures. As soon as they leave the executive positions, these benefits are usually taken away from the executives.

There is considerable evidence for the existence of large private benefits of corporate control elsewhere. Johnson et al. (1985) show that stock prices rise significantly upon the deaths of the firms' aged CEOs. Morck, Shleifer, and Vishny (1988b) show that high managerial ownership in certain U.S. firms is associated with depressed public share prices. Barclay and Holderness (1989) show that control blocks trade at higher prices than small transactions. Dyck and Zingales (2004) show that this effect is greater in more corrupt countries. All of these studies are consistent with the existence of large private benefits of control. The finding of Dyck and Zingales in particular suggests that the size of private benefits is related to corruption, and it thus favors the view that these benefits involve the consumption of corporate wealth by the controlling shareholder.

The importance of maintaining control was evident in the house charters of the great *zaibatsu* families and in the autobiographical writings of Yoshisuke Aikawa (1934), the founder of the Nissan *zaibatsu*. Morck and Yeung (2003) argue that the extraction of private benefits of control is less dependent on talent than is genuine entrepreneurship, and that leaving one's heirs opportunities to extract such benefits is therefore a preferred way of providing for them.

A fixation on preserving control rights can lead to inefficiently risk-averse investment decisions. Thus, Miyajima (2000) reports that firms belonging to the three major *zaibatsu* exhibit greater risk aversion than firms belonging to newer *zaibatsu*. One explanation for this is more extensive private benefits of control for the principals of the established groups, though there are certainly others too.

In short, private benefits of control probably figured large in the formation of *zaibatsu* and *keiretsu*. This leaves open, however, the question of what other considerations might also have been important.

7.8.4   Insulation from Market Pressures

Another possibility is that corporate groups benefit the economy overall but that group firms nonetheless exhibit inferior performance in the eyes of investors. Much literature contemporaneous with the *zaibatsu* stresses their ability to ignore shareholders. For example, a Meiji-era report on the Kyushu Railway deplores how the company was "dominated from the start by the vulgar view that it had to economize on building outlays." This refers to a conflict described by Ushiba (1909) between "the stockholders desiring an increase in dividends even to the point of reducing the business, and the directors insisting on expanding the business even if it means cutting dividends." Ericson (1989) describes how a large shareholder, the banker Imamura Seinosuke, tried not only to curtail the railway's vast expansion plans but to force it to downsize in response to the economic downturn of 1890.

Ericson (1989) applauds the railway's "substantial progress [*sic*] in separating management from ownership" and the professionalism of its president, Sengoku Mitsugu, who owned little stock and could therefore go "on pursuing his positive policies, thrusting aside a second attempt by disgruntled stockholders to interfere with his program in 1902." But Ericson concedes that such "sophistication" was the exception. The Kyushu and Sanyo railroads were Mitsubishi companies, and Mitsubishi "differed from most railway owners in its primary concern for indirect benefits of railway investment." That is, the Mitsubishi railroads were not intended to maximize shareholder value but to assist other Mitsubishi companies in transporting inputs and outputs.

The foregoing is a somewhat convoluted way of saying that the *zaibatsu* railways were forced to overexpand to reduce the shipping costs of other Mitsubishi companies, in a clear instance of "self-dealing" or "tunneling." However, this may not have been economically inefficient. Since railways have a public good component, it is possible that shareholder value maximization would lead to a suboptimal investment. Tunneling by the *zaibatsu* to overbuild might actually improve social welfare, though at the expense of the railways' other shareholders. By 1905, banks and insurance companies had emerged as the major shareholders in most railroads, and such self-sacrifice by railroad shareholders was at an end. The railroads were nationalized in 1906 and 1907, perhaps permitting more self-sacrifice by them.

Governments elsewhere took advantage of large corporate groups as preexisting command and control devices for implementing industrial policies. For example, Korea, Malaysia, and Sweden appear to have encouraged pyramidal groups so that government officials could influence the corporate sector by dealing directly with a few individuals—the patriarchs in charge of the pyramids.[93] The governments in question seem to have believed, perhaps correctly, that these small group interactions allowed a highly effective transmission of government policies and a better coordination of private- and public-sector initiatives.

Certainly, the *zaibatsu* were more agile and willing than freestanding firms to change direction rapidly in order to accommodate changing government policy objectives. By rapidly expanding one firm with capital from others, the *zaibatsu* could quickly change direction and focus. Their large established capital bases also let them enter new industries quickly. Postwar *keiretsu* were also favored as vehicles through which industrial policy might be implemented (Komiya, Okuno, and Suzumura 1988; Okimoto 1989).

This agility was clearly beneficial in terms of endearing the *zaibatsu* and *keiretsu* to certain government officials. However, it did not always enrich the groups involved. The *zaibatsu* families lost out heavily after, and per-

---

93. See Högfeldt (chap. 9 in this volume) for details regarding Sweden. Morck and Yeung (2004) make the argument more generally.

haps during, the war despite their groups' agility in expanding munitions production. More generally, deviating from value-maximizing behavior has dynamic costs that disadvantage the group over time, as in Morck and Nakamura (1999). This may explain the weakness of the *keiretsu* firms in present-day Japan.

7.8.5   Economies of Scale and Scope in Political Rent Seeking

A final possibility is that the close relationships corporate groups develop with government generated financial returns that compensated for profits lost while pursuing government objectives. Morck, Stangeland, and Yeung (2000), in discussing pyramidal groups throughout the world, argue that government officials and great mercantile family patriarchs, who come to know and trust each other, are likely to engage in mutual back scratching, favor trading, and other forms of corruption that, while beneficial for the family group of firms, can greatly damage the economy. Morck, Stangeland, and Yeung, Fisman (2001), Johnson and Mitton (2003), Rajan and Zingales (2003), and others present empirical evidence consistent with this more skeptical view.

There is considerable evidence that business-government relations in both prewar and postwar Japan were largely organized around rent seeking. Morikawa (1992, pp. 3–4) argues that political entrepreneurship, the use of ties to powerful political figures to obtain government favors, reaped huge returns in the provision of goods and services to the state and to state-owned enterprises in the Meiji period.

The great *zaibatsu* of prewar Japan all obtained a leg up on their competitors due to government favors. The Sumitomo obtained their cash-cow copper mines because of their close association with the Tokugawa regime. The Mitsui and Mitsubishi *zaibatsu* obtained cash-cow mining operations in questionably competitive privatizations by the Meiji government. All three prospered in prewar Japan in part because of their ability to give the government what it wanted when it wanted it. If the government decided Japan needed to export, the *zaibatsu* could move into export-oriented businesses. If the government decided Japan needed technology, the *zaibatsu* could rev up their machinery production. In short, the *zaibatsu* seemed able to react to the changing whims of government policymakers with greater nimbleness and forcefulness than other firms could manage.

In postwar Japan, the *keiretsu* firms and their main banks also appear to have been generously subsidized for their enthusiasm about industrial policy programs (Okimoto 1989). Indeed, Beason and Weinstein (1996) show that the greater part of Japan's postwar industrial subsidies went to mining firms, most of which were members of the large horizontal *keiretsu*. In contrast, independent companies like Honda were denied subsidies for deliberately contravening industrial policy plans by, for example, producing automobiles when told not to.

The importance of rent seeking in postwar Japan is perhaps evident in the status accruing to employment in government. This status existed largely because of the attractions of a career path involving *amakudari*—literally, "descent from heaven." *Amakudari* involves an older, high-ranking government official leaving his post to become a senior manager in industry, and was a common path to the boardroom in postwar Japan. This practice may have made sense in the immediate postwar period, when there was perhaps a serious shortage of talent due to the purging of senior executives who had cooperated with the military government.

However, Van Rixtel (2002) and others argue that *amakudari* subsequently devolved into a system of regulatory capture, as in Stigler (1971). This was largely because of the *genkyoku* principle, whereby specific ministries claimed exclusive regulatory power over specific industries. Since civil servants in these ministries were prime candidates for *amakudari*, the ministries rapidly became vocal advocates within the government for the interests of their industries. For example, in the race for industrial promotion of biotechnology, the Ministry of Health wanted to participate in policymaking explicitly on behalf of the pharmaceutical industry, its traditional *amakudari* partner. Since the great *keiretsu* firms included the most attractive *amakudari* landing spots and were the most enthusiastic about *amakudari*, these groups may have enjoyed an advantage, in the short term at least, due to their better connections with government.

This regulatory capture is now thought by some researchers to have contributed to Japan's current economic and governance problems.[94] Bureaucrats uncritically advanced industry agendas, hopeful of *amakudari* opportunities. Corporate executives, former bureaucrats, realized that their talents were in influencing government rather than overseeing new research and development programs. The result was an unhealthy regulatory morass that came to surround many established industries in Japan, and that is now the subject of much criticism.

7.9   Conclusions

During Japan's modern history, beginning in 1868, its corporate sector was first organized into great family pyramids, or *zaibatsu*, then subjected to Soviet-style central planning, then reorganized into widely held firms, and finally restructured into *keiretsu* corporate groups. While many lessons lie in Japan's complicated development story, a few that have to do with the interaction between the corporate sector and Japan's institutions are especially noteworthy.

Although Japan specialists often write of *zaibatsu* as uniquely Japanese

94. See Horiuchi and Shimizu (2001) for a discussion of the role of *amakudari* in Japan's current economic downturn.

constructs, they are typical of the family-controlled pyramidal groups that the other chapters in this volume show dominating the corporate sectors of most other countries. The postwar *keiretsu,* in contrast, are more uniquely Japanese. *Zaibatsu* were probably sensible structures for sidestepping Japan's early, and probably poorly functioning, markets. By doing business mainly with each other, *zaibatsu* firms could avoid being cheated or otherwise harmed in inefficient and opaque markets for goods, labor, and capital. The postwar *keiretsu* may have been, in part at least, a similar response to the chaotic early postwar years.

But both *zaibatsu* and *keiretsu* were also devices for entrenching insiders. *Zaibatsu* let great mercantile families and entrepreneurial individuals direct vast amounts of public investor capital yet retain full control of all the ventures so funded. *Keiretsu* probably formed to stop hostile takeovers and tenure professional managers. That insiders sought such entrenchment indicates that they received private benefits of control.

The passage of time exposed weaknesses of corporate groups.

One popular argument for groups is that group banks can finance group firms, avoiding information asymmetry problems and other capital market failures. Japanese history shows that such arrangements invite moral hazard and agency problems. *Zaibatsu,* like Suzuki, that followed this model, failed during the depression era. The current problems of the great horizontal *keiretsu* also seem to stem from a history of inefficient capital allocation.

Although *zaibatsu* and *keiretsu* might initially have been devices for extracting economies of scale from scarce talented managers, by entrenching insiders they ultimately kept talented outsiders out of boardrooms. This certainly affected firm-level performance. But it may have retarded macroeconomic growth as well. Morikawa (1980, 1992) argues that entrenched *zaibatsu* families' risk aversion and aversion to external financing to preserve family control retarded prewar Japan's growth. He argues that few projects for Japan's industrialization were initiated by *zaibatsu.* Morck, Nakamura, and Shivdasani (2000) argue that oversight by entrenched bankers may have had a similar effect on *keiretsu* firms.

Yet despite these and other weaknesses, corporate groups persisted.

In part this may have been because they retained genuine economies of scale and scope. *Zaibatsu* in particular funneled foreign technology into Japan, probably continually renewing their economies of scale.

But both *zaibatsu* and *keiretsu* probably also altered Japanese institutions to favor their continued importance. Both supported Japan's political elite vigorously at critical historical junctures. By participating enthusiastically in government industrial policies, no matter how wrongheaded, *zaibatsu* and *keiretsu* nurtured relationships that generated both subsidies and political influence. This influence was often instrumental in securing lasting advantages over the competition, as when the early *zaibatsu* families obtained tax-farming concessions, mines, and government contracts. The cooperation of *zaibatsu* and *keiretsu* with industrial policies probably led to captive regulator problems. Entire ministries were likely captured by industrial groups through *genkyoku* and *amakudari*. This undermined the state's ability to regulate prudently the economy and the financial system, and locked in favoritism to established large firms that "played the game." The collapse of the Suzuki *zaibatsu* because of its *lack* of political connections is the exception to prove this rule. In the postwar period, *keiretsu* banks and firms also benefited disproportionately from regulatory favoritism and overt subsidies. By lobbying for the suppression of the corporate bond market in postwar Japan, main *keiretsu* banks seriously weakened the financial system overall.

Thus, *zaibatsu* and *keiretsu* survived the institutional conditions that gave them birth. By investing heavily in political connections, they prolonged their competitive advantage even as the institutional deficiencies underlying their formation faded. But this political rent seeking prolonged some institutional weaknesses and engendered others.

Murphy, Shleifer, and Vishny (1991) and many others show pervasive rent seeking to impede growth. This is because it diverts talented individuals from genuine entrepreneurship toward more lucrative careers in rent seeking. Both rent seeking and innovation have increasing returns to scale for individuals and firms. However, rent seeking is a zero or negative-sum game, while innovation is a positive-sum game. Diverting talent into ever more lucrative rent seeking diverts ever greater resources into zero or negative-sum games, and thus slows growth.

We do not argue that groups are wholly bad. Rather, Japan's history exposes how groups in general, and groups that rely on internal capital markets in particular, can distort institutional development.

References

Acemoglu, Daron, Simon Johnson, and James Robinson. 2001. The colonial origins of comparative development: An empirical investigation. *American Economic Review* 91 (5): 1369–1422.

Aikawa, Yoshisuke. 1934. *New capitalism and holding companies.* Tokyo: Tokyo Bankers Association.

Allen, Franklin, and Douglas Gale. 2000. *Comparing financial systems.* Cambridge: MIT Press.

Aoki, Masahiko. 1988. *Information, incentives, and bargaining in the Japanese economy.* Cambridge, MA: Cambridge University Press.

———. 1994. Monitoring characteristics of the main bank system: An analytical and developmental view. In *The Japanese main bank system: Its relevancy for developing and transforming economies,* ed. Masahiko Aoki and Hugh Patrick, 109–41. Oxford and New York: Oxford University Press.

Aoki, Masahiko, and Paul Sheard. 1992. The role of the main bank in the corporate governance structure in Japan. Paper presented at conference Corporate Governance: New Problems and New Solutions Structure in Japan. 1–2 May, Stanford, California.

Asajima, Shoichi. 1984. Financing of the Japanese *zaibatsu*. In *Family business in the era of industrial growth,* ed. Akio Okochi and Shigeaki Yasuoka, 95–117. Tokyo: University of Tokyo Press.

Asashima, Shoichi. 1982. *Senkanki Sumitomo zaibarsu keieishi* [Inter-war period Sumitomo *zaibatsu* business history]. Tokyo: University of Tokyo Press.

Barclay, Michael, and Clifford Holderness. 1989. Private benefits from control of corporations. *Journal of Financial Economics* 25:371–95.

Beale, Adolf, and Gardiner Means. 1932. *The modern corporation and private property.* New York: Macmillan.

Beason, Richard, and David E. Weinstein. 1996. Growth, economies of scale, and targeting in Japan (1955–1990). *Review of Economics and Statistics* (78) 2:286–95.

Bertrand, M. P., P. Mehra, and S. Mullainathan. 2002. Ferreting out tunneling: An application to Indian business groups. *Quarterly Journal of Economics* 117:121–48.

Bisson, T. 1954. Zaibatsu *dissolution in Japan.* Berkeley: University of California Press.

Blinder, Alan S. 1991. A Japanese buddy system that could benefit U.S. business. *Business Week,* October 14, 32.

Boot, Arnoud, and Anjan Thakor. 2000. Can relationship banking survive competitions? *Journal of Finance* 55:679–713.

Bremer, Marc, and Richard Pettway. 2002. Information and the market's perceptions of Japanese bank crisis: Regulation, environment, and disclosure. *Pacific Basin Finance Journal* 10:119–39.

Caves, Richard. 1982. *Multinational enterprise and economic analysis.* Cambridge: Cambridge University Press.

Caves, Richard, and Masu Uekusa. 1976. *Industrial organization in Japan.* Washington, DC: Brookings Institution.

Cha, Myung Soo. 2001. The origins of the Japanese banking panic of 1927. Institute of Economic Research Discussion Paper Series A no. 408. Tokyo: Hitotsubashi University.

Chan, Su, John Martin, and John Kensinger. 1990. Corporate research and development expenditures and share values. *Journal of Financial Economics* 26:255–66.

Claessens, Stijn, Simeon Djankov, Joseph Fan, and Larry Lang. 2002. Disentangling the incentive and entrenchment effects of large shareholdings. *Journal of Finance* 57 (6): 2741–71.

Claessens, Stijn, Simeon Djankov, Larry H. P. Lang. 2000. The separation of ownership and control in East Asian corporations. *Journal of Financial Economics* 58 (1–2): 81–112.

Dower, John. 2000. *Embracing defeat: Japan in the aftermath of World War II.* East Rutherford, NJ: Penguin Books.

Dyck, Alexander, and Luigi Zingales. 2004. Private benefits of control: An international comparison. *Journal of Finance* 59 (2): 537–601.

Ericson, Steven. 1989. Private railroads in the Meiji Era: Forerunners of modern Japanese management. In *Japanese management in historical perspective,* ed. Tsunehiko Yui and Keiichiro Nakagawa, 51–77. Tokyo: University of Tokyo Press.

Faccio, Mara, and Larry H. P. Lang. 2003. The separation of ownership and control: An analysis of ultimate ownership in Western European countries. *Journal of Financial Economics* 65 (3): 365–95.

Fisman, Raymond. 2001. Estimating the value of political connections. *American Economic Review* 91 (4): 1095–1103.

Fletcher, William Miles III. 1989. *The Japanese business community and national trade policy 1920–1942.* Chapel Hill: University of North Carolina Press.

Fouraker, L. 2002. Precursors of convergence in interwar Japan: Kaneko Naokichi and the Suzuki Trading Company. Paper presented at Media in Transition 2: Globalization and Convergence. 10–12 May, Cambridge, Massachusetts.

Fraser, Donald, S. Ghon Rhee, and Guen Hwan Shin. 2002. The impact of interbank and capital market competition on relationship banking: Evidence from the Japanese experience. University of Hawaii, College of Business Administration. Working Paper.

Fruin, W. Mark. 1983. *Kikkoman: Company, clan, and community.* Cambridge, MA: Harvard University Press.

———. 1992. *The Japanese enterprise system: Competitive strategies and cooperative structures.* New York: Oxford University Press.

Fukuzawa, T. 1930. *Zaikai jinbutsu gakan* [Business leaders: Personal views]. Tokyo: Daiamondsha.

Gerlach, Michael L. 1992. *Alliance capitalism: The social organization of Japanese business.* Berkeley: University of California Press.

Glaeser, Edward, and Andrei Shleifer. 2002. Legal Origins. *Quarterly Journal of Economics* 117 (4): 1193.

Gompers, Paul, and Josh Lerner. 2002. *The venture capital cycle.* Cambridge: MIT Press.

Goto, Akira. 1982. Business groups in a market economy. *European Economic Review* 19:53–70.

Haber, Stephen. 1989. *Industry and underdevelopment: The industrialization of Mexico, 1890–1940.* Stanford, CA: Stanford University Press.

Hadley, Eleanor. 1970. *Antitrust in Japan.* Princeton, NJ: Princeton University Press.

Hamada, Koichi. 1998. The incentive structure of a managed market economy: Can it survive the millennium? *American Economic Review* 88 (2): 417–21.

Hanazaki, Masuharu, and Akiyoshi Horiuchi. 2000. Is Japan's financial system efficient? *Oxford Review of Economic Policy* 16 (2): 61–73.

———. 2001. A vacuum of governance in the Japanese bank management. In *Banking, capital markets and Corporate Governance,* ed. H. Osano and T. Tachibanaki, 133–80. London and New York: Palgrave.

———. 2003. A review of Japan's bank crisis from the governance perspective. Hitotsubashi University, Institute of Economic Research. Working Paper.

———. 2004. Can the financial restraint theory explain the postwar experience of Japan's financial system? In *Designing financial systems in East Asia and Japan,* ed. Joseph P. H. Fan, Masuharu Hanezaki, and Juro Teranishi, 19–46. London: Routledge-Curzon.

Hasegawa, Yasubei. 1938. *Kabushiki Kaisha no Shomondai* [Various issues of joint stock companies]. Tokyo: Tokyo Taibunsha.

Hashimoto, J. 1997. Japanese industrial enterprises and the financial market between the two World Wars. In *Finance in the age of the corporate economy: The third Anglo-Japanese business history conference,* ed. P. L. Cottrell, A. Teichova, and T. Yuzawa, 94–117. Hants, UK: Ashgate.

Hayashi, Fumio. 2000. The main bank system and corporate investment: An empirical assessment. In *Finance, governance, and competitiveness in Japan,* ed.

Masahiko Aoki and Gary Saxonhouse, 81–97. Oxford and New York: Oxford University Press.

He, Kathy, Randall Morck, and Bernard Yeung. 2004. Stability. University of Alberta, School of Business. Working Paper.

Hellman, Thomas, Kevin Murdock, and Joseph Stiglitz. 2000. Liberalization, moral hazard in banking, and prudent regulation: Are capital requirements enough? *American Economic Review* 90 (1): 147–65.

Hirschmeier, Johannes. 1964. *The origins of entrepreneurship in Japan.* Cambridge, MA: Harvard University Press.

Hirschmeier, Johannes, and Tsunehiko Yui. 1981. *The development of Japanese business.* 2nd ed. London: Allen and Unwin.

Holding Companies Liquidation Commission (HCLC). 1950. *Nihon zaibatsu to sono katai* [Japanese *zaibatsu* and its dissolution]. Tokyo: Shinyohen.

Horiuchi, Akiyoshi. 1999. Nihonni okeru kinyu kozo no kiso: Tenbo [The basis of Japan's financial structure: A survey]. *Japanese Ministry of Finance Research Institute Financial Review* (June): 1–32.

Horiuchi, Akiyoshi, and Katsutoshi Shimizu. 2001. Did Amakudari undermine the effectiveness of regulator monitoring in Japan? *Journal of Banking and Finance* 25 (3): 573–96.

Hoshi, Takeo. 1995. Cleaning up the balance sheets: Japanese experience in the post-war reconstruction period. In *Corporate governance in transitional economies: Insider control and the role of banks,* ed. M. Aoki and H.-K. Kim, 303–59. Washington, DC: World Bank.

Hoshi, Takeo, and Anil Kashyap. 2001. *Corporate financing and governance in Japan: The road to the future.* Cambridge: MIT Press.

Hoshi, Takeo, Anil Kashyap, and David Scharfstein. 1990a. Bank monitoring and investment: Evidence from the changing structure of Japanese corporate banking relationship. In *Asymmetric information, corporate finance, and investment,* ed. Glenn Hubbard, 67–88. Chicago: University of Chicago Press.

———. 1990b. The role of banks in reducing the costs of financial distress in Japan. *Journal of Financial Economics* 27:67–88.

———. 1991. Corporate structure, liquidity, and investment: Evidence from Japanese industrial groups. *Quarterly Journal of Economics* 106:33–60.

Hoshi, Takeo, Anil Kashyap, and David Scharfstein. 1993. The choice between public and private debt: An analysis of post-deregulation corporate financing in Japan. Massachusetts Institute of Technology, Sloan School of Management. Unpublished manuscript.

Hoskins, Geoffrey. 1992. *The first socialist state. A history of the Soviet Union from within.* 2nd ed. Cambridge, MA: Harvard University Press.

Huson, Mark, and Dhananjay Nanda. 1995. The impact of just-in-time manufacturing on firm performance in the US. *Journal of Operations Management* 12 (3–4): 297–311.

Ito, Masanao. 2001. Showashonen no kinyu system kiki: Sono kozo to taio [The financial system crisis in the 1920s: The structure and responses]. Institute of Monetary and Economic Studies Paper no. 2001-J-24. Tokyo: Bank of Japan.

Jensen, Michael, and William Meckling. 1976. The theory of the firm: Managerial behavior, agency costs and ownership structure. *Journal of Financial Economics* 3:305–60.

Johnson, Simon, Rafael La Porta, Florencio López-de-Silanes, and Andrei Shleifer. 2000. Tunneling. *American Economic Review* 90 (2): 22–27.

Johnson, Simon, and Todd Mitton. 2003. Cronyism and capital controls: Evidence from Malaysia. *Journal of Financial Economics* 67 (2): 351–82.

Johnson, W. Bruce, Robert P. Magee, Nandu J. Nagarajan, and Henry A. Newman.

1985. An analysis of the stock price reaction to sudden executive deaths: Implications for the management labor model. *Journal of Accounting and Economics* 7 (1–3): 151–74.

Kaneko, Naokichi. 1928. Suzuki okoku [The Suzuki Kingdom]. *Osaka Asahi Shimbun,* 19–21 April.

Kaplan, Steven, and Bernadette Minton. 1992. Outside intervention in Japanese companies: Its determinants and its implications for managers. *Journal of Financial Economics* 36:225–58.

Kato, T. 1957. *Honpo ginkoshiron* [History of banks in Japan]. Tokyo: University of Tokyo Press.

Katsura, Yoshio. 1976. Failure in *zaibatsu* making: Suzuki Shoten. In *Nihonno zaibatsu* [Japanese *zaibatsu*], ed. Shigeaki Yasuoka, 177–223. Tokyo: Nikkie.

Khanna, Tarun, and Krishna Palepu. 2000. Is group affiliation profitable in emerging markets? An analysis of diversified Indian business groups. *Journal of Finance* 55 (2): 867–93.

Kobayashi, Masaski. 1985. Japan's early industrialization and the transfer of government enterprises: Government and business. *Japanese Yearbook on Business History: 1985* 2:54–80.

Kojima, Kenji. 1997. Japanese corporate governance. Kobe University, Research Institute for Economics and Business Administration. Working Paper.

Komiya, Ryutaro, Masahiro Okuno, and Kotaro Suzumura, eds. 1988. *Industrial policy of Japan.* New York: Academic Press.

La Porta, Rafael, Florencio López-de-Silanes, Andrei Shleifer, and Robert Vishny. 1999. Corporate ownership around the world. *Journal of Finance* 54 (2): 471–520.

Lang, Larry, and René Stulz. 1994. Tobin's *q,* corporate diversification, and firm performance. *Journal of Political Economy* 102:1248–80.

Lincoln, J., M. Gerlach, and C. Ahmadjian. 1996. *Keiretsu* networks and corporate performance in Japan. *American Sociological Review* 61:67–88.

Lincoln, J., M. Gerlach, and P. Takahashi. 1992. *Keiretsu* networks in the Japanese economy: A dyad analysis of intercorporate ties. *American Sociological Review* 57:561–85.

McMillan, Charles. 1984. *The Japanese industrial system.* Berlin: De Gruyter.

Ministry of Finance. 1983. *Hojin kigyo tokei* [Incorporate businesses statistics]. Tokyo: Ministry of Finance.

Mishima, Y., ed. 1981. *The Mitsubishi* zaibatsu [in Japanese]. Tokyo: Nikkei.

Mitsubishi Bank. 1954. *Mitsubishi ginkoshi* [History of the Mitsubishi bank]. Tokyo: Mitsubishi Bank.

Miwa, Yoshiro, and J. Mark Ramseyer. 2002. The fable of the *keiretsu. Journal of Economics and Management Strategy* 11:169–224.

Miyajima, Hideaki. 1994. Transformation of *zaibatsu* to postwar corporate groups: From hierarchically integrated groups to horizontally integrated groups. *Journal of the Japanese and International Economies* 8:293–328.

———. 1999. Presidential turnover and performance in the Japanese firm: The evolution and change of the contingent governance structure under the main bank system. In *Japanese management in the low growth era: Between external shocks and internal evolution,* ed. Daniel Dirks, Jean-Francois Huchet, and Thierry Ribault, 121–44. Heidelberg: Springer.

———. 2000. Nihon kigyono shoyukozo, shihon kosei, setsubitoshi: Senkanki to kodo seichokino kozo hikaku [Ownership structure, capital structure and investment of Japanese corporations: Comparison between the inter-war period and high-growth period]. Waseda University (Tokyo), Faculty of Commerce. Mimeograph.

Miyamoto, Matao. 1984. The position and role of family business in the development of the Japanese company system. In *Family business in the era of industrial growth,* ed. Akio Okochi and Shigeaki Yasuoka, 39–91. Tokyo: University of Tokyo Press.

Morck, Randall. 2005. How to eliminate pyramidal business groups: The double taxation of inter-corporate dividends and other incisive uses of tax policy. In *Tax policy and the economy,* ed. James Poterba. Cambridge: MIT Press, forthcoming.

Morck, Randall, and Masao Nakamura. 1999. Banks and corporate control in Japan. *Journal of Finance* 54:319–39.

———. 2001. Japanese corporate governance and macroeconomic problems. In *The Japanese business and economic system: History and prospects for the 21st century,* ed. Masao Nakamura, 325–49. New York: Palgrave Macmillan.

Morck, Randall, Masao Nakamura, and Anil Shivdasani. 2000. Banks, ownership structure, and firm value in Japan. *Journal of Business* 73:539–69.

Morck, Randall, Andrei Shleifer, and Robert Vishny. 1988a. Characteristics of targets of hostile and friendly takeovers. In *Corporate takeovers: Causes and consequences,* ed. Allan Auerbach, 101–29. Chicago: University of Chicago Press.

———. 1988b. Management ownership and market valuation: An empirical analysis. *Journal of Financial Economics* 20 (1–2): 293–315.

———. 1989. Alternative mechanisms for corporate control. *American Economic Review* 79 (4): 842–52.

———. 1990. Do managerial objectives drive bad acquisitions? *Journal of Finance* 45 (1): 31–48.

Morck, Randall, David A. Stangeland, and Bernard Yeung. 2000. Inherited wealth, corporate control, and economic growth: The Canadian disease. In *Concentrated corporate ownership,* ed. Randall Morck, 319–69. Chicago: University of Chicago Press.

Morck, Randall, and Bernard Yeung. 2003. Agency problems in large family business groups. *Entrepreneurship Theory and Practice* 27 (4): 367–82.

———. 2004. Family firms and the rent seeking society. *Entrepreneurship Theory and Practice* 28 (4): 391–409.

Morikawa, Hidemasa. 1976. Chiho zaibatsu [Local *zaibatsu*]. In *Nihonno zaibatsu* [Japanese *zaibatsu*], ed. S. Yasuoka, 146–75. Tokyo: Nikkei.

———. 1980. *Zaibatsuno keieishiteki kenkyu* [Business history research of *zaibatsu*]. Tokyo: Toyo Keizai.

———. 1992. *Zaibatsu: The rise and fall of family enterprise groups in Japan.* Tokyo: University of Tokyo Press.

Murphy, Kevin, Andrei Shleifer, and Robert Vishny. 1989. Industrialization and the big push. *Journal of Political Economy* 97:1003–26.

———. 1991. The allocation of talent: Implications for growth. *Quarterly Journal of Economics* 106 (2): 503–30.

Nakamura, Takafusa, and Konosuke Odaka, eds. 2003. *The economic history of Japan: 1914–1955–a dual structure.* Oxford, UK: Oxford University Press.

Nissho. 1968. *Nissho 40nen no Ayumi* [History of Nissho's 40 years]. Tokyo: Nissho.

Noguchi, Yukio. 1998. The 1940 system: Japan under the wartime economy. *American Economic Review Papers and Proceedings* 88 (May): 404–6.

Ogura, S. 2002. *Banking, the state and industrial promotion in developing Japan, 1900–73.* Houndmills, UK: Palgrave.

Okazaki, Tetsuji. 1994. The Japanese firm under the wartime planned economy. In *The Japanese firm: Sources of competitive strength,* ed. Masahiko Aoki and Ronald Dore, 350–75. Oxford University Press.

———. 1999. *Mochikabu kaishano keizaishi: Zaibatsuto kigyo tochi* [Economic history of the holding company: Zaibatau and corporate governance]. Tokyo: Chikuma Shobo.

Okazaki, Tetsuji, and Masahiro Okuno-Fujiwara. 1993. *Gendai Nihon Keizai Sisutemu no Genryu* [The origin of the contemporary Japanese economic system]. Tokyo: Toyo Keizai.

Okazaki, Tetsuji, and Kazuki Yokoyama. 2001. Governance and performance of banks in prewar Japan: Testing the "organ bank" hypothesis quantitatively. Center for International Research on the Japanese Economy Discussion Paper no. CJRJE-F-111. University of Tokyo, April.

Okimoto, Daniel. 1989. *Between MITI and the market*. Stanford, CA: Stanford University Press.

Okumura, H. 1976. *Nihonno rokudai kigyo shudan* [Six major Japanese corporate groups]. Tokyo: Diamondsha.

Patrick, Hugh. 1967. Japan. In *Banking in the early stages of industrialization,* ed. Rondo Cameron, Olga Crisp, Hugh T. Patrick, and Richard Tilly, 239–89. Oxford University Press.

Porter, Michael. 1990. *The competitive advantage of nations.* New York: Free Press.

Rajan, Raghuram. 1992. Insiders and outsiders: The choice between relationship and arm's length debt. *Journal of Finance* 47:1367–1400.

Rajan, Raghuram, and Luigi Zingales. 2003. The great reversals: The politics of financial development in the twentieth century. *Journal of Financial Economics* 69 (1): 5.

Reischauer, Edwin O. 1988. *The Japanese today: Change and continuity.* Cambridge, MA: Harvard University Press.

Sataka, Makoto. 1994. *Sengo kigyo jikenshi* [Postwar corporate events]. Tokyo: Kodansha.

Sheard, Paul. 1991. The economics of interlocking shareholding in Japan. *Richerche Economiche* 45:421–48.

———. 1994. Interlocking shareholdings and corporate governance. In *The Japanese firm: Sources of competitive strength,* ed. Masahiko Aoki and Ronald Dore, 310–49. Oxford University Press.

Shiomi, Saburo. 1957. *Japan's finance and taxation: 1940–1956.* New York: Columbia University Press.

Shogyo Koshinsho. 1930. *Mitsui zaibatsu.* Tokyo: Shogyo Koshinsho.

Stigler, George. 1971. The theory of economic regulation. *Bell Journal of Economics and Management Science* 2 (Spring): 3–21.

Takahashi, Kamekichi. 1930a. *Kabushiki Gaisha Bokokuron* [The stock company: A cause of national decay]. Tokyo: Banrikaku Shobo.

———. 1930b. *Nihon zaibatsu no kaibo* [Analysis of Japanese *zaibatsu*]. Tokyo: Chuokoronsha.

Takahashi, Kamekichi, and J. Aoyama. 1938. *Nihon zaibatsu ron* [The Japanese *zaibatsu*]. Tokyo: Shunjusha.

Takeda, Haruhito. 1995. Daikigyo no kozo to zaibatsu [The structures of large firms and *zaibatsu*]. In *Daikigyo jidai no torai* [Arrival of large corporations], ed. T. Yui and E. Daito, 79–115. Tokyo: Iwanami.

Tamaki, Hajime. 1976. *Nihon zaibatsushi* [History of Japanese *zaibatsu*]. Tokyo: Shakai Shisosha.

Tamaki, Norio. 1995. *Japanese banking: A history, 1859–1959.* Cambridge: Cambridge University Press.

Teranishi, Juro. 1999. The main bank system. In *The Japanese economic system and its historical origins,* ed. Tetsuji Okazaki and Masahiro Okuno-Fujiwara, 63–96. Oxford University Press.

————. 2000. The fall of the Taisho economic system. In *Finance governance and competitiveness in Japan,* ed. Masahiko Aoki and Gary Saxonhouse, 43–63. Oxford University Press.

————. 2003. *Nihon no keizai system.* Tokyo: Iwanami.

Toyo Keizai. 1991. *Kigyo Keiretsu Soran '92* [Company *keiretsu* groupings 1992]. Tokyo: Toyo Keizai Shimposha.

Udagawa, M. 1976. Shinko zaibatsu [New *zaibatsu*]. In *Nihonno zaibatsu* [Japanese *zaibatsu*], ed. S. Yasuoka, 107–44. Tokyo: Nikkei.

Ushiba, Takuzo. 1909. Tetsudo eigyo no hoshin [Policies in railway management]. In *10 nen Kinen no Tetsudo* [The 10-year-old Japanese railway], ed. R. Kinoshita, 274–86. Tokyo: Jiho Kyoku. Previously published in *Tetsudo jiho* 14 (1899).

Weinstein, David, and Yishay Yafeh. 1998. On the costs of a bank centered financial system: Evidence from the changing main bank relations in Japan. *Journal of Finance* 9:154–73.

Yafeh, Yishay. 1995. Corporate ownership, profitability, and bank-firm ties: Evidence from the American occupation reforms in Japan. *Journal of the Japanese and International Economies* 9:154–73.

————. 2000. Corporate governance in Japan: Past performance and future prospects. *Oxford Review of Economic Policy* 16 (2): 74–84.

————. 2004. Japan's corporate groups: Some international and historical perspectives. In *Structural impediments to growth in Japan,* ed. M. Blomstrom, J. Corbett, F. Hayashi, and A. Kashyap. Chicago: University of Chicago Press.

Yamamura, Kozo. 1976. General trading companies in Japan: Their origins and growth. In *Japanese industrialization and its social consequences,* ed. Hugh Patrick, 161–99. Berkeley: University of California Press.

Yamazaki, H. 1988. The development of large enterprises in Japan: An analysis of the top 50 enterprises in the profit ranking table (1929–1984). *Japanese Yearbook on Business History* 5:12–55.

Yasuoka, Shigeaki, ed. 1976. *Nihonno zaibatsu* [Japanese *zaibatsu*]. Tokyo: Nikkei.

————. 1984. Capital ownership in family companies: Japanese firms compared with those in other countries. In *Family business in the era of industrial growth,* ed. Akio Okochi and Shigeaki Yasuoka, 1–32. Tokyo: University of Tokyo Press.

Comment   Sheldon Garon

In their chapter, Randall Morck and Masao Nakamura write that "Japan's corporate sector has, over the past century, been reorganized according to every major corporate governance model." Nearly the same could be said for the shifting *interpretations* of corporate governance in Japan—particularly those of the combines known as *zaibatsu* before 1945 and the business groups called *keiretsu* following World War II. Prewar Marxists criticized the *zaibatsu* for their concentration of wealth, while rightists attacked (sometimes literally) *zaibatsu* leaders for their profit-making, unpatriotic behavior. To the Americans who occupied a defeated Japan between 1945

Sheldon Garon is a professor of Japanese history at Princeton University.

and 1952, the *zaibatsu* constituted the most formidable obstacle to building economic democracy in the New Japan. Arguing that the *zaibatsu* had abetted wartime militarism and stunted the growth of a healthy small-business sector, the occupation broke the big four *zaibatsu* into scores of independent firms. Or so the Americans thought. The old *zaibatsu* units and other firms soon regrouped into the more loosely constituted *keiretsu.* As Japan achieved its "economic miracle" in the 1950s and 1960s and increasingly challenged U.S. business interests, historical evaluations of the *zaibatsu* and *keiretsu* shifted again, from criticism to admiration. Chalmers Johnson (1982) judged that the *zaibatsu* had contributed to prewar economic development with their economies of scale, their pioneering role in commercializing modern technologies, their close cooperation with the state's developmental agenda, and above all their "introduction of a needed measure of competition into the [state's] plan-rational system" (p. 23). Johnson similarly lauded the bank-centered *keiretsu* for their contribution to postwar economic growth (pp. 204–6). When the Japanese economy sunk into its long decade of slow growth and no-growth after 1991, observers generally concluded that Japan's corporate governance—so recently praised—had for a long time in fact impeded economic growth. Or as Morck and Nakamura state here, the *zaibatsu* and especially the *keiretsu* enthusiastically engaged in rent seeking that "probably retarded financial development and created long-term economic problems."

Their chapter offers a sweeping historical analysis of the changes in corporate ownership of the *zaibatsu* and *keiretsu,* beginning with era of the Tokugawa shoguns (1603–1868). For students of Japanese economic history, the most valuable contribution may be the detailed structural analysis of ownership and governance within a variety of the major combines both before and after 1945. The authors also challenge the thesis of "transwar" continuity, or in Yukio Noguchi's formulation, the "1940 system." Johnson, Noguchi, and others describe how Japanese enterprises, which before the 1930s depended significantly on equity markets, became heavily reliant on banking capital during World War II, and they suggest that this pattern of bank-centered finance continued unabated into the postwar era (Noguchi 1995, pp. 8–9). Morck and Nakamura instead reveal the reappearance of a vibrant equity market following the occupation's dissolution of the big *zaibatsu* in the late 1940s. The ensuing wave of corporate raids and attempts at hostile takeovers, the authors cogently argue, prompted the former *zaibatsu* firms to defend themselves by restoring some of their ties in the form of *keiretsu* and by instituting cross-shareholding against the raiders.

By adopting a long-range historical perspective, the authors provide a set of persuasive explanations for the rise and persistence of the prewar *zaibatsu* and the postwar *keiretsu.* These explanations cluster around (a) the combines' advantages in environments of weak markets, low trust, and scarce managerial talent, (b) the ongoing quest for control of the firms and pyramids by the family owners and sometimes their trusted managers, and (c) the combines' symbiotic relations with the state.

The paper, moreover, offers useful ways of defining and understanding the *zaibatsu*. Amid the confusion over what constituted a *zaibatsu*, the U.S. occupation ended up restricting the category—and thus its dissolution policy—to only the big four combines: Mitsui, Mitsubishi, Sumitomo, and Yasuda. However, there is much utility in the authors' inclusive definition of a *zaibatsu* as any "large pyramidal group of publicly traded firms." By opting for a more expansive definition, the paper ably revisits the question of whether there were substantial differences between the so-called old and new *zaibatsu* in the 1920s and 1930s. The authors demonstrate that these distinctions may have been more apparent than real, as the old *zaibatsu* moved into military-related chemical and heavy industry—much as the new *zaibatsu* were doing—and these operations constituted rapidly growing shares of each concern's profits. Furthermore, the old *zaibatsu* resembled the new *zaibatsu* in financing their heavy/chemical industrial firms by relying on equity.

The chapter's contributions notwithstanding, the argument could have been strengthened in several areas. I begin with questions about the overall analysis. The title is baffling because it obscures the agency of the actors in this story. Are we to assume that leaders of Japanese corporations, like the proverbial frog in the title, only viewed their reflection at the bottom of the well and remained ignorant of the world? Or, in the authors' words, have "the Japanese literally searched the world for the best institutions of capitalism, and changed their institutions more radically . . . than in any other major industrial economy"? And if so, *who*, precisely, played the key roles in changing these institutions—the U.S. occupation, the Japanese state, or the *zaibatsu/keiretsu*? Second, the chapter is subtitled "A History of Corporate Ownership in Japan," yet the paper presents little evidence of alternative models of ownership outside the *zaibatsu* and *keiretsu*. One wonders about ownership patterns within the small- and medium-business sector, which employed many more people and was central to the prewar export sector (more so than the *zaibatsu*). By the 1920s and 1930s, small businesses had organized themselves effectively as a political bloc and were influencing government policy. In the 1950s, curiously, the man who unified the small-business associations was none other than Aikawa Yoshisuke (also written Ayukawa Gisuke), pioneer of the prewar Nissan *zaibatsu* (Garon and Mochizuki 1993, pp. 145–66; Samuels 2003, p. 236). Although this chapter focuses on the *zaibatsu/keiretsu*, we must note that the big combines coexisted in uneasy political and economic relationships with smaller firms.

Because the paper covers the century-and-a-half evolution of the *zaibatsu* and *keiretsu*, it is also appropriate to raise several historically based questions about the analysis. The authors have not read widely in the general historiography of modern Japan, and several of their historical judgments rest on decades-old interpretations or the anachronistic assumptions of present-day economists. One of the more egregious anachronisms appears in their statement that the Tokugawa shogunate's "antiglobalization backlash continued to hermetically isolate Japan" between the 1630s and the 1850s. Globalization is hardly the apt term to describe the world of European monopolistic trading companies, nor did the shoguns "hermetically" isolate Japan, which continued to trade with the Dutch, Koreans, and Chinese.

The chapter's most serious historiographical problems lie in the analysis of the wartime economic order (1931–45) and its legacies for postwar corporate governance. The authors insist that wartime Japan was a "rigidly centrally planned economy," in which the state "de facto nationalized all its major corporations, subordinating them to central planners." By 1945, they conclude, "Japan had an economy little different from that of Russia in the 1920s," and the nation, "though a former right-wing dictatorship, was nonetheless virtually as centrally planned as many Eastern European countries were in 1989." By 1938, claim Morck and Nakamura, "most senior economic planners under the military government were Soviet trained." As further evidence, they cite the wartime compulsory cartels known as "control associations" (tōseikai), arguing that the cartels' "control committees, of course, would end up staffed by military personnel." Referring to the weakening influence of the zaibatsu families due to the wartime regime's controlled economy, the authors describe the drama as one of "marching into serfdom"—the comfortable scions apparently playing the role of the serfs.

These are extraordinary statements. Rarely are they totally wrong, but in all cases they suffer from exaggeration or inadequate evidence. Let us begin with how the zaibatsu fared under wartime controls. By nearly all accounts, the zaibatsu not only prospered during World War II but increased their domination over the economy. Despite some attempts by the army to diminish their influence in the early 1930s, the zaibatsu—both "new" and "old"—benefited tremendously from the exploitation of the militarily occupied territories of Manchuria, China, and Southeast Asia. Although the zaibatsu often protested state intervention in the economy, in practice they took advantage of wartime controls to strengthen themselves against rivals. The U.S. occupation's foremost authorities on the subject emphatically concluded that the industrywide control associations had permitted the zaibatsu to reserve for themselves the lion's share of resources and finance, thereby weakening and even destroying smaller firms within each cartel. The control associations, noted T. A. Bisson (1954), were "manned almost exclusively by top Zaibatsu personnel"—not military men—and "in essence they merely added government sanction to the kind of behavior practiced by the combines when on their own" (p. 13). The big employers also used the bureaucratically imposed labor-management councils in each workplace to decimate the remnants of organized labor (Garon 1987, chap. 6).

In addition, the authors remain unclear about the fate of dividends. They assert that "dividends were restricted so that earnings could be reinvested patriotically." At other points, they suggest that dividends for *zaibatsu* families were "apparently now sharply curtailed," and the most recent draft claimed the wartime dividends were "outlawed." A little more research would have shown that state policies toward dividends were less revolutionary than the chapter supposes. To be sure, a 1938 law controlled dividends, but it hardly eliminated them. A firm that planned to pay more than a 10 percent dividend needed to obtain a permit from the Ministry of Finance (Okazaki 1994, p. 364). Moreover, concludes Johnson (1982) in his well-researched study, "dividends on equity shares continued to be paid until virtually the end of the Pacific War," and "these *zaibatsu* ownership rights turned out to be virtually the only civilian rights that were respected throughout the wartime period" (p. 139).

Indeed, it is difficult to square the wartime regime's maintenance of the *zaibatsu*'s rights of private ownership with the chapter's insistence that the Japanese state's controls should be considered in the same category as Soviet central planning. Admittedly, wartime bureaucrats and economists studied Soviet planning. It is also true that the government's Planning Board (Kikakuin) included some relatively socialistic bureaucrats, and many wartime planners disliked the *zaibatsu* for their allegedly selfish, patriotic behavior. However, wartime planners were much more taken by their extensive surveys of Nazi German controls (and, to a lesser extent, the Italian Fascist and even New Deal models). If one looks at the actual policies adopted vis-à-vis capital and labor, they more closely resembled Nazi policies than Soviet programs. This is hardly surprising. Like the Japanese officials, the Nazis denigrated shareholders in favor of workers and managers, yet maintained private ownership by big business. The German corporation law of 1937 likewise permitted the payment of dividends, while diminishing governance by shareholders and reinvesting more of the profits in the companies. Japanese bureaucrats, of course, enjoyed greater access to information on the policies of its German ally than it did to the hostile Soviet Union. As for the influence of the Socialist-leaning experts, many were arrested or removed in 1941 as the result of pressure from big business (Johnson 1982, chap. 4).[1] In short, the *zaibatsu* in wartime should not be likened to their Russian counterparts who were obliterated under Soviet rule. They remind us more of Nazi-era big business, which some

---

1. On the importance of German and fascist models, see Garon (1987), chapter 6, and Fletcher (1982).

have compared to "the conductor of a runaway bus who has no control over the actions of the driver but keeps collecting the passengers' fares right up to the final crash" (Grunberger 1971, p. 184; see also p. 177).

Moreover, the authors misjudge the nature of the wartime state and pay scant attention to the "transwar" role of the civilian bureaucracy in economic policy. They subscribe to the dated view that the "military assumed dictatorial powers over the economy." Accordingly, they miss what the mainstream scholarship on the Japanese political economy has highlighted for the past two decades: the enormous wartime influence of the "economic bureaucrats" located in the Ministry of Commerce and Industry and its successors.[2] It was these officials, not military men, who devised the industrial policies that promoted the development of heavy and chemical industries, placed small firms under the control of the *zaibatsu,* and weakened shareholder control in favor of the managers. These bureaucrats were also forced to conclude that they could not fully subordinate the *zaibatsu* to state control. The result was not the reduction of the *zaibatsu* to "serfdom," but rather the evolution of cooperative relationships between the bureaucrats and big business that continued after 1945. Significantly, the economic bureaucrats generally escaped the U.S. occupation's purges and actually saw their authority over the economy strengthened as the Americans supported the continuation of state intervention to revive the economy. The economic bureaucrats gained a powerful base with the formation of the Ministry of International Trade and Industry (MITI) in 1949.

The inclusion of the economic bureaucrats would have nuanced the authors' interesting analysis of the emergence of the postwar *keiretsu.* As it stands, their chapter explains the rise of *keiretsu* primarily in terms of the companies' joint defense against corporate raiders in 1952–53. In so doing, however, they ignore the formidable role of the state in the immediate postwar years. They particularly overlook transwar continuities in the thinking of the economic bureaucrats, who sought to diminish the influence of the *zaibatsu* families and the equity market in favor of bank-centered finance and the state's use of the financial system to promote certain types of industrial development. Long before the attempted hostile takeovers of the early 1950s, the economic bureaucrats were already nudging the dissolved *zaibatsu* companies toward reconsolidating themselves around banks, rather than the old family holding companies (Johnson 1982, pp. 174, 199, 204–6).

Finally, after a detailed, historical examination of corporate governance, the chapter suggests that the prewar *zaibatsu* and postwar *keiretsu* "may have retarded macroeconomic growth." This is an intriguing question, yet there is little in the present essay that rigorously and historically relates cor-

---

2. See Johnson (1982).

porate governance to overall growth. Curiously, the authors chose not to critique (or even cite) Chalmers Johnson's influential history of Japanese industrial policy, which placed the *zaibatsu* and *keiretsu* at the center of Japan's economic growth before 1975.

References

Bisson, T. A. 1954. Zaibatsu *dissolution in Japan.* Berkeley: University of California Press.

Fletcher, William Miles III. 1982. *The search for a new order: Intellectuals and fascism in prewar Japan.* Chapel Hill: University of North Carolina Press.

Garon, Sheldon. 1987. *State and labor in modern Japan.* Berkeley: University of California Press.

Garon, Sheldon, and Mike Mochizuki. 1993. Negotiating social contracts. In *Postwar Japan as history,* ed. Andrew Gordon, 145–66. Berkeley: University of California Press.

Grunberger, Richard. 1971. *The 12-year reich: A social history of Nazi Germany, 1933–1945.* New York: Holt, Reinhart.

Johnson, Chalmers. 1982. *MITI and the Japanese miracle: The growth of industrial policy, 1925–1975.* Stanford, CA: Stanford University Press.

Noguchi, Yukio. 1995. *1940 nen taisei* [1940 system]. Tokyo: Toyo keizai shinposha.

Okazaki, Tetsuji. 1994. The Japanese firm under the wartime planned economy. In *The Japanese firm,* ed. Masahiko Aoki and Ronald Dore, 350–77. Oxford: Oxford University Press.

Samuels, Richard J. 2003. *Machiavelli's children: Leaders and their legacies in Italy and Japan.* Ithaca, NY: Cornell University Press.

8

Financing and Control in The Netherlands
A Historical Perspective

Abe de Jong and Ailsa Röell

L'ambition de la république est de s'enrichir et non de s'agrandir.
—Denis Diderot, *Voyage en Hollande*, 1780

Introduction

The goal of this paper is to place the current structure of Dutch ownership and control in a historical perspective. The historical development of Dutch financial markets and institutions is somewhat idiosyncratic. It mixes elements such as a stock exchange culture dating back to the Dutch golden age of seaborne trading dominance, a legal system handed down from a brief period of French occupation, and strong influences from neighboring Germany as well as England and the United States. The paper first sets out, in section 8.1, to describe in brief the historical development of Dutch industrial finance. The remainder of the paper then turns to a comparative analysis of Dutch listed firms over the course of the twentieth century by focusing on three years spaced at thirty-five-year intervals: 1923, 1958, and 1993. A general description of the data and their sources is given in section 8.2, focusing on a wide array of financial characteristics of the firms. This is followed in section 8.3 by a closer analysis of corporate control mechanisms and, in particular, shareholder rights and defenses against hostile takeovers. Networks of influence are the focus of section 8.4, and the main themes discussed in that section are the nature and composition of the supervisory and management boards: the degree to which there are interlocking directorships with banks and other industrial firms,

Abe de Jong is an associate professor in the Department of Financial Management at Erasmus University, Rotterdam. Ailsa Röell is professor of finance at Tilburg University and a senior research scholar at Princeton University.

We would like to thank Randall Morck, Jan Luiten van Zanden, and an anonymous referee for helpful comments. We thank Henry van Beusichem and Esther Koomen for excellent research assistance.

and the presence of identifiable founding-family members on the board. Section 8.5 concludes.

8.1   Historical Overview

8.1.1   General Introduction

The Dutch have some claim to a pioneering role in stock exchange capitalism. The first shareholdings in a Dutch corporation came into being in 1602, when the Vereenigde Oostindische Compagnie (VOC), the first great limited-liability joint stock company in the world, was founded. The initial investors were, in 1602, unaware of their destiny: ostensibly, they were contributing money to a limited-term partnership that would send out a series of merchant ships to the East Indies, with a liquidating dividend promised at the end of twenty years. To the investors' dismay (and despite their vociferous protests), in 1622 the company's directors (who reported to the government rather than to the shareholders) decided to prolong the company's charter, thus shelving the liquidation and keeping this astonishingly lucrative[1] enterprise going for many years.

By the middle of the seventeenth century the Netherlands had developed an active shareholding culture, with speculation in VOC shares and even derivatives trading a widespread popular pursuit. In the eighteenth century, the fortunes of the Dutch East India trade declined, and the VOC finally went under in 1799. Even so, the wealth amassed by the Dutch during the Golden Age was still largely undissipated and primarily invested in a wide range of international government securities. A spate of defaults, notably by the French government, reduced this wealth and seriously undermined confidence in securities investment, but even in the nineteenth century there were still many wealthy rentier families whose riches were primarily held in the form of securities.[2]

In the early nineteenth century the Dutch nation emerged from the French occupation of 1795–1813; it assumed its present geographical contours with the separation of Belgium from the Netherlands in 1830. The first half of the nineteenth century was a period of continued economic stagnation: Dutch investment in infrastructure and the new steam-driven manufacturing technologies was minimal, and the country's industrial development lagged far, far behind that of Belgium, Germany, France, and,

---

1. By the time of its last dividend in 1782, an initial investment of f 100 in the VOC would have yielded f 360,033.33 in payouts (Steensgaard 1982). Steensgaard gives an insightful discussion of how the novel corporate form of the VOC made this enduring profitability possible—for example, by facilitating long-term investments in the military protection of trading routes and monopolies.

2. The rentier class were popularly referred to as coupon-cutters: "ces rentiers hollandais que le peuple appelle ironiquement *coupon-knippers,* parce qu'ils n'ont rien à faire, sauf à détacher les coupons semestriels de leurs fonds publics" (de Laveleye 1864, p. 329).

of course, England. This period of retarded growth has been studied intensively by economic historians, and the consensus now seems to be that it cannot be attributed to a shortage of capital or to Dutch investors' supposed preference for foreign investments above domestic industry. Other factors seem more likely culprits. One was the disarray of government finances: the new Kingdom of the Netherlands inherited from the French a crushing debt burden of 420 percent of net national income, with concomitantly high interest rates on government paper; the situation was not brought under control until around 1850 (see Jonker 1996). Another was the need to redefine the traditional division of labor within the low countries: the southern provinces, now Belgium, had traditionally specialized in manufacturing while the North focused on commerce. Thus, there was no strong manufacturing base to build on. Then there were the steep transport costs related to the extra cost of providing a proper infrastructure, with adequate drainage and flood defenses, in such low-lying and waterlogged territory; and various other factors such as the high cost of raw materials, and the high wage levels and the poor education of the citizenry.

Industrial development started coming to life in the second half of the nineteenth century, with new shareholder capital raised for a number of enterprises such as railway construction, albeit rather laboriously, buffeted by the vicissitudes of international political developments and the business cycle. The main source of capital for industry during that period seems to have been retained earnings, supplemented with contributions by members of the founding families and closely connected wealthy individuals. Interestingly, the rather meager contribution of publicly raised equity was not offset by long-term bank loan finance: such financing was also very scarce throughout the country's industrialization.

The long period of stagnation of the eighteenth and early nineteenth centuries, and the short period of French hegemony, create a natural break in capital market traditions and institutions. Only in the late nineteenth century did substantive modern industrial development get off the ground. Although several institutions were already present in the Dutch Golden Age, we take this revival as a starting point for our analysis. We turn now to a few specific themes that are of central importance for the genesis of today's landscape of corporate finance and control: first, the evolution of the Dutch framework of company law, and second, the role of the stock exchange, banks, and private financing in providing capital for industry.

8.1.2   Evolution of the Public Limited Company

Public shareholder finance requires an appropriate legal basis, and at the start of the seventeenth century, there was little in the way of precedent to draw upon. The earliest Dutch joint-stock enterprises of the seventeenth century (in addition to the VOC, several other trading companies and a number of insurance companies emerged) were explicitly created to further the public interest, with trading monopolies granted by the government and control exercised by public appointees. Almost from the start, Dutch shareholding culture was embroiled in a series of corporate governance skirmishes, as conflicts of interest became apparent and their resolution was hammered out.[3]

The legal form of the Dutch corporation evolved over time from the early days of the VOC.[4] Around 1720, the legal status of the limited company or *naamloze vennootschap* (NV for short) was largely remodeled along the precedent set by English company law; and the setting up of companies whose primary purpose was private profit, rather than the service of the public interest, became the norm. By and large, the companies set up at the time in Holland were reputable, unlike some of their English counterparts spawned by the prevailing stock market bubble. One Dutch innovation of the time was the Amsterdam broker Abraham van Ketwich's creation, in 1774, of the world's first investment trust:[5] the Negotiatie onder de Zinspreuk "Eendraagt Maakt Magt" (Investment under the Motto "Unity Is Strength"). The subsequent collapse of company profits and share prices led to a slowdown in the creation of new limited companies (and of new investment trusts: after 1779, there was a ninety-year hiatus).

Following the French occupation of the turn of the nineteenth century, Dutch civil law was codified along lines closely following the French civil code of 1804. The Wetboek van Koophandel (commercial code) of 1838 set the legal parameters for public limited companies. From the start, it was felt to be inadequate to its purpose. At first, there was particular resistance to the "foreign" notion that the founding of a public limited company

---

3. These disputes bear an amusing resemblance to the issues that are still being debated today. Those initial VOC shareholders who were not actively involved in the running of the company—known as the long-suffering or *dolerende* shareholders—had many reasons for complaint. Their objections are vividly preserved in the company's archives. The initial complaints centered around payout policy (when the interim dividend payouts were passed or fell short of the amount stipulated in the company's charter, and when the promised liquidating dividend of 1622 was shelved) and the murkiness of the company's accounts: letters and pamphlets calling for financial disclosure and speaking of abuses and damaging disorders were circulated, but they were ignored by the *Heeren* XVII—the "seventeen gentlemen" directors—until the strength of shareholder outrage prompted the government to require full and open accounts for 1622. Even so, a groundswell of protest about inadequate financial disclosure continued for decades after. Later documents regulate the conflation of management's personal interests with those of the company proper (there were numerous company directives reminding its employees that they were under no circumstances allowed to transport or trade goods on own account, and the *Heeren* XVII brought out a report in 1741 on abuses by company management at home and abroad). There is even the seventeenth-century equivalent of the corporate jet (directors' travel on company business by inland yacht, and the declaration of travel expenses, was carefully regulated—for example, in a document dating from 1698). See Frentrop (2003) for an English-language history of Dutch corporate governance.

4. Our description is based on the introductory chapter of van der Heijden's (1992) handbook of Dutch company law.

5. Albeit one containing a somewhat curious lottery element, intended to stimulate speculative interest.

Fig. 8.1   Caricature of a Dutch supervisory board, by J. Braakensiek, 1898 (currently in the Gemeente Archief Amsterdam)
Commissioner A (*to his neighbor*): "Is everything in order over there, with that safe. . . . ?"
Commissioner B: "Now listen here, that is up to the management. We have our hands full supervising the company; if we have to start looking after the safe as well . . ."

would require royal approval, even if the conditions that would ensure such approval were set down in the law. Camfferman (2000) mentions that, in particular, the relevant government ministry's practice of asking that financial accounts be sent in on an annual basis was very unpopular. The law also failed to address a number of issues such as the personal liability of founders, issuers, management, and directors; the shareholders' obligations with regard to paying in their capital,[6] and nonmonetary contributions to the company. The last quarter of the nineteenth century saw a spate of company bankruptcies, some of which involved the outright looting of company funds. The weaknesses of corporate governance safeguards in protecting investors, and in particular the inadequacies of monitoring by boards of directors, was already an open matter of public concern, as evidenced by figure 8.1, an 1898 cartoon depicting a supervisory board in action.

After a very long period of public debate, with legislative proposals submitted, withdrawn, and resubmitted regularly from 1871 onward, a new, more comprehensive and flexible company law was finally enacted in 1928. Preventive government scrutiny was retained: the minister of justice would vet the proposed charter of an NV before it could be registered with the

---

6. For example, in the case of the NCS railway initial public offering (IPO) in 1860, described in the appendix 1.

chamber of commerce and thereby officially founded. The new regime was based on four principles (Van der Heijden 1992, para. 28, p. 19):

1. Preventive government monitoring, including the possibility of judicial suppression
2. Transparency of the internal organization and division of powers (including financial reporting)
3. Protection of the capital against excessive payouts to shareholders
4. Strengthened liability of founders, management, and directors

One of the most controversial issues was the openness requirement, in particular the obligation to publish full annual accounts (a balance sheet and a profit and loss statement) open to the general public. Traditionally many companies had kept this information private within a small inner circle—for example, by allowing only a small number of shareholder delegates to look at the accounts. Almost immediately, a commission was set up to examine if the obligation to publish accounts could be weakened. The law was criticized for not distinguishing between large, open companies that placed securities with the general public and closed or family companies that did not. Others countered that limited liability requires, in principle, openness of the financial situation of both kinds of NV. Other objections concerned the law's restrictions on oligarchic clauses, the rights of redress awarded to minority shareholders, and the strengthened liability of management and directors.

Company law was again fully revised in 1970–71. The main impetus was twofold.

Firstly, there was the need to adjust to the European Economic Community's First Directive on Company Law of 1968. The biggest change in this regard was to create a new, separate type of limited company, following the law of surrounding countries (Germany, France, and Belgium): the *besloten vennootschap* (BV) or closed company, in addition to the traditional NV. The impact of this change was immediate. The great majority of smaller companies converted from NV to BV, primarily as a result of the lower level of financial disclosure required of the latter (NVs were now required to make their annual accounts readily available to the public at large by depositing them at the offices of the *handelsregister*). In addition, new arrangements were set in motion for the protection of minority shareholders (through *enquêterecht:* the right to ask for a judicial enquiry under certain conditions).

The second force driving change was the wish to increase the influence of employees. Dutch attitudes to the role of corporations had evolved over the course of the twentieth century. In the beginning of the century, corporations were seen as vehicles for shareholder wealth creation. Over the course of the century, firms became seen as more independent entities oriented toward continuity, stability, and the interests of multiple stakeholders, as expressed in a salient Hoge Raad (Supreme Court) decision of 1949. It is perhaps the relative homogeneity of the Dutch population that has fostered a sense of solidarity, expressed in a preference for consensus decision-making and a generous welfare system. The corporatist model of centralized, consensual economic decision-making, known as the *poldermodel,* was very successful in the reconstruction of the Dutch economy after World War II. In particular, centralized collective bargaining made possible a lengthy period of wage restraint that contributed substantially to economic growth. In return, employee representation in decisions regarding job security and employment is considered appropriate. And indeed, any corporate restructuring that involves the loss of jobs imposes a significant cost on the public purse in the form of unemployment and/or disability pay. This means that corporate decision making has a direct public interest dimension. Not surprisingly, the stakeholder view of corporate governance, which sees shareholders as just one of many interested parties entitled to a say in decision making, dominates Dutch public opinion.

The *structuurregime* or "structured regime," introduced in 1971, was designed to increase worker participation by imposing a carefully defined control structure on all larger firms (roughly speaking, those with at least 100 employees). Such firms must set up an *ondernemingsraad* (OR) or company council, a body created to represent and consult the views of employees.[7] These and other large firms (those with capital and reserves of at least f 25 million) are also obliged to set up a supervisory board (*raad van commissarissen,* RvC) with some powers that might otherwise be held by the shareholders' meeting. Such a board appoints new members itself by co-optation (unless the shareholders' meeting or council objects), and the statutes may determine that one or more are to be government appointees. The board supervises important managerial decisions, appoints and dismisses the management board (*raad van bestuur,* RvB), and establishes and approves the yearly accounts (De Jong et al. 2004).

A perhaps unintended side effect of the *structuurregime* is that, because it gives shareholders almost no say in the appointment or removal of supervisory board members and management, it protects entrenched management to an excessive degree. The co-optation system is currently the topic of intense public debate and is unlikely to survive in its current form.

The most recent developments in the Netherlands are two best practices codes for publicly listed firms. The first code is a product of the Peters Committee, named after former Aegon chief executive officer (CEO) Jaap Pe-

---

7. It has a right to relevant information, a right to advise on major decisions (e.g., transfers of ownership, relocation, and important investments); it can delay decisions it disagrees with for one month and appeal to the *ondernemingskamer* (company chamber) of the Amsterdam Court. Its permission is required for changes to social arrangements (pensions, working hours, wages, safety rules), and if it disagrees the employer must obtain a local judge's decision to go ahead.

ters. This code contains forty recommendations, about the role of management, supervisory boards, and, most important, a reconsideration of the role of capital in governance. As thirty-nine (out of the forty) recommendations did not involve legal changes, the code's implementation draws on self-regulation. De Jong et al. (2004) show that this effort failed, as no observable changes were present and stock market reactions, if present, were negative. After the irregularities with Ahold an initiative was taken to restore investors' confidence in the Dutch market. In March 2003 a committee chaired by Morris Tabaksblat, former CEO of Unilever, started a new code and had already released the final draft in December 2003. Following the successful U.K. codes, the comply-or-complain principle is introduced, forcing firms to explain to shareholders any deviations from the best practice. Although the contents of the code largely overlap with Peters's ideas, the enforcement is more promising.

8.1.3   Equity Financing and the Role of the Stock Market in Industrial Finance

The Amsterdam stock exchange was a sophisticated and active market throughout the nineteenth century. The *prolongatie* system funneled large amounts of savings to the market. The market was overcrowded, open and competitive: the principle of unrestricted public access was carefully upheld by the city authorities, and premises were shared with commodities trading. However, the stock exchange did not initially play much of a direct role in the financing of industry. The bulk of the official list seems to have been made up of foreign state loans, American railway stocks, American industrial shares, and colonial securities. The first date at which domestic industrial stock was officially listed on the Amsterdam stock exchange is generally reported to be a brewery listing in 1889, though Jonker (1996) suggests this date is misleading; four industrial issues (from a sugar refinery, a shipyard, and an engineering firm) were already quoted in the early 1880s. In any case a listing meant little before 1903, when listing requirements and a vetting process by the Vereeniging voor Effectenhandel (set up in 1876 to oversee the market and instill investor confidence) were formalized.

Meanwhile there was a large and active unlisted securities market on which domestic securities were both auctioned and directly placed; an example of a prime unlisted stock traded there during the last decades of the nineteenth century is Heineken. Shares were often initially privately placed, and Jonker (1996) cautions that a lack of domestic industrial stock exchange listings should not be interpreted as a definitive indicator of investor disinterest. A number of NVs set up in the 1840s and 1850s found ready backers; they did not seek a listing until the end of the century. By 1937–39, private placements still encompassed 16.6 percent of bond issues and 4.8 percent of equity issues, and private "underhand" loans remained important right up until the eve of World War II: in 1938, institutional investors' portfolios still contained equal amounts of underhand loans and listed securities (Renooij 1951, pp. 186 and 190). Clearly, then, the Amsterdam stock exchange was not the sole venue for primary issues or for secondary trading. The dearth of domestic industrial listings cannot be interpreted as a sign of structural impediments to equity financing.

Van Zanden (1987, 1998) points out that external finance, albeit not obtained from the general public, played a major part in the industrialization of Amsterdam. Initially, money for capital-intensive new ventures would be supplied by the city's traditional trading elite. For example, merchants set up two companies for steamship transport and shipbuilding in hopes of stimulating trade. Similarly, rich and successful entrepreneurial dynasties would move into related industries: for example, the profits from sugar refining were plowed back into beer brewing and flour milling concerns. Meanwhile, the government and King William I at times provided crucial credit lines. And in 1883 Amsterdam's financial elite contributed a capital of f 0.5 million for a banking venture, the Finantieele Maatschappij voor Nijverheidsondernemingen, whose explicit purpose was to provide finance for industry in the form of credit, in anticipation of repayment when a public share issue was completed.

Still, it is fair to say that infusions from a network of family, friends, and business associates, complemented by retained earnings, were, in the Netherlands as in most other countries, the dominant source of risk capital for much of industry in the late nineteenth century. For example, the textile industry developing in the East and South of the country was almost exclusively financed in this way. The exception, rather than the rule, were large, capital-intensive infrastructure projects like railways, which typically relied on an initial primary issue of shares to the general public, sometimes combined with some form of limited government support, to get off the ground. The appendix describes the initial share ownership structure following four nineteenth-century railway flotations.

8.1.4 The Role of Banks

A surprising feature of Dutch financial history (particularly when contrasted with the emergence of powerful universal banks in Germany in the late nineteenth century) is the limited role played by banks in the financing of industrial growth, not just in the early period of industrialization of the late nineteenth century but well into the twentieth century. Dutch economic historians attribute the patchy record of late nineteenth-century banking initiatives—banks were set up, but many failed, and the industry remained exceedingly fragmented well into the twentieth century—to a number of causes.

One major cause was the dominance of the *prolongatie* system of financing, which flourished throughout the late nineteenth and early twentieth centuries. *Prolongatie* refers to short-term callable margin loans, on the face of it a rather unlikely source of industrial finance. As a legacy from the successes of the Golden Age, the nineteenth-century Netherlands still had a strong stock market culture and a well-developed network of local agents (notaries, lawyers, and brokers) who would collect savings from wealthy individuals and channel them to the stock exchange. Much of the money was not invested in securities directly but made available to firms or other investors in the form of short-term margin loans. These, though of course callable at short notice, were typically rolled over or "prolonged," whence their name. They were backed by securities, commodities, or other exchange-traded collateral. Thus industry and trade in effect obtained direct short-term capital in a very fragmented way, via margin loans provided by investors without the intermediation of a banking system. The *prolongatie* loans were considered safe; the interest rate was attractive and roughly tracked the London discount rate (hovering between 3 and 5 percent between 1820 and 1860; see Jonker 1996, figure 12.4, p. 96). The system worked so smoothly that intermediation and liquidity transformation by a nascent banking system was effectively crowded out. This remained the case well into the twentieth century, as argued by Jonker (1995). On the eve of World War I, the amount outstanding on *prolongatie* at any point in time was around 400 million guilders, more than double the known deposits of all the banks taken together. Jonker (1996; see figure 9.2, p. 191) points out that the short-term interest rate on the Amsterdam exchange remained at or above the yield on government bonds until nearly 1920, effectively precluding substantive profitable deposit taking by banks. The *prolongatie* market did not disappear until short rates fell dramatically toward the end of the 1920s.

Another brake on banking development was Dutch savers' distrust of financial institutions. The sovereign bond defaults of the late eighteenth century and the parlous state of government finances in the early nineteenth century (with government debt hovering around a staggering 400 percent of national income) meant that even the paper money circulated by the Nederlandsche Bank (set up in 1814 at the behest of King Willem I, an energetic supporter of initiatives to revive the Dutch economy) was long considered an unsafe substitute for specie. Private banking institutions were considered even more dubious, a view confirmed when the first wave of new banking ventures of the 1860s was followed by several banking failures in the long recessionary period starting in 1870.

The industrial boom that started in 1895 precipitated a period of intense interest in industrial finance in the early twentieth century, right up until 1920. During this period many new companies were listed and public share offerings were readily absorbed. Banks, for this short period only, were prepared to offer long-term financing to industry. Meanwhile, a wave of banking consolidation from 1911 onward, together with a major shakeout of minor and regional banks in the crisis that started in 1920 (in 1920–22 a total of bad debts amounting to nearly 10 percent of the assets of the biggest five banks was written off), left the general banking industry dominated by the "Big Five" banks.

Financing for industry completely dried up in the deflationary 1920s and did not revive until after World War II. Banks' reluctance to provide long-term financing for industry was the subject of intense debate; while large companies could fill the gap by issuing stocks and bonds, small and medium-sized enterprises were seriously constrained. The government went so far as to attempt to set up a bank for industrial finance in 1935 (it succumbed to the bad economic climate). The banks limited their role to collecting deposits (though, as Jonker 1995 shows, in the interbellum years Dutch banking deposits, and in particular time deposits, were still extraordinarily low relative to the total money supply compared with neighboring countries), making short-term loans (maturities of over three months were avoided as much as possible), and underwriting new issues. While they dominated the new issue market from the 1930s onward, they acted only as a conduit, never retaining equity stakes in industry or making long-term loan commitments.

In short, the Dutch banks most resembled the British banks, not the universal banks of neighboring Belgium and Germany, as stressed in Van Goor and Koelewijn's (1995) overview of Dutch banking in the twentieth century. Dutch bankers focused on mercantile finance and consistently veered away from long-term commitments. As "general" banks they did do a lot of underwriting and investment banking business (also carried out by some private specialized firms); there was no counterpart of the Glass-Steagall Act formally mandating the separation of commercial and investment banking.

In 1945, the Herstelbank (bank for reconstruction), a joint venture between the government and the financial sector, was set up to fill the perceived gap in finance for long-term investment by providing long-term loans (a subsidiary, the Nationale Participatie Maatschappij, was created to take equity stakes). It played an important role in the recovery of Dutch industry over the decade following World War II. Perhaps its example (and that of its various successors), together with other government policies, stimulated the commercial banks' slow evolution toward medium- and long-term lending in the 1950–60 period. Meanwhile, banks did adhere to the fundamental principle of nonengagement in industry; indeed, industry spokesmen at the time explicitly expressed reservations about bank influence on commercial and strategic decision making.

The boom years of 1955 to 1970 saw a period of increased diversification, as specialized institutions such as the mortgage banks lost ground. A spate of large-scale bank mergers led to a fear that banks had too much market power and were exposing themselves to an unacceptably wide range of risks. Thus, starting in 1971 the Nederlandsche Bank, as industry regulator, put out a number of unofficial directives (some of which were later codified in the Wet Toezicht Kredietwezen 1978) that prohibited mergers of general banks with insurance companies or mortgage banks, restricted bank participation in the equity of other companies (financial or nonfinancial) to 5 percent without explicit permission from the NB, and limited the value of share stakes held by banks to 60 percent of their capital.

The 1980s were a difficult period of retrenchment for the banks, and again the accusations that banks were excessively cautious led to the adoption of various government measures (such as loan guarantees) to encourage the provision of risk-taking capital. Meanwhile the international expansion of Dutch industry brought with it a continuing trend toward the formation of large banking conglomerates offering a wider range of financial services.

In 1990 banking and insurance regulation was radically loosened. Participation in the European Union (EU) has meant that Dutch banks' market power is no longer considered a threat. As an immediate consequence, more mergers in 1991 created the three current giant banks (ABN-Amro, ING Bank, and Rabobank). And restrictions on banking-insurance alliances were lifted in accordance with EU practice. This has led to the formation of conglomerate groups holding substantial share stakes in large numbers of companies. Thus, a gradual trend away from the Anglo-Saxon model and toward a more Continental style of banking is in evidence.

8.1.5   Nonbank Institutional Investors: Insurance Companies and Pension Funds

Insurance companies and pension funds have played a role in taking equity stakes, absorbing bond issues, and providing long-term loans at least since the beginning of the twentieth century. Our data for 1993 show that both the ING Bank and the Aegon insurance group had substantial long-term stakes in other companies (note that ING was formed in 1991 by a merger involving, among others, the large insurance company Nationale Nederlanden).

Institutional investors rose to a prominent place in the Dutch capital markets during the early decades of the twentieth century.[8] Traditionally, nineteenth-century life insurers had invested primarily in securities that

---

8. Renooij (1951, p. 63) reports figures illustrating the rising importance of such investors: between 1900 and 1939, deposits with private savings banks rose from f 80 to f 515 million and those with the state Rijkspostspaarbank from f 85 to f 670 million, while the capital of the life insurance companies rose from f 130 to f 1,359 million. Meanwhile, various social insurance funds were founded in the first quarter of the century in response to social legislation, and by 1939 the Algemeen Burgerlijk Pensioenfonds (the government employees' pension fund) held f 794 million in assets, the railway workers' and miners' pension funds held a combined f 203 million, and private industry's Ongevallenfonds and Invaliditeits- en Ouderdomsfonds together some f 491 million, while the self-employed workers' voluntary Ouderdomsfonds B held f 68 million.

were judged to be particularly safe and liquid; many of them invested exclusively in Dutch government bonds, and indeed many were restricted to do so by their statutes. The twentieth century saw a gradual lifting of these restrictions, but investment in private issuers' securities remained only a small fraction of their investments. In the pre–World War I burst of enthusiasm for industrialization, a typical life insurer, Eerste Nederlandsche, invested as much as 4 percent of its assets in banking and 7 percent in manufacturing securities; these were predominantly bonds rather than equity. Interest in privately issued securities then dwindled down to almost zero, until it revived in the late 1930s; by 1939, the precursor companies of Aegon held about 5 percent of their assets in manufacturing company securities, while over time the balance had shifted from bonds to equity (Gales 1986). Still, around 1950 life insurers' investment in industrial securities remained modest, indeed, the proportion was lower than at the turn of the century. Insurers did also make some contributions to industrial finance in the form of direct long-term loans (*onderhandse leningen*)[9] and mortgages. But the trend toward equity and nongovernment bonds did not gather force until the second half of the twentieth century.

Regarding pension funds, to illustrate their contribution to equity financing, consider the combined Philips pension funds, founded in 1913, described in appendix 2d of Van Nederveen Meerkerk and Peet (2002). Equity comprised a mere 2 percent of the fund's total investment in 1925; most of the fund was invested in (government) bonds. By 1950, equity took a 7 percent share, rising to 28 percent in 1975 and 46 percent in 2000. By then, the Philips pension fund was holding f 16,771 million in equity, together with f 106 million in venture participations. Here again we see very modest interest in risk-bearing capital in the first half of the century, with a marked shift toward investment in corporate equity in the second half of the century.

In any case, it does not seem to be the case that institutional equity ownership has been matched by an active role in corporate decision making. The discussion surrounding the recent management crises at Ahold and other major Dutch companies gives some insight into why the independent, public-sector employee pension fund Algemeen Burgerlijk Pensioenfonds (ABP) is one of the few Dutch institutional investors to attempt an activist stance. As pointed out by an insurance company spokesman, banks and insurance companies are not only shareholders; for them, the firm in which they invest is at the same time a (potential) client: "You are in a difficult position if you want to present a new contract to the management board whilst you have voted against one of their proposals the day be-

---

9. These were exempt from stamp duty until 1939 and hence a popular substitute for bonds in the interwar period. The major place taken by direct long-term private loans in institutional investors' portfolios is distinctive to the Netherlands and Germany.

fore."[10] Meanwhile, activism by private companies' pension funds is likely to be reined in by the parent company's management, in return for reciprocal restraint by their counterparts' pension funds. Institutional shareholder activism thus remains somewhat limited in scope and potential.

8.2 Empirical Analysis: The Data

8.2.1 The Sample of Firms

Our study focuses on all domestic firms that have equity officially listed on the Amsterdam Stock Exchange in the years examined. It should be pointed out that this concept is somewhat different from the usual definition of "listed firms" for the Netherlands, which also includes firms whose bonds only are listed. Traditionally, many of the security issues listed and traded on the Amsterdam exchange have been bonds; though the proportion of listed firms that list only their bonds and not their stock as well is relatively small (for example, 17 percent in 1910). One reason to exclude these firms from our sample is that they are somewhat less likely to comply with the obligation to publish annual accounts.

The universe of firms for which we present data also excludes the financial sector. In 1923 this sector comprised mainly banks and mortgage banks. In the second half of the century insurance firms and collective investment vehicles such as mutual funds are important additional constituents of this group. Our main data sources for information about the nonfinancial firms are Van Oss's *Effectenboek* for 1923 and 1958 (Van Oss 1924, 1959) and the electronic database REACH (Review and Analysis of Companies in Holland) for 1993.

It should be noted that many of the largest Dutch firms are not listed, so that our sample cannot be said to represent all the most important Dutch companies. Sluyterman and Winkelman (1993) identify the 100 largest Dutch firms in terms of their assets. Even though they point out that their methodology probably underrepresents privately held firms because their balance sheet data are harder to obtain and their accounting practices are generally more conservative, they still find that only about three-fourths of these firms are listed. Agricultural firms (and their food-processing outgrowths) in particular are often organized as cooperatives, as are the banks that specialize in agricultural loans (the Rabobank and its precursors).

8.2.2 The Three Sample Years

Our data were gathered for three years spaced at thirty-five-year intervals: 1923, 1958, and 1993. In choosing these particular years we were influenced by three considerations.

---

10. The speaker is D. Brilleslijper, Delta Lloyd spokesman, in *FEM Business,* 20 September 2003.

First, we would like to have years that were in some sense typical of an epoch. The year 1923 comes toward the end of the first great boom in industrial development; it is still a year of relative prosperity, predating the subsequent collapse in share prices, the Depression, and the Second World War. In 1958 the economic dislocation wrought by the war has receded: postwar reconstruction is virtually complete, and a new era of prosperity and growth has set in. Meanwhile, 1993 is a year in which the impact of EU membership has already shaped many developments.

A second consideration is the availability of data. For example, large ownership stakes were only available following the 1991 disclosure law (Wet Melding Zeggenschapsrecht), which came into effect in February 1992 (De Jong et al. 2001). This makes 1993 an interesting year to study.

Finally, our aim was to try to pick years that as much as possible enabled us to complement rather than duplicate the available body of work on Dutch economic history.

8.2.3   Data Availability

For most limited-liability companies, the publication of annual accounts was not legally required in the Netherlands until 1928. However, from 1909 the stock exchange's Fondensreglement required all companies that wished to list their stocks or bonds to make available to shareholders annual published accounts comprising the balance sheet and profit- and loss statements. By 1910, about 80 percent of listed firms complied in whole or in part, though the level of compliance was considerably lower (around 50 percent) among manufacturing firms. By 1923, our first sample year, compliance (as measured by the availability of accounts in Van Oss' Effectenboek) had risen considerably.

Information on share ownership prior to the share ownership disclosure law of 1991, the Wet Melding Zeggenschapsrecht (WMZ), is very hard to obtain because as a rule Dutch public listed companies issue bearer, not registered, shares, and we have no easy access to public registries to trace share ownership. In principle, some information about share ownership can be retrieved from company archives. In particular the records of shareholder meetings would give insight into, at least, the identities of shareholders actively involved in decisions about the company. Such archival research, however, is far beyond the scope of this paper.

Thus, for 1923 and 1958 the only way we investigate family influence and control is by tracking the identities of the management and the board of directors, both available for much of the late nineteenth and the twentieth centuries from published sources.[11]

---

11. This information is in principle available for all public limited companies (*naamloze vennootschappen*) from both the yearbooks of NVs compiled by Van Nierop and Baak over the period 1880–1948 and from the yearbooks relating to listed securities, Van Oss's *Effectenboek* 1903–78 (later continued as Effectenboek).

8.2.4   Summary Statistics

As shown in table 8.1, the number of firms on the Amsterdam Stock Exchange's official list has actually declined over the last few decades studied. The decline in numbers is offset by a substantial increase in size; the average book value of assets increased more than a hundredfold over the sev-

Table 8.1   Summary statistics

	1923	1958	1993
Book value total assets (× f 1,000)	13,673	79,700	2,286,000
	(3,158)	(9,314)	(360,000)
Past three-year growth book value total assets	−0.077	0.161	0.170
	(−0.074)	(0.102)	(0.080)
No. of observations	303	318	141
Tobin's q	0.372	0.421	1.270
	(0.338)	(0.411)	(1.132)
No. of observations	214	245	143
Return on assets	0.073	0.159	0.073
	(0.047)	(0.113)	(0.074)
No. of observations	317	321	143
Four-year standard deviation ROA		0.037	0.032
	n.a.	(0.024)	(0.023)
No. of observations		298	141
Payout ratio	0.375	0.716	0.369
	(0.311)	(0.440)	(0.363)
No. of observations	300	323	143
Debt to total assets	0.300	0.339	0.535
	(0.280)	(0.325)	(0.536)
Fixed assets to total assets	0.552	0.404	0.381
	(0.578)	(0.352)	(0.355)
Cash and liquid assets to total assets	0.114	0.124	0.107
	(0.050)	(0.084)	(0.041)
Age	21.80	47.12	48.75
	(18)	(46)	(36)
No. of observations	317	333	84
Managerial board size	2.158	2.318	2.776
	(2)	(2)	(2)
Supervisory board size	4.874	4.540	5.167
	(5)	(4)	(5)
Family firm: (former) firm name equals board member's surname (%)	28.1	27.6	6.3
Family firm: at least two board members with same surname (%)	31.5	29.1	5.6
Family firm based on both criteria (%)	16.4	16.2	1.3
Family firm based on at least one criterion (%)	43.2	40.5	10.4
No. of firms	317	333	143

Notes: Medians are reported in parentheses below the means. n.a. = not available. ROA = return on assets.

enty years from 1923 to 1993, a period during which prices (as measured by the gross domestic product [GDP] deflator) rose by a factor of 12. To some extent these trends are attributable to mergers and consolidation, but a tendency to limit the exchange's official list to very large and liquid companies may also play a role.

The data regarding the three-year growth in assets show that 1923 followed upon a difficult period; indeed, there had been a serious economic downturn, and overall stock market equity prices had fallen by about one-half during the immediately preceding decade.

That Tobin's q was extremely low in 1923 is not surprising; however, the low average value of 0.421 for 1958 is less easily explained. Tobin's q is measured as the ratio of market value of total assets to book value of total assets. The market value of total assets is measured as book value of total assets minus book value of equity plus market value of equity. A problem arises here, because the book and market values of equity need to be "comparable." Especially in 1923, many firms have multiple types of equity. The market value is not available for each type of equity. In 1923 and 1958, we leave the types of equity for which we have no market prices in book value terms and attributed reserves to equity types on a pro rata and book value basis.

The median return on assets (ROA) fluctuated between a low of 4.7 percent in 1923 and a high of 11.3 percent in 1958, down to 7.4 percent in 1993. The ROA in 1923 is the ratio of net profits to equity; in other years it is operating income to book value total assets.

The median payout ratio of 0.31 that we obtain for 1923 is somewhat on the low side in both historical and international perspective. In the nineteenth century, the norm was to pay out most or all of earnings, perhaps with some retentions from extraordinary profits to create a reserve for use in smoothing dividends in bad years. In the first two decades of the twentieth century, it gradually became accepted practice to retain earnings for the purpose of expansion. However, payout ratios were generally still very high, and Post (1972, table 5) cites a payout ratio of 0.78 in 1923 for all Dutch NVs (not just listed ones). One point to note is that 1923 was not a good year for the economy, coming at the end of the depression of 1921–23. Many of the firms in our data set made losses, and nearly half of the firms passed their dividend; the median payout ratio for the firms that did pay out a nonzero dividend was 0.75, which is very close to Post's figure.

Our data source, Van Oss' Effectenboek, sometimes gives fairly detailed information about the disposition of profits, both as stipulated in the company charters and as carried out ex post. A striking feature of the 1923 data is the substantial proportion that is statutorily destined for the executives and directors in the form of *tantièmes* or profit-sharing agreements. The norm for statutory payouts of this nature is in the region of 15 percent of profits, which suggests that such payments should perhaps be interpreted in part as a reflection of the ownership rights of the individuals concerned rather than just as remuneration for executive effort. But in practice the actual payments made often fall far short of the profit-sharing payouts stipulated ex ante in the company statutes.

By 1958 the mean (median) payout ratio was 0.72 (0.44), declining to 0.37 (0.36) in 1993. Payout ratios declined secularly until the 1980s, as firms chose to retain earnings to finance expansion. A probable contributing factor was the introduction of a corporation tax, phased in around 1941. A classical system is in force: corporate earnings are taxed at 35 percent, whether distributed or not, and dividends are subsequently taxed as personal income at a heavy 60 percent marginal rate, while there is no capital gains tax. Indeed, of the thirty-three countries studied by La Porta et al. (2000), the Netherlands tax regime has the rock-bottom ratio of net-of-tax payout from dividends relative to capital gains. Accordingly, one would expect Dutch personal investors to have little enthusiasm for dividend payouts and a preference for retained earnings. Such a preference would be less likely on the part of those institutional investors that are exempted from income tax. While the Dutch tax system does not attempt to mitigate the double taxation of dividends at the corporate and personal income tax levels, it has traditionally been exceptionally careful in ensuring that intercorporate dividends are not double-taxed at the corporate level. This feature of the tax regime is one reason why the Netherlands (and in particular the Netherlands Antilles) is popular as a base for international holding companies.

Leverage as measured by the ratio of debt to total assets exhibits a marked increase from a median of 0.32 in 1958 to 0.54 in 1993. Again, the corporate tax shield from debt may explain this increase in leverage in the postwar half-century.

The sizes of the managerial and supervisory boards remained fairly constant over the seventy-year period studied.

Meanwhile, founding family influence seems to have declined dramatically. Our proxies for family influence are two: one is the presence of board members with the founding family surname; the other is multiple board members with a common surname. These indicators of family presence declined only slightly from 1923 to 1958, but there was a large reduction from 1958 to 1993. Both criteria for family influence dropped by a factor of about 5, from roughly 30 percent to 6 percent, leaving a total of only 10.4 percent of firms in 1993 still exhibiting one or both indicators of family influence.

8.3   Oligarchic Clauses and Takeover Defenses

8.3.1   Description of Takeover Defenses and Shareholder Rights

Dutch corporations are insulated against the threat of hostile takeovers by an array of unusually strong and somewhat idiosyncratic defense mechanisms. In this section we will describe the main devices currently in use[12] and attempt to trace their historical origins. It should be pointed out at the outset that ever since 1881, Dutch corporate law does not permit the use of nonvoting or lower-voting shares, thus ruling out one obvious means of detaching control from ownership. Moreover, early Dutch corporate law from 1838 onward mandated voting caps in order to protect minority shareholders from oppression by a dominant shareholder: one person should not have more than six (three) votes in a company with more (less) than a hundred shares. This means that before the new law of 1928, pyramids or large majority stakes were not a secure means of entrenching control, necessitating the development of alternative safeguards.

As a small country surrounded by powerful and at times warring neighbors, it should not be surprising that vulnerability to foreign influence has always been a source of serious concern among Dutch industrialists, particularly in the early part of the twentieth century. A number of defensive measures have been rationalized on this basis. As mentioned earlier, the Dutch stakeholder model (*poldermodel*) also induced a movement that shifted shareholder power to independent supervisory board members.

Statutory Defenses

By *statutory defenses* we mean those that are enshrined in the company's statutes. Among the statutory defenses, those that restrict the powers of the *algemene vergadering van aandeelhouders* (AVA) or shareholders' meeting are known as *oligarchische regelingen* (oligarchic measures/arrangements/devices). Such clauses give all or part of the control of the company to others than to the shareholders representing the majority of the capital at the shareholder meetings.

The most prominent oligarchic device is the use of *prioriteitsaandelen* or *priority shares*[13] with statutorily defined extra powers of decision within the corporation. Such shares were first introduced in 1898, when the main Dutch oil company operating in the Netherlands Indies (the progenitor of Royal Dutch/Shell) changed its statutes to ward off the threat of foreign influence. Such shares are often associated with a right of *bindende voordracht* (binding proposal) in the nomination of management and directors. Other oligarchic devices include arrangements to allocate decision-making powers to another organ of the company (such as the board or the priority shareholders) for explicitly specified important classes of decisions that would normally require shareholder approval: such matters can include the composition of management and board, their remuneration, dividend payout policy, modification of company statutes, or dissolution

---

12. Our description is based on Voogd's (1989) detailed investigation of Dutch companies' statutory defenses.

13. Confusingly, such shares were initially known as "preference shares," but this usage is now no longer allowed. They are also sometimes called "founders' shares" or, say, "A-shares."

of the company. Finally, there are devices such as voting restrictions and strengthened supermajority and quorum requirements for shareholder meeting decision making.

Since World War II the *issue of shares into friendly hands,* and in particular of *preference shares* (*preferente aandelen*), has developed into a major defensive strategy. This is a nonoligarchic statutory device in that it attempts to influence the composition of the shareholder meeting rather than restricting its powers. From 1949 to 1981 there were some twenty-six instances where companies defensively issued ordinary shares to friendly individuals, banks, institutional investors, potential merger partners, or allied foundations. The motive for such defensive issues was to dilute the power of large shareholders, preserve independence in the face of a hostile takeover attempt, or ensure takeover by a white knight. The use of ordinary shares for defensive purposes waned after the mid-1970s because the issue of ordinary shares is costly in terms of cash requirements (the issue price must be fair to existing shareholders, and for registered shares, a down payment of at least 25 percent of the nominal value plus 100 percent of the *agio,* the difference between the issue price and the nominal value, is required), frowned upon by legal commentators, and much circumscribed by the adjustments to Dutch company law made in 1981 to implement the Second European Directive on Company Law. In particular, the new law gave preemptive rights to participate in ordinary share issues to existing shareholders, unless the shareholders' meeting explicitly waived the right; and a five-year expiration limit was placed on any allocation of the power to make issue decisions to organs other than the shareholders' meeting.[14]

In the early 1970s preference shares quickly replaced ordinary shares as the instrument of choice for defensive issues. Provisions for issuing preference shares for defensive purposes first appeared in the statutes of a Dutch company, Rijn-Schelde, in 1969. There were two reasons for the switch to preference shares. First, under the new law, ordinary shareholders do not automatically have preemption rights to new issues of preference shares (though the stock exchange did attempt to impose on listed companies a shareholder approval requirement for issues of preference shares of more than 50 percent of the existing capital). Second, preference shares can be designed to provide a much larger ratio of voting power to paid-in capital than ordinary shares; indeed, the net outlay can be made essentially negligible. Preference shares can be issued more or less at par, if liquidation

14. Even so, Voogd (1989) finds that on January 1, 1988, 59 percent of the companies on the stock exchange's official list had statutes empowering an organ other than the shareholders' meeting to issue ordinary shares (in 76 percent of these cases, the management; in 15 percent, the priority shareholders; in 8 percent, the board of directors; and in 1 percent, the board and management jointly), while 51 percent of companies had made similar arrangements for the power to deny preemptive rights to shareholders (distributed 74 percent, 17 percent, 8 percent, and 1 percent respectively among the various alternative organs).

rights are limited to the paid-in capital and the preferred dividend is suitably tied to the market interest rate. If the legal minimum of 25 percent of par value is paid in, the number of votes obtained for any paid-in sum of money is maximized. But that is not all. The preference shares are generally placed with financial institutions, institutional investors, or a foundation specially set up for the purpose. For such a foundation to be self-financing it would need to borrow the amount required for paid-in capital; therefore the dividend on the preference shares must be carefully tied to the required interest on the loan, and cumulative preference rights are necessary to ensure that the foundation can reasonably be expected to meet its obligations. Voogd (1989) found that 48 percent of the listed companies he examined had *defensive preference shares,* defined as preference shares that were *op naam* (registered) and not *aan toonder* (bearer) shares, not fully paid in, with limited dividend and liquidation rights, and with dividend rights tied to the market interest rate. Of the companies issuing defensive preference shares, 66 percent had issued preference shares equal to 100 percent of the authorized ordinary shares, thus carrying 50 percent of voting power (20 percent of companies had preference shares ranging between 50 and 100 percent of the ordinary shares, and only 14 percent of companies issued 50 percent or less).

A further device for influencing the composition of the shareholder base is the issue of registered (*op naam*) shares[15] together with limitations on the transfer or ownership of such shares. Such *blocking devices* (*blokkeringsregeling*) can include a requirement for permission from a company organ for the transfer of shares, a requirement to offer shares to fellow shareholders before selling them to third parties, or statutory limitations on who can own the shares (Dutch nationals, residents, etc.).

Finally, an important statutory defensive device is the *X percent rule* (*X percent-regeling*), which limits the ownership of shares (usually the ordinary shares, which are normally the ones that are listed and that thus change hands often) by a single shareholder. Voogd (1989) finds that 25 percent of listed companies (excluding mutual funds) have such a rule in their statutes. Usually the company's shares are registered (*op naam*) and placed with a specially created foundation or *administratiekantoor,* which issues nonvoting bearer certificates that are listed on the stock exchange. These are freely exchangeable into voting shares, but only up to the specified X percent boundary.

Other less common statutory defensive measures include *voting limits,* though as these can be circumvented by the use of straw men, they are now out of favor. All twelve officially listed companies that included voting caps in their statutes in early 1988 were ones already in existence before 1929;

---

15. Such shares cannot be listed; typically, these companies issue bearer certificates that are traded on the stock exchange.

taken together, these companies represented around 40 percent of the market value of Amsterdam listed companies (Voogd 1989). Some corporate statutes include a varied brew of other measures limiting voting rights to long-term shareholders, Dutch nationals, and so on.

Nonstatutory Defenses

A classic and quite common nonstatutory defense mechanism is the use of an *administratiekantoor* (AK), typically a special-purpose foundation that owns all or most of the company's shares and issues nonvoting *certificates* to the general public. The certificates carry all the underlying shares' economic rights (dividends, liquidation value, etc.) but no control rights. Especially in cases where these certificates are *niet royeerbaar*—that is, not exchangeable for ordinary vote-carrying shares—the effect is to give all voting power to the trustees of the AK, who are typically closely intertwined with the company's management, although the stock exchange imposes some independence requirements on the AK.[16] From the mid-fifties onward the increasing use of certification of this kind has been roundly criticized from many quarters, including the legal profession and the Vereniging voor de Effectenhandel, the securities dealers' association running the stock exchange. Since 1992, listings of *niet-royeerbare* certificates are not allowed anymore. In a recent adaption of Dutch company law, all certificate holders are allowed to vote by proxy with their certificates. Only under special circumstances (in case voting by certificate holders interferes with the general interests of the firm) can the proxy voting be refused or limited.

The use of *pyramidal holding companies* to concentrate control is relatively rare in the Netherlands, given that certification is a readily available means of securing control without any appreciable outlay of capital. However, a small number of such holding company constructions do exist,[17] and with certification likely to be phased out, pyramids may become more prevalent. Similarly, *cross-shareholdings* along the French model are unusual but not unknown in the Netherlands.

The Structured Regime

In 1971, the "structured regime" was imposed on all large companies with a large number of employees in the Netherlands. The primary reason for its introduction was to give workers some power of consultation and in-

16. For example, at a chaotic shareholder meeting for Ahold in September 2003, 97 percent of votes supported a remuneration package for the incoming CEO that was widely denounced as excessively generous. No representatives of the AK were present; before even knowing the broad scope of the remuneration proposal, they had already authorized the secretary of the management board to exercise their votes, representing 50 percent of the total.

17. Most notably, Heineken, where the Heineken family has 50.01 percent control of the unlisted Heineken Holding NV, which in turn controls the listed firm Heineken NV with 50.01 percent.

fluence through the *ondernemingsraad* (workers' council). In addition, some of the powers normally given to the shareholders' meeting (such as management appointments and the approval of the annual accounts), as well as the power to approve a set of other important management decisions, were vested in the *raad van commissarissen* (supervisory board), which appointed its own members by a system of co-optation that basically bypassed any shareholder influence. An exemption for the structured regime is allowed for multinational companies with a majority of employees working abroad. Also, companies that do not meet the criteria for compulsory subjection to the structured regime can still voluntarily apply it. Many have chosen to adopt the regime voluntarily or not to abolish the regime when as a result of international expansion the percentage of foreign workers passed the 50 percent threshold. The structured regime gives corporate insiders much more freedom at the expense of shareholder rights. Under very specific conditions firms have to adopt the mitigated structured regime, where the powers to appoint management and approve annual accounts would normally remain with the shareholders' meeting, although the co-optation system for supervisory board appointments remains in place.

Recently, the structured regime has been a topic of public debate. The influence given to employees via the *ondernemingsraad* is quite weak; a recently adopted proposal for the revision of the regime includes reserving positions on the supervisory board for employee appointees, a move that will clearly enhance worker power. At the same time the structured regime's allocation of shareholders' normal powers to an unaccountable, self-perpetuating supervisory board is the target of heavy criticism. A prominent Dutch legal scholar, Jaap Winter, has gone so far as to describe the structured regime as a "cynical compromise"[18] that transfers shareholder rights to corporate insiders without giving employees or shareholders any real decision-making powers.

8.3.2 Data and Analysis

Our data enable us to give an overview in table 8.2 of the takeover defenses employed by the companies in our sample; in the Netherlands, takeover protection has traditionally been very strong. Our sources are Van Oss's *Effectenboek* for 1923 and 1958 (S. F. van Oss 1924, 1959) and for 1993 the *Gids bij de Officiële Prijscourant* (J. H. de Bussy 1993a).

One of the most prominent mechanisms, priority shares, has increased dramatically in importance; by 1993 43 percent of firms had such shares.[19]

18. "The starting point was the idea that labor and capital were equally valuable, and both should have equal power. In reality a cynical compromise was reached: the heart of their powers has been taken away from the shareholders, while little more was received by employees" (*FEM Business,* 13 September 2004).

19. The low figure for 1923 should be treated with some caution, as the nomenclature for priority or founders' shares was somewhat less clearly established.

Table 8.2   Takeover defenses and ownership structure (%)

	1923	1958	1993
Priority shares	2.52	28.23	42.66
Voting limits	(By law)	0.30	6.29
Certificates	11.67	24.92	38.46
Limited or fully exchangeable certificates	8.52	18.02	
Not exchangeable		5.71	3.50
X arrangement			10.49
Certificates and traded ordinary shares	10.76	21.62	2.10
Joint ownership construction		2.10	3.50
Preference shares (antitakeover)			60.14
Structured regime			53.15
Compulsory			41.96
Voluntary			9.79
Mitigated			1.40
Ownership concentration			
Largest outside blockholder			24.49
All outside blockholders			43.10
Ownership identity of blocks			
Banks			7.16
			(77 nonzero)
Insurance companies			2.75
			(50 nonzero)
Pension funds			0.73
			(11 nonzero)
State			0.61
			(3 nonzero)
Industrial firms			12.58
			(51 nonzero)
Managerial board members			5.31
			(20 nonzero)
Supervisory board members			2.47
			(12 nonzero)
No. of firms	317	333	143

Meanwhile, voting limits were, in 1923, still a feature of all firms by law. Their prevalence in the statutes of listed firms had fallen to 6.3 percent by 1993, and in most cases these were firms surviving from the pre-1928 period when statutory voting limits were mandatory.[20]

The use of certificates or depository receipts has increased substantially over time; 38 percent of firms had some measure of certification present in 1993, rising steadily from 12 percent in 1923. A joint ownership construction was present in 3.5 percent of firms by 1993.

20. In 1958 it is possible that Van Oss does not contain complete information about voting limits. Therefore, the percentage reported is likely to underestimate the actual presence.

The issue of preference shares is a crucial defensive strategy in takeover situations. The use of preference shares for defensive purposes was initiated in 1969; by 1993, 60 percent of listed industrial firms had this defensive mechanism in place.

The structured regime, which gives some influence to the workers' council and devolves much of the authority of the shareholders' meeting to a self-constituted supervisory board, was introduced in 1971. By 1993, 53 percent of listed industrial firms were subject to the structured regime, and 10 percent of these had voluntarily chosen to have the structured regime apply.

Table 8.7 in section 8.4.3 compares and contrasts the prevalence of takeover defenses in family and nonfamily firms. The main distinction is that in family firms there are more likely to be priority shares, conferring upon the holders of these shares a varying set of decision-making powers that would otherwise fall upon the ordinary shareholders' meeting.

For 1993, ownership data are available, and it is possible to investigate the interactions between takeover defenses and ownership structure. Table 8.8 in section 8.4.3 shows that, on the whole, takeover defenses and concentrated ownership are substitute control mechanisms and thus negatively correlated. Large outside block holders are negatively correlated with all defense mechanisms considered, and significantly so with the use of defensive preference shares and priority shares. Similarly, when management board members hold large stakes, certificates are less likely to be used. The results regarding the structured regime need to be interpreted with caution as it is generally compulsory for the largest firms. Such firms are less likely to be heavily management owned and more likely to be partially owned by a bank. The finding that takeover defenses and concentrated ownership are substitutes rather than complements agrees with earlier work by De Jong and Moerland (1999).

Table 8.9 in section 8.4.3 explores the impact of takeover defenses on corporate performance by regressing Tobin's q cross-sectionally on dummies for the presence of the various common defense mechanisms (the third column of results for each of the three sample years in table 8.9). Earlier research by De Jong, Moerland, and Nijman (2000) on a cross section of fifty listed Dutch firms suggests that defense mechanisms such as certificates, defensive preference shares, and, most significantly, the structured regime do reduce other performance measures such as the stock market return and the return on equity; they find that only the size of the supervisory board has a significant, negative impact on Tobin's q. De Jong et al. (2004) confirm these results for a sample of all Dutch listed firms over 1993–99. In our larger sample, again, there is not much evidence of an impact of defense mechanisms on q, though in 1958 the presence of priority shares seems somewhat detrimental.

8.4   Networks of Influence: Interlocking Board Memberships

8.4.1   Boards and Networks

In this section we will focus on the phenomenon of interlocking directorates—that is, of having the same individual occupy board seats in multiple firms. Two aspects of this practice will be looked at.

First, the number of appointments per board member is studied. Members with multiple appointments may have reputational capital; that is, they may be excellent managers or monitors. On the other hand, multiple appointments may reduce the time available for individual firms, reducing the effectiveness. Ferris, Jagannathan, and Pritchard (2003) provide recent evidence in U.S. firms and find no negative effects of multiple appointments. For the Netherlands, there is no evidence relating network relationships to firm performance but a wealth of descriptive evidence regarding interlocking directorates. To name but two prominent studies, Schijf (1993) describes networks in 1886 and 1902 and Stokman, Wasseur, and Elsas (1985) focus on networks in 1976 in the context of an international comparative project.

A second aspect of interlocking directorates that is of particular interest is the relation between banks and nonfinancial firms. Bank relations may bring expertise to the board of nonfinancial firms. Besides, bank relations may offer monitoring, which reduces contracting costs. On the other hand, banks may abuse their power and information to expropriate wealth from other lenders and shareholders; recent studies on U.S. firms are Booth and Deli (1999) and Kroszner and Strahan (2001). The relations between banks and nonfinancials have been studied in the Netherlands by, among others, Van den Broeke (1988) and Jonker (1989). Van den Broeke selects four industrial firms and one bank and describes the interlocking directorships. The bank, Rotterdamsche Bankvereeniging, has joint board members with three out of four firms through eight interlocks in the period 1918–39, even though throughout this period it did not make a single long-term loan to any of the firms concerned, in line with Dutch banking practice at the time. Jonker (1989) selects eight banks and measures interlocks with nonfinancial exchange-listed firms in 1910, 1923, 1931, and 1940. For example, in 1923, the eight banks had forty-three board members and these persons held 431 board positions outside the banks.

Interlocking directorships can involve both executive and supervisory board members. Dutch firms have dual board systems on the German model. The first tier comprises the executive board (*Directeuren* or *Raad van Bestuur*), the management team that is responsible for the firm's strategy and daily operations. These executives are supervised by the second tier, the supervisory board (*Raad van Commissarissen* or *Raad van Toezicht*).

In 1923, supervisory boards were not a legal requirement (Bos 1923, p. 34). Nonetheless, all exchange-listed firms in 1923 do have a supervisory board. The members are normally appointed by the shareholders' meeting. In special cases, the owners of preferred shares, priority shares, or bonds have the right to appoint all or a limited number of supervisors. Intermediate arrangements existed where other parties than the shareholders propose members, while the shareholders can reject the proposal.

In 1993, a supervisory board is a legal obligation for firms that adopt the so-called *structuurregeling* or structured regime, introduced in 1971. This regime is compulsory for firms that meet size criteria (in particular, those that have more than a cutoff number of domestic employees). In 1993, again, all the listed firms have supervisory boards.

8.4.2   Data Sources

Our aim is to describe the relevance of interlocks for nonfinancial firms. First, we describe the interlocks with other nonfinancial firms. Second, we focus on interlocks between banks and nonfinancials.

The focus for nonfinancial firms is simply on all exchange-listed firms. For 1923 and 1958 we use Van Oss's *Effectenboek* (S. F. van Oss 1924, 1959). For 1993 we mainly use REACH and *Jaarboek van Nederlandse Ondernemingen* (J. H. de Bussy 1993b).

For the identification of board members of banks we do not want to restrict ourselves to listed banks because, especially in 1923, several important banks were unlisted partnerships. Therefore we select the largest banks. For 1923 we use the *Financieel Adresboek voor Nederland* issued by J. H. de Bussy (1923). This book contains the section *Financiëele instellingen in Nederland,* which includes for each financial institution its name, its placed equity and reserves, and the names of its board members. The book includes listed and nonlisted institutions. For 1958 we use the same book (J. H. de Bussy 1958) and collect bank information from the section *Bank- en credietwezen.* For 1993 we use *Omzetcijfers 1993,* issued in 1994 by Het Financieele Dagblad. This guide contains the banks and other financial institutions in the Netherlands, including total assets. The board members of most banks are in the *Jaarboek van Nederlandse Ondernemingen* and, if not, are obtained from annual reports.

For 1923 we identify 504 banks, of which 423 banks have available a book value of equity (placed equity plus reserves). Total equity value is 1,319 million guilders. The first 60 firms have 1,213 million guilders of equity value, or 92 percent of the total. The smallest firm in the selection of 60 has equity worth 200,000 guilders. Of these 60, 32 are listed on the Amsterdam stock exchange. The 5 largest banks have 49 percent of the total equity value, and the 10 largest have 67 percent.

In 1958, we traced 148 banks, with total equity value of 1,099 million guilders. The largest 50 banks have 96 percent (1,061 million guilders). The

5 largest banks have 48 percent of the total equity value, and the 10 largest have 69 percent.

In 1993, we have seventy-one banks (general and savings banks), and for fifty-six we have a book value of total assets. Total value is 1,309,788 million guilders. We select the ten largest banks but exclude two banks for governmental financing. We also include three smaller banks that are known for long-standing relations with nonfinancials. The eleven banks have a total asset value of 1,084,151 guilders, or 91 percent (excluding governmental banks). The difference with 1923 is striking and in particular caused by the dominance of three large banks: ABN-AMRO, Rabobank, and ING.

8.4.3   Results and Analysis

Table 8.3 describes the interlocks of board members of nonfinancial listed firms for 1923, 1958, and 1993.

The first six rows in table 8.3 describe our sample of (nonfinancial) firms and banks. The average board size has fluctuated somewhat: the average total number of board members per firm decreased slightly from 7.03 in 1923 to 6.86 in 1958, increasing by 1 to 7.94 by 1993. It is important to notice that the number of banks in our sample declines from fifty-seven to

Table 8.3   Boards and interlocks

	1923	1958	1993
Number of firms	317	333	143
Number of managerial board members	684	772	397
Number of supervisory board members	1,545	1,512	739
Number of banks	57	50	12
Number of managerial board members	238	159	60
Number of supervisory board members	432	361	122
Firms: number of managerial board members			
With one interlock	137	127	38
With two interlocks	56	38	13
With three interlocks	32	21	6
With four interlocks	39	6	3
With five interlocks	11	19	0
With more than five interlocks	61	25	0
Total interlocks	1,248	599	94
Average number of interlocks	1.82	0.78	0.24
Firms: number of supervisory board members			
With one interlock	371	328	170
With two interlocks	205	175	89
With three interlocks	136	131	90
With four interlocks	141	69	32
With five interlocks	49	77	6
With more than five interlocks	170	220	0
Total interlocks	3,440	3,606	776
Average number of interlocks	2.23	2.39	1.05

twelve over the seventy-year period studied; as mentioned in our discussion of the data selection procedure, ongoing concentration in the banking system means that the proportion of total banking equity value represented by our sample remains roughly constant at over 90 percent. Not surprisingly, as the banks in the 1993 sample are so much larger, they have more board members: 15.2 on average, as opposed to 11.7 (10.4) in 1923 (1958). Meanwhile, for both banks and industrial firms, the ratio of supervisory board members to management board members remained fairly steady, ranging between 1.82 and 2.27.

Table 8.3 shows us whether board members have more or less additional board seats. For managerial board members (including the chairman), our findings indicate that members in 1923 held many more positions than in 1958 or 1993: the average number of interlocks dropped from 1.82 in 1923 down to 0.24 in 1993. For supervisory board members the average number of interlocks decreased less dramatically: in the postwar period the average number fell by roughly one-half. In 1923 we also find quite a few board members with more than five interlocks; by 1993, no board member had more than five additional seats.

In the remainder of this section we focus on industrial-firm board members who have affiliations with banks.

Table 8.4 contains the frequency distributions of bank interlocks in firms. Banking interlocks were more widespread in the earlier periods of our investigation: the proportion of firms with no bank interlocks was 40 percent (39 percent) in 1923 (1958), rising to 55 percent in 1993. Thus, in 1923 and 1958, the presence of bankers was more widespread than in 1993. In 1923, twelve firms even had ten or more bankers on the board. The average number of board members with a bank affiliation decreases from 0.60 (0.61) in 1923 (1958) to 0.45 in 1993. However, it should be noted that the significant concentration in the banking industry over the 1958–93 pe-

Table 8.4	Frequency distribution bank interlocks		
% of firms with:	1923	1958	1993
No bank interlocks	40.38	39.34	55.24
One bank interlock	22.08	26.43	25.87
Two bank interlocks	12.30	13.81	9.09
Three bank interlocks	7.89	6.61	5.59
Four bank interlocks	5.05	5.11	3.50
Five bank interlocks	4.42	3.00	0.70
Six bank interlocks	1.26	0.90	0
Seven bank interlocks	0	1.20	0
Eight bank interlocks	0.63	0.60	0
Nine bank interlocks	2.21	0.90	0
Ten or more bank interlocks	3.79	2.10	0
Average number of bank interlocks	0.596	0.607	0.447

Table 8.5   Banks and their interlocks

Banks	Interlocks
1923 (over 15)	
Rotterdamsche Bankvereeniging	119
Nationale Bankvereeniging	56
Bank voor Indië	55
De Twentsche Bank	50
Nederlandsche Handel-Maatschappij	43
Hollandsche Bank voor Zuid-Amerika	31
Koloniale Bank	31
De Nederlandsche Bank	26
Kas-Vereeniging	26
Amsterdamsche Bank	19
Bank-Associatie Wertheim & Gompertz 1834 en Credietvereeniging 1853	18
Nederlandsch Indische Handelsbank	16
1958 (over 10)	
Rotterdamsche Bank N.V.	149
De Nederlandsche Bank N.V.	73
De Twentsche Bank N.V.	63
Nederlandsche Handel-Maatschappij N.V.	51
Amsterdamsche Bank N.V.	46
Nationale Handelsbank N.V.	20
Bank voor Handel en Scheepvaart N.V.	20
N.V. Export-Financiering-Maatschappij	19
N.V. Nederlandsche Bankinstelling voor Waarden belast met Vruchtgebruik en Periodieke Uitkeringen	19
Van Mierlo en Zoon N.V.	19
Nederlandse Overzee Bank N.V.	14
N.V. Hollandsche Disconteeringsmaatschappij van 1939	12
N.V. Hollandsche Koopmansbank	12
Kas-Associatie N.V.	11
Maatschappij voor Middellang Crediet N.V.	11
Hollandsche Bank Unie N.V.	11
1993 (over 10)	
Abn-Amro	34
Internationale Nederlanden Bank (ING)	18
Nationale Investeringsbank	18
MeesPierson	14

riod would have led to a decline in the number of bank board members available for positions on industrial firm boards.

The use of interlocks by banks is illustrated in table 8.5, which lists all banks with at least ten (fifteen) interlocks in 1958 or 1993 (1923). It is clear that there has been a substantial decline in the latter period of the century in the number of major-bank board members who sit directly on industrial-firm boards.[21]

---

21. Our data do not allow us to determine whether all or part of this decline may be offset by the placement of bank officials from below the board level on industrial firm boards.

Table 8.6	Interlocks at firm level			
Own firm—other firm—type of other firm		1923	1958	1993
Supervisory board—supervisory board—industrial		5.997 (83.9)	6.327 (79.9)	3.441 (74.1)
Supervisory board—management board—industrial		1.079 (46.7)	0.901 (42.3)	0.454 (37.8)
Management board—supervisory board—industrial		1.530 (31.5)	0.921 (24.6)	0.454 (20.3)
Management board—management board—industrial		1.000 (25.6)	0.366 (12.3)	0 (0)
Supervisory board—supervisory board—bank		1.202 (46.7)	1.285 (53.7)	0.622 (40.6)
Supervisory board—management board—bank		0.461 (29.0)	0.198 (17.4)	0.077 (7.7)
Management board—supervisory board—bank		0.293 (11.4)	0.201 (8.4)	0.084 (7.7)
Management board—management board—bank		0.287 (3.8)	0.012 (0.9)	0 (0)

Note: Average number of interlock and in parentheses percentage of firms with at least one interlock.

Table 8.6 further documents the decline in interlocks, contrasting banks' and other industrial firms' board members' roles on industrial-firm boards. Industrial-firm interlocks have declined steeply over the seventy years of our investigation; the overall decline in the average number of interlocks is by roughly a half. While multiple supervisory board memberships are still very common, interlocks involving management board members in particular have fallen steeply. Indeed, by 1993 there was no industrial firm in our sample sharing a common management board member with a bank or other industrial firm.

Meanwhile, the role of banks in industrial firm board interlocks was falling even more rapidly than that of industrial peers. Again, bank-industry interlocks involving a management board member fell very steeply, far more so than those involving two supervisory boards. A further decline in bank interlocks over the period 1976–96 is documented by Heemskerk, Mokken, and Fennema (2003), who find that finance-industry interlocks declined by almost 40 percent over that period, outpacing the 25 percent decline in overall interlocks.

Table 8.7 compares and contrasts the prevalence of interlocks in family and nonfamily firms; the criterion used to define family firms in this table is a board member with a surname that matches the firm's original name. In 1928, the only significant difference was that members of the management board of nonfamily firms were much more likely to be on the board of other industrial firms. By 1958, this difference had largely disappeared, as nonfamily firms' board members became more like those of family firms. In 1993, the situation had reversed, as the management board

Table 8.7   Characteristics of family firms

	1923		1958		1993	
	Family	No family	Family	No family	Family	No family
Book value total assets	12,043	14,309	67,937	84,190	1,885,229	2,312,999
Past three-year growth book value assets	−0.151	−0.048*	0.289	0.112***	0.372	0.159
Tobin's q	0.400	0.362	0.464	0.405**	1.284	1.269
Return on assets	0.030	0.090**	0.152	0.162	0.076	0.073
Four-year standard deviation ROA			0.040	0.035	0.036	0.032
Payout ratio	0.331	0.392	0.511	0.795	0.257	0.376
Debt to total assets	0.306	0.298	0.398	0.316***	0.537	0.534
Fixed assets to total assets	0.436	0.596***	0.331	0.432***	0.417	0.379
Cash and liquid assets to total assets	0.093	0.122	0.080	0.140***	0.068	0.109
Age	13.57	25.01***	37.28	50.88***	65.80	47.67
RvB size	2.52	2.02***	2.91	2.09***	2.67	2.78
RvC size	4.52	5.01*	4.36	4.61	4.22	5.23
Dummy certificates	0.090	0.130	0.20	0.27	0.22	0.40
Dummy priority shares	0.045	0.018	0.450	0.220***	0.56	0.42
Dummy preferred shares					0.44	0.61
Dummy structured regime					0.33	0.54
Dummy interlock RvC— RvC/industrial	0.87	0.83	0.80	0.80	0.56	0.75
Dummy interlock RvC— RvB/industrial	0.42	0.49	0.39	0.44	0.44	0.37
Dummy interlock RvB— RvC/industrial	0.18	0.37***	0.20	0.27	0.44	0.19**
Dummy interlock RvB— RvB/industrial	0.08	0.33***	0.09	0.14	0.00	0.00
Dummy interlock RvC— RvC/bank	0.43	0.48	0.51	0.55	0.33	0.41
Dummy interlock RvC— RvB/bank	0.36	0.26	0.18	0.17	0.11	0.07
Dummy interlock RvB— RvC/bank	0.08	0.13	0.11	0.07	0.11	0.07
Dummy interlock RvB— RvB/bank	0.02	0.04	0.00	0.01	0.00	0.00
Ownership largest outside blockholder					22.27	24.64
Ownership all outside blockholders					34.67	43.67
Ownership banks					7.79	7.12
Ownership RvB members					20.00	4.32***
Ownership RvC members					10.32	1.94**
No. of observations	89	228	92	241	9	134

***Significant at the 1 percent level.
**Significant at the 5 percent level.
*Significant at the 10 percent level.

Table 8.8   Relations between takeover defenses and interlocks and ownership

	1923	1958		1993			
	Certificates	Certificates	Priority shares	Certificates	Priority shares	Preferred shares	Structured regime
Dummy certificates	1.000	1.000	-0.007	1.000	-0.188**	-0.120	0.080
Dummy priority shares		-0.007	1.000	-0.188**	1.000	0.009	-0.012
Dummy preferred shares				-0.120	0.009	1.000	0.323**
Dummy structured regime				0.080	-0.012	0.323***	1.000
Dummy interlock RvC— RvC/industrial	0.079	0.099	0.065	0.106	-0.072	0.171**	0.341**
Dummy interlock RvC— RvB/industrial	0.093	0.068	-0.024	0.066	-0.001	0.074	0.240**
Dummy interlock RvB— RvC/industrial	0.218***	0.202***	-0.018	-0.184**	0.163	0.055	0.195**
Dummy interlock RvB— RvB/industrial	0.144**	0.059	-0.052				
Dummy interlock RvC— RvC/bank	0.113**	0.186**	-0.061	0.079	-0.050	0.207**	0.205*
Dummy interlock RvC— RvB/bank	0.071	0.065	0.011	-0.012	0.016	0.074	0.061
Dummy interlock RvB— RvC/bank	0.087	0.351***	0.026	-0.066	0.069	0.074	0.166**
Dummy interlock RvB— RvB/bank	0.134**	0.019	0.081				
Ownership largest outside blockholder				-0.155	-0.155	-0.182**	-0.082
Ownership all outside blockholders				-0.084	-0.195**	-0.173**	-0.024
Ownership banks				-0.005	-0.241***	0.153	0.198**
Ownership RvB members				-0.165**	-0.006	-0.022	-0.273***
Ownership RvC members				-0.038	0.057	-0.083	-0.085

***Significant at the 1 percent level.
**Significant at the 5 percent level.

members of nonfamily firms became even less likely to hold supervisory board positions elsewhere.

To complete our description of the prevalence of interlocks, table 8.8 illustrates their relation to takeover defense mechanisms. In both 1923 and 1958 interlocking directorships, especially those of the management board, show a strong positive association with certification of shares. By 1993 this was no longer the case. Instead, supervisory board cross-directorships were associated with the use of defensive preferred shares, and most types of interlocks were associated with subjection to the structured regime, which may simply indicate that these are the larger and less multinationally oriented firms.

As an exploratory enquiry into the impact of interlocks on industrial performance, in table 8.9 the second of each year's set of regressions considers the impact of interlocks on Tobin's q. The impact is insignificant in 1993, but in the two earlier years the association between interlocks and q

Table 8.9   Q regressions

	1923 (1)	1923 (2)	1923 (3)	1958 (1)	1958 (2)	1958 (3)	1993 (1)	1993 (2)	1993 (3)
Intercept	0.078 (1.65)	0.057 (1.09)	0.062 (1.22)	0.184*** (2.68)	0.236*** (3.46)	0.208*** (2.71)	1.126*** (5.09)	1.015*** (3.82)	1.191*** (5.08)
Log (book value)	0.009* (1.73)	0.012* (1.86)	0.011* (1.68)	-0.007 (1.18)	-0.012 (-1.61)	-0.012* (-1.70)	0.061** (2.08)	0.062** (2.17)	0.028 (0.95)
Debt to total assets	0.846*** (19.9)	0.841*** (19.14)	0.858*** (20.10)	0.951*** (18.29)	0.948*** (18.49)	0.958*** (17.61)	-0.028 (-0.11)	0.074 (0.27)	0.030 (0.11)
Past three-year growth book value total assets	-0.015 (-0.94)	-0.016 (-1.01)	-0.019 (-1.06)	0.012 (0.84)	0.010 (0.64)	0.008 (0.52)	0.125 (1.23)	0.106 (1.02)	0.162 (1.45)
Fixed assets to total assets	-0.009 (-0.30)	-0.007 (-0.27)	-0.004 (-0.12)	0.078*** (2.73)	0.068** (2.52)	0.073** (2.41)	-0.642*** (-2.27)	-0.602** (-2.09)	-0.569* (-2.21)
Log (age)	-0.009 (-0.92)	-0.009 (-0.90)	-0.008 (-0.72)	-0.018 (-.87)	-0.020 (-0.87)	-0.017 (-0.87)			
Cash and liquid assets to total assets	0.035 (0.93)	0.037 (0.95)	0.058 (1.42)	0.158* (1.83)	0.145* (1.70)	0.144 (1.53)	-0.037 (-0.10)	0.133 (0.40)	0.045 (0.13)
Payout ratio	0.001 (0.16)	0.0001 (0.02)	-0.002 (-0.25)	-0.002 (-0.88)	-0.003 (-1.05)	-0.002 (-0.83)	0.040 (0.67)	0.033 (0.54)	0.051 (0.74)
Dummy certificates		-0.018 (-1.23)			0.045 (1.63)			0.092 (0.90)	
Dummy priority shares					-0.023* (-1.72)			-0.068 (-0.89)	
Dummy preferred shares								0.092 (1.05)	

Dummy structured regime									−0.072 (−0.97)	
Dummy interlock RvC—RvC/industrial	0.005 (0.22)							0.009 (0.48)		−0.012 (0.11)
Dummy interlock RvC—RvB/industrial	−0.033** (−2.06)							0.015 (0.93)		0.002 (0.02)
Dummy interlock RvB—RvC/industrial	0.016 (0.86)							0.014 (0.60)		−0.130 (0.83)
Dummy interlock RvB—RvB/industrial	−0.003 (−0.19)							−0.042** (2.33)		
Dummy interlock RvC—RvC/bank	0.011 (0.60)							0.005 (0.36)		0.117 (1.22)
Dummy interlock RvC—RvB/bank	−0.027* (−1.75)							−0.012 (0.89)		−0.041 (0.20)
Dummy interlock RvB—RvC/bank	−0.015 (−0.64)							0.033 (1.22)		0.514 (1.08)
Dummy interlock RvB—RvB/bank	−0.008 (0.30)							−0.041 (1.43)		
Dummy family firm	0.002 (0.12)							0.002 (0.17)		0.057 (0.37)
Adj. R^2	0.78	0.78	0.78	0.74	0.75	0.74	0.07	0.74	0.06	0.08
No. of observations	193	193	193	224	224	224	139	224	139	139

Notes: White heteroskedasticity-consistent *t*-values. Observations with payout <0 removed.

***Significant at the 1 percent level.

**Significant at the 5 percent level.

*Significant at the 10 percent level.

is negative whenever it is significant. This is weak evidence that interlocks, and especially those that involve management board members of other industrial firms or banks, were not beneficial in 1923 and 1958.

8.5   Conclusions

Our paper gives a bird's-eye overview of financing and control of Dutch listed firms over the past century. Regarding the influence of families in firms, our data suggest a clear trend toward professional management taking hold in the second half of the twentieth century. The role of banks in the control and financing of Dutch industry seems to have been rather secondary, and more British than German in nature. While employees have been given some voice in corporate decision making in the last few decades of the century, again, their power is not as strong as in Germany. Real decision-making power currently seems to rest very strongly with a set of self-perpetuating management insiders, entrenched behind a quite formidable array of takeover defenses. But the ongoing process of convergence toward a common European model is slowly but surely eliminating some of the idiosyncrasies of Dutch corporate governance.

Appendix

Railway Finance in the Nineteenth Century

The flotation of a number of railway issues in the middle of the nineteenth century seems to have been fairly easy, with the exception of the Nederlandse Centraalspoorweg Maatschappij in 1860, which many industry insiders realized in advance would be unprofitable because it did not connect major industries or population centers.

These flotations are of additional interest because the disposition of the shares has been investigated, giving some insight into their initial ownership structure. Van den Broeke (1983, 1985) documents in detail how initial finance was raised. As a case in point, take the 1863 flotation of the Maatschappij tot Exploitatie van Staatsspoorwegen. The initial shareholders were 244 in number, holding a total of 24,000 shares of f 250 each (f 6 million in total). The largest stake reported by Van den Broeke is 3,000 shares held by a Paris bank, Hottinguer & Cie; the second largest, 2,765 shares, by Wurfbain en Zoon, an Amsterdam securities brokerage house. Four other stakes of 1,000 shares and above are mentioned, all held by banks in Amsterdam, London, and Brussels.

There is no sign that any of these shareholders were motivated by a desire to take a controlling stake in the venture: the largest stake was no more than 12.5 percent. The largest stakes were all held by banking houses or securities firms. Many of these were based abroad and therefore in no position to exercise meaningful control. In total, 74.5 percent of the capital was taken up by the banking/financial sector, and the Dutch banks never developed an active role in the management of industry as in the German model.

Nor is there any sign that the government saw shareholding as an attractive means of ensuring control. The king and his entourage, and various politicians, government officials and members of the judiciary contributed for less than 600 shares in total. When efforts to raise a further f 6 million in the subsequent five years seemed to founder, the government repeatedly declined to step in and only came up with a loan of f 2.5 million, to be paid off as soon as new equity was raised.[22] There seem to have been a couple of shareholders with direct commercial ties to the railway business: a shipping line connecting England to Vlissingen (Flushing), for example.

22. Even this very modest form of government support was considered too much in some quarters, to judge by a pamphlet published in Breda in 1866, entitled *May the money, that is contributed by the Dutch citizen as taxes, be lent to a private company for its own profit? A word to the Dutch people, by Someone (Mag het Geld, dat door den Nederlandschen Burger als Belasting Wordt Opgebragt, Worden Geleend aan eene Maatschappij van Partikulieren, Tot Haar Eigen Winstbejag? Een Woord aan het Nederlandsche Volk, van Iemand)*.

Table 8A.1   Dutch railway finance

	Hollandsche Ijzeren Spoorweg Maatschappij	Nederlandsche Rhijnspoorweg Maatschappij	Nederlandse Centraalspoorweg (NCS) Maatschappij[a]	Maatschappij tot Exploitatie van Staatsspoorwegen
Year founded[b]	1837	1845	1860	1863
Initial equity capital (placed)	f 1.24 million[c]	f 24 million	f 5 million (authorized), f 4.1 million (subscribed)	f 6 million
Number of shares	1,240	100,000	20,000	24,000
Nominal value	f 1,000	f 240	f 250	f 250
No. of initial shareholders	140	35	105	244
No. of stakes $\geq$ 2%	9	9	at least 2	9(?)
Largest stake	11.3%	14%	at least 16%	12.5%
Largest shareholders and no. of shares held	140 stockbroker Amsterdam 110 stockbroker Amsterdam 79 stockbroker Amsterdam 66 stockbroker Amsterdam 65 stockbroker Amsterdam 49 stockbroker Amsterdam 35 manufacture Amsterdam 25 trade Amsterdam 25 unknown Amsterdam	14,000 merchants London 14,000 merchants London 14,000 merchants/bankers London 14,000 manufacturers The Hague 14,000 manufacturers Haarlem 12,500 directors SWRail London 6,250 bankers London 6,250 bankers Liverpool 3,545 merchants Amsterdam	3,200 railway construction Paris 1,600 businessmen Paris	3,000 bank Paris 2,765 stockbrokers Amsterdam 2,000 bank Amsterdam 2,000 bank London 1,730 bank Amsterdam 1,400 railway equipment company Utrecht 1,000 bank Brussels 500 bank Frankfurt 500 bank Basel
Foreign ownership	2.4%	67.0%	> 90%	35.2%
Leverage (total capital)[d]				
1850	0.66 (f 10.8 million)	0.49 (f 14.0 million)	—	
1860	0.71 (f 11.1 million)	0.38 (f 26.5 million)	—	
1870	0.89 (f 17.2 million)	0.41 (f 41.6 million)	1.90 (f 10.0 million)	0.75 (f 10.5 million)
1880	1.50 (f 37.5 million)	0.64 (f 49.9 million)	5.26 (f 9.9 million)	0.43 (f 18.0 million)
1890	1.68 (f 60.4 million)	0.84 (f 56.2 million)	2.35 (f 11.4 million)	1.31 (f 40.2 million)

Source: Van den Broeke (1985).

[a]The data for NCS are less meaningful because the initial offering was undersubscribed, and many initial shareholders subsequently reneged on their obligation to fully pay up. Stakes are those attending/represented at shareholder meetings. The French stakes were somewhat involuntary, as they were payments for construction services and materials.

[b]The year given is the date of incorporation and of raising capital (or attempting to) from the public. Concessions were generally granted a few years in advance to a small group of entrepreneurial individuals (*concessionarissen*) who then set up the company and raised capital.

[c]Raised to f 6.2 million within the same year by a 4-for-1 rights issue that was heavily oversubscribed and entirely taken up by the initial shareholders.

[d]Debt is measured as long-term debt; equity excludes reserves. Leverage is debt-equity ratio; total capital is the sum of debt and equity.

References

Booth, J. R., and D. N. Deli. 1999. On executives of financial institutions as outside directors. *Journal of Corporate Finance* 5:227–50.

Bos, J. W. 1923. Over commissarissen van naamlooze vennootschappen. PhD diss., Rijksuniversiteit Groningen.

Broeke, W. van den. 1983. De financiering en de financiers van de spoorwegen in Nederland: De Maatschappij tot Exploitatie van Staatsspoorwegen 1863–1870. *Economisch- en Sociaal-Historisch Jaarboek* 46:26–44.

———. 1985. *Financiën en financiers van de Nederlandse spoorwegen 1837–1890.* Zwolle, The Netherlands: Uitgeverij Waanders.

———. 1988. Vermogensstructuren en netwerkrelaties in het Nederlandse bedrijfsleven 1890–1940. *Jaarboek voor de geschiedenis van bedrijf en techniek* 5:154–71.

Camfferman, Kees. 2000. Jaarrekeningpublicatie door beursgenoteerde naamloze vennootschappen in Nederland tot 1910. Nederlandsch Economisch-Historish Archief (NEHA *Jaarboek,* 71–103.

De Jong, A., and P. W. Moerland. 1999. Beheersingsmechanismen in Nederland: Substituut of complement? *Maandblad Accountancy en Bedrijfskunde* 73:499–512.

De Jong, A., P. W. Moerland, and T. Nijman. 2000. Zeggenschapsverhoudingen en financiële prestaties. *Economisch-Statistische Berichten* 85:368–71.

De Jong, Abe, Doug DeJong, Gerard Mertens, and Charles Wasley. 2004. The role of self-regulation in corporate governance: Evidence and implications from the Netherlands. *Journal of Corporate Finance,* forthcoming.

De Jong, Abe, Rezaul Kabir, Teye Marra, and Ailsa Röell. 2001. Ownership and control in the Netherlands. In *The control of corporate Europe,* ed. Fabrizio Barca and Marco Becht, 188–206. Oxford, UK: Oxford University Press.

Ferris, S. P., M. Jagannathan, and A. C. Pritchard. 2003. Too busy to mind the business? Monitoring by directors with multiple board appointments. *Journal of Finance* 58:1087–1111.

Frentrop, Paul. 2003. *A history of corporate governance 1602–2002.* Haarlem: Deminor.

Gales, B. P. A. 1986. Werken aan zekerheid: Een terugblik over de schouder van AEGON op twee eeuwen verzekeringsgeschiedenis. The Hague: Aegon Verzekeringen.

Goor, Linda van, and Jaap Koelewijn. 1995. Le système bancaire néerlandais: Étude rétrospective. In *Les banques en Europe de l'Ouest de 1920 à nos jours,* ed. Maurice Lévy-Leboyer, 153–75. Paris: Ministère de l'Économie et des Finances, Comité pour l'histoire économique et financière.

Heemskerk, E., R. Mokken, and M. Fennema. 2003. From stakeholders to shareholders? Corporate governance networks in the Netherlands 1976–1996. University of Amsterdam, Amsterdam School for Social Science Research. Unpublished manuscript. http://users.fmg.uva.nl/heemskerk/publications/stakeholder Preprint_2003.pdf.

Heijden, E. J. J. van der. 1992. Handboek voor de naamloze en de besloten vennootschap. 12th ed. Adapted by W. C. L. van der Grinten. Zwolle: W. E. J. Tjeenk Willink.

J. H. de Bussy. 1923. *Financieel adresboek voor Nederland* [Financial address book for the Netherlands]. Amsterdam: J. H. de Bussy.

———. 1958. *Financieel adresboek voor Nederland* [Financial address book for the Netherlands]. Amsterdam: J. H. de Bussy.

———. 1993a. *Gids bij de officiële prijscourant van de Amsterdamse Effectenbeurs*

1993 [Guide with the official price list of the Amsterdam Securities Exchange 1993]. Amsterdam: J. H. de Bussy.

————. 1993b. *Jaarboek van Nederlandse ondernemingen 1992–93* [Yearbook of Dutch companies 1992–93]. Amsterdam: J. H. de Bussy.

Jonker, Joost. 1989. Waterdragers van het kapitalisme: Nevenfuncties van Nederlandse bankiers en de verhouding tussen bankwezen en bedrijfsleven, 1910–1940. *Jaarboek voor de geschiedenis van bedrijf en techniek* 6:158–90.

————. 1995. Spoilt for choice? Statistical speculations on banking concentration and the structure of the Dutch money market, 1900–1940. In *The evolution of financial institutions and markets in twentieth-century Europe,* ed. Y. Cassis, G. D. Feldman, and U. Olsson, 187–208. Aldershot, UK: Scolar Press.

————. 1996. *Merchants, bankers, middlemen: The Amsterdam money market during the first half of the nineteenth century.* Amsterdam: NEHA.

Kroszner, R. S., and P. E. Strahan. 2001. Bankers on the boards: Monitoring, conflicts of interest, and lender liability. *Journal of Financial Economics* 62:415–52.

La Porta, R., F. López-de-Silanes, A. Shleifer, and R. W. Vishny. 2000. Agency problems and dividend policies around the world. *Journal of Finance* 55:1–33.

Laveleye, Emile de. 1864. L'économie rurale en Néerlande. *Revue des Deux Mondes* 49.

Nederveen Meerkerk, Elise van, and Jan Peet. 2002. *Een peertje voor de dorst: Geschiedenis van het Philips pensioenfonds.* Amsterdam: Aksant.

Post, J. G. 1972. *Besparingen in Nederland 1923–1970: Omvang en verdeling.* PhD diss., University of Amsterdam.

Renooij, Dirk Cornelis. 1951. *De Nederlandse emissiemarkt van 1904–1939.* Amsterdam: J. H. de Bussy.

S. F. van Oss. 1924. *Effectenboek voor 1924: Binnenland* [Securities guide for 1924: Domestic]. The Hague: S. F. van Oss.

————. 1959. *Effectenboek voor 1959: Binnenland* [Securities guide for 1959: Domestic]. The Hague: S. F. van Oss.

Schijf, Huibert. 1993. *Netwerken van een financieel-economische elite: Personele verbindingen in het Nederlandse bedrijfsleven aan het eind van de 19e eeuw.* Amsterdam: Het Spinhuis.

Sluyterman, Keetie E., and Hélène J. M. Winkelman. 1993. The Dutch family firm confronted with Chandler's dynamics of industrial capitalism, 1890–1940. *Business History* 35 (4): 152–83.

Steensgaard, Niels. 1982. The Dutch East India Company as an institutional innovation. In *Dutch capitalism and world capitalism,* ed. Maurice Aymard, 235–57. Cambridge: Cambridge University Press.

Stokman, Frans N., Frans W. Wasseur, and Donald Elsas. 1985. The Dutch network: Types of interlocks and network structure. In *Networks of corporate power: A comparative analysis of ten countries,* ed. Frans N. Stokman, Rolf Ziegler, and John Scott, 112–30. Cambridge, UK: Polity Press.

Voogd, R. P. 1989. *Statutaire beschermingsmiddelen bij beursvennootschappen.* Kluwer: Deventer.

Zanden, Jan L. van. 1987. *De industrialisatie in Amsterdam 1825–1914.* Bergen: Octavo.

————. 1998. *The economic history of the Netherlands 1914–1995: A small open economy in the "long" twentieth century.* London: Routledge.

Comment   Peter Högfeldt

It is natural to compare the Netherlands and Sweden since they are the two smallest countries surveyed in this volume, but also because their financial systems and corporate control structures have developed along different historical paths from initial points that could hardly have been further apart. The free city of Amsterdam provided the fertile ground for the first modern hub of international financial markets and advanced intermediation that, for example, helped underdeveloped Sweden to finance imperial wars against neighboring countries. The Swedish students, sailors, and businessmen who visited Amsterdam in the seventeenth and eighteenth centuries were attracted by the city's openness and dynamics. The philosopher René Descartes, who went the other way to enlighten the court of Queen Christina, was taken by the poverty, isolation, and coldness of Stockholm compared to the opulence and modernity of Amsterdam, even if the initial shock was not the immediate cause of his death in the winter of 1650 shortly after his arrival.

When the political map of Europe was significantly redrawn during the following centuries, the relative decline of Amsterdam and the fast industrialization of peaceful but very poor Sweden after 1870 evened out the economic differences between the two countries. Today the two countries are small, open, and export-oriented economies dominated by very large transnational companies. But the conspicuous institutional differences between the two countries' financial systems and corporate control structures reflect the strong, historical path dependence of their developments. Abe de Jong and Ailsa Röell's chapter illustrates this very nicely by painting a broad picture of the Dutch financial developments that is suitable for a comparative analysis with Sweden. They also present interesting analyses of how characteristics (for example, leverage, payout ratios, and Tobin's q) of firms listed on the Amsterdam Stock Exchange have changed over time and of interlocking board memberships. Given the thick veil of secrecy that by tradition protects Dutch firms, the authors have done an excellent job when collecting their data.

Even if God's hand may be in the details, I will focus my comparative analysis on three major characteristics of the Dutch financial system and discuss possible causal links in the historical development using Sweden as an alternative institutional setting.

Peter Högfeldt is a research associate of the European Corporate Governance Institute (ECGI) and an associate professor in the Department of Finance, Stockholm School of Economics.

The Limited Role of Banks in Corporate Financing

For an outside observer perhaps the most surprising feature of the Dutch financial system is "the limited role played by the banks in the financing of industrial growth" throughout the industrialization as well as later. Although the banks were not prohibited from operating as universal banks, they specialized in the traditional short-term mercantile financing like British banks and stayed out of long-term, industrial financing, and did not hold equity stakes in their clients. This started a long tradition of bank noninterventionism in Dutch corporate governance. Instead, the industrial firms' demand for capital was satisfied via the *prolongatie* system of short-term callable margin loans collected from wealthy private persons through an old, local network of agents outside the banking system.

At first sight this seems the most unlikely source of long-term industrial financing, but it was evidently competitive enough to preempt the banks from entering the market for a long time. The semi-market character of the decentralized system seemed to have circumvented the general public's distrust of financial institutions due to very bad experiences in the past. The wealth accumulated in the Golden Ages and controlled by wealthy rentier families thus financed investments several centuries later. This is a nice example of path dependence in the development of a financial system, despite the turmoil created by the Napoleonic Wars. The Dutch case thus shows that development of a universal banking system is *not necessary* for financing of industrial growth when the private, pecuniary wealth of a country is in the hands of a small but sufficiently large number of wealthy families that *also* have access to nonintermediated networks for investments.

The story becomes more intriguing when we compare it to what happened in Belgium, the industrialized and relatively poorer southern part, after the separation from the Netherlands. Despite initially having the same legal origin and identical banking laws as well as the same corporate law, universal banking became the Belgian solution, and, unlike in the Netherlands, pyramiding became extensive. Although the stronger French influence in Belgium points in the direction of universal banking, I conjecture that the lack of a larger class of very wealthy families *combined* with a substantial demand for long-term industrial investments explains why collection of savings from the broader base of all people in the society via a universal banking system became the solution. A well-developed deposit banking system may collect the necessary savings at a relatively low cost but may not be able to intermediate efficiently without developing special competencies in industrial financing. Direct equity ownership may be one way to make the monitoring of clients more efficient, but recurrent industrial crises may also explain why banks became owners of large equity positions. When dual-class shares are prohibited, pyramiding may be an attractive solution to control firms for both banks and other interests, as the Belgian example shows.

The development of Swedish banking from a pure deposit system to a universal banking system when the demand for industrial financing increased substantially at the beginning of the twentieth century illustrates this very nicely. Lacking a sufficiently broad base of wealthy people, the national political debate was about how to collect the citizens' savings via a national banking system in order to finance the necessary industrial investments; the infrastructural investments were primarily financed via international public bonds. Down the road the banks later became the controlling owners of the largest industrial firms in Sweden via pyramiding, most often combined with the use of dual-class shares.

If the financial system in general and the stock markets in particular are underdeveloped due to lack of a sufficiently large group of wealthy individuals at the early stage of industrialization, corporate financing via universal banking may thus become the dominating interface instead of stock market–based corporate financing. While universal banking seems to point in the direction of bank and shareholder control via separation of ownership from control through use of either dual-class shares or pyramiding or both, the Dutch case without universal banking seems to lead to dispersed ownership but with very entrenched managerial control via use of other legal devices to separate ownership from control when dual-class shares are prohibited. It thus seems to be the *combination* of a wealthy class of investors with investment options outside the banking system, and the prohibition of dual-class shares that in the Dutch case implies managerial control with dispersed ownership. The passive rentier attitude of Dutch equity investors has perhaps reinforced this effect. By being counterfactual to the convention in Continental Europe, the Dutch case thus in effect supports the causal link between universal banking and shareholder corporate control via separation of ownership and control.

I thus conjecture that when the initial level of wealth in a country is low and nonintermediated forms of financing are rare or nonexistent, intermediation of industrial financing via a universal banking system is more likely to occur, which seems to later imply shareholder control via strong separation of ownership and control. The Dutch case seems to be the exception that supports the generality of this conjecture.

The Bulwark of Takeover Defenses

While it seems relatively straightforward to identify *when* the Dutch tradition to use very elaborate entrenchment devices started, it is much more difficult to understand *why* it happened. It would have been very interesting to have more information and analysis of the political background to the corporate law of 1881, and to know *why* it did not permit "the use of nonvoting or lower-voting shares, thus ruling out one obvious mean of detaching control from ownership," in particular since the future corporate laws have consistently used the same design principle. Since the earlier corporate law of 1838 that mandated voting caps in order to protect minority shareholders and also became the standard feature of later corporate laws, there seems to have been a common underlying principle to limit the power of large block shareholders. But why did this early and strong aversion against shareholder control occur?

Was it a delayed reaction to the manifest and persistent expropriation of noncontrolling shareholders in the Vereenigde Oostindische Compagnie (VOC)—the Dutch East India Company—or was it an attempt to protect the Dutch firms from hostile takeovers by German and French firms, as the authors suggest? The latter alternative is less plausible as it does not explain why the use of dual-class shares, the single most efficient anti-takeover defense, was prohibited or what would stop the new controlling owners from getting around the law by taking the firm private or forming a merger. Or was it because the ordinary shareholders viewed themselves as passive rentiers primarily interested in dividends that are shared in proportion to their capital contribution, and not in corporate control? It seems as if the Dutch investors behaved more like long-term bondholders rather than as typical shareholders because of their large and old private wealth.

I have no specific answer to these questions, but it seems pivotal to understand *why* if we want to understand the current Dutch control structure since the first corporate laws that carefully limited the larger shareholders' opportunities to maintain and exert corporate control set the standard for the future laws and, thus, shaped the future control structures through path dependence. For example, were the legislators and the larger shareholders, who probably exerted political influence, (fully) aware at the time that the corporate law down the road opened up for co-optive managerial control protected by a plethora of antitakeover devices, which became a Dutch specialty long before U.S. lawyers perfected it in recent decades with the help of the state of Delaware? If they were aware of the consequences, why the manifest intention to limit the power not only of the controlling shareholders but also de facto of the noncontrolling ones?

The relatively strong protection of minority shareholders against expropriation by controlling shareholders in the Dutch corporate laws thus implies both (a) (relatively) dispersed ownership and (b) very strong managerial entrenchment via direct control often without ownership. The first implication appears consistent with Burkart, Panunzi, and Shleifer's (2003) legal minority protection theory of corporate ownership, while the second is inconsistent since the shareholders are poorly protected against managerial expropriation as well as against inefficient decisions by the management (agency costs); hostile takeovers are hardly efficient threats! The missing *nonlegal* element in the Dutch case seems to be that banks were passive and did not get involved in long-term industrial financing and corporate ownership, which opened up for managerial control instead. Hence, strong legal protection of minority shareholders does not rule out exceptionally strong managerial entrenchment through co-option.

There is a fundamental difference between (a) mechanisms that primarily *protect* the large shareholders' interests by separating ownership from control, like dual-class shares, pyramiding, and cross-shareholding, and (b) other devices like the *administratiekantoor,* preference shares, the X rule, voting limits, and so on that entrench management control by *diluting* and *limiting* the value of shareholder control. The first type of defenses implies reinforced shareholder control via separation of ownership and control, while the latter type opens up for and supports managerial control by weakening shareholder control. The two sets of protective mechanisms are, however, substitutes in the following sense: if a Swedish or a U.S. IPO firm uses dual-class shares it uses none or very few of the other mechanisms, while firms without such shares often have a long list of complementary antitakeover defenses, but not as extensive a list as the Dutch arsenal; see Field and Karpoff (2002) and Holmén and Högfeldt (2004). The empirical results thus imply that because of the long-standing prohibition of dual-class shares, the single most powerful mechanism against takeovers, the Dutch firms use a diversified portfolio of other, weaker antitakeover defenses; pyramiding is of limited use since it supports shareholder control.

As a comparison, table 8C.1 shows the extreme simplicity and trans-

Table 8C.1   **Use of control mechanisms by controlling owner (%; from Agnblad et al. 2001)**

Sample (% of total)	Dual-class shares	Right of preemption	Voting restriction	Mandatory bid rule	Shareholder agreement
Whole sample (100)	63	13	4	1	5
Bank (1)	50	0	0	0	0
Buyout investor (1)	0	0	0	0	0
Family (62)	71	16	3	0.5	6
Foreign (8)	46	8	13	4	4
Foundation (0.3)	100	0	0	0	0
Insurance (1)	33	0	0	0	0
Mutual fund (6)	32	5	0	0	0
Other (8)	71	13	0	0	0
Public (2)	29	0	0	0	0
Sphere (10)	61	7	10	7	3

Source: Aktiemarknadsbevakning (AMB), Sundin and Sundqvist (1998), company charters, and Patent- och Registreringsverket (PRV).

Notes: Table shows frequency of different control mechanisms for 304 firms listed on the Stockholm Stock Exchange and the Stockholm Börsinformation list in October 1998. The sample is split into subsamples based on the characteristics of the controlling shareholder and type of mechanism.

parency of the control structure of Swedish firms listed on the Stockholm Stock Exchange; see Agnblad et al. (2001). The dual-class share design is the most commonly used mechanism to control firms, in particular for family firms, since 63 percent of the listed firms use it. Only 13 percent of the firms have the right to preemptively redeem nonlisted A-shares that have been passed on to a new owner. This is the second most common control mechanism; the others are very infrequently used. The use of dual-class shares to separate ownership from control has very strong political support in Sweden since it is a very efficient protection against foreign takeovers; see Holmén and Högfeldt (2004).

Another important element of the Dutch control structure is the strategic use of co-optive (family) foundations that by legal design are very opaque, almost impenetrable for an outsider like the tax authorities, and not subject to taxation on corporate dividends. This is an important advantage since dividends to regular shareholders are disadvantaged by a relatively high tax, which implies a low payout ratio of profits and support for use of retained earnings as a primary source of financing. Since shareholders discount the levered and opaque control structure when the firms need to raise external capital from the capital markets, the relatively high tax on dividends seems like a logical element of the Dutch control structure to lock in capital into the existing firms.

The strong legal support and protection of the very secretive foundations is another example of the extreme nature of the Dutch control structure. The historical preference 'for secretive, private decision making among a small number of business partners and for co-optive control already in place in the golden days of Amsterdam seems to have been propagated through time and taken to its extreme—another interesting example of path dependence. The strong aversion for centuries to making annual reports and accounting information available to general shareholders and to the public is another example.

It is thus logical that the founding families of the two most successful firms founded in Sweden during the last fifty to sixty years, IKEA (the Kamprads) and Tetra Pak (the Rausings), have moved their fortunes out of reach of the Swedish tax authorities and have kept their firms fully private by using the very favorable Dutch legislation for private foundations as holding entities before paying out rents to personal foundations for the family members in Liechtenstein. The heavy entrenchment, very comfortable secrecy (no questions asked), and low or nonexistent taxes on corporate dividends are thus very convenient features of the Dutch foundations, also for foreign families interested in locking in control for generations.

The historical irony in the case of the Netherlands is that the strong public aversion against corporate power in the hands of large shareholders as well as in the hands of financial institutions like banks has generated perhaps the most extreme concentration of corporate power in the hands of very heavily entrenched and co-optive management teams and foundations that operate behind a legal veil of secrecy. But where did all the shareholders go, and why did they give up their power so easily without a fight? The answer seems to lie in the original character of the Dutch financial system and the strong historical path dependency in its development.

The Politics of Corporate Control

Since political ideologies and decisions shape and affect the development of a country's corporate control system, a deeper understanding requires an analysis of how politics and corporate financing interact. The public acceptance of a corporate governance structure in a society ultimately depends on its politically viability; without manifest political support, an extreme control structure will not survive. An analysis of the politics of Dutch corporate governance would thus have been even more interesting. The authors have, however, decided to leave this out of their already very rich chapter. But they stress that the small Dutch welfare society, like the even smaller Swedish society, is strongly consensus oriented. Despite this political affinity, the two countries' control structures have developed along different paths over the past thirty to forty years.

There is, however, a common theme. The vigorous political ambitions in both countries since the late 1960s to reform the traditional control structures and make them more "democratic" by giving firms' stakeholders more voice has had the opposite result: the entrenchment of the controlling interests has increased in recent decades. But the two countries followed very different roads. In the Netherlands the trade unions did not unexpectedly join forces with the management and short shrift the shareholders by transferring pivotal decision-making powers from the shareholders' annual meeting to a co-optive (corporative) supervisory board dominated by management and labor appointees. The already entrenched managerial power was thus reinforced by a political measure that was supposed to achieve the opposite. Were there any strong political protests voiced against the *structured regime,* or was it done in consensus behind a veil of secrecy? It would have been interesting to know how this actually happened since it seems to have been a relatively recent, pivotal event.

In Sweden employees were granted formal representation in the boards but with very limited decision-making power; the primary motivation was to have access to pertinent corporate information and an opportunity to give voice. The traditional skepticism toward managerial capitalism because of its perceived short-sightedness, combined with the political consensus between the leading capitalism and the Social Democrats, instead resulted in stronger political support for the incumbent owners in control. The new corporate law as well as the political rhetoric stressed the pivotal importance of firms having well-defined and strong owners in control; increased use of dual-class shares was the primary means to obtain the objective. A more realistic and sinister objective was to ascertain that the leading listed firms remained under Swedish control when capital markets became deregulated and capital demands increased as the international competition became more vigorous.

The two consensus-oriented welfare societies thus handled the new historical situation very differently by (not unexpectedly) reinforcing the incumbent management in the Netherlands and the controlling shareholders in Sweden. The path dependence in the development of the two countries' control structures was therefore reinforced rather than weakened. The longer historical perspective that pinpoints the path dependence, however, also accentuates rather than moderates the impression of how much has happened in recent decades! In both countries, however, the historical compass points in the direction of more entrenched control structures rather than toward more flexible ones.

Final Thoughts

The case of the Netherlands is very interesting by itself because Amsterdam gave birth to the first modern, advanced financial system. I think, however, that the Dutch case is even more interesting since it nicely illustrates how its historical roots via path dependence have shaped future developments *without* making the outcomes predictable: a mixture of random and nonrandom factors representing Anglo-Saxon, German, and French influences of a political, legal, and economic nature has affected the actual path followed by a small country at the geographical crossroads. For example, there was managerial control of the largest listed firms like in the United States, although with a distinctive Dutch control twist, and a banking system that focused on short-term mercantile financing as in the United Kingdom rather than universal banking with long-term industrial financing as in continental Europe. The Dutch financial system is thus not a *clean* example that easily fits into the civil law country camp. The standard dichotomy is simply too coarse when we really want to understand the development and characteristics of the Dutch financial system; the differences versus other civil law countries like Sweden are simply more interesting than the similarities. It is thus not surprising that the EU, dominated by civil law countries, has failed conspicuously to harmonize takeover codes and eliminate antitakeover defenses despite ambitious attempts.

The comparison between the Netherlands and Sweden, however, shows that the developments of the national control structures over time have a common element—the strong historical path dependence since established control structures reproduce and even reinforce themselves over time despite changing conditions—but the Dutch case takes it to the extreme. Civil law countries seem to be conducive to such dependencies and causalities since their political organization and decision-making processes are often very centralized. The early political support in the Netherlands for prohibition of dual-class shares in the corporate law as well as of pyramiding seems down the road to (logically) imply managerial control protected by a plethora of antitakeover defenses. There is significant political support in Sweden to instead allow and even encourage the use of control mechanisms that rigidly separate votes from capital, which points in the future direction of maintained shareholder control via increased separation of ownership from control over time but without using any other special antitakeover devices. It is thus not surprising that large listed firms in the Netherlands are controlled by co-optive management teams while in Sweden the controlling owners ultimately make the pivotal decisions.

Since the Dutch case is an extreme exception to the typical continental European corporate control structure, I am still puzzled by three enigmas: First, why have shareholders passively accepted that their control powers have been transferred to co-optive and heavily entrenched management teams often without direct ownership? Second, how efficient is such a rigid and opaque corporate control structure over time, in particular when subject to structural changes in a competitive international environment? And third, why were dual-class shares prohibited in the first Dutch corporate laws, and how has this affected the development of the Dutch corporate control structure?

References

Agnblad, Jonas, Erik Berglöf, Peter Högfeldt, and Helena Svancar. 2001. Ownership and control in Sweden: Strong owners, weak minorities, and social control. In *The control of corporate Europe,* ed. Fabrizio Barca and Marco Becht, 228–58. Oxford: Oxford University Press.

Burkart, Mike, Fausto Panunzi, and Andrei Shleifer. 2003. Family firms. *Journal of Finance* 58:2167–2202.

Field, Laura C., and Jonathan M. Karpoff. 2002. Takeover defenses at IPO firms. *Journal of Finance* 57:1857–89.

Holmén, Martin, and Peter Högfeldt. 2004. A law and finance analysis of initial public offerings. *Journal of Financial Intermediation* 13:324–58.

Sundin, Anneli, and Sven-Ivan Sundqvist. 1998 *Owners and power in Sweden's listed companies.* Stockholm: Dagens Nyheter.

9

The History and Politics of Corporate Ownership in Sweden

Peter Högfeldt

One of the ironies of European business history of the twentieth century is the relative stability (resiliency) of corporate ownership structures despite the unprecedented political turmoil with devastating wars and the interregnum of Socialism. It is, however, still impossible to understand the strong historical path dependence without analyzing how political factors have profoundly affected the development of corporate ownership by first setting the stage and then changing the conditions in systematic ways (see, e.g., Roe 2002a,b)—not only through the design of the legal system (regimes) and corporate laws, and the efficiency of legal enforcement and supervision, but also by changing the balance of interests between labor and capital by regulation of labor, product and capital markets, and development of tax-financed public welfare systems with egalitarian ambitions to redistribute resources and opportunities.

Another historical irony is that previous adversarial relations between capital and labor have given way to a corporatist society where heavily en-

Peter Högfeldt is associate professor of finance at the Stockholm School of Economics and a research associate of the European Corporate Governance Institute (ECGI).

Special thanks to Martin Holmén for help and comments and to Jan Glete for providing data. I have benefited from constructive discussions and comments by Marco Becht, Lennart Erixon, Silvia Giacomelli, Colin Mayer, Randall K. Morck, Marco Pagano, Krishna Palepu, Raghuram G. Rajan, Ailsa Röell, Örjan Sjöberg, and Steen Thomsen, as well as from participants at the University of Alberta Business School and National Bureau of Economic Research (NBER) conference at Lake Louise, Alberta, Canada, June 21–22, 2003, and participants at the Center for Economic Policy Research (CEPR)/ECGI/INSEAD/NBER/ University of Alberta joint conference on the Evolution of Corporate Governance and Family Firms in Fontainebleau January 30–31, 2004, for valuable comments. I also appreciate the generosity of The Bank of Sweden Tercentenary Foundation. An article based on this paper was published in the European and U.S. editions of *Financial Times* on October 16, 2003: "Socialist Ideal That Tied Up Swedish Riches."

trenched private ownership of the largest listed firms coexists and cooperates with labor unions whose members enjoy strong employee protection and are represented on the board (see Pagano and Volpin 2001). Since financial markets are conducive to structural changes, which often run counter to the status quo interests of incumbent labor and capital, they tend to be less developed in corporatist countries, and firms also tend to be less dependent on external financing through equity markets (see, e.g., Rajan and Zingales 2003a). This is particularly true in Continental Europe and in Scandinavia, where proportional voting systems tend to favor formation of minority or coalition governments and consensus decision making, which fosters political rent seeking by the firms' stakeholders, and larger public sectors.[1] Corporate ownership in a country therefore rests not only on the corporate law and on the legal regime but ultimately on the political acceptance at large of entrenched private ownership. The structure of corporate ownership and governance, and the development of the financial system, are thus very much integrated parts of a country's political history.

But how do the economic, political, legal, and historical conditions interact? The challenge in comparative historical analysis of corporate ownership is to try to separate which factors are primarily exogenous and which are predominantly endogenously determined, and then evaluate their relative importance and causal relations by comparing the realized historical paths across countries. History is of course not deterministic, since the actual equilibrium path is only one of many possible ones, and temporary random events like financial crises and subsequent regulatory responses may have long-term effects through path dependence (see Rajan and Zingales 2003b). The underlying assumption is thus that there is enough structural stability in societies for the comparative analysis to map out the major decisive factors of corporate ownership over time.

This is of course a very tall order, but fortunately some institutions and factors (e.g., constitutions, legal regimes and enforcement, economic geography) are surprisingly stable over time and therefore natural candidates as exogenous determinants in the causal historical analysis. Protection of property rights, freedom of contracting, and the openness of the civic society have basically been exogenous factors over a longer time period but have sometimes been exposed to the strong winds of political change.

---

1. In a cross-country analysis of the relation between political institutions and policy outcomes, Persson and Tabellini (2003) find that presidential regimes have smaller governments than parliamentary systems. Majoritarian elections induce smaller governments, less welfare spending, and smaller deficits than do proportional elections. In particular, they report systematic differences in spending patterns: "Proportional and parliamentary democracies alone display a ratchet effect in spending, with government outlays as a percentage of GDP rising in recessions, but not reverting in booms. All countries cut taxes in election years. Presidential regimes postpone fiscal contractions until after the elections, while parliamentary regimes do not; welfare-state programs are expanded in the proximity of elections, but only in democracies with proportional elections."

Changes in external competition and major technological changes are also primarily exogenous, in particular for a small open market economy, and often catalysts for structural changes. Other pivotal factors have a much less exogenous character since they are more influenced by changing economic and political conditions—for example, the domestic economy's openness to trade and capital flows and the choice of exchange rate regimes and policies to promote flexible labor markets and development of financial markets. The strongest endogenous factor in the twentieth century has definitely been how political ideology (e.g., socialism or egalitarianism) in general, and the voice of parties and organized stakeholders, in particular labor, have rallied political support for and implemented policies that absorb and assuage effects of brute, tempestuous markets forces.

This paper contributes to the comparative historic analysis by analyzing which factors (economic, legal, historical, and political) were decisive in the historical development of corporate ownership (listed firms) in Sweden. In fact, Sweden is a rather suitable case for a causal analysis since several economic factors are exogenously determined by the fact that it is a small and export-oriented economy that has exploited its base of natural resources and supplied Europe with raw materials and manufacturing goods. Institutional and political conditions have also been very stable since the country benefited politically and economically by staying out of the two wars. In particular, the political stability has been unprecedented among Western democracies.

The Social Democratic Party (SAP) has been in power since 1932 except for nine years between 1976 and 1982 and between 1991 and 1994 but predominantly as a single-party minority government with passive support from the Communist Party (SKP, VPK, and Vänsterpartiet [Socialist Party]), and more recently also from the Environmental Party (Miljöpartiet) or in coalition or with support from the Farmers' Party (Bondeförbundet, later Centerpartiet). Consistent with the corporatist spirit in society, the relation between the well-organized interests of capital and labor has in general been cooperative and consensus oriented, and property rights have been respected. The exceptions to this rule are two major political conflicts in the late 1940s (about a far-reaching governmental interventionist program for a more planned economy to fight an expected postwar depression) and in the late 1970s and early 1980s (about a proposal for partial transfer of corporate control to the labor unions), which both resulted in electoral setbacks for the Social Democrats and in implementation of significantly watered-down programs that later were terminated.

Despite recurrent financial and industrial crises, and increasing capital demands, corporate control of the largest firms has been remarkably stable and increasingly concentrated since the 1930s. The political intervention and general influence in the economy at large has, however, been significant, and embodied in an unusually large tax-financed public sector that redistributes resources and opportunities between citizens in a very ambitious manner. The mixture of institutional stability, persistent Social Democratic policies, and stable, concentrated corporate ownership in a small open economy exposed to international competitive pressure makes Sweden a particularly interesting case.

I focus on three major questions about the history and politics of corporate ownership. First, given the changing economic and political conditions, which factors caused the ownership of the largest listed firms to become so concentrated and stable over time? And which are the economic consequences thereof? Since stability breeds complacency, lock-in of inherited capital, and political rent seeking, in particular if firms are controlled by families and banks, it is important to track the effects on investments, research and development (R&D), overall growth, and creation of new firms; where does the new entrepreneurial blood come from? (See, e.g., Morck, Stangeland, and Yeung 2000 and He, Morck, and Yeung 2003.)

Second, the relation between labor and capital has not been without tension, but why did the very strong egalitarian ambitions of the labor movement (the blue-collar union LO and the Social Democratic Party [SAP]) make a halt at private ownership and accept that the control of the largest firms via pyramids and extensive use of dual-class shares rests with a very small elite of old families and professional managers? Why does one of the most egalitarian societies accept one of the most unequal distributions of power over large corporations? Neither lasting influence of an antithetical political ideology nor ambitious redesign by occupational powers (Germany and Japan) seems thus to hinder established mechanisms of corporate control from reproducing (replicating) themselves in democracies. But why are the control mechanisms so strong that they survive the whirlwinds of political and social change?

The third question concerns how the structure of the financial system has influenced and shaped corporate ownership and how ownership in turn has affected the development of the financial system, in particular of the primary equity markets. The question is of course motivated by the influential literature on law and finance that finds correlations between e.g. civil law origin dummy (significant regression coefficient), more concentrated ownership and less developed financial markets (see, e.g., La Porta, López-de-Silanes, and Shleifer 1999 and La Porta et al. 2000). Are there other factors besides the degree of legal protection of minority shareholders that explain why ownership did not become dispersed in Sweden? Does, for example, Mark Roe's idea that ownership and control do not separate in Continental Europe because the pressure of *social democracy* (in a wide sense, not necessarily a political party) also applies to perhaps the most social democratic society in Europe, Sweden?

I provide an integrated answer to the three closely related questions by focusing on a narrow financial perspective: how did the firms finance their investments? Or, more specifically, how dependent have listed firms been on external capital from the primary equity market?[2] The importance of political, social, and external economic factors will be analyzed from the perspective of how they have influenced and shaped the firm's dependence on external equity financing. The basic idea is that ownership will become dispersed only if firms need to raise a significant part of their capital in the external equity markets, and that political decisions will determine how dependent firms are on external financing. Political support for use of pyramids and dual-class shares that separate votes from capital will limit the controlling owners' as well as the firm's dependence on equity markets. This occurs because the separation of ownership from control drives a significant wedge between the costs of internal and external capital as new external shareholders demand compensation (discounts) for the associated agency costs. But the firm's internal capital is comparatively inexpensive for the controlling owners, as they have access to and exert power over all of the firm's internal cash flows via a relatively small (less than proportional) capital investment. This generates an *enhanced* pecking order of financing: strong reliance on retained earnings and borrowing but avoidance of equity issues, in particular of large public offers, as they would dilute control and also be extra costly due to the discounts to new outside shareholders (see Holmén and Högfeldt 2004b).[3] The enhanced pecking order is reinforced by the key political decision to allow banks to directly

2. My ideas have been inspired by Rajan and Zingales (2003a,b) and their interest group theory of financial development where incumbents oppose development when it breeds competition. My analysis of the Swedish case may be regarded as an application and elaboration of their basic framework by its focus on the interaction between political ideology and corporate ownership. Another great inspiration is Mark Roe's political theory about social democracy (Roe 2002a) and his views on corporate law and corporate governance (Roe 2002b), although I disagree on some points. My analysis deviates from the interesting approach to a new political economy surveyed and developed by Pagano and Volpin (2001, 2004), respectively, since I emphasize the importance of political ideology more strongly than differences in electoral systems, but their analysis has been thought provoking. Erixon (1997) has been an important inspiration, and my financial approach may be regarded as complementary to his real analysis of the Swedish industrial development. I have also benefited from Henrekson and Jakobsson (2001, 2003a,b), who emphasize the negative effect of taxes on corporate ownership and the threat of Socialism to private ownership. But they completely ignore that the existence of pyramids presupposes that intercorporate dividends as well as capital gains are not taxed; see Morck (2003). Social Democratic governments have over the years implemented such tax policies that are conducive to pyramiding; see Holmén and Högfeldt (2004b). Applying Rajan and Zingales's general reasoning, however, I develop a political theory of corporate ownership and financial markets that generates the diametrically opposite conclusion. The Social Democrats have been the guarantor rather than the threat to entrenched corporate ownership since the political and corporate incumbencies have been united over time by strong common interests. Glete's (1994) historical description and analysis of corporate networks have significantly contributed to my knowledge and ideas about corporate ownership in Sweden.

3. The pecking order is enhanced since it is caused by agency costs *inherent* to the ownership structure and not primarily by asymmetric information costs, and since public offers are very strongly avoided; see Högfeldt and Oborenko (2004).

or indirectly own equity, as the banks are more likely to provide new debt when their closely related firms need capital. The close connections between banks and large listed firms have had profound and lasting effects on corporate financing and ownership in Sweden over the last 100 years.

If capital for investments can be supplied primarily through retained earnings, by borrowing in banks, or by infusion of private capital, firms have no immediate need to go through the strictures of equity offers and place a larger fraction of shares with new investors that may dilute the value of their private benefits of control and disperse ownership. The Social Democrats have in particular pursued three policies that tend to reinforce entrenchment of incumbent owners: (a) allowing bank ownership of equity; (b) providing strong support for control structures that rigidly separate votes from capital, for a long time also combined with rigorous restrictions on foreign ownership of equity; and (c) persistently giving retained earnings and borrowing a tax advantage over equity. The policies have de facto disfavored the formation of new, fast-growing firms over incumbent firms as well as outside equity financing by supporting an enhanced pecking order of financing in established firms.

The real irony is thus that corporate ownership in Sweden is very concentrated not despite, but because of, persistent Social Democratic policies since the Great Reversal in 1932. The Social Democrats have in fact been the guarantor rather than the terminator of private capitalism since the political and corporate incumbencies have been united by strong common interests. Incumbent owners need the political support to legitimize that their corporate power rests on extensive use of dual-class shares and pyramiding, while the Social Democrats only get the necessary resources and indirect support for their social and economic policies from the private sector if the largest firms remain under Swedish control so that capital does not migrate.

Before elaborating on these ideas, I start by presenting a general picture of how corporate ownership has developed historically. After an analytical description of how the ideology and policies of the Social Democrats have affected corporate ownership, I develop my simple political theory of why ownership did not separate widely in Sweden, which focuses on the interaction between corporate ownership and development of the primary equity markets. Before presenting an integrated answer to the three main questions of this chapter, I critically evaluate the Swedish model of corporate ownership. To extract some general implications about how history and politics interact, I speculate about the major exogenous and endogenous factors that caused corporate ownership to follow the path it did in Sweden. I conclude by putting my analysis in a wider historical context.

9.1   A Stylized History of Corporate Ownership in Sweden

Starting with economic reforms in the 1860s (e.g., freedom to establish new firms for men and women and liberalization of foreign trade), Sweden followed a trajectory of fast industrialization with the highest recorded rate of productivity growth between 1870 and 1913; the productivity level was the second-lowest in Europe in 1970 (Maddison 1982). The export-oriented raw material sector expanded very fast as it supplied the booming Western Europe with timber and iron ore. A first wave of (domestic) innovations provided the foundation for new (genius) firms specialized in engineering and manufacturing that became the basis of large export of investment goods: Atlas Copco (1873), L. M. Ericsson (1876), Alfa-Laval (1883), ASEA (1883), AGA (1904), and SKF (1907). Already before 1914 the newly founded firms represented half of the production value in Swedish engineering. The very rapid industrialization until 1914 took place behind a tariff barrier that averaged about 15 percent. In a second wave of innovations, primarily international ones adapted to domestic conditions, new firms with domestic consumer goods orientation were founded: Electrolux, Scania-Vabis, Volvo, and SAAB.

The long expansion from 1870, in particular from the 1890s, to 1914 resulted in radical transformation of all facets of society. Sweden is a good early example of successful export-led growth. The public sector, both at the central level and in municipalities, raised very significant amounts of capital in international bond issues (primarily from France and Germany) to finance the large infrastructural investments in, for example, railroads, harbors, cities, and housing. Because of very favorable circumstances, the loans were repaid during World War I. As part of the structural reforms, a banking system on the Scottish model with deposit banks that issued notes was built. The new firms used almost exclusively retained earnings (about 40 percent of profits were reinvested), trade credits, short-term credit notes, and later short-term bank loans combined with bond financing of machinery and buildings (see Gårdlund 1947). Firms were controlled by a very small circle of shareholders around the founder and his or her family (see Jörberg 1988).

Commercial banks (equity backed) developed fast from the 1870s, when the regulation of interest rates was abandoned. But bank loans did not become an important source of industrial financing until around 1900. The banking industry was well organized and had political support since an efficient banking system was regarded as crucial for the development of a relatively poor country. Because of the large export-led industrial expansion after 1900, a relatively large external equity financing became necessary. More organized and regular trading started at the Stockholm Stock Exchange in 1901 as equity replaced the traditional bond financing, and borrowing from banks increased rapidly in response to the increasing demand for capital. The development of the financial system in Sweden seems to be demand driven as new institutions and regulation adjusted to the changing conditions.

However, despite significant increase in demand for investment capital from the rapidly growing export-oriented industries (manufacturing and raw material–based industries), after 1900 when the equity market became more important, the capital flows were mainly directed through the banking system. After heavy lobbying from the banking industry, the Banking Act of 1911 allowed banks to directly own shares and operate as investment banks; the leading bankers controlled the public commission that wrote the law (see Fritz 1990). The German banking system was now the role model since significant infusion of new capital via the (universal) banking system was argued to be the key to the German economic success. The banks fueled the speculative stock market boom of the 1910s and 1920s both by helping clients to lever up their portfolios and by buying most of the relatively frequent equity issues via highly leveraged, stock-financed so-called Issuing Companies (Emissionsbolag) that were very closely affiliated with the banks (see Östlind 1945). The established relation-based banking system thereby extended its influence and control also to the new equity market that developed too late to become a large independent supplier of risk capital before the financial markets de facto closed down in the 1930s.

After the crises in the early 1920s the banks owned a significant number of shares in the major listed firms and became the controlling owner; see table 9.1. However, since the innovators that founded the first generation of firms were not equally successful as businessmen, they often lost control, particularly after financial crises, or the control of their family was diluted. Given the rather advanced technical character of the firms, an outside professional manager with background in engineering and management was often hired to run the firm. That the banks became controlling owners reinforced this tendency, as they lacked the competence to run the firms themselves. The previously privately controlled firms that already dispersed their ownership when issuing new equity to finance their investments in the 1910s and 1920s in effect came to be run by the management under supervision of the controlling bank. It is thus no surprise that the overwhelming majority of the twenty-five largest firms in 1925 are de facto run by the chief executive officer (CEO). In fact, an interesting feature of corporate ownership in Sweden until after World War II is the very strong position of the CEO, who most often did not own any shares but often had a significant support from minority shareholders. There are examples where the CEO won battles with the largest owners by accumulating the votes of the minority shareholders. The firms were frequently identified more with their CEO than with their controlling owners; there are several cases where the CEO built a dynasty by letting his son or son-in-law succeed him.[4]

After the financial crises in the 1930s when banks owned very large portfolios of listed stocks and de facto controlled the largest listed firms, the

---

4. For example, three generations of Laurin were CEOs of PLM without owning any shares and despite the fact that one father warned the owners to let his son succeed him.

Table 9.1   **Ownership and controlling owners in the twenty-five largest industrial firms in Sweden in 1925**

Firm	No. of Employees	Controlling owner	Type of control
ASEA	7,000		M
Stora Kopparberg	7,000	Wallenberg	E (M)
Svenska Tändsticks AB	5,000	Ivar Kreuger	F
Grängesberg/LKAB	5,200		M
SKF	5,200	Mark/Carlander Wallenberg Skandinavbanken	M
Uddeholm	4,100		M
Höganäs-Billesholm	3,900		M
L. M. Ericsson	3,500	K. E. Wincrantz Ivar Kreuger	FE
Husqvarna	3,300		M
Tobaksmonopolet	3,200	Government	M
Sockerbolaget	3,000		M
Ytterstforss-Munksund	3,000	Svenska Handelsbanken	M
Holmens Bruk	3,000	Wahren	M
Gimo-Österby	3,000	Svenska Handelsbanken	M
Sandviken	3,000	Göransson/Magnusson	F
Skånska Cement	2,600	Wehtje	FM
Götaverken	2,500	Broström	ME
Separator	2,300	Cross-holdings	M
NOHAB	2,300	Göteborgs Handelsbank	M
Billerud	2,200		M
Bergvik & Ala	2,200	Svenska Handelsbanken	M
A. K. Fernström	2,100	Fernström	F
Iggesund	2,000	Trygger/Von Sydow	ME
Skönvik	2,000	Bunsow Svenska Handelsbanken	M
Malmö Yllefabrik	1,900	Schmitz Skandinavbanken	F

Source: Glete (1994).
Notes: Type of controlling owners: F (family control and CEO member of the founding family); E (entrepreneurial control; controlling owner appoints the CEO and is active in the board); and M (management independent of owners).

Swedish 1934 (light) version of Glass-Steagall prohibited them from directly owning equity, but a few years later they were allowed to transfer their assets to holding companies if the shares were distributed to the bank's shareholders. The controlling owners of the banks thus maintained control and, in effect, reinforced it, since the holding companies were formally separated from the banks but were organized as (listed) closed-end investment funds (CEIFs), which became the pivotal entity around which the typical three-level Swedish ownership pyramid is built: a controlling family or bank foundation at the apex and the listed portfolio firms at the bottom, which are controlled via the CEIF at the intermediate level. Figure 9.1 illustrates the transparent three-level structure of the Wallenberg ownership pyramid in 1996 with Investor in the middle as the pivotal

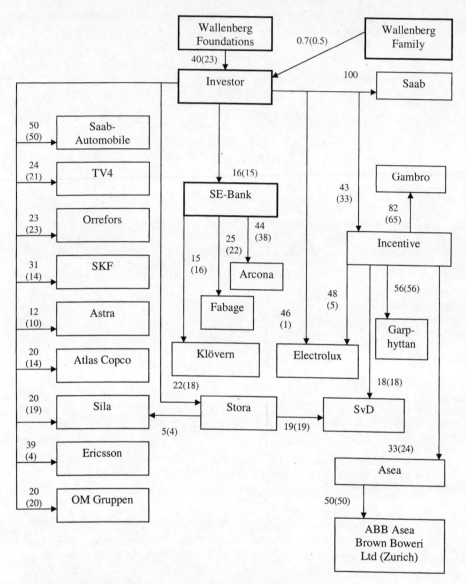

Fig. 9.1 The Wallenberg sphere in January 1996

Source: Reproduced from Sundin and Sundqvist (1996).

Note: Vote ownership is reported with equity ownership in parentheses.

control vehicle of the largest listed firms in Sweden, and the tax-exempt family foundations at the top.

Investor was founded by the Wallenberg-controlled Stockholms Enskilda Bank (today SEB) while Industrivärden, the other leading holding company (CEIF), was founded by the management-controlled Svenska Handelsbanken (SHB). Starting already in the 1920s, the banks exercised more influence as shareholders and sometimes also as controlling owners at the same time as being the major provider of loans. Since the equity markets de facto closed down in the 1930s, the banking law made the financial capital the dominant supplier of capital, and the bankers became business leaders even if the CEOs had a strong position without owning shares. The banks restructured the financially distressed Swedish industrials using intermediated capital and active management of their portfolio (see Larsson 2002). A combination of political conditions and financial crises reversed the road to dispersed ownership.

It is particularly interesting to observe that the two pivotal reforms of bank ownership in 1911 and 1934 both had the strong support of the Social Democrats; without their votes, together with those of the Liberals in 1911, there would not have been any reform.[5] They wrote the new law in 1934 after gaining power in 1932. When the Social Democrats formed their first minority government in 1920, Hjalmar Branting appointed Johannes Hellner, head of the legal department at Stockholms Enskilda Bank, to finance minister.

Because of a sequence of pivotal political decisions, supported by both the Social Democrats and the political voice of leading capitalists, listed firms in Sweden have primarily relied on retained earnings—the traditional but also significantly tax-subsidized way of financing—and bank loans but have only to a very limited extent issued new shares. The largest firms were linked to their main bank as supplier of credits while the firms deposited money and did their banking with their hausbank. Analyzing credit contracts between listed firms and large banks between 1916 and 1947, Sjögren (1995) finds that forty-six of fifty nonfinancial listed firms entered contracts that lasted for at least five years. Of the listed firms, 40 percent had contracts that lasted for the whole period. More than 30 percent of the firms had credit, ownership, deposit, and bond issuance contracts with only one bank. But the other side of financial interaction was a tight network of pivotal persons around the bank; the controlling owners or CEOs of the listed firms were often represented on the bank's board while representatives of the bank had seats in the firms' boards. Figure 9.2 illustrates the alliances

5. In 1905 Marcus Wallenberg senior argued that Sweden had great untapped resources, able engineers, and good workers but lacked entrepreneurs. His remedy was to start a business school and allow banks to buy shares in listed companies. His family helped found Stockholm's School of Economics in 1909. And his elder half-brother K. A. Wallenberg, chief executive of Stockholm's Enskilda Bank, chairman of the Swedish Bankers' Association, and member of Parliament, spearheaded an initiative to allow the largest commercial banks to own shares and to begin acting as investment banks. Against the will of the Conservative government but with the support of the Social Democrats, his proposal was adopted in 1911.

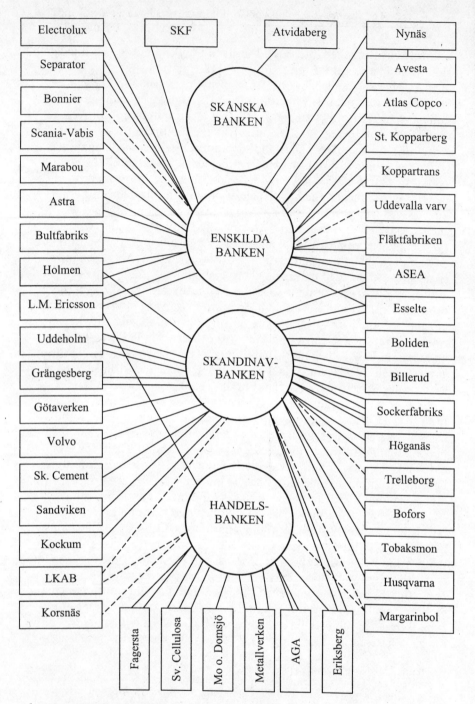

Fig. 9.2   The banks and the largest firms in 1960

Source: Hermansson (1965, p. 190).

Notes: The full line indicates that managing directors and/or board members of the bank are also board members of large firms that do their major borrowing and other financial activities with the bank. The dotted lines show that there is only an indirect relation as old managers or nonboard members affiliated with the bank are also board members of client firms.

and very close relations between leading representatives of the major banks, in particular the three largest ones—Enskilda Banken (Wallenberg), Skandinavbanken, and Handelsbanken—and industrial firms in 1960 (see Hermansson [1965], former leader of the Communist Party in Sweden). The lines (dotted lines) indicate a direct (indirect) link between the banks and the main borrowers as the banks' managing directors or board members are members of the board of their main industrial clients.

Table 9.2 shows the ownership and control of the largest listed firms right after the war in 1945. The size of the firms has become significantly larger, and owners, in particular the Wallenberg group, have advanced their position even if management control under bank supervision is the norm while control by founding firms has diminished further. Using a Swedish Census on equity ownership from 1945, Lindgren (1953) reports that 6 to 7 percent of shareholders controlled 65 to 70 percent of the market value. Analyzing records from the shareholders' general meetings, he finds that a single in-

Table 9.2   Ownership and controlling owners in the twenty-five largest industrial firms in Sweden in 1945

Firm	No. of Employees	Controlling owner	Type of control
ASEA	23,200	Wallenberg	ME
Uddeholm	11,000		M
Bofors	9,200	Axel Wenner-Gren	M
SKF	8,500	Mark/Carlander Wallenberg	(E)
L. M. Ericsson	7,500	ITT, SHB-Group Wallenberg	E
Stora Kopparberg	7,500	Wallenberg	E
SCA	7,000	SHB-Gruppen	M
Esselte	6,700		M
Fagersta	6,400	SHB-Gruppen	M
Svenska Tändsticks AB	6,200	Wallenberg	E
Grängesberg/LKAB	6,200		M
Götaverken	6,000	AB Gillius (Management)	M
Sandviken	5,900	Göransson/Magnusson	F
Husqvarna	5,800		M
Hellefors Bruk	5,300	Custos	M
Skånska Cementgjuteriet	4,500	Wehtje	E
Skånska Cement/IFÖ	4,500	Wehtje	F
Sockerbolaget	4,000		M
Volvo	3,700		M
Svenska Metallverken	3,500		M
Billerud	3,500		M
Boliden	3,500	Skandinaviska Banken	M
Separator	3,300	Wallenberg	ME
Höganäs-Billesholm	3,100		M
Kockums Mek Verkstad	3,000	Kockum	E

Source: Glete (1994).
Notes: See table 9.1 notes.

dividual represented the majority of votes in 60 percent of the large firms (more than 500 employees) while three or fewer owners constituted the majority in over 90 percent of these firms. In regularly quoted firms, a single individual represented the majority in 53 percent of the cases, while in 85 percent of the firms the two largest owners represented more than 50 percent of the votes.

Figure 9.3 shows the so-called *fifteen families* and their controlling interests and financial networks in 1960, which Hermansson (1965) identified as the ultimate controlling owners of the listed firms in Sweden. Of the fifty largest industrial firms, forty-one are controlled by these families (nine are controlled by the state or by cooperatives or municipalities). The government commission on ownership and influence in private industry (Statens Offentliga Utredningar [SOU] 1968a) analyzed the situation in 1963 and identified the same fifteen families as well as two bank-related groups as the controlling owners. It is interesting to observe that the nine families that were closely tied to Handelsbanken and Skadinavbanken do not exert any power today or are significantly marginalized; an exception might be the Klingspors, who, through their association with the Stenbeck Group, still exert power. Of the families with very close personal ties to Enskilda Banken and Investor, the main family, the Wallenbergs, is still in control, even if their control has become diluted in recent years due to large international mergers (ABB, AstraZeneca, and Stora Enso) and concentration of their portfolio investments. The Bonnier and Johnsson families have been rejuvenated in the fifth generation and are still influential even if their relative position has declined. The Wehtje and Throne-Holst families, and to a lesser extent the Söderberg family, have been marginalized since 1967 or exert no power today.

But already in 1967 the very rapid growth and international expansion of the leading firms in the 1950s and 1960s had undercut the family control of the largest listed firms even if the families more frequently changed to a dual-class structure in order to maintain control when raising new capital. Only 18 percent of the largest listed firms used such a control structure in 1950, but almost one-third used it in 1968. However, as table 9.3 illustrates, the financial capital became dominant and the Wallenberg group in particular had the financial muscle when the equity markets were dormant. The increasing capital demands to establish a large ownership position is also evident from table 9.4, which shows the frequency of ownership positions sorted both by size of ownership (by capital—not votes) and by size of the 100 largest firms in terms of employment in 1950, 1963, 1978, and 1985. The frequency of small but identifiable holdings has decreased very significantly over the years, while the number of larger positions has increased, particularly in the larger firms, which indicates that owners with more capital resources have become more dominant, even without considering their extra voting power due to the frequent use of dual-class shares.

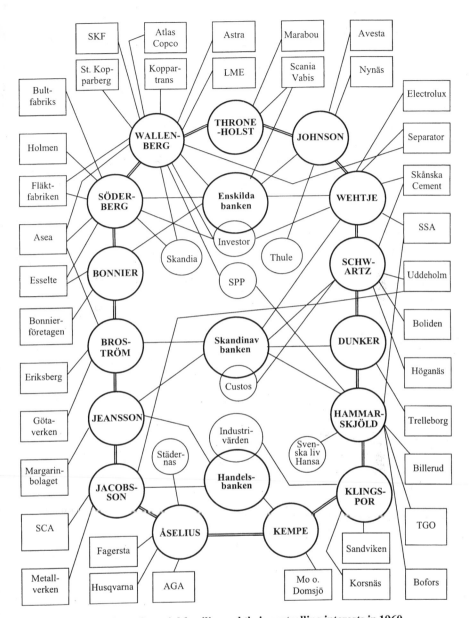

Fig. 9.3   The fifteen financial families and their controlling interests in 1960

Source: Hermansson (1965, p. 289).

Note: This figure shows the network between the financial families and the firms they control, as well as their relations with the three major banks (Enskilda Banken, Skandinavbanken, and Handelsbanken) and with holding companies (closed-end investment funds like Investor, Custos, and Industrivärden) associated with the banks and with insurance companies (e.g., Skandia, Thule, and SPP).

Table 9.3   Ownership and controlling owners in the twenty-five largest industrial
                   firms in Sweden in 1967

Firm	No. of Employees	Controlling owner	Type of control
SKF	64,759	Wallenberg, Asken	M (E)
L. M. Ericsson	46,400	Wallenberg SHB-Gruppen	E
ASEA	32,401	Wallenberg	E
Svenska Tändsticks AB	31,800	Wallenberg	E
Volvo	24,268		M
Electrolux	20,964	Wallenberg	E
Alfa-Laval	17,837	Wallenberg	E
Skånska Cementgjuteriet	17,518	Skånska Cement	M
Grängesberg	16,010		M
Uddeholm	15,812	Custos	M
Sandviken	14,850	Klingspor/Stenbeck	E
SCA	14,121	SHB-Gruppen	M
SAAB	13,699	Wallenberg	E
BPA	13,000	TUC	M
Facit	12,832	Ericsson	M
Bofors	12,300		M
AGA	12,244	SHB-Gruppen	M
Stora Kopparberg	11,371	Wallenberg	E
Atlas Copco	11,196	Wallenberg	E
Skånska Cement	9,638		M
Scania Vabis	9,280	Wallenberg	E
Götaverken	8,274	AB Gillius (Management)	M
Mo & Domsjö	8,017	Kempe/Carlgren	F
Svenska Metallverken	7,775	SHB-Gruppen	F
Esselte	7,668		M

Source: Glete (1994).
Notes: See table 9.1 notes.

Table 9.5 shows that in 1990 the largest firms have become significantly larger due mergers and acquisitions while the Wallenbergs remained in control. However, the number of management-controlled firms is still high, in particular since three of the most important—Sandvik, Skanska, and Volvo—developed an elaborate system of cross-shareholdings to fend off potential hostile takeovers as more developed liquid markets facilitated such endeavors. New financial operators became active during the 1980s— Anders Wall, Erik Penser, and Sven-Olof Johansson, to name a few—but their importance vanished during the 1990s. More recent additions are Carl Bennet, Gustaf Douglas, Sven Hagströmer, Mats Qviberg, Fredrik Lundberg, Melker Schörling, and Jan Stenbeck who have built and rebuilt existing firms into controlling groups using entrepreneurial financial skills.

In recent years the Wallenberg power sphere has let go of control in Alfa-Laval, Esab, KemaNobel, SAAB Automobile, Swedish Match, and partially of Scania and most parts of the Incentive conglomerate and of Dili-

Table 9.4   **Frequency of ownership positions sorted both by size of ownership (capital) and by size of the 100 largest firms in terms of employment in 1950, 1963, 1978, and 1985 (%)**

	< 2.0	2.0–5.0	5.0–10.0	10.0–25.0	25.0–50.0	50.0–100
1950						
Firms 1–25	347	34	13	5	5	2
Firms 26–50	149	48	14	23	6	4
Firms 51–75	128	25	14	19	8	9
Firms 76–100	70	33	15	7	8	12
1963						
Firms 1–25	388	63	21	5	7	3
Firms 26–50	336	67	19	9	6	1
Firms 51–75	169	77	24	16	6	7
Firms 76–100	140	66	23	18	4	11
1978						
Firms 1–25	10	89	18	16	5	2
Firms 26–50	14	81	35	17	4	3
Firms 51–75	1	43	31	15	10	7
Firms 76–100	2	53	11	9	12	11
1985						
Firms 1–25	28	89	39	21	9	3
Firms 26–50	14	81	44	17	10	4
Firms 51–75	14	51	32	21	14	9
Firms 76–100	4	57	17	17	17	8

Source: Studieförbundet Näringsliv och Samhälle (SNS) Ownership Project (1988).

gentia, while establishing control of Gambro, WM-Data, and a portfolio of smaller firms. The group has also been instrumental in abolishing shares with a 1:1000 voting differential in Electrolux and SKF but not in Ericsson until 2004, when the A-shares were finally converted to a new differential of 1:10 as the other controlling owner, Industrivärden, (finally) accepted the negotiated compensation for old A-shares. Instead of a joint voting strength of over 80 percent in Ericsson, they now only control around 40 percent of the votes.

The long-run survival of controlling families in Sweden looks as follows. Four (Wallenberg, Bonnier, Johnson, and Söderberg) of the fourteen families that established control before 1920 are still exerting control, while six (Rausing, Kamprad, Olsson, Wallenius, Persson, and Stenbeck) of the twenty-three families that founded firms between 1920 and 1965 are still significant and active owners today. Other vanished slowly and maintained positions until the 1980s: Kempe/Carlgren, Salén, Edstrand, Roos, Malmros, von Kantzow, Throne-Holst, Philipson, and Wendt. These families were well connected, but most likely the entrepreneurial spirit ran out—and so did their financial resources. Newer additions have shown much worse survival rates. The addition in recent years of new family-controlled firms that have grown large very fast has been very limited indeed; the very old firms

Table 9.5   Ownership and controlling owners in the twenty-five largest industrial firms in Sweden in 1990

Firm	No. of Employees	Controlling owner	Type of control
ASEA Brown Boveri	215,154	Wallenberg Brown Boveri	E (M)
Electrolux	150,892	Wallenberg	E
Volvo	72,213	Volvo-Skanska Cross-Shareholding	M
Stora	69,700	Wallenberg	E
Ericsson	66,138	Wallenberg SHB-Gruppen	ME
SKF	49,305	Wallenberg Skanska	ME
Procordia	45,193	Government/Volvo	ME
Skanska	31,746	Volvo-Skanska Cross Shareholding	M
SCA	30,139	SHB-Gruppen	M
Saab Scania	29,388	Wallenberg	E
Nobel Industrier	26,654	Penser	E
Sandvik	26,373	Skanska	M
NCC	23,178	Johnsson's Foundations	E
Trelleborg	21,939	Dunker's Foundation	M
Atlas Copco	21,507	Wallenberg	E
Alfa-Laval	20,809	Wallenberg	E
Esselte	19,545	Lindholm	E
ASEA	18,066	Wallenberg	E
BPA	17,948	TUC	M
AGA	14,559	SHB-Gruppen	M
Cardo	14,080	Volvo	M
MoDo	12,961	Kempe/Carlgren (SCA)	E
Svenskt Stål AB	12,014	Government	ME
SIAB	9,814	Lundberg	E
FFV	9,709	Government	ME

Source: Glete (1994).
Notes: See table 9.1 notes.

still dominate, even if the number of family-controlled firms among initial public offerings (IPOs) had been high (see Holmén and Högfeldt 2004a).

Significant legal restrictions on foreign ownership have been an important ingredient of the Swedish ownership model. Starting with the ban on foreigners' owning real estate and mines in the nineteenth century, foreign ownership was in 1916 limited to 20 percent of voting rights in Swedish firms owning natural resources. In the 1930s foreign ownership in listed firms was limited to so-called unrestricted shares (representing at most 20 percent of the voting rights), while *restricted* shares could only be owned by Swedish individuals and institutions.[6] There has been a dramatic in-

6. To circumvent the 20 percent voting restriction on foreign ownership in order to raise large amounts of equity capital in the U.S. capital markets in the late 1920s, firms controlled by Ivar Kreuger, like Ericsson and SKF, introduced B-shares with a 1/1000 voting right. In 1983 the restriction on foreign ownership of natural resources was adjusted to the dual system for foreign ownership of shares in listed firms in the Corporate Purchase Act (Företagsförvärvslagen).

crease in foreign ownership of listed shares since 1993, when the restrictions on foreign ownership were abolished. Anticipating that direct foreign ownership of equity will be allowed as part of the process to join the European Union (EU), many family-controlled firms started to use dual-class shares in the 1980s; an overwhelming majority of them used them in the early 1990s.

Looking further back at trends, direct ownership of listed shares by Swedish households decreased from 75 percent in 1950 to about 25 percent in 1990, while ownership by Swedish institutions increased from about 20 percent in 1950 to 70 percent in 1990; foreign ownership was well below 10 percent during this period but is currently around 35 percent. These types of portfolio investments are primarily in B-shares. The original owners have therefore most frequently managed to remain in control by using dual-class shares more efficiently. But the institutional capital has definitely become much more important in Sweden and has recently, somewhat reluctantly, started to exert responsibility and power as large providers of capital but not necessarily as controlling owners.

Table 9.6 shows that almost seventy years after the formal legal separation from the banks, the two closed-end funds—Investor and Industrivärden—are still the major controlling owners of the largest listed firms. Even if the pyramids are shallow, the combined effect with dual-class shares creates a substantial *control multiplier:* total equity value of firms controlled by CEIFs divided by value of capital invested by controlling owners. For example, panel A shows that in year 2000 the controlling owners' investments in the CEIFs were worth 80 billion Svenska Kronor (SEK), which amounts to 2.6 percent of the market capitalization of the Stockholm Stock Exchange. The total market value of listed firms de facto controlled by the CEIFs (largest fraction of votes) was 1,786 billion SEK, which is 57 percent of the market capitalization of 3,135 billion SEK (excluding the market value of CEIFs).[7] The control multiplier was thus 22 (57/2.6) in 2000 and has grown over time.

Panel B shows the dominance of the two most powerful CEIFs—Investor and Industrivärden—where the pivotal owners controlled almost 50 percent of the market capitalization by investing only 2 percent of the market capitalization. The control multiplier for the two combined was thus 23.[8]

The firms controlled by CEIFs do not only dominate the stock market capitalization. They are also extremely important for general economic

7. At the end of 2000, four (twelve) of the ten (twenty) largest firms (market value equity) in Sweden were controlled by CEIFs.

8. The dramatic increase in the CEIF control multiplier in 1991 is due to intragroup takeovers. Industrivärden acquired Bahco (previously named Promotion), the other CEIF controlled by the SHB group, while Investor acquired another Wallenberg-controlled CEIF, Providentia. The value under control remained roughly the same, but the value of the controlling owners' listed investments decreased. The same year Investor also acquired Saab, where the Wallenbergs had a large direct ownership. In 1994 Investor also acquired Export-Invest, another CEIF within the Wallenberg sphere.

Table 9.6   Closed-end investment funds' control of the Stockholm Stock Exchange (SSE), 1986–2000

Year	Value under CEIF control	Value of SSE (CEIFs excluded)	% of SSE value (CEIFs excluded) under CEIF control	Personal investments on SSE by the controlling owners of the CEIFs	Personal investments as % of SSE value	Control/capital
			A. Value under CEIF control			
1986	284,328	405,505	70.1	25,008	6.2	11.4
1987	235,598	402,100	58.6	21,063	5.2	11.2
1988	342,266	566,403	60.4	31,218	5.5	11.0
1989	447,512	701,360	63.8	41,022	5.8	10.9
1990	296,758	504,560	58.8	31,054	6.2	9.6
1991	352,133	516,247	68.2	20,444	4.0	17.2
1992	368,878	505,439	73.0	20,050	4.0	18.4
1993	691,817	831,846	83.2	40,135	4.8	17.2
1994	587,787	964,558	60.9	33,394	3.5	17.6
1995	743,420	1,137,772	65.3	41,223	3.6	18.0
1996	1,067,296	1,743,868	61.2	60,963	3.5	17.5
1997	1,343,580	1,984,227	67.7	75,378	3.8	17.8
1998	1,373,303	2,249,611	61.0	73,156	3.3	18.8
1999	2,151,551	3,644,555	59.0	106,431	2.9	20.2
2000	1,786,520	3,134,973	57.0	80,259	2.6	22.3

B. Total market value controlled by Investor and Industrivärden

	Value under Wallenberg or SHB control	Market value of SSE (CEIFs excluded)	% of SSE value under Wallenberg or SHB control	Personal investments on SSE by the Wallenbergs and SHB	Personal investments as % of SSE value	Control/capital
1986	214,167	405,505	47.6	14,467	3.2	14.8
1987	188,426	402,130	42.9	12,659	2.9	14.9
1988	284,120	566,403	46.0	20,589	3.3	13.8
1989	378,846	701,360	48.9	27,034	3.5	14.0
1990	275,475	504,560	50.3	21,935	4.0	12.6
1991	294,597	516,247	53.4	14,691	2.7	20.1
1992	310,584	505,439	56.8	15,459	2.8	20.1
1993	561,866	831,846	62.9	32,699	3.7	17.2
1994	560,923	964,558	54.6	28,911	2.8	19.4
1995	702,468	1,137,772	58.1	36,073	3.0	19.5
1996	1,004,736	1,743,868	54.4	52,806	2.9	19.0
1997	1,340,257	1,984,227	63.4	66,426	3.1	20.2
1998	1,341,042	2,249,511	56.6	63,944	2.7	21.0
1999	2,088,542	3,644,555	55.0	96,148	2.5	21.7
2000	1,632,428	3,134,973	49.3	69,707	2.2	23.4

Source: Holmén and Högfeldt (2004b).

Notes: This table shows the total market value of equity controlled by closed-end investment funds (CEIFs) and as a percentage of the SSE market capitalization (market value of CEIFs excluded), the personal investments (investments by foundations controlled by the family/organization included) by the controlling owners of the CEIFs (i.e., the capital amount the owners themselves have invested), the percentage of total market capitalization invested by the controlling owners of the CEIFs, and the ratio between value under control and the net capital investment by the controlling owners of the CEIF. Panel A shows value under CEIF control (sum of firm values in which a CEIF is part of the controlling block; i.e., the largest voting block) in million SEK, value of SSE in million SEK with CEIFs excluded, the market value of the personal investments by the controlling owners of the CEIFs (controlled foundations included). Panel B shows total market value controlled by Investor and Industrivärden (sum of firm equity values in which Investor or Industrivärden is part of the controlling block; i.e., the largest voting block) in million SEK, market capitalization of SSE (million SEK with CEIFs excluded), and personal equity investments on the SSE by the Wallenbergs and the SHB (foundations included), either through the CEIFs (Investor [Providentia, Export Invest] or via Industrivärden [Promotion/Bahco]) or through direct investments.

activity in Sweden. In 2000 CEIF-controlled firms generated 38 percent of the Swedish gross domestic product (GDP).[9] And in 1999 their investments constituted 28 percent of the gross capital formation in the business sector. By controlling a large share of the corporate capital in Sweden, the pyramids' investment decisions thus have significant impact on the overall allocation of economic resources. Even if the separation of ownership and control in pyramid structures is a well-established international phenomenon, the very large control multiplier in CEIFs may thus have wider economic implications in Sweden.[10]

Via Investor the Wallenbergs also exert significant political influence both externally and within the business community, for example, by being the controlling owners (together with the government) of the Stockholm Stock Exchange (SSE) and by in effect setting their own standards for listing requirements and for ethical codes—the Swedish version of self-regulation. After the equity markets were reactivated in the 1980s and firms needed more capital as the size of firms grew rapidly, the two funds' control has in fact increased because of very extensive use of dual-class shares. Overall entrenchment of corporate ownership has increased since other listed firms as well as newly listed IPO firms have also used dual-class shares in an unprecedented way to maintain control; around 60 percent of the listed firms use dual-class shares. Despite the very significant increase of institutional capital and foreign capital, corporate ownership is as entrenched as ever in Sweden since the largest firms are still controlled by an old financial nobility of families in the third to fifth generation and by banks, but to a much lesser extent by institutions that provide the majority of the capital.

The conflict between private control and increasing capital demands is thus handled in Sweden by strategic pyramiding and more frequent use of dual-class shares that increases the separation between control and ownership over time. The pivotal corporate control of the largest listed firms thus remains in Swedish hands while the capital becomes more institutionalized and international. The rest of the paper is an attempt to explain why this happened and what the long-term consequences are. It is a highly political story!

9.2   Social Democracy and Capitalism

The historical agenda of the Social Democrats had three stages: first, the fight for *political democracy* (suffrage), then use of parliamentary power to

9. GDP and capital formation numbers are collected from Statistiska Centralbyrån (SCB, Statistics Sweden).

10. The Social Democrats have demonstrated an active interest in the development of ownership concentration in the private industry, in particular in the banking sector, as evident from a string of governmental reports from the 1960s to the end of the 1980s (SOU 1968a,b, 1988; Statens Industriverk [SIND] 1980:5), when domestic capital markets as well as international capital flows were heavily regulated.

implement *social democracy* (an egalitarian welfare state), and finally *economic democracy,* wherein economic decisions within firms are not based on strict private rationality but reflect the wider social interest of the firm's stakeholders and society at large. The electoral victory in 1932 initiated implementation of the social democracy. The existing industrial structure with relatively large-scale production in a few export-oriented firms, often with a well-defined controlling owner or a strong manager, suited their vision of the road to economic democracy quite well. They did not envision direct nationalization of industries but a stakeholder form of socialism that was more efficient than pure capitalism because it contained elements of rational planning that would eliminate the waste that irrational, short-sighted markets create, like unemployment and volatile investment cycles. The necessary economic changes would also be faster and more efficiency-enhancing if they took place in ways that were more socially acceptable for workers. Egalitarianism and economic efficiency were thus not necessarily contradictory concepts.

The ideological motivation was the almost existential conflict built into capitalism between private ownership of capital (firms) and the ever-growing social character of production; workers are not only a production factor but also members of society with social needs, and private economic decisions within firms will have a wider and deeper impact on society at large. The immediate needs of the workers within the firm would be protected by their union's negotiating with the employer about compensation and working conditions without governmental intervention (except for basic regulation); that is, the adversarial relations between labor and capital would be respected without board representation of labor. Their more general social interests outside the firm (e.g., employment, pension, education, and housing) would be protected via Social Democratic political initiatives to build a tax-financed public sector that redistributed resources between individuals and families and provided social services and insurance. The overriding objective was, however, to create a full employment economy by promoting growth-enhancing policies that stimulated labor mobility as well as investments and restructuring within the industrial sector. Higher growth would not only generate higher wages but also increase welfare by financing the public sector.

The Social Democrats' vision of economic growth was large-scale production with ever-growing firm size, as resources are better used within a planned hierarchy than in markets; in particular, allocations to large investments and to large-scale R&D are more efficient (see, e.g., Wigforss 1980, vol. I). To realize the idea of a more efficient, higher stage of capitalism the pivotal factor was to induce capitalists to invest more, particularly in long-term capital-intensive production; a good capitalist is one who fulfills his or her basic economic function of investing. The increasing dependence of very large firms would also make the social character of production more obvious, and thus also the need to let the firm's stakeholders and wider societal concerns affect the private economic decisions within the firm. This was in effect a vision of a corporatist society with capitalistic firms without capitalists, as their decision power would be cut back to the decision to invest; capital would remain within the firm as investments financed by retained earnings were heavily tax subsidized. Firms would be run in the interests of society at large and not in the narrow, private economic interests of essentially nominal owners. Or to use the words of Ernst Wigforss (1980), the leading ideologue and minister of finance from 1932 to 1949, "social firms without owners." Taming of capitalism thus did not imply immediate takeover of private ownership as long as the capitalists invested.

The existing corporate structure of relatively few but large, export-oriented firms closely affiliated with and often controlled by the major banks actually fitted the corporatist vision very well. Banks are intrinsically relatively more important than individual firms, as they are pivotal nodes in the network that allocates capital across firms and individuals, which may make it easier for them to assume wider societal concerns. However, perhaps more important, being both major lenders and providers of equity capital to the often highly leveraged firms, the controlling banks in effect acted more like bondholders with focus on long-term survival than as thoroughbred, risk-taking capitalists. They are therefore more inclined to adopt a long-term perspective with less focus on myopic profits and are more ready to accept social considerations when firing and hiring people. In particular, they are more likely to finance large, capital-intensive investments that are also socially desirable. Such owners are also more conducive to respond to tax-based policies that strongly stimulate reinvestment of retained earnings in the large, established firms.[11]

The idea of social firms without owners was part of a greater vision of a socially planned (democratic) economy that consisted of an integrated set of policies: for example, tax-based policies to promote and direct investments, and regulations to channel household savings to politically controlled funds that allocate capital to socially desirable objectives like investment in housing, infrastructure and education. But this set of policies also included programs to stimulate growth by promotion of innovations, labor market mobility, and extensive research in cooperation with the leading capitalists and their firms. The pivotal element was to generate a higher overall growth rate by policies that stimulated savings and allocated investments more efficiently by also incorporating wider societal objectives.

11. In the 1950s Galbraith's book from 1956—*American Capitalism: The Concept of Countervailing Power*—and later his 1967 book, *The New Industrial State,* had a strong influence on the leading Social Democrats with its blessing of large-scale production. He was invited by the prime minister for a two-day conference with leading representatives of the Swedish society.

The higher growth might then be used to finance the social reform agenda. The programs would be implemented by the Social Democrats but in close cooperation with the capitalists. How was it done?

9.2.1 The First Step on the Road to Economic Democracy: Cooperation in Corporatist Spirit

For two reasons, 1938 is a pivotal year. First, to avoid political intervention and legislation to regulate the tempestuous labor market relations but also to appease unions that voiced more radical political demands, the Swedish Confederation of Employers (SAF) initiated talks with LO (the TUC) that resulted in a general accord—Saltsjöbadsavtalet—that regulated their interactions. It contained rules for negations and conflict resolution, procedures for how to fire and lay off workers, and procedures for how to limit the detrimental effects on third parties and society at large. The implicit trade-off in the agreement was that SAF recognized the LO as a full and equal counterparty representing all workers, while LO accepted the employers' right to unilaterally direct and assign the work load between workers. The accord had a distinct corporatist character and established a spirit of consensus and cooperation in labor market relations that stressed common economic goals—saltsjöbadsandan—and lasted for almost forty years, until 1976, when LO abandoned the accord. It was particularly strong after the mid-1950s, when SAF initiated centralized wage negotiations between the parties (perhaps due to an increased labor shortage).

The second pivotal event in 1938 was the reform of corporate taxes to grant free depreciation allowances for machines and equipment. This system benefited large, profitable, and capital-intensive firms, as historical profits (retained earnings) determine future investments. Since the rules were also very generous by international standards, the previous hostility toward Social Democratic policies from leading CEOs of ASEA, Electrolux, L. M. Ericsson, Separator (Alfa-Laval), and SKF (called the Big Five [TBF]) subsided, even if this political pressure group existed until 1953. Starting in 1958, the corporate tax system allowed *accelerated* depreciation for machines and equipment (maximum 40 percent of profits before taxes in an investment fund) while at the same time depositing 46 percent of the depreciation allowance in an account in the Central Bank that did not pay any interest and could only be used if approved by the bank as part of general business-cycle policies.

These two major changes in 1938 made *cooperation* between labor and capital the norm for interaction in the corporatist society but biased the firms' investment criterion, as retained earnings became the major tax-subsidized source of financing. Almost concurrently, the major banks were allowed to transfer the significant corporate assets they held after the crises in the early 1930s to holding companies organized as closed-end investment funds. By making their temporary ownership in the aftermath of the crisis permanent, the leading banks became the major owners of the largest listed firms, even if formally only at arm's length. These three changes shaped what might be called the Swedish model and had long-run implications for the future political and economic developments.

9.2.2   The Second Step: The Corporatist Innovation Model

The Social Democratic vision of the social firm was a large, capital-intensive firm that invests heavily, particularly in R&D, in order to be more productive and to grow larger. The basic idea is that innovations are best developed in and commercially implemented by very large export-oriented firms. Small firms may innovate but are of limited importance and can be appropriated by the larger ones that undertake R&D in a more rational systematic way and can carry the large fixed costs because of their size. The importance of entrepreneurs who develop innovations commercially by founding new, viable, and rapidly growing firms was heavily discounted by the leading Social Democrats, as they argued that capitalism had reached a higher and more advanced stage of large-scale production and innovation. Entrepreneurship was thus implicitly assumed to be exogenously given despite the fact that the leading Swedish firms were founded not so long ago by innovators who turned entrepreneurs.

In fact, the Swedish model has two innovation systems (see Erixon 1997). In the *fundamental system* the large, mature firms in engineering and manufacturing produce or acquire new ideas through their international contacts and transmit them to their domestic plants and other firms. Exposure to foreign competition and demanding customers abroad forces the export-oriented firms to assimilate and develop new ideas into commercial products. These innovations are not of breakthrough character that establishes new firms; rather, they shape or reshape existing firms to maintain their competitive edge. This innovation system is thus an integrated part of the large export-oriented firms, as it both feeds on the international network and is a prerequisite to remain internationally competitive.

The *regulated system of innovations* is more domestically oriented and is based on the cooperative interaction between public authorities (not primarily universities) and large domestic firms mainly producing investment goods and advanced products. The authorities may stimulate innovations through public procurements (military orders), technical cooperation with authorities (between Ericsson [telecommunication systems] and Televerket [monopoly operator]), through regulation and setting of standards (housing, energy transmission and consumption, safety, and environment), and through tax policies like the free allowance of R&D expenditures (more than 90 percent of the R&D spending in the Swedish manufacturing industry during the postwar period was financed within the firm).

The regulated innovation system has probably been the more important since it amounts to a rather direct form of economic support of the largest firms using the taxpayers' money, and in particular since it was part of "planned" economy with coordinated public policies. For example, behind tariffs and import restrictions, and with support of tax subsidies for firms to buy trucks and cars, and heavy public investments in the national traffic system, the transportation industry developed very fast during the early postwar period. Using regional subsidies, SAAB and in particular Volvo integrated backward and developed an elaborate network of decentralized suppliers; the transportation industry became a very large employer and a significant export industry. The saying "what is good for Volvo is good for Sweden" was commonly accepted. But without the protection and support of specially designed public policies Sweden would not be the domicile of two (Scania and Volvo) of the three largest manufacturers of heavy trucks in the world. Without the public support from universities (elaborate education of engineers and advanced research), regional subsidies, and large advance public orders Ericsson would not have become the largest supplier of telecommunication systems in the world. Similar programs were developed for huge investments in energy production and systems, for highways and for housing: the Million Program between 1965 and 1974.

This cooperation in large-scale projects between public authorities and the largest firms had a significant corporatist and somewhat nationalistic flavor as the unions actively participated and the coordinated efforts were heralded as part of the national project to build the country in a spirit of strong consensus under Social Democratic leadership. It is striking how strong the coordination and integration of the policies (industrial, regional, tax, and labor market policies) were toward a common goal of developing a more rational, social economy that satisfied the people's needs through significant interventionism, in particular by directing and coordinating large-scale investments with significant externalities.

The very large public investment projects were financed by taxes but also by the channeling of savings to public pension funds (the Allmän Tjänstepension [ATP] system with three original Allmänna Pensionsfonderna [AP] funds; later supplemented by a fourth fund that also invested in equity) that invested in public bonds. Since the equity markets in effect were closed down until the early 1980s and the Central Bank and the Ministry of Finance controlled the capital flows in the financial system, banks and insurance companies were forced to invest very heavily in public bonds, in particular to finance the very large housing program. To channel household savings to collective funds and direct their investments was a very important part of the policies to implement a social democracy and use political power to direct investments. These policies in effect made the large listed firms even more dependent on retained earnings to finance investments; the volume of bank loans was regulated and capped while the equity markets were not operational.

9.2.3   The Third Step: The Labor Market Model

An important part of the growth policies was the so-called active labor market policies initiated by LO in 1951: the Rehn-Meidner model (see Hedborg and Meidner 1984 and Korpi 1978). To sustain a full-employment economy that grows without inflation, that idea was to support reallocation of resources and employment away from industries that are not internationally competitive to more productive industries with sustainable growth opportunities. Through solidaristic wage policies that compress the wage differential at a high average level that maintains the international competitiveness of the export-oriented sector, the overall productivity would increase by speeding up the closing down of firms in less productive industries while in effect inducing firms in more competitive industries to become more efficient by investing in more capital-intensive technologies. The model tends to generate excess profits in the most competitive firms, as they pay relatively low wages. Combined with labor market policies that retrain workers and stimulate their geographic and occupational mobility by compensating them for loss of income and extra costs when relocating, the model enhances the dynamic efficiency in the economy without causing too high inflationary pressure. The public sector would thus support and pay for the higher labor mobility. The model combines an egalitarian ambition with support for reinforced dynamic restructuring in order to maintain competitiveness, a higher growth rate, and higher wages.

When the negative social consequences of the higher mobility (regional unemployment, disparate regional economic development and unemployment, increasing geographic concentration of jobs to the largest firms' plants) became too costly politically in the early 1970s, the labor market policies changed from encouraging mobility to supporting lock-in of employees with the current employer as the new labor market legislation focused on job tenure. At the same time the overall unemployment rate tended to increase because of the stiffer international competition.

9.2.4   The Result: The Swedish Model

The Social Democrats accepted the private control of the largest firms while the leading capitalists accepted their political dominance. Based on mutual acceptance, an elaborate cooperation in corporatist spirit developed around large infrastructural and industrial projects that benefited the largest export-oriented firms in engineering and manufacturing. Tax-based policies were put in place to stimulate a high investment level, particularly in the transnational firms, by subsidizing investments in machinery, buildings, and R&D, and to give priority to retained earnings and bank loans as the major sources for financing—institutionalized saving in collective funds. Labor market relations are peaceful and cooperative but with respect for adversarial interests; there is no codetermination. The policies stimulated and supported a high growth rate and propagated the established large-scale industrial firms with concentrated private ownership but deliberately ignored the formation of new firms and the importance of small firms: a dynamic but aging social economy with a large public sector.

9.2.5   More Radical Policies to Implement Economic Democracy

Profound political, social, and economic changes designate the years around 1970 as the defining moment for the Swedish model; what might be termed its Golden Age came to an end, and its negative effects became all too apparent in a very short space of time. In response to very fierce critique against the political incumbency, both from within and from outside the labor movement, LO and SAP became more radical by proposing strongly egalitarian policies with more redistribution of incomes and opportunities via the public sector that grew very fast during the 1970s and resulted in the highest taxes in the world.[12] More than half of the average income was paid in taxes, but a significant part was directly paid back to the households through redistribution programs, in particular to families with children, students, and pensioners, but also indirectly as subsidized consumption. At the party congress in 1975 Olof Palme initiated the third stage of the historical agenda: economic democracy. The timing could hardly have been worse: the Bretton Woods system—the anchor of the strongly interventionist economic policies with control over capital flows—was collapsing, and the oil crises had triggered the deepest economic crises since the 1930s. The new constitution adopted in 1973 used strictly proportional elections (which tend to and did breed unstable minority governments), and SAP was about to lose the 1976 election after forty-four years in power.

The basic principle of nonintervention by the government in labor market relations was abandoned in 1974 with the Employment Security Act (LAS), which was written and enacted in response to direct demands from LO. It provided employees with an elaborate protection against dismissal and application of a strict last in–first out principle (LIFO); the only two legal grounds for dismissal were gross misconduct and redundancies. The 1976 Codetermination Act granted labor union representatives (strict minority) board representation. The laws were designed with the conditions of the largest firms in mind, and the needs and demands of small firms for more flexible adjustment were ignored. Since tenure to the current employer became more important for job security than actual skills and effort

---

12. In retrospect, perhaps the most important event was the long, bitter, and very politicized illegal strike in the North in 1969 against poor and unequal working conditions in the mines of the state-run corporation LKAB. It triggered a fierce debate with uncompromising critique against the political incumbency as it made the inequalities visible (see Korpi 1978 and Hedborg and Meidner 1984).

with the LIFO principle, the costs of dynamic mismatches increased, both in the general labor market and within the firms, as workers de facto became more locked in with firms. To alleviate the higher costs of LAS for small firms, new and more flexible rules were enacted in 1997.[13]

But the most radical proposal was the 1976 decision by the LO congress to implement Ernst Wigforss's vision of *social firms without owners* by a gradual transfer of ownership of all firms with more than fifty employees to wage-earner funds with trade union and other stakeholder representatives collectively exercising the funds' voting and other ownership rights. The actual transfer of shares would occur by private placements to the funds corresponding to 20 percent of the firm's annual profit (Meidner 1978). The more profitable the firm was, the faster the transfer of control— at a profit rate of 10 percent it took thirty-five years for a fund to establish a majority control. Consistent with the established line of ideas, the fund's capital would stay within the firm and not be reallocated. The combined effect of the labor market laws and wage-earner funds would thus be an even stronger lock-in of both capital and labor within firms.

The proposal had the lukewarm support of the SAP leadership and was the catalyst that united all members and organizations to the right of the labor movement in the most vociferous protests ever. A watered-down and rather tame version was enacted in 1984 after the Social Democrats returned to power in 1982, but was abolished by the Center-Right government in 1992 and not reintroduced by subsequent Social Democratic governments.[14] The controversy over wage-earner funds is the only time that private ownership has been really questioned. The debate has been silent since then.

9.2.6 The Orthogonal Trajectory Away from Economic Democracy

It is fair to assume that outside observers of Swedish society around 1980 would have predicted a bumpy road ahead to economic democracy with more interventionism and stronger political control over the economy. But the real historical irony is that the actual trajectory chosen by the Social Democrats when returning to power was orthogonal to the conjectured one, as it entailed a radical break with past policies: far-reaching deregulation of the banking system, dismantling of capital flow controls,

---

13. For example, by the use of *prearranged temporary employment contracts* all firms have the unconditional right to employ up to five persons for a maximum of one year; the possibility for local collective contracts to replace the stipulations in the law and sidestep the LIFO principle in case of dismissal; annul the right of reemployment for dismissed workers and to extend the temporary employment beyond a year. In case of redundancies, firms with no more than ten employees are allowed to except two workers from the LIFO principle by a new law in 2001.

14. The five wage-earner funds were financed by a 0.2 percent payroll tax and a 20 percent tax on real profits above SEK 1 million during seven years. When abolished the funds' capital was distributed to research and venture capital funds to promote new firms.

privatization of state-owned firms and policies that promoted market competitiveness, and reactivation of equity markets that were liberalized with unrestricted foreign ownership of shares. The chosen road led to more market economy, not to more socialism.

A similar radical across-the-board break with the old also happened in France with a Socialist government (see Helleiner 1994). Given the centralist nature of both Swedish and French political governance structures, the turnaround behavior is broadly consistent with Rajan and Zingales's (2003a,b) political theory of incumbency.[15] But perhaps a more direct interpretation of the Swedish case is that it shows the profoundly pragmatic character of an encompassing party that has been heavily entrenched for decades and almost inseparable from the state bureaucracy: to win elections in order to exercise power is the primary objective. But to win elections the economy has to be in order. The very radical change of policies was perceived as necessary to get the economy in order and promote growth.

9.2.7   Necessary Condition for the Swedish Model of Corporate Ownership: Organized Labor and Capital

One important part of the Swedish model of corporate ownership is that it presupposed the existence of two identifiable, well-organized parties—labor and capital—that both had a political and a trade-based, corporative representation. At one level it is of course trivial to characterize the society as corporatist, but why did it become corporatist, and why was it so important, in particular for the Social Democrats?[16] My answer pinpoints both external (exogenous) and ideological factors. The fact that industrial production was comparatively capital intensive and organized in relatively few, large, and geographically concentrated units in firms controlled by families and part of networks around the leading banks facilitated organization of both employers and employees. So did the smallness of the culturally homogeneous society, and the fact that industrialization came relatively late but was then very fast. The other crucial exogenous factor was the strongly export-oriented character of the largest firms, which made both capital and labor heavily dependent on the business cycles and fostered a sense of fighting the economic elements together. For example, after the deep crisis in the early 1920s, the strategies of both SAP and LO changed to become less adversarial and more focused on employment and

---

15. Henrekson and Jakobsson (2003a,b) present an alternative interpretation that emphasizes the break in policies but does not provide a consistent explanation, as they seem to argue that the threat from Socialism is as unrelenting as ever.

16. Reiter (2003) argues that the crucial importance of Saltsjöbadsavtalet 1938 was that "it gave the Social Democratic Party an identifiable counter-party in the country's export-oriented industrialization and the construction of the welfare state" but does not provide any arguments or theory that explains why.

higher wages, which during the long, unprecedented expansion since the 1890s had been taken for granted.

The ideological factor is the idea that labor and capital are the two natural adversaries in a capitalistic economy but that capitalists are crucial for the development of an advanced social democracy because of their strategic control over investments and thereby growth in the private sector. It was thus not inconsistent with the Social Democratic ideology to accept and respect (at least for the time being) private ownership, and even reinforce the entrenchment of well-defined private owners by political support for the use of dual-class shares and pyramiding. In exchange, the capitalists did not move their capital or refuse to invest but accepted the political supremacy, in particular since it involved an elaborate and profitable collaboration with the government and the unions. The objective of social firms without owners could thus be implemented (at least partially) via negotiations between the firms' two major stakeholders with the (often passive) support of the government (state). The fact that both the workers and the leading capitalists already were united in encompassing national and centralized organizations that stressed overriding goals facilitated consensus-based outcomes, which fitted the ideological view that society is progressively changed via many small and peaceful steps.

This combination of exogenous and ideological factors does not fit the political (nonideological) theory of Pagano and Volpin (2004) of a corporatist political equilibrium where low investor protection that benefits controlling owners is exchanged for high employment protection for labor. This outcome is more likely under a proportional voting system, as it fosters the formation of homogeneous blocks of voters, in particular if the wealth distribution is unequal or the production technology has low capital intensity.[17] The listed firms in Sweden did, however, (on average) use relatively capital-intensive technologies and were primarily dependent on banks for their financing, not on equity financing as their theory seems to suggest. The strong dependence on a relation-based banking system thus implies that neither an unequal wealth distribution nor low-capital-intensity technologies are necessary conditions.[18] Interestingly, only since the Swedish voting system became fully proportional in 1973 have governments without the participation of the Social Democratic Party been formed for the first time since 1932.

17. "The intuition behind this result is that proportional voting pushes political parties to cater more to the preferences of social groups with homogeneous preferences, that is, entrepreneurs and employees. This is because under this voting rule the additional mass of voters that can be attracted by shifting a party's platform is greater if the shift favors a homogeneous constituency" (Pagano and Volpin 2004).

18. In a more literal sense it is also difficult to imagine that shareholder minority protection should be on the top of the minds of controlling owners and that workers should have any reason to develop preferences about such protection—in particular since they did not own any shares and stock markets were closed down at the time when corporatism reigned.

The one-sided emphasis on equity markets, in particular on the primary function, in theories of political economy of corporate ownership (governance) is difficult to reconcile with the limited dependence of such markets in Continental Europe for most of the previous century. Ownership is not more concentrated there because of weaker legal protection of minority shareholders, as the theory seems to presuppose (see also Burkart, Panunzi, and Shleifer 2003), but primarily because of political support for the use of mechanisms to separate votes from capital (dual-class shares, cross-shareholdings, and pyramiding; see Holmén and Högfeldt 2004a). Politically motivated concessions, both to the government and to the workers, are easier to obtain when firms have a well-defined private owner in control as they are visible in the public arena. It is therefore not surprising that concentrated private ownership seems to cluster with well-organized labor unions and formation of major parties along the left-right spectrum. Rather than focusing on formal minority protection, it seems more natural to pinpoint the political support for concentrated ownership built on separation of ownership from control and determine how this systematically affects corporate financing and worker protection.

I sum up this section by answering one of my main questions: why did the Social Democrats not only accept but de facto support that control of the large listed firms and of the pivotal banks remained in private hands? A possible and plausible answer has three parts. First, the party's ideologically and economically pivotal objective to influence or control the large listed firms' investment behavior could be achieved through means that did not assume the eclipse of private ownership. Second, since old family fortunes remained within the firms as working capital and became foundations (institutions) because of the tax policies, the private capital in effect became more social and institutionalized, in particular the bank capital; the remaining "private" character of capital was not a primary problem. Moreover, since formation of large, private fortunes in newly founded firms via equity financing was limited and controlled by tax policies and regulations, the wealth distribution did not threaten to become too dispersed.

Third, implementation of the Social Democrats' social agenda did not necessitate a takeover of control of large listed private firms but could be realized through reforms and policies that redistributed resources and opportunities via the public sector with strong and persistent electoral support. Their more radical agenda for economic democracy, on the other hand, was more ideological and abstract and did not generate enough popular support. Besides more tactical considerations, the heavy and unprecedented entrenchment of the party in general and the fact that individual careers are closely tied to being in control of the public bureaucracy in particular de facto narrowed the primary objective to winning elections to remain in power and running the economy in a competent and stable way to finance reforms.

9.3   Corporate Ownership and Development of Financial Markets

Why did corporate ownership in Sweden not separate widely, as in the Anglo-Saxon countries? The leading answer in the literature would be that it was because of weak formal minority protection (see, e.g., La Porta et al. 2000 and Burkart, Panunzi, and Shleifer 2003). Good protection encourages both outsiders to invest and founding families to sell out a larger fraction in an IPO since formal rules limit extraction of pecuniary benefits by management when the firm becomes widely held; both factors stimulate development of advanced financial markets. Lower protection thus causes founders to maintain a larger fraction of shares to avoid being exploited, which predicts a negative relation between formal minority protection on the one hand, and ownership concentration and size of (pecuniary) private benefits of controlling owners, respectively, on the other. But this line of reasoning does not square well with the history and politics of corporate ownership in Sweden for several reasons.

The empirical estimates of Dyck and Zingales (2004) suggest that, contrary to predictions, the size of private benefits in Sweden are of about the same size as in the Anglo-Saxon countries that are perceived to have a better formal (legal) minority protection. In particular, there is no positive relationship between ownership concentration and size of private benefits or a negative relation with the level of minority protection (see Holmén and Högfeldt 2004a). Inconsistent with the leading theory, the only legal regime dummy that is significant is the negative coefficient (lower private benefits) for Scandinavian origin. Other behavioral factors that are related to the culture and norms of the society, like degree of tax compliance, level of corruption, openness, and crime rates, eliminate the explanatory power of legal regimes and of level of minority protection (see Dyck and Zingales 2004). Stock market capitalization in relation to GDP, number of listed firms per million inhabitants, frequency of IPOs, and household frequency of equity ownership (around 55–60 percent) are if not higher at least comparable to the Anglo-Saxon countries and higher than for Continental Europe (see Holmén and Högfeldt 2004a). The potential for transfer of corporate assets to the controlling owners is perhaps largest in pyramiding, but unlike Bertrand, Mehta, and Mullainathan (2002) for Indian pyramids, Holmén and Högfeldt (2004b) find no evidence of tunneling in Swedish pyramids.

Lack of minority protection did not hinder the development of active financial markets before WWI (see Rajan and Zingales 2003a). Neither was it a prerequisite for the stock market boom in recent decades, as protection was improved in the early 1990s after public scandals involving self-dealings, particularly in management-controlled firms with cross-shareholdings. The differences in formal minority protection between advanced countries seem too small to explain the very significant discrepancies in ownership concentration; see also Roe (2002a,b).

Implicitly, the leading explanation seems to assume that the size of private benefits of control is larger if the firm becomes listed than if it remains privately held because of the pecuniary extraction from minority shareholders. But the two most successful firms in Sweden founded after WWII—IKEA (founded by Ingvar Kamprad) and Tetra Laval (the Rausing family)—have both (aggressively) avoided going public with the explicit argument that their private value of control would be diluted, both because of the listing (information and transparency) requirements, and since their long-run strategy (patiently building an empire) may be compromised by the perceived myopic character of the stock market. The third most successful firm, H&M (an international chain of clothing stores founded by Erling Persson), went public in the 1970s in order to finance its future growth, in particular its international expansion. But since H&M has consistently generated high enough profits to fully finance its investments by retained earnings, Stefan Persson, the head of the family and chairman of the board (former CEO), has officially announced that the family regrets the listing, saying it would have been better to stay private. Private benefits of control may thus have less to do with pecuniary extraction of minority shareholders than with the value of being in control (power) per se, which is maximized when staying fully private. Since a public listing dilutes the private benefits of control, a family-controlled firm goes public only when it needs new capital. More generally, Holmén and Högfeldt (2004a) find that Swedish IPO firms in general, but family firms in particular, have a strong preference for maintained control, and their behavior is consistent with the control theories (see Bebchuk 1999 and Bebchuk, Kraakman, and Triantis 1999).

9.3.1 Roe's Political Theory

Mark Roe's alternative political theory that ownership does not separate widely in Continental Europe since it is not politically and socially acceptable in the Social Democracies is summarized in his Clarendon Lectures (Roe 2002a):

> It [ownership] is concentrated in no small measure because the delicate threads that tie managers to shareholders in the public firm fray easily in common political environments, such as those in the Continental European social democracies. Social democracies press managers to stabilize employment, to forgo some profit-maximizing risks with the firm, and to use up capital in place rather than downsize when markets no longer are aligned with the firm's production capabilities. Since managers must have discretion in the public firm, how they use that discretion is crucial to stockholders, and social democratic pressures induce managers to

stray further than otherwise from their shareholders' profit-maximizing goals. A crucial political prerequisite to the rise of the public firm in the United States is the weakness of social democratic pressures on the American business firm.

The dual side of this compelling set of arguments is thus that Social Democracies in Roe's wider sense presuppose concentrated corporate ownership but will be less efficient as necessary changes are delayed or do not take place. The first implication is generally in line with my arguments, but the second one does not fit the history and politics of corporate ownership in Sweden, perhaps the quintessential Social Democratic society, very well. For example, Roe's arguments do not recognize the pivotal effect in a small open economy of the international competitive exposure on labor market relations and conditions within the firm. Being determined by outside conditions, it is perceived as an objective, exogenous factor that defines the necessary adjustments and limits the set of possible actions in order to remain competitive and be paid a higher wage in the current or in another job. As an *encompassing* union, the well-established tradition within the LO has been not to fight changes motivated by rational economic arguments but to accept and actually facilitate them in order for the whole economy to maintain its competitiveness and growth. In fact, the general economic policy, in particular the labor market policies, that the Social Democrats pursued with the active backing of the LO were at least until the 1970s very growth oriented, as they stimulated structural changes and rationalizations, promoted labor mobility, and provided ambitious retraining and educational programs for the unemployed. Local unions may voice protests but are not known to obstruct or aggressively fight back if negotiations about layoffs and close-downs are done in an orderly manner. Looking through the Swedish lens, Roe ignores the crucial importance of a public sector that provides an *outside* protection via insurance, education, and benefit programs that assuages the hardships of unemployment, which seems to facilitate rather than obstruct necessary economic changes.

Despite corporatist tendencies and a spirit of cooperation, the adversarial interests of labor and capital have not been mixed and diluted by codetermination since unions did not get legal rights to elect board representatives until the 1970s. It is a strict minority representation; there are no dual boards, and unions have no right to veto a firm's decisions. Unlike in Germany, codetermination was not designed to appease aggressive unions and to fight social and political instability. Moreover, the general rule has been that politicians should not intervene but let the representatives of labor and capital settle disputes and other matters by negotiations.

Overall, Mark Roe paints a picture in too stark colors that exaggerates the differences between Continental Europe and the United States by implying that necessary economic adjustments will not be efficiently implemented in Social Democracies.[19] The Swedish experience suggests that efficiency-enhancing changes will be undertaken but in a different, more orderly, and fair manner, perhaps somewhat delayed due to negotiations but often with more far-reaching consequences when they occur.[20] The effect of international exposure, a large welfare sector, and different labor market institutions (encompassing, well-organized unions) and ownership structures leads to outcomes that differ perhaps more in form than in substance. The more negative institutional aspects of the Scandinavian model are the significant lock-in effects of both labor (e.g., strict application of the LIFO rule) and capital within the old, established firms that will be stable and relatively efficient while the addition of new growing firms will be hampered.

9.3.2 An Alternative Political Theory of Why Ownership Does Not Separate Widely

My analysis of the history of Swedish corporate ownership, however, suggests another political theory as to why ownership does not separate widely: listed firms do not have to disperse ownership and dilute private benefits of control in order to raise new capital since their dependence on the equity market is limited because of political decisions and institutional factors. This is particularly true for the largest listed firms with well-established networks. The focus is on the equity markets' primary function—provision of capital—and its political sensitivity, not on liquidity provision. The basic idea is that political decisions will determine how dependent firms are on external financing: if capital for investments can be supplied primarily through retained earnings, by borrowing in banks, or by infusion of private capital, firms have no immediate need to go through the strictures of equity offers and place a larger fraction of shares in a wider group of investors and dilute private benefits of control in the process.

My political theory of corporate financing starts with the assumption

---

19. Roe's arguments presuppose that shareholder value maximization has consistently been the single, hard objective in the United States while the firm's objective has been diluted by stakeholder concerns in Europe. A reasonable interpretation is that because of primarily political reasons maximization of shareholder value has been accepted only in certain time periods in the United States but not uniformly, and that the importance of stakeholder value in Europe has also varied substantially with the political tides. Implicit in Mark Roe's theory about the negative effects of Social Democracy is also the idea that the relation between labor and management is more adversarial than that between labor and controlling owners. If anything, however, the Swedish experience seems to suggest that the union representatives are closer to the management and that the relations are based on consensus and trust as long as the firm pursues a reliable long-term strategy.

20. An illustrative example is the dramatic downsizing of Ericsson in recent years from 110,000 employees worldwide to less than 50,000. A significant fraction of the employees worked in Sweden, but very few if any protests were voiced, as it was done in an orderly, negotiated way. The unions did not obstruct but helped to accommodate the changes, as they were perceived as necessary in order for Ericsson to survive in the long run.

that corporate control based on separation of control from ownership via mechanisms to separate votes from capital, like dual-class shares and pyramiding, presupposes political support to be socially acceptable. In the Swedish case, the political legitimacy of entrenched private ownership is traded off against the implicit guarantee that the largest listed firms do not migrate and that they continue to invest, thereby generating economic resources to finance the political reform agenda. The separation of control from ownership has a profound effect on corporate financing, however, as it drives a significant wedge between the costs of internal and external capital. New external shareholders demand compensation (discounts) for the agency costs inherent in the separation, which makes external equity more expensive. Shareholders seem to attach significant discounts to privately controlled firms using dual-class shares (10–15 percent) and to pyramid holding companies (25–30 percent) to separate votes from capital (see Holmén and Högfeldt 2004b). But internal capital is relatively inexpensive for the controlling owners since they have access to all of the firm's cash flows via a small (less than proportional) capital investment.

The wedge caused by the separation of control from ownership therefore generates an *enhanced* (political) pecking order of financing: strong reliance on retained earnings and borrowing but avoidance of equity issues, in particular of large public offers, as they would dilute control and also be extra costly due to the discounts to new outside shareholders (see Holmén and Högfeldt 2004b). The pecking order is enhanced since it is caused by agency costs *inherent* to the ownership structure and not primarily by asymmetric information costs, and since it predicts the absence or strong avoidance of public offers (see Högfeldt and Oborenko 2004). This is the key mechanism that explains why firms in countries with prevalent use of dual-class shares and pyramiding like Sweden have more concentrated ownership but are also much less dependent on the primary equity markets and why they do not need to disperse ownership.

The connection between the politics of corporate ownership and financing is particularly conspicuous in the regulation of banks' ownership of equity since the 1930s. When the Swedish version of the Glass-Steagal Act was enacted in 1934, commercial banks were no longer allowed to *directly* own shares in other firms (a right granted them in 1911 because of pivotal support from the Social Democrats). Reflecting the strong political and economic interests of leading bankers but with the support of the Social Democrats, banks were, however, allowed a few years later to transfer their portfolios of controlling interests to holding companies that were organized as CEIFs and distribute the funds' shares to the banks' existing shareholders. The controlling owners of the commercial banks at the apex of the pyramid thus controlled the largest firms at the bottom via CEIFs at the intermediary level that were listed. Since pyramiding was combined with use of dual-class shares, the separation between votes and capital was multiplicative.

The new laws in effect made two dominating banks (SEB and Svenska Handelsbanken) the controlling owners of the largest listed firms, and bank loans the major way to finance the firms' investments besides retained earnings, in particular in the decades when the equity markets were dormant. Corporate control was therefore via political decisions directly linked to the control over intermediated capital, which tend to make equity financing much less likely. Unlike in the United States, the pyramids were politically supported via the tax system: intercorporate dividends as well as reinvested capital gains were de facto tax exempt (see Holmén and Högfeldt 2004b). Since this preferential tax treatment is pivotal for the existence of pyramids (see Morck 2003), it is the critical element in the Social Democrats' consistent support of the very heavy entrenched private ownership of the largest listed firms in Sweden. It is perhaps also the very reason why capital did not migrate.

More generally, since for ideological reasons the Social Democrats focused on the largest established firms and supported both retained earnings via tax benefits and a relation-based banking system, the two major ways to finance investments both had strong political support. They were also in general very skeptical toward the turbulent equity markets that are conducive to economic and social changes, which is antithetical to their political ambitions to provide stability and social reforms in an orderly, planned manner. But for egalitarian reasons they were, and still are, even more skeptical toward the equity markets' primary function. The combination of entrepreneurship and equity financing will facilitate creation of large private fortunes and break the social status quo—that is, it will limit the possibilities for social control and for redistribution. Since a well-functioning primary market will widen the income distribution but in particular the distribution of wealth and ownership of assets, new equity issues have consistently been disfavored by a tax disadvantage. Reactive financing via retained earnings that benefits incumbent owners by locking in the capital in the existing firms was preferred to a more proactive and aggressive financing mode via the primary equity market, which is more likely to implement faster and more drastic changes that are likely to challenge the incumbents' power. This outcome is also the most likely since the new entrepreneurs and firms lack political power while the well-organized incumbents are united by common interests and have political voice.

As long as this closely integrated system of ownership and financing is stable, firms do not need to raise substantial amounts of new capital from the equity markets. And when firms were highly leveraged in the 1970s and needed more equity capital as both profits and credits were squeezed and more restructuring takeovers occurred, there was strong political support for the incumbent (often capital-constrained) owners to use dual-class shares to separate votes from capital contribution in order to maintain control also after issues of equity.[21] Hence, for a combination of political and institutional reasons, ownership does not separate widely since listed firms are not directly dependent on equity markets to finance their investments.

My alternative political theory of corporate financing has several testable implications. The first one is that the very entrenched and relation-based banking system will block the development of arm's-length markets for corporate bonds; if they exist they will not be well developed. Hence, it should not come as a surprise that there are no domestic corporate bond markets in Sweden and that the largest listed firms use the international bond markets, but only to a limited extent.

The second prediction of the theory is that the volume of IPOs and seasoned equity offerings [SEOs] on average should be very small. Figure 9.4 shows that the annual volume (2002 prices) of new equity and bond issues on average corresponds to about 10 percent of gross domestic capital formation before 1931 but averages only about 1 percent since then. The peak in 1917–18 is a result of the speculative war economy fuelled by excessive buying of new issues by the highly leveraged and bank-affiliated issuing companies before they were forced to close down after the deep financial crises in the early 1920s (Fritz 1990 and Östlind 1944).[22] During 1927–29 Ivar Kreuger capitalized heavily on the exuberant market sentiments by issuing equity and, in particular, debentures (unsecured bonds) both domestically and internationally to save his highly leveraged and very opaque empire before it collapsed after he shot himself in Paris in 1932 and triggered the worst financial crises in Sweden.

The more recent peak in 1992 around 5 percent is the result of extremely low investments due to very high interest rates in the wake of the second-worst financial crises when a speculative real estate bubble burst. It was fuelled by excessive credit expansion by the recently deregulated banks. The large volume in 1999 is, of course, due to a record number of information

---

21. The legislators' motivation for the use of dual-class shares in the new corporate law (Proposition 1997/98:99, p. 120; my translation) illustrates the political support: "The use of shares with different voting rights has a long tradition in Swedish law. Dual-class shares are very common among listed companies in Sweden. The dual-class share system has significant advantages. It makes it possible (facilitates) to have a strong and stable ownership function even in very large companies, thereby creating the necessary conditions for an efficient management as well as for the long-term planning of the firm's activities. Shares with different voting rights also facilitate for growing companies to raise new capital without the original owners losing control. There is no evidence that the dual-class share system has caused any noticeable negative effects. . . . Dual-class shares can significantly promote the efficiency and development of individual firms as well as of the business sector in general."

22. The SEO volume in 1917–18 corresponds to about 2.5 percent of the total stock market value, while the volume in 1927–29 is about 7 percent of the market cap.

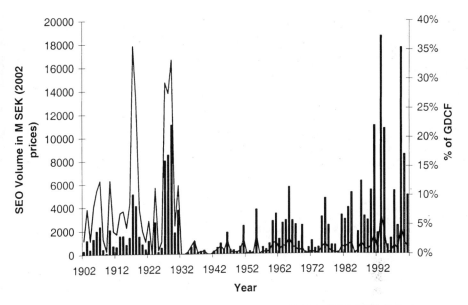

Fig. 9.4 **Seasoned equity offering (SEO) activity in Sweden 1902–2002: Relative to gross domestic capital formation (GDCF)**
Sources: For 1902–87 Althaimer (1988), and for 1988–2002 Holmén and Högfeldt (2004b).

technology (IT)–related IPOs, particularly related to mobile internet and IT-based services. For comparative purposes, the table does not include the 30 billion SEK rights issue in 2002 by the financially distressed Ericsson since it is the largest SEO ever. It is particularly interesting to note that this single issue corresponds to 13 percent of the total volume of all SEOs (2002 prices) during the last 100 years, 25 percent of all SEOs since 1970, and 40 percent of all SEOs during the exuberant 1990s (about 10 billion dollars). The listed firms' dependence on the equity markets for new capital has thus been very limited indeed in Sweden.

Because of the strong preference for control, in particular among family firms, a third implication is that dual-class shares should be used very frequently and that SEOs should follow a specific pecking order ranked by the extent to which they dilute control: first rights issues, then private placements, followed by directed issues (stock-financed acquisitions), and finally public offers that are strongly avoided. Moreover, the issues should be relatively small and only offer low voting B-shares. Rights issues should have the largest size since they dilute control the least. The empirical evidence from 233 IPOs between 1980 and 1997 in Holmén and Högfeldt (2004a) and from Swedish SEOs since 1984 in Högfeldt and Oborenko (2004) are consistent with this implication, since almost 90 percent of the privately controlled IPO firms use dual-class shares and there is a well-defined pecking order of SEOs. In particular, the amounts raised are very small, and rights issues are by far the largest. The fastest-growing IPO firms are controlled by the founder/entrepreneur and finance their expansion by rights issues, normally within eighteen months after the listing.[23]

It is particularly interesting to observe the absence of public offers, which are both the most common and the largest offers in the United States but infrequently used outside the Anglo-Saxon countries. Relatively large public offers are especially important in the financing of newly founded firms that grow very quickly ("gazelles"). But they are also instrumental to disperse ownership widely at and after the IPO. The very infrequent use of public offers may thus explain both why ownership does not disperse widely and why very few young firms grow to become really large in Sweden. To understand why public offers are uncommon in, say, civil law countries may also explain why financial markets in general and primary equity markets in particular are less developed there.[24] My theory suggests that because of the politically supported control structure combined with the strong preference for maintained private control, public offers are last in the enhanced pecking order since by their larger size they dilute control the most and are most costly because of the required discounts to new shareholders.

More generally, my theory predicts the following stylized facts about the corporate system cluster: (a) concentrated ownership because of extensive use of devices to separate votes form capital; (b) secondary markets relatively well developed if dual-class shares are frequently used (B-shares provide liquidity) but primary markets particularly politically vulnerable and underdeveloped; (c) equity financing of investments far less important than borrowing and use of retained earnings (small volume of IPOs and SEOs) and limited market timing; (d) pecking order also of SEOs, with rights issues (largest) and private placements most frequent while public offers are absent or exceptionally few; (e) very few young firms grow fast to become really large; (f) undeveloped markets for corporate bonds (due to the strong relation-based banking system); and (g) relatively equal distribution of wealth and income. Because the separation of ownership from control drives a wedge between the costs of internal and external capital, my theory predicts that firms controlled by pyramids or via extensive use

23. If the founders relinquish control, they do so by selling their control block before the IPO but keep the block intact both at the IPO and afterwards until they sell it. Family-controlled firms often finance relatively small acquisitions by issuing B-shares (see Holmén and Högfeldt 2004b and Högfeldt and Oborenko 2004).

24. Even if trading volumes and market caps are less developed than in the Anglo-Saxon countries because of the extensive use of dual-class shares, the liquidity provided by trading of B-shares may still be large: the number of IPOs is not necessarily small since dual-class shares facilitate maintained family control after the IPO and stock-financed acquisitions.

of dual-class shares will have higher investment–cash flow sensitivities; see Holmén and Högfeldt (2004b) for supporting empirical evidence.

The reasons why ownership did not separate widely in Sweden are thus according to my theory profoundly political: use of dual-class shares and pyramiding, which are politically supported, drives a wedge between the costs of internal and external capital that causes an enhanced (political) pecking order of corporate financing. The political support for separation of control from ownership and for nonequity financing benefits established firms and in effect aligns the interests of the incumbent political power with incumbent capital (in particular the leading banks) as corporate control is maintained and actually reinforced—despite increasing needs for new capital—while formation and growth of new firms by equity financing are effectively disfavored for egalitarian reasons.

9.4   A Critical Evaluation of the Swedish Model of Corporate Ownership

At this point it is convenient to oversimplify and pinpoint three constituent parts of the Swedish model of corporate ownership. The first is the primarily exogenous character of production: capital-intensive, large-scale, export-oriented production (raw materials, manufacturing, and engineering) by relatively few large, transnational, and privately controlled firms. The second is the changing international market conditions due to political, economic (competition), and technological factors. The final is the endogenous effects of prolonged Social Democratic policies. We focus on the long-run economic effects by looking at the impact of three major Social Democratic policies: (a) political support for a relation-based banking system and control of the largest listed firms via bank-controlled closed-end investment funds; (b) political support for dual-class shares and other devices to separate votes and capital in order to facilitate maintained private control with well-defined owners despite increasing capital needs and institutionalization of ownership; and (c) consistent political focus on the largest listed firms and strong preference for retained earnings and bank loans as the major ways to finance investment while in particular disfavoring equity financing and equity markets in general. These policies jointly create the foundation for the enhanced political pecking order of financing and have three major long-run effects.

9.4.1   Overinvestment by Large Firms in Old Industries and Underinvestment of New Firms in Growing Industries, Biased Distribution of Firm Size and Age, and Lower Overall Growth

The strong dependence on retained earnings and debt in the enhanced pecking order, reinforced by the preferential tax treatment, implies that firms' investment criterion has been systematically biased since past profits to a significant degree influence or determine the allocation of investments, not expected future profits.[25] This benefits firms in old, established, and capital-intensive industries with large real assets that have consistently been profitable and are part of a leading bank's network. But the policies disfavor young firms in new lines of business based on human capital and services with strong growth potential and in need of risk capital. Since incumbent firms have access to relatively inexpensive internal capital while new firms are hampered since they use the primary equity markets only to a limited extent, the biased investment criterion is likely to create systematic under- and overinvestment problems that tend to have a negative effect on the overall growth in the economy. The largest firms that will tend to invest too much are in mature industries with lower future growth potential, while the new and smaller firms tend to invest too little and are likely to be in lines of business with higher growth potential. These effects are reinforced by the fact that, for control reasons, IPO firms are not inclined to use large public offers to grow fast, and older firms that finance their investments via retained earnings tend to have realized returns that are significantly below their cost of capital; investments financed via debt or equity do not seem to systematically underperform (see Holmén and Högfeldt 2004b). The free cash flow problem thus seems to be particularly serious for firms that have a well-defined owner in control and rely on retained earnings; they also tend to have higher investment–cash flow sensitivity. Inefficient investments due to (free) access to retained earnings may be the very reason why firms with strong separation of control and ownership are traded at a discount.

Since the labor market laws in recent decades have promoted tenure with an employer, the combined effect of investment and labor market policies is therefore a significant lock-in of both labor and capital within the existing large firms and their controlling owners. The biased investment criterion and the lock-in effects endogenously create stronger path dependency as the firms' future developments (size, investments, and growth) are more directly tied to past performance. The long-run effects on the firm structure will be a survival and growth bias: an overrepresentation of very large and old firms in mature industries and an underrepresentation of new and fast-

---

25. The corporate and ownership tax policies are not the direct cause behind the enhanced pecking order of financing since they are primarily supportive of the ownership policies that promote separation of control from ownership. The tax policies have at the margin disfavored direct ownership by households and benefited institutional ownership, and disfavored equity as a source of capital, in particular when the inflation rate is high, while favoring debt and retained earnings. Table 9.7 shows the effective marginal tax rates for different type of owners and sources of financing at points in time when taxes were revised. A negative marginal tax rate indicates that the rate of return is greater than before: a marginal tax rate of –83 percent for a debt-financed investment by a tax-exempt institution transforms to 10 percent real return before tax to 18.3 percent return after tax. The taxes on debt, equity, and retained earnings were rather differentiated before the big tax reform in 1991 but have become more harmonized since then. Note that the most negative tax effects on equity ownership by households occurred before 1985, when the equity markets were dormant in Sweden.

Table 9.7   **Effective marginal tax rates for different combinations of owners and sources of finance in 1960, 1970, and 1980 (real pretax rate of return 10 percent at actual inflation rates) and in 1985, 1991, and 1999 at different inflations rates for listed firms**

	Debt	New share issues	Retained earnings
1960			
Households	27.2	92.7	48.2
Tax-exempt institutions	−32.2	31.4	31.2
Insurance companies	−21.7	41.6	34.0
1970			
Households	51.3	122.1	57.1
Tax-exempt institutions	−64.8	15.9	32.7
Insurance companies	−45.1	42.4	41.2
1980			
Households	58.2	136.6	51.9
Tax-exempt institutions	−83.4	−11.6	11.2
Insurance companies	−54.9	38.4	28.7
1985			
0% inflation rate	50.4	43.7	46.0
5%	75.0	87.6	58.8
10%	102.1	129.2	68.8
1991			
0% inflation rate	29.0	17.6	40.3
5%	38.8	46.4	51.5
10%	47.7	76.6	60.4
1999			
0% inflation rate	36.2	56.2	47.3
5%	49.1	79.2	60.2
10%	61.9	103.1	70.5

Source: Södersten (1984) and Öberg (2003).

Notes: All calculations are based on the actual asset composition in manufacturing and conform to the general framework developed by King and Fullerton (1984). The average holding period is assumed to be ten years. A negative tax rate implies that the rate of return after tax is greater than before tax. For instance, a tax rate of −83 percent for a debt-financed investment owned by a tax-exempt institution in 1980 tells us that a real rate of return of 10 percent before tax becomes 18.3 percent taking the tax effects into account.

growing firms in new industries. Broadly consistent with this conjecture, Sweden has one of the most skewed distributions with an extreme dominance of very large and very old multinational firms still controlled by Investor and Industrivärden, and very limited addition of new fast-growing firms. Figure 9.5 shows, for example, that thirty-one of the fifty largest firms in 2000 were founded before 1914. No firm founded after 1970 has been added to the list. Moreover, measured by number of the *Fortune* 500 firms in 1991, Sweden ranked as number six with fifteen firms on the list and with the highest number of firms per GDP unit (one billion USD, purchasing power parity adjusted): 0.104 (see Jagrén 1993). The size distribution of Swedish firms (small, medium, and large) is 84.1 percent, 12.1 per-

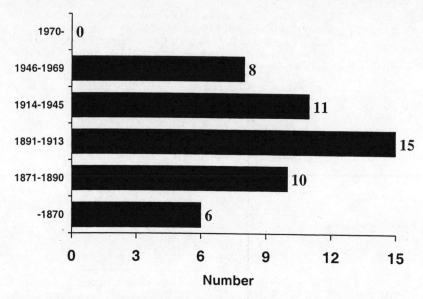

Fig. 9.5   Fifty largest firms in 2000 sorted by the period when they were founded
Source: NUTEK and ALMI (2001).

cent, and 3.7 percent, respectively, compared to an international average size distribution of 87.5 percent, 10.2 percent, and 2.2 percent, respectively, which shows the bias toward larger firms (see Henrekson and Jakobsson 2001).

He, Morck, and Yeung (2003) find that greater instability in the ranking over time of a country's largest firms is associated with faster economic growth.[26] Economic growth is thus more likely to be caused by the rise of new large firms than by the prosperity of established large firms. Sweden has one of the most stable rankings over time but really stands out in their analysis as the only country where the continuity of control over time actually increases.[27] That lock-in of family control for generations may have negative effects is a well-known phenomenon. For example, Holmén and Högfeldt (2004b) report a robust 14 percent discount for large listed firms that are heir controlled. The conjecture that incumbency tends to breed complacency and stagnation, in particular when investments are financed via retained earnings, is consistent with Morck, Stangeland, and Yeung's

26. "The faster growth is primarily due to faster growth in total factor productivity in industrialized countries, and faster capital accumulation in developing countries" (He, Morck, and Yeung 2003).

27. They observe a very interesting fact: "Note that control continuity is always less than corporate stability, except in the case of Sweden. This is because the Wallenberg family took control prior to 1996 of two new top ten firms that arose between 1975 and 1996. These two new top ten firms thus have a continuity of control. This situation arises in no other country" (He, Morck, and Yeung 2003).

(2000) finding in a cross-country analysis that countries with a larger fraction of heir-controlled firms tend to have a significantly lower overall growth rate. The dominance of the same firms among the very largest for decades as well as the extreme continuity of control in Sweden is thus consistent with a lower overall growth rate in the economy.

The strong path dependency is particularly conspicuous for the very important closed-end investment funds that control the largest listed firms, since their shares trade at a significant discount (on average 25–30 percent) relative to their portfolio, which in effect makes it economically impossible for them to raise new equity capital via SEOs. The funds thus prefer that their portfolio firms primarily finance their investments by retained earnings and loans since these sources are relatively cheap, although the firms are traded at a 10 percent discount because of being controlled via a pyramid (see Holmén and Högfeldt 2004b). Since intercorporate dividends are not taxed if they just pass through the pyramid holding company (the closed-end investment fund) on their way from the portfolio firms to the ultimate shareholders, the controlling owners are even more inclined to retain earnings in the portfolio firms. Since realized capital gains are not taxed if reinvested, the pyramid holding companies avoid paying dividends themselves. The combined effect of the preferential tax treatment and the pyramid control structure is therefore that the portfolio firms systematically pay out less dividends and tend to overinvest, which the significantly higher investment–cash flow sensitivity and the significantly lower realized return on investments financed via retained earnings for pyramid firms shows (Holmén and Högfeldt 2004b). Moreover, since the two leading banks are both controlling owners of the most important pyramids and the major providers of loans to the portfolio firms, they tend to behave more like bondholders: accumulating hidden reserves and choosing conservative investment strategies that focus on long-run survival and stable cash flows, not on risk taking and entrepreneurship.

The lock-in effect and the biased investment criterion have especially negative long-run effects since the portfolio firms are in old and often capital-intensive industries. In particular, these firms tend to invest heavily in R&D, often along the narrow trajectory previously chosen by a specializing strategy (few and highly specialized areas with relatively large production volumes), and not in a diversifying direction in alternative technologies (see Erixon 1997). The old, established firms have their comparative advantage in the commercial implementation and marketing of large-scale research projects, not in major breakthrough patents and innovations. While neither R&D investments nor the number of resulting patents is necessarily small, the endogenous effect is that it perpetuates a development path that leads to an even smaller and narrower base of highly specialized firms that might not generate high growth and that may also be economically vulnerable due to shifts in technology. An interesting fact is that of

100 major innovations in the Swedish industry during the postwar period more than 80 occurred in large firms (see Granstrand and Alänge 1995).

Through strong path dependency, the old, established, large-scale industrial structure is thus pushed to its limits by political and endogenous economic decisions that determine the investment strategies and how they are financed. After 100 years of unprecedented growth (among the three highest-growth countries ever recorded for a 100-year period), Sweden ranked as one of the three wealthiest Organization for Economic Cooperation and Development (OECD) countries in 1970. Due to lack of resiliency of the stale economic and political structures, as well as recurrent and prolonged adjustment problems in the aftermath of the oil crises (six devaluations), growth has been significantly lower during the last thirty years, and Sweden now ranks behind neighboring countries. The relationships presented here between the characteristics of heavily entrenched corporate control and growth provide a more plausible and direct explanation of why the Swedish economy has shown signs of stagnation than the alternative theory that pinpoints the negative effects of higher taxes and of a larger public sector (see Lindbeck 1997).[28]

9.4.2   Private Control Maintained by Increasing Separation of Votes from Capital, Which Makes the Capital Base Too Small and Increases Agency Costs and Inefficiencies

When the increased international competitive pressure in the 1960s and 1970s forced highly leveraged Swedish firms to invest more, particularly in R&D, and needed to finance takeovers and mergers to exploit scale advantages, the volume of SEOs increased considerably for the first time since the 1930s. Because of the strong preference for maintained control, the frequency of listed firms that use dual-class shares increased significantly, from 18 percent in 1950 to 32 percent in 1968, to 54 percent in 1981, and peaked at around 80 percent in 1992 to settle at 63 percent in 1998 and below 60 percent after the IT bubble burst (see Agnblad et al. 2001; Holmén and Högfeldt 2004a; and Henreksson and Jakobsson 2003a,b).[29] The high frequency of dual-class shares to separate votes from capital is thus a fairly recent phenomenon and most prevalent among family-controlled firms (see Agnblad et al.). This development has received political support since firms with well-defined private owners in control are believed to be more efficient; families have a long-term commitment, as the growth of private fortune is tied to the firm's development. In the 1980s and particularly after 1993, when all restrictions on foreign ownership of shares were abol-

---

28. It is ironic that since 1997, when Lindbeck presented his dire and one-sided predictions about the future development of the Swedish economy, the macroeconomic performance and growth have at least equaled if not surpassed that of comparable EU countries.

29. In 1950 only 18% of 100 largest firms used dual-class shares: 29% in 1963; and 42% in 1978.

ished, the political ambition (sometimes explicit but most often implicit) has been to promote maintained control in order to keep corporate headquarters—specifically R&D, marketing, and strategic functions—in Sweden. This illustrates the political foundation and sensitivity of corporate control in Sweden. The political support for extensive use of dual-class shares and pyramiding is traded off against the indirect (direct) promise that the largest firms continue to invest in Sweden and do not migrate. Dual-class shares and pyramiding are in fact the very cornerstones of the Social Democratic model of corporate ownership.[30]

Despite much larger foreign ownership (35 percent of outstanding shares), almost exclusively via B-shares, and much more institutional ownership, the old families and closed-end investment funds have been able to maintain a somewhat diluted control by increasing use of dual-class shares combined with reinforced protection of incumbent owners via mandatory bid rules and more stringent takeover rules that de facto increase entrenchment. However, in very large international mergers motivated by scale effects and very large R&D costs, the separation of votes and capital has not been enough to maintain control; Investor lost control of Stora (pulp and paper) and Astra (pharmaceuticals) in mergers with Enso and Zeneca, and earlier it lost control of ASEA in a merger with Brown Boveri—ABB. Despite some dilution of control and much larger capital needs, it is remarkable that established families and closed-end funds are still very often in control. But the increased separation between votes and capital undercuts the very justification for capitalistic firms, as a small capital contribution generates control over all other investors' capital, in particular as the vote lever is often justified on historical grounds. The system therefore also becomes more politically vulnerable, as, for example, the recent EU initiative to abolish dual-class shares shows.

The strong separation between votes and capital generates two principal types of costs that are primarily borne by the noncontrolling shareholders: costs due to extraction of pecuniary benefits (self-dealing) by the controlling owners, and agency costs due to bad (inefficient) decision making. Since the corporate law is designed to handle the problems with self-dealing, and legal enforcement as well as tax enforcement is stringent, agency costs are the most likely reason behind the discounts on firms with leveraged control structure (see Roe 2002a). For example, Holmén and Högfeldt (2004b) did not find any indication of tunneling (corporate steal-

---

30. A public inquiry about voting rights stated explicitly that dual-class shares could be useful to ascertain that "Swedish firms remain controlled by Swedish interests" (see SOU 1986:23). More recently, the fight against EU proposals to in effect abolish the use of dual-class shares has been spearheaded by the Wallenberg family via Investor, whose shareholders paid for the campaign. The Social Democratic government announced that it would do everything within its power to back the Wallenbergs and fight the proposal. The right to use dual-class shares is declared to be a national interest. If dual-class shares were prohibited in the future, it is very likely that the Swedish model as we know it would disintegrate.

ing) in Swedish pyramids that have the most leveraged control structures. Moreover, the increased use of dual-class shares to maintain control implies that the capital base for control becomes smaller: that is, the leverage effect in votes increases, which tends to increase the agency costs as the difference between the power to make pivotal decisions and the private value at risk for controlling owners increases. This effect is amplified by the lock-in of control for generations by the same family. In Schumpeterian spirit, such dynamic agency costs can be substantial, as the entrepreneurial genes and drive do not replicate easily; see Holmén and Högfeldt (2004a). The discounts on family-controlled firms thus most likely gauge such agency costs due to misallocation of control rights to heirs who make inefficient decisions, due, for example, to significantly lower returns on investments financed via retained earnings (see Cronqvist and Nilsson 2003 and Villalonga and Amit 2004).

The importance of agency costs due to a significant lock-in of control over the largest firms for a very long time can best be illustrated by the very large discounts on CEIFs, the pyramid holding companies; see Holmén and Högfeldt (2004b). The vote lever is particularly large since Swedish funds combine separation via pyramiding and dual-class shares, which generates a multiplicative effect. Since Investor has a voting differential of 1:10, while Ericsson was the only listed firm on the SSE (until 2004) that had a 1:1000 differential, the multiplier for the ownership of the Wallenberg family in Ericsson is 125—their own contribution is only about 0.8 percent of Ericsson's capital while they control over 80 percent of the votes jointly with Industrivärden. After the reform, the two major owners controlled around 40 percent of the votes.

Figure 9.6 shows that the discount on Investor's share price relative to the fund's net asset value from 1930 to 2002 has been substantial (averaging about 30 percent), in particular in the 1970s, when it was around 40 percent. After being cut to almost 20 percent in the early 1990s, the discount is now back at around 35 percent. In addition, the portfolio firms have a 10 percent discount due to being under pyramidal control. Analyzing all CEIFs, Holmén and Högfeldt (2004b) find that the discount increases linearly with the controlling owner's degree of separation between votes and capital in the fund and with the number of years the present owner has been in control. The discount is thus significantly higher for founder-controlled pyramids: that is, it gauges the cost of pyramidal power as it becomes more leveraged and more entrenched. The results are consistent with controlling owners' becoming more dependent on the multiplicative separation between votes and capital over time. Pyramidal separation is thus not a static phenomenon, since the use of dual-class shares is intensified in order to maintain control.

The discounts are primarily explained by dynamic agency costs (inefficient decisions) associated with the heavily entrenched power. For ex-

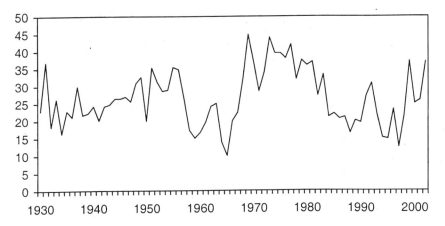

Fig. 9.6   Discount (%) on Investor 1930–2002: Share price relative to net asset value (NAV)
Sources: For 1930–91, Lindgren (1994, pp. 93, 149, 177, and 255), and for 1992–2002 Holmén and Högfeldt (2004b).

ample, Holmén and Högfeldt (2004b) report that the CEIFs' active portfolio management generates a return that is significantly below their cost of capital when capital gains are reinvested instead of being distributed. In particular, a passive portfolio management by just holding the portfolio generates a significantly higher return than actively managing it according to the pivotal owners' specific interests. This in effect limits their investments to projects in which they have a controlling interest, which in turn often implies that bad projects are supported too long; the soft return requirements on retained earnings reinforce these effects. The lower returns translate to into a loss (outflow) in the shareholders' return stream from the investment.

A standard neoclassical model predicts that the discount is simply the ratio of the capitalized value of the outflow, which does not go to the CEIF's shareholders, to the total value of *all* outflows from the CEIF (i.e,, including the dividends going to the shareholders; see Ross 2002). Holmén and Högfeldt's (2004b) empirical estimate of this *theoretical* ratio—the fraction of all outflows that does not go to the shareholders—gives a discount of 25.3 percent compared to the *actual* average discount of 26 percent. The size of the agency costs is on average 0.7 percent of the CEIF's portfolio value, and increases with separation between votes and capital in the CEIF. Since the size of the discount is directly linked to the control structure and power of the controlling owners, the model in effect explains the large discounts in Sweden and provides a solution to the *closed-end fund puzzle.*

Shareholders are in principle privately compensated for the costs of pyramidal ownership through the discounts, but pyramiding also has a negative impact on the efficiency of the capital allocation in the economy that is probably significantly larger. Almeida and Wolfenzon (2004) have developed an interesting model of the equilibrium allocation of capital when the comparative advantage of capital markets in reallocating capital, especially in time of change, is not at work. They show that the overall efficiency may decrease in the presence of *conglomerates,* even when capital is allocated efficiently within the conglomerate. The reason is that local efficiency within a subset of firms does not correspond to global efficiency, as capital is not efficiently allocated between *all* firms.

Unlike with conglomerates, the problem with pyramidal control is not inefficient internal capital markets, since no *direct* capital transfers between pyramid firms are possible. The major problem is instead that too much capital is locked into the separate firms within the pyramid and not redistributed, since the highly leveraged control structure causes an enhanced (political) pecking order because external capital is significantly more expensive than internal capital.[31] Firms controlled by pyramids are thus likely to be *overcapitalized* by relatively cheap internal capital, which may lead to overinvestment, particularly in fixed assets (PPE) and R&D, and lower returns than required by the market (cost of capital). Pyramids may thus have a strategic negative impact on corporate financing and investments because of their limited dependence on the primary equity markets and because they retain too much earnings in firms that are primarily in mature industries.[32] Since not enough of the old capital (for control reasons) is reallocated via the external equity markets to (for example) fledgling firms in new, growing industries, pyramiding hampers both the development of financial markets and the overall growth. These negative effects may be particularly significant in Sweden since the pyramids have had strategic control over the largest and oldest listed firms for decades.

9.4.3 Preference for Maintained Control, Which Implies Limited Use of Equity Financing and That Too Few Firms Grow to Become Large

Egalitarianism may be conducive to dynamic changes, as is evident from the labor market policies that were designed to promote mobility and structural changes in more socially acceptable forms. But when the objective to promote or contain a less dispersed distribution of wealth disfavors equity financing in general, and, in particular, limits the possibilities for newly

31. Unlike the discount on conglomerates, the large discount on pyramid holding companies cannot be explained by inefficiencies in the portfolio firms since this is already reflected in the value of the holding firm's portfolio.

32. The reason why pyramids exist is profoundly political; see Morck (2003) and Holmén and Högfeldt (2004b). However, their structure is not primarily explained by the controlling owners' desire to exert power as such but to get control over a large and relatively cheap source of financing, or control over very large cash flows via a small but strategic investment; see Holmén and Högfeldt (2004b).

founded firms to grow fast using equity financing, there exists a conflict between egalitarianism and dynamic growth. The opportunities for entrepreneurs to build private fortunes by developing new firms have been limited because of tax reasons but also since the strong preference for maintained control in effect limits the volume of equity financing and, in particular, the use of public offers. This preference might be primarily a cultural trait but is more likely to be an equilibrium outcome that is endogenously generated by the corporate ownership model reinforced by the design of the tax system—that is, by the enhanced political pecking order of financing. The preference for control implies limited use of equity financing because it disperses ownership and slow growth rate since the capital infusions are relatively small—too few firms grow quickly to become large. The political disfavoring of equity financing and favoring of retained earnings and loans have reinforced this effect. Hence, there are effects both on the demand and on the supply side that limit equity financing in equilibrium.

In line with the pecking order theory of SEOs, the largest offers for IPO firms are rights issues that dilute control the least (see Holmén and Högfeldt 2004b). However, they are still too small to generate a high growth rate for newly listed firms controlled by the founding entrepreneur. In general, family-controlled IPO firms are undercapitalized because of the preference for control. The strong preference for maintained control and use of retained earnings as the preferred method of financing also limits the growth rate of small and medium-sized enterprises (SMEs). For a sample of 1,248 firms with five to forty-nine employees, Wiklund, Davidsson, and Delmar (2003) report that entrepreneur's prioritize growth only if they do not lose control and independence of other stakeholders while the well-being of their employees is not compromised. They strongly prefer financing via retained earnings even if they are aware that the firm will follow a trajectory with lower growth than with equity financing. Forty-four percent say that they would rather sell the whole firm than share control even if it would improve performance and growth. Moreover, firms where the founder's family owns a smaller fraction and/or have more ownership categories are more likely to grow faster.

Since the formation of new firms has been relatively low and decreasing until the mid-1990s, the addition of new firms that grow quickly has been limited. Together with the limited use of equity financing to support fast-growing firms, this implies a skewed size and age distribution of firms with negative effects on future growth. The incapacity to use equity financing to promote the growth of new firms in advancing industries may be the real Achilles' heel of the Swedish model.

9.4.4   A Summary: An Integrated Answer

An integrated, general answer to the three questions about how corporate ownership developed in Sweden, why the Social Democrats accepted a very concentrated private ownership and control over listed firms, and why ownership did not separate widely in Sweden is structured as follows.

The Swedish corporate ownership model is built on a basic understanding between the Social Democrats (labor) and capital: political support and legitimacy of heavy entrenched private ownership is traded off against the implicit guarantee that the largest listed firms do not migrate and that they continue to invest. The strong separation of ownership and control causes an enhanced (political) pecking order of financing that is endogenously supported by the interests of the two incumbencies.

The incumbent capital's strong preference for maintained control of listed firms implies a priority for financing via retained earnings and loans, and only limited use of equity financing when needed, since this would disperse ownership and eventually control, in particular if public offers are used. For different reasons, the political ordering of financing alternatives by the Social Democrats was the same. The ideological focus on the largest listed firms and their investments combined with skepticism toward equity markets in general, and the primary markets in particular for egalitarian reasons, implied a strong preference for retained earnings and loans. The existing strongly relation-based banking system supported this ordering, and so did the explicit political support for use of devices to separate votes from capital via pyramids and specifically for dual-class shares when the firms needed more equity financing. As the incumbent capital became more institutionalized, while creation of large private fortunes in new firms via significant equity financing is limited and does not threaten to disperse the distribution of wealth too much, the order was also politically acceptable. It is worth emphasizing that this line of argument pinpoints the political sensitivity of the equity markets' primary function and not their secondary function to provide liquidity, which is more standard.

The resulting equilibrium perpetuates and reinforces the initially concentrated ownership of the largest listed firms since ownership does not have to disperse because of significant need for equity financing—ownership becomes more entrenched as separation of votes and capital increases over time. Since historical profits determine future investments and not expected future profits, the equilibrium entails a strong path dependency: dominance of very large and old firms in mature industries that tend to overinvest while there are relatively few new and fast-growing firms in advancing lines of business. Since the labor market policies promote tenure with the existing employer, both labor and corporate control are locked in with the existing firms. The old industrial structure is thus taken to its limits by the strong path dependency of corporate control, investments, labor, and political power. The almost innate entrenchment of both the political and the corporate powers breeds economic stagnation as well as lack of social dynamics.

9.5   Why did corporate ownership in Sweden follow this particular historical path?

The purpose of this section is to very briefly outline some general factors and the correlations between them that have been particularly important determinants of the development of corporate ownership in Sweden. My conjectures are of course subjective, very speculative, and incomplete, as I focus on the overall picture from a specific financial perspective, but the institutional and political stability makes it perhaps both easier and at the same time more interesting to outline a hypothetical answer. I conjecture that the following causal chain between some of these categories (factors) has been particularly important.[33]

When Sweden started its modern economic development about 150 years ago, the country was relatively well endowed with natural resources (e.g., minerals, forests, and water power), mainly located in the northern part of the country, but large capital investments were needed to fully exploit the endowments. The lack of domestic capital and of a sufficiently large group of wealthy people left two alternative ways to raise the necessary capital: collection of many people's small savings via a domestic system of saving and deposit banks and borrowing via the issuing of bond loans abroad (perhaps also the migration of wealthy persons and entrepreneurs). The very large emigration wave to North America increased the political pressure to modernize the very poor country. The reasons behind the country's poverty and the question of what to do about it were the major political issues. How to organize an efficient banking system and how to reform it as the financing demands changed were hotly debated questions for many decades. Political reforms paved the way for a banking system of Scottish type, and very large bond loans to finance infrastructural investments were sold to French and German but also to English investors.

Economic geography is very important since the country is located on the northern rim of Europe but has a very long costal line. Since the Hanseatic times, Sweden has been connected with Continental Europe and partly integrated via the Baltic Sea, but also connected with the British Isles, Amsterdam, and Hamburg via the North Sea, and later also part of a North At-

33. In general, I think (without explicitly motivating it here) that an empirically relevant theory of the historical development of corporate ownership and its importance for financial development and growth should consider (at least) seven broad categories: (a) endowments (natural resources, geography, and population) and production technologies; (b) level and distribution of wealth (poverty); (c) openness of society (transparency and competitiveness); (d) legal system and enforcement; (e) political system (ideology, electoral system, tax system); (f) structure of financial system (relation based—arm's length); and (g) major "random" events (e.g., wars and the Great Reversal). The order is convenient and does not reflect the categories' relative importance. The two literatures on finance and growth (see, e.g., Beck, Levine, and Loayza 2000 and Carlin and Mayer 2003) and on the political economy of corporate finance (see, e.g., Pagano and Volpin 2001) have identified specific factors crucial for financial development, but it would take me too far astray to discuss them now.

lantic economy after the great emigration. The export of raw materials had gone on for centuries, which developed an awareness of being part of an international market economy and fostered market discipline. Financial transfers had also been crucial; for example, Sweden's wars were financed out of Hamburg and Amsterdam. Trade credits and short-term borrowing were later used efficiently as they de facto became long-term capital. As people migrated to develop their know-how and skills abroad, cultural values, ideas, technological knowledge, and market knowledge were transferred to Sweden when they returned. Because it is a small country, the national culture is the cumulative result of influences from several different cultures. Despite an underdeveloped civic society, the country was thus relatively open; the tensions within the elites were between the international modernity and the parochial Swedish traditionalism. The longtime international integration into a larger market economy provided the necessary basis for the late but fast and successful industrialization of Sweden. The early formation of several new firms based on breakthrough innovations that are still important today would probably not have taken place if the engineers and entrepreneurs had not traveled and been internationally connected and if the basic skills and training had not already been in place via the long experience of export-oriented production.

When the capital demands for large-scale industrial investments increased about 100 years ago, the financial system could in principle have developed into a market-based system of equity and bond financing, but the political power of the commercial banks, combined with support from the Social Democrats, instead extended the intermediated system into equity financing by the banking law of 1911 that permitted banks to operate as investment banks and directly own equity. The fledgling stock market was too speculative to become an alternative source of outside financing. The relatively large equity issues in the 1910s and 1920s were primarily financed by the leveraged issuing companies controlled by banks at very short arm's length, and not via public offers.

Without the bank law of 1911 it is likely that corporate ownership would have developed quite differently; the law was the pivotal reason banks ended up holding large equity portfolios of very financially distressed firms in the early 1930s. When the new bank law of 1934 prohibited banks to directly own equity, they were allowed to transfer them to closed-end investment funds instead of being forced to sooner or later sell these assets back to the market when prices rebounded. The leading banks could thus continue to exert control over the largest listed firms, even if it formerly was at arm's length. Unlike in the United States, the banks were not the problem in Sweden but the solution to the problem of how to create financial and social stability and to restructure the large industrials. The main banks were financially healthy enough, were experienced as investment bankers, and had developed the political contacts.

As in the United States, the policies after the deep financial crises shaped the future developments through a strong political and regulatory path dependency. This large random event, however, had an even larger impact in Sweden, as the crises were the start of *both* the political hegemony of the Social Democrats and the political model of entrenched corporate ownership with the banks as the pivotal nodes for corporate control; financial intermediation was de facto extended into highly leveraged corporate control via pyramiding. A short-term and acute solution to the poorly functioning financial markets was extended for decades through the political hegemony and the basic understanding between labor and capital. Corporate ownership is thus very political indeed.

In the early 1980s when deregulation of financial markets started and stock markets were reactivated, the increased use of dual-class shares was backed by strong political support. The B-shares provided the necessary liquidity and dispersion of ownership (capital) while the control rested firmly with the traditional private owners, who increased their separation between control and ownership when market values and capital demands increased. Because of the control structure, the primary market for equity did not develop fully, and the system in effect continued to be very dependent on intermediated financing and retained earnings (a reactive financing mode) even though the tensions between ownership and control were growing and attracting attention from politicians who would reform the system.

I thus think it is possible to identify a simple causal chain that explains why the Swedish financial system has not developed into a fully market-based financial system with very active primary markets and dispersed corporate ownership. Given the poverty and lack of wealthy individuals, and the use of relatively capital-intensive technologies and large-scale production, a system of intermediated financing was politically chosen to collect and allocate the capital. The defining moments for the developments of the financial system are 1911, 1934–37, and 1984, when the intermediated system was extended into equity financing (banks were allowed to directly own shares), when banks became the pivotal controlling owners of the largest firms, and when the equity markets were reactivated (the Great Reversal was reversed) but the heavily entrenched control structure was maintained and reinforced by increased use of dual-class shares, respectively. At these three turning points the development of the financial system as well as of corporate ownership and control could have followed other paths if the political decisions had been different. Because of the strong path dependency in an intermediated financial system when it is supported by political powers united by common interests, a genuinely market-based financial system has not developed in Sweden.

However, it is almost impossible to underestimate the persistent effects even today of the major random event: the crises in the early 1930s that were the catalyst of both the political hegemony of the Social Democrats and the very strong and growing entrenchment of private corporate control. Even if these two phenomena are not always analyzed as being causally connected, it is almost inevitable not to regard them as Siamese twins in an analysis of the development of corporate ownership in Sweden, as I have done in this paper.

9.6   Conclusions

One hundred years ago modernity in Sweden was spearheaded by the rapidly advancing industrial sector and carried by its two new social groups—capital and labor—which reshaped the economic, political, and social arenas. A relatively small group of leading industrialists and bankers, most often recruited outside the establishment, represented the commercial interests, had a pronounced Anglo-Saxon orientation, and were politically active with a stress on rational reforms to promote changes. The well-organized labor movement (SAP and LO) transformed its more radical, original revolutionary objectives into a reformist agenda pursued by democratic, parliamentary means, and viewed itself as the carrier of future social and economic changes of historical proportions. Despite significant ideological influence from Germany, the leadership was primarily stimulated by ideas from the British labor movement that could be implemented politically. Even though labor and capital had adversarial interests, they shared a common sense of being harbingers of modernity. Together with the Liberal Party, the Social Democrats successfully fought for general and equal suffrage (implemented in 1921) against the Old Right, which was organized around the (autocratic) king and supported by the nobility, the church, the military, the leading civil servants, and the large farmers. The Right had by tradition looked toward Germany for guidance and emphasized social and cultural values embodied in strong Lutheranism, nationalism, and traditionalism, with support for the monarchy and social order, mixed with disdain for the commercial Anglo-Saxon countries and their (lack of) values.

Unlike in Germany, where the Old Right was fueled by revenge after WWI and where the transition to modernity was violent, resulting in the direst consequences for Europe, the transition in Sweden was peaceful despite the weak governments and economic crises of the 1920s and early 1930s. In 1932 the Social Democratic vision of the Good Home (Folkhemmet) was not only the political answer to the turbulent economic and political times with its focus on full employment policies but also represented the democratic modernity, with strong emphasis on egalitarian values and encompassing policies based on social and economic rationality with a (benevolent) paternalistic flavor mixed with some mild nationalism. To implement the vision of the good society, the economic policies promoted growth and full employment, particularly in the postwar period until the

1970s, and the development of a large public sector. Embodied in the elaborate welfare state and in the political hegemony of the Social Democrats, it is the most successful and long-lived political vision ever in a democracy.

But when the industrial society reached its peak in the mid-1970s, and forty years of strong growth turned into almost thirty years of relative stagnation, recurrent economic, financial, and budget deficit crises, and significant loss of economic welfare, the weaknesses became all too apparent: the lack of resilience of a too-small base of very large, old, and highly specialized firms in stagnating industries and lack of new growing firms in advancing industries. On ideological grounds the Social Democrats focused on the largest listed firms, in particular their investments and R&D spending, and promoted policies that supported financing via retained earnings and borrowing from a strongly relation-based banking system but disfavored equity markets as suppliers of capital for egalitarian reasons. Their political support for use of dual-class shares and pyramiding in effect aligned the interests of the incumbent political power with incumbent capital (in particular the leading banks) as corporate control is maintained and actually reinforced. Capital is locked in with the incumbent firms since the separation of control from ownership drives a wedge between the costs of internal and external capital that causes an enhanced (political) pecking order of corporate financing. Investments are thus primarily determined by historical profits, not by expected future profits.

Listed firms have indeed not been dependent on the primary equity markets, while the formation of private fortunes tied to new, fast-growing firms fueled by equity market financing has been very limited. This explains both why ownership did not disperse and why the addition of new firms has been so poor. Since labor market rules are designed to protect incumbent workers, both labor and control over capital are therefore locked into the existing corporate structure while the Social Democrats have locked in the political sector. The real problem with the Swedish model of corporate ownership is thus the lack of economic and social dynamics—modernity has become stale and embedded.

The strong historical and political path dependency is apparent in the fact that the two socioeconomic groups that spearheaded modernity 100 years ago—leading capitalists and organized labor—are still the heavily entrenched incumbencies even if the importance of the industrial society has been declining for decades.[34] The real irony is that corporate control, although diluted in recent years by increased institutional ownership, is still in the hands of a very few well-established families and banks, not despite but because of Social Democratic policies.

The Social Democrats in effect became the guarantor of heavily en-

34. Path dependency is here used in a wider, more general sense than in, e.g., Bebchuk and Roe (1999).

trenched private corporate ownership rather than the terminator of capitalism, since the political and corporate incumbencies have been united by strong common interests. Incumbent owners need the political support to legitimize that their corporate power rests on extensive use of dual-class shares and pyramiding. At the same time, the Social Democrats only get the necessary resources and indirect support for their social and economic policies from the private sector if the largest firms remain under Swedish control so that capital does not migrate. By not encouraging outsiders to create new firms and fortunes, and by not fully activating the primary equity markets, the heavy politicized system has redistributed incomes but not property rights and wealth. The result is an aging economic system with an unusually large proportion of very old and very large firms with well-defined owners in control.

References

Agnblad, Jonas, Erik Berglöf, Peter Högfeldt, and Helena Svancar. 2001. Ownership and control in Sweden: Strong owners, weak minorities, and social control. In *The control of corporate Europe,* ed. Fabrizio Barca and Marco Becht, 228–58. Oxford: Oxford University Press.
Almeida, Heitor, and Daniel Wolfenzon. 2004. Equilibrium costs of efficient internal capital markets. New York University, Stern School of Business. Working paper.
Althaimer, Hans. 1988. Börsen och företagens nyemissioner [New equity issues on the Stockholm Stock Exchange 1902–1986]. In *Stockholms Fondbörs: Riskkapitalmarknad i omvandling,* ed. Ingemund Hägg, 39–56. Stockholm: SNS Förlag.
Bebchuk, Lucian A. 1999. A rent-protection theory of corporate ownership and control. NBER Working Paper no. 7203. Cambridge, MA: National Bureau of Economic Research.
Bebchuk, Lucian A., Reinier Kraakman, and George Triantis. 1999. Stock pyramids, cross-ownership, and dual class equity: The creation and agency costs of separating control from cash flow rights. NBER Working Paper no. 6951. Cambridge, MA: National Bureau of Economic Research.
Bebchuk, Lucian A., and Mark J. Roe. 1999. A theory of path dependency in corporate governance and ownership. *Stanford Law Review* 52:127–70.
Beck, Thorsten, Ross Levine, and N. Loayza. 2000. Finance and the sources of growth. *Journal of Financial Economics* 58:261–300.
Bertrand, Marianne, Paras Mehta, and Sendhil Mullainathan. 2002. Ferreting out tunnelling: An application to Indian business groups. *Quarterly Journal of Economics* 117:121–48.
Burkart, Mike, Fausto Panunzi, and Andrei Shleifer. 2003. Family firms. *Journal of Finance* 58:2167–2202.
Carlin, Wendy, and Colin Mayer. 2003. Finance, investment, and growth. *Journal of Financial Economics* 69:191–226.
Cronqvist, Henrik, and Mattias Nilsson. 2003. Agency costs of controlling minority shareholders. *Journal of Financial and Quantitative Analysis* 38:695–719.

Dyck, Alexander, and Luigi Zingales. 2004. Private benefits of control: An international comparison. *Journal of Finance* 59:537–600.

Erixon, Lennart. 1997. The golden age of the Swedish Model: The coherence between capital accumulation and economic policy in Sweden in the early postwar period. Report 97:9. Oslo: Institute for Social Research.

Fritz, Sven. 1990. *Affärsbankernas aktieförvärvsrätt under 1900-talets första decennier* [The right of commercial banks to acquire shares during the first decades of the 20th century]. Acta Universitatis Stockholmiensis; Stockholm Studies in Economic History 14. Stockholm: Almqvist and Wicksell International.

Glete, Jan. 1994. *Nätverk i näringslivet: Ägande och industriell omvandling i det mogna industri-samhället 1920–1990* [Corporate networks: Ownership and industrial restructuring in the mature industrial society]. Stockholm: SNS Förlag.

Granstrand, Ove, and Sverker Alänge. 1995. The evolution of corporate entrepreneurship in Swedish industry: Was Schumpeter wrong? *Journal of Evolutionary Economics* 5:133–56.

Gårdlund, Torsten. 1947. *Svensk industrifinansiering under genombrottsskedet 1830–1913* [Financing of Swedish firms during the formative years 1830–1913]. Stockholm: Svenska Bankföreningen.

He, Kathy S., Randall Morck, and Bernard Yeung. 2003. Corporate stability and economic growth. University of Alberta School of Business. Working paper.

Hedborg, Anna, and Rudolf Meidner. 1984. *Folkhemsmodellen* [The Swedish model]. Stockholm: Rabén & Sjögren.

Helleiner, E. 1994. *States and the reemergence of global finance: From Bretton Woods to the 1990s.* Ithaca, NY: Cornell University Press.

Henrekson, Magnus, and Ulf Jakobsson. 2001. Where Schumpeter was nearly right: The Swedish model and capitalism, Socialism and democracy. *Journal of Evolutionary Economics* 11:331–58.

———. 2003a. The Swedish model of corporate control in transition. SSE/EFI Working Paper no. 521. Stockholm: Stockholm School of Economics.

———. 2003b. The transformation of ownership policy and structure in Sweden: Convergence towards the Anglo-Saxon model? *New Political Economy* 8:73–102.

Hermansson, Carl-Henrik. 1965. *Monopol och storfinans: De 15 familjerna* [Monopoly and leading capitalists: The fifteen families]. Stockholm: Rabén och Sjögren.

Högfeldt, Peter, and Andris Oborenko. 2004. Does market timing or enhanced pecking order determine the capital structure? Stockholm School of Economics. Working paper.

Holmén, Martin, and Peter Högfeldt. 2004a. A law and finance analysis of initial public offerings. *Journal of Financial Intermediation* 13:324–58.

———. 2004b. Pyramidal discounts: Tunneling or overinvestment? European Corporate Governance Institute and Stockholm School of Economics. Working paper.

Jagrén, Lars. 1993. De dominerande storföretagen [The domineering transnational firms]. In *Den långa vägen: Den ekonomiska politikens begränsningar och möjligheter att föra Sverige ur 1990-talets kris* [The long road: The limitations and possibilities for economic policy measures to lead Sweden out of the crisis in the 1990s], ed. Thomas Andersson. Stockholm: IUI Foundation.

Jörberg, Lennart. 1988. *Svenska företagare under industrialismens genombrott 1870–1885* [Swedish entrepreneurs during the industrial breakthrough 1870–1885]. Lund Studies in Economics and Management 2. Lund, Sweden: Lund University Press.

King, M. A., and D. Fullerton, eds. 1984. *The taxation of income from capital: A comparative study of the United States, the United Kingdom, Sweden, and West Germany.* Chicago: University of Chicago Press.

Korpi, Walter. 1978. *The working class in welfare capitalism: Work, union and politics in Sweden.* London: Routledge & Kegan Paul.

La Porta, Rafael, Florencio López-de-Silanes, and Andrei Shleifer. 1999. Corporate ownership around the world. *Journal of Finance* 54:471–517.

La Porta, Rafael, Florencio López-de-Silanes, Andrei Shleifer, and Robert Vishny. 2000. Investor protection and corporate governance. *Journal of Financial Economics* 59:3–27.

Larsson, Mats. 2002. Storföretagande och industrikoncentration [Mergers and acquisitions among large listed firms in Sweden 1913–38]. In *Industrialismens tid: Ekonomisk-historiska perspektiv på svensk industriell omvandling under 200 år,* ed. Maths Isacson and Mats Morell. Stockholm: SNS Förlag.

Lindbeck, Assar. 1997. The Swedish experiment. *Journal of Economic Literature* 35:1273–1319.

Lindgren, Gunnar. 1953. Shareholders and shareholder participation in the larger companies' meetings in Sweden. *Weltwirtschaftliches Archiv* 71:281–98.

Lindgren, Håkan. 1994. *Aktivt ägande:Investor under växlande konjunkturer* [Active ownership: Investor in variegating business cycles since 1916]. Stockholm: Stockholm School of Economics, Institute for Research in Economic History.

Maddison, A. 1982. *Phases of capitalist development.* Oxford: Oxford University Press.

Meidner, Rudolf. 1978. *Employee investment funds: An approach to collective capital formation.* London: Allen and Unwin.

Morck, Randall. 2003. Why some double taxation might make sense: The special case of intercorporate dividends. NBER Working Paper no. 9651. Cambridge, MA: National Bureau of Economic Research.

Morck, Randall K., David A. Stangeland, and Bernard Yeung. 2000. Inherited wealth, corporate control, and economic growth: The Canadian disease. In *Concentrated corporate ownership,* ed. Randall K. Morck. Chicago: University of Chicago Press.

NUTEK and ALMI. 2001. *Tre näringspolitiska utmaningar: Allianser för hållbar tillväxt* [Three challenges for the industrial policy: Alliances for sustainable growth]. Stockholm: NUTEK Förlag.

Öberg, Ann. 2003. Essays on capital income taxation in the corporate and housing sectors. PhD diss., Uppsala University.

Östlind, Anders. 1945. Svensk samhällsekonomi 1914–1922: Med särskild hänsyn till industrin [The Swedish economy 1914–1922, in particular the industrial sector]. Stockholm: Svenska bankföreningen.

Pagano, Marco, and Paolo Volpin. 2001. The political economy of finance. *Oxford Review of Economic Policy* 17:502–19.

———. 2004. The political economy of corporate governance. Forthcoming in *American Economic Review.*

Persson, Torsten, and Guido Tabellini. 2003. Political institutions and policy outcomes: What are the stylized facts? IIES working paper. Stockholm University.

Rajan, Raghuram G., and Luigi Zingales. 2003a. The great reversals: The politics of financial development in the 20th century. *Journal of Financial Economics* 69:5–50.

———. 2003b. *Saving capitalism from the capitalists: Unleashing the power of financial markets to create wealth and spread opportunity.* New York: Crown Business.

Reiter, J. 2003. Changing the microfoundations of corporatism: The impact of financial globalization on Swedish corporate ownership. *New Political Economy* 8:103–26.

Roe, Mark J. 2002a. Corporate law's limits. *Journal of Legal Studies* 31:233–71.
———. 2002b. *Political determinants of corporate governance: Political context, corporate impact.* Clarendon Lectures in Management Studies. Oxford: Oxford University Press.
Ross, Stephen A. 2002. Neoclassical finance, alternative finance and the closed-end fund puzzle. *European Financial Management* 8:129–37.
Sjögren, Hans. 1995. Long-term financial contracts in the bank-oriented financial system. *Scandinavian Journal of Management* 10:315–30.
Statens Offentliga Utredningar (SOU). 1968a. Koncentrationsutredningen I. Stockholm: Finansdepartementet.
———. 1968b. *Kreditmarknadens struktur och funktionssätt.* Koncentrationsutredningen II. Stockholm: Finansdepartementet.
———. 1986. *Aktiers röstvärde.* Betänkande av röstvärdeskommittén. Stockholm: Liber.
———. 1988. *Ägande och inflytande i svenskt näringsliv: Huvudbetänkande från ägarutredningen.* Stockholm: Industridepartementet.
Statens Industriverk (SIND). 1980. *Ägandet i det privata näringslivet.* Stockholm: Statens Industriverk.
Studieförbundet Näringsliv och Samhälle (SNS) Ownership Project. 1988. Special reports by Ragnar Boman, Anna-Karin Eliasson, and Barbro Sköldebrand. Stockholm: SNS Förlag.
Södersten, Jan. 1984. Sweden. In *The taxation of income from capital: A comparative study of the United States, the United Kingdom, Sweden and West Germany,* ed. M. A. King and D. Fullerton. Chicago: University of Chicago Press.
Sundin, Ann-Marie, and Sven-Ivan Sundqvist. 1996. *Owners and power in Sweden's listed companies.* Stockholm: Dagens Nyheter.
Villalonga, Belen, and Raphael Amit. 2004. How do family ownership, management, and control affect firm value? Harvard Business School. Working paper.
Wigforss, Ernst. 1980. *Ernst Wigforss skrifter i urval I-IX* [A collection of Ernst Wigforss's writings]. Stockholm: Tidens Förlag.
Wiklund, Johan, Per Davidsson, and Fredric Delmar. 2003. What do they think and feel about growth? An expectancy-value approach to small business managers' attitudes toward growth. *Entrepreneurship Theory and Practice* 27 (3): 247–70.

Comment   Ailsa Röell

What makes Peter Högfeldt's analysis of Swedish corporate ownership particularly compelling is its focus on how politics has shaped the Swedish corporate finance landscape. The paper sweeps through the twentieth century, interrelating political change and developments in financial institutions, and providing a theoretical perspective.

From the viewpoint of an observer of the Dutch situation, I am struck by the question of how two such similar countries as Sweden and the

Ailsa Röell is professor of finance at Tilburg University and a senior research scholar at Princeton University.

Netherlands could have developed in such a divergent way. Both are small, open economies with a fairly homogeneous population that industrialized relatively late; both use proportional voting; and both developed into social democracies with a strong emphasis on social cohesion, consensus, and corporatist economic management in the second half of the twentieth century. In both cases, the unions traded wage moderation in the postwar expansion for a series of reforms in the 1970s designed to protect job security and worker rights. In both cases, the corporatist compromise meant that shareholder value maximization could not be the sole business objective. But it is fair to say that in both countries, workers did not achieve real power over corporate decision making. Yet at the same time, shareholder voice was significantly curtailed.

It is here that the two countries differ dramatically: in the manner in which ownership and control were separated. In Sweden the widespread use of dual-class shares, combined with a set of powerful bank-controlled investment trusts inherited from the reforms of the 1930s, enabled a tiny set of influential players to enduringly control much of Swedish industry. In the Netherlands, the French-origin corporate law did not permit the use of dual-class or nonvoting shares (and indeed, until the 1920s, it imposed voting caps on large stakes); moreover, the commercial banks had never played a large role in long-term financing. Thus, the Swedish pyramidal group structure did not take hold. Instead, power in the largest companies, insofar as it was not already in the hands of controlling interests, was given to self-perpetuating boards that represented neither shareholders nor employees.

The flaws of the Dutch system are now manifest in a series of scandals related to fraud, mismanagement, and excessive executive pay. Corporate management, not formally accountable to any one constituency, is daily on trial in the court of public opinion, not to mention in the real courts. Political reforms are overdue and likely.

In Sweden the potential costs come in the form of misallocated capital, ossification, and reduced innovation, as well as higher consumer prices due to the oligopolistic nature of the ownership structures. How high are these costs, and to what extent has economic growth been impaired? Sweden has fallen back from its enviable position in 1970, with the highest per capita GDP in Europe, to seventh place in 2003 (at current exchange rates, eleventh in terms of purchasing power parity!). The extent to which the interplay of political imperatives and the corporate ownership structure is responsible for this decline is a topic of ongoing debate to which the current paper contributes fresh insights.

10

Spending Less Time with the Family
The Decline of Family Ownership
in the United Kingdom

Julian Franks, Colin Mayer, and Stefano Rossi

Entrebrawneurial Britain
  I strut around my stately life
Hand in hand with lover and wife.
  I even own a share or two
In a family firm my father grew.

Of course I have not the slightest view
On what this firm is supposed to do.
  Nor have I any reason to care
Since *in absentia* I sit in a Chair,
Of a Board that yesterday I chose to hire
And tomorrow I've decided that I will fire.

Julian Franks is professor of finance at the London Business School. Colin Mayer is the Peter Moores Professor of Finance in the Saïd Business School, University of Oxford. Stefano Rossi is a Ph.D. candidate in finance at the London Business School.

We are grateful for helpful suggestions on this and a companion paper ("The Origination and Evolution of Ownership and Control") from participants at conferences at the American Finance Association meetings in Washington DC, January 2003, the National Bureau of Economic Research Program on the Evolution of Family Ownership conference in Boston, INSEAD and Lake Louise, the Political Economy of Financial Markets Conference at Princeton, September 2003, and the Research Institute of Economy, Trade, and Industry (RIETI) Conference on Comparative Corporate Governance: Changing Profiles of National Diversity in Tokyo, January 2003, and at seminars at the Bank of England, the Bank of Italy, Cambridge University, the London Business School, the London School of Economics, Studieförbundet Näringsliv och Samhälle (SNS), Stockholm, the Stern School, New York University, Université Libre de Bruxelles, University of Bologna, and University of California, Los Angeles. We have received helpful comments from Brian Cheffins, Barry Eichengreen, Charles Hadlock, Leslie Hannah, Cliff Holderness, Gregory Jackson, Kose John, Hideaki Miyajima, Randall Morck, Hyun Song Shin, Oren Sussman, Elu von Thadden, and Xavier Vives.

10.1   Introduction

The United Kingdom is a strange country. It does not have concentrated ownership; most countries do. It does not have pyramid structures; most countries do. Family ownership is of limited significance; in most countries it is extensive. There are few dual-class shares; in many countries they are extensive. It has an active market in corporate control; elsewhere, it is largely nonexistent.

By way of a measure of its peculiarity, Becht and Mayer (2001) report that in a majority of listed Austrian, German, and Italian firms there is a single voting block of shares that commands a majority of votes in these companies. Families account for 45 percent of blocks in Austria, 32 percent in Germany, and 30 percent in Italy. The average size of the blocks is 26 percent in Austria, 27 percent in Germany, and 20 percent in Italy. In the United Kingdom, on average the largest voting block will usually cast under 10 percent of votes, while less than 5 percent of blocks are attributable to families, and the average size of their blocks is only 5 percent. There is a stark contrast in the significance of families in corporate control between the United Kingdom and the rest of Europe.

Even by the standards of the United States, the United Kingdom is odd. Dual-class shares are by no means absent from the United States. Powerful families established some of the largest corporations in the United States, and pyramids were, at least at one stage, widespread. The United States may be odd, but Britain is even more peculiar.

Why is the United Kingdom so different? Was it always so deviant? The British business history literature would seem to suggest not. Family ownership has been a dominant theme in British business history. Alfred Chandler developed a thesis of comparative industrial performance around differences between managerial capitalism in North America and family organizations in Europe. He argued that the United Kingdom was held back at the turn of the century by a continuing reliance on family as against professional managerial capitalism. Successes were restricted to industries in which there were modest investment requirements, most notably branded packaged goods. Companies such as Beechams, Cadbury, Colman, Reckitt, and Rowntree were dominated by their owners and had little professional management. The consequences were most seriously felt in those industries that required large-scale investments—chemicals, electrical equipment, and metals; these declined markedly in relation to their German and U.S. competitors. David Landes (1965, pp. 536–64) described the stereotypical image of the British family firm as being an organization founded by fanatical fathers and succeeded by squabbling siblings who "worked at play and played at work."

According to this view, at the beginning of the twentieth century, as in most other countries, powerful families dominated the British corporate sector. They may have been incompetent, but at least they were there, and presumably their extinction was a consequence of their incompetence. As a result, the origins of the British corporate system are quite conventional, and its current anomalous status is a consequence of the normal workings of market forces.

Plausible though this story is, we argue in this paper that it is probably not an accurate and certainly not a complete description of what transpired. At the very least, it does not capture the rich interaction that occurred between financial markets and companies in the United Kingdom.

There are many aspects of this that are misleading. The first is that while families were important at the beginning of the twentieth century, their significance did not in general derive from long-term large-scale ownership of British companies. By way of ownership, families were rapidly marginalized. The pattern of ownership, which we report above as characterizing corporate British today, emerged early in the twentieth century.

Instead, the significance of family influence claimed by Chandler comes from a different source. While families rapidly relinquished ownership, they retained control through their positions on the boards of directors. They often held the all-important position of chairman of the board, and even if they did not, then their board representation was frequently disproportionate to their ownership stakes. This is quite different from the pattern observed in Continental European countries of extensive family ownership with delegated managerial control. In Britain families exerted power without responsibility, whereas in most countries they had responsibility with at least limited power.

Still more interesting than the nature of ownership and control was the process by which it came about. Family ownership did not for the most part decline because families sold out. They did not typically abandon firms through company flotations or share sales. Instead, their holdings were diluted in the process of issuing shares to finance growth. In a sample of firms that we will describe below, we estimate that issues of shares associated with acquisitions, rights issues, and placings accounted for almost two-thirds of the decline in directors' shareholdings over the period 1900 to 1950. A majority of this issuance arose from one particular activity of firms, namely acquisitions. More than half of the dilution (36.2 percent) of the 61.6 percent is associated with issues of shares for acquisitions. Shares were not primarily issued to finance internal investments but rather to acquire other firms.

The changing pattern of ownership of British firms during the century was primarily a product of the immense amount of takeover activity that occurred during the twentieth century. Hannah (1976), for example, documents the three major merger waves that occurred around 1900, 1920, and 1930. Many of these mergers were consolidations of several companies, establishing the corporate groupings that dominated the rest of the century.

What is remarkable about this process of ownership dilution is that it occurred in largely unregulated equity markets with little protection to minority investors. In this paper we explore this acquisition process. We document how it went through various stages. In the first half of the twentieth century there was no market for corporate control. All mergers were the result of an agreement between the two or more boards of the merging companies. Often a holding company was created to buy all the shares of the combining firms, with the old boards of directors forming a new board. Mergers were the result of cooperation rather than competition between companies for a target in an auction market.

During the 1940s and 1950s there were important changes in the U.K. capital markets. First, following a number of scandals, minority investor protection was strengthened at the end of the 1940s. Disclosure was improved, and antidirector provisions were introduced. Second, there was a sharp increase in institutional ownership. By 1960, institutions were the largest shareholder in more than a third of the companies in our sample. Third, and most significantly, a market for corporate control emerged: "For the first time it became popular for the ownership of public companies to be determined simply by stock market transactions and for control to pass thereby to parties previously unconnected with the firm" (Roberts 1992, p. 183).

Charles Clore launched the first hostile takeover in 1953 for a large shoe chain called J. Sears Holdings. This bid introduced the concept of paying a significant premium for the shares of target firms. Whereas before 1950 there was little difference in cost between partial and full acquisitions, the emergence of hostile takeovers substantially increased the cost of acquiring full ownership. As a consequence, it became attractive to make partial rather than full bids for companies.

Companies responded by attempting to protect themselves and their minority shareholders against the takeover threat. We estimate that within a period of fifteen years about 7.5 percent of listed companies had issued dual-class shares with discriminatory voting rights. In others, they sought protection under the wing of a friendly parent. In particular, in the brewing industry, Whitbread provided protection through large stakes to several local brewers under what became known as "the Whitbread umbrella."

Partial acquisitions, dual-class shares, and strategic block holdings gave rise, at least temporarily, to shareholding patterns that are currently commonplace on the Continent but were previously rare in the United Kingdom. This is a particularly interesting stage in the development of the British corporation because it could at this point have switched into Continental European mode with dual-class shares and pyramids. In Japan, similar takeovers threats in the post-WW2 period prompted the erection of elaborate defenses in the form of cross-shareholdings that have persisted until today. But this did not happen in Britain. Financial institutions had become steadily more influential investors in equities by the 1950s and 1960s, and with the agreement of the stock exchanges they were able to deny these firms access to the capital markets. The result was the dismantling of the protective measures until they were virtually extinguished by the 1980s. The elimination of dual-class shares and pyramids in the United Kingdom was therefore due to the dominance of institutional investors. In other countries, corporations were more significant holders of corporate equity[1] and derived benefits from the retention of mechanisms such as pyramids and dual-class shares for sustaining control.

Instead, the more enduring response to the emergence of a market for corporate control was regulatory. The Takeover Panel was established in 1968. Its first rules included mandatory bid and equal price requirements ensuring that offers would be made at the same price to all shareholders once 30 percent of a target had been purchased. These two rules had the effect of preventing both discriminatory price offers and the buildup of large share blocks.

By the beginning of the 1970s the key features of current U.K. corporate ownership and control were in place: substantial institutional shareholdings, a hostile takeover market, and extensive minority investor protection. Together they had the effect of establishing active markets in corporate control.

In a companion paper, we have documented that dilution of family ownership has been a feature of the whole of the twentieth century, in large part due to share acquisitions. But not only was acquisition the main cause of the dilution, it was also its main effect. At the start of the century families could expect to retain control over extended periods as directors, if not owners, of their firms, and their approval was required before changes in control through takeover could take place. By the end of the century, family board representation was not sufficient to ensure continuity of control in the face of hostile takeovers. This had two consequences. First, the feature that Chandler had noted of the dominance of management by families was less evident by the end of the century. Second, dilution of ownership had control as well as cash-flow consequences for families. Management had therefore become more professional, and families were unable to preserve the continuity of control that they enjoyed in the first half of the century.

As Davies and Hopt (2004) note, despite similarities in the structure of their capital markets and the common law nature of their legal systems, the United Kingdom and United States today allocate decision rights regarding takeover offers in very different ways. In the United Kingdom they reside with the target shareholders, whereas in those state jurisdictions in the United States that are sympathetic to the use of poison pills as takeover de-

1. See, for example, Franks and Mayer (2001) for data on corporate holdings in Germany.

fenses, most notably in Delaware, they reside with the target management. The exposure of target management to hostile takeovers in the United Kingdom is not therefore simply a product of its common law or dispersed ownership system. Politics, in the guise of the growing influence of institutional investors in the second half of the twentieth century, may have been at least as important in establishing the United Kingdom's unusually active market in corporate control.

In section 10.2 we describe the data sets that we employ in this chapter. In section 10.3, we record the evolution of family ownership, board representation, and the rise of institutional share ownership. Section 10.4 describes the merger and acquisitions process in the first of the century. Section 10.6 looks at how a takeover market emerged in the second half of the twentieth century. Section 10.7 concludes the chapter and examines the implications of these developments for family control of British companies.

10.2   Data

We employ three data sets in this chapter. The first comprises individual firm data on the ownership and board representation of samples of firms incorporated around 1900 and 1960. There were twenty firms that were incorporated or reincorporated between 1897 and 1903 and were still in existence in 2001 and twenty firms that were incorporated between 1958 and 1962 and were still in existence in 2001; we have collected data on all of these. To avoid the obvious bias that might arise from the greater longevity of the 1900 than the 1960 sample, we collected a third sample of twenty firms incorporated around 1900 that are no longer in existence today. We compare the evolution of ownership and control of the 1960 sample with both the surviving and nonsurviving 1900 samples.

The data have been assembled from (a) archives of company accounts and share registers (including names and size of shareholdings) stored at Companies House in Cardiff, and at the Public Records in Kew, Richmond (Surrey);[2] (b) new issue prospectuses at the Guildhall Library in London; (c) annual issues of the *Stock Exchange Year Book,* which lists names of directors and the sources of any changes in issued capital; and (d) official lists of trading of securities from the British Library in London. Share registers provided evidence of annual ownership changes, and the annual returns to

2. Since the beginning of the twentieth century, firms in the United Kingdom have been required to file information at a central depository called Companies House, now situated in Cardiff, Wales. This is a remarkable and largely unique long-run source of data on firms. However, it suffers from one deficiency: Companies House retains complete records on all firms that are still in existence today but discards information on most, but not all, dead companies. We therefore supplemented data from Companies House with a second source of public information from the Public Records in Kew, Richmond (Surrey), which keeps some information on dead companies.

Companies House gave details of resignations of existing directors and appointments of new directors.

From these data, we collected names of directors, their shareholdings (including those of their families), the date and amounts of capital issued in acquisitions, new share issues via public and private placements, and other changes in share capital, such as capitalizations of reserves. We traced the founding family ownership from incorporation until the last family member left the board by recording shareholdings and place of residence of family members, taking account of name changes across generations when, for example, the daughter of a founder married. We also traced shareholdings through intermediary firms. For outside shareholdings, we limited ourselves to stakes greater than 1 percent of ordinary capital. We used newspaper archives to document evidence of tender offers and trading in provincial stock exchanges, especially in the early 1900s.

The second data set collected for this study includes information on antitakeover defenses (dual-class shares, voting right restrictions, and insider block holdings) for about 1,800 listed firms in two London Stock Exchange (LSE) industry classifications, breweries and industrials and commercials.

The third data set comes from Hannah's (1974a) list of takeovers over the period 1919 to 1939 and includes announcement dates of takeovers from the *Financial Times* newspaper, the medium of exchange, dividend changes and board turnover from the *Stock Exchange Year Book,* and share prices from the daily official list (at the Guildhall Library). Newspaper archives are used to document evidence on the hostility of takeover activity, particularly during the 1950s and early 1960s.

10.3   Ownership and Board Representation

10.3.1   Ownership

According to Rajan and Zingales (2003), the United Kingdom has had one of the largest stock markets in the world throughout the twentieth century. Table 10.1 reports the number of companies listed on the LSE and the market value of listed securities for the period 1853 to 1939. As the stock exchange did not collect aggregate statistics over this period, several other sources have had to be used. According to Killick and Thomas (1970) and Michie (1999), around 1850, provincial stock exchanges had more listed companies than the LSE—490 as against 200. Hart and Prais (1956) record a large expansion of listed companies on the LSE over the period 1885 to 1939, although their data refer only to industrial and commercial companies. From 1963, the LSE has kept a continuous series of aggregate equity market values, including preference and dual-class shares. One of the most striking features is the marked decline in the number of listed firms that has occurred over the past forty years (see table 10.1).

| Table 10.1 | The number of companies and market capitalization of companies listed on the London Stock Exchange (LSE) | | |

| | No. listed companies | | |
Date	LSE	Provincial	Source
	A. Pre-1950		
1847		490[b]	Killick and Thomas (1970)
1853	200		Michie (1999)
1885	70[a]		Hart and Prais (1956)
1907	571[a]		Hart and Prais (1956)
1913	1,700		Rajan and Zingales (2003)
1939	1,712[a]		Hart and Prais (1956)

| | United Kingdom | | | | | International | |
	No. of companies	No. of equity securities	Market value (£/M)	GDP current prices	Market development (GDP/MV)	No. of companies	Market value (£/M)
	B. 1963–2000						
1963	4,409	4,064	32,204				
1970	3,418	3,197	37,793	44,200	0.86	387	57,135
1980	2,747	2,283	86,720	201,000	0.43	394	183,846
1990	2,006	2,081	450,544	479,000	0.94	553	1,124,131
2000	1,904	2,272	1,796,811			501	3,525,701

Notes: This table reports London Stock Exchange statistics on a number of listed companies and market capitalization from various sources.

[a]Industrial companies only (Hart and Prais).

[b]Manchester, Newcastle, Liverpool, and Leeds.

Table 10.2 records family shareholdings of a sample of twenty companies incorporated around 1900 and twenty incorporated around 1960 that were still in existence in 2001 (the "survivors") and a sample of twenty companies incorporated around 1900 that died during the century ("nonsurvivors"). It documents the number of companies where the founding family's shareholding passes a particular threshold of 25 percent, 50 percent, and 75 percent of equity. Franks, Mayer, and Rossi (2004) report that insider ownership declined rapidly and at similar rates in the first and second halves of the century. Rates of ownership dispersion were similar in samples of companies incorporated in 1900 and 1960. Table 10.2 confirms that family ownership was rapidly diluted throughout the century. By 1940, forty years after incorporation, the number of firms in which families owned more than 25 percent of shares had declined from thirteen to four among the survivors. Family ownership was initially even less pronounced among the nonsurvivors (nine out of twenty companies passed the 25 percent threshold), but pro rata to the number of survivors it then declined less rapidly to four out of twelve survivors in 1940.

Table 10.2   **Family shareholdings and ownership thresholds**

	Survivors				Nonsurvivors				No. of
	25%	50%	75%	N	25%	50%	75%	N	observations
1900 sample									
1900	13	9	8	20	9	8	6	20	40
1910	10	7	7	20	9	8	5	20	40
1920	11	8	7	20	8	6	4	17	37
1930	7	4	3	20	8	4	3	16	36
1940	4	3	3	20	4	4	3	12	32
1950	3	3	2	20	4	3	3	10	30
1960	2	1	1	20	3	2	1	4	24
1970	0	0	0	20	2	1	1	3	23
1980	0	0	0	20	1	1	1	2	22
1990	0	0	0	20	0	0	0	1	21
2000	0	0	0	20	0	0	0	0	20

	25%	50%	75%	No. of observations
1960 sample				
1960	16	15	7	20
1970	8	5	3	20
1980	7	2	1	20
1990	1	1	0	20
2000	0	0	0	20

Source: Own calculations.
Note: This table reports the number of companies in our sample where the founding family owns more than 25 percent, 50 percent, and 75 percent of issued ordinary share capital, respectively.

Table 10.2 shows that this dilution of family ownership was even more noticeable in the 1960 than in the 1900 sample. For example, forty years after incorporation, there was no company in the 1960 sample in which family ownership passed the 25 percent threshold. Family ownership therefore diminished rapidly throughout the century but much more so in the second half of the century.

Table 10.3 documents how financial institutions emerged to take the place of families as dominant owners of corporate Britain around the middle of the twentieth century. It reports the number of cases where a financial institution was the largest shareholder of our sample of firms. Forty years after incorporation, there were four cases in the 1900 survivor sample where a financial institution was the largest shareholder, compared with thirteen in 1990 for the 1960 sample. The average size of institutional stakes was also larger in the second half of the century. The average stake of the four financial institutions that were the largest shareholders in the 1900 sample was 5.9 percent in 1940, compared with an average stake of 16.2 percent in the thirteen companies in the 1960 sample in 2000. Thus, in

Table 10.3   **Is the largest shareholder an institution?**

	Survivors			Nonsurvivors		
	Institution	Block size	No. of observations	Institution	Block size	No. of observations
1900 sample						
1900	0		20	0		20
1910	1	5.00	20	0		20
1920	0		20	0		17
1930	0		20	1	6.90	16
1940	4	5.89	20	1	0.90	12
1950	7	3.73	20	3	8.95	10
1960	8	4.18	20	0		4
1970	9	5.35	20	0		3
1980	8	6.46	20	0		2
1990	16	10.77	20	1	11.70	1
2000	17	12.85	20	0		0

	Institution	Block size	No. of observations
1960 sample			
1960	0		20
1970	4	4.88	20
1980	5	16.27	20
1990	10	15.39	20
2000	13	16.20	20

Source: Own calculations.

Note: This table reports the number of companies where the largest shareholder is an institution, along with the average size of these largest block holdings.

the first half of the century institutional shareholdings were largely absent, and where they were present they were quite small. In contrast, in the second half of the century, there were a larger number of stakes held by institutions, and they were much more significant in size.

In summary, family ownership declined rapidly in the first half of the twentieth century, and institutions emerged to take the place of families from the middle of the century.

10.3.2   Board Representation

Table 10.4 shows that family representation on boards persisted for much longer than their ownership. It documents the profile of board representation for the two samples of firms at ten-year intervals. Over forty years from 1900 to 1940, the percentage of board seats held by outside (nonfamily) shareholders in the sample of survivor firms (panel A) increased from 46 percent in 1900 to 64 percent in 1940. The proportion of firms in which families occupied the position of chief executive officer (CEO) of the board

Table 10.4 **Board composition**

	Board size		Family CEO	Board members outside founding family (%)		No. of observations
	Mean	Median		Mean	Median	
A. 1900 sample, survivors						
1900	5.40	5.00	16	45.46	41.45	20
1910	5.80	5.00	17	44.48	52.75	20
1920	5.95	5.00	13	59.75	66.60	20
1930	6.45	6.00	10	64.37	72.35	20
1940	6.65	6.00	10	64.16	71.55	20
1950	6.90	6.50	9	71.10	87.50	20
1960	7.20	7.00	4	76.15	100.00	20
1970	9.15	8.00	2	81.88	100.00	20
1980	7.95	7.00	2	86.71	100.00	20
1990	8.25	8.00	2	90.68	100.00	20
2000	7.90	7.00	2	92.51	100.00	20
Mean	7.05		7.91	70.66		
B. 1900 sample, nonsurvivors						
1900	4.93	4.00	11	68.23	100.00	20
1910	5.33	5.00	10	76.44	100.00	20
1920	5.92	5.50	9	70.34	72.90	17
1930	5.82	5.00	8	72.82	77.70	16
1940	4.86	6.00	5	92.84	100.00	12
1950	3.50	3.50	3	95.83	100.00	10
1960	9.67	8.00	3	100.00	100.00	4
1970	5.50	5.50	2	100.00	100.00	3
1980	7.00	7.00	2	100.00	100.00	2
1990	4.00	4.00	0	100.00	100.00	1
2000			0	100.00	100.00	0
Mean	5.06		7.74	79.42		
C. 1960 sample						
1960	2.80	3.00	16	43.15	41.65	20
1970	5.55	5.00	12	66.48	77.50	20
1980	6.47	6.00	8	74.94	86.65	20
1990	7.35	7.00	4	82.55	100.00	20
2000	7.00	6.00	3	83.62	100.00	20
Mean	5.83		10.90	70.15		

Source: Author calculations.
Note: This table reports board size and the percentage of board members that do not come from the founding family.

declined from 80 percent (i.e., sixteen out of twenty) to 50 percent (i.e., ten out of twenty). As table 10.2 recorded, the proportion of survivor firms in which families held more than 25 percent of shares declined much more rapidly by 45 percent from 65 percent (i.e., thirteen out of twenty) in 1900 to 20 percent (i.e., four out of twenty) in 1940. Family representation on the boards did not therefore decline as rapidly as their ownership.

Table 10.5 provides a summary measure of this. It reports separation of family ownership and control as measured by the difference between family representation on the boards of firms and family ownership of shares. A positive number means that family board representation is disproportionate to family ownership. Table 10.5 shows that at the beginning of the century, family ownership was in excess of family board representation, but by 1940 it had become disproportionately high.

Panel B of table 10.4 reports lower family board representation among

Table 10.5   **Separation of ownership and control**

	Survivors	No. of Survivors	Nonsurvivors	No. of Nonsurvivors	Full sample	No. of observations
1900 sample						
1900	−1.16	20	5.69	20	1.86	40
1910	6.78	20	2.00	20	4.67	40
1920	−7.87	20	9.88	17	−1.00	37
1930	8.97	20	14.25	16	10.91	36
1940	15.60	20	6.17	12	13.16	32
1950	13.15	20	4.02	10	11.04	30
1960	14.99	20	0.00	4	12.45	24
1970	15.04	20	0.00	3	12.60	23
1980	12.03	20	0.00	2	11.13	22
1990	9.15	20	0.00	1	8.71	21
2000	6.69	20		0	6.69	20
Mean	8.50		6.94		8.13	

	Mean	No. of observations
1960 sample		
1960	−1.52	20
1970	3.13	20
1980	6.70	20
1990	10.50	20
2000	11.94	20
Mean	6.15	

Source: Author calculations.

Notes: This table reports mean and median separation of ownership and control. Separation is defined as the difference between the proportion of founding family members on the board and family shareholdings. A negative value indicates that there is a greater proportion of family ownership than board representation.

the 1900 nonsurvivors than the survivors. Family board representation was only 32 percent in 1900, in comparison to 55 percent among the survivors, and it declined to 7 percent in 1940. There was therefore less family ownership and less family board representation among the nonsurvivors than the survivors in 1900, and families failed to retain board positions among nonsurvivors to the degree that they did in survivors. Table 10.5 confirms that family board representation did not increase to the same extent relative to ownership among nonsurvivors as among survivors. So families retained neither ownership nor board positions among nonsurvivors. Whether the decline of families on the boards as well as in the ownership of nonsurvivors was a cause or a consequence of their demise is not a question to which we attempt to provide an answer here. All we do is to note that the difference in family ownership and board representation among surviving and nonsurviving firms may be an interesting approach to evaluating the contribution of families to corporate performance.

In the second half of the century, family representation on boards declined more rapidly. Forty years after incorporation, a family member was chairman/CEO in three companies in the 1960 sample, in comparison to ten in the 1900 survivors. Likewise, the proportion of seats on the boards occupied by families declined to 16 percent forty years after incorporation in the 1960 sample, in comparison to 36 percent in the 1900 sample. Thus, family representation on boards as well as ownership declined more rapidly in the second than in the first half of the century.

Table 10.4 shows that, relative to their ownership stakes, family representation on boards moved in a very similar way in the 1960 sample compared to the 1900 survivors, starting from slightly more ownership than board representation in 1960 and ending with markedly more board representation than ownership forty years after incorporation in 2000. Thus, families did not match the very rapid decline in their ownership in the second half of the century with their share of seats on boards of firms.

In summary, dilution of family ownership occurred rapidly throughout the twentieth century. As the next section describes, this was primarily due to growth through acquisition. However, in the first half of the century families were able to retain control in surviving firms through representation on the boards of firms. In the second half, board control as well as ownership was rapidly extinguished. A new form of ownership, institutions, emerged in the middle of the century to replace families, and, as we document in section 10.5, a new form of corporate control, the hostile takeover, appeared to replace that exerted by families.

10.4 Mergers and Acquisitions in the First Half of the Century

Franks, Mayer, and Rossi (2004) argue that the main cause of dispersion of ownership during the twentieth century was equity issuance. In particular, their sample of firms grew rapidly through acquisition and in the process issued equity to outside shareholders, thereby diluting insiders' shareholdings. Franks, Mayer, and Rossi report that insider holdings were diluted over the period 1900 to 1950 at an average rate of 12.6 percent per annum. Of this, none was attributable to initial public offerings (IPOs), 4.6 percent to rights issues, 20.8 percent to placings, and 36.2 percent to mergers and acquisitions.[3]

During the first half of the century, mergers and acquisitions were usually made by the bidder approaching the directors and agreeing to purchase their shares: "An approach through the directors, followed by controlled stock transfers on the recommendations of the directors (rather than contested takeover raids) remained the norm in these years" (Hannah 1974b, p. 68). A price was negotiated, and management wrote to the shareholders stating that "the offer has been unanimously accepted by the Directors of your company for the whole of their individual shares, and they have no hesitation in recommending its acceptance to the shareholders" (*Financial Times,* 19 January 1920). The same terms were offered to outside shareholders as the directors.

As Hannah (1974b) has noted, "The loyalty of shareholders to directors was strong, and the directors of other companies had a natural aversion to challenging it. Even if a direct bid were to be made, the directors of the victim firm remained in a strong position relative to their own shareholders. In practice the shareholders would recognize the superiority of the directors' information and tend to take their advice on the true value of the company in relation to the bid price" (pp. 70–71); "Directors felt a responsibility to recommend offers to their shareholders when the bid price was pitched reasonably" (pp. 68–69). It is therefore unsurprising that there was a complete absence of hostile takeover bids in the first half of the century.

The continuing presence of families on boards, in particular in the position of chairman, even in the absence of ownership, may have been important in upholding reputations. So too were titled directors. Florence (1953) reports that there were 654 English peers as active members of city firms in 1932. Titled directors were particularly common in the largest companies, although "at a rough estimate almost half the titled directors inherited their title or acquired it by prowess in the fighting services or sport and not in business" (Florence, p. 245). Florence notes that "one well-known insurance company in 1937 had among sixteen directors, three knights, one baron, one marquis, one earl and two dukes" (p. 245). Likewise, May (1939) reports that of 654 British peers, 189 of them were directors of companies

3. In the first half of the century shares were often traded without a prospectus. Shares would simply be issued and sold directly by the company to subscribers or be sold through advertisements in the press. The IPO event was much more formal after 1948, when prospectuses were compulsory and their content strictly regulated prior to trading on recognized stock exchanges such as the LSE.

and held 562 directorates between them: "Sometimes a man with a 'good name,' knowing nothing about the business and even without residence in the country, is set up as chairman with the principal duty of reading the annual speech, which has been written out for him, to the shareholders" (May, p. 145). As Lord Justice Scrutton said in the Court of Appeal in the judgment on Combined Pulp and Paper Mills Ltd. 1932, "The company promoter wants a man whose name will appeal to the public and who does not know too much about the business. The name will attract capital—the company promoter will do the rest" (pp. 35–36 of the transcript).

In tables 10.6 and 10.7 we examine the workings of the acquisitions market in the first half of the century. We undertook a series of tests on bid premia, changes in boards, and dividend responses of targets similar to those that are now routinely performed on recent acquisitions in the United Kingdom and United States. We report data on forty-one mergers and acquisitions (M&As) in the United Kingdom over the period 1919 to 1939. This is the entire population of M&As that met three criteria: the market value of target assets exceeded £1 million, the targets were listed on the LSE, and they were classified by the LSE as being in one of three industries—breweries and distilleries; industrial and commercial; or iron, coal, and steel.

Table 10.6 shows the proportion of target directors who were retained on the board after the merger, the number of cases in which the chairman was removed, and the change in dividends around the announcement of the mergers. On average, two-thirds of the target directors remained on the target's board after the acquisition. In fourteen of forty-one cases (approximately one-third of the total), the chairman was removed. In comparison, in a study of thirty-five successful hostile takeovers in 1985 and 1986, Franks and Mayer (1996) report that 90 percent of directors were replaced within two years of the bid's being consummated. The equivalent figure for

Table 10.6	Takeovers in the United Kingdom, 1919–39: Target board turnover and dividend changes			
Time period	Proportion of target board resigning after takeover (%)	Chairman resigned	Dividend constant	No. of observations
1919–23	5.36	0	10	11
1924–28	33.76	3	11	12
1929–33	16.68	2	7	7
1934–39	57.80	9	8	10
Total	30.28	14		40

Sources: Hannah (1974b) and author calculations.

Notes: This table reports the proportion of target directors that resign after a takeover, the number of target companies where the chairman resigns and the proportion of target companies keeping the dividend constant two years prior to the takeover for a sample of 40 takeovers over the period 1919–39.

Table 10.7   **Bid premia in the United Kingdom**

Time period	No.	Months −4 to +1 (%) EW	Month 0 (%) EW	Total market value (£/millions)
		A. 1919–39		
1919–23	11	−10.02	−3.34	31.5
1924–28	12	+14.69	+0.55	43.3
1929–33	7	−2.45	−1.13	19.0
1934–39	10	+14.84	+0.22	26.6
Mean		+4.93	−0.90	

	Target	Months −4 to +1 (%) EW	Month 0 (%) EW	
		B. Hostile takeovers, 1953–58		
1953	J. Sears	122.22	90.48	
1958	Savoy Hotel	87.00	19.53	
1958	British Aluminum	39.53	17.47	
Mean		82.92	42.49	

	No.	Months −4 to +1 (%) EW	VW	Month 0 (%) EW	VW	Total market value (£/billions)
			C. 1955–85			
1955–59	151	28	25	16	11	0.5
1960–64	190	24	26	18	14	1.4
1965–69	262	27	24	19	12	3.7
1970–74	196	35	41	25	23	2.8
1975–79	383	38	34	30	22	3.8
1980–84	281	27	27	25	30	10.0
Mean		30	30	22	19	

Notes: This table reports the bid premia for the United Kingdom in the twentieth century. Panel A considers 40 U.K. takeovers over the period 1919–39 and computes premia as the raw (unadjusted) stock returns for targets over the periods (−4 to +1) months and month 0, where month 0 is the announcement month. Panel B refers to the first three hostile takeover bids of the 1950s, as reported in Roberts (1992), and computes premia as in panel A. Panel C refers to 1,463 U.K. takeovers in the period 1955–85 and computes premia as the market-adjusted stock returns for targets over the periods (−4 to +1) months and month 0, where month 0 is the announcement month. The source for panel C is Franks and Harris (1989).

thirty-five accepted bids was 50 percent. Board turnover was appreciably lower in the first half of the century in comparison with both accepted and hostile bids in the second.[4]

4. This might indicate greater private benefits accruing to target directors in the early part of the century.

Table 10.6 also shows very little change in dividends in the year of the bid compared to the previous year in the 1919 to 1939 sample. In comparison, Franks and Mayer (1996) report that dividends were increased in a substantial proportion of both hostile and accepted takeovers in 1985 and 1986. They were increased in 76 percent of targets of successful hostile takeovers in the year before the bid and in 73 percent of targets two years before the bid.

But it is in relation to bid premia that the differences are most pronounced. Panel A of table 10.7 records that in the sample of forty targets target shareholders received bid premia of −0.9 percent during the month of the bid (i.e., "month 0"), calculated on an equal weighted basis. These bid premia are raw equity returns with no adjustment for market movements or risk. Bid premia for months −4 to +1 on the same basis were 4.9 percent. Bid premia were therefore little different from zero. In contrast, Franks and Mayer (1996) report bid premia of between 20 and 30 percent for hostile and agreed bids during 1985 and 1986 in the United Kingdom.

The picture that emerges is one of cooperative consolidations between merging firms in the first half of the century. The support of management was required for approval by shareholders. Bid premia were low, the medium of exchange usually involved share exchanges, management was frequently kept on the target board, and dividend changes were modest. Since acquisitions frequently involved share exchanges, acquiring firms avoided the devaluation of their currency that dual-class shares would have entailed. The absence of dual-class shares in the first half of the century may therefore have been intimately linked to the importance of takeovers and their form of financing.

This picture of cooperation and little competition was dramatically altered in the 1950s, as we will describe in section 10.6.

10.5   Three Case Studies

This section describes three cases that illustrate the way in which three prominent British firms expanded during the eighteenth, nineteenth, and twentieth centuries; the contribution of acquisitions to their growth; the changing nature of family ownership and board representation; and the contribution of incorporation and mergers to that process.

10.5.1   Case Study of GKN

Dowlais Iron Company was set up in 1759 in the village of Dowlais near Merthyr Tydfil in South Wales. John Guest was appointed as manager of Dowlais in 1767, and his grandson became the company's sole owner in 1851. The Dowlais Iron Company was at this stage the largest ironworks in the world, operating eighteen blast furnaces and employing more than 7,300 people. The business was the first licensee of the Bessemer process, constructing the world's most powerful rolling mill in 1857, and producing its first Bessemer steel in 1865.

The Keen family established the Patent Nut and Bolt Company in 1856 in Smethwick, England. In July 1900, Guest, Keen, and Company Limited was incorporated in Birmingham with the purpose of taking over the Dowlais Iron Company and the Patent Nut and Bolt Co., Ltd. The shareholders of the two companies received 250,000 ordinary shares. At the same time, 400,000 ordinary shares were issued via public subscription, and the company was floated with 546 ordinary shareholders and more than 2,000 preference shareholders. Both classes of shares were traded on the London and Birmingham Stock Exchanges. There was no evidence of the company's being dispersed before 1900: the company history suggests that both Dowlais Iron Co. and the Patent Nut and Bolt were 100 percent owned by directors and their families. Evidence for this comes from a comparison of directors' holdings with the shareholdings of the two companies before the merger. Since directors' holdings after the flotation were 33.6 percent of the ordinary shares, and the newly issued shares were 400,000, compared with a pre-issue total of 250,000 we can compute a lower bound of directors' ownership pre-issue of 87.3 percent.

In 1902 the company acquired Nettlefold and Company, one of the world's leading manufacturers of screws and fasteners, which set up in Smethwick in 1854, by issuing 315,000 new ordinary shares. The new company name then became Guest, Keen, and Nettlefolds Limited, and Mr. Edward Nettlefold joined the board. By 1910, the directors held 26.4 percent of issued ordinary shares. In 1920, shares in Guest, Keen, and Nettlefolds Ltd. (GKN) were quoted at Birmingham, Bristol, Cardiff, Edinburgh, Glasgow, Liverpool, Manchester, and Sheffield, while the prices of the transactions were marked (i.e., reported) on the official list of the LSE.

A crucial decade in the evolution of ownership and control of GKN was then about to begin. First, the company acquired John Lysaght Limited of Bristol (also quoted in Bristol and London) in one of the largest tender offers of the decade.[5] In November 1923 GKN then undertook two other major tender offers, acquiring D. Davis and Sons and Consolidated Cambrian of Cardiff.

As a consequence of these acquisitions there was a huge increase in the number of shareholders: GKN had about 1,000 shareholders before 1920, and more than 20,000 in 1924. At this stage, GKN was one of the largest manufacturing businesses in the world, involved in every stage of manufacturing from coal and ore extraction to iron and steel making and finally

5. Details of the deal are as follows: in January 1920, GKN issued 1,989,919 new ordinary shares and 2,652,331 preference shares. Ordinary shareholders of John Lysaght Ltd. were offered four new second preference and three new ordinary shares in GKN for every three ordinary shares held.

to finished products including the nuts, bolts, screws, and fasteners, for which it was renowned during this period.

On June 14, 1946, GKN formally listed on the LSE. By then the directors owned a negligible stake, and the largest shareholder of the period was the Royal Bank of Scotland, with 2.37 percent of issued ordinary shares. In the second half of the century, Prudential Assurance, Norwich Union Life Insurance, Schroder Investment Management, and Scottish Widows Investment Management, among others, alternated as the largest shareholders, with stakes varying from 3 percent to 5.25 percent of issued equity capital.

The picture that emerges from GKN is of a firm whose shares were initially traded on local provincial exchanges, that expanded rapidly through acquisitions and broadened its shareholder base both numerically and geographically in the process, and that by the beginning of the second half of the twentieth century was widely held primarily by institutional shareholders.

10.5.2   Case Study of Schweppes

In 1783, forty-three-year-old German-born Jean Jacob Schweppe invented an efficient system for the manufacture of mineral water. In 1790, he entered a partnership to expand the business and established a factory in London. Around 1800 he changed his and the business's name to Schweppes, while continuing to expand on a national scale. By 1831, J. Schweppes and Co. became the Supplier of Soda Water to the Royal Household. In 1834, John Kemp-Welch and William Evill bought J. Schweppes and Co. and extended the product range to include flavored soda drinks such as lemonade. The following year the firm was awarded the royal warrant by Queen Victoria, and in 1851 it won the contract to supply "Temperance" beverages at the Great Exhibition in the United Kingdom. By 1870, the firm's product range included tonic water and ginger ale. The former rapidly became popular with the British in India, as it contained quinine, which was used as a preventive measure against malaria. In 1877 the firm opened its first factory in Sydney, Australia, and seven years later a factory in Brooklyn, New York.

The sudden death of John Kemp-Welch in 1885 precipitated the formation of Schweppes as a limited company in the following year. Although no direct evidence exists on the ownership structure at this stage, it would appear that the company was 100 percent owned by the directors until its public flotation in London on March 6, 1897. After flotation the directors and their families held collectively 27.2 percent of the 300,000 ordinary shares. The new company, Schweppes plc, was incorporated to acquire the business of J. Schweppe and Co. established in 1783, and a total of £1,250,000 new capital (of which £300,000 was perpetual debenture stock issued to the directors and £950,000 was a public subscription, in the form of 300,000 ordinary shares, 300,000 preference shares, and 350,000 deferred shares).

The public flotation was extremely successful and oversubscribed. At the end of 1897, there were more than 1,650 ordinary shareholders and 750 preference shareholders. There was evidence of the company's shares being traded in Manchester.

In 1919 the Kemp-Welch family relinquished the chairmanship (although two members remained on the board until the early 1940s), and under the new chairman, Sir Ivor Phillips, the company started a new period of expansion. Overseas development was conducted through a newly formed fully owned subsidiary, Schweppes (Colonial and Foreign) Ltd. The strategy was to manufacture locally in the overseas countries, in order to reduce the group's reliance on exports. At the end of Sir Phillips's chairmanship in 1940, the company had more than 2,700 ordinary shareholders, and it was formally listed on the LSE on December 19, 1942.

During the 1950s there were several major acquisitions paid in shares: L. Rose and Co. acquired in 1957 with 1,544,400 new ordinary shares, and Chivers and Sons, W. P. Hartley, and W. Moorhouse all acquired in 1959 with together 4,000,000 new ordinary shares. In 1969, Schweppes plc merged with the Cadbury Group to form Cadbury-Schweppes.

10.5.3   Case Study of Cadbury

In 1794, Richard Cadbury, a prominent Quaker, moved from the West Country in Britain to Birmingham. Thirty years later his son John opened a shop at 93 Bull Street, then a fashionable part of Birmingham, to sell tea, coffee, hops, mustard, and a new sideline—cocoa and drinking chocolate, which John prepared himself using a mortar and a pestle.

In 1847 John Cadbury took his brother Benjamin into partnership in 1847, changing the name of the business to Cadbury Brothers of Birmingham, and renting a new factory in Bridge Street in the center of Birmingham. Thanks to a reduction in tax on imported cocoa beans, the business expanded and received the first of a series of royal warrants of appointment by Queen Victoria.

The Cadbury Brothers moved their manufacturing operations to Bournville, United Kingdom, and established the Bournville factory and village, which became an important addition to the U.K. industrial landscape. By the time that Cadbury Brothers was incorporated as a limited company (on June 16, 1899), and the Bournville factory had 2,600 employees. At that stage, Richard and George Cadbury, the sons of the late John Cadbury, owned 100 percent of the ordinary shares.

A crucial year in the company history was 1919, when Cadbury Brothers merged with J. S. Fry and Sons of Bristol, whose product range (e.g., Turkish delight) complemented Cadbury's chocolates. After the merger, the new company was registered as British Cocoa and Chocolate on May 19, 1919, with a capital of £2,500,000. The two families shared both board seats and company ownership, with the Frys holding four seats on the board as well as the chairmanship and 45.44 percent of ordinary shares, and the Cadburys holding the rest (six seats on the board, and 54.56 percent of ordinary shares). Another former director of Fry also sat on the board.

As the company's operations expanded and factories opened around the world, the Fry family board representation declined, while Cadbury's increased. Shortly before the merger with Schweppes plc in 1969, the Cadbury family held the chairmanship and seven of the thirteen seats of the board of directors, while only one Fry remained on the board. The Cadbury family held slightly more than 50 percent of the ordinary shares, while the Fry family held just over 10 percent. The rest was dispersed among more than 200 ordinary shareholders. There was evidence of trade on both London and Birmingham Stock Exchanges of ordinary and preference shares before the merger with Schweppes in 1969.

These three case studies illustrate the speed with which ownership was dispersed and how much of the dilution of the original family's ownership was due to acquisitions for share exchanges. They also show how one of the founding families came to dominate the merged entity even where the merger was apparently between equals. This dominance persisted as the ownership of the founding family dwindled.

10.6 Takeovers in the Second Half of the Century

In the spring of 1953, Charles Clore, a self-made millionaire from business and property ventures, launched a bid for J. Sears and Co., the parent company of a shoe shop chain, Freeman, Hardy, and Willis. Instead of following the conventional approach of negotiating with target management, Clore mailed offer documents directly to Sears's shareholders over the heads of management. Roberts (1992) writes, "The Sears directors, who were taken entirely unawares, retaliated by announcing the tripling of the dividend. Shareholders were astonished by this sudden largesse, which was perceived as a desperate and irresponsible act on the part of the management. Faith in the incumbent board being thoroughly undermined, there was a rush to sell to Clore, who quickly acquired control of the company. 'We never thought anything like this would happen to us', were the Parthian words of the outgoing Sears' chairman" (p. 186).

The unconventional nature of the approach was reflected in exceptional financial features of the bid. In contrast to the observation made above that dividends did not in general change around acquisitions, the Sears directors responded to the bid by tripling the value of their dividend. While the average value of bid premia had historically been around zero, the bid premium for Sears was 90 percent in the month of the bid and 122 percent in the five months from month -4 to $+1$.

As table 10.7 shows, there were then several bids that recorded bid premia that were very large by previous standards. In the case of the bid by Land Securities Investment Trust in autumn 1953 for the Savoy Hotel Co., owners of the Savoy, Claridge's, and Simpson's in the Strand, the bid premium was 19 percent in the month of the bid and 87 percent in the five months around the bid. In the bid for British Aluminum by Reynolds Metals of Virginia in 1958, the month-zero bid premium was 17 percent and the five-month bid premium was 17 percent.

It is not entirely clear why the takeover market emerged at this juncture in Britain. Alfred Chandler associates the emergence of a market for corporate control in the United States with the rise in institutional shareholding (Chandler 1990). But, as table 10.3 shows, in the United Kingdom the market for corporate control predated the accumulation of most institutional shareholdings. A more plausible explanation is that the tighter financial disclosures required of company accounts by the 1948 Companies Act provided the basis on which corporate predators could for the first time make reasonably accurate estimates of asset values and earnings, and thus launch bids without the cooperation of the target (Hannah 1974b). In Charles Clore's takeover of Sears, Roberts (1992) reports that "Clore launched his attack on being informed by a partner in the estates agent Healey & Baker that Sears' balance sheet under-estimated the real estate value of the firm's 900 high street stores by £10 million" (p. 186).

The response of the corporate sector was to seek protection against the rapidly emerging takeover market. It initially received a sympathetic ear from the government and the Bank of England, which were concerned about the impact of hostile acquisitions on the corporate sector and the government's policy of dividend restraint (Roberts 1992). All levels of government were involved—including, in the case of the bid for the Savoy, the prime minister, Winston Churchill, who was worried about the possible impact of the bid on his favorite dining club at the Savoy. But while it found this form of buccaneering capitalism distasteful and ungentlemanly, the government felt impotent to do much about it, and in any event, by the time of the next merger wave at the end of the 1950s, it had come around to the view that "Mr. Clore appears to have improved the retail shoe trade of the country."

Unable to gain protection from the government, the corporate sector began to erect its own defenses. Table 10.8 reports incidence of antitakeover measures in three years: 1950, 1965, and 1975. In the case of 1965 and 1975 the table also shows changes (adoptions of antitakeover defenses in existing companies, emergence of new companies with antitakeover defenses, and abandonment by existing companies) from 1950 and 1965, respectively. Antitakeover measures are said to exist if any of the following are present: dual-class shares, voting restrictions, or share blocks by insiders in excess of 50 percent. Statistics are reported for three LSE sector classifications: commercial and industrial, breweries and distilleries, and iron, coal, and steel, which totals more than 2,000 companies.

Table 10.8   **Incidence of antitakeover measures**

	No. of companies	% of listed companies				
A. 1950						
Commercial and industrial	56	3.60				
Breweries and distilleries	13	6.30				
Iron, coal, and steel	4	1.82				
Total	73	3.68				

	Static analysis		Dynamic analysis (since 1950)			
	No. of companies	% of listed companies	Adoptions	New companies	Delisting	
B. 1965						
Commercial and industrial	236	11.80	98	86	4	
Breweries and distilleries	10	10.20	2	4	9	
Iron, coal, and steel	3	2.21	0	2	3	
Total	249	11.15	100	92	16	

	Static analysis		Dynamic analysis (since 1965)			
	No. of companies	% of listed companies	Adoptions	New companies	Dropped	Delisting
C. 1975						
Commercial and industrial	145	7.25	18	7	32	84
Breweries and distilleries	6	6.06	1	0	1	4
Iron, coal, and steel	1	2.08	0	0	1	1
Total	152	7.08	19	7	34	89

Source: Own calculations.

Note: This table reports the incidence of antitakeover measures (dual-class voting, voting restrictions and insider ownership greater than 50 percent) in the United Kingdom in 1950 in panel A, 1965 in panel B, and 1975 in panel C.

Table 10.8 reports that the number of companies with antitakeover measures increased from 73 in 1950 to 249 in 1965. This represents an increase in incidence of antitakeover measures from 3.7 percent of the sample to 11.1 percent between 1950 and 1965. There were 100 new adoptions by companies that were already in existence in 1950, and ninety-two new companies were formed with antitakeover defenses.[6] The incidence of takeover defenses therefore increased substantially during the 1950s and 1960s.[7]

A further form of takeover defense that emerged was to seek protection

6. There is a residual of sixteen companies that were delisted.
7. The companies with antitakeover measures were nonacquisitive companies and did not therefore expect to use their own shares to purchase other companies.

under the wing of a friendly company. The brewing industry was particularly fragmented, with a large number of small local brewers. Whitbread took share stakes in several of these as a way of providing protection against hostile bidders.

For a brief period during the 1950s and 1960s, the landscape of corporate Britain began to resemble that of Continental Europe. There was an unregulated takeover market with the potential for acquiring control through purchases of partial share stakes and discriminatory offers. Companies responded by introducing dual-class shares and voting right restrictions, and pyramid structures emerged as companies sought protection under the wing of others.

But these takeover defenses met with stiff opposition from an influential quarter—the institutional investors and the LSE. They were concerned about the interference with the takeover process, the ability of management to entrench itself behind takeover defenses, and the withdrawal of their voting rights. Under pressure from the institutions, the stock exchange made it known that it disapproved of the use of dual-class shares and would not permit their use in new equity issues.

The intervention of the institutions and the stock exchange proved decisive, and during the 1970s and 1980s companies steadily withdrew dual-class shares. Panel C of table 10.8 reports that by 1975 the proportion of listed companies with dual-class shares in the three sectors had declined from 11.1 percent to 7.1 percent. The number of companies in the commercial and industrial sector that dropped dual-class shares between 1965 and 1975 was well in excess of those that adopted them. By the late 1980s there were only a handful of companies with dual-class shares left among listed companies in the United Kingdom.

Meanwhile, under prompting from the Bank of England, in 1959 the city established a working party to produce a code of conduct for takeovers. This initially yielded a series of ineffectual recommendations, but, in the face of several prominent takeover scandals[8] and under the looming threat of legislation, in 1967 it produced the City Code on Take-Overs and Mergers and created the Panel on Take-Overs and Mergers to enforce it.[9] This in due course established the principle of equal treatment of all shareholders, the requirement of acquiring firms to disclose their shareholdings and reveal their intentions, and the obligation to make offers for all shares at highest prices once 30 percent of the target firm's shares had been acquired. In other words, it re-created by self-regulation the equal price treatment that had prevailed by convention without regulation in the first half of the century before hostile takeovers.

8. One example of this was the Jasper Affair in 1959, involving takeover malpractice and the misuse of building society funds.
9. The power of the panel to sanction firms that do not comply with the code has proved to be highly effective.

What is striking about these developments is the fact that the political process was not at the end of the day guided by the interests of the corporate sector, which sought to limit hostile bids and to erect takeover defenses, but by those of the financial institutions. It was the institutions that prevented firms from implementing dual-class shares and the institutions that drew up the rules by which takeovers were subsequently conducted. It was therefore the financial sector that prevented the United Kingdom from drifting into a Continental-style corporate structure with dual-class shares, pyramids, and limitations on takeovers, and that set the ground rules by which an active market in corporate control could develop. Through the takeover code and panel, the financial sector also prevented the corporate sector from erecting the takeover defenses, in particular poison pills, that became commonplace in the United States. The distinct nature of the U.K. corporate sector is therefore in part a consequence of the dominance of equity institutions that placed shareholder returns above the private interests of either corporate shareholders or management.

10.7   Conclusions

This paper has documented the rapid erosion of family ownership of U.K. corporations during the twentieth century. The dispersed ownership that characterizes the U.K. corporate system today emerged early in the twentieth century. The United Kingdom did not start off life in the twentieth century like Germany or Italy today. In terms of ownership concentration and the involvement of families, it looked more like the United Kingdom today than Germany or Italy.

The observations on the dominance of families in the running of firms are a reflection of their board representation rather than their ownership. Board participation by families became disproportionate to their ownership stakes. There were good reasons for being concerned about this development. The divergence between ownership and control undermined the efficient running of corporations, as documented by Chandler.

But what was remarkable about this was the process by which it came about. The decline in family ownership was not for the most part a consequence of families' selling out but a result of equity issues. These equity issues were not primarily used to finance internal growth (there was rather little use of equity for this purpose in the first half of the twentieth century) but to acquire other companies. Equity-financed acquisitions accounted for a high proportion of the dilution of family holdings.

What is equally striking is the fact that these substantial equity issues took place against the background of informal, largely unregulated stock markets. Nevertheless, shareholders trusted directors to uphold principles of equal price treatment for all. There was little evidence of the partial share offers and price discrimination that characterizes the takeover market in many countries today.

Why directors abided by this and were not tempted to accept cheaper partial offers at the expense of minority investors is not entirely clear. But one clue comes from the significance of acquisitions and equity issuance to the growth of corporations. Large British companies were particularly reliant on the stock market to fund growth. This may reflect the absence of a local banking system of a type that exists in many other countries and through which companies in those countries are able to establish close relations and borrow on an ongoing basis. To be able to access the stock market, companies in the United Kingdom had to sustain the trust of their shareholders, which in part revolved around ensuring that they were equally treated in new share issues. Discriminatory offers might reduce the costs of particular acquisitions, but these were more than offset by the higher cost of using equity in subsequent acquisitions. Regulation was not therefore required since it was in the self-interest of directors to ensure the fair treatment of their shareholders.

The nondiscriminatory treatment of shareholders in takeovers also goes some way toward explaining the absence of pyramids in the United Kingdom. Acquirers were not able to purchase the partial share stakes in companies that would have allowed them to create pyramids. Target firms were absorbed into the merged company and essentially disappeared as separate listed entities.

However, this collaborative arrangement broke down in the middle of the century in the face of a hostile takeover market. Target directors were no longer in a position to enforce equal price rules since acquirers could go behind their backs and appeal directly to controlling shareholders. Directors initially tried to protect themselves and their minority investors by erecting takeover defenses. For a brief period, the United Kingdom took on the appearance of Continental Europe, with dual-class shares, pyramids, and discriminatory price acquisitions. But the takeover defenses incurred the wrath of the institutions, which mounted a successful attack on them through the stock exchange and succeeded in devising the rules by which takeovers were to be conducted.

Once again the development of the U.K. corporate sector was determined by the interests of shareholders to a degree that probably did not occur in most other countries. At an optimistic level, the reason for the oddity of the United Kingdom noted at the start is the well-developed and efficient nature of its stock market and the dominance of financial institutions that eschewed the private benefits of Continental Europe. Equally plausibly, it is a consequence of its centralized banking system and the unusual reliance of its corporate sector on the stock market during the twentieth century.

References

Becht, Marco, and Colin P. Mayer. 2001. Introduction. In *The control of corporate Europe,* ed. Fabrizio Barca and Marco Becht, 1–45. Oxford: Oxford University Press.

Chandler, Alfred D. 1990. *Scale and scope: The dynamics of industrial capitalism.* Cambridge, MA: Harvard University Press.

Davies, Paul, and Klaus J. Hopt. 2004. Control transactions. In *The anatomy of corporate law,* ed. Reinier Kraakman, Gerard Hertig, Paul Davies, Henry Hansmann, and Klaus J. Hopt, 157–91. Oxford: Oxford University Press.

Florence, P. Sargant. 1953. *The logic of British and American industry.* London: Routledge & Kegan Paul.

Franks, Julian R., and Robert S. Harris. 1989. Shareholder wealth effect of corporate takeovers: The U.K. experience 1955–1985. *Journal of Financial Economics* 23:225–49.

Franks, Julian R., and Colin P. Mayer. 1996. Hostile takeovers and the correction of managerial failure. *Journal of Financial Economics* 40:163–81.

———. 2001. Ownership and control of German corporations. *Review of Financial Studies* 14:943–77.

Franks, Julian R., Colin P. Mayer, and Stefano Rossi. 2004. Ownership: Evolution and regulation. London Business School and Saïd Business School, University of Oxford. Mimeograph.

Hannah, Leslie. 1974a. Mergers in British manufacturing industry 1880–1918. *Oxford Economic Papers* 26:1–20.

———. 1974b. Takeover bids in Britain before 1950: An exercise in business "prehistory." *Business History* 16:65–77.

———. 1976. *The rise of the corporate economy.* London: Methuen.

Hart, P. E., and S. J. Prais. 1956. The analysis of business concentration: A statistical approach. *Journal of the Royal Statistical Society* 119:150–91.

Killick, John R., and William A. Thomas. 1970. The provincial stock exchanges, 1830–1870. *Economic History Review* 23:96–111.

Landes, David. 1965. Technological change and development in Western Europe 1750–1914. In *Cambridge economic history of Europe, Vol. VI: The Industrial Revolution and after,* ed. H. J. Habakkuk and M. Postan, 536–64. Cambridge: Cambridge University Press.

May, Wilfred. 1939. Financial regulation abroad: The contrasts with American technique. *Journal of Political Economy* 47:457–96.

Michie, Ranald C. 1999. *The London stock exchange: A history.* Oxford: Oxford University Press.

Rajan, Raghuram G., and Luigi Zingales. 2003. The great reversals: The politics of financial development in the 20th century. *Journal of Financial Economics* 69:5–50.

Roberts, Richard. 1992. Regulatory responses to the rise of the market for corporate control in Britain in the 1950s. *Business History* 34:183–200.

Comment   Barry Eichengreen

In this paper Franks, Mayer, and Rossi significantly advance our understanding of the history of corporate ownership in the United Kingdom. To be sure, the first phenomenon they trace, the decline of family ownership, is well known. The modest capital requirements, limited scale, and family-based ownership structure of early nineteenth-century manufacturing enterprise are staples of the history of the British industrial revolution. In the 1820s the typical Manchester cotton mill employed 100 to 200 operatives and required capital investment of perhaps £9,000. Neither shared ownership nor separation between ownership and control were essential for establishing or operating such an enterprise. But by the middle of the nineteenth century, with changes in technology and the extent of the market, the representative cotton mill had grown larger, often by several orders of magnitude. Increasingly, specialized management and complex modes of raising capital became the order of the day. Responding to this reality, first joint-stock companies and then limited liability were sanctioned by Parliament in 1844 and 1856.[1] Companies sold shares to individual investors as a way of raising funds for now more extensive investment. They established boards of directors to help run these more complex organizations. With the second industrial revolution centered on the steel, chemical, and engineering industries at the end of the nineteenth century, the importance of scale, scope, and therefore fixed investment and outside finance grew more important still. Share issuance and professional management became the rule rather than the exception. In this way the forward march of technology and markets progressively diluted family ownership and control.

In addition, there is a prominent strand of historical writing on Britain's loss of its early nineteenth-century economic preeminence (the "clogs to clogs in three generations" interpretation) that blames the grandsons of the founding generation of industrialists for effectively running into the ground the firms that their forbears had so diligently worked to create. Educated in the humanities rather than management, the third generation poured its energies—and financial resources—into politics and landed estates rather than the further development of the family firm. The minority of early nineteenth-century firms that survived were sold off to other owners with more narrowly economic objectives.[2]

Barry Eichengreen is George C. Pardee and Helen N. Pardee Professor of Economics and Political Science at the University of California, Berkeley, and a research associate of the National Bureau of Economic Research.

1. These had been available previously through private acts of Parliament, but more restrictively.
2. An influential interpretation along these lines is Landes (1969, p. 336 and following). To quote, "Thus the Britain of the late nineteenth century basked complacently in the sunset of economic hegemony. In many firms, the grandfather who started the business and built it by

While not speaking directly to this interpretation of Britain's so-called relative economic decline, Franks, Mayer, and Rossi shed considerable new light on the dynamics of ownership and control. They show that loss of family control was often the price of public share issues floated to raise finance not for internal investment but to finance expansion through mergers with competing firms. Although there are hints of this finding in, inter alia, Hannah (1976), it has not been documented as thoroughly before. Another of the authors' findings, which appears to be entirely new, is that families, even while having their ownership position diluted, were able to retain control to a surprising extent by occupying a disproportionate number of seats on the board of what was no longer the family firm (often even chairing the board). Moreover, most directors of the company that was the target of the acquisition, and even the chairman, retained a position on the new board. Adherents of the "clogs to clogs in three generations" thesis will nod their heads at this finding, although this is not a connection that the present authors pursue.

Franks, Mayer, and Rossi then document the gradual erosion of disproportionate family control in the second half of the twentieth century, reflecting the growing influence of hostile takeovers and institutional investors. Indeed, what they document is not merely an erosion but a transformation. Whereas families possessed board representation disproportionate to their ownership at the beginning of the twentieth century, by the end of the century substantial family-controlled voting blocks were even less common than in other advanced economies. In the United Kingdom today, dual-class shares through which block holders—often, in other countries, family members—share ownership but not control are virtually unknown.

What explains this transformation? Franks, Mayer, and Rossi argue that disproportionate family representation on the boards of the merged public companies was made possible by the weakness of minority investors' rights. This is consistent with the older historical literature critical of late nineteenth- and early twentieth century stock flotations and mergers, through which minority investors were often ripped off.[3] But, partly in response to earlier scandals, protection for minority investors was strengthened after World War II. Important reforms included strengthened disclosure requirements through the adoption of the 1948 Companies Act. The

---

unremitting application and by thrift bordering on miserliness had long died; the father who took over a solid enterprise and, starting with larger ambitions, raised it to undreamed-of-heights, has passed on the reins; now it was the turn of the third generation, the children of affluence, tired of the tedium of trade and flushed with the bucolic aspiration of the country gentlemen. (One might more accurately speak of 'shirtsleeves to hunting jacket—or dress coat, or ermine robes—in three generations'.) Many of them retired and forced the conversion of their firms into joint-stock companies. Others stayed on and went through the motions of entrepreneurship between the long weekends."

3. See, for example, Macrosty (1907).

ability of minority investors to vote with their feet and the ability of firms to launch takeovers on the basis of publicly available information (and thus without the cooperation of the potential target) led to the development of a market in corporate control that threatened the entrenched position of board members. The latter attempted to defend themselves by building large block holdings, developing strategic alliances, and issuing dual-class shares on a significant scale for the first time in British history. But that defense proved temporary: institutional investors, who worked hand in glove with the stock exchange, were able to impose sanctions against firms that engaged in such practices, denying them access to outside finance, if, for example, they sought to use dual-class issues in new equity flotations. The city was able to strengthen sanctions against directors who did not advance the interests of all shareholders, including minority investors, with its Code on Take-Overs and Mergers in 1967. Regulation, notably as a result of the establishment of the Takeover Panel in 1968, cemented this new equilibrium.[4]

It is worth observing that this account is not obviously consistent with the currently fashionable literature emphasizing Britain's common-law tradition as an explanation for the precocious development of its financial markets.[5] Protection for minority investors went from relatively weak in the second half of the nineteenth century to relatively strong in the second half of the twentieth despite no obvious change in legal inheritance. Rather, legal and institutional reforms protecting minority investors responded to past scandals; thus, they may have had an element of path dependence. They also responded to politics and policy in the manner argued by Rajan and Zingales (2003). The openness of the British economy to trade and finance prevented entrenched interests from closing down its financial markets in response to the crisis of the 1930s and thereby diminishing the markets' influence, in the manner of other countries. As a result, the market power and political sway of the institutional-investor community—and the big financial institutions in particular—sufficed to force through reforms strengthening minority investor rights and creating a true market in corporate control.

At this point the reader, his appetite having been whetted, wants to learn more. He wants to know about the nature of the changes in British financial markets and the economy, presumably produced by the crisis of the 1930s and World War II, that enhanced the power of the big financial institutions, allowing them to effectively discipline directors and protect minority investors where they had not been able to do so before. He wants to know why big financial institutions, which were certainly not unrepre-

---

4. Although the authors only imply, as opposed to arguing, that this too was a consequence of the growing influence of institutional investors.

5. See, for example, LaPorta et al. (1998).

sented in countries like Germany, Japan, and France, did not have a similar tendency to suppress big block holdings, family control, and director autonomy. If it is the precocious development of British financial markets that accounts for the influence of institutional investors, one wonders whether a legal tradition conducive to financial deepening may have been responsible for these developments after all. Or was the emergence of large institutional investors itself a response to the weakness of minority shareholder rights and the shortcomings of investor protection? If inadequate information disclosure and the absence of sanctions against self-interested directors are the explanations for why there did not exist a thriving market in corporate control until the second half of the twentieth century, as the authors argue, then how is one to understand Sylla and Smith's (1995) emphasis on the Directors Liability Act of 1890 (which made company directors liable for statements in prospectuses soliciting buyers for company shares) and the Companies Act of 1900, which strengthened the principle of compulsory corporate disclosure, as the explanation for why British financial markets developed so rapidly around the turn of the century, to the point where they quickly overtook those of the United States? At a minimum, this suggests that the 1948 Companies Act and the 1967 Code on Take-Overs and Mergers were not radical departures from the status quo ante; rather, they had a prehistory whose economic archeology deserves to be uncovered.

References

Hannah, Leslie. 1976. *The rise of the corporate economy.* Baltimore: Johns Hopkins University Press.

Landes, David. 1969. *The unbound Prometheus.* Cambridge: Cambridge University Press.

LaPorta, Rafael, Florencio López-de-Silanes, Andre Shleifer, and Robert Vishny. 1998. Law and finance. *Journal of Political Economy* 106:1113–55.

Macrosty, H. W. 1907. *The trust movement in British industry.* London: Longmans Green.

Rajan, Raghuram, and Luigi Zingales. 2003. The great reversals: The politics of financial development in the 20th century. *Journal of Financial Economics* 69: 5–50.

Sylla, Richard, and George David Smith. 1995. Information and capital market regulation in Anglo-American finance. In *Anglo-American financial systems,* ed. Michael Bordo and Richard Sylla, 179–208. New York: Irwin.

Why Has There Been So Little Block Holding in America?

Marco Becht and J. Bradford DeLong

11.1 Introduction

A century ago European academics like Werner Sombart worried why the United States was exceptional, in that it had no socialism. Today we academics worry about a different form of American exceptionalism: why is there so little block holding in the United States?

Most other countries have powerful family groups that control substantial numbers of corporations through large blocks, some held through pyramids of holding companies and special classes of shares with extraordinary voting rights. The United States, by and large, does not. Most other countries have holding or other parent companies that maintain substantial control over the affairs of publicly traded and listed operating corporations. The United States, by and large, does not: large parent companies do not have listed subsidiaries. Many other countries have large blocks of shares in individual corporations held or voted by financial intermediaries that play a key role in monitoring and supervising corporate managers. The United States, by and large, does not.

The pattern found in the United Kingdom is in some ways closest to the United States. In the United Kingdom, like the United States, ownership is

Marco Becht is a professor of finance and economics at Université Libre de Bruxelles (ULB), a resident fellow at the European Center for Advanced Research in Economics and Statistics (ECARES) at ULB, and the executive director of the European Corporate Governance Institute (ECGI). J. Bradford DeLong is a professor of economics at the University of California, Berkeley, and a research associate of the National Bureau of Economic Research (NBER).

We would like to thank Fabrizio Barca, Lucien Bebchuk, Patrick Bolton, Chris DeLong, Barry Eichengreen, Randall Morck, Carlos Ramirez, Mark Roe, Ailsa Röell, Andrei Shleifer, participants in seminars at Berkeley, ECARES, INSEAD, and the NBER, and many others for helpful discussions and comments.

diffused. Yet in the United Kingdom institutional shareholders are powerful. In the United States they are not.[1] In most countries the market for corporate control follows the U.K. model—tender offers are rapidly put to a shareholder vote, with the board condemned to passivity. In the United States active boards bargain with bidders, motivated by fiduciary duties, stock options, severance pay packages, and other considerations.[2] In the United Kingdom shareholders rarely litigate. In the United States class-action lawyers are looking for new cases they can bring all the time.

America's peculiarity is made even more striking by the fact that it is not a long-standing historical tradition. America's corporate control exceptionalism has emerged in the past century. Before 1900 America did not lack for powerful family groups, for parent companies, or for financial intermediaries that aggressively embraced the role of monitoring and supervising corporate managers. Turn-of-the-last-century analyst John Moody—founder of the firm that is still one of America's two leading bond-rating agencies—wrote a very influential book, *The Truth about the Trusts,* in 1904, which detailed his understanding of the small and powerful networks of financiers and investors who controlled the governance of America's corporations.

Moody looked forward to a future in which America would have effectively delegated complete control over the "commanding heights" of its economy to an alliance made up of one single family group and one single financial intermediary. The family group was the Rockefellers, who had leveraged their initial Standard Oil fortune into control of a broad range of America's industry. The financial intermediary was the investment banking partnership of J. P. Morgan and Company, which had transformed J. P. Morgan's father's position as the seller of American railroad bonds to British investors into a role as *the* gatekeeper for access to America's capital markets.

Moody wrote his book to persuade American investors and politicians that the future he saw was a good thing. In Moody's view, the personalized

---

1. Institutional investors in the United Kingdom often operate behind the scenes. Thus, their influence is relatively hard to measure (see Black and Coffee 1994). Their power did become highly visible in the advisory votes on executive remuneration during the 2003 annual meeting season. By contrast, relative impotence of institutional investors in the United States is well documented; see Black (1998), Gillan and Starks (1998), Karpoff (1998), and Romano (2001) for recent surveys. Outside a fully fledged proxy fight, shareholders in U.S. corporations have little say in the selection of corporate directors (Bebchuk 2003; Posen 2003). Forcing the long-standing chairman and chief executive officer of Walt Disney, Michael Eisner, to relinquish his chairman position—after years of below-average performance and above-average remuneration—has been hailed as a major victory for institutional shareholders (*Financial Times,* 14 March 2004).

2. Of course, shareholders may profit from being represented by a board committee that can behave strategically. Burrough and Helyar (1990) narrate the case of RJR-Nabisco, in which the board committee first demanded "final offers" from the bidders, and then reopened the bidding—successfully extracting higher prices for its shareholders' stock.

oligarchic financial capitalism of controlling blocks held by Rockefellers and other plutocrats would be a profitable, effective, and productive organization of American finance. And, indeed, American capitalism at the start of the twentieth century was one in which *family* was very important.

But the organization that Moody foresaw did not come to pass, or to the extent it did come to pass it was proved ephemeral. Sixty years later John Kenneth Galbraith (1967) marveled at the speed with which American capitalism had become impersonal:

> Seventy years ago the corporation was the instrument of its owners and a projection of their personalities. The names of those principals— Carnegie, Rockefeller, Harriman, Mellon, Guggenheim, Ford—were known across the land. . . . The men who now head the great corporations are unknown . . . [and] own no appreciable share of the enterprise. . . . They are selected not by the shareholders but, in the common case, by a Board of Directors which narcissistically they selected themselves.

But for Americans as of the middle of the twentieth century, "Guggenheim" was an art museum—not a family dynasty of mines and natural resources. "Rockefellers" were politicians and a stray banker—not the lords of petroleum and transport. "Carnegie" meant an endowment for international peace and a large number of libraries—not the controllers of the steel industry.

John D. Rockefeller and his immediate associates *controlled* Standard Oil, and much else, in 1900. But by 1930 Gardiner Means (1930, 1931) is looking at a world in which ownership is greatly dispersed, and is trying to think through the consequences of a financial world in which it is nearly impossible to assemble a block of shareholder votes large enough to credibly threaten the incumbents who have control.[3]

---

3. Of course, 1932 sees the publication of Adolf Berle and Gardiner Means's (1932) *The Modern Corporation and Private Property.* There are interesting differences between the arguments of Means by himself and those of Berle and Means, or at least our perception of the latter's arguments. The "Berle and Means corporation" is controlled by its professional managers, an arrangement that arises from an inevitable (and—in Berle and Means—undesirable) "separation of ownership and control" in the giant corporation. Means (1930) documents a "remarkable diffusion of ownership from 1917 to 1921" that he concludes is "primarily the result of the heavy surtaxes of the war period, a nonrecurring phenomenon" he likens to the one-off increase in small landholdings after the French Revolution. More significantly, Means (1930) suggests that the WWI surtax "concentrated the attention of the former owners of industry on the possibility of retaining control without important ownership, either through the wide diffusion of stock or through various legal devices [footnote: nonvoting common stock, voting trusts, pyramided holding companies etc.] and thereby accelerating that separation of ownership and control" (Means 1930, p. 592), a situation not unlike those found in some other countries of the world where powerful families exert a degree of power disproportionate to their ownership. Means (1931) characterizes "control as something apart from ownership on one hand and from management on the other." The real puzzle of the U.S. corporation, then, is how and why professional managers managed to wrest control from the former owners—who could have stayed in control had they taken steps to set up devices to do so.

At the end of 1929 only 11 percent of the 200 largest corporations in the United States were still controlled by large block holders, while 44 percent were controlled by incumbents with much reduced ownership interest. In another 44 percent of cases management was alleged to have taken over control and to have established itself as a self-perpetuating body that Means saw as resembling more than anything else the organizational structure of the Catholic Church, where "the Pope selects the Cardinals and the College of the Cardinals in turn select the succeeding Pope" (Means 1931, p. 87, footnote 7).[4]

We believe that the origins of American shareholding exceptionalism come a generation before *The Modern Corporation and Private Property.* Immediately after 1900—and in a few cases before—the diffusion of shareholding and the shift of power to salaried managers begin. Thus, we believe Galbraith and Means and even Moody were overly optimistic about the Vanderbilts, Carnegies, and Guggenheims as classic block holders. The American exception, the separation of ownership and control, started early. It was spurred by trust promotion, by antitrust policy, and by the ability of investment bankers like J. P. Morgan to successfully sell large blocks of stock to a wide public.

J. P. Morgan successfully sold William Henry Vanderbilt's majority block in the New York Central Railway to the market in 1879 (Chernow 1990, p. 42).[5] In steel, Andrew Carnegie sold his majority block in the Carnegie Steel Corporation in 1901 as U.S. Steel was assembled. In smelting and refining, the Guggenheims sold their majority block in the American Smelting and Refining Company (ASARCO) in 1908–9.

William Vanderbilt and the Guggenheims *wanted* to separate ownership and control. They believed that they could maintain control through their informal influence over the boards of directors and could invest the proceeds of the sales in new diversified ventures. They believed that they had found a way to achieve the benefits of diversification and the ability to en-

---

4. In corporations, "control will tend to be in the hands of those who select the proxy [nomination] committee by whom, in turn, the election of directors for the ensuing period may be made. Since this committee is appointed by the existing management, the latter can virtually dictate their own successors. Where ownership is sufficiently subdivided, the management can thus become a self-perpetuating body even though its share in the ownership is negligible" (Means 1931, p. 87). This basic mechanism is largely unchanged, and Yermack (1999) recently found evidence that U.S. chief executive officers (CEOs) continue in this tradition and select their own directors. The point was also well made by Kenneth Lay, then CEO of Enron, in a speech given at an April 1999 Houston conference titled "Corporate Governance: Ethics across the Board": "Of course, the CEO, as well as the board, is very much involved in choosing appropriate board members. The process of building an effective board typically reflects what the CEO thinks the company needs at that point in time." Lay appears to have believed that what Enron did not need was an aggressive board-level audit committee.

5. Carnegie took bonds and no stock from U.S. Steel because he thought the new steel near-monopoly was overvalued. He was sorry.

ter new sectors, all without loosing de facto control over their original enterprises.[6]

> In selling off majority control of ASARCO, the Guggenheims were following advice from their lawyers and bankers that was popular at that time and remained popular for the next half-century. This theory held that it was neither necessary nor possible for individuals or a family to retain actual majority ownership of a large enterprise. Control could be as easily maintained by splitting the stock up into small lots and selling to a broad segment of the public. . . . Morgan showed Vanderbilt how it could be done. He proceeded to show hundreds of other capitalists how they could do the same. (Hoyt 1967, p. 193)

Among the 200 largest U.S. corporations in 1937, few had families with majorities of the voting shares. Many had families that dominated the boards of directors.

And today? La Porta, López-de-Silanes, and Shleifer (1999), ECGN (1997), and Barca and Becht (2001), among others, find that the United States is exceptional in the limited influence and small size of its major block shareholders.[7] Among the 200 largest U.S. corporations in 2004, the Ford family and the Ford Motor Company are exceptions to the exception, just as they were in 1937. In the short run of years the owners who believed that they could use the services of J. P. Morgan and Company to achieve

---

6. Carnegie sold out to the J. Pierpont Morgan–promoted U.S. Steel trust, which had a J. P. Morgan–dominated board and was run by Carnegie's own professional manager, Charles Schwab. Carnegie did not reinvest the proceeds of the sale for profit but in philanthropic enterprises.

7. La Porta, López-de-Silanes, and Shleifer (1999) rationalize the pattern of block holding around the world as a result of nations' small-investor protections, or lack thereof. One sacrifices the benefits of diversification and takes on extraordinary amounts of idiosyncratic risk when one fears that the legal system will allow the effective expropriation of small shareholders. Thus they would expect to—and they do—find more block holding where legal protections of small shareholders are weak.

It is not clear to us whether this general worldwide argument can explain all of America's absence of block holding, for legal protections against formal expropriation and explicit tunneling appear to us to be insufficient to fully resolve the principal-agent problem first identified by Berle and Means. It is true that today the risk that in the United States small shareholders will be illegally expropriated by managers or large blockholders is small, despite an avalanche of successful class action suits. But (illegal) expropriation is only one danger to shareholder wealth. For example, Bebchuk (2002) makes a powerful and convincing (to us at least) argument that recent American compensation practices amount to shareholder wealth expropriation, a view that is widely shared among institutional shareholders, the general public, and the press. Equally, Moeller, Schlingemann, and Stulz (2002) argue that acquisitions at the end of the 1990s have destroyed billions of dollars of shareholder wealth. However, both views are contested by Holmstrom and Kaplan (2003). Managerial groupthink generated over time as managers choose like-minded sycophants to be their successors provides another reason for shareholders to fear American-style managerial capitalism. Legal protections cannot guard against this source of reduction in shareholder value, which may be a more important spur to block holding and shareholder voice.

diversification and maintain control were probably right. In the long run of generations they were wrong.

This lack of block holders appears to have had important and powerful consequences for American corporate governance. Mark Roe begins his 1994 *Strong Managers, Weak Owners* with an anecdote about General Motors (GM). At the start of the 1990s, the two largest shareholders of GM wanted to express their views on how GM should select its new CEO. The GM Corporation paid no attention to them at all—a degree of managerial autonomy that is hard to imagine being the rule in almost any other industrial economy (Roe 1994, p. xiii).

Becht, Bolton, and Röell (2002) maintain that the key issue is to find the point of balance between managerial discretion and small shareholder protection: too much concern for protecting small shareholders from block holders allows managers to reinterpret their end of the corporate contract. Too much power on the part of large shareholders, and small shareholders are left vulnerable to expropriation, while managers are monitored too closely. If the experience of other industrial countries is any guide, America is way to one side of the point of balance. This suggests that it may well be paying heavy costs as a result of its institutional failure to minimize the damage done when shareholders fail to monitor and enforce their open-ended contracts with top corporate managers.[8]

Mark Roe (1994) believes that America evolved its exceptional form of non-block holding and its exceptional forms of corporate control due to "politics." Ever since the age of Andrew Jackson in the 1830s, Americans have loved the market but hated monopolists. Americans love the market because it makes them free and gives them the power to say no: if you don't like the deal you are being offered here, simply walk down the street a block and bargain with the next potential seller. But suppose that there is only one monopolist? Then you are not free but controlled.

In Roe's political interpretation, those seeking to limit and curb financial concentration and control—whether small rural bankers, corporate managers, or others—found that their arguments struck this deep chord in and resonated with Americans' basic way of viewing the world. By asserting the existence of a "money trust," they mobilized American politics to destroy every effective financial institution that might have held blocks and exerted control over American managers. In Roe's view, technology created the necessity for hundreds of thousands of shareholders. Politics crippled the institutions—*grossbanken,* insurance companies, mutual funds, pension funds—that would otherwise have taken their supervisory and

---

8. However, the extraordinary relative success of the American economy over the course of the twentieth century does make one much less confident about making judgments of large-scale century-long failure in America's markets for corporate control. This might be due, at least in part, to finance economists' exaggeration of the importance of the widely held managerial corporation in the economy as a whole.

control functions seriously and reduced the magnitude of the shareholder-manager principal-agent problem in corporate finance.

Roe's argument is eloquent, powerful, and largely convincing. But it seems to us that it has four holes. First, the victory of American populism and progressivism in the struggle over the organization of corporate finance was not foreordained. Populists lost in the turn-of-the-twentieth-century struggle over the American monetary system. Progressives won a partial victory in the struggle over the role of unions in the mid-1930s, but that partial victory was itself substantially rolled back little more than a decade later—and ever since then American private-sector unions have been in an inexorable decline. Roe has a hard time answering why "politics" in its American populist-progressive tenor was so strong in corporate finance yet weaker in labor-management relations and completely powerless in monetary affairs.

Second, there are two ways that block holders can function. The block holder can be a financial institution that aggregates the small shareholdings of a great deal of individuals into a block. The block holder can be a plutocratic family that wishes as a matter of family policy to have voting control. Roe (1994) makes a strong case that specific financial regulation prevented financial institutions—banks, insurance companies, pension funds, and mutual funds—from holding blocks, as they allegedly do in German and Japan. Families were not subject to these legal restrictions. What other regulation, if any, prevented families from holding large blocks, as the Ford family has successfully done for more than a century?

Third, in *The Visible Hand,* Alfred Chandler (1977) argues that *ownership* separated from *management* because of technical progress. Roe (1994) follows this argument. Chandler brushed aside the possibility that ownership separated from control and control was also separate from management. We agree with Chandler and Roe that the desire for diversification is a powerful force that can and should induce families to disperse ownership, but we raise the question why control was not separated from both ownership *and* management.

Diversification is a very valuable thing: go drink coffee at Il Fornaio in Palo Alto some weekday morning, and you may see some people—people who failed to diversify—who were worth more than a billion dollars four years ago and are worth some ten million today. But there are ways of dispersing ownership without putting control into the hands of professional managers. The fortune- and control-holding families of other countries have built institutions to retain corporate control with dispersed ownership, even when hiring a professional manager: through pyramids of holding companies and special supervoting classes of stock, they have managed to effectively diversify their portfolios enough to remove most of the idiosyncratic risk without sacrificing effective control. Why didn't the major plutocratic families of turn-of-the-twentieth-century America take this road? Did they believe that the solution J. Pierpont Morgan had pioneered for William Vanderbilt was an effective way of dispersing ownership while retaining effective control? Were they not worried about proxy contests? Could they not foresee that the only reliable means of preventing a corporate palace revolution is voting control?

Fourth, diversification is not the only economic force that can cause dispersion. American corporations could have used debt finance or retained earnings, instead of diluting their founders' stakes through new equity issues and equity-financed acquisitions. Why did America's family-controlled corporations rely so much on equity-based finance and growth through acquisitions? Was it the financial system and the need to transport capital over large distances that drove corporate America to Wall Street? Was it regulation that made Wall Street inevitable for corporate America?

Thus our task in this paper is to fill in these gaps in the story of Roe (1994). We do so in five stages. After this first, introductory section, in section 11.2 we briefly paint a picture of industrializing America's corporate finance in the first decade of the twentieth century, arguing that America then looked like a normal developing family- and finance-capitalist economy as far as corporate oversight and control was concerned. Section 11.3 considers the remarkable democratization of shareholding that took place between World War I and the end of World War II: the benefits of sacrificing control for diversification hinge on how deep the market into which you are trying to sell your controlling block is, and a number of factors from the high-pressure war bond sales campaigns of 1917–18 to the writings in popular magazines of share ownership advocates like Edgar L. Smith (1924) to the media coverage of Wall Street celebrity culture in the 1920s made U.S. markets much deeper—and thus the sacrifice of diversification for control in the United States much more attractive—than elsewhere. It also discusses the attempts by block holders to find durable institutional instruments through which to exercise control, and the government's pursuit of such block holders through the thickets of law and institutions: the original "voting trusts" were replaced by "holding companies"; companies with multiple classes of stock had difficulty getting listed on exchanges (but is that cause or effect?); antitrust regulators sought to put controls on holding companies and pyramids. The coup de grace, however, was dealt by an accidental outside shock: the great crash and the Great Depression. The Insull and Van Sweringen pyramidal empires were completely bankrupted when what had been seen as prudent leverage proved disastrous in the Great Depression itself.

Section 11.4 looks back from the end of the 1930s: no more "money trust," few blockholders, and the approach of managerial capitalism. Section 11.5 then concludes.

Our conclusions do not make as neat a story as we would wish, at least not when we put on our hats as economists. We would wish for a single straight-line narrative: *America's populist-progressive politics made large-scale block holding impossible;* or *America's continental size made its firms enormous, and block holding extremely expensive in terms of the sacrifice of diversification it entailed;* or *the competence of America's managerial class combined with strong protections for small shareholdings greatly diminished the relative benefits of block holding;* or *the early and extraordinary taste on the part of Americans for shareholdings made the relative benefits of diversification much larger in America.*

Yet the story as we have to tell it is messier. The populist-progressive political tradition in America exerted pressure against finance capitalism, but the populist-progressives were not the main current of American politics. Recall that for more than half a century before 1948, the only way a Democrat got into the presidency was (a) in the Great Depression itself and (b) when Theodore Roosevelt's feud with William H. Taft led Roosevelt to split the Republican Party and the Republican vote.

America's continental size made its firms enormous, but it also made its entrepreneurial fortunes enormous as well: the Rockefellers, the Carnegies, the Mellons, even the Morgans had very few peers in Europe. Certainly many American holders of control blocks gradually peeled off shares and watched their influence shrink because they had confidence in their managers, but shouldn't they have been thinking more long term? Were New Jersey's, and later Delaware's, protections for shareholders that much better than anywhere else? Were America's markets really that much deeper and that much more able to absorb diversification than anywhere else?

If Mark Roe's story is one of "politics" (plus the economics that made immense corporations efficient due to their massive economies of scale and the requirement for hundreds of thousands of shareholders), our story is one of fast-growing corporations in a large country with a large single market and a vast appetite for capital—"frenzied finance"—plus a large number of contingent historical accidents, rather than convergence to a "rational" system of corporate governance and control. During the 1990s, when the U.S. Internet boom seemed unstoppable, it was fashionable to predict that corporate governance around the world would soon mirror the U.S. model: private executives would receive high-power incentive pay in the form of stock options, and they would be kept in check chiefly by the specter of mergers or takeovers resulting from low stock prices. Labor unions, major-institution shareholders, and rich-family financiers—key influences in corporate control in other countries—would become less important.

Some signs supported the convergence view. Managers in other countries looked enviously at the magnitude of the capital flowing through U.S. financial markets and the easy terms on which funds could be raised. Corporate governance in Europe, Japan, and emerging markets appeared to be shifting in the U.S. direction, as foreign firms that wanted to be listed on U.S. stock exchanges tried to make their systems appealing to American investors. In at least one aspect—the number of shareholders per firm—convergence is probable. Firms with a broad shareholder base have an easier time tapping pension fund money via the New York and London markets.

But to the extent that the U.S. system is the result of a number of historical accidents that eroded the power of pyramid-dominating families and large institutional investors, perhaps the convergence we can expect in the future is more likely to be toward a mixed model. Recall that widely distributed ownership is compatible with strong institutions that vote large share blocks through proxies, as well as with dispersed voting rights and contestable board control, as in the United Kingdom. And recall that it is just as compatible with uncontestable board control nominally exercised in the interest of shareholders—as in the United States, with their poison pills and entrenched directors, or as with the Netherlands' priority shareholders, who possess the sole right to nominate directors for election to corporate boards.

It is not clear that the next generation of the Gates family will have as little influence on American corporate control as the current generation of the Rockefeller family does. It is not clear that the large American financial institutions of the twenty-first century—two of which are still likely to bear the name of "Morgan"—will have as little influence on American corporate control as the firms of the mid-twentieth century did.

11.2   Rockefellers and Morgans: American Financial Capitalism at the Start of the Twentieth Century

In 1904 John Moody—then perhaps the most respected commentator on and analyst of Wall Street—wrote *The Truth about the Trusts* to give his view of the extraordinary wave of economic development and industrial concentration in turn-of-the-last-century America. John Moody argued that big business was here to stay and was getting bigger. "Trusts" were here to stay.[9] Moreover, "trusts" were by and large good things: economies of scale meant that big business—large hierarchical Chandlerian[10] corporations—were efficient and productive, and they delivered goods to consumers at low cost. It was true that trusts came with elements of monopoly

---

9. The word *trust* originally referred to the voting trust set up by Standard Oil's lawyer S. C. T. Dodd to bring the various Standard Oil companies operating in different states (and holding corporate charters issued in different states) under centralized control; see Dodd (1893). Moody pioneered the modern usage of the word, referring to any form of industrial combination with an impact on product market power, irrespective of the legal technique used. Hence Moody's "trusts" include voting trusts proper, holding companies, amalgamations, and other types of horizontal combinations.

10. See Chandler (1977).

power attached. But the monopoly element was a necessary cost in order to obtain the enormous economies of scale. Furthermore, the monopoly element was not all bad, for competition led to instability and turmoil, while the higher costs of monopolized markets were somewhat offset by the regularization of supply that large-scale planning by a dominant firm made possible. As Moody wrote (p. xix), "monopoly is the mother of our entire modern industrial civilization. It is institutional and men must reckon with it."

Moody's case was not completely false. After all, muckraker Ida Tarbell's principal objection to the Standard Oil Trust was not that it charged consumers prices that were too high. It was that Standard Oil used its *monopsony* power to force railroads to charge it lower prices for shipping oil, and used its *scale* to reduce manufacturing costs. It thus drove smaller and less efficient oil refiners out of business. From Tarbell's point of view, the prices that Standard Oil charged customers were not too high, but too low.[11] From Moody's point of view, the Progressivist attraction to Tarbell's advocacy of small business was very dangerous for the future of the American economy. For economic progress depended on efficiency. And efficiency depended on trusts: large, hierarchical, integrated corporations with monopoly power that served as islands of efficient central planning within the market economy.[12]

For our purposes, however, the most important part of Moody's argument is what comes next in Moody's logical sequence: his claim that America owes an enormous debt for its industrial development to one extended family (and its partners and allies)—the Rockefellers:

---

11. See Tarbell (1904). One of the great fights in the early twentieth century was over whether the antitrust laws existed to protect consumers from rapacious monopolies charging them high prices or to protect small-scale business against more-efficient large-scale businesses that threatened to charge customers low prices. In the first half of the twentieth century, this political struggle largely ended in a draw: the answer was "both." Only in the years after the 1970s, in one of the greatest and most extraordinary projects of activist judge-made law in American legal history, did the aggressive and activist judges of Chicago remake antitrust law and give it an explicit rationale: that of maximizing economic surplus. See Bork (1978).

12. In a side argument, Moody (1904) defends the trusts against an alternative critique also made by Progressives: that the trusts cheated investors by being *unsuccessful* and failing to be good enough monopolists to produce the promised dividends. In the decade of the 1900s initial and post–initial public offering (IPO) investors in Morgan's International Mercantile Marine and in the Rockefellers' Amalgamated Copper (see Lawson 1905) lost their shirts, and even investors in Morgan's U.S. Steel took a severe haircut. But Moody writes (p. xxi): "In the majority of instances, however, they no doubt went in with their eyes more or less open. The average man who buys industrial issues . . . knew or ought to have known that he was going into a gamble . . . stocks yielding from 8% to 15% when prevailing interest rates were only 4% to 5%. No sympathy need be wasted on the many noisy speculators who are now condemning all Trusts because they themselves happened to be caught in the speculative crash." Although there is then some backtracking: "Of a different nature, of course, are . . . widows, orphans . . . induced to transfer their hard-earned savings into stocks like Steel common . . . by trusted advisors who ought to have known better."

The large diagram facing the Introduction [of *The Truth about the Trusts*] gives an indication of the extent to which the Greater Trusts are dominated by that remarkable group of men known as the "Standard Oil" or Rockefeller financiers. These men . . . entirely control or make their influence felt to a marked degree . . . [in] all the Greater trusts. They are in fact the real fathers of the Trust idea. . . . Standard Oil. . . . But it is not merely in oil and its allied industries . . . [that] Rockefeller interests are dominant. . . . [The] Copper Trust and the Smelters' Trust . . . closely identified with the mammoth Tobacco Trust . . . a marked influence in the great Morgan properties . . . U.S. Steel . . . hundreds of smaller Industrial Trusts, the Rockefeller interests are conspicuous . . . different members of the Standard group of financiers . . . identified with a great many of the prominent Trusts. . . . [I]ndirect influence is of great importance in many other industrial consolidations. (p. 490)

Moreover, Moody sees the power of the Rockefeller family and its partners to control the American economy on a steady upward growth curve. In railroads, for example, Moody sees

S[tandard] O[il] interests . . . [as] steadily increasing their influence. . . . [The] Gould-Rockefeller [group of railroads] . . . is, of course, directly dominated by them; but . . . Standard [Oil] influence [is already] felt . . . forcefully in all the Railroad groups, and . . . is showing a steady growth throughout the entire steam railroad field. (p. 491)

Moody ends his discussion of railroad finance by saying that it is "freely predicted in Wall Street" that within a decade the United States will see the "Rockefeller interests [become] the single dominating force in . . . railway finance and control."

Moreover, Moody sees the Rockefeller interests as only part—although definitely the senior partner part—of the finance capitalists who he expects to see controlling nearly all large American corporations within the near future. First, there are the other major robber baron families that made their fortunes during the Gilded Age and that now work hand in glove with the Rockefellers (p. 493): "smaller groups of . . . Pennsylvania Railroad interests . . . Vanderbilts and . . . Goulds . . . closely allied with the Rockefellers . . . on most harmonious terms with the Moore's of the Rock Island system, and the latter are allied in interest quite closely with . . . Harriman." The picture painted is not one in which rich families typically clash: in Moody's view, the era of the great struggles for control between different robber baron factions was over.[13] The picture painted is one much closer to that of Silicon Valley venture capitalists in the 1990s, where each of a number of venture capitalist firms would contribute capital to one another's

---

13. He was not completely correct. The great Northern Securities Panic of 1904 occurred while Moody's book was in press. And the late 1920s saw more struggles for control erupt as the stock market bubble grew.

deals, but in which challenges for the lead role as principal financier and advisor appeared to be very rare—and to be thought of as not quite kosher, as breaking the rules of the game as played by gentlemen.

Second, there was the House of Morgan, assisted by the smaller investment banks of the early twentieth century. Here again Moody saw the community of interest among financiers as overwhelming (p. 493):

> It should not be supposed, however, that these two great groups of capitalists and financiers [the Rockefeller and the Morgan interests] are in any real sense rivals or competitors for power, or that such a thing as "war" exists between them. . . . [T]hey are not only friendly, but they are allied . . . harmonious in nearly all particulars. . . . These two mammoth groups jointly . . . constitute the heart of the business and commercial life of the nation, the others all being the arteries which permeate in a thousand ways our whole national life, making their influence felt in every home and hamlet, yet all connected with and dependent on this great central source, the influence and policy of which dominates them all.

Indeed, if the Rockefeller family after its extraordinary upward ride in wealth via Standard Oil possessed the wealth to buy control of whatever company or group of companies it chose, the House of Morgan—and the few other smaller investment banking partnerships—held a near lock on the ability to sell large blocks of bonds and equities into the not-yet-terribly-thick New York and London markets. Morgan had acquired its reputation by being over decades a reasonably honest broker in advising potential British investors about which American railroads were uncorrupt (and by participating in reorganizations to try to guarantee that the newly recapitalized railroad company would remain uncorrupt). It had competitors, but they were few. When questioned by Pujo Investigating Committee Chief Counsel Samuel Untermyer in 1912, Morgan's close associate George F. Baker (president of New York's First National Bank) could not name "a single [securities] issue of as much as $10 million . . . that had been made within ten years without the participation or cooperation" of J. P. Morgan; Kuhn, Loeb; Kidder, Peabody; or Lee, Higginson.[14] With American securities issues then running at a pace of about $500 million a year, that is an extraordinary degree of concentration.

The fact of the matter is that if you wanted to establish or operate a large enterprise—whether railroad, municipal utility, or industrial—in the United States at the start of the twentieth century, you had to work through or please one of a very small number of gatekeepers: the Rockefellers or one of their largely allied families (Elkinses, Wideners, Vanderbilts) for key blocks of capital, and Morgan or one of the other few investment banks for the seal of approval that would gain one's securities a market. These groups appear not to have competed against each other: when capital-stressed

14. See DeLong (1991).

AT&T went looking for rescue during the panic of 1907, it found that Morgan lieutenant George F. Baker offered it take-it-or-leave-it terms: either throw out your president and change your entire corporate strategy, or go bankrupt. AT&T's incumbent management was unable to find another negotiating partner, and acceded to Baker's terms.[15]

11.2.1   Standard Oil

The early history of Rockefeller's Standard Oil illustrates the influence of legal innovations and antitrust regulation on the evolution of ownership and corporate organization in the pre-WWI period.

1865–67: Partnership

Standard Oil has its origins in a partnership set up by John D. Rockefeller and the English engineer Sam Andrews in Cleveland in 1865 trading under the name "Rockefeller and Andrews."[16] On 4 March 1867 they were joined by Henry M. Flagler, whom Rockefeller liked and who gave him access to financing from the wealthy Cleveland businessman Stephen V. Harkness.[17] William Rockefeller, John D.'s brother, provided a Wall Street connection. The expanding "Rockefeller, Andrews, and Flagler" partnership was soon in need of further capital and confronted with problem of bringing in outside investors without losing control.

1870–78: Ohio Corporation

It was Flagler who found the solution: in 1870 the Standard Oil Company (Ohio) was incorporated, with Rockefeller family members holding 50 percent of the shares, as shown in table 11.1: John D. Rockefeller (the president) held 26.7 percent, William Rockefeller (the vice president) 13.3 percent, and William Rockefeller's brother-in-law, Oliver B. Jennings, another 10 percent. Flagler (the secretary and treasurer) held 13.3 percent, his relative S. W. Harkness 13.3 percent, and Sam Andrews 13.3 percent.[18]

Over the course of the next decade the shareholdings of Standard Oil be-

---

15. See DeLong (1991): "The investment bankers' price for continuing to finance the company was that its next president should be . . . Theodore N. Vail . . . [because] George F. Baker had been very much impressed with Vail's performance in other dealings" and that it should adopt Vail's previously proposed strategy of "rapid nationwide expansion . . . to a true nationwide telephone system."

16. Rockefeller and Andrews were breaking away from a previous partnership with the Maurice, James, and Richard Clark (Andrews, Clark, and Co.), whom Rockefeller did not get on with and who had the majority of the votes in the partnership (Chernow 1998, p. 85). Rockefeller, the junior partner, essentially eliminated the three Clarks from the partnership that continued as "Rockefeller & Andrews" (Chernow, pp. 87–88).

17. Harkness had made his money with liquor deals, but this did not seem to disturb puritan Rockefeller (Chernow 1998, p. 106).

18. Chernow (1998, p. 133) states that the remaining 10 percent were "divided among the former partners of Rockefeller, Andrews and Flagler," which seems to imply that the partnership had other partners. We have not yet tracked down the original structure.

Table 11.1   Standard Oil shareholders, 1870

Name of shareholder	Shares	%
John D. Rockefeller	2,667	26.7
Henry M. Flagler	1,333	13.3
Sam Andrews	1,333	13.3
William Rockefeller	1,333	13.3
Stephen Harkness	1,334	13.3
Oliver B. Jennings	1,000	10.0
Former partners	1,000	10.0
Total	10,000	

Source: Chernow (1998).

came more complex, as shown in table 11.2. Principals gave some of their shares to family members. Other executives and local Cleveland financiers acquired stakes. And the enterprise grew at staggering speed.

1879–82: Ohio Trust

Under Ohio corporation law the Standard Oil Company (Ohio) could not own stock in other corporations and operate outside the state. In reality the Standard Oil companies were run from 26 Broadway in New York. In 1879 a first legal solution to this problem was found, a trust agreement that gives us a second glimpse at the shareholder structure of Standard Oil. Three middle-management employees of Standard Oil Ohio were made to hold the shares of the Standard Oil companies outside the state of Ohio in trust (Messrs. Myron R. Keith, George F. Chester, and George H. Vilas). Dividends received were passed on to the thirty-seven shareholders of Standard Oil Ohio, in proportion to their holding (see table 11.2).[19] The group of shareholders had grown to thirty-seven, but the Rockefellers were still holding a 30 percent block that put them in a position of control.[20]

1882–92: New York Trust

The 1879 trust agreement solved the problem of interstate ownership and control but was not suitable for expanding the shareholder base while keeping control in Rockefeller hands. Standard Oil's solicitor, Samuel C. T. Dodd, devised the second trust agreement, which was a legal masterpiece and extremely influential.[21] The shares of all Standard Oil companies were

19. For a facsimile of the 1879 trust agreement see Stevens (1913).
20. Sam Andrews is no longer on the list. In 1878, after a disagreement over payout policy (Rockefeller wanted high retained earnings, Andrews wanted more dividends), John D. Rockefeller bought out Andrews's stake (Chernow 1998, p. 181).
21. As we have seen, the word *trust* became synonymous with all types of major industrial combinations no matter what legal instrument was used and has survived as "antitrust" to this day and age.

Table 11.2   **Standard Oil shareholders, 1878**

Name of shareholder	No. of parts in trust (proportional to shares held in Standard Oil of Ohio)	%
W. C. Andrews	990	2.8
John D. Archbold	350	1.0
F. A. Arter	35	0.1
J. A. Bostwick	1,872	5.3
D. Brewster	409	1.2
Daniel Bushnell	97	0.3
J. N. Camden	132	0.4
H. M. Flagler	3,000	8.6
Hanna & Chapin	263	0.8
S. V. Harkness	2,925	8.4
D. M. Harkness	323	0.9
L. G. Harkness	178	0.5
Gustave Heye	178	0.5
John Huntington	584	1.7
Horace A. Hutchins	111	0.3
Estate of Josiah Macy	892	2.5
Chas. Lockhart	1,408	4.0
W. H. Macy	59	0.2
W. H. Macy, Jr.	28	0.1
A. M. McGregor	118	0.3
O. H. Payne	2,637	7.5
H. W. Payne	292	0.8
O. H. Payne, trustee	61	0.2
A. J. Pouch	178	0.5
Charles Pratt	2,700	7.7
C. M. Pratt	200	0.6
Horace A. Pratt	15	0.0
John D. Rockefeller	8,984	25.7
Wm. Rockefeller	1,600	4.6
O. B. Jennings	818	2.3
Henry H. Rogers	910	2.6
W. P. Thompson	200	0.6
J. J. Vandergrift	500	1.4
W. T. Wardell	78	0.2
W. G. Warden	1,292	3.7
Jos. L. Warden	98	0.3
Warden, Frew & Co.	485	1.4
Total	35,000	100.0

Source: 1878 Trust Agreement (reproduced in Stevens 1913).

placed in a single trust with nine trustees, who exerted central control over all Standard Oil companies but formally did not own anything. As before, dividends were distributed to the holders of the trust certificates in proportion to their holdings. The holders of the trust certificates appointed the trustees in a vote, but the Rockefellers, Flagler, Payne, and Harkness continued to hold a majority of the certificates, and the trustees were appointed for a staggered term.[22] In fact, Dodd had managed to create a takeover-proof holding company operating an interstate business out of New York, an arrangement that conformed with the letter of the law, but not the spirit.

1892–98: "Community of Interest"

The regulators responded. In 1889 several states passed antitrust laws, and in 1890 Congress passed the Federal Sherman Antitrust Act, marking the beginning of an ongoing struggle between Standard Oil, antitrust reformers, and antitrust enforcers at the federal and the state level.[23] The first (apparent) setback came on 2 March 1892, when the Supreme Court of Ohio ruled that the Standard Oil trust agreement violated the law, and on 10 March 1992 the Standard Oil trust announced that it would dissolve, exchanging trust certificates in proportional amounts of shares in each of the constituent companies. This gives us the next opportunity for observing that the nine trustees jointly held more than 50 percent of the trust certificates. John D. Rockefeller alone held a 26.4 percent stake, allowing him and his associates to exert majority control in all Standard Oil companies.[24]

1898–1911: New Jersey Holding Company

Between 1888 and 1893 the state of New Jersey reformed its corporate law, explicitly allowing New Jersey corporations to own stock in corporations in other states of the Union. As a result, new incorporations (and state income from fees) shot up, and New Jersey became known as "the home of the trusts" (read, holding company; Stoke 1930). Standard Oil followed suit in 1898, and the "community of interest" was replaced by the Standard Oil of New Jersey, turning itself into a New Jersey holding company and owning the stock of the Standard Oil companies in the other states.

Standard Oil was no exception. With regulation and active attorneys depriving the trusts of their original legal instrument, they turned to the legal instruments that were still available: the "community of interest," the hold-

---

22. The 1882 trust agreement is also reproduced in Stevens (1913).
23. See Thorelli (1955) for a detailed account of the political history leading up to the passage of the act.
24. Curiously, it took a considerable amount of time before the other certificate holders performed the exchange. In this period, the trustees continued to control the old trust and voted almost all the exchanged shares in the constituent companies (Hidy and Hidy 1955, p. 226).

ing company, and outright fusion. The holding company was used as often as outright fusion, including well-known names like Eastman Kodak, U.S. Steel, and the E. I. du Pont de Nemours Powder Company (Bonbright and Means 1932, pp. 68–72).

But again, the enforcers caught up. In 1904 the Supreme Court culled the J. P. Morgan–led merger of the great transatlantic railroads through the Northern Securities Holding company (Ripley 1915), casting serious doubts on the effectiveness of the holding company as a vehicle for circumventing antitrust regulation in the context of horizontal combinations. Worse, in 1911 the Supreme Court ruled that the American Tobacco Company, which had been created through outright fusion, was also in violation of the antitrust laws.[25] The landmark ruling breaking up Standard Oil into its constituent companies was pronounced in the same year, marking the de facto end of Rockefeller rule over the oil industry.

Thus, if we can take John Moody as a reliable observer,[26] American corporate control at the start of the twentieth century appears to have looked remarkably "normal," where "normal" is understood as "like other coun-

25. See Stevens (1913) for a facsimile of the court's decision.
26. We believe that we can take Moody as a reliable observer. While historians like Fritz Redlich (1951) take Moody and others (like C. W. Barron, as reported in Pound and Moore 1931, or Frank Vanderlip, as reported in Vanderlip and Sparkes 1935) at face value, some other historians of American finance do not. Financial historian Vincent Carosso (1970) argue that Pujo Committee Chief Counsel Louis Untermyer could only claim there was a "money trust" by redefining it as a "loose, elastic" term meaning not a formal organization of any kind but an "understanding," and that even so investment bankers could not exercise "control" because they were always less numerous than the non–Wall Street directors (pp. 139, 151–52). Huertas and Cleveland's history of Citibank (1987) argues that the investment banking market at the start of the twentieth century was a contestable one: that had a railroad executive like C. W. Mellen wished to use other partnerships than J. P. Morgan and Company to float securities for his railroad's expansion, he would have found no obstacles to doing so. Had other firms wished to compete with J. P. Morgan for, say, the underwriting of U.S. Steel, they would have found it possible to do so. But profits are small in contestable markets, and the underwriting profits from U.S. Steel were as large a share of their economy then as $30 billion would be for us now (DeLong 1991).
There is, however, no doubt that there are other issues than concern for the public interest in many Progressives' attacks on the money trust. Perhaps Louis Brandeis was more—or as—interested in protecting the property of his Boston railroad financier clients and allies from competition from Morgan-financed railroads as he was in advancing the public interest. Certainly Samuel Untermyer had found cooperation with the "Money Trust" more advantageous than criticism of it. Huertas and Cleveland (1987) write that Untermyer was an "aspiring politician" for whom the Pujo media spotlight was a wonderful opportunity. He thus changed his position 180 degrees, for in 1910 Untermyer had dismissed monopolization as a nonproblem in American industry and had attacked demagogues who hoped to use it as an issue. Huertas and Cleveland cite Kolko (1963, p. 359).
The situation seems to us analogous to that of the late Roman Republic's parties of *optimates* and *populares.* Just as Untermyer changed sides, and just as Progressive Money Trust–hating congressman Charles Lindbergh's son Charles, the aviator, was to marry Morgan partner Dwight Morrow's daughter Anne, so Rome's feuding elite patrician factions fought viciously over political control between time-outs for marriages and realignments. But this does not mean that there were not real issues involved in *optimates'* and *populares'* disputes over land settlement policy for veterans and imperial expansion.

tries." Immensely wealthy families with powerful voting blocks. Stock locked up in "trusts" (voting trusts, holding companies, amalgamated corporations) whose trustees and boards closely scrutinize managers. Large financial institutions that see it as their business to choose and unchoose corporate managers, and that by and large respect each other's relative spheres of industrial influence. As Charles Mellen, president of the New York, New Haven, and Hartford Railroad, put it in a private conversation with journalist C. W. Barron, he was a thrall of J. P. Morgan and company: "I wear the Morgan collar, but I am proud of it."[27]

But then it began to fall apart.

As Mark Roe (1994) details, the American "money trust" was subjected to a powerful political attack in the first two decades of the twentieth century. A Democratic Party anchored in the west and south with leaders like William Jennings Bryan and Woodrow Wilson fought hard to claim the banner of "Progressivism" for its own and to reduce the illegitimate power over the nation's economy wielded by the bankers, financiers, and industrialists of that strange and un-American city that was New York.[28] Theodore Roosevelt tried first to co-opt that Progressive movement and then to split the Republican Party by joining the attack against America's "malefactors of great wealth."

The Progressive critique focused on two sets of issues. The first was the simple existence of *economic power*—a situation in which someone's economic future depended on their pleasing one particular gatekeeper. In the view of Progressive leader Louis Brandeis, this dammed entrepreneurship and initiative. Who would dare to cross or to question the judgment of a Morgan or a Rockefeller? As Brandeis told Morgan lieutenant Thomas Lamont at a private meeting in 1913, "You may not realize it, but you are feared."[29] And, Brandeis added, this fear was a very unhealthy thing: "I believe the effect of your position is toward paralysis rather than expansion."[30]

Second, the Progressives' belief in fair play was outraged by the fact that the Rockefeller, Morgan, and allied groups at the top of America's finance capitalist pyramid turned conflict of interest into a lifestyle. Investment bankers and insider block holders were principals themselves, were the bosses of corporate managers who had fiduciary duties to try to sell off securities at as high a price as possible, and also were the bosses of or exercised substantial control over the managers of financial intermediaries

27. See Pound and Moore (1931, p. 273).
28. See Hofstadter (1964).
29. As Brandeis said he had discovered from his own personal experience with the financing of the New York, New Haven, and Hartford Railroad: "I went to some of the leading Boston bankers. . . . I said . . . 'Won't you please act . . . [?] Their reply . . . was that they would not dare to . . . that it would be as much as their financial life was worth to try to poke their fingers in." See Lamont (1913).
30. See Lamont (1913).

who had the exact opposite interest. They thus had the freedom to sacrifice the interests of one set of principals to another, or to sacrifice both of the other sets of interests to their own private profit—for they themselves were both principals as block holders and middlemen as the key intermediaries in large-scale transactions. Few moments in the history of congressional investigations are more eye-opening than George W. Perkins, partner in J. P. Morgan and company and vice president of New York Life, arguing to Arsene Pujo's congressional investigative committee and its chief counsel Samuel Untermyer that there was no conflict of interest: that even though Morgan was selling the securities and New York Life was buying them, he knew at every moment whether he was a principal (in his role as partner of Morgan) with an interest in selling at a high price or an agent of the policy holders (in his role as vice president of New York Life) with an interest in buying at a low price, and could act accordingly (Pujo Committee 1913b).

From the Progressives' point of view, this was mendacious nonsense. Louis Brandeis (1913) invoked the authority of Jesus Christ to condemn it as he pushed for financial reforms that would (p. 56) "give full legal sanction to the fundamental law that 'No man can serve two masters'. . . . No rule of law has been more rigorously applied than that which prohibits a trustee from occupying inconsistent positions. . . . A director . . . is . . . a trustee." National City Bank President Frank Vanderlip[31]—one of the "insiders" of the Money Trust—reminisced about the times:

> I opposed underwriting fees because I felt that they were too high. As a [Union Pacific] director . . . my obligation . . . ran to the stockholders . . . not to Harriman. I have in mind recollections of occasions when it was pointed out to me, in a hurt tone, that the City Bank was sharing in those underwriting profits that I thought were too fat. (pp. 204–5)

Conflict of interest and malfeasance cannot be the whole story. If so, why would both the McCormick and the Deering families have been so anxious to let Morgan partner George W. Perkins be an honest broker and set the respective prices at which their interests were to be combined into International Harvester?[32] Nevertheless, Progressivism was strong enough and powerful enough in the first two decades of the twentieth century to make life as a finance capitalist intermediary or block holder unpleasant.

Even before 1900, there was at least one family that had decided that the political pressure and the lack of diversification were together too large risks to run. As Carosso (1970) recounts the story, in 1879 William Vanderbilt decided that he wanted to sell off the control block in the New York

---

31. See Vanderlip and Sparkes (1935).

32. See DeLong (1991), p. 212. It does look like the McCormicks and the Deerings were a little bit naive. Carstensen (1989) makes a convincing case that George W. Perkins did attempt a (small) sacrifice of International Harvester's interests to enrich the House of Morgan's main project at the time, U.S. Steel.

Railroad that he had inherited from his father, the Commodore. Hoyt (1967) quotes William Vanderbilt as saying, "We get kicked and cuffed by Congressional committees, legislatures and the public and I feel inclined to have others take some of it, instead of taking it all myself."

How do you sell off a control block in one of the leading enterprises of the age, when nothing like it had been attempted before? Junius Spencer Morgan and his son, John Pierpont Morgan, had a plan. The principal market for the shares was to be England, where J. S. Morgan lived and did most of his business. English investors would be offered a share in a well-run railroad that had good track and a clear line from the port of New York all the way to Chicago. How could English investors be sure that the railroad line would continue to be well run? When J. S. Morgan sold them their shares, they would sign the proxies over to his son J. P. Morgan, who lived in the United States, would represent them on the New York Railroad's board, and would vote their proxies. A combination of (a) political pressure and (b) the promise of a wide and diversified market that would purchase the control block at a good price together induced this first step toward Berle-Means-style finance fifty years before they wrote this book.

There is more to the story. For the Progressive movement led not just to smoke or noise but to one definitive major government intervention in the commanding heights of the economy: the antitrust suit against and then the breakup of Standard Oil.

11.3   The Coming of Shareholder Diversification

In 1911, the Supreme Court ordered the breakup of Standard Oil. In 1912 the Pujo Committee investigated the "Money Trust." In 1914 Louis Brandeis inveighed against the power of the "Money Trust" in an attempt to make it one of the key issues for Wilson administration policy activism. In 1914 the passage of the Clayton Act also took place, with its section 7 prohibiting corporations from holding controlling stakes in competing corporations. In 1932 Adolf Berle and Gardiner Means published their book *The Modern Corporation and Private Property,* trying to think through the consequences of a world in which block holders were few and shareholders many and without means of communication and organization. In 1933 the Glass-Steagall Act separated commercial from investment banking. In 1935 the Public Utility Company Holding Act eliminated any possibility of a pyramidal utility empire. In 1948 the federal government shied away from attempting to break up GM but nevertheless pursued the smaller task of getting rid of GM's large remaining block holder: DuPont. Mark Roe (1994) tells this process of fragmentation as the triumph of politics: Populists, Progressives, and their heirs, striking a deep chord in their attacks on the personal exercise of economic power in America, pursue stockholders through the law and through institutions, in the

Table 11.3   Large Standard Oil shareholders, 1911

Name of shareholder	% holding
Rockefeller, J. D., Sr.	24.9
C. W. Harkness	4.4
Payne	4.1
Flagler	1.5
Rockefeller, William	0.8
Archbold	0.6
Pratt	0.5
Jennings	0.4

Source: Hidy and Hidy (1955).

process eliminating every way that dispersed owners can organize the monitor and supervise entrenched managers. And, indeed, practically all of what Roe writes is accurate and insightful.

11.3.1   Standard Oil

But more is going on. Consider the flagship company of the post-1911 Rockefeller fortune: Standard Oil of New Jersey (now Exxon). In 1912 John D. Rockefeller senior alone owned a quarter of Standard Oil (New Jersey), as table 11.3 shows. The top 1.5 percent of shareholders owned 72 percent of the company's shares. The Rockefellers and their allies both *owned* and *controlled* Standard Oil (New Jersey). Yet over the subsequent generation and a half, ownership of Standard Oil (New Jersey) became remarkably dispersed.

We have data year by year from 1912 to 1950 on the number of shares and shareholders, on the number of shareholders owning more than one thousand shares, and on the cumulative holdings of such "large" shareholders of Standard Oil (New Jersey).[33] Unfortunately, "1,000 shares" does not mean the same thing in 1912 as it does in 1950. In 1912 1,000 shares is 0.1 percent of the company, a one one-thousandth stake. In 1950 1,000 shares is only one thirty-thousandth of the company's capital stock. There are only 5,832 holders of Standard Oil (New Jersey) stock in 1912. By 1950 there are 222,064, more than 35 times as many.

With this limited data, even putting them on a roughly comparable basis requires heroic assumptions. We make them. We make the heroic assumption that the distribution of the upper tail of shareholdings of Standard Oil (New Jersey) follows a power-law distribution:[34] that the share S

33. From Gibb and Knowlton (1976).
34. See Krugman (1996) and Piketty and Saez (2001). Krugman advances various arguments for what kinds of circumstances and generating processes might lead one to expect a power-law relation to hold. Piketty and Saez estimate power-law distributions for top income fractions.

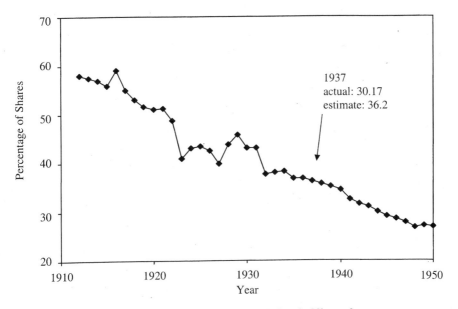

Fig. 11.1   Standard Oil of New Jersey: Estimated shareholdings of top twenty shareholders
Source: Authors' calculations from data from Gibb and Knowlton (1976).

of stock shares held by the top share B of shareholders at any moment in time follows the equation $S = A(B^p)$. We use our data to obtain a log least-squares estimated value of 1.43 for A.[35]

Given this estimated value for A, we generate an estimate of p for each year to fit that year's data point on the percent of shareholders with more than 1,000 shares and the percent of shares that such shareholders own. Thus—if the power-law assumption holds—we put our data on Standard Oil on a consistent basis. The most interesting ways to present the data are two: first, year-by-year estimates of the rough share of Standard Oil owned by the top twenty shareholders; second, year-by-year rough estimates of the smallest number of Standard Oil shareholders you would need to assemble in order to control more than 50 percent of the company's stock. Figures 11.1 and 11.2 present our results.

Figure 11.1 shows that the erosion of concentration across the one and a half generations from 1912 to 1950 is impressive. It also shows that our estimate is surprisingly accurate for the year we can observe the actual percentage holding of the largest twenty owners (from the Temporary Na-

35. With a *t*-statistic of 5.43. The identifying variance in this regression is dominated by the two splits of Standard Oil of New Jersey in this time period: a tripling of the number of issued shares in 1921 and a further fivefold multiplication in 1923.

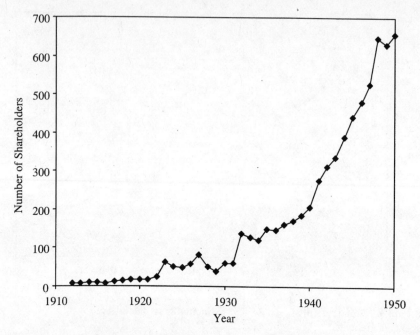

Fig. 11.2   Standard Oil of New Jersey: Estimated number of shareholders required to hold more than 50 percent of stock

Source: Authors' calculations from data from Gibb and Knowlton (1976).

tional Economic Committee study). Our estimate is 36.2 percent; the actual concentration was 30.2 percent.

It is possible to turn the question around. What is the smallest coalition of shareholders that could be assembled to vote 50 percent of the stock of Standard Oil of New Jersey? In 1912 our rough power-law-derived estimate is eight: the largest eight shareholders own more than half of Standard Oil of New Jersey. By 1920 a fair amount of dispersion has taken place: our estimate is that you need the eighteen rather than the eight largest shareholders to make up a majority.

Further diversification by major owners leads to an estimate of between forty and eighty by the late 1920s, and then the turmoil of the multiyear crash and stock market declines of the Great Depression carries the number up to 150 by the mid-1930s. By 1950, or so our power-law-derived estimates tell us, you would need to assemble the six hundred largest shareholders to control 50 percent of the outstanding shares of Standard Oil of New Jersey.

These estimates are, of course, vulnerable to the heroic assumption of a power-law distribution for shareholdings. At the most basic level, the underlying facts are these: In 1912 105 shareholders—1.8 percent of all

Standard Oil of New Jersey shareholders—owned 75 percent of Standard Oil of New Jersey stock. In 1950 2,142 shareholders—0.9 percent of a vastly expanded number of Standard Oil of New Jersey shareholders—together owned 62 percent of Standard Oil of New Jersey stock. In 1950 you would have had to assemble not a majority but a considerable fraction of those 2,142 "large" shareholders to assemble a majority of shares. In 1912 you could have assembled a majority of shares by simply picking the biggest holders from the 105. The assumption that the upper tail of share-holdings follows a power-law distribution aids our comprehension of the shape of the process of share dispersion, and is probably not far from the truth. It does not generate the fact of dispersion.

Note that none of the "political" factors stressed by Roe (1994) were at work in this dispersion of Standard Oil (New Jersey) shareholdings, and the resulting increase in the likely power of established managers and de-crease in the power of owners over decisions about corporate direction and managerial succession. Incumbent shareholders sold off their shares, see-ing the value of diversification in reducing the expected cost of the idio-syncratic risk borne by holding large blocks as worth more than the loss of the ability to easily assemble a controlling voice at annual meetings should one want to challenge or replace management. And over the course of a generation and a half this process of diversification proved to be remark-ably powerful in its effects.

11.3.2   Politics

The effects of the drift away from control and toward diversification that we have seen at work were, of course, reinforced by the workings of the political factors stressed by Roe (1994). In striking contrast to banking elsewhere, American banking *was* fragmented—by the inability to branch across state lines, and often by the inability to branch at all.[36] The earlier national banks and the later members of the Federal Reserve system could not own shares of stock.[37] The Armstrong investigation of 1905–6 knocked out insurance companies as possible attractive locuses for the exercise of supervision, monitoring, and control.[38] As mutual funds developed, they were regulated in such a way as to make 5 percent block ownership or the possession of a seat on a board the cause of substantial restrictions in liq-uidity. As pension funds developed, they too were encouraged to become

36. See White (1982).
37. It is important not to overstate the power of the pre-1933 restrictions on American banks. Banks could not branch across state lines, but the importance of New York meant that they hardly needed to: the National City Bank of James Stillman and Frank Vanderlip and the First National Bank of George F. Baker were doing fine as nationwide financial interme-diaries from their Manhattan bases. Banks could not own equities, but their "security affili-ates" could—and as long as the ownership and management of a bank's security affiliate was identical to that of the bank itself, there was little hazard.
38. See Roe (1994), chapter 7.

passive investors rather than active block holders.[39] Attempts by banks to navigate around the restrictions imposed on them to become truly large and powerful financial intermediaries were prevented by a series of legal restrictions. As Roe (1994) puts it (p. 101),

> The modern banking laws—McFadden, Glass-Steagall, the FDIC [Federal Deposit Insurance Corporation] Act, and the Bank Holding Company Act—should not be seen as fragmenting the banking system . . . [but as] stop[ping] the . . . finesse . . . of [previous] laws. . . . Glass-Steagall stopped another finesse of the rules, but it should not be seen as shattering a truly powerful, stockholding intermediary. . . . [T]he United States declin[ed] to build and refine a system of powerful intermediaries that could have come to counterbalance managerial power in large public firms.

11.3.3   General Motors

But there is more to it than that. Where there were substantial block holdings, circumstances conspired to cut them down to size. Consider the investment that DuPont (the chemical corporation) made in GM. After the end of World War I a former DuPont treasurer, John J. Raskob, persuaded the DuPont company to invest $25 million in GM as a way of creating a possible automotive market for DuPont's artificial fabric, paint, and plastic products. The relationship grew remarkably close: Pierre S. du Pont became GM's president in 1920. In the 1920s DuPont's GM stockholdings amounted to one-third of GM's outstanding stock. And DuPont and GM worked together in the 1920s to develop coolants and gasoline additives. More important, however, the DuPont interests backed the restructuring plan of Alfred P. Sloan that made GM the dominant automobile company in America—and in the world.[40]

Come the late 1940s the federal government began thinking about whether it wanted to try to dissolve GM in order to increase competition in the automobile industry. In the end the government decided not to pursue a breakup of GM. However, the close links between the DuPont chemical company and GM produced by the large DuPont holdings did come under scrutiny. And in *U.S. v. DuPont* the Supreme Court held in 1957 that DuPont's GM shareholdings were indeed a violation of the previously almost-unused section 7 of the Clayton Antitrust Act. The court ruled that DuPont's acquisition of GM shares was motivated by a desire to obtain "an illegal preference over its competitors in the sale to General Motors of its products, and a further illegal preference in the development of chemical discoveries made by General Motors."[41] The fact of influence coupled

39. See Roe (1994), chapter 9. Here, however, Roe argues that the decisive factor was less likely to be Populist-Progressivist fear of "malefactors of great wealth" than managerial fear of pension-fund socialism à la Drucker (1976).
40. See Sloan (1964).
41. See Harbeson (1958).

with the fact that at least some of GM's purchases of DuPont's products were motivated by a desire by GM to keep its owner happy was enough to call for divestiture. The days when GM had a single large, active shareholder powerful enough to monitor and overawe management had come to an end.

11.4   The View from the End of the 1930s

It was actually[42] Gardiner Means (1931) who wrote that

> It is apparent that, with the increasing dispersion of stock ownership in the largest corporations, a new condition has developed with regard to their control. . . . No longer are the individuals in control of most of these corporations the dominant owners. Rather, there are no dominant owners, and control is maintained in large measure separate from ownership.

Empirically, this insight was based on an analysis of the growth in the number of stockholders between 1900 and 1928 (Means 1930, updating Warshow 1924) and the distribution of ownership blocks among the largest 200 U.S. corporations at the end of 1929 (Means 1931).[43]

Means (and, a year later, Berle and Means) was certainly right in seeing a substantial diffusion of shareownership. Figure 11.3 shows the number of shareholders in America's three largest corporations. By the end of the 1920s AT&T had nearly half a million shareholders. The Pennsylvania Railroad had 150,000. Table 11.4 reports Means's numbers on the growth of shareholding for a broader range of companies. The pattern is the same: wide diversification is well under way.

Means attempted a fivefold classification of "the separation of power over corporate resources and ownership interests therein." The spectrum ran from (a) almost complete ownership through (b) majority control, (c) control through a legal device (a pyramid, nonvoting preferred or common stock, voting trusts), (d) minority control through a stock interest, down to (e) management control.[44]

The key to control with little (or no) ownership was the rules governing board elections. In Germany votes attached to bearer shares typically fell into the hands of depository banks; in the United States proxy voting by

---

42. Nevertheless, almost every modern article on corporate ownership cites Berle and Means (1932).

43. A shortened version of Means (1930) became chapter 1 of book I in Berle and Means (1932); Means (1931) became chapter 5. Chapter 3 of book I is a shortened version of Means (1931b). More generally, it appears that Means was responsible for book I and Berle for book II.

44. Management control arises when "ownership is so widely distributed that no individual or small group has even a minority interest large enough to dominate the affairs of the company" (p. 83).

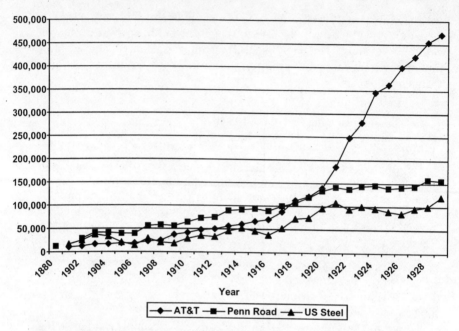

Fig. 11.3   Number of shareholders in the three largest U.S. corporations—AT&T, the Pennsylvania Railroad, and U.S. Steel
Source: Authors' calculations from data from Means (1930).

mail and record ownership put these votes de facto into the hands of the incumbent board of directors:

> Ordinarily, at an election, the shareholder has three alternatives. He can refrain from voting, he can attend the annual meeting and personally vote his stock [or appoint a personal proxy to attend], or he can sign a proxy transferring his power to certain individuals selected by the management of the corporations, the proxy committee. . . . [C]ontrol will tend to be in the hands of those who select the proxy committee by whom, in turn, the election of directors for the ensuing period may be made. Since this committee is appointed by the existing management, the latter can virtually dictate their own successors.

It is no coincidence that the proxy process was a major concern of the drafters of 1933 Securities and Exchange Act[45] and continues to be so to this day.[46]

---

45. Thomas Corcoran, one of Felix Frankfurter's "Happy Hot Dogs" brought in from Harvard to draft the 1933 Securities and Exchange Act, shared this view: "Proxies, as solicitations are now, are a joke. The persons who control the machinery for sending out proxies, with practically no interest in the corporation, can simply keep other people from organizing [and] get enough proxies to run the Company" (Seligman 1982, p. 87).

46. The 1933 act contained specific provisions on the proxy voting process, but to date these provisions have not changed the nature of U.S. board elections in a fundamental way: "Share-

Table 11.4   **Growth in number of shareholders, 1900–28**

Name of company	1900	1910	1913	1917	1920	1923	1928	Growth (%)
Industrial								
Union Bag and Paper	1,950	2,250	2,800	1,592	1,856	2,263	1,278	−34.5
General Asphalt	2,089	2,294	2,184	2,112	1,879	2,383	1,537	−26.4
Gt. North. Iron Ore	3,762	4,419	4,685	4,855	6,747	9,313	7,456	98.2
Am. Sugar Refin.	10,816	19,551	18,149	19,758	22,311	26,781	22,376	106.9
Am. Car and Foundry	7,747	9,912	10,402	9,223	13,229	16,090	17,152	121.4
U.S. Steel Corporation	54,016	94,934	123,891	131,210	176,310	179,090	154,243	185.6
United Shoe Machy	4,500	7,400	8,366	6,547	8,762	10,935	18,051	301.1
Am. Smelt. and Refin.	3,398	9,464	10,459	12,244	15,237	18,583	15,040	342.6
U.S. Rubber	3,000	3,500	12,846	17,419	20,866	34,024	26,057	768.6
International Paper	2,245	4,096	3,929	4,509	3,903	4,522	23,767	958.7
Am. Locomotive	1,700	8,198	8,578	8,490	9,957	10,596	19,369	1,039.4
Swift and Co.	3,400	18,000	20,000	20,000	35,000	46,000	47,000	1,282.4
Stand. Oil of N.J.	3,832	5,847	6,104	7,351	8,074	51,070	62,317	1,526.2
General Electric	2,900	9,486	12,271	12,950	17,338	36,008	51,883	1,689.1
DuPont Powder	809	2,050	2,697	6,593	11,624	14,141	21,248	2,526.5
United Fruit	971	6,181	7,641	9,653	11,849	20,469	26,219	2,600.2
Proctor & Gamble	1,098	1,606	1,881	2,448	9,157	11,392	37,000	3,269.8
Total Industrial	108,233	209,188	256,883	276,954	374,099	493,660	551,993	410.0
Utilities								
Brooklyn Union Gas	1,313	1,593	1,646	1,834	1,985	1,879	2,841	116.4
Western Union	9,134	12,731	12,790	20,434	23,911	26,276	26,234	187.2
Commonwealth Edison	1,255	1,780	2,045	4,582	11,580	34,526	40,000	3,087.3
Am. Tel. & Tel.	7,535	40,381	55,983	86,699	139,448	281,149	454,596	5,933.1
Total Utilities	19,237	56,485	72,464	113,549	176,924	343,830	523,671	2,622.2
Railroads								
Reading	6,388	5,781	6,624	8,397	9,701	11,687	9,844	54.1
N.Y.N.H. & Hartford	9,521	17,573	26,240	25,343	25,272	24,983	27,267	186.4
Illinois Central	7,025	9,790	10,776	10,302	12,870	19,470	21,147	201.0
Pennsylvania	51,543	65,283	88,586	100,038	133,068	144,228	157,650	205.9
Union Pacific	14,256	20,282	26,761	33,875	47,339	51,022	47,933	236.2
Chicago and Northwestern	4,907	8,023	11,111	13,735	19,383	21,555	16,948	245.4
Del. Lack. and Western	1,896	1,699	1,959	2,615	3,276	6,650	7,957	319.7
Atlantic Coast Line	702	2,278	2,727	3,404	4,422	5,162	4,213	500.1
Chesapeake and Ohio	1,145	2,268	6,281	6,103	8,111	13,010	6,885	501.3
Great Northern	1,690	16,298	19,540	26,716	40,195	44,523	43,741	2,488.2
Total Railroads	99,073	149,275	200,605	230,528	303,637	342,290	343,585	246.8

Source: Means (1930, table II) and authors' calculations.
Note: Growth column shows growth between 1900 and 1928.

Figures 11.4 and 11.5 show Means's classification of corporate control for large corporations at the end of the 1920s for both "immediate" and

---

holders typically are provided proxies allowing a vote only on company-nominated candidates, and disclosure in company proxy material is limited to those candidates. Also, most companies use plurality rather than majority voting for director elections, so candidates are elected regardless of whether a minimum percentage of shareholders approve. Therefore, company nominees are nearly always elected to the board, regardless of the number of shareholders who object to their candidacy" (from Securities and Exchange Commission [SEC] chairman William Donaldson's introductory remarks at the 8 October 2003 open meeting on the SEC's proxy access proposal). On the SEC's 2003 reform proposals see also Bebchuk (2003, 2004).

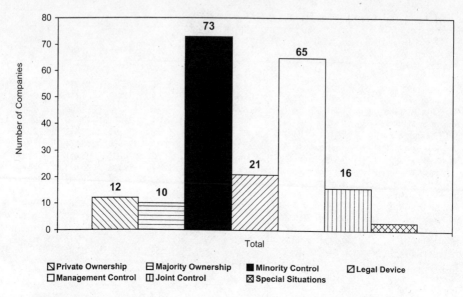

Fig. 11.4   Immediate corporate control in the 200 largest American corporations in 1930

Source: Means (1931).

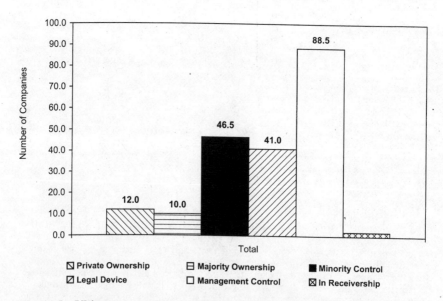

Fig. 11.5   Ultimate corporate control in the 200 largest American corporations in 1930

Source: Means (1931).

"ultimate" control, tracing control to the company that had ultimate control over corporate assets. In terms of ultimate control, management control had become the dominant force in corporate control in America.

From our perspective, Means's assessment of corporate control at the end of 1929 is not satisfactory. First of all, conceptually, his classification does not distinguish between control by a CEO-as-president who dominates a board of "yes men," and family control with little ownership that is exerted via a family dominated, self-appointing board.[47] Two, the data in Means (1931) and Berle and Means (1932) do not allow us to make the distinction between family control through ownership, family control through boards, and management control. Three, the data compiled by Means (1931a) were not complete and not entirely reliable.

To investigate family control, we turn to the earliest comprehensive and reliable cross section of blockholder control in the largest 200 U.S. corporations—the Temporary National Economic Committee's (TNEC) "Investigation of Concentration of Economic Power."[48] The TNEC report was laboriously compiled from SEC filings and questionnaire surveys by SEC staff and was considered to permit one, "for the first time, to determine with some precision the magnitude of the largest holdings in each of a wide group of giant corporations" (Gordon 1945, p. 31).[49] The TNEC (1940) report reflects the general ownership situation around the end of 1937 and, for each of the largest 200 corporations, listed and nonlisted, contains information on record ownership, beneficial ownership, share classes, and the names and holdings of directors. More important, the TNEC volume contains a control classification that is more suitable to our investigation than Means (1931). The TNEC classification is also based on the size of the largest block of voting shares, but it also considers the distribution of other blocks and the presence of shareholders on the boards.[50]

47. The same is true for the other separation categories. A voting trust could be controlled by a family and the company run by a family member or a professional manager, or the trust could be controlled by a professional manager outright.

48. The TNEC has not been intensively used. Two exceptions are Gordon (1945), who made extensive use of the TNEC data to investigate managerial ownership and, more particularly, ownership by "control groups"; and Leech (1987), who studied potential block holder coalitions using power indices.

49. Holderness, Kroszner, and Sheehan (1999) use an even earlier cross section compiled from section 16 reports of insider holdings for 31 December 1935 covering more than 1,500 publicly listed corporations, but not nonlisted companies. The SEC report contains data on direct ownership and beneficial ownership of individual officers and directors, but it does not contain information on the holdings of outside block holders and, hence, corporate control. In the 1930s the data were used extensively by Gordon (1936, 1938). Comparing the SEC's 1935 and the TNEC (1940) data, Gordon (1945, p. 25) considers the TNEC (1940) data more reliable, but Holderness, Kroszner, and Sheehan (1999, p. 447) show that a comparison of insider ownership for the 169 firms in both samples gives very similar results.

50. The basic TNEC classification distinguishes between four control groups: majority control, predominant minority (30–50 percent of voting stock), substantial minority (10–30 percent), and substantial minority control (less than 10 percent of voting stock). The remaining cases are prudently classified as "companies without apparent dominant stock interest."

Table 11.5   American corporate control in 1938

Control group	Manufacturing	Railroads	Utilities	Other	All Companies
Single family group	28	1	5	9	43
Two or more family groups	23	2	3	8	34
Family and corporate groups	5	0	0	1	6
Single corporate group	4	8	25	5	42
Two or more corporate groups	2	3	8	1	14
No dominant stockholding group	34	15	4	8	81
50–100%	10	6	20	4	42
30–50%	17	7	7	8	37
10–30%	28	1	12	9	47
Under 10%	9	0	2	3	13
No block	34	15	4	8	61
Total	96	29	45	30	200

	Manufacturing (%)	Railroads (%)	Utilities (%)	Other (%)	All Companies (%)
Single family group	29.2	3.4	11.1	30.0	21.5
Two or more family groups	24.0	6.9	6.7	20.0	17.0
Family and corporate groups	5.2	0.0	0.0	3.3	3.0
Single corporate group	4.2	27.6	55.6	16.7	21.0
Two or more corporate groups	2.1	10.3	17.8	3.3	7.0
No dominant stockholding group	35.4	51.7	8.9	26.7	30.5
50–100%	10.4	20.7	44.4	13.3	21.0
30–50%	17.7	24.1	15.6	20.0	18.5
10–30%	27.1	3.4	26.7	30.0	23.5
Under 10%	9.4	0.0	4.4	10.0	6.5
No block	35.4	51.7	8.9	26.7	30.5
Total	100.0	100.0	100.0	100.0	100.0

Source: TNEC data and authors' calculations.

Table 11.5 reports the distribution of control in terms of numbers of companies and as percentages of total assets. Figure 11.6 reports the size of the largest share block for the TNEC companies, and figure 11.7 characterizes the type of the potential control share block. Note the important differences, shown in figure 11.8, between utility companies and others: utility companies had the most diversified ownership by far, and attempts to gather utilities into a more centralized control structure were defeated by the combination of finance and politics—the Morgan-led raid and carveup of Samuel Insull's utility empire, and then the Public Utility Holding Company Act of 1938. Utility companies also explain much of Means's (1931) original result. Pyramiding was a phenomenon that was largely confined to the utilities sector. The utilities sector was also the sector where the companies at the top of the pyramids were widely held.

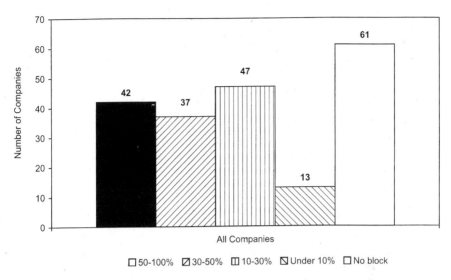

Fig. 11.6   The size of direct stakes in 1938

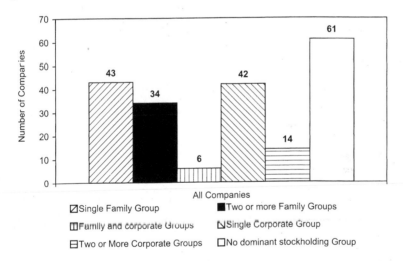

Fig. 11.7   Control groups in 1938

Hence, it was the special type of pyramiding in the utilities sector that led the marked increase in dispersion when considering "ultimate" ownership.

The TNEC (1940) list of the largest 200 corporations includes companies that are subsidiaries of other companies on the list (complex and pyramidal holdings). Gordon (1945) argued that this induced an upward bias into ownership concentration statistics and excluded the twenty-four sub-

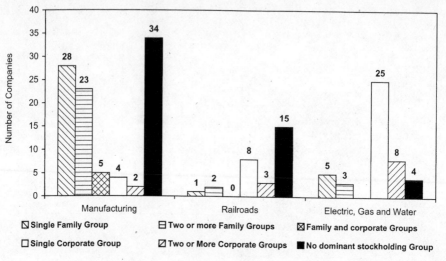

Fig. 11.8   The special place of utilities in 1938

sidiaries from the sample (twenty-one companies with majority ownership by a corporation and three leased lines).

11.4.1   Where did the founders go?

The TNEC sample gives us the data that we need to answer our key question: where did all the founders go? In the TNEC 1938 cross section, 96 of the largest 200 U.S. corporations were in the manufacturing sector, and 34 (35.4 percent) of those had no dominant block holder. The largest investors were Dutch institutional investors[51] and the Sun Life Assurance Company of Canada, holding small blocks under 5 percent. We have traced the origins of the thirty-four industrial companies without a dominant ownership interest back in time. The results suggest that the origin of the "modern corporation" in 1939 is found in the first horizontal merger wave, trust promotion, and antitrust measures.

Tables 11.6, 11.7, and 11.8 show the links between the TNEC cross section of manufacturing corporations without a dominant block holder, and John Moody's original list of trusts in 1904. In twenty cases there is a direct link through the company name. In three cases the companies changed their names: Atlantic Refining and Continental Oil had been part of the

---

51. See De Jong and Röell (chap. 8 in this volume) for a history of ownership and control in the Netherlands. The major Dutch investors were Hubrecht van Harencarspel Maatschappij, Broes and Gosman Maatschappij, Nederlandsch Administratieen Trustkantoor, Wertheim and Gompertz Westendorp Maatschappij, Administratiekantoor van Binnen en Buitsenlandsche Fondsen. Broekmans Administratiekantoor, and Niew-Amsterdamch Administratiekantoor (TNEC 1940, pp. 1502–4).

Table 11.6   TNEC industrial corporations without dominant ownership interest, and with trust origins

Name of company	Name and page in Moody/comment	Incorporation date	State
Allis-Chalmers Manufacturing Co.	Allis-Chalmers Company (p. 454)	1901	NJ
American Car & Foundry Co.	American Car & Foundry Co. (p. 455)	1899	NJ
American Radiator & Standard Sanitary Corporation	American Radiator Company (p. 456)	1899	NJ
American Smelting & Refining Co. (ASARCO)	American Smelting and Refining Company (and affiliated companies) (Greater Trust; p. 45)	1891	NJ
American Sugar Refining Co.	American Sugar Refining Company (and affiliated companies) (Greater Trust)	1891	NJ
American Tobacco Co.	Consolidated Tobacco Company (and affiliated companies) (Greater Trust; p. 69)	1901	NJ
American Woolen Co.	American Woolen Company (p. 457; p. 236)	1899	NJ
Anaconda Copper Mining Co.	Amalgamated Copper Company (Greater Trust)	1899	NJ
Armour and Co.	Armour, Swift, National Packing, Cudahy (and affiliated interests) (p. 457)	1868	NJ
Atlantic Refining Co.	Standard Oil Company (Standard Oil, Greater Trust)	1899	NJ
Bethlehem Steel Corporation (Delaware)	United States Shipbuilding Company (p. 344; part of ship-building trust)	1902	NJ
Borden Co.	Borden's Condensed Milk Company (p. 458)	1899	NJ
California Packing Corporation	California Fruit Canner's Association	1900	CA
Continental Oil Co.	Standard Oil Company (Conoco, Standard Oil)	1911	NJ
Corn Products Refining Co.	Corn Products Company (p. 459)	1902	NJ
Eastman Kodak Co.	Eastman Kodak Company (p. 460)	1901	NJ
General Electric Co.	General Electric Company (p. 460)	1892	NY
Pullman Inc.	Pullman Company (p. 464)	1897	IL
Pure Oil Co.	Pure Oil Company (p. 464)	1895	NJ
Union Carbide & Carbon Corporation	Union Carbide Company (p. 465)	1898	VA
Union Oil of California (UNOCAL)	Not in Moody. Independent oil company.	1890	CA
United Fruit Co.	United Fruit Company (p. 465)	1899	NJ
United States Steel Corporation	United States Steel Corporation (Greater Trust)	1901	NJ
United States Smelting, Refining & Mining Co.		1899	
Westinghouse Electric Manufacturing Co.	Westinghouse Companies (p. 466)	1899	IL

Sources: TNEC (1940, pp. 1502–4) and Moody (1907, pp. 453–78).

Table 11.7   TNEC industrial corporations without dominant ownership interest, and without clear trust origins

Name of company	Comment	Incorporation date	State
American Rolling Mill Co. (ARMCO)		1901	
B. F. Goodrich Co.		1870	
Continental Can Co. Inc.	Incorporated after horizontal merger wave	1913	
Goodyear Tire & Rubber Co.	Went into receivership in 1921, with creditors taking over control, forcing out founders and dispersing ownership	1898	OH
Kennecott Copper Corporation	Consolidation of Guggenheim and other interests	1914	
Mid-Continent Petroleum Corporation	No information found		
National Distillers Products Corporation	No information found		
Texas Corporation (Texaco)	Independent oil company	1902	
Wilson & Co. Inc.	Meat packing company		

Sources: TNEC (1940, pp. 1502–4) and Moody (1907, pp. 453–78); Allen (1949) for Goodyear.

Standard Oil Trust, which was broken up in 1911; the Anaconda Mining Company was a previously acquired subsidiary of the Amalgamated Copper Company; in 1901 Bethlehem Steel was part of the United States Shipbuilding Trust—although its rapid expansion came afterward. For ten companies no direct trust origin could be established. Nevertheless, it is striking that two-thirds of the manufacturing corporations without large blocks in the late 1930s had been part of Moody's finance-capitalist corps a generation earlier.

Why did trust formation lead to widely held ownership? Looking at the history of the twenty-four widely held manufacturing companies with trust origins, we identify three principal reasons.

1. The original dominant shareholders were bought out by trust promoters who sought to cash in and reduce leverage by floating the combination on the stock exchange. The most prominent example is U.S. Steel, with J. P. Morgan buying out Andrew Carnegie.

2. Trust promoters who kept dominant ownership positions in the trusts were forced to relinquish control by antitrust action. The outstanding example is the Standard Oil of New Jersey holding company, which was dissolved in 1911. Although the Rockefellers were given equal ownership blocks in the individual postbreakup companies, it was clear that further antitrust action would have resulted had they sought to influence or

Table 11.8   Moody's greater industrial trusts, as of 1 January 1904

Name of company	Incorporation date	State	Number of plants acquired or controlled	Total capitalization, stocks and bonds outstanding	Status 1939
Amalgamated Copper Co.	1899	NJ	11	175,000,000	Among 200 largest
American Smelting and Refining Co.	1899	NJ	121	201,550,400	Among 200 largest
American Sugar Refining Co.	1891	NJ	(about) 55	145,000,000	Among 200 largest
Consolidated Tobacco Co.	1901	NJ	(about) 150	502,915,700	Among 200 largest
International Mercantile Marine Co.	1902	NJ	6	170,786,000	Defunct
Standard Oil Co.	1899	NJ	(about) 400	97,500,000	Broken up
United States Steel Co.	1901	NJ	(about) 785	1,370,000,000	Among 200 largest

Sources: Moody (1907, p. 453); TNEC, and companies' histories.

coordinate the activities of these companies in a major way. Antitrust action against influential owners was also important in some other cases, in particular when families held blocks in related businesses. The classic example is a 23 percent block the Du Pont family acquired in General Motors via the E. I. du Pont de Nemours chemical company in 1917–19. Du Pont was forced to sell the block as a result of civil action brought by the government under the Clayton Act of 1914.[52]

3. The original owners and/or the trust promoters sold their ownership stakes but sought to keep control of the trusts by dominating the boards through family-affiliated directors. An outstanding example of the former is ASARCO, where the Guggenheims had carved out a near 50 percent ownership stake they sold after a few years, while retaining board control (at least for a while). A prime example of the latter is, again, U.S. Steel, where four J. P. Morgan partners came to sit on the board of the newly formed trust (Chernow 1990). This mechanism was also important in some of the widely held companies without clear trust origins, like B. F. Goodrich (David Goodrich was chairman), Wilson and Co. (Edward Foss Wilson was president and director; Thomas E. Wilson chairman of the board) and Kennecott Copper (three members of the Guggenheim family were members of the board).

In all of the thirty-four companies without dominant ownership, the separation of ownership and control emphasized by Means (1931) and Berle and Means (1932) was complete by the late 1930s.

Why did the original owners and the trust promoters sell their control blocks in the first place? One reason—stressed by Dewing (1919)—was that the American stock market gave them an opportunity to sell the stock for more than it was worth. "Physicians, teachers, dentists, and clergymen" constituted "the happy hunting ground" of the "sucker list," where people were persuaded to buy "highly speculative and worthless securities" by "devious and dubious" methods. A second reason was the very success of Morgan and his peers—George F. Baker, James Stillman, Frank Vanderlip, and company—not at swindling the investing public but at persuading the investing public, through a good track record, that they would not be swindled. As DeLong (1991) calculated, large industrial combinations promoted and organized by J. P. Morgan were by and large quite good investments. Giving founders peace of mind through special or preferred stock, merging competitors, maintaining a presence on the board of directors, and putting the weight of the Morgan name behind the newly diversified enterprise all raised the price that founding families could get for their con-

---

52. The 23 percent block was bought in 1917–19, the federal government took civil action under section 15 of the Clayton Act to enjoin violations of section 7 of that act in 1949, the case was initially dismissed by the district court but upheld by the Supreme Court in 1957, and the block was sold in 1961.

trol blocks. Moreover, this strategy appeared to involve no inevitable loss of control—or so it looked for a while, until the Morgan partners and the founders died or rotated off the board and were replaced by managerial picks.

Thus Vanderbilt and Carnegie were bought out by attractive offers for their shares they could not refuse; Havemeyer, Rockefeller, and Du Pont were forced out by government antitrust policy; the Guggenheims diversified while attempting to keep control of the board. And sooner or later many of them turned to philanthropy. The fact that America was not supposed to be a land of aristocracy, combined with Teddy Roosevelt's crack about "malefactors of great wealth," stung. So Rockefeller endowed the University of Chicago and Rockefeller University. Carnegie built 3,000 libraries, bought 4,100 church organs, and built Carnegie Hall, the Carnegie Institute, and the Peace Palace at the Hague. And he said, "He who dies rich dies disgraced." As the founding families turned their interests elsewhere, control slipped bit by bit into the hands of the managers.

The process continued, and families continued to fade, after World War II. Consider Coca-Cola. In 1919 the Woodruff family buys the company. In 1923 George Woodruff becomes CEO. In 1938 Woodruffs own 39 percent of the stock, directly and indirectly, chair the board, and have one additional director seat. Today? Berkshire-Hathaway and the SunTrust bank are the only 5 percent shareholders. No Woodruff sits on the board of directors.

11.5   Conclusion

Thus the story we have to tell turns out not to be a neat one. America is indeed exceptional. But the causes of its exceptionalism are not at all simple. Mark Roe is right: politics mattered a lot. Antitrust policy, the campaigns against the "money trust" and the "power trust," muckraking, and populism meant that to be concentrated was to be a target. Why not (a) avoid being a target and (b) pick up the benefits of diversification, even if the cost is some extra slack between the interests of owners and the actions of managers?

But other things mattered too, and probably mattered more. The turn of the American upper class of the Gilded Age to philanthropy, for example, was clearly important. And so—possibly—was the role played by inheritance taxes. The sophistication of American investment banking and the large size of the pool of potential stock owners appear to have made it possible for founding families to divest themselves of their control blocks without paying a substantial price penalty. How important were the legal shareholder protections emphasized by La Porta and company in creating this opportunity to sell out with only a small (or no) discount, and how important were other factors? We wish that we knew.

We do know that the ability of trust promoters and investment bankers to place large amounts of stock with ever wider circles of investors was an important driver of ownership dispersion. We also found anecdotal evidence that "frenzied finance," the belief that one can get rich quickly by investing in a bull market, contributed to this ability—just as it did during the Internet boom and the mergers and acquisitions wave of the late 1990s.

Also important was the fact that few if any among the founding families thought that they were giving up control to salaried managers. They believed that they would be able to maintain their dominance over the boards of what they still saw as their own companies indefinitely. Perhaps they expected the diversified shareholders to follow their lead and vote for them in board elections? The illusion that control could be maintained even without a controlling block proved a durable one, but it was an illusion. At the end of the 1920s even John D. Rockefeller himself found it an enormous struggle to fire the president of Standard Oil of Indiana.

The basic problems of corporate governance—how to make managers accountable to investors, protect small investors from large ones, provide managers with the right incentives, and manage conflicts of interest—are common, but there is "stunning international variety" in the solutions. Moreover, no one system seems durably and obviously superior, not even that of the United States, as is clear in the wake of the Enron scandal and the alleged rigging of corporate elections by Hewlett-Packard management.

The costs of changing corporate governance structures are high, the likelihood of gains uncertain, and claims of the U.S. system's macroeconomic advantages are as likely to last as did the claims two decades ago for the superiority of Japan's system. Political differences, organizational inertia, and the absence of clear, durable superiority in efficiency will preserve a wide divergence of models.

It is probably right to believe that diversity in corporate control will persist. But in one aspect—the number of shareholders per firm—some convergence among listed companies is likely. Firms with a broad shareholder base have an easier time tapping pension fund money via the New York and London markets. An aging population, particularly in Europe, and the consequent need to convert at least part of pay-as-you-go pension plans into capitalized ones have driven a trend toward a greater role for the stock market. Stock index providers are increasingly "punishing" companies with large block holders by limiting the weight in the index to the size and value of the "free float."

But even if firms with many shareholders become more prevalent, they need not all be governed alike. Such widely distributed ownership is compatible with dispersed voting rights and contestable board control, as in the United Kingdom. But it is just as compatible with uncontestable board control nominally exercised in the interest of shareholders—as in the

United States, with their poison pills and entrenched directors, or as with the Netherlands' priority shareholders, who possess the sole right to nominate directors for election to corporate boards.

In their ideal world, institutional investors and professors would probably root for convergence with the U.K. model—not the U.S. one. There are reasons to believe everybody will be disclosing on which side of the road they are driving under International Accounting and Disclosure Standards, but it is unlikely they will all end up driving on the left.

Appendix

Dual-Class Shares

Dual-class share capitalizations with differential voting rights are powerful instruments for securing voting control of corporations with relatively proportionally less and often little ownership. The most widely used arrangement involves the combination of voting and nonvoting shares, with voting ratios—the ratio of votes to the capital that must be invested to secure them—that depend on the relative amounts of shares issued.[53] Dual-class structures with voting ratios of 1:10 are common in Denmark (Neumann 2003), Norway (Bohren and Odegaard 2001), and Sweden (Högfeldt 2004; Agnblad et al. 2001).[54] In the Netherlands (and in the United Kingdom) it is possible to issue priority (or deferred) shares that have special rights vested in them—for example, the sole right to make binding nominations for board election. It is also possible to list voting trust certificates without voting rights (De Jong et al. 2001).

The United States today is not exceptional in its rules. The law of many states allows corporations to issue shares with no voting rights, limited voting rights, contingent voting rights, or multiple voting rights. In practice, U.S. corporations are more indulgent than their U.K. peers, but they show more restraint than corporate Canada. There were 100 dual-class firms in the United States with at least one class listed in 1994, rising steadily to 215

53. Under German law up to 50 percent of par value can be issued as nonvoting stock. In theory, owning all the voting stock gives 100 percent of the voting rights with 50 percent ownership of the total equity. Today the only German company that is known to attain the maximum 1:2 voting ratio using this arrangement is Porsche AG (Becht and Mayer 2001). In the United Kingdom there are no limits on the ratio of nonvoting to voting stock. Although such capitalizations are very rare today, and have been rare historically (Frank, Mayer, and Rossi 2004), in the case of DMGT plc a 4 percent ownership stake can secure 67 percent of the voting rights (Becht 2003).

54. In the Nordic countries today voting ratios are limited to 1:10 by law. Historically, voting ratios of 1:1000 or higher were used. In Sweden the equity base of Ericsson is a grandfathered survivor of this era.

in 2001. The most common voting ratio is 1:10, but in some cases it can be higher (Gompers, Ishii, and Metrick 2004, table 3).[55] Well-known examples of dual-class share companies include Berkshire Hathaway, Viacom, Comcast, the Ford Motor Company, Wrigley, and Hershey Foods, among others.

However, historically, the United States has been exceptional in the virtual absence of dual-class share capitalizations of *common stock* with differential voting rights. This absence has been attributed to the restrictions imposed by the New York Stock Exchange's listing rules, which discouraged deviations from "one-share-one-vote" and other practices that would violate what the New York Stock Exchange (NYSE) considered appropriate standards in "corporate democracy, responsibility, integrity and accountability to shareholders" (Seligman 1986, p. 689). Until 1985 the relevant section of the NYSE's listing manual clearly stated that "since 1926, The New York Stock Exchange has refused to list non-voting *common stock*" (NYSE 1983, 313.00[A]; cited in Seligman 1986, p. 690). The NYSE was also "of the view that any allocation of voting power under normal conditions to classes of stock other than common stock should be in reasonable relationship to the equity interests of such classes" (NYSE 1983, 313.00[D]). The NYSE also believed that preferred stockholders should have the right to appoint at least two directors when dividend payments were not met in six consecutive quarters (NYSE 1983, 313.00[E]).[56] More

55. The authors identify dual-class companies by combining data from three different databases: the Securities Data Company (SDC), the Center for Research in Security Prices (CRSP), and the Investor Responsibility Research Center (IRRC).

56. More generally the NYSE was critical of all devices that propel voting rights beyond ownership, refusing to list voting trust certificates, classes of shares with unusual voting provisions, and shares of companies that give out irrevocable proxies or have voting pool arrangements. It is not entirely clear when the additional provisions cited were put into the listings manual. For a detailed description of the NYSE's stance on this issue in 1983 see Seligman (1986, pp. 689–90). The AMEX and NASDAQ were not as choosy, and Seligman (1986) argues that this was the reason the NYSE abandoned its restrictive policy in 1985–86. The current provisions of section 313 of the listing rules read as follows:

(B) *Non-Voting Common Stock.* The Exchange's voting rights policy permits the listing of the voting common stock of a company which also has outstanding a non-voting common stock as well as the listing of non-voting common stock. However, certain safeguards must be provided to holders of a listed non-voting common stock:

(1) Any class of non-voting common stock that is listed on the Exchange must meet all original listing standards. The rights of the holders of the non-voting common stock should, except for voting rights, be substantially the same as those of the holders of the company's voting common stock.

(2) The requirement that listed companies publish at least once a year and submit to shareholders an annual report (Para. 203.01) applies equally to holders of voting common stock and to holders of listed non-voting common stock.

(3) In addition, although the holders of shares of listed non-voting common stock are not entitled to vote generally on matters submitted for shareholder action, holders of any listed non-voting common stock must receive all communications, including proxy material, sent generally to the holders of the voting securities of the listed company.

fundamentally, we would like to know why the NYSE took such a firm stance against families and promoters who sought to retain voting control by issuing common stock without voting rights. But before we turn to this question, we first explore how widely used nonvoting shares actually were before 1926.

The capital stock of U.S. corporations is traditionally divided into preferred stock and common stock.[57] Although there were not general rules, preferred stock generally had "a prior lien on assets, a prior lien on earnings and the right to cumulative dividends" (Dewing 1934, p. 137). Nonvoting preferred stock was issued with full voting rights, no voting rights, or contingent voting rights, only acquiring voting rights when certain conditions were met (or not), for example, if dividends were not paid.[58] Classified common stock only came into use from 1917 onward (Dewing 1934, p. 195). Class B was subordinated to Class A in receiving noncumulative dividends, if the management so decided, while Class B retained full voting control (Dewing 1934, pp. 196–97).[59] Empirically, the 200 largest U.S. corporations in 1937–39 (TNEC 1940) had issued 404 different types of stock: 208 common stock issues and 196 preferred stock issues. Among the preferred stock issued, 61 issues had contingent voting and only 21 were nonvoting.[60] Among common stock issues, we found only 8 nonvoting common stock issues, and only three times was it used to secure corporate control.[61] Both findings are consistent with the literature: "as in the case of the preferred stocks [there were] only relatively few industrial shares which were entirely non-voting" (Stevens 1926, p. 360). Why then was nonvoting *common stock* so controversial, and why did the older and more frequent nonvoting preferred not cause the same controversy? To answer this ques-

---

(C) *Preferred Stock, Minimum Voting Rights Required.* Preferred stock, voting as a class, should have the right to elect a minimum of two directors upon default of the equivalent of six quarterly dividends. The right to elect directors should accrue regardless of whether defaulted dividends occurred in consecutive periods.
(NYSE Listing Manual, 313.00 Voting Rights, last modified 10/01/1998)

57. Dewing (1934, p. 138) also discusses "guaranteed stock," which was issued by promoters in consolidations and claims that are similar to unsecured debt.

58. The rights of each stock were defined in the corporation's charter and bylaws, written on the stock certificate, and the variety of documented flavors is astonishing.

59. For Dewing (1934, p. 198), "from all angles [a class common stock] appears as a kind of weakened preferred stock; it is another attempt to lure the investor into accepting lessened security in the hope of a speculative profit."

60. Own calculations based on TNEC (1940, pp. 206–30). Stevens (1926) found sixteen issues of completely nonvoting preferred among 350 corporations. Dewing (1934) reports similar results for a cross section of 1,048 preference stock issues between 1925 and 1930.

61. In practice, nonvoting stock can be an important tool for securing family and/or incumbent control, but it is equally important to understand the rules of corporate elections. In this respect, U.S. corporate law provided for potential variety: voting could be by shares or class; with equal or unequal voting rights; with simple majority voting, supermajority voting, or cumulative voting (for directors); conditional or unconditional. Stevens (1938) showed that the general assessment is not changed by these considerations—nonvoting stock was not an important tool of corporate control.

tion a small excursion into the pre-1926 history of thinking behind the capital structure of U.S. corporations is required. Starting with the horizontal combinations we have stressed in earlier parts of this paper, capitalization, in particular "overcapitalization" ("stock watering") was a subject for leading corporate finance textbooks (Mead 1926; Dewing 1918, 1934), muckrakers (Lawson 1906), outraged professors (Ripley 1927), the financial press, politicians, and regulators.[62] Are securities issued against anything but the equivalent of the replacement value of tangible assets "water"? What securities can and should be issued against "goodwill"? When does goodwill become water? How much free cash-flow should investors put in the hands of the promoters and the management? How should one value intangible assets?

The issue is well illustrated by the F. W. Woolworth initial public offering highlighted in Graham and Dodd (1934).[63] The asset side of the company's balance sheet was divided in tangible assets and "goodwill." The latter was valued at $50,000,000. On the liabilities side there were 500,000 shares of common stock with a par value of $100 each offsetting the goodwill, and preferred stock offsetting the value of the tangible assets. The goodwill was written down to $1 by 1925, out of earnings and profits. The presence and degree of stock watering depended on the valuation of the tangible assets, the intangible assets, and which type of security was issued against which asset class.[64]

For traditionalists like Ripley, who had built a reputation as the leading scholar of railroad finance, some of the "modern" techniques of corporate finance were getting out of hand. The increased use of Class A common stock without voting rights was the peak of an unacceptable development. Investors were giving up all their control rights and creating a "birthright for pottage" (Ripley 1927, p. 78). In Ripley's, Mead's, Stevens's, and Dewing's view assets were claims on cash flow with (contingent) control rights. Without having knowledge of the insights of modern contract theory, they argued that claims on certain asset classes should be matched with certain (contingent) control rights for bond- and shareholders. Ripley's opposition to dual-class common share issues was motivated by his beliefs of what

62. The term "watered stock" referred "definitely and explicitly to the large issues of common stock brought into existence at the time of promotion against which existed no property value except 'goodwill'" (Dewing 1934, p. 84). An alternative definition stated that "stock watering may be defined as the issuance of full-paid stock in an amount exceeding the value of the assets against which the stock has been issued" (Dodd 1930).

63. The "stock watering" debate is rooted in more fundamental debate over par-value versus non-par-value stock: "This whole discussion of the significance of no-par stock rests on the presumption that the stockholder is interested primarily in the rights to earnings. And a corollary of this is that he is not interested in the original cost of the property which is creating the earnings. If this is so, then the term *watered stock* loses all its significance" (Dewing 1934, p. 84).

64. The market value of the common stock was $20,000,000 in 1911 and $354,182,000 in 1937, divided into 9,703,610 shares (TNEC 1940, p. 230).

a "sound" capitalization should look like. Under traditional railway finance, common stock was issued against goodwill, and its value was crucially dependent on the quality of management. Hence common stockholders demanded, and were given, voting rights. Depriving common stockholders of the right to appoint the board, and hence participate in the selection of management, at least in theory, was considered an outrage.

It was against this background that Ripley (1927) declared that the rise of Class A (nonvoting) common stock issues in 1924–25 would make these twelve months "go down in history—like the Year of the Plague, or the Year of the Big Wind—as the Year of the Split Common Stock and the Vanishing Stockholder." Ripley's view, forcefully expressed in an address to the Academy of Political Science (28 October 1925), caused a remarkable echo. It was published in the *Nation* and the *Atlantic Monthly* and amplified in the *New York Times*. The public and official mood was such that, with few exceptions, between 1926 and 1986 the NYSE did not list nonvoting common stock issues (Seligman 1986, pp. 695–97).

The nonvoting stock episode lends support to Roe's (1994) "fragmented finance" view. Ripley's (1927) main line of attack was directed again the investment banking houses that were the motors behind the undesirable developments in American corporate financed he condemned so forcefully in "Main Street and Wall Street." However, to be entirely sure about what motivated the NYSE's decision, more clinical research is required.[65]

References

Barca, Fabrizio, and Marco Becht, eds. 2001. The Control of Corporate Europe. *The control of corporate Europe.* Oxford: Oxford University Press.

Bebchuk, Lucian Arye. 2003. Symposium on corporate elections. Harvard Law and Economics Discussion Paper no. 448. November. http://ssrn.com/abstract =471640.

Bebchuk, Lucian Arye, and Jesse M. Fried. 2003. Executive compensation as an agency problem. *Journal of Economic Perspectives* 17:71–92.

Becht, Marco, Patrick Bolton, and Ailsa A. Röell. 2002. Corporate governance and control. ECGI Finance Working Paper no. 02/2002. European Corporate Governance Institute. http://ssrn.com/abstract=343461.

Berle, Adolf, and Gardiner Means. 1932. *The modern corporation and private property.* New York: Macmillan.

Black, Bernard S. 1998. Shareholder activism and corporate governance in the U.S. In *The New Palgrave Dictionary of Economics and the Law,* ed. Peter Newman. London: Macmillan.

Black, Bernard S., and John C. Coffee, Jr. 1994. Hail Britannia? Institutional investor behavior under limited regulation. *Michigan Law Review* 92:1997–2087.

65. This being said, Seligman (1986) does provide numerous references that firmly point in the direction of a populist backlash against bankers and "their" nonvoting shares.

Bonbright, J. C., and G. C. Means. 1932. *The holding company: Its public signifi-cance and its regulation.* New York: McGraw-Hill.

Bork, Robert. 1978. *The antitrust paradox.* New York: Free Press.

Brandeis, Louis. 1913. *Other people's money—and how the bankers use it.* New York: Stokes.

Burrough, Bryan, and John Helyar. 1990. *Barbarians at the gate: The fall of RJR-Nabisco.* New York: Harper Collins.

Carosso, Vincent. 1970. *Investment banking in America.* Cambridge, MA: Harvard University Press.

Carosso, Vincent P., and Rose C. Carosso. 1987. *The Morgans: Private international bankers, 1854–1913.* Cambridge, MA: Harvard University Press.

Carstensen, Fred. 1989. A dishonest man is at least prudent: George W. Perkins and the International Harvester Steel properties. Storrs, CT: University of Connecticut.

Chandler, Alfred. 1977. *The visible hand: The managerial revolution in American business.* Cambridge: Harvard University Press.

Chernow, Ronald. 1990. *The house of Morgan.* Boston: Atlantic Monthly Press.

Davis, Stephen. 2004. Culture shift shakes corporate America. *Financial Times,* March 14.

DeLong, J. Bradford. 1991. Did J. P. Morgan's men add value? A historical perspective on financial capitalism. In *Inside the business enterprise,* ed. Peter Temin. Chicago: University of Chicago Press.

Dewing, Arthur S. 1919. The financial policy of corporations. New York: Ronald Press.

Dodd, S. C. T. 1893. The present legal status of trusts. *Harvard Law Review* (November).

Donaldson, William H. 2003. Introductory remarks at the October 8 open meeting: Proxy access proposal. U.S. Securities and Exchange Commission. Washington, D.C., October 8.

Douglas, William O., and James Allen. 1940. *Democracy and finance: The addresses and public statements of William O. Douglas as member and chairman of the Securities and Exchange Commission.* New Haven, CT: Yale University Press.

Drucker, Peter. 1976. *The unseen revolution: How pension fund Socialism came to America.* New York: W. W. Norton.

Dunlavy, C. A. 1998. Corporate governance in late 19th century Europe and the U.S.: The case of shareholder voting rights. In *Comparative corporate governance: The state of the art and emerging research,* ed. K. J. Hopt, H. Kanda, M. J. Roe, E. Wymeersch, and S. Prigge. Oxford: Oxford University Press.

Galbraith, John Kenneth. 1967. *The new industrial state.* New York: Houghton Mifflin.

Garraty, John. 1960. *Right-hand man: The life of George W. Perkins.* New York: Harper and Brothers.

Gerschenkron, Alexander. 1962. *Economic backwardness in historical perspective.* Cambridge: Harvard University Press.

Gibb, George, and Evelyn Knowlton. 1976. *History of the Standard Oil Company.* New York: Harper.

Gillan, Stuart, and Laura Starks. 1998. A survey of shareholder activism: Motivation and empirical evidence. *Contemporary Finance Digest* 2:10–34.

Harbeson, Robert W. 1958. The Clayton Act: Sleeping giant of antitrust? *American Economic Review* 48 (1): 92–104.

Hawley, Ellis Wayne. 1966. *The New Deal and the problem of monopoly: A study in economic ambivalence.* Princeton, NJ: Princeton University Press.

Hofstadter, Richard. 1964. The paranoid style in American politics. *Harper's Magazine.*

Holderness, Clifford G., Randall S. Kroszner, and Dennis P. Sheehan. 1999. Were the good old days that good? Changes in managerial stock ownership since the Great Depression. *Journal of Finance* 54:435–69.

Holmstrom, Bengt, and Steven N. Kaplan. 2001. Corporate governance and merger activity in the United States: Making sense of the 1980s and 1990s. *Journal of Economic Perspectives* 15:121–44.

Hoyt, Edwin Palmer. 1967. *The Guggenheims and the American dream.* New York: Funk & Wagnalls.

Huertas, Thomas, and Harold Cleveland. 1987. *Citibank.* Cambridge, MA: Harvard University Press.

Karpoff, Jonathan M. 1998. The impact of shareholder activism on target companies: A survey of empirical findings. University of Washington School of Business.

Krugman, Paul. 1996. *The self-organizing economy.* Cambridge, MA: Blackwell.

La Porta, Rafael, Florencio López-de-Silanes, and Andrei Shleifer. 1999. Corporate ownership around the world. *Journal of Finance* 54 (2): 471–517.

Lamont, Thomas. 1913. *The Brandeis talk.* Thomas W. Lamont Papers, Box 84. Boston: Harvard Graduate School of Business.

Lawson, Thomas. 1905. *Frenzied finance: The crime of Amalgamated.* New York: Greenwood.

Leech, Dennis. 1987. Ownership concentration and control in large U.S. corporations in the 1930s: An analysis of the TNEC sample. *Journal of Industrial Economics* 35:333–42.

Means, Gardiner C. 1930. The diffusion of stock ownership in the U.S. *Quarterly Journal of Economics* 44:561–600.

———. 1931. The separation of ownership and control in American industry. *Quarterly Journal of Economics* 46:68–100.

Moeller, Sara B., Frederik Paul Schlingemann, and Rene M. Stulz. Wealth destruction on a massive scale? A study of acquiring-firm returns in the recent merger wave. *Journal of Finance,* Forthcoming http://ssrn.com/abstract=571064.

Moody, John. 1904. *The truth about the trusts.* New York: Moody.

Paine, Albert. 1921. *Theodore N. Vail: A biography.* New York: N.p.g.

Piketty, Thomas, and Emmanuel Saez. 2001. Income inequality in the United States, 1913–1998. University of California at Berkeley, Department of Economics.

Pound, Arthur, and Samuel Moore, eds. 1931. *More they told Barron.* New York: Harper and Brothers.

Pujo Committee. U.S. Congress. House. Committee on Banking and Currency. 1913a. *Minority Report of the Committee . . . to Investigate the Concentration of Control of Money and Credit.* Washington, DC: Government Printing Office.

———. 1913b. *Money Trust Investigation.* Washington, DC: Government Printing Office.

Redlich, Fritz. 1951. *The molding of American banking.* New York: Hafner.

Reed, William J. 2001. The Pareto, Zipf, and other power laws. *Economics Letters* 74:15–19.

Ripley, William Z. 1915. *The railroads: Finance and organization.* New York: Longmans Green.

Roe, Mark. 1994. *Strong managers, weak owners: The political roots of American corporate finance.* Princeton, NJ: Princeton University Press.

Romano. 2001. Less is more: Making institutional investor activism a valuable mechanism for corporate governance. *Yale Journal of Regulation* 175–250.

Seligman, Joel. 1982. *The transformation of Wall Street: A history of the SEC.* Boston: Houghton Mifflin.

Shleifer, Andrei, and Lawrence Summers. 1988. Breach of trust in hostile takeovers. In *Corporate takeovers,* ed. Alan Auerbach. Chicago: University of Chicago Press.

Shleifer, Andrei, and Robert Vishny. 1986. Large shareholders and corporate control. *Journal of Political Economy* 94 (2): 461–88.

———. 1997. A survey of corporate governance. *Journal of Finance* 52:737–80.

Smith, Edgar L. 1924. *Common stocks as long-term investments.* New York: Macmillan.

Smith, George, and Richard Sylla. 1993. The transformation of financial capitalism: An essay on the history of American capital markets.

Sloan, Alfred P. 1964. *My Years with General Motors.*

Sombart, Werner. 1904. *Why is there no Socialism in the United States?* New York: M. E. Sharpe.

Stevens, William, ed. 1913. *Industrial combinations and trusts.* New York: Macmillan.

Stoke, Harold W. 1930. Economic influences upon the corporation laws of New Jersey. *The Journal of Political Economy* 38 (5): 551–79.

Sylla, Richard. 1992. The progressive era and the political economy of big government. *Critical Review* 5.

Tarbell, I. M. 1904. *The history of the Standard Oil Company.* New York: McClure Phillips & Co.

Temporary National Economic Committee (TNEC). 1940. *The distribution of ownership in the 200 largest nonfinancial corporations.* Washington, DC: Government Printing Office.

Thorelli, H. B. 1955. The Federal antitrust policy: Origination of an American tradition. Baltimore, MD: Johns Hopkins Press.

Untermyer, Samuel. 1915. Speculation on the stock exchanges. *American Economic Review* 5 (1): 24–68.

Vanderlip, Frank, and Boyden Sparkes. 1935. *From farm-boy to financier.* New York: Appleton Century.

Warshow, H. T. 1924. The distribution of corporate ownership in the U.S. *Quarterly Journal of Economics* 39:15–38.

White, Eugene. 1982. The political economy of banking regulation. *Journal of Economic History* 42.

White, Eugene. 1989. *Regulation, taxes, and the financing of American business 1860–1960.* New Brunswick, NJ: Rutgers University.

Willis, Parker, and John Bogen. 1929. *Investment banking.* New York: Harper and Row.

Comment   Richard Sylla

Two recent essays place the history of the American business corporation in a comparative context. One is the chapter here, "Why Has There Been So Little Blockholding in America?" by Becht and DeLong. The other is a synopsis and two draft chapters of a forthcoming book by Colleen Dun-

Richard Sylla is Henry Kaufman Professor of the History of Financial Institutions and Markets, professor of economics at the Stern School of Business at New York University, and a research associate of the National Bureau of Economic Research.

lavy, *Shareholder Democracy: The Forgotten History* (Dunlavy 2004, forthcoming). Each essay argues that the United States developed patterns and practices of corporate governance that were exceptional rather than typical of the patterns and practices of other nations.

Becht and DeLong contend that around 1900 the United States was not exceptional—corporate control, they say, was "relatively 'normal'"—because families and large financial institutions held controlling blocks of stock in corporations, as in other industrialized economies, and could ride herd on corporate managers. During the next three to four decades, however, they argue that the United States became exceptional as wealthy families sold off their controlling blocks to numerous smaller investors and as large financial institutions retreated from, or were forced to retreat from, exercising monitoring and control functions over corporate management. Thus was born the "Berle-Means corporation" with its widely dispersed stockholdings giving rise to a separation of ownership from control, and leaving management firmly in control. Since this did not happen to nearly the same extent in other countries, where families and/or financial institutions continued to retain greater control over management, the United States became an exception to the usual pattern of corporate control.

Colleen Dunlavy, in contrast to Becht and DeLong, contends that around 1900 the United States was already exceptional in having "plutocratic" voting rights as the norm for corporate shareholders. By that she means that shareholder voting rights in U.S. corporations typically were one share, one vote, giving large shareholders much more say in corporate affairs than small shareholders. In other countries, such as Great Britain, France, and Germany, shareholder voting rights were more "democratic" in limiting the power of large shareholders, the block holders of Becht and DeLong, to control corporate affairs. Earlier in history, the voting rights of shareholders had been more democratic in the United States as well. But they took a "plutocratic turn" toward one share, one vote in the middle decades of the nineteenth century. Dunlavy explores several explanations for the U.S. plutocratic turn, tentatively settling on one holding that the competition for capital was more intense in the United States than in the leading European economies.[1] By adopting plutocratic voting rights for shareholders, American corporations could gain advantages in the competition for capital, and so they did.

---

1. Dunlavy's tentative explanation is plausible. The United States was growing more rapidly than the European countries, and unlike them it was importing both people and capital. The European states were exporting people and capital, often to the United States. These considerations, as well as higher interest rates and bond yields in the United States than in Europe, suggest that at the margin, competition for capital was greater in America. But all of these considerations likely applied before the plutocratic turn in shareholder voting. Why did the competition for capital in the United States become more intense in the middle decades? Was it from the demand side, perhaps related to the advent of railroads? Or was it possibly from the supply side, perhaps from a decline of capital inflow after the state debt defaults and repudiations of the early 1840s? Or both?

Was corporate governance in the United States around 1900 like that in
Europe, as Becht and DeLong say? Or was it not, as Dunlavy contends?
Differences in the two positions perhaps are not as great as they might
seem. Becht and DeLong look forward from 1900 into the twentieth century and explore the change from finance capitalism to managerial capitalism. Dunlavy in a sense looks backward from 1900, beginning her study
a century or so earlier and exploring the transition from "democratic"
shareholder capitalism to "plutocratic" shareholder capitalism in the
United States, and its persistence in Europe. She agrees with Becht and De-
Long that after 1900 managerial capitalism displaced shareholder capitalism in the United States. She also indicates that in the twentieth century
shareholder voting rights in Europe followed the American lead and became more plutocratic. This perhaps explains why Becht and DeLong do
not find it necessary to say much about cross-national differences in voting
rights, and why almost everyone now considers one share, one vote as normal or natural in corporate governance.

But one share, one vote was hardly the norm in the early history of corporations. Pure democracy in voting for directors and on other corporate
matters would imply one shareholder, one vote, regardless of whether the
shareholder held one or a thousand shares. That would seem odd by current norms, but it was not so odd two centuries ago. Then it seemed to be
the Anglo-American common-law presumption if no other voting rights
scheme was specified in a corporate charter. More often than not in
Britain, France, Germany, and the United States, some other voting rights
scheme was specified. And more often than not, it was not one share, one
vote. It was another scheme—somewhere between one shareholder, one
vote and one share, one vote—that limited the influence of large shareholders in corporate governance. Dunlavy calls such schemes "a prudent
mean," a term borrowed from Alexander Hamilton, who used it to describe
the shareholder voting scheme he proposed in 1790 for the Bank of the
United States, and which became a part of the bank's charter as drafted by
Hamilton and adopted by Congress in 1791.

Picking up on Dunlavy's lead, I looked into the origins of Hamilton's
idea of prudent-mean voting rights, his rationale for it, and its influence on
early U.S. corporate charters. These matters are of some historical importance. Although the United States did not invent the idea of the business
corporation, from the 1790s to the 1850s it developed the corporation as a
form of competitive enterprise to a far greater extent than did European
nations. U.S. federalism played a large role because corporate chartering
was almost entirely a function of U.S. state governments, of which there
were many, rather than centralized at the national level as in Europe.

The prudent-mean concept of shareholder voting rights appears to have
originated with Hamilton, although more study of previous and contemporary business charters would be necessary in order to determine whether

his formulation of it was a new idea or reflected customary practices. Before there were any U.S. banks and while he was still a colonel in the Continental Army, Hamilton in three letters to American leaders in 1779–81 had proposed a national bank to help finance the war effort. Two of those letters outlined bank charters but did not take up the matters of corporate governance such as shareholder voting rights. One of the letters was to Robert Morris in spring 1781, and Morris, Congress's newly appointed superintendent of finance, was simultaneously preparing his own proposal for the charter of the Bank of North America. The fifth article of Morris's plan proposed the voting scheme that we now regard as normal, namely "that every Holder of a share . . . may have as many Votes as he holds shares" (Morris 1973, pp. 68–69). Congress approved Morris's plan, and the Bank of North America, the first modern bank in the United States, opened for business at the start of 1782.

Two years later in New York, Hamilton—by then a lawyer—helped found the Bank of New York, wrote its constitution, and served as one its original thirteen directors. Article 5 of Hamilton's 1784 Constitution of the Bank of New York stated: "that every holder of one or more shares, to the number of four, shall have one vote for each share. A subscriber of six shares shall have five votes; eight shares, six votes; and ten shares, seven votes; and one vote for every five shares above ten" (Domett 1884, p. 12).[2] No rationale is given for this voting scheme, but since it differed from that of Morris's bank, with which Hamilton was familiar, and since the Bank of New York was the second—or third, the Bank of Massachusetts with the Morris scheme of one share, one vote appearing nearly simultaneously—the idea of limiting the voting rights of large shareholders in a banking corporation must have been Hamilton's. The Bank of New York commenced operating under Hamilton's constitution, and it applied to the state legislature for a charter of incorporation several times before one was finally granted in 1791. The 1791 charter retained Hamilton's voting scheme and "was substantially the model upon which all the bank charters granted in the State of New York were framed prior to 1825" (Domett 1884, p. 35).[3]

For the rationale of Hamilton's restriction on the power of large shareholders, we have to turn to his 1790 proposal, made as secretary of the treasury, for a Bank of the United States. In the *Report on a National Bank,* Hamilton gives a number of reasons why the Bank of North America that Congress in 1781 (and subsequently several states) had chartered would not do as a national bank. Among them is this:

> A further consideration in favour of a change, is the improper rule, by which the right of voting for Directors is regulated in the plan, upon which the Bank of North America was originally constituted, namely a

---

2. The entire constitution is on pp. 11–15 of Domett (1884).

3. The 1791 New York charter is contained in an appendix to Domett, pp. 127–34.

vote for each share, and the want of a rule in the last charter [granted by Pennsylvania]; unless the silence of it, on that point, may signify that every Stockholder is to have an equal and a single vote, which would be a rule in a different extreme not less erroneous. It is of importance that a rule should be established, on this head, as it is one of those things, which ought not to be left to discretion; and it is consequently, of equal importance, that the rule should be a proper one.

A vote for each share renders a combination, between a few principal Stockholders, to monopolise the power and benefits of the Bank too easy. An equal vote to each Stockholder, however great or small his interest in the institution, allows not that degree of weight to large stockholders, which it is reasonable they should have, and which perhaps their security and that of the bank require. A prudent mean is to be preferred. (Hamilton 1963, p. 328)

Later in the *Report,* when he outlines a constitution or charter for the Bank of the United States, Hamilton in article 11 makes his prudent mean idea more concrete:

The number of votes, to which each Stockholder shall be entitled, shall be according to the number of shares he shall hold in the proportions following, that is to say, for one share and no more than two shares one vote; for every two shares, above two and not exceeding ten, one vote; for every four shares above ten and not exceeding thirty, one vote; for every six shares above thirty and not exceeding sixty, one vote; for every eight shares above sixty and not exceeding one hundred, one vote; and for every ten shares above one hundred, one vote; but no person, copartnership, or body politic, shall be entitled to a greater number than thirty votes. (Hamilton 1963, p. 335)

It is interesting to speculate, in the manner of Becht and DeLong, on how many shareholders with such a voting scheme would be needed to constitute a majority block for control. The Bank of the United States was a large corporation, capitalized at $10 million in twenty-five thousand shares of $400 each, par value. The U.S. government subscribed for five thousand shares, leaving twenty thousand shares in the hands of private shareholders. At one extreme, if each of the private shareholders held one share, there would be twenty thousand private votes plus thirty votes for the federal government. A controlling block without the government would then be 10,016 individuals and shares.

At the other extreme, if all private shareholders held 200 shares, the number of shares that allowed the maximum of 30 votes, there would be 100 private shareholders and 3,030 votes counting the 30 votes of the government. A private controlling block would then be 51 private shareholders. This number is in the range that Becht and DeLong estimate as the number of large shareholders that it would have taken to control Standard Oil of New Jersey in the late 1920s, after its share ownership had undergone considerable deconcentration since the heyday of John D. Rockefeller. One might almost say that Alexander Hamilton, with or without realizing it, had invented the Berle-Means corporation fourteen decades before those authors rediscovered it. But that would not quite be correct, for Hamilton also wrote into the Bank of the United States charter that the secretary of the treasury on behalf of the federal government could require the bank to report to him on its condition as often as once a week. So the bank's management was rather continually monitored by its largest shareholder-regulator.

Colleen Dunlavy finds in Hamilton's statement that an equal vote to each stockholder "allows not that degree of weight to large stockholders, which it is reasonable they should have, and which perhaps their security and that of the bank require" the germ of her explanation of why the plutocratic turn toward one share, one vote came to the United States in the middle decades of the nineteenth century. As the competition for capital heated up, corporations wanting to survive and thrive had to give more weight and security to large shareholders. Before that happened, Hamilton's prudent-mean notion of shareholder voting rights was more democratic, less plutocratic. Since his charters were emulated widely, they became influential in early U.S. banking and corporate development.

I conclude that we need to know a lot more about the history of the corporation, a subject that seems curiously neglected given its importance in modern economic history. Becht and DeLong suggest that we might leave managerial capitalism behind and return to the "initial" conditions around 1900, when families and finance capitalists controlled corporations: "It is not clear that the next generation of the Gates family will have as little influence on American corporate control as the current generation of the Rockefeller family does. It is not clear that the large American financial institutions of the twenty-first century . . . will have as little influence on American corporate control as the firms of the mid-twentieth century did." But these are not the only alternatives to managerial capitalism. Taking a longer view of the history of the corporation, it seems evident that there were other, even earlier initial conditions that might also be considered as models for corporate control and governance. They extend back at least to the late eighteenth century, when the competitive business corporation first emerged in the United States, and to the early practices of other countries as well.

References

Domett, Henry W. 1884. *A history of the Bank of New York, 1784–1884.* 3rd ed. Cambridge, MA: Riverside Press.

Dunlavy, Colleen. 2004. The plutocratic turn in 19th-century shareholder voting rights: Why the U.S. but not Britain, France, or Germany? Paper presented at seminar at Harvard University Charles Warren Center for Studies in American History. 19 April, Cambridge, Massachusetts.

————. Forthcoming. *Shareholder democracy: The forgotten history.* Cambridge, MA: Harvard University Press.

Hamilton, Alexander. 1963. *The papers of Alexander Hamilton.* Vol. 7. Ed. Harold C. Syrett. New York: Columbia University Press.

Morris, Robert. 1973. *The papers of Robert Morris, 1781–1784.* Vol. 1. Ed. E. James Ferguson. Pittsburgh: University of Pittsburgh Press.

Contributors

Alexander Aganin
Cornerstone Research
1000 El Camino Real
Suite 250
Menlo Park, CA 94025-4327

Marco Becht
European Centre for Advanced
  Research in Economics and
  Statistics (ECARES)
Université Libre de Bruxelles
Avenue F.D. Roosevelt 50, CP114
1050 Brussels, Belgium

J. Bradford DeLong
Department of Economics
601 Evans Hall
University of California, Berkeley
Berkeley, CA 94720-3880

Alexander Dyck
Joseph L. Rotman School of
  Management
University of Toronto
105 St. George Street
Toronto, Ontario M5S 3E6 Canada

Barry Eichengreen
Department of Economics
University of California
549 Evans Hall 3880
Berkeley, CA 94720-3880

Caroline Fohlin
Department of Economics
Johns Hopkins University
3400 North Charles Street
Baltimore, MD 21218

Julian Franks
London Business School
Regent's Park
London NW1 4SA England

Sheldon Garon
History Department
Princeton University
Princeton, NJ 08544

William Goetzmann
School of Management
Yale University
Box 208200
New Haven, CT 06520-8200

Peter Högfeldt
Department of Finance
Stockholm School of Economics
Box 6501
SE-113 83 Stockholm, Sweden

Abe de Jong
Faculteit Bedrijfskunde, Dept Fin
    Mgmt
Erasmus University Rotterdam
Room F4-32, PO Box 1738
3000 DR Rotterdam, The Netherlands

Tarun Khanna
Harvard Business School
Morgan Hall 221
Soldier's Field Road
Boston, MA 02163

Elisabeth Köll
Department of History
Case Western Reserve University
10900 Euclid Avenue
Cleveland, Ohio 44106-7107

Colin Mayer
Saïd Business School
Oxford University
Park End Street
Oxford OX1 1HP England

Ashoka Mody
European Department
International Monetary Fund
700 19th Street, NW
Washington, DC 20431

Randall K. Morck
School of Business
University of Alberta
Edmonton, Alberta T6G 2R6 Canada

Antoin E. Murphy
Department of Economics
Trinity College
Dublin 2 Ireland

Masao Nakamura
Sauder School of Business
The University of British Columbia
2053 Main Mall
Vancouver, British Columbia V6T 1Z2
    Canada

Krishna G. Palepu
Harvard Business School
Soldiers Field Road
Boston, MA 02163

Michael Percy
School of Business
University of Alberta
Edmonton, Alberta T6G 2R6
    Canada

Dwight H. Perkins
Department of Economics
Harvard University
Littauer M-12
Cambridge, MA 02138

Daniel Raff
Department of Management
The Wharton School
University of Pennsylvania
Philadelphia, PA 19104-6370

Ailsa Röell
Bendheim Center for Finance
Princeton University
26 Prospect Avenue
Princeton, NJ 08540-5296

Stefano Rossi
London Business School
Regent's Park
London NW1 4SA England

Jordan Siegel
Harvard Business School
Morgan Hall 231
Soldiers Field Road
Boston, MA 02163

Lloyd Steier
School of Business
University of Alberta
Edmonton, Alberta T6G 2R6
    Canada

Richard Sylla
Stern School of Business, Economics
New York University
44 West 4th Street
New York, NY 10012-1126

Gloria Tian
School of Business
University of Alberta
Edmonton, Alberta T6G 2R6
    Canada

Paolo Volpin
Institute of Finance and Accounting
London Business School
Regent's Park
London NW1 4SA England

Daniel Wolfenzon
Leonard Stern School of Business
New York University
Kaufman Management Center
44 West 4th Street, KMC 9-87
New York, NY 10012

Bernard Yeung
Leonard Stern School of Business
New York University
Kaufman Management Center
44 West 4th Street, KMC 7-65
New York, NY 10012

Author Index

Acemoglu, Daron, 45, 46, 68, 71, 71n4, 83, 135, 136
Adams, Michael, 244n24, 246n29, 256n48
Agnblad, Jonas, 512, 564
Ahmadjian, C., 434n72
Alänge, Sverker, 564
Albach, Horst, 252
Aleotti, Aldo, 336
Allen, Franklin, 442
Almeida, Heitor, 362, 363, 568
Amatori, Franco, 332, 359
Amit, Raphael, 566
Amsden, Alice, 141, 142
Anderson, Malcom, 188
Aoki, Masahiko, 33n10, 52, 249n32, 434n72, 442, 442n85, 443, 443n88, 444n89
Armstrong, Christopher, 120, 120n34, 122n39
Arrow, Kenneth, 35
Asajima, Shoichi, 373n12
Asashima, Shoichi, 444n90
Audretsch, David, 269
Axelrod, Robert, 34

Bae, Kee-Hong, 33n9
Baia Curioni, Stefano, 334, 335
Barca, Fabrizio, 33n9, 325, 329n2, 330, 343, 359, 617
Barclay, Michael, 447
Baskerville, Peter, 70, 79n15, 101n27
Baumol, William J., 136

Baums, Theodor, 2n1, 244n24, 257, 264n69
Beale, Adolf, 435
Beason, Richard, 449
Bebchuk, Lucien, 4, 33n9, 343, 344, 551, 614n1, 617n17
Becht, Marco, 33n9, 49, 236, 236n13, 264n69, 265n70, 523n58, 582, 617, 618
Beck, Thorsten, 571n33
Benelli, Guiseppe, 264n69
Berkowitz, Daniel, 41n18, 48
Berle, Adolf, 4, 615n3, 633, 639, 639n42, 643, 650
Bertrand, Marianne, 33n9, 297, 550
Beyer, Jürgen, 245n27
Bhagwatti, Jagdish, 95, 297
Bhattacharya, Utpal, 340
Biais, Bruno, 53, 340
Bisson, T. A., 462
Black, Bernard S., 614n1
Blinder, Alan S., 443n88
Bliss, Michael, 68, 69, 70, 74n7, 79, 80, 101n27, 114, 115, 124
Bloch, Laurence, 188
Blondel, Christine, 189, 206, 236n13
Boehmer, Ekkehard, 236, 236n13, 246n29
Böhm, Jürgen, 252, 257, 258n55
Bokelmann, Bettina, 252
Bolton, Patrick, 49, 264n69, 265n70, 618
Bonin, Hubert, 203
Boorman, Howard L., 166n14
Boot, Arnoud, 442n85
Booth, J. R., 492

Boothman, Barry, 120n34
Bork, Robert, 623n11
Bos, J. W., 493
Boycko, Maxim, 53
Bradach, Jeffrey, 35n11
Braeutigam, Ronald, 54
Bragantini, Salvatore, 325
Brandeis, Louis, 632
Braun, Matias, 363
Bremer, Marc, 445
Brickwell, Daniel M., 232, 244, 246n29, 256n48
Brioschi, Francesco, 332, 359
Bris, Arturo, 121n38
Broeke, J. W. van, 492
Burkart, Mike, 31, 32, 68, 120, 136, 363, 510, 549, 550
Burrough, Bryan, 614n1
Burt, Ron S., 36
Buss, Georg, 260

Cable, John, 258n55, 269
Calomiris, Charles, 238n15
Cameron, Rondo, 198, 199, 200
Cameron, Steve, 123n40
Camfferman, Kees, 471
Cantillon, Richard, 201–2
Carlin, Wendy, 571n33
Carlson, Ellsworth, 155n2, 167
Carosso, Vincent, 630n26, 632
Carstensen, Fred, 632n32
Caves, Richard, 441–42, 443
Chan, Su, 446
Chan, Wellington K. K., 152n1, 157n4, 171n22
Chandler, Alfred D., 238n15, 359, 602, 619, 622n10
Cheffins, Brian, 38n15
Chen, Chih-Jou Jay, 177
Cheng, Linsum, 168
Chernow, Ronald, 616, 626n16, 626n17, 626n18, 627n20
Chirinko, Robert, 255n43
Choi, Chi-cheung, 152n1, 175
Chung, Stephanie, 172
Ciofi, Paolo, 359
Claessens, Stjin, 2, 4, 33n9
Clay, Karen, 41n18
Cleveland, Harold, 630n26
Coase, Ronald, 35n11
Coble, Parks, 164n11

Cochran, Sherman, 175n26
Coffee, John, 42, 614n1
Coleman, James S., 35n11
Colli, Andrea, 359
Colojanni, Napoleone, 359
Commons, John R., 54
Cronqvist, Henrik, 566

Däbritz, Walther, 243
Daniels, Ron, 33n9
Daouk, Hazeem, 340
Das, Gurcharan, 31, 296, 297, 301
Davidsson, Per, 569
Davies, Paul, 585
Davis, James H., 35
Day, Richard H., 56
De Jong, Abe, 473, 474, 481, 491, 646n51
Deli, D. N., 492
Delmar, Fredric, 569
DeLong, J. Bradford, 625n14, 626n15, 630n26, 632n32
De Long, Thomas, 309n10, 315, 423n58
De Luca, Giuseppe, 334, 337, 359
Demsetz, Harold, 115
Desai, A., 322
Dewenter, Kathryn, 53
Diamond, Jared, 43, 44n25
Director's Liability Act (1890) (United Kingdom), 25
Dittmar, Amy, 327
Djankov, Simeon, 2, 4, 33n9
Dodd, S. C. T., 622n9
Domett, Henry W., 663, 663n2, 663n3
Dower, John, 423n57
Du, Xuncheng, 160
Dunlavy, Collen, 27, 48, 260n62, 661, 661n1, 665
Du Tot, Nicolas, 194
Dyck, Alexander, 269, 327, 447, 550
Dyer, Jeffrey H., 36

Easterly, William, 71, 71n4, 83, 130
Eastman, Lloyd E., 153
Eccles, Robert, 35n11
Edwards, Jeremy, 258, 269
Elsas, Donald, 492
Elston, Julie Ann, 255n43, 269
Emmerich, Markus, 263n66, 264n67
Engberg, Holger L., 252n36
Engerman, Stanley, 71, 71n4, 83, 136
Enriques, Luca, 41, 43, 334n8, 338, 340

Ericson, Steven, 447–48
Erixon, Lennart, 521n2, 563

Faccio, Mara, 33n9, 54, 235n9, 235n10,
    236n13, 237
Falkenhausen, Bernhard Freiherr von,
    265n73, 266n74, 266n76, 266n77
Faure, David, 155, 156, 160n9, 161, 175
Feldenkirchen, Wilfred, 238, 238n17
Fennema, M., 497
Ferguson, Niall, 285
Ferris, S. P., 492
Feuerwerker, Albert, 153, 154, 155, 155n2,
    158, 158n6, 167
Fey, Gerrit, 263n66
Field, Laura C., 511
Fisman, Raymond, 449
Flandreau, Marc, 198
Fletcher, William Miles, III, 419n49, 463
Fohlin, Caroline, 239n19, 240n20, 247,
    247n30, 250n33, 251n35, 255, 255n45,
    259n60, 269n81
Francis, Dianne, 68, 101n27, 123n40
Franks, Julian, 244, 269, 585n1, 588, 593,
    595, 597
Fraser, Donald, 442n85
Fraune, Christian, 244n24, 257
Frentrop, Paul, 28, 42, 43, 46, 49, 470n3
Frick, B., 264n69
Fritz, Sven, 556
Fruin, W. Mark, 445
Fukuyama, Francis, 35, 35n11

Gadgil, D. R., 287, 322, 323
Gailbraith, Kenneth, 615
Gale, Douglas, 442
Gales, B. P. A., 479
Gao, Zhiyu, 170
Gardella, Robert, 162n10
Gärlund, Torsten, 523
Garon, Sheldon, 461, 463, 463n1
Gerlach, Michael L., 434n72
Gerschnkron, Alexander, 238, 238n16
Gessler, Ernst, 266n78
Ghemawat, Pankaj, 16, 33n9, 53, 294
Ghon Rhee, S., 442n85
Gibb, George, 634n33
Gillian, Stuart, 614n1
Glaeser, Edward, 40n16, 40n17
Globerman, Steven, 134, 135
Goetzmann, William N., 157n3

Goldstein, Andrea, 330
Gömmel, Rainer, 229, 259
Goor, Linda van, 477
Gorton, Gary, 237, 269
Goto, Akira, 443
Gottschalk, Arno, 257, 257n49
Granovetter, Mark, 33n9, 34
Granstrand, Ove, 564
Greif, Avner, 143, 301
Grifone, Pietro, 359
Grunberger, Richard, 464
Guerin, Daniel, 21
Gueslin, André, 200, 203

Haas, Wolfgang, 245
Haber, Stephen, 33, 44, 45, 85n22, 446
Hadley, Eleanor, 426
Hamada, Koichi, 439n79
Hamilton, Gary G., 176, 176n27
Hamilton, William, 34
Hanazaki, Masuharu, 440, 441, 442, 445
Hannah, Leslie, 583, 587, 593, 602, 609
Hayashi, Fumio, 444n91
Hayek, Friedrich, 40n16, 41n19
Hazari, R. K., 287, 297
Ilc, Kathy, 435n73, 520, 562, 562n26,
    562n27
Healy, Paul M., 186n1
Hedley, James, 68
Heeks, Richard, 304
Heemskerk, E., 493
Heijden, E. J. J. van der, 472
Heiner, Ronald A., 56
Helleiner, E., 547
Hellman, Thomas, 442, 442n85
Helyar, John, 614n1
Henning, Friedrich-Wilhelm, 259
Henrekson, Magnus, 521n2, 547n15, 564
Henry, Peter Blair, 95
Hermansson, Carl-Henrik, 530
Hertz, Ellen, 168n16
Hikino, Takashi, 359
Hilferding, Rudolph, 238n17
Hirschmeier, Johannes, 157n4, 370
Hoffman, Philip T., 195, 196
Hofstadter, Richard, 631n28
Högfeldt, Peter, 511, 512, 521, 521n2,
    521n3, 549, 550, 551, 554, 555, 557,
    558n23, 559, 560, 562, 563, 564, 565,
    566, 567, 568, 569
Holderness, Clifford, 447, 643n49

Holmén, Martin, 511, 512, 521, 521n2, 549, 550, 551, 554, 555, 557, 558n23, 559, 560, 562, 563, 564, 565, 566, 567, 568n32, 569
Holmstrom, Bengt, 617n7
Hopt, Klaus J., 252, 260, 266n75, 267n79, 585
Horiuchi, Akiyoshi, 422n55, 440, 441, 442, 445, 450n94
Hoshi, Takeo, 33n10, 429, 439n78, 439n79, 442n84, 444, 444n90
Hosking, Geoffrey, 21
Hoyt, Edwin Palmer, 617, 633
Huertas, Thomas, 630n26
Hüffer, Wilhelm, 266n74

Iber, Bernhard, 234n7, 236n13, 237, 269
Ito, Masanao, 409n41

Jagannathan, M., 492
Jakobsson, Ulf, 521n2, 547n15, 564
James, Harold, 229
Jeidels, Otto, 237–38
Jenkinson, Tim, 246n29
Jensen, Michael, 115, 168, 443
Johnson, Chalmers, 463, 464, 464n2
Johnson, Simon, 45, 46, 68, 71, 71n4, 83, 135, 136, 449
Johnson, W. Bruce, 447
Joly, Hervé, 235, 235n11
Jones, Geoffrey, 316, 317
Jonker, Joost, 469, 474, 475, 476
Jörberg, Lennart, 523

Kahneman, Daniel, 54
Kang, Jun-Koo, 33n9
Kao, Cheng-shu, 176n27
Kaplan, Steven, 52, 444n89, 617n7
Karpoff, Jonathan M., 511, 614n1
Kaserer, Christoph, 244n24
Kashyap, Anil, 33n10, 439n78, 439n79, 442n84, 444, 444n90
Kato, T., 413
Kennedy, Robert E., 309n10, 313n14
Kennedy, William P., 238n16
Kensinger, John, 446
Khanna, Tarun, 2, 16, 33n9, 34, 35, 36, 45, 51, 53, 66, 68, 135, 141, 142, 283, 286n1, 287n2, 287n3, 294, 297, 298, 300, 313, 315, 316, 317, 318, 445
Khemani, R. S., 101n27
Killick, John R., 587

Kim, Jin-Mo, 33n9
Kindleberger, Charles, 28n5, 198, 204
King, Robert G., 50, 72, 92
Kirby, William, 170
Kleeberg, John, 50, 52
Klein, Sabine, 236, 236n13
Kless, Heinz-Peter, 252
Knowlton, Evelyn, 634n33
Kocka, Jürgen, 238n17
Koelewijn, Jaap, 477
Kojima, Kenji, 434n72
Köke, Jens, 233, 236n13, 244n24, 246n29, 265, 269
Köll, Elisabeth, 165n12, 168, 170, 174n25, 175
Komiya, Ryutaro, 448
Kraakman, Reinier, 4, 33n9, 344, 551
Kremp, Elizabeth, 188
Kroszner, R. S., 492, 643n49
Krueger, Anne, 53, 136
Krugman, Paul, 145, 634n34
Kübler, Friedrich, 265n72, 266
Kuemmerle, Walter, 309n10
Kunze, W., 238n17
Kuran, Timur, 54
Kwan, Man Bun, 152

Lafaurie, Jean, 198
Lai, Chi-kong, 155n2, 158, 158n6
Lamb, Helen B., 301
Lamont, Thomas, 631n29, 631n30
Lamoreaux, Naomi, 57n32
Landes, David S., 13, 36, 124, 582, 608n2
Lang, Larry H. P., 2, 4, 33n9, 235n9, 235n10, 236n13, 237, 443n88
La Porta, Rafael, 2, 2n1, 6, 24, 28, 31, 32, 35n11, 37, 37n12, 38, 41n19, 43, 43n24, 72, 84, 85, 120, 135, 141, 185, 187, 278, 308n9, 325, 327, 333n7, 338, 340, 343, 362, 520, 550, 610n5, 617, 617n7
Larsson, Mats, 527
Laux, Frank, 259n58
Lavington, F. E., 238n16
Lee, En-han, 160–61
Leff, N., 298
Lehmann, Erik, 236n13
Lehn, Kenneth, 115
Leuz, Christian, 268, 327
Levine, Ross, 50, 71, 71n4, 72, 83, 92, 130, 571n33
Lévy-Leboyer, Maurice, 189, 198, 202, 238n17

Liefmann, Robert, 260
Lin, Nan, 177–78
Lincoln, J., 434n72
Lindbeck, Assar, 564
Ljungqvist, Alexander, 246n29
Loayza, N., 571n33
Loderer, Claudio, 264n69
López-de-Silanes, Florencio, 37n12, 43, 84,
    120, 135, 185, 187, 327, 520, 617, 617n7
Lys, Thomas, 264n69

Macaulay, Stewart, 35
Macrosty, H. W., 609
Maddisson, A., 278, 523
Mahoney, Paul, 41n19
Mahrt-Smith, Jan, 327
Malatesta, Paul, 53
Marchildon, Gregory, 69
Martin, John, 446
März, E., 238n17
Maule, Christopher J., 69, 101n27
Mauro, Paulo, 89
May, Wilfred, 594
Mayer, Colin, 238n16, 244, 269, 571n33,
    582, 585n1, 588, 593, 595, 597
Mayer, Roger C., 35
McElderry, Andrea, 155, 157n3, 168n19
McMillan, Charles, 370
Means, Gardiner, 4, 435, 615, 615n3, 616,
    616n4, 633, 639, 639n42, 639n43, 643,
    644, 650
Meckling, William, 115, 443
Mehta, Paras, 33n9, 297, 550
Meier, Johann Christian, 260
Menke, Joachim, 263n65
Merryman, John, 40
Metzger, Thomas A., 157n5
Michie, William A., 587
Milgram, Stanley, 54
Minton, Bernadette, 444n89
Mishima, Y., 391n26, 392n28
Mitton, Todd, 449
Miwa, Yoshiro, 434
Miyajima, Hideaki, 425, 431n64, 432n66,
    440n83, 444, 447
Mochizuki, Mike, 461
Mody, A., 321
Moeller, Sara B., 617n7
Moerland, P. W., 491
Mokken, R., 497
Mokyr, Joel, 43
Moody, John, 25, 622, 622n12, 623n12

Moore, Samuel, 631n27
Morck, Randall K., 4, 33, 33n9, 34, 37n13,
    45, 52, 53n29, 66, 68, 124, 132, 136,
    141, 308n9, 363, 423n58, 432n67, 434,
    434n70, 435n73, 440, 442n84, 443,
    443n88, 444, 444n89, 447, 448n93, 449,
    451, 520, 521n2, 555, 562, 562n26,
    562n27, 568n32
Morikawa, Hidemasa, 385, 421n52, 444,
    451
Morris, Robert, 663
Mosca, Gaetano, 143
Mullainathan, Senhil, 33n9, 297, 550
Murdock, Kevin, 442, 442n85
Murphy, Antoin E., 191
Murphy, Kevin, 85, 89, 136, 452
Myers, Gustavus, 68–69, 70, 75n8, 77n11,
    77n12, 79, 81n19, 82n21

Nakamura, Masao, 34, 52, 370, 434, 440,
    442n84, 443, 444, 444n89, 451
Nakatani, Iwao, 33n10
Nakazato, Minoru, 41
Nanda, Dhananjay, 268, 309n10, 315, 327,
    443
Naylor, R. Thomas, 69, 70, 82, 92, 101n27
Nederveen Meerkerk, Elise van, 479
Nenova, Tatiana, 327
Newman, Peter, 108n29, 109–10
Nibler, Marcus, 258, 269
Nijman, T., 491
Nilsson, Mattias, 566
Noguchi, Yukio, 425, 460
Nussbaum, Arthur, 260n61

Oborenko, Andris, 521n3, 554, 557, 558n23
Ocko, Jonathan K., 162n10
Odaka, Konosuke, 370
Ogura, S., 414n47
Oi, Jean C., 177n28
Okazaki, Tetsuji, 369n3, 413, 414n46, 420,
    422, 439, 444n90, 463
Okimoto, Daniel, 448, 449
Okumura, H., 438, 439
Okuno, Masahiro, 448
Okuno-Fujiwara, Masahiro, 439
Olson, Mancur, 33, 44n26, 45, 46, 54
Östlind, Anders, 524, 556
Owen, Bruce M., 54

Pagano, Marco, 51, 53, 337, 338, 340, 518,
    521n2, 548, 548n17, 571n33

Palepu, G. Krishna, 141, 142, 186n1, 283,
    287n3, 297, 298, 300, 313, 315, 316,
    317, 445
Palepu, Krishna, 16, 33n9, 34, 35, 36, 45,
    51, 66, 68, 135
Panetta, Fabio, 51, 337, 338
Panunzi, Fausto, 31, 32, 68, 120, 136, 363,
    510, 549, 550
Papenheim-Tockhorn, Heike, 252
Pareto, Vilfredo, 143
Parkman, Francis, 69, 123n41
Patrick, Hugh, 418n48
Peet, Jan, 479
Perlitz, Manfred, 258n55
Perotti, Enrico, 53, 340
Persson, Torsten, 518n1
Pettway, Richard, 445
Pfannschmidt, Arno, 252
Pfeiffer, Eric, 315
Piketty, Thomas, 634n34
Piramal, Gita, 295, 296, 297, 300, 301
Pistor, Katharina, 40n17, 48
Pohl, Hans, 227, 229, 238n17
Pollard, Sidney, 203, 238n16
Porter, John, 85, 107
Porter, Michael, 434
Portes, Alejandro, 34, 36
Postel-Vinay, Gilles, 195, 196
Pound, Arthur, 631n27
Powell, Walter W., 35n11
Pritchard, A. C., 492
Pross, Helge, 227, 228, 229, 234, 262,
    264n67
Putnam, Robert, 35n11, 36

Raddatz, Claudio, 363
Rajan, Raghuram, 33, 38, 49, 50, 53, 71n4,
    111, 133, 136, 203, 340, 341, 363, 377,
    441, 449, 518, 521n2, 547, 550, 587,
    610
Ramamurti, Ravi, 315
Ramseyer, J. Mark, 41, 434
Rawski, Thomas G., 168
Redlich, Fritz, 630n26
Reischauer, Edwin O., 421
Reiter, J., 547
Renooij, Dirk Cornelis, 475, 478n8
Reynolds, Lloyd, 116
Richard, Jean-Francois, 48
Riesser, Jakob, 238n15, 239
Ripley, William Z., 630
Rivkin, Jan, 2, 287n2
Roberts, Richard, 584, 601, 602

Robinson, James A., 45, 46, 68, 71, 71n4,
    83, 135, 136
Roe, Mark, 117, 120, 136, 264n68, 265, 517,
    520, 521n2, 551–53, 565, 618–19, 620,
    631, 633, 637, 637n38, 638
Röell, Alisa A., 49, 264n69, 265n70, 618,
    646n51
Rosenthal, Jean-Laurent, 57n32, 195, 196
Ross, Stephen A., 567
Rossi, Stefano, 327, 588, 593

Saez, Emmanuel, 634n34
Safarian, A. E., 133
Sahlmn, William A., 35n11
Samuels, Richard J., 461
Santucci, Tanja, 244n25
Savoie, Donald, 66, 123n40
Scalfari, Eugenio, 359
Scharfstein, David, 33n10, 442n85, 444,
    444n90
Schijf, Huibert, 492
Schlingemann, Frederik Paul, 617n7
Schmid, Frank A., 237, 269
Schoorman, F. David, 35
Schreyögg, Georg, 252
Schulz, W., 260
Schumpter, Joseph A., 32–33, 50, 238n15,
    238n16
Seger, Frank, 258n55
Seligman, Joel, 640n45
Servaes, Henry, 327
Shangwu, Yinshuguan Bianyisuo, 163, 167,
    170
Shapiro, D. M., 101n27
Sheard, Paul, 432n66, 434n71, 442n85
Sheehan, Brett, 168, 643n49
Shimizu, Katsutoshi, 450n94
Shin, Guen Hwan, 442n85
Shiomi, Saburo, 421
Shivdasani, Anil, 451
Shleifer, Andrei, 31, 32, 37, 37n12, 40n16,
    40n17, 43, 49, 50, 53, 54, 68, 84, 85, 89,
    120, 135, 136, 185, 187, 308n9, 327,
    338, 343, 346, 362, 363, 432n68,
    434n70, 443n88, 447, 452, 510, 520,
    549, 550, 617, 617n7
Siciliano, 335
Siegel, Jordan, 143
Siegrist, Hans, 227, 227n3, 228
Silverman, Dan, 21
Singh, Harbir, 36
Sjögren, Hans, 527
Sluyterman, Keetie E., 480

Smith, Edgar L., 620
Smith, George David, 25, 37, 38n15, 43, 611
Smith, Thomas C., 157n4
Sokoloff, Kenneth, 71n4, 83, 136
Sparkes, Boyden, 630n26, 632n31
Stanbury, W. T., 101n27
Stangeland, David A., 4, 33n9, 52, 132, 443, 449, 520, 562–63
Starks, Laura, 614n1
Steier, Lloyd, 35n11
Stevens, William, 627n19, 629n22, 630n25
Stigler, George, 450
Stiglitz, Joseph, 442, 442n85
Stinchcombe, Arthur L., 35n11
Stoke, Harold W., 629
Stokman, Frans N., 492
Strachan, H., 298
Strahan, P. E., 492
Stulz, René, 44, 443n88
Stulz, Rene M., 617n7
Sundin, Anneli, 511
Sundqvist, Sven-Ivan, 511
Suzumura, Kotaro, 448
Svejnar, Jan, 264n69
Swamy, Subramanian, 285
Swatsky, John, 123n40, 128
Sylla, Richard, 25, 37, 38n15, 43, 611

Tabellini, Guido, 518n1
Takahashi, Kamekichi, 419–20
Takahashi, P., 434n72
Tamaki, Hajime, 418n48, 425n60, 427n62, 436n74, 436n75
Tarbell, Ida, 623, 623n11
Taylor, Graham, 70, 101n27
Teranishi, Juro, 370, 414, 440
Thakor, Anjan, 442n85
Thakurdas, P., 323
Thorelli, H. B., 629
Thurow, Lester C., 33
Tilly, Richard, 238n15, 238n17
Timothy, Hamilton, 82n20
Trento, Sandro, 329n2, 330
Treue, Wilhelm, 227, 229
Triantis, George, 4, 33n9, 344, 551
Tulchinsky, Gerald, 69
Turani, Giuseppe, 359
Turgot, Anne Robert Jacques, 204
Tversky, Amos, 54

Uekusa, Masu, 441–42
Ukhov, Audrey, 157n3
Ushiba, Takuzo, 447

Van der Heyden, Ludo, 189, 206
Vanderlip, Frank, 630n26, 632n31
Vargas, Ingrid, 317
Villalonga, Belen, 566
Vishny, Robert, 49, 53, 85, 89, 136, 308n9, 432n68, 434n70, 443n88, 447, 452
Volpin, Paolo, 53, 327, 340, 518, 521n2, 548, 548n17, 571n33
Voogd, R. P., 485n12, 486n14, 487

Walder, Andrew G., 177n28
Wallich, Paul, 238n15
Wasseur, Frans W., 492
Watson, Alan, 40n17
Weber, Max, 44, 72
Wehler, Hans Ulrich, 227n3
Weigand, Jürgen, 236n13, 269
Weinstein, David, 444, 449
Weiss, Gunther, 41n19
Welhöner, Volker, 238n18
Wengenroth, Ulrich, 238n18
Wenger, Ekkehard, 244n24
Wessel, Horst A., 238n18
Whale, P. Barret, 238n15, 258n56
White, Eugene, 198, 637n36
Wiener, Fritz A., 260
Wigforss, Ernst, 539, 540
Wiklund, Johan, 569
Wilhelmini, Hans, 265n71
Williams, E. T., 163
Williamson, Oliver, 35n11
Williamson, Rohan, 44
Winkleman, Hélène J. M., 480
Wójcik, Dariusz, 245
Wolfenzon, Daniel, 33, 37, 45, 50, 53n29, 308n9, 338, 343–44, 346, 362, 363, 365, 568
Wright, Mary Clabaugh, 153, 154
Wu, Melito, 300
Wurgler, Jeffrey, 277, 327
Wysocki, Peter D., 268, 327

Yafeh, Yishay, 370, 423n56, 425, 429, 431n64, 434n70, 442n86, 443, 443n87, 444
Yasuoka, Shigeaki, 373n11, 382n27
Yeung, Bernard, 4, 33, 45, 52, 53n29, 66, 68, 124, 132, 136, 141, 363, 435n73, 443, 447, 448n93, 449, 520, 562, 562n26, 562n27
Yokoyama, Kazuki, 413
Young, Leslie, 33n9
Yui, Tsunehiko, 370

Zanden, Jan L. van, 475
Zelin, Madeline, 152, 162n10
Zhang, Guodhui, 158
Zhongguo, Di'er Lishi Dang'anguan, 170
Zhu, Ning, 157n3
Zhu, Ying, 163

Zhu, Yingui, 157n3
Ziegler, Dieter, 228, 229, 238n16
Zingales, Luigi, 33, 38, 49, 50, 51, 53, 71n4,
    111, 133, 136, 203, 269, 325, 327, 337,
    338, 340, 341, 363, 377, 447, 449, 518,
    521n2, 547, 550, 587, 610

Subject Index

Acquisitions. *See* Mergers and acquisitions
Adaptation process, in China, 153
Agnelli family, 39, 335
Aikawa, Yoshisuike, 394–97, 447
Air Canada, 125, 128
Aitkin, Max (Lord Beaverbrook), 93, 97–98, 101, 119
Allan, Hugh, 79, 88, 92
Allan Line, 79, 79n14
Ambani group (India), 301
Amsterdam stock exchange, 474–75
Andrews, Sam, 626
Anti-Combines Act (1989) (Canada), 117
Anti-Combines Law (1889) (Canada), 115–16
Anti-Monopoly Law (1947) (Japan), 431
Apex firms, 377
Argentina, corporations in, 2
Argus Group, 106–7
Assignants, 12, 39, 187, 197–200
Auto Pact, 134

Bank capitalism, 6
Bank groups, 34
Banking system: competition in Canadian, 115–16; development of, in Canada, 111–13; establishment of Canadian, 78–79; evolution of, in France, 191–95; Great Depression and, in Italy, 328
Bank of England, 198
Banks: ill-trusted stock markets and, 51; as monitors, 52; role of, capital allocation

and, 6; role of German, in corporate ownership, 237–46; *zaibatsu*, 439–42
Banque de France, 198, 199
Bennet, R. B., 116, 118–19, 124
Billes, John and Alfred, 105
Birla family (India), 15–16, 17, 297, 301
Black, Conrad, 108
Black, George, 106–7
Block holders, 618, 619
Bombardier, Armand, 105
Brandeis, Louis, 30
Britain. *See* United Kingdom
British East India Company, 12, 28
Bronfman family, 108, 110
Bubble Act (1722), 11, 28, 201
Buchanan, Isaac, 80
Buchanan, Peter, 80
Business groups, 57; corporate governance and, 33–35; postwar, in Japan, 369; trust and, 36–37
Business planning, 55

Cadbury Brothers, case study of, 600–601
Caisse de Dépôt et Placement du Québec, 126, 130
Canada: agriculture in, 91; British control of, 76–78; canal building in, 80; colonial, 67; colonial mercantilist heritage of, 123–30; competition policy in, 115–17; corporate governance in, 120–21; corporate groups in, 66–67; corruption and big push in, 89–92; corruption in,

Canada (*continued*)
81–82, 84; data sources for corporate ownership in, 68–70; development of financial systems in, 92–95, 111–13; economic growth in, 86f; establishment of banking system in, 78–79; establishment of Province of, 80–81; establishment of steamship lines in, 79; ethnic divisions in, 130–31; on eve of industrialization, 83–85; evolution of corporate ownership in, 98–111; factors contributing to large widely held freestanding firms in, 67–68; as French colony, 72–75; fur trade in, 73, 78, 83; Great Depression and, 104–5; hierarchy in, 84–85; immigration boom of, 85; industrialization in, 85–98; influence of Great Depression in, 31; information industries in, 91–92; initial corporate ownership structures in, 97–98; institutional change in, 47; insurance companies in, 89; labor rights in, 117–20; land reform in, 82–83; literature on colonial economies and, 71–72; mergers and acquisitions in, 93–95, 94f, 97–98, 101–11; mining industries in, 91, 92–93, 104–5, 106; multinational firms in, 101; nationalism and, 67; National Policy of, 95–96; overview of changes in corporate ownership in, 65–68; overview of corporate governance in, 8–9; ownership structures in, 98, 99f; Patent Act of 1872 and, 95; preparing for "big push" and, 87–89; prime ministers and governments in, 103t; pyramids in, 9, 103–7; railroad building in, 80–82, 87–89; retailing in, 91; shareholder rights in, 120–23; smuggling and, 96; state capitalism in, 7; state control of corporate assets in, 99–101; tax system in, 113–15; trade barriers and, 131–35; trade openness in, 95–97; transplants and, 47–48. *See also* Quebec
Canada Business Corporations Act, 122
Canada Development Corporation (CDC), 127, 134
Canadian Pacific Railroad (CPR), 88, 91, 92, 96
Canal building, in Canada, 80
Capital, savings and, 4–5
Capitalism: creative destruction as principle of, 33; defined, 4–5; living standards and, 5–6; varieties of, 1–2. *See also* Bank capitalism; Family capitalism; Shareholder capitalism; State capitalism
Capital markets: changes in, in United Kingdom, 584–85; in China, 155–57
Carnegie, Andrew, 616
Cartier, Jacques, 72
Case de Dépôt et Placement du Québec, 53
Chaebol, 368
Champlain, Samuel de, 73
Chateau Clique, 77, 78
Chief executive officers (CEOs), corporate, 1–2, 66–67; in the Netherlands, 23
Chile, 316
China: capital markets in, 155–57; characteristics of corporate ownership in, 175–78; Company Law (1904) legislation, 161–63; corporate ownership and control in early twentieth century, 171–75; cultural factors and corporate governance in, 45; dividend payments in, 168, 168n16; establishment of industrial enterprises in, 154–55; family businesses in, 152; foreign corporate enterprises in, 152–53; government-sponsored enterprises in, 157–60; impact of company law on Dasheng cotton mills, 164–69; joint-stock companies in, 155–57; large private enterprises in, 152; light industry enterprises in, 159–60; mining enterprises in, 160; overview of corporate governance in, 9–11; path dependent processes and, 28, 29; precedents of corporate governance, 150–51; processes of adaptation in, 153; railway companies in, 160–61; responses by business to Company Law in, 163–64; Self-Strengthening Movement in, 153–55; Taiping Rebellion and, 153–54; transplants and, 48
China Merchants' Steamship Navigation Company, 154–55, 158, 162
Choten Corp., 381–82
Chrétien, Jean, 109–10, 123, 129–30
Civil law, 57–58; vs. common law, 39–41
Claude-Henri, comte de Saint-Simon, 12
Clayton Act, 633
Clore, Charles, 584
Closed companies (BVs), in the Netherlands, 472

Coca-Cola, 305
Colbert, Jean-Baptiste, 67, 72, 73–74, 187
Colonial economies, literature on, 71–72
Common law, 57–58; vs. civil law, 39–41; corporate governance and, 37–38; uncertainty and, 42–43
Companies Act (1900) (United Kingdom), 25
Company Law (1904) (China), 161–63; impact of, on Dasheng No. 1 Cotton Mill, 164–69; responses by businesses to, 163–64
Company Law (1870) (Germany), 13
Company Law (1884) (Germany), 13
Company of the West, 191–92. *See also* Mississippi Company
Competition, in Canada, 115–17
Corporate governance: business groups and, 33–35; in Canada, 120–21; cultural factors and, 45; entrenchment by elites and, 54–56; families and, 31–33; in Germany, 260–61; government involvement and, 52–54; importance, 5; importance of ideas and, 29–31; institutional change and, 46–47; large outside shareholders and, 48–50; law and, 37–43; monitoring quality of, 5; path dependent processes and, 28–29; preindustrial economies of nations and, 43–46; stock markets and, 50–51; transplant effect and, 47–48; trust and, 35–37
Corporate Governance Codex, 268
Corporate groups, in Canada, 66–67
Corporate ownership: in Canada, 65–70, 97–111; in China, 171–78; of Dasheng No. 1 Cotton Mill, 171–75; in France, 186–90, 204–7; in Germany, 266–70; in India, 284–94; role of German banks and, 237–46; in Sweden, 517–38, 550–59; in United Kingdom, 585
Corporations: control of world's, 2–4, 3f; early, 8; family-controlled, 2–4; pyramid structure of, 4
Corporations Law (1904), 10
Corruption, in Canada, 81–82, 84; big push and, 89–92
Cox, George, 93
Creative destruction, as principle of capitalism, 33
Crédit Mobilier, 12–13, 28, 39, 51, 187, 199–200, 205

Cultural factors, corporate governance and, 45
Cunard, Abraham, 78
Cunard, Samuel, 79
Cunard Line, 78, 79

Daladier, Edouard, 188
Dasheng No. 1 Cotton Mill, 10; corporate ownership and control of, 171–75; impact of company law on, 164–69
Deja.com, 5
Didot publishing company, 206
Diefenbaker, John, 106, 108, 126, 133
Directly controlled subsidiaries, 377
Diversification, 619–20
Dodd, S. C. T., 627, 629
Dual-class shares, 653–57
DuPont company, 638–39
Dutch East Indies Company, 21–22, 46

East India Company, 191
Eaton, Timothy, 91
Edper group, 108
England. *See* United Kingdom
Ente Nazionale Idrocarburi (ENI), 18, 328
Ente Partecippazioni e Finanziamento Industrial Manifatturiera (EFIM), 18
Entrenchment, by elites, corporate governance and, 54–56
Entrepreneurship, in India, 298–302
Establishments, 33
Ethnic divisions, Canada and, 130–31

Family business groups, 57–58; advantages of, 66–68; in China, 152; corporate governance and, 31–33, 135; in Italy, 326. *See also Keiretsu; Zaibatsu; specific families*
Family capitalism, 6; shortcomings of, 6; in United States, 26, 615–17
Family Compact, 77, 80, 116, 123
Family-controlled corporations, in poor countries, 2–4
Family ownership, in United Kingdom, 582–83, 590–93
Feder, Gottfried, 29
FIAT, 335
Financial development, 52, 58
Flagler, Henry M., 626–29
Foreign Investment Review Agency (FIRA), 127, 134, 135

France: *assignats* experiment in, 197–200; capitalism in, 7; capital market developments in, 201–4; current corporate ownership structure in, 188–89; emergence of credit-based banking system in, 199–200; evolution of banking system in, 191–95; factors influencing corporate ownership structure in, 186–88, 186f; historical elements influencing corporate ownership in, 204–7; history and corporate ownership in, 189–90; inheritance laws in, 205–6; jurisprudence in, 40; Limited Liability Acts, 202; overview of corporate governance in, 11–13; path dependent processes and, 28; role of *notaires* in, 195–97; simple and limited partnerships in, 201–2

Free Trade Agreement (FTA), 132

Führerprinzip, 14

Fujinami, Kyujiro, 533

Fur trade, 73, 78, 83

Galt, Alexander T., 81, 92

Galt, John, 79–80

Gandhi, Indira, 16, 17, 295, 297

Gandhi, Rajiv, 295

General Motors, shareholder diversification and, 638–39

Germany, 223–24; bank control laws in, 265–68; board structures in, 260–61; cartels in, 227; consequences of corporate ownership and control in, 268–70; corporate governance in, 260–61; corporate ownership and recent reforms in, 267–68; corporate ownership and reforms of 1965 in, 266–67; general patterns of ownership in, 224–27; history of share companies (AGs) in, 258–60; influence of Great Depression in, 30; institutional change in, 47; interlocking directorates in, 246–54; overview of corporate governance in, 13–15; ownership patterns during Nazi regime, 230–31; ownership patterns during postwar years, 231–37; ownership patterns during Weimar Republic, 229–30; ownership patterns in early twentieth century, 227–29; path dependent processes and, 28–29; postindustrialization developments for corporate governance in, 261–68; proxy

voting in, 254–58; pyramiding in, 14–15; relationship between share ownership and voting rights in, 262–65; role of banks in, 6; role of banks in corporate ownership in, 237–46; Shareholder Law of 1937 in, 14, 265–66; state capitalism in, 7; transplants and, 47

GKN (Guest, Keen, and Nettlefolds Limited), case study of, 597–99

Glass-Steagall Act (1933) (United States), 26, 51, 633

Google, 5

Gordon, Walter, 134

Governance. See Corporate governance

Government involvement, corporate governance and, 52–54

Great Britain. See United Kingdom

Great Depression, 620; Canada, 104–5; in Germany, 261–62; influence of, on corporate governance, 29–31; institutional reform and, 56; in Italy, 328

Greenmail, 20

Harkness, Stephen V., 626–29

Harris, Robert, 80

Head, Francis Bond, 80

Hendry, John, 92

Hincks, Francis, 81, 82

Holding Company Liquidation Commission (HCLC), 425–26

Holland. See Netherlands, the

Honda, 438–39

Hong Kong, corporations in, 2

Hongzhang, Li, 154, 158, 159–60

Horizontal *keiretsu,* 435, 436f

Horsey, William, 106

Howe, Clarence Decateur (C. D.), 67, 105–6, 116–17, 119, 121, 125–26, 128, 133

Howe, Joseph, 79

Hudson's Bay Company, 12, 28, 75–76, 77, 78, 83, 85, 87; annual dividends of, 76f, 77; ownership structure of, 97

Hydro One, 69n2, 103

IBM, 305

Ideas, 57

India, 283–84; business-government relations in, 294–96; business groups and governments in power in, 296–98; business groups and institutional voids in, 298–302; cultural factors and corporate governance in, 45–46; entrepre-

neurship in, 298–302; ethnic groups and entrepreneurship in, 300–301; group companies in, 286–88, 290–91t; history of corporate ownership in, 284–94; IBM in, 305; License Raj in, 297, 297n4; multinational corporations in, 286–87, 302, 305; overview of corporate governance in, 15–17; path dependent processes and, 29; persistence of concentrated ownership in, 285–89; persistence of dominance of business groups in, 289–94, 294t; recent evolution of groups and markets in, 302–3; rent seeking by business groups, 297; Securities and Exchange Board of India and, 302–3; social usefulness of persistence of concentrated ownership in, 315–18; software industry in, 303–15; state capitalism in, 7
Indigenous institutions, 58
Indirectly controlled subsidiaries, 377
Industrial *zaibatsu,* 392–94
Infosys Technologies, 313, 314–15
Inheritance laws, 187; in France, 205–6
Institutional change, corporate governance and, 46–47
Institutional ownership, in United Kingdom, 584
Institutional reform, 55–56
Institutional stability, 55
Institutions, indigenous, 58
Instituto per la Ricostruzione Industriale (IRI), 328, 329, 336
Insurance companies, in Canada, 89
Interlocking directorates, in Germany, 246–54
Irving, Kenneth Collin (K. C.), 105
Israel, corporations in, 2
Italy: characteristics of corporate governance in, 325–27; economic policy in, 328–30; effect of Great Depression on stock market in, 335–36, 336f; enforcement and stock market development in, 340; evolution of investor protection in, 331t; family-owned companies in, 350–57; financing of economic growth during 1950s and 1960s in, 342–43; Great Depression in, and banking system, 328; independent public offerings (IPOs) in, 341–42; influence of Great Depression in, 30; institutional change in, 47; investor pro-

tection and development of stock market in, 338–39; legal and regulatory environment in, 330–34; market competition in, 330; nationalization of electric industry in, 329–30; openness of trade and financial development in, 340–41; overview of corporate governance in, 18–19; ownership structure of firms in, 343–50; path dependent processes and, 29; politics and stock market development in, 340; state capitalism in, 7; state-controlled pyramidal groups and 1990s economic crisis in, 53; state-owned enterprises in, 330; stock markets in, 334–38

Japan: centrally planned economy under military government of, 413–23; early industrialization following Meiji restoration in, 373–74; industrialization in, 368; influence of Great Depression in, 30–31; institutional change in, 47; *keiretsu* groups in, 367–68; legal framework for shareholders in, 431–32; MacArthur and Anglo-American capitalism in, 423–34; overview of corporate governance in, 19–21; ownership changes during depressions in, 402; path dependent processes and, 29; Planning Agency during WWII in, 368–69; postwar attempts to dissolve *zaibatsus* in, 425–31; postwar business groups, 369; rent seeking in, 449–50; role of banks in, 6; state capitalism in, 7; Tokugawa economy of, 370–73. See also *Keiretsu; Zaibatsu*
Jian, Zhang, 10
Jiangnan Arsenal, 154
Jodrey, Roy, 105

Kaiping Coal Mines, 154, 158
Kaneko, Naokichi, 403–13
Keiretsu, 21, 33, 34, 39, 54, 367–69, 431, 432–34, 445–46, 450–52; definitional ambiguities of, 438–39; economies of scope and scale and, 442–45; horizontal, 435, 436f; insulation from market pressures and, 447–49; organization of, 434; political rent seeking and, 449–50; private benefits of control and, 446–47; role of, 434–35; vertical, 436–37. *See also* Family business groups; *Zaibatsu*

Keiretsu defense, 432–35
Kikakuin, 368–69, 422–23
King, Mackenzie, 116, 118, 119, 121, 124

Labor rights, in Canada, 117–20
Land reform, in Canada, 82–83
Latin America, oligarchic institutions in, 45
Laurier, Wilfred, 67, 85, 92, 124
Law, 57–58. *See also* Civil law; Common law
Law, John, 11, 12, 28, 187, 191–95, 201
License Raj, 53
Limited companies (NVs), in the Nether-
    lands, 469–74
Limited Liability Acts (1867) (France), 202
Limited-liability share companies (AGs)
    (German), 225–27, 226t; in early twen-
    tieth century, 227–29; in industrializa-
    tion period (1870–1913), 258–60; dur-
    ing Nazi regime, 230–31; in postwar
    years, 231–37; during Weimar Repub-
    lic, 229–30
Living standards, capitalism and, 5–6
London Stock Exchange (LSE), 587–88
L'Oréal, 206, 210–11
Lower Canada, 77–78; Chateau Clique in,
    77, 78

MacArthur, Douglas, 423–25
Macclean, John Bayne, 91–92
MacDonald, John A., 82, 87, 88, 92, 95, 117
Manitoba: establishment of, 78; Republic
    of, 87
Martin, Paul, 123
Mercantilism, 73–74; as defining feature of
    Canada, 123–24; evolution of, in
    Canada, 125–30
Mergers and acquisitions: in Canada, 93–
    95, 94f, 97–98, 101–11; in first half of
    century in United Kingdom, 593–97;
    in United Kingdom, 583–84
Merritt, William Hamilton, 80
Mexico, 446; corporations in, 2
Michelin, 206, 207–9
Milan Stock Exchange, 335
Mining industries, in Canada, 91, 92–93,
    104–5, 106
Mississippi Company, 11, 39, 187, 192–94,
    201. *See also* Company of the West
Mitsubishi family, 19, 410; *zaibatsu,* 391–92,
    393f
Mitsui family, 36, 371–72, 378–81, 410;
    pyramid structure and, 383–87, 388f
Molson, John, 79

Monopolies, 1; Canada and, 115–17
Montreal, Bank of, 78–79
Montreal Stock Exchange, 80
Moody, John, 614–15, 622–25, 622n9, 630
Morgan, J. P., 616, 633
Mulroney, Brian, 109, 117, 128, 132–33
Multinational firms: in Canada, 101; in
    India, 286–87, 302, 305
Multiple voting shares, 14
Munk, Peter, 110

National Economic Policy (Canada), 117
National Energy Policy (1981) (Canada),
    127–28
Nationalism, Canada and, 67
National Policy (Canada), 95–96
National Product Marketing Act (1934)
    (Canada), 116
Nehru, Jawarharlal, 16, 296
Netherlands, the, 467–68; CEOs in, 23; cul-
    tural factors and corporate governance
    in, 44; empirical analysis of firms in,
    480–84; equity financing in, 474–75;
    evolution of public limited companies
    in, 469–74; history of development of
    industrial finance in, 468–69; influence
    of boards and networks in, 492–93; in-
    fluence of boards and networks in, data
    on, 493–94; influence of boards and
    networks in, results and analysis on,
    494–502; insurance companies and fi-
    nancing of industrial growth in, 478–
    79; nineteenth-century railway finance
    in, 502–7; overview of corporate gover-
    nance in, 21–23; path dependent pro-
    cesses and, 29; pension funds and
    financing of industrial growth in, 479–
    80; pyramid holding companies in,
    488; role of banks in financing indus-
    trial growth in, 475–78; role of stock
    markets in industrial finance in, 474–
    75; "structured regime" in, 488–89;
    takeover defenses in, 484–88; takeover
    defenses in, data on, 489–91; trans-
    plants and, 47; voting power of large
    outside shareholders in, 49
Networks, 36
New Deal, 30
New Democratic Party, 119
Nissan group, 394–97
North American Free Trade Area
    (NAFTA), 132n48
Northwest Company, 77

Notaires, 195–97
Nova Scotia, Bank of, 79

Oligarchic devices, 23
Oligarchic institutions, 45
Oligarchies, 33
Oppression Remedy, 122
Organ bank hypothesis, 413

Palme, Olof, 545
Patent Act (1872) (Canada), 95
Path dependence, 29, 71; in China, 28; in
     Sweden, 563–64, 575
Pattison, Jimmy, 110
Pearson, Lester, 107–8, 132, 133
Pereire, Emile and Isaac, 12
Pesenti group, 350–53
Peugeot (PSA Peugeot Citroen), 206, 211–14
Phillips, Eric, 106
Phyn, Ellice, and Co., House of, 78
Plutocratic voting, 48
Political rent seeking, 123; in India, 294–98;
     in Japan, 449–50
Politics, 58; corporate governance and, 52–
     54; effects of, in U.S., 637–38; lack of
     block holders in U.S. and, 618–19
Power group, 108, 110
Preference shares, 23
Priority shares, 23
Progressive movement, 26, 631–32
Prospect theory, 54–55
Proxy voting, 237; in Germany, 254–58
PSA Peugeot Citroen, 206, 211–14
Public Utility Company Holding Compa-
     nies Act (1935) (United States), 26, 633
Public Utility Holding Company Act
     (1938), 644
Pyramid structure, of corporations, 4;
     American utility companies and, 644–
     45; in Canada, 9, 103–7; in Germany,
     14–15, 237; in Italy, 18, 325–26; in
     Japan, 19–20; in the Netherlands, 488;
     in Sweden, 563; in United Kingdom,
     24–25; in United States, 26–27; *zai-
     batsu* and, 376–77, 381–83

Quebec: founding of, 72–73; Révolution
     Tranquille and, 126, 130. *See also*
     Canada
QWERTY effect, 56

Railroads, in Canada, 80–81, 87–89
Rao, Narasimha, 295

Real bills doctrine, 51
Rent seeking. *See* Political rent seeking
Richelieu, Cardinal, 73
Rockefeller, John D., 615, 626–29
Rockefeller, William, 626
Roman, Stephen, 106
Rowell, N., 189

Savings: capital and, 4–5; methods of, 5–7
Schacht, Hjalmar Horace Greeley, 29
Schweppes, case study of, 599–600
Securities and Exchange Board of India,
     302–3
Securities and Exchanges Act (1934)
     (United States), 27, 41, 121
Securities Trading Act (1948) (Japan),
     431
Shanghai Cotton Cloth Mill, 158
Shareholder capitalism, 5
Shareholder Law (1937) (Germany), 14,
     265–66
Shareholder rights: in Canada, 120–23;
     common law and, 38–39; insecure,
     trust and, 51
Shareholders, large outside, corporate gov-
     ernance and, 48–50
Share ownership, voting rights and, in Ger-
     many, 262–65
Sherbrooke Cotton Mill, 81
Simpson, George, 87
Social Democratic Party (Sweden), 30, 519;
     bank reforms and, 527; historical
     agenda of, 538–41
Socialism, 7
Società di Gestioni e Partecipazioni Indis-
     turtriali (GEPI), 18
Software industry, in India, 303–15; distri-
     bution of companies by revenues in,
     306–8, 307t; industrial organization of,
     306–8; success of, 308–12; top-twenty
     companies in, 307t
Sony, 438
South Sea Bubble, 11, 28
South Sea Company, 191, 201
Standard Oil, 626–30; breakup of, 633; di-
     versification of shares and, 634–37;
     shareholder diversification and, 634–37
State capitalism, 7
Steamship lines, Canadian, 79
Stock markets: corporate governance and,
     50–51; ill-trusted, banks and, 51; in
     Italy, 334–40, 336f; in the Netherlands,
     474–75

Sumitomo family, 19, 372–73, 380–81, 410;
pyramid structure and, 388, 389f
Suzuki family, 19–20; rise and fall of, 402–
13
Sweden: alliances between banks and industrial firms in, 527–29, 528f; business-
government relations in, 36–37; close-
end funds as owners of largest listed
firms in, 535–38; controlling families
in, 529–34; controlling interests of the
fifteen families in, 530, 531f; corporate
ownership and development of financial markets in, 550–59; corporations
in, 2; corporatist innovation model in,
542–44; critical evaluation of Swedish
model of corporate ownership in, 559–
70; direct ownership of listed shares by
households in, 535; entrepreneurship
in, 542; general accord of 1938, 541–
42; history of corporate ownership in,
522–38; influence of Great Depression
in, 30; institutional change in, 47; labor
market polices in, 544; necessary conditions for Swedish model of corporate
ownership in, 547–49; orthogonal trajectory away from economic democracy in, 546–47; overview of corporate
governance in, 23–24; overview of history and corporate ownership in, 517–
22; ownership and control of largest
firms in 1945, 529–30, 529t; ownership
and control of largest firms in 1967,
532t, 533t, 630; ownership and control
of largest firms in 1990, 532–33, 534t;
path dependent processes and, 29;
public investment projects in, 543; radical policies to implement economic
democracy in, 545–46; reasons for historical path of corporate ownership in,
571–74; reform of corporate taxes in
1938, 541–42; Social Democratic Party
in, 30, 519, 527, 538–41; Swedish
model in, 544–45; transplants and, 47;
transportation industry in, 543
Swedish model of capitalism, 8

Takahata, Seiichi, 403–4
Talon, Jean, 74
Tariffs, Canada and, 131
Tata Consultancy Services (TCS), 304–5,
312–14, 315, 317
Tata family (India), 15, 17, 289, 296, 298–

300, 303, 317; software industry and,
304; time line of entry into new busi-
ness by, 299f
Tax systems, in Canada, 113–15
Taylor, Edward Plunkett, 105, 106
Temporary National Economic Committee
(TNEC), 643, 643n48, 643n49, 643n50
Thompson, Roy, 105, 106
Thornton, Henry, 198
Timber barons, 78
Toronto Stock Exchange, 82
Toyoda, Sakichi, 400–401
Toyota, 438
Trade openness, in Canada, 95–97
Transplant effect, corporate governance
and, 47–48, 58
Trudeau, Charles, 105
Trudeau, Pierre Elliott, 105, 108–9, 117,
126–27, 134
Trust: business groups and, 36–37; corpo-
rate governance and, 35–37; insecure
shareholder rights and, 51

Uniform Commercial Code, 41
Union Générale, 187
Unions, in Canada, 117–20
United Kingdom: case study of Cadbury
Brothers, 600–601; case study of GKN,
597–99; case study of Schweppes, 599–
600; changes in capital markets during
1940s and 1950s in, 584–85; control of
corporations in, 4; cultural factors and
corporate governance in, 44; data for,
586–87; family ownership in, 582–83;
family representation on boards in,
590–93; hostile takeovers in, 584; institutional investors in, 49, 584–85;
jurisprudence in, 40; key features of
current corporate ownership in, 585;
mergers and acquisitions in, 583–84,
593–97; overview of corporate governance in, 24–25; path dependent processes and, 28; peculiarity of, 582–83;
rates of family ownership in, 587–90;
shareholder capitalism in, 5; state capitalism in, 7; takeover offers in, 585–86;
Takeover Panel in, 585; takeovers in
second half of century, 601–5
United States: block holdings, introduction
on, 613–22; capitalism in, 1; civil codes
in, 41–42; control of corporations in, 4;
distribution of corporate control in,

644–45, 644t; effects of politics on block holdings in, 637–38; explanations for disappearance of company's founders for, 646–51; family capitalism in, 26, 615–17; financial capitalism at start of twentieth century in, 622–33; growth in number of shareholders in, 641t; immediate corporate control in 200 largest American corporations in 1930, 641–43, 642f; institutional change in, 47; institutional reform in, 56; number of shareholders in three largest corporations in, 640f; overview of corporate governance in, 25–27; Progressive Movement in, 26; proxy voting in, 639–43; shareholder capitalism in, 5; shareholder diversification in, 633–39; state capitalism in, 7; takeover offers in, 585–86; top fifty firms in, 292–93t; ultimate corporate control in 200 largest American corporations in 1930, 641–43, 642f
Upper Canada, 77–78
Upper Canada, Bank of, 79–80

Vajjpayee, Atal Behari, 295
Vanderbilt, William, 616, 620, 632–33
Veblen, Thorsten, 30
Vertical *keiretsu,* 436–37
Voting caps: in Germany, 14; in the Netherlands, 23
Voting power, large outside shareholders and, 48–50
Voting rights, share ownership and, in Germany, 262–65

Wallenberg family, 30, 47, 525–27, 530, 532–33, 538
Weimar Republic, corporate ownership patterns during, 229–30
White knight defense, 532
White squires, 369, 369n4
Wipro software company, 315
Wolvin, Roy, 118

Yasuda *zaibatsu,* 388–91
Yokoi, Hideki, 432–33

Zaibatsu, 19, 20, 21, 36, 54, 368, 369–70, 450–52; banks, 439–42; Big Four, 383–92; break up of, by Supreme Commander of Allied Powers (SCAP), 424–25; centrally planned economy under military government and, 413–23; defined, 374–77; economies of scope and scale and, 442–45; formation of, 377; independent companies and, 400–402; industrial, 392–94; insulation from market pressures and, 447–49; local, 398–400; Mitsubishi, 391–92, 393f; Mitsui, 383–87; organ banks of, 413; political rent seeking and, 449–50; post-WWII attempts to dissolve, 425–31; preserving insider control and, 377–81; prewar local, 437–38; private benefits of control and, 446–47; pyramids and, 381–83; Sumitomo, 388, 389f; Suzuki, 402–13; weak institutions and, 445–46; widely held, 394–97; Yasuda, 388–91. *See also* Family business groups; Japan; *Keiretsu*